Uganda's Human Resource Challenge

Uganda's Human Resource Challenge

Training, Business Culture and Economic Development

Jörg Wiegratz

FOUNTAIN PUBLISHERS
Kampala

Fountain Publishers
P. O. Box 488
Kampala - Uganda
E-mail: sales@fountainpublishers.co.ug
publishing@fountainpublishers.co.ug
Website: www.fountainpublishers.co.ug

Innovations at Makerere Committee
Makerere Universtiy
P. O. Box 7062
Kampala, Uganda
E-mail: iatmak@utlonline.co.ug
Tel: 256-41-531067/9
Fax: 256-41-531069

Distributed in Europe and Commonwealth countries
outside Africa by:
African Books Collective Ltd,
P. O. Box 721,
Oxford OX1 9EN, UK.
Tel/Fax: +44(0) 1869 349110
E-mail: orders@africanbookscollective.com
Website: www.africanbookscollective.com

Distributed in North America by:
Michigan State University Press
1405 South Harrison Road
25 Manly Miles Building
East Lansing, MI 48823-5245
E-mail: msupress@msu.edu
Website: www.msupress.msu.edu

First published 2009

ISBN 978-9970-02-968-1

Contents

Acronyms

AfDB	African Development Bank
AGOA	African Growth and Opportunity Act
AJOBAC	Africa Journal of Business and law
APER	Agricultural Productivity Enhancement Programme
APPP	Africa Power and Politics Programme
ARSCP	African Roundtable on Sustainable Consumption and Production
ATAIN	Agribusiness Training and Input Network
ATFC	Applied Eropical floriculture courses
APEP	Agricultural Productivity Enhancement Program
ATFC	Applied Tropical Floriculture Courses
b	billion
BDS	Business Development Services
BMO	Business Membership Organisation
BMU	Beach Management Unit
BMZ	Federal Ministry for Economic Cooperation and Development (Germany)
BNP	Bee Natural Product
BTVET	Business, Technical and Vocational Education and Training
BUDS-EDS	Business Uganda Development Scheme- Enterprise Development Support
CBR	Centre for Basic Research
CDO	Cotton Development Organisation
c.p.	Ceteris paribus (all other things being equal)
CIM	Centrum for International Migration and Development
CICS	Competitiveness and Investment Climate Strategy
CODESRIA	Council for the Development of Social Science Research in Africa
COMESA	Common Market for Eastern and Southern Africa
CP	Cleaner Production
CPC	Cleaner Production Centres
CPRC	Chronic Poverty Research Centre
CSOs	Civil Society Organisations
CSR	Corporate Social Responsibility
CTA	Chief Technical Advisor
DANIDA	Danish International Development Agency
DCs	Developing Countries
DDA	Dairy Development Authority

DFID	Department for International Development
DFST	Department of Food Science and Technology
DLP	Growth in Average Labour Productivity (Output/Labour ratio)
DVC	Domestic Value Chain
DVCD	Domestic Value Chain Development
EACCU	East African Community Customs Union
EAC	East African Community
EB	European Buyer
EBA	Everything but Arms
EFAG	Education Funding Agencies Group
EMS	Environmental Management Systems
EPRC	Economic Policy Research Centre
ESIP	Education Strategic Investment Plan
ESSP	Education Sector Strategic Plan
EST	Environmentally Sound Technologies
E&T	Education and Training
ETS	Education and Training System
EU	European Union
EUg	Enterprise Uganda
EYA	Employer of the Year Award
FAL	Functional Adult Literacy
FDI	Foreign Direct Investment
FEMA	Faculty of Economics and Management
FI	Financial Institutions
FUE	Federation of Uganda Employers
FV	Fruits and Vegetables
FY	Financial Year
GCC	Global Commodity Chains
GDP	Gross Domestic Product
GDP(mp)	GDP at market price
GEM	Global Entrepreneurship Monitor
GHPs	Good Hygiene Practices
GNS	Gross National Savings
GOU	Government of Uganda
GPN	Global Production Network
GTZ	German Technical Cooperation
GVC	Global Value Chain
HACCP	Hazard Analysis and Critical Control Point
HCI	Human Capital Index
HR	Human Resource
HRD	Human Resource Development
HRM	Human Resource Management
HRMAU	Human Resource Managers Association of Uganda
ICI	Innovation Capability Index

ICT	Information and Communication Technology
IDEA	Investment in Developing Export Agriculture
IDP	Internally Displaced Persons
IDR	Industrial Development Report
IFIs	International Financial Institutions
IDRC	International Development Research Centre
IGG	Inspectorate General of Government
ILO	International Labour Organization
IMF	International Monetary Fund
INEF	Institute for Development and Peace
IPS	Integrated Productive Skills
IS	Informal Sector
JICA	Japan International Cooperation Agency
LDC	Least Developed Country
LF	Labour Force
Lf	Lead firm
LFA	Lead farmer
LG	Learning Group
LIS	Learning and Innovation System
LLL	Linking, Leveraging and Learning
LSD	Local Skills Development
m	million
MAAIF	Ministry of Agriculture, Animal Agriculture and Fisheries
MAPS	Marketing and Agro-Processing Strategy
MCP	Master Craftsman Programme
MD	Managing Director
MDGs	Millennium Development Goals
MEAs	Multilateral Environmental Agreements
MEMD	Ministry of Energy and Mineral Development
MFI	Micro Finance Institutions
MFPED	Ministry of Finance, Planning and Economic Development
MGLSD	Ministry of Gender, Labour and Social Development
MOES	Ministry of Education & Sports
MOLG	Ministry for Local Government
MPS	Milieu Programma Sierteelt
MSEs	Micro and Small Enterprises
MSI	Millennium Science Initiative
MSMEs	Micro, Small and Medium Enterprises
MTCS	Medium Term Competitiveness Strategy
MTTI	Ministry of Tourism, Trade and Industry
MUBS	Makerere University Business School
MUK	Makerere University
MVA	Manufacturing Value Added
MWLE	Ministry of Water, Land and Environment
NAADS	National Agricultural Advisory Services

NARO	National Agricultural Research Organisation
NARS	National Agricultural Research System
NCDC	National Curriculum Development Centre
NSCG	Non-Sectoral Conditional Grant
NEMA	National Environment Management Authority
NGO	Non-governmental Organisation
NHCC	National Housing & Construction Company
NIS	National Innovation System
NICs	Newly Industrialising Countries
NIEs	Newly Industrialising Economies
NLS	National Learning System
NORAG	Norwegian Agency for Development Cooperation
NURRU	Network of Ugandan Researchers and Research Users
NUSAF	Northern Uganda Social Action Fund
OA	Organic Agriculture
OD	Organisation Development
ODA	Official Development Assistance
ODI	Overseas Development Institute
OECD	Organisation for Economic Co-operation and Development
OHS	Occupational Health and Safety
OPM	Oxford Policy Management
OSSREA	Organisation for Social Science Research in Eastern and Southern Africa
p.c.	per capita
PCY	Promotion of Children and Youth
PE	Primary Education
PEAP	Poverty Eradication Action Plan
PEVOT	Programme of Employment Oriented Vocational and Technical Training
PLE	Primary Leaving Examination
PIRT	Presidential Investors Roundtable
PMA	Plan for Modernisation of Agriculture
PPE	Post Primary Education
PPET	Post-Primary Education and Training
PPG	Pro-Poor Growth
PPP	Public-Private Partnership
PSCP	Private Sector Competitiveness Programme
PSD	Private Sector Development
PSDG	Private Sector Donor Group
PSFU	Private Sector Foundation Uganda
PSI	Population Services International
PSP	Private Service Providers
PWD	People with Disabilities
R&D	Research and Development
RDS	Rural Development Strategy

ROI	Return on investment
SACCOs	Savings and credit cooperative organisations
SAP	Structural Adjustment Policies
SoC	Social Capital
SCs	Supply Chains
SCF	Soft competitiveness factors
SCOPE	Strengthening the Competitiveness of Private Enterprise
SCP	Sustainable Consumption and Production
SE	Secondary Education
SEP	Strategic Exports Programme
SESEMAT	Secondary Science and Mathematics Teacher
SHF	Smallholder farmer
SI	Support institution
SID	Support industry
SIDA	Swedish International Development Cooperation Agency
SITC	Standardised Industrial Trade Classification
SMEs	Small and Medium Enterprises
SNV	Netherlands Development Organisation
SPS	Sanitary and Phytosanitary
S&T	Science and Technology
SSEs	Small Scale Enterprises
SV	Supervisor
TAF	Technology Acquisition Fund
TAI	Technological Activity Index
TCFC	Training and Common Facility Centre
TE	Tertiary Education
TEXDA	Textile Development Agency
TFP	Total Factor Productivity
TNCs	Transnational Corporations
TOT	Terms of Trade
VET	Vocational Education and Training
UBA	Uganda Bankers Association
UBOS	Uganda Bureau of Statistics
UCDA	Uganda Coffee Development Authority
UCE	Uganda Commodity Exchange
UCPC	Uganda Cleaner Production Centre
UEPB	Uganda Export Promotion Board
UF	Ugandan firm
UFEA	Uganda Flower Exporters Association
UFPEA	Uganda Fish Processors and Exporters Association
UGAPRIVI	Uganda Association of Private Vocational Institutions
UGT	Uganda Gatsby Trust
UIA	Uganda Investment Authority
UIRI	Uganda Industrial Research Institute

UIP	Uganda Integrated Programme of UNIDO
ULAIA	Uganda Leather and Allied Industries Association
UMA	Uganda Manufacturers Association
UMIDA	Uganda Metal Industries Development Association
UNBS	Uganda National Bureau of Standards
UNCST	Uganda National Council for Science and Technology
UNEB	Uganda National Examinations Board
UNEP	United Nations Environment Programme
UNHCR	United Nations High Commissioner for Refugees
UNHS	Uganda National Household Survey
UNICEF	United Nations Children's Fund
UNIDO	United Nations Industrial Development Organization
UNU-WIDER	UN University, World Institute for Development Economics Research
UPE	Universal Primary Education
UPPET	Universal Post Primary Education and Training
UPTOP	Uganda Programme for Trade Opportunities and Policy
USAID	United States Agency for International Development
USE	Universal Secondary Education
USSIA	Uganda Small Scale Industry Association
UVETA	Uganda Vocational Education and Training Authority
UVQF	Uganda Vocational Qualifications Framework
UWEAL	Uganda Women Entrepreneurs Association
VCs	Value Chains
VCD	Value Chain Development
VE	Vocational Education
VET	Vocational Education and Training
VT	Vocational Training
VTC	Vocational Training Centre
WB	World Bank
WFP	World Food Programme
WRS	Warehouse Receipt System
WIDER	World Institute for Development Economics Research
WTF	World Technology Frontier

Foreword

This book explores salient issues of Uganda's economic development process, linking the analysis to the theme of human resource development (HRD). The book focuses on aspects of HRD which are related to the building and deepening of capabilities, and the skills, knowledge, know-how and experience relevant to enhanced economic development. HRD, as used throughout the book, stands for education but especially training and day-to-day, on-the-job learning in broad terms. It argues that HRD is crucial for Uganda if the country is to address the challenges and opportunities of economic development and work towards her targets for poverty reduction, accelerated economic transformation and growth, and private sector development (PSD), to which Uganda aspires. Efforts to enhance economic development and PSD in Uganda need to go beyond basic infrastructure provision such as roads and electricity or the provision of adequate finance and the conventional pillars of what is called 'an enabling environment'. More emphasis needs to be put on HRD, especially training, workplace learning and related aspects of (the politics, sociology and economics of) business practices and norms in the country. The book also discusses implications and develops recommendations to enhance the contribution that the business, technical and vocational education and training (BTVET) sector can make in addressing human resource needs in Uganda.

In doing so, the book presents (a) main arguments, findings, conclusions, and recommendations of an extensive research and in-depth analysis process carried out for the German Technical Cooperation (GTZ) in the first half of 2006 (Wiegratz 2006a, 2006b), and (b) empirical studies on value chain governance that the author carried out with a team of colleagues in 2006-2007 for the government of Uganda (Wiegratz et al. 2007a, 2007b). In this book, the author attempts to analyse matters as they unfolded up to 2006. Statistical and other updates of the period thereafter have been minimal, mainly because, first, the arguments made in the book are not overly time-sensitive (hence not outdated), and, second, because the purpose of the report is to make sense of the pre-2007 period, e.g. prior to the rise of agricultural and fuel prices around the world (including Uganda), the weather (drought, floods) and energy problems, the discovery of oil reserves in Uganda, and, most recently, the global financial crisis. An understanding of the central arguments of the book can help the reader to navigate analytically more recent as well as the coming years.[1]

This research and the writing of the book was carried out with the intention of providing a comprehensive view on some key PSD matters that have a direct or indirect link with HRD. The focus of related government policies and programmes as well as donor support - including implementation priorities and performance - was reviewed with the intention of examining the extent to which their priorities capture such salient aspects. The overall analysis of this book - the findings, views and ideas presented - can be seen as a range of background inputs for a general debate about HRD and PSD and the linkages between the two.

1 The author has tried though to provide up-to-date references up to early 2009.

The research for this book considered a range of recent survey and other research findings. This helped to generate updated insights about aspects of the HRD situation in the economy and thus come up with some new issues for consideration by HRD proponents, which can complement their current work focus, where appropriate. Overall, it is hoped that the book will contribute to the debate on Uganda's economic development and provide an analysis of aspects of the related human resource dimension. As any other book, this one also has its limits in terms of research scope and analysis: the book does not tackle (in depth) a range of matters related to its theme, e.g. issues of politics, political economy, history, sociology, social policy and so on.

Throughout the book there will be some reference to the concepts and work of the United Nations Industrial Development Organization (UNIDO), including its programme in Uganda. This is due to the author's work for UNIDO in Uganda between 2004 and 2005 - as a junior consultant in industrial competitiveness in the Ministry of Trade, Tourism, and Industry (MTTI)[2] - and his consequent familiarity with UNIDO's research and technical programmes. UNIDO is one of the agencies in Uganda that is active in the area of skills development for industrial activities in small, medium and large enterprises. Reference to UNIDO's training interventions and effects in Uganda is given where appropriate and illustrative for the general arguments presented in the book. Overall, due to the author's work on industrial development matters in Uganda, the book is geared towards exploring HRD issues mainly in the *non-agricultural* (e.g. industrial) sectors. However, reference to agriculture is made as well, where appropriate.

J.W.
Kampala, 2009

2 This work was part of UNIDO's assistance to the GOU in the context of developing an industrial policy and strengthening research capacities in the MTTI.

Acknowledgement

This book is based extensively on research work of the author done for GTZ PEVOT (Programme of Employment Oriented Vocational and Technical Training). The study comprised desk research, a limited number of interviews, as well as written responses by informants to related questions. A summary of the background report on HRD in Uganda was published by GTZ under the title 'Capabilities for catching-up: Economic development and competitiveness in Uganda: Implications for Human Resource Development with particular focus on Technical and Vocational Education and Training in Uganda', edited by Eva Castaner and Matthias Giersche (see Wiegratz 2006b). We acknowledge GTZ PEVOT as initiator of this study and thank GTZ for agreeing that part of the work be published in this book. The Deutsche Gesellschaft für technische Zusammenarbeit (GTZ) GmbH, Postfach 5180, 65726 Eschborn, Germany (www.gtz.de) is coordinating the German cooperation programme for the Promotion of Employment-oriented Vocational and Technical Training (PEVOT) I Development of the BTVET System on the basis of a commission from the German Federal Ministry for Economic Cooperation and Development (BMZ). The opinions and analyses expressed in this book do not necessarily reflect the views and official policies of PEVOT or GTZ. For background information on PEVOT's activities see Box 57 (Appendix 34).

Further, research by the author and his colleagues in the period 2006-2007 on value chain matters in the Ugandan context - findings of which are included in this book - was funded by the Uganda Programme for Trade Opportunities and Policy (UPTOP), a joint programme of the government of Uganda and the European Union (EU). Co-funding was provided by Secretariat of the Competitiveness and Investment Climate Strategy in the Ministry of Finance, Planning and Economic Development, Uganda Sustainable Tourism Development Programme (EU), Makerere University Business School (MUBS) and Land O'Lakes International Development. Early findings from the author's PhD research (2007-2010, Studentship from the University of Sheffield) are also included in the book.

A special expression of gratitude goes to the MTTI and the Economic Policy Research Centre (EPRC) for supporting the author with office space and collegial support during his time of work in Uganda, and the I@MAK project and Fountain Publishers (especially Alex Bangirana and Hettie Human) for making this publication possible. The support provided by the Faculty of Economics and Management (FEMA), Makerere University (MUK) is also appreciated. Gratitude to Paschal Nyabuntu (freelance consultant) and Charles Omagor (MUBS) for allowing the author to include in this book some of the findings of their joint studies on matters of value chain governance in the Ugandan context. The author is grateful for the support provided by colleagues in the past years as well as the inputs and comments provided by respondents and informants who contributed to this book. They are too many to be named in this foreword. Yet the research for and work on this book would certainly not have been possible without the initial thrust of Remie Toure (then UNIDO), Dr. Victor

Richardson (consultant), Joseph S. Kitamirike (then MTTI, now NHCC), Matthias Giersche, Hans-Günter Schröter (both GTZ), Eva Castañer (consultant), and the colleagues at the MTTI and UNIDO. A final thanks to Rose Nakayi and other supportive family members and friends in Germany, Uganda, the UK, and elsewhere.

Remaining mistakes are entirely those of the author. Comments are very much appreciated.

J.W.
Kampala, 2009

Introduction

Productive capacities and capabilities for enhanced competitiveness

The global setting for domestic economic development and industrialisation - as envisaged by Uganda - has changed significantly over the last two decades: rapid, pervasive and continuous technical progress, liberalisation, shrinking economic distance, intensified competition for markets and export-oriented Foreign Direct Investment (FDI), new systems of production and trade, and new rules and regulations are all accelerating the globalisation of production and trade and changing the way in which both are organised and coordinated (UNIDO 2002). This affects the prospects for producers from developing countries who aspire to compete in the global economy. Producers face price, wage and productivity pressures as well as increasing requirements for: (a) consistency in product quality, quantity, labelling, packaging, and uniformity (taste, appearance, in some cases on a year-round basis), (b) speed, flexibility, efficiency, reliability, technology and innovativeness in production, marketing, delivery and value chain management, and (c) compliance to relevant quality, safety, technical, environmental and sanitary standards/regulations (e.g. traceability).

Around the world, some firms and nations have been able to respond to these challenges and make use of the emerging opportunities of the global economy. Others have been marginalised and excluded further; often they do not have sufficient productive and trade-related capacities and capabilities to respond vigorously to new trends and requirements, and participate gainfully in the global economy. In any case, countries at all levels of development face the challenge of ensuring that enterprises become and remain competitive. The pace of population growth and urbanisation in developing countries supports the case for establishing competitive firms that can offer jobs and incomes, and drive the structural change of their respective domestic economy (ibid).

Effective innovation and learning vital for advanced productivity and competitiveness

Under the conditions of current globalisation, intensified competition[3], fast-changing global specialisation, persistent technological change[4] and regulatory harmonisation and standardisation, firms will have to advance their competitiveness and productivity sufficiently, in particular through effective *innovation* and *learning*. Often this would mean learning to improve and upgrade *products, processes* and *organisations* (organisational techniques) continuously as well as, where appropriate, enter, over time, into high value-added activities with more skill-and/or technology-intensive production profiles and stronger productivity growth (shift from agriculture to industry and services). Adopting and mastering respective

3 This is partly due to global excess production capacity in some manufacturing sectors, leading to a downward pressure on prices.

4 For instance, innovation in terms of increasingly science-based production technologies.

forms of fast-changing technology is inherent in the course of action. This process is driven among others by a cumulative effort to develop, deepen (or upgrade) and apply a critical mass of a range of relevant ***capabilities***, especially entrepreneurial, investment, design, industrial, technical, technological, production, product, marketing, managerial, organisational, learning, social, linkage, interactive and institutional capabilities (ibid, Lall 2001a, Morrison et al. 2006).

Different authors use a different mix of the above terms to classify capabilities. Sanjay Lall, for instance, emphasises the capabilities "to operate plants [or generally, capacities] at competitive levels, raise quality, introduce new products and diversify into higher value-added activities and to attract FDI into such activities" (2005, 37). Capacity here can refer to 'hardware' (production plants, equipment, etc.) or 'software' (information, knowledge, skills). In this book, the term *capabilities* is used to refer to an *evolving set of knowledge, information, experience and skills (institutional, individual, etc.)* specific to the processes undertaken by a particular firm, sector, and/or value chain (Morrison et al. 2006, Wiegratz 2006a, 2006b).[5]

Support institutions (SIs) are vital for building and deepening capabilities. SIs are regarded as institutions or agencies charged with education and training (E&T), technology transfer and support, linkage and network-building, entrepreneurship development, clustering and value chain development, export promotion, research and development (R&D), human resource management support, and, generally, the provision of information and other services for PSD. These institutions need to build capabilities, for example in technology use, business planning, market research, product development, testing, marketing, innovation activities, as well as value chain development and coordination; capabilities that are very relevant for value adding in, for example, modern agro-industry (Lall 2002, 2004a).

Correspondingly, a low level of capabilities in an economy - at micro and meso level, e.g. in firms and (training) SIs - holds back a significant and sustained supply response to the new challenges of competition, technical change, growing skills needs and shrinking economic distances in increasingly competitive and technology-oriented markets. This is largely the situation in many economies and industries in Africa which have been 'dropping out' from - or remaining integrated only in an adverse way into - the dynamics of global industrial activity (Lall 2005, 35-6, 2002, 2). In the case of African economies, they continue to be included in the global economy mainly as primary resource suppliers, not as manufacturers, marketers, and logistic nodes. As Lall writes, "just opening up to global markets, technology and capital flows, without a base of capabilities, means that economies cannot competitively handle new

5 In the book, for the sake of convenience, these terms are used or understood somewhat interchangeably. For instance, when the author refers to a specific capability he also has in mind the respective skills, knowledge, know-how, information and experience. In the same vein, the author uses the terms *GOU*, *state*, and *public sector technocrats, bureaucrats* and *officials* interchangeably. The term GOU (which is used mostly in the book), for instance, comprises the state bureaucracy as well. In the same way, the author uses the term *donors* in a sense that includes, for instance, implementing development agencies who are actually not donors in the strict sense. Further, the term *training* usually refers to both on-the job (firm/farm level) and institutionalised training and education, including BTVET. The term *firm* usually includes the meaning *enterprise*, including *firms* and (commercial) *farms*. With *Africa*, we refer to sub-Saharan Africa (SSA) excluding South Africa. Finally, where appropriate, abbreviations are used when referencing to institutions, e.g. UNIDO for United Nations Industrial Development Organization. In the reference list, the title is listed under the full name of the publishing institutions.

industrial technologies. If they cannot, they risk marginalisation in a globally integrated market" (ibid, 2). This scenario leads to a continuation of the growing economic (especially industrial) and technological divide between Africa and other developing regions. In this context, the capability and knowledge gap is considered to be one of the main reasons for the economic performance and income gap (Yumkella 2005, UNIDO 2005c, UNCTAD 2003).[6]

Further, estimates by UNIDO suggest that almost 60% of the difference in income between SSA countries and advanced industrial countries (year 2000) can be attributed to gaps in the - broadly defined - *stock of knowledge* (2005c). "Accumulation of knowledge coupled with increases in other capabilities, particularly in governance and finance, stand out as the most critical factors in taking advantage of the catching-up potential" (ibid, 17). It is thus highly relevant (i) to invest in generation of knowledge and domestic capabilities, for instance, to better access and use available knowledge in locally innovative activities, and (ii) to ensure a support system that fosters this process. According to UNIDO, "existing local knowledge and competences largely determine how effectively an organisation can master inflows of technological knowledge" (2005d, 6). This view is in line with arguments about the importance of *creating 'new' endowments* of an economy, such as human resources or public institutions - or systems for education, training, learning, innovation, and public service delivery - and thus 'new' forms of competitive advantage for advancements in economic development (Ferranti et al. 2002).[7]

Box 1 reflects the complex challenges of building domestic capabilities for economic development, in particular industrial development, and points to the importance of tacit knowledge, skills, attitudes and experience as well as social and institutional capital. The process of capability building is a *long-term and cumulative venture and is rife with pervasive market and institutional failures* - especially in latecomer, or late-latecomer economies in LDCs - such as Uganda - that entered the global industrial scene more recently. Latecomers have to catch up with the advanced levels of capabilities, productivity, technology, infrastructure, learning and support institutions, and business networks in other economies, that enjoy the 'first mover advantage' of their earlier entry into the global economy. These first-movers benefit from accumulated advantages. Also, they often find a comparatively high level of education and strong support systems in their host economies. This allows them to improve their operations and capabilities relatively fast: latecomer firms from countries such as Uganda then have to catch up against a moving target (Lall 2004a, Lall et al. 2004a, 2004b, Mathews 2006).

While the process of capability formation can generally be considered as a long-term, risky, costly, path-dependent, and cumulative venture, in the particular case of LDCs it also faces market and institutional failures - such as technological, information, and coordination externalities, and uncertainty - which lower impetus for firms to invest in capabilities. In

6 This book does not cover a *political-economic* analysis of Africa's position in the global economy and her related economic development features.

7 Traditional factor endowments are land, labour, capital, and natural resources. In the context of exploring interrelationships between resource-based and knowledge-intensive sectors and economies, a World Bank analysis of economies in Latin America and the Caribbean concludes: "[T]he statistical evidence shows that, especially for manufactures but also for certain agricultural products, the 'new' endowments explain a larger share of the international differences in comparative advantage than traditional endowments. … Public policy has a large role in building up such endowments" (Ferranti et al. 2002, 5, 3).

this context, governments have a role to help latecomer enterprises overcome the various disadvantages and market failures (Lall 2001a, 2001b, 2004a). In principle, the remarks below have relevance for capability building in commercial agriculture, industry and services.

Box 1: Building domestic capabilities for industrial development in a liberalising economy

"Africa can enjoy sustained growth of incomes, employment and exports provided that its enterprises can raise productivity to competitive levels, and keep it there.* While raising productivity is desirable per se, this is not enough to ensure growth in a liberalizing world if the level of productivity (even after adjusting for lower wages) is below that needed to compete. Some activities may survive at lower productivity levels if they do not face direct foreign competition (for instance, they may be protected by high transport costs or access to cheap local raw materials, or they may serve niche markets that imports cannot threaten easily). Such protected or niche activities have largely driven Africa's recent (anaemic) industrial growth in countries that have allowed import competition. But such activities will not suffice to deliver the rates of growth required by the MDGs because they are confined to small markets and, most importantly, cannot provide the foreign earnings Africa badly needs. African enterprises must enter the larger arena, both at home and abroad, if they are to provide significant industrial growth. The key to raising productivity to competitive levels lies in improving industrial capabilities. But what are industrial 'capabilities'? They are not production capacities in the sense of physical plant, equipment and buildings; it is relatively easy to acquire or build capacity, at least if the financial resources are available. Capability - *the ability to make capacity operate competitively* - requires something more: the tacit knowledge, skills and experience related to specific technologies that is collected by enterprises and cannot be imported or bought in. The process involves creating new skills, partly by formal education but, usually more importantly, by training and the experience of new technologies. It requires obtaining technical information, assimilating it and improving upon it. It entails building institutional rather than individual capital, with new managerial and organizational methods, new ways of storing and disseminating information and of managing internal hierarchies. It also needs intense interaction between enterprises - firms do not learn on their own - and between enterprises and support institutions. Finally, it requires the factor markets that provide skills, technology, finance, export marketing and infrastructure to respond to the new needs of enterprises. The process of capability building has to be continuous, not once-for-all, because technologies and market conditions change constantly, and responding to these changes requires new skills and knowledge. Building competitive capabilities needs policies to overcome these market failures.** The story of industrial success in the developing world is in fact the story of how effectively governments have helped their enterprises to overcome such failures in capability building.

* Productivity here is interpreted broadly to include not just production but also quality, design, delivery and marketing.

** Policies have to address market failures at three levels. The **first** is within the firm, in terms of promoting investment in complex new technologies when faced with costly and risky learning costs (infant industry promotion). The **second** is between firms and industries (coordination of investments in activities linked by externalities, needing the promotion of value chains or geographical clusters). The **third** is between firms and factor markets and institutions (coordination at the higher level)."

Source: *UNIDO (2004a, 6, emphasis added), based on Lall (2001a). See also Abramowitz (1986) and Biggs et al. (1995).* [8]

8 The notion of technological capabilities in Biggs et al. (1995) comprises "the skills and information required to establish and operate modern machinery, and the learning ability to upgrade these skills when needed ... [T]hese capabilities are categorized into three functional groups: investment capabilities, production capabilities, and learning mechanisms ... [In this view, l]earning mechanisms constitute the most important category of technological capabilities since they enable firms to augment their endowments of the other two types of capabilities" (WB 1996).

Local innovation and learning: Improving processes, products and organisations and mastering technologies

Importantly, innovation in most developing country' firms, also in Uganda, does not mean to develop products, technologies or organisational methods that are new-to-the-world (innovating at the 'world frontier') but new to the local company (and often local economy), e.g. incremental improvements in machines, tools, production processes or quality management practices for an existing product, improved inventory control systems or practices in HRD, e.g. training methods. A major part of such innovative efforts goes into adopting, adapting, using and building upon imported (hence already *existing*) product and process technologies - in an environment that has become increasingly competitive. All these forms of local innovation and learning are closely related to respective skills-availability which allows such improvements. Fostering innovative efforts of firms and farms is thus vital given that low diffusion of basic and advanced technology from outside is one of the main problems in SSA economies (UNIDO 2002).

Some domestic firms will innovate and learn in flexible and interactive relationship arrangements with foreign partners (e.g. "learning from buyers") which have the technologies, knowledge, know-how, skills, capital, and markets[9] that domestic firms need in order to advance their production and products, meet market requirements, and nurture scale and learning economies (ibid). *Marrying effectively the available internal and external sources of competitiveness and growth* is one of the key strategies for a competitive latecomer economic development and industrialisation. It can help to address domestic inputs' deficiencies and technological constraints that impede this process and thus foster or unlock realisation of the domestic growth potential (ibid, 2004a, 2005d, Mathews 2006, Lall 2004a). "Today industrialization is not driven by resource endowments alone, but by technology, knowledge, skills, information, innovation, research and development, and networking. ... Productivity growth stems from enhanced adaptive capabilities to use modern technology and commercialize new knowledge" (UNIDO 2005a, 3). Important in this process are functioning, efficient, responsive and interactive SIs which help firms to develop and upgrade local capabilities, and support them in their effort to *link, leverage* and *learn* (*LLL-approach,* UNIDO 2002) from foreign/advanced sources of information, knowledge, technology and skills. In this view, a vital approach to foster Uganda's economic development would be strengthening local capabilities, attracting foreign mobile capabilities and learning in relationships with foreign partners (e.g. buyers/ consumers, service providers, experts, etc.); and indeed, a vital part of Uganda's economic policy is attracting FDI.[10]

9 E.g. branding, distribution and after-sales servicing systems, which are costly and difficult to build independently by the local exporting firm.

10 See also Amsden's (1992) discussion of 'industrialisation through learning'.

Relevant new features of the global production and trade

Before we turn to Chapter 1, it is important to review six *important features of contemporary global markets* which play a contextual role in what follows in the rest of the book:

- The evolution and sophistication of cross-border, value-adding networks of production and trade (of a "network-centered global economy", Gereffi 2005, 166), in particular global value chains (GVCs[11]) and Global production networks (GPNs). This is a result of amplified cross-border fragmentation, relocation and coordination - led mainly by transnational corporations (TNCs) - of global production and trade in both goods and services (the organisation of value-adding activities in *network relationships*), among other things.
- The increasing importance of large global buyers (retailers, wholesalers, branded marketers, supermarkets, other intermediaries) and their market power and requirements for quality, chain management, or reliability. The same applies to concentration in other stages of global industry, e.g. concentration in food processing. It is estimated that around two-thirds of visible world trade is handled by TNCs, and of this about one-third, the dynamic segment, is within TNCs' systems (internal production systems: affiliates-parents, or among affiliates) and not on open markets. Overall, manufacturing accounts for 90% of visible world trade (Lall 2005, 4, 24).
- The shifting modes of transnational governance structures - the coordination and control of dispersed activities - of these global production systems by lead firms, often TNCs, which is related to dynamics in competition (including profit rates), technical progress, and standards.
- The increasing importance of China and India as drivers of change and competitive pressures.
- The importance of global rules and standards.
- The significance of a relatively small group of market dynamic products in world merchandise trade: the 40 most dynamic products in the period 1985-2000 have increased their world market share collectively from 22% to 37%. Notably, 39 of the 40 most dynamic products are manufacturers (Gereffi et al. 2005, 78-9, Gereffi 2005, Humphrey 2005, 1-10, Zalk 2004, 10, Kaplinsky and Morris 2006b).[12]

Analysing the new forms of organisation and ownership of production and trade - for example, the modes of interaction between nominally independent local producers and foreign buyers, and how this affects the possibilities of advancement of local firms (prospects of jobs, wages, skills and value creation) - is vital for any national strategy and policy that aims at building local capacities and capabilities for increased production and trade, and thus relates to: corresponding issues of market access, product diversification and improvement, as well

11 Or, global commodity chains (GCC).

12 The most dynamic products are those which have experienced the highest and most sustained growth in world trade over the period in terms of their growth in world market share. Notably, a large part of the top products are produced under the auspices of TNC-controlled GVCs, particularly in electronics, cars, and apparel. The analysis excludes products with a very small share - less than 0.33% - in world trade as well as oil-based commodities. The analysis is at the Standardised Industrial Trade Classification (SITC) four-digit level (Zalk 2004, 24).

as competitiveness of domestic firms, value chains and clusters, and support institutions. Generally, new forms of production and trade create new forms of skills requirements: in other words, change creates new skills gaps in firms/farms that have to be tackled accordingly (Humphrey 2005).[13]

Note, throughout this book this author will at times quote significant statements, views and findings of other sources at some length: The intention is to allow the reader to appreciate relevant contributions to the theme of the book. The hope is that this will contribute adequately to the deliberations on HRD in Uganda.

13 See Box 40 (Appendix 1) for insights on recent drivers of competitive advantage in relation to fragmentation and relocation processes in the global economy.

1

Macroeconomic Analysis of the Ugandan Economy

The post-1986 growth episode

The main pillars of the growth period

The period of political turmoil and widespread armed conflicts in Uganda prior to 1986 caused severe losses in economic and human resources and led to structural deterioration of all sectors. The Ugandan economy, starting from a low base of a mainly (semi-) subsistence economy after the years of civil war, has experienced high economic growth rates - well above the Sub-Saharan African average - since 1986. The growth episode is separated conventionally into the following main pillars and episodes (Kappel et al. 2004, IMF 2005, Ssemogerere 2005)[14]:

- The process of general economic recovery and rehabilitation after the years of civil war, including the reactivation of existing production capacities (which were underutilised or not-utilised during previous years) and the return of financial capital as well as human capital (including entrepreneurs) namely Ugandan-Asians and Ugandans who were abroad during the years of civil war.
- The policy reform strategy of the GOU with a focus on: internal security, stabilisation/fiscal discipline, liberalisation of key markets and sectors (e.g. reduction of tariffs, abolition of the marketing boards for coffee, tea and cotton, reforms in foreign exchange markets and the banking sector), privatisation (of more than 100 state companies in telecommunications, electricity, etc.), supply-side incentives and institutional reforms, in particular the restructuring of public administration and decentralisation.
- The high growth rates of the 1990s are also due to favourable world market prices during the period 1992-1997 for the country's major export commodity at that time, coffee, which led to high growth rates in the agricultural sector, and remarkable and historically unprecedented inflows of official development assistance (ODA) that encouraged the recovery and growth process. The significant donor money flows have continued to date, making Uganda a strongly aid-dependent country.

14 See also Hansen and Twaddle (1988, 1991, 1998), Mamdani (1996b, 1995, 1994), Langseth et al. (1995), Belshaw and Lawrence (1999), Mugaju (1999), Kasekende and Atingi-Ego (1999), Ssemogerere (1999), Dijkstra and van Donge (2001), Holmgren et al. (2001), Reinikka and Collier (2001a), Tangri and Mwenda (2001), Black et al. (2002), Brock et al. (2002), Brock et al. (2003), Musisi and Dodge (2002), Oloka-Onyango (2004), Harrison (2005a, 2005c), Hickey (2005, 2003), Ssewakiryanga (2005, 2004a, 2004b, 2004c), Mbabazi and Taylor (2005), Kiiza et al. (2006), Rubongoya (2007), Okidi et al. (2007), UNDP (2007b), and OPM (2008) for more details on the economic and social reform processes in Uganda during the post-1986 period.

Recent growth rates: Reflection of a slowdown in transformation and catch-up?

Between 1986/87 and 2004/05, the average annual gross national product (GDP) growth rate was 6.3%[15]; with a certain slowdown of annual growth rates - although still remaining positive and reasonably high - in recent years. For example, the average growth rate for the period 1990/91-94/95 was 7% vs. 6.6% for 1995/96-1999/2000 and 5.6% for 2000/01-2004/05. Notably, all three sectors - agriculture, industry and services - experienced a growth slowdown in the later period compared to the situation in the 1990s (Tables 1 and 2, related Figures 1 and 2).[16]

In terms of per capita growth, during the 1990s, "Uganda attained one of the highest per capita real GDP growth rates in the world - albeit from a low base - of 2.8 percent, compared with 1.7 percent for all developing countries" (World Bank/WB 2006a, viii). More recently, there was a slowdown in GDP per capita growth: the rate was about 3.0% p.a. for the total period 1986/87-2004/05 with a level of about 2.6% p.a. for the more recent years of that period (MFPED 2006). At the time when the slowdown became statistically apparent, views were expressed that the slowdown in GDP growth would put at risk the economic sustainability and poverty reduction goals of GOU: "With annual per capita growth rates falling ... concerns are being raised about the sustainability of the needed high economic growth to further reduce poverty" (IMF 2005, 5). In terms of future years, to achieve its growth and poverty reduction aspirations, the country would need a p.c. income growth of around 4%. This is a very difficult project. Even if this income growth is achieved, Uganda would still be grouped as a low or lower-middle income country (Bevan et al. 2003).[17]

The International Financial Institutions (IFIs) argue that the reported slowdown is to be expected in advanced post-conflict economies such as that of Uganda (WB 2006a, IMF 2006).[18]

---

15 In comparison, the average GDP growth rate for SSA was about 2.8% for 1990-2003 (Citigroup 2006, 2).

16 Uganda's medium term target GDP growth rate is 7%, while GDP growth rates of 7-8% p.a. are considered to be required to make an impact on poverty.

17 According to Bevan et al. (2003), Uganda's aspiration of achieving on average 7% GDP growth p.a. - while population growth is around 3% - would require a p.c. income growth of around 4%. "While rates of this sort have been achieved for extended periods in a handful of countries, they remain exceptional, and recent work on Uganda's growth prospects suggests that they will be very difficult to emulate. ...[A] reasonable projection if the programme of policy reforms is implemented energetically might be on the order of 3% per annum. However, if there is some policy slippage, or if the economy suffers adverse trade, aid or security shocks, it could be substantially less than this. ...[E]ven on the most optimistic assumption of sustained 4% per capita income growth, the conventional measure only reaches US$740 in constant US $ 2000 by 2023 [with US$300 as initial position in 2000], and remains below US$755, the current threshold between low and lower-middle income countries. Unless the growth performance of the next couple of decades is truly spectacular, Uganda will remain a low income country throughout this period, and realistically must expect to do so for considerably longer" (Bevan et al. 2003, 20).

18 Recent WB analysis suggests that the GDP growth rate slowdown might mainly be due to a reduction in private consumption - while investments and exports increase their contributions to growth. Accordingly, a lower role of consumption is not uncommon after higher levels in the immediate post-conflict period (2006a, viii, see also IMF 2006). In detail, the WB assessment is as follows: "The recent slowdown in growth is due entirely to the slow-down in private consumption, while contributions to growth from private investment and exports have increased. This change in the source of growth is a positive development: private investment and export-led growth would clearly be more sustainable than private consumption-led growth. Moreover, the slow-down in private consumption likely reflects a return to more normal trends after high levels in the post-

According to observers, the growth impetus and opportunities of the immediate recovery and stabilisation period (and related reforms) had been captured substantially by the early 2000s; and what remains will be exhausted gradually over the next few years (Bevan et al. 2003, Collier and Reinikka 2001).[19] Indeed, some new sources of economic growth and development are needed; and thus, a renewed and broadened focus of the very policies and support measures that target PSD. In this book it is argued that HRD-for-PSD ought to be a vital part of future interventions.

The fastest growing sectors since the early 1990s were *industry* (manufacturing/agro-industry, construction), and *services* (wholesale/retail trade fuelled by increasing imports, tourism-related services, telecommunication and, in particular, community/public services), with *agriculture* performing below the average growth rate. Between the years 2000-2005 in particular, industry revealed higher or similar growth rates - from a smaller base though - compared to services (e.g. 10.6% vs. 7.7% in 2004/05). The dynamics in these two sectors compensated for the positive but below-average performance of agriculture, which grew at below 2% (2004/05). Raising *agricultural productivity* remains difficult: the output growth in agriculture in the recent past was, according to the IMF, "primarily due to an expansion of the amount of land under cultivation, while productivity gains were limited" (IMF 2005, 5). Economic growth "remains vulnerable to external and natural shocks - including rainfall - because of the large share of agriculture in the economy" (2006, 5).

Main drivers of the growth episode in the 1990s include (a) *private investment* (from both domestic and foreign sources) in industry and construction,[20] and (b) *increased donor supported public spending* on community services such as education, health and government services. The extent to which growth - and also the reduction in poverty - was driven by donor support and money (e.g. through the community service leverage) is notable (Okidi et al. 2004). Estimates suggest that *almost one-third* of the related improvements could be due to the direct foreign aid impacts (Reinikka and Collier 2001b, 38-44).[21]

In fact, ODA - especially to finance economic recovery following civil wars - has been estimated to be the most important factor fuelling rapid growth episodes in *outputs, capital deepening* and *labour productivity* in Uganda in the four decades since the 1960s (Ssemogerere 2005, ix-x).[22] Yet, "most of the ODA financed essential infrastructure to support resumption of

---

conflict period. These developments, however, do bring into the fore the need to ensure continued and higher growth in private investment and exports" (2006a, viii). The IMF notes regarding the slow-down in GDP growth rates that this is actually "a pattern also observed in other postconflict countries" (2006, 5, see Collier and Hoeffler 2002, emphasis added).

19 Note, by the year 2000, Uganda had only roughly recovered the pc. income "that the economy experienced when achieving independence in 1962, but it has not yet reached the peak level of 1970 (Collier and Reinikka 2001, 453-4). There is thus still some room for continued recovery-based growth (e.g. further growth of primary commodity exports and manufacturing for local demand) (ibid, 457).

20 This has translated into growth in capital inputs (capital accumulation).

21 Reinikka and Collier (2001b, 43-4) estimate that the direct contribution of foreign aid (e.g. without consideration of impact on policy reforms) is about 30% of the realised GDP growth rate p.c. and of the decline in poverty incidence (1992-1997).

22 Based on a study commissioned by UNIDO, on productivity performance in Uganda in the period 1961-2000; the study uses various materials including data from the UNIDO productivity database (Ssemogerere 2005). Accordingly, in the post-1986 period in particular, ODA has financed relief/rehabilitation and later capacity building/technical assistance to prepare for the Structural Adjustment Policies (SAP) regime. It has further helped to limit adverse effects of unfavourable

growth, rather than ongoing capital deepening to raise productivity, especially in the private sector ... Until the recent past, the focus of this ODA was not specifically on capital formation or labour quality accumulation and this limited the otherwise positive contributions of capital deepening and labour productivity to economic growth" (ibid, 7, 18). Remarkably, since the late 1990s donor money rose relative to key indices of the economy: "donor inflows, net of debt-service payments, increased by 5 percentage points of GDP, reaching about 12 percent of GDP in 2003/04; flows of direct budget support rose from about 1 percent of GDP to nearly 6 percent of GDP" (IMF 2005, 4). By around 2005-06, donors had been financing about half of the national budget, making Uganda one of highest donor-dependent African countries.[23] The dependency of sections of the economy on ODA inflows can be a fragile arrangement.

The more recent stronger emphasis of GOU on policies and reforms in health and education - e.g. focus on HIV/AIDS, Universal Primary Education (UPE), increased private financing of education - is generally considered a crucial beginning of increased HRD interventions, although apparently "it is too early yet to see their systematic benefits [in the respective economic performance figures]" (Ssemogerere 2005, 18).

Table 1: Annual GDP Growth Rates (%), 1995/96-2004/05

Sectors/FY	95/96	96/97	97/98	98/99	99/00	00/01	01/02	02/03	03/04	04/05
Agriculture	4.4	1.2	5.8	5.8	5.6	4.6	3.9	2.3	1.6	1.9
Industry	21.1	11.9	12.6	12.6	4.2	6.0	8.2	6.7	8.2	10.6
Services	8.2	5.9	7.6	7.6	6.6	5.2	8.2	5.7	8.2	7.7
GDP (MP)	9.8	4.9	4.7	8.2	5.4	5.0	6.4	4.7	5.7	6.2

Source: *MFPED (2006). Data from February 2006.*

TOT shocks, and has continued to support the recovery process. It peaked in 1995 at 871mUS$ (ibid, ix). The study ranks other main driving forces - besides ODA - for periods of rapid output growth as follows: (1) high gross national savings (GNS) and export earnings supporting early growth following independence, (2) exogenous favourable TOT (windfall gains), and (3) the post SAP economic policies in the 1990s (macro-economic stability and investment climate) which start to show positive effects (FDI etc.). Regarding capital deepening, besides ODA other main factors are, in order of relevance: (a) results of favourable economic policies (in early and late 1960s as well as late 1990s, causing for instance in the latter case rising FDI inflows and GNS), and (b) exogenous positive terms of trade (TOT) shock (1992-95) (ibid, ix-x). Slumps in overall output and capital deepening were related to poor policies that precipitated civil wars and exogenous TOT (ibid, x).

23 Note: "projections of long term donor aid requirements indicate that the annual requirement for donor aid for central government will average just under $800 million during the 2004/05 to 2013/14 period, which is only slightly higher than the average aid inflow over the last four fiscal years of around $766 million" (MFPED 2004, 211).

Figure 1: Annual GDP Growth Rates (%), 1995/96-2004/05

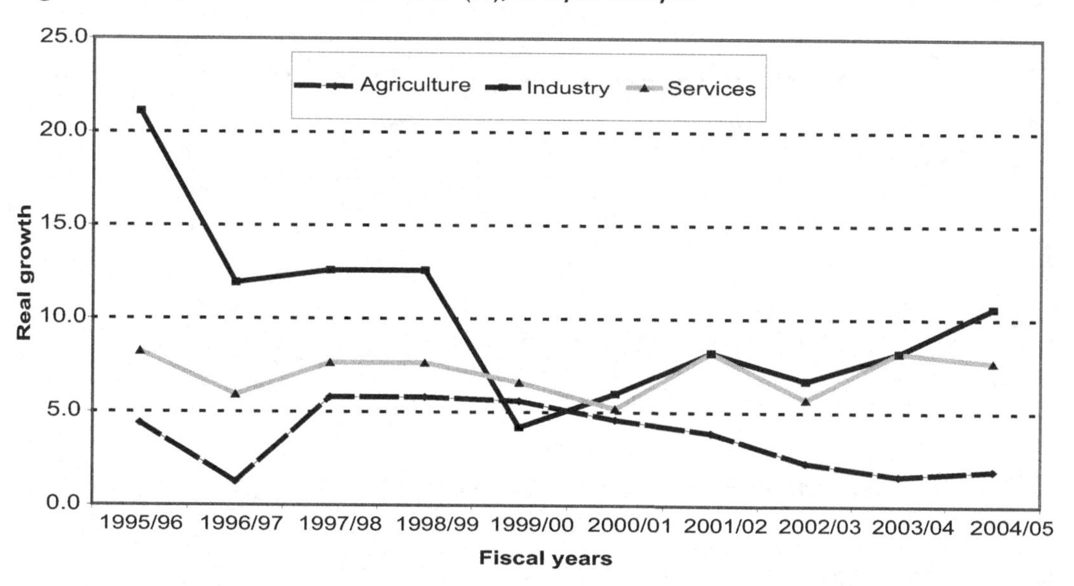

Source: *MFPED (2006).*

Table 2: GDP Growth Rates (%), Average for five-year period, 1990/91-2004/05

Sectors/Period	1990/91-94/95	1995/96-1999/2000	2000/01-2004/05
Agriculture	4.0	3.8	2.9
Industry	11.4	11.2	7.9
Services	8.2	7.0	7.0
GDP (MP)	7.0	6.6	5.6

Source: *MFPED (2006).*

Figure 2: GDP Growth Rates (%), Average for five-year period, 1990/91-2004/05

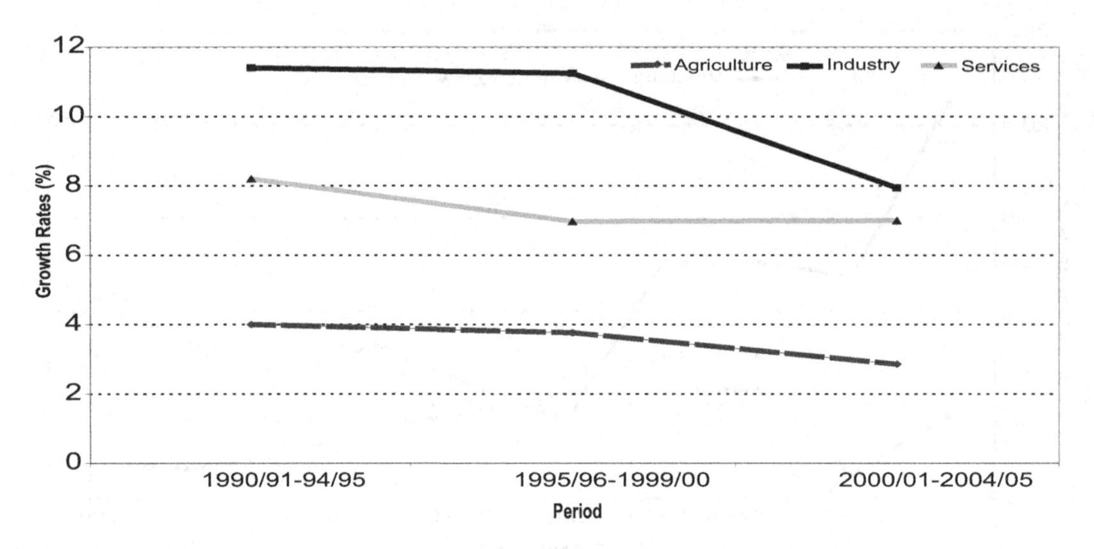

Source: *MFPED (2006).*

Table 3 illustrates details of the sectoral growth rates for recent years. In FY 2004/05, the three fastest growing sub-sectors were: transport and communication (18.7%), construction (14.8%), and manufacturing (8.5%, due to good performance in the following sub-sectors: beverages and tobacco, food processing as well as textiles, clothing and footwear, basic metal and metal products, and non-metallic materials).

Table 3: Details of sectoral growth (%), 2000/01-2004/05

Industry Group	**2000/01**	**2001/02**	**2002/03**	**2003/04**	**2004/05**
Agriculture	**4.6**	**3.9**	**2.3**	**1.6**	**1.9**
Monetary	4.5	5.7	3.9	1.6	2.7
Cash crops	-4.9	7.4	4.6	0.3	3.1
Food crops	8.2	5.7	3.7	1.7	1.7
Livestock	3.8	4.4	3.9	1.1	4.5
Forestry	8.5	6.2	5.6	5.6	5.6
Fishing	4.0	3.5	3.2	3.4	4.0
Non-monetary	**4.6**	**1.7**	**0.1**	**1.6**	**0.8**
Food crops	4.6	1.0	-0.9	1.4	-0.3
Livestock	5.6	6.2	5.8	1.0	6.9
Forestry	4.2	3.2	3.5	3.5	3.5
Fishing	4.0	3.5	3.2	3.4	4.0
Industry	**6.0**	**8.2**	**6.7**	**8.2**	**10.6**
Mining & Quarrying	10.1	11.0	1.2	8.6	7.2
Manufacturing	8.9	5.3	4.3	4.5	8.5
Electricity & water	8.2	5.4	4.6	6.8	6.1
Construction	1.3	13.4	11.6	13.8	14.8
Construction (non-monetary)	3.4	3.4	3.5	3.4	3.4
Services	**5.2**	**8.2**	**5.7**	**8.2**	**7.7**
Wholesale & retail trade	6.5	6.2	4.7	3.6	6.5
Hotels & restaurants	7.1	18.1	7.5	19.1	4.1
Transport & communication	9.6	12.4	16.8	21.1	18.7
Road	5.8	7.2	5.6	7.2	7.1
Rail	4.9	1.9	-1.6	1.0	2.5
Air & supportive services	-4.4	1.6	16.1	11.9	13.1
Posts & telecommunications	32.3	33.9	48.0	50.3	35.7
Owner-occupied dwellings (non-monetary)	8.0	7.0	6.5	6.0	6.0
Community services	2.4	7.0	2.7	5.5	5.2
General government	0.2	8.7	-7.8	7.5	-0.7
Education	2.7	7.2	5.2	7.5	6.6
Health	-4.9	7.8	7.3	1.7	8.3
Rents	4.8	5.2	4.9	4.6	4.7
Miscellaneous	6.1	6.6	4.7	3.5	7.6

Source: *MFPED (2006).*

Recent growth figures in the years up to 2007/08 were mixed: In FY 2005/06, there were "two domestic shocks; the prolonged drought, which affected agriculture production, and the reduction in hydro electricity generation capacity at Jinja, which resulted in major load shedding in the second half of the year" (GOU 2006, 11). Consequently, agriculture and manufacturing experienced a decline in growth rates, while service[24] and monetary construction continued to perform well and support overall growth. Accordingly, the annual growth rate of the agricultural sector was just above 0% which was the lowest rate for the sector since FY 1991/92. Further, growth in industry almost halved from about 11% in FY 2004/05 to about 5% in FY 2005/06 (ibid, 4-7). "Hardest hit is the formal manufacturing

24 Especially road transport, telecommunications, finance, hotels/restaurants and support services.

sector, where growth has fallen sharply from 13.5 percent to -3.5 percent. Most manufacturers have either been forced to reduce production, revert to 24-hour shift work patterns or use diesel generators, which has increased their costs of production" (ibid, 6-7). However, plans to improve thermal electricity generation in the short-term and increased agro prices raised expectations that production in both industry/manufacturing and agriculture would recover (ibid, 5, 8).

Indeed, figures for the years 2007 and 2008 indicate that the growth slow-down trend of the early 2000s has not continued. Positively, growth dynamics picked up again and have increased to a remarkable 7.9% (2006/07) and 9.8% (2007/08) (GOU 2008b). Dynamics that seem to have played a role in this regard include: (i) growth in sectors such as manufacturing, wholesale/retail trade, transport and communication, and financial services, (ii) regional trade dynamics, (iii) the increase in prices for coffee and other agricultural exports (also due to the rise in global food prices), (iv) the interest of (new and established) firms to invest in Uganda as their service and logistics hubs for the region, and (v) the expectations of oil production. Some local agro-processing firms, for instance, are penetrating new regional markets and increasing their respective networks, and accumulating valuable experience. In particular, export figures have increased considerably post-2005, for instance Uganda's regional exports to Southern Sudan, DR Congo, and Kenya. The COMESA (Common Market for Eastern and Southern Africa) is now the leading export destination (39%) followed by the EU (28%).[25] Further, services exports, especially tourism, education and labour remittances, also boost the export records of the country. "The value of exports of merchandise goods and services increased from $2b in Financial Year 2006/07 to $2.4b in 2007/08. The value of merchandise exports in 2007/08 amounted to US$ 1.8 billion while export of services amounted to US$ 540million ... [R]emittances ... amounted to $476m in 2007/08 compared to $ 430m in 2006/07. FDI increased to $946m in 2007/08, from $695 in 2006/07. Coffee exports increased from $229m in 2006/07 to $348m in 2007/08. Partly as a result of this good export performance, the level of Uganda's international reserves increased to $2.7b in June 2008" (GOU 2009).

The recent positive figures and trends in some sectors are remarkable, but do not make the matters to be discussed in this book of less concern: HRD, productivity, technological upgrading, collective action, value chain development, and SIs need to be addressed adequately in future; efforts to enhance PSD need to go beyond basic infrastructure provision.[26]

Sectoral growth sources: Services and industry account for 90% of growth

Dynamics in services and industry used to be the key sectoral sources of growth. In the FY 2004/05, services (3.3%) and industry (2.1%) together contributed *almost 90%* (53%/34%) to national GDP growth. Monetary agriculture drives the rather small contribution (0.7%/11%) of the agricultural sector. Overall, the services sector contributed most to the growth episode of the last decade (Tables 4-6, and Figure 3).[27]

---

25 A detailed analysis of these recent trends is beyond the scope of this book.

26 The in-depth analysis in this research, which was developed mainly in February-May 2006, does not significantly cover the developments beyond 2005/06, e.g. the effects of the global financial crisis on Uganda's economy.

27 Note that despite the low contribution to growth, the agricultural sector remains a vital source of livelihood provision, food security (export-oriented) industry input, and (domestic, regional, international) trade.

Table 4: Sectoral contribution to GDP growth (%, based on Factor Costs GDP), 1995/96-2004/05

Sector/FY	95/96	96/97	97/98	98/99	99/00	00/01	01/02	02/03	03/04	04/05
Agriculture	2.0	0.6	0.8	2.4	2.3	1.9	1.6	0.9	0.6	0.7
Industry	3.1	2.0	1.1	2.2	0.8	1.1	1.5	1.3	1.6	2.1
Services	3.2	2.3	2.5	3.1	2.7	2.1	3.3	2.4	3.4	3.3
Indirect taxes	1.4	0.0	0.3	0.4	-0.3	-0.1	0.0	0.2	0.1	0.1
GDP(mp)	**9.8**	**4.9**	**4.7**	**8.2**	**5.4**	**5.0**	**6.4**	**4.7**	**5.7**	**6.2**

Source: *MFPED (2006).*

Figure 3: Sectoral contribution to GDP growth (%, factor costs), 1995/96-2004/05

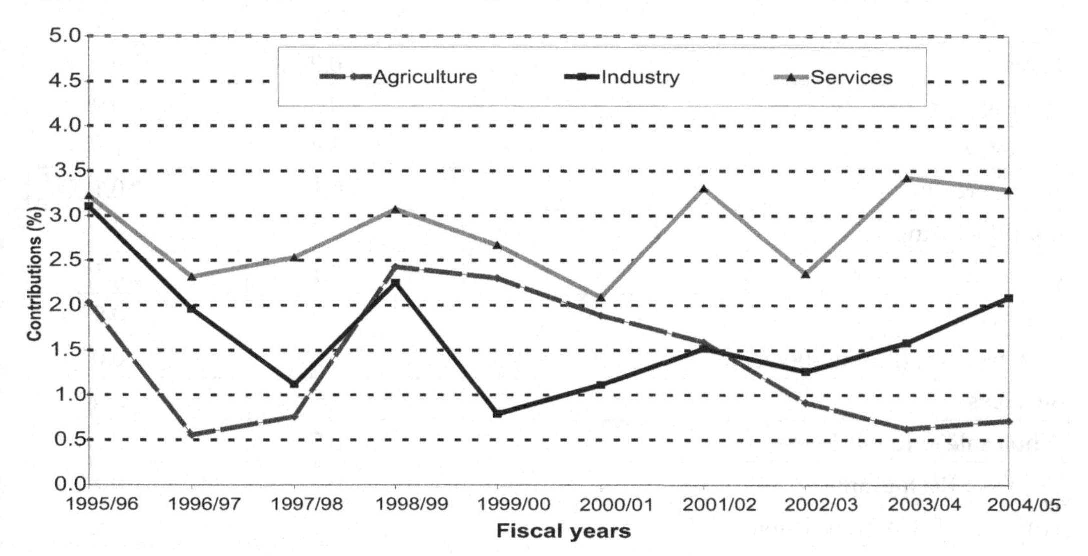

Source: *MFPED (2006).*

Table 5: Sectoral contribution to GDP growth (%), average for five year period, 1990/91-2004/05

Sector/Period	1990/91-94/95	1995/96-1999/2000	2000/01-2004/05
Agriculture	**2.0**	**1.6**	**1.1**
Industry	1.5	1.8	**1.5**
Services	**3.1**	**2.8**	**2.9**

Source: *MFPED (2006).*

Table 6: Details of sectoral contribution to GDP growth (%, basic price GDP), Average for five-year period, 1995/96-2004/05

Sector/Period	1995/96-1999/00	2000/01-2003/04
Agriculture	**1.6**	**1.1**
Monetary	1.2	0.8
Cash crops	0.4	0.2
Food crops	0.5	0.4
Livestock	0.2	0.1
Forestry	0.0	0.0
Fishing	0.1	0.1
Non-monetary	0.4	0.2
Food crops	0.2	0.0
Livestock	0.1	0.1
Forestry	0.0	0.0
Fishing	0.0	0.0
Industry	**1.8**	**1.5**
Mining & quarrying	0.1	0.1
Manufacturing	1.0	0.5
Electricity & water	0.1	0.1
Construction	0.6	0.9
Construction (non-monetary)	0.0	0.0
Services	**2.8**	**2.9**
Wholesale & Retail Trade	0.7	0.6
Hotels & Restaurants	0.2	0.3
Transport & Communication	0.4	0.9
Road	0.3	0.2
Rail	0.0	0.0
Air & supportive Services	0.0	0.0
Posts & Telecommunications	0.1	0.6
Owner-occupied Dwellings (non-monetary)	0.3	0.2
Community services	1.1	0.8

Source: *MFPED (2006).*

The relatively low growth performance in *agriculture* in the past years is an indicator of unfavourable international prices in the late 1990s/early 2000s,[28] inadequate market integration, and low productivity levels in the sector. The decreasing average contribution of *industry* to GDP growth in 5-year-period comparisons (1995/96-1999/2000 vs. 2000/01-2004/05) is also noteworthy given the *potential* relative advantage of this sector to use technology, advance

28 Price deteriorations were particularly strong in the coffee sector where coffee prices fell by 70% in the late 1990s/early 2000s. Since then, coffee prices and thus the terms of trade of the country have partially recovered (IMF 2005, 4)

and apply skills and realise productivity gains quickly, and increase output. In particular, the contribution of manufacturing firms to growth has decreased from 1.0% to 0.5% (Tables 5 and 6), which is worrying given the country's ambition to industrialise, and the importance of a dynamic manufacturing sector for strong overall GDP growth in the future (Bevan et al. 2003). Apparently, the manufacturing sector has difficulties realising the potential for *productivity improvements and sectoral growth* (product diversification, market penetration). Part of this appears to be related to (a) inadequacies in industrial, technological as well as managerial, organisational and entrepreneurial skills and capabilities, (b) insufficient SIs (e.g. those that would form a national learning or innovation system) which would provide required skills and capabilities and boost industrial and technological learning and upgrading. These inadequacies undermine the competitiveness drive of the industrial and related sectors.

Difficulties of job creation in formal sector

Was the growth episode of the last 15 years employment-intensive? One way to look at it is considering accumulated figures of actual employment for formal sector investment projects. The Uganda Investment Authority (UIA) licensed around 300-400 projects p.a. in 1993-1997, and around 140 projects p.a. since 2000[29]. According to different *firm surveys*, an accumulated actual investment of USD 1.446 million has created around 80,000-90,000 jobs in total on the ground (early 1990s to end of 2001). Hence, on average there were around 8,000-10,000 new jobs p.a. This is around 60% of what firms had initially stated in their plans. The main reasons for the reported abundance of investment projects were failure to service loans, failure to secure finance, high competition and lack of market (UIA 2004, BOU et al. 2004).[30]

Surveys among manufacturing firms report an average growth in permanent full-time employment in these firms of about 5% over a three-year interval (firms surveyed for period 1995-97) and 4% (period 2000-02) (WB 2004b, 53). Another study, using Government data[31] on the manufacturing sector, points to an overall stagnation of employment levels in the sector for the period 1987-2000: The *average* annual growth rate of employment was only 0.4% constituting "practically zero [increase in] demand for labour" (Ssemogerere 2005, 14). The employment level in this sector remained at about 17,000 employees (with ups and downs over the years) while the number of establishments rose from 79 to 122. Notably, the index of industrial production increased significantly from 100% (1987) to 541% (2000) in the same period with an average output growth of 14.1% p.a. The study suggests the adoption of

29 Getting a license from UIA requires a minimum investment of 50,000US$ and 100,000US$ for local and foreign investors respectively; local investors, however, can also proceed with the investment without licensing from UIA.

30 A recent investment survey (2001) covered 765 enterprises, mainly from the manufacturing sector (31%, 238 firms), wholesale & retail trade (21%) and financing (14%), but also from agriculture, hunting, forestry and fishing (9%), transport, storage & communication (7%), and construction (5%). Around 54% of the firms were domestically owned (more than 50% of shares were owned by Ugandans), while 46% were foreign-owned. Accordingly, there is an almost equal share of domestic and foreign companies in total investment (51%/49%) and employment (45%/55%). Most of the actual investment took place in form of plant and machinery (37%) and land and buildings (33%). The finance and the manufacturing sectors accounted for 24% and 23% of investment respectively. Moreover, the manufacturing sector recorded 26,875 jobs, thus contributing 33% to the total employment covered by the survey. Others were agriculture (19%), financing 14%, wholesale 11%, and construction 10% (BOU et al. 2004).

31 Data is taken from UBOS (statistical abstract, industrial production index) and the MFPED (Background to the Budget 2002/03).

more capital-intensive modern technology and the scrapping of more labour-intensive older technology to be among the main reasons for the stagnation in overall employment levels (low labour demand) during the period of concern (ibid, 14-5).[32] Further possible reasons could be the limited level of competitiveness, entrepreneurship and export ability of the young manufacturing sector, while it faces competitive pressures in a liberalised economy. The overall employment creation problems of the manufacturing sector should be noted.

Further, according to UBOS, the employment level in selected manufacturing firms has increased in recent years: from about 17,000 (2001) to around 29,000 (2004); with 131 and 157 establishments covered by the statistics respectively. Employment growth was particularly strong in 2002-04, with an increase in the number of employees of about 50% (19,000 to 29,000) (2005, 17). Notably, the severe electricity crisis which started in 2006 has likely resulted in a lowering of employment levels in the manufacturing sector.

Overall, the data presented gives an idea of the difficulties of job creation related to *formal* investments and private sector activity in Uganda. The overall experience of the last decade in this respect has lowered confidence in the job-creation capacity of new investment in the formal sector, especially when the investment comes with capital-intensive/labour-saving technology (see e.g. MGLSD 2004). Note, in this context, that a UNIDO study on productivity concluded that the technological change in the world in the last four decades (1960-2000), which however mainly took place in the industrialised countries, "has not been neutral regarding capital and labour; it has been labour saving" (Isaksson et al. 2005, 55).

This mix of challenges regarding formal sector employment growth, especially in the manufacturing sector (due to use of more capital-intensive modern technology in this sector), will likely remain present in the Ugandan economy. However, as will be shown below, GOU has to date not fully exploited certain support avenues for PSD in the country, e.g. with respect to sector-specific training and productivity measures which - had they been in place already - might have increased the speed and scope of job creation in the recent past.[33] Either way, (informal/formal) economic activities in *all* the sectors – agriculture, industry, trade and services - will remain vital for Uganda in terms of employment, income creation, HRD and thus economic and social development.

Structural transformation

Services is the biggest sector and contributes almost half to GDP

As a consequence of sectoral growth dynamics in the context of the country's economic and social recovery, structural transformation in the Ugandan economy has started to take place since the mid 1980s, in particular in the first reform decade (before 1997/98), with shifts in

32 Ssemogerere suggests that the "forces responsible for this stagnation included the adoption of more capital-intensive modern technology through privatization, the scrapping of more labour intensive older technologies, either due to lack of spare parts or repair and maintenance skills and computerization which started in Uganda in the 1990s, and, finally, the preference for semi-automated processes to reduce production errors from less skilled labour" (2005, 14). Ssemogerere also refers to findings of a Master's Dissertation, Makerere University, which conducted and analysed interviews with about 50 manufacturing firms (see Lutwama, 2004). According to Lutwama (2004) firms reported the use of capital-intensive methods of production to be the biggest constraint to employment growth (low labour absorption rate); this was followed by the level of demand for manufactured products.

33 See discussion of the flower sector in Box 3 as an illustration of the argument.

sectoral shares of GDP. Foremost were improvements in industry and services. Since then, there has been a relative slowdown in the pace of structural transformation (Bevan et al. 2003).[34] However, the trend remains: industry (20.6% of GDP in FY 04/05) and services (43.4%) increase their share of the Ugandan economy to about two-thirds of GDP. Services is the biggest sector at present, ahead of agriculture (36%) which experienced constantly declining shares (Tables 7 and 8, and Figure 4).

Table 7: Sectoral shares of GDP (%), 1986/87-2004/05

Sector/ FY	86/87	90/91	95/96	96/97	97/98	98/99	99/00	00/01	01/02	02/03	03/04	04/05
Agriculture	53.1	50.9	44.5	43.0	41.9	41.1	41.0	40.8	39.9	39.0	37.5	36.0
Industry	11.0	12.3	16.4	17.5	17.9	18.7	18.4	18.6	18.9	19.3	19.8	20.6
Services	36.0	36.8	39.1	39.5	40.3	40.2	40.5	40.6	41.2	41.7	42.7	43.4

Source: *MFPED (2006).*

Figure 4: Sectoral shares of GDP (%), 1995/96-2004/05

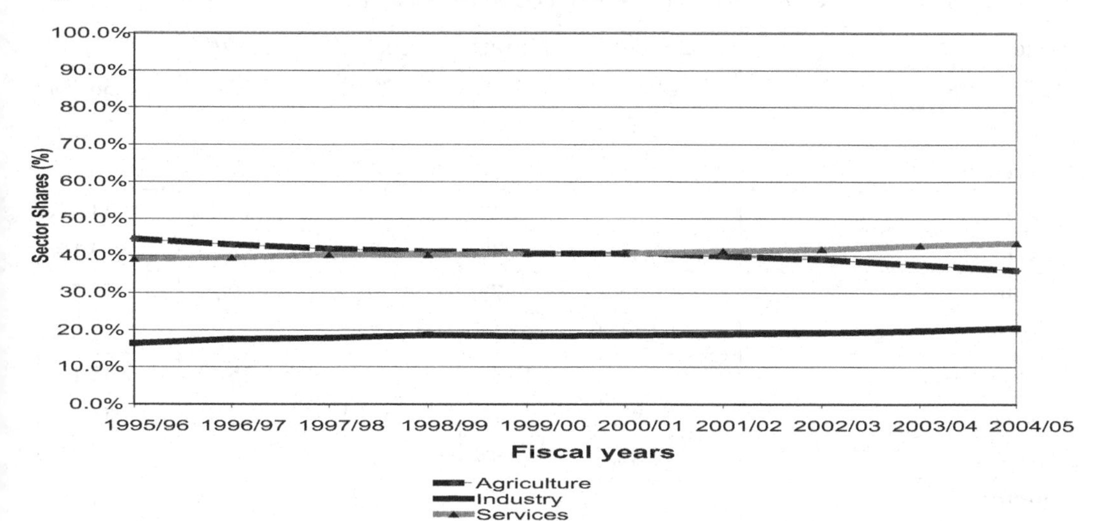

Source: *MFPED (2006).*

34 Collier and Reinikka are of the view that the sectoral changes (between mid 1980s and the end of 1990s) have "reflected recovery [from very low post-conflict to a normal level] rather than [actual] transformation" (2001, 457).

Table 8: Sectoral shares of GDP (%), average for five-year period, 1990/91-2004/05

Sector/Period	1990/91-1994/95	1995/96-1999/00	2000/01-2004/05
Agriculture	48.6	42.3%	38.7%
Industry	13.4	17.8%	18.2%
Services	38.0	39.9%	40.2%

Source: *MFPED (2006).*

Looking at the sectoral details in Table 9, especially for 2004/05, monetary agriculture (mainly cash and food crops) and non-monetary agriculture (food crops, livestock) contribute 21% and 15.1% to GDP respectively; manufacturing is at 9.6%, monetary construction 8.3%; wholesale/ retail trade 10.9%, transport and communication 7.7%, and community services 17.9%. Around one-fifth of the economy is reported to be non-monetary (non-monetary agriculture/ construction) creating a challenge for the authorities' agenda to increase commercialisation and market integration (e.g. market connectedness) of this part of the economy.

Table 9: Details of sectoral shares of GDP (%), 2000/01-2004/05

Sector	2000/01	2001/02	2002/03	2003/04	2004/05
Agriculture	40.8%	39.9%	**39.0%**	**37.5%**	**36.0%**
Monetary	22.8%	22.6%	22.5%	21.6%	21.0%
Cash crops	4.2%	4.2%	4.2%	4.0%	3.9%
Food crops	12.4%	12.4%	12.3%	11.8%	11.3%
Livestock	3.3%	3.3%	3.3%	3.1%	3.1%
Forestry	0.7%	0.7%	0.7%	0.7%	0.7%
Fishing	2.1%	2.1%	2.0%	2.0%	1.9%
Non-monetary	18.0%	17.3%	16.5%	15.9%	15.1%
Food crops	14.8%	14.1%	13.4%	12.8%	12.0%
Livestock	1.8%	1.8%	1.8%	1.7%	1.8%
Forestry	1.1%	1.1%	1.1%	1.1%	1.0%
Fishing	0.3%	0.3%	0.3%	0.3%	0.2%
Industry	**18.6%**	**18.9%**	**19.3%**	**19.8%**	**20.6%**
Mining & Quarrying	0.8%	0.8%	0.8%	0.8%	0.8%
Manufacturing	9.6%	9.5%	9.4%	9.3%	9.6%
Electricity & Water	1.4%	1.4%	1.4%	1.4%	1.4%
Construction	6.2%	6.6%	7.1%	7.6%	8.3%
Construction (non-monetary)	0.6%	0.6%	0.6%	0.6%	0.5%
Services	**40.6%**	**41.2%**	**41.7%**	**42.7%**	**43.4%**
Wholesale & Retail Trade	11.1%	11.1%	11.1%	10.9%	10.9%
Hotels & Restaurants	2.5%	2.8%	2.9%	3.2%	3.2%

Transport & communication	5.1%	5.4%	6.0%	6.9%	7.7%
Road	3.5%	3.5%	3.6%	3.6%	3.7%
Rail	0.2%	0.2%	0.1%	0.1%	0.1%
Air & supportive services	0.3%	0.3%	0.4%	0.4%	0.4%
Posts & Telecommunications	1.1%	1.4%	1.9%	2.7%	3.5%
Owner-occupied Dwellings (non-monetary)	3.6%	3.6%	3.7%	3.7%	3.7%
Community services	18.3%	18.4%	18.0%	18.0%	17.9%
Total monetary	77.8%	78.6%	79.2%	79.9%	80.7%
Total Non-monetary	**22.2%**	**21.4%**	**20.8%**	**20.1%**	**19.3%**

Source: *MFPED (2006).*

Comparing the details of the sub-sectoral shares of the GDP in five-year periods (Table 10) reveals that structural transformation at the sub-sectoral level was gradual; notably, manufacturing could not expand its share significantly and remains below 10%. This might be due to the fact that some sub-sectors are dependent on the domestic and regional market (relatively low purchasing power, low dynamics), and/or experience supply side difficulties to increase their outputs considerably and deliver competitively to export markets in the higher-value product range.

Table 10: Details of sectoral shares of GDP (%), average for five-year period, 1995/96-2004/05

Sector/Period	**1995/96-1999/00**	**2000/01-2004/05**
Agriculture	**42.3%**	**41.6%**
Monetary	23.4%	23.2%
Cash crops	4.6%	4.6%
Food crops	12.3%	12.2%
Livestock	3.5%	3.5%
Forestry	0.7%	0.7%
Fishing	2.3%	2.3%
Non-monetary	18.9%	18.4%
Food crops	15.6%	15.1%
Livestock	1.8%	1.8%
Forestry	1.2%	1.2%
Fishing	0.3%	0.3%
Industry	**17.8%**	**18.2%**
Mining & quarrying	0.6%	0.7%
Manufacturing	8.9%	9.2%
Electricity & Water	1.4%	1.4%
Construction	6.2%	6.3%
Construction (Non monetary)	0.6%	0.6%
Services	**39.9%**	**40.2%**
Wholesale & Retail Trade	11.1%	11.1%
Hotels & Restaurants	2.2%	2.3%

Transport & Communication	4.7%	4.8%
Road	3.4%	3.5%
Rail	0.2%	0.2%
Air & Support. Services	0.4%	0.4%
Posts & Telecommunications	0.7%	0.8%
Owner-occupied Dwellings (non monetary)	3.4%	3.4%
Community services	18.6%	18.6%
Total Monetary	72.7%	73.9%
Total Non-monetary	**27.3%**	**26.1%**

Source: *MFPED (2006).*

Notably, Bevan et al. (2003) point to the *major scale of transformation* required to achieve the p.c. income levels that are targeted for Uganda by 2023. Accordingly, this would imply agriculture shrinking to 18% of GDP, and industry and services rising to 35% (manufacturing to 22%) and 47% of GDP respectively. Sectoral growth rates in dynamic sectors such as industry would have to be substantial, i.e. around 10% in manufacturing, for a consistent 4% p.c. income growth. Implications include labour moving out of agriculture and agricultural productivity increasing (ibid).[35] Naturally, increased productivity and competitiveness is required for all sectors to foster transformation.

Upgraded set of skills and capabilities needed to continue transformation

The sectoral growth trends reviewed above suggest there is a need for improved *implementation*/or *revised* growth-related strategies and policies including PSD and HRD policies in order to allow structural transformation to continue dynamically. Supporting the emergence and stabilisation of a certain profit-investment-nexus in various sectors to attract additional investments and thus spur growth will be one of the challenges. Importantly, entrepreneurs would be better equipped to succeed in their investment plans if they have available the required skills and capabilities at the level of firms and SIs.[36] Tackling broad investment climate issues (security, infrastructure, etc.), as GOU and donors currently try to do, is vital to support private sector growth.

However, Lall's remarks about industrialisation prospects in Africa - which can also be used as a description of the Ugandan case - illustrate the *decisive role of human resources in industrial development and structural transformation.* An economic policy mix that is chiefly based on liberalisation and investment climate policies is insufficient and (potentially) harmful[37] - GOU needs to put more emphasis on building and deepening the range of capabilities needed by the economic transformation agenda.

35 Listed 'benchmarks' in the study are based on comparison with a number of countries that had previously experienced the p.c. income growth - and reached target income level - that is envisaged by Uganda. Further benchmarks (as % of GDP) include: exports at 25%, imports 29%, investment 26% (fuelled mainly by domestic investment), savings 23%, private credit 38%, aid 4% and domestic revenue 20%. Higher secondary enrolment and urbanisation (rural population at 65%) are others (Bevan et al. 2003).

36 The discussion on HRD requirements for economic development in Uganda will be deepened below.

37 At least for some sub-sectors and/or for some time.

> The basic problem of African industrial competitiveness lies not in market access to rich countries or the investment climate but in the low level of industrial capabilities that hold back a significant and sustained supply response. Africa cannot industrialise using its ample resources unless it develops the capabilities to handle ... complex technologies efficiently ... Many processing activities need advanced capital- and skill-intensive technologies to meet the rigorous standards of export markets; food products are particularly demanding because of sanitary requirements ... Africa thus needs to do much more than open up and improve the investment climate. Liberalization *can* spur efficiency, but where capabilities are too weak to cope with international competition, it can simply lead to the destruction of capacity and the dispersal of existing capabilities. In these conditions, local firms will not set up new facilities in areas where they face full international competition; nor will foreign investors enter. This is precisely the experience of much of Africa. A vigorous supply response is possible only if governments help new industrial capabilities to develop. Without this, the investment response of the private sector (local and foreign) is bound to be hesitant and inadequate (2005, 35-6, italic in original).

Environmental sustainability

The speed and level of economic growth and transformation have consequences for the level of environmental degradation and pollution in the country. For instance, the contribution of industrial firms to the pollution of the environment has been growing rapidly; they use obsolete equipment and environmentally inappropriate technologies, or discharge their effluent directly into their immediate ecosystems, especially open waters. Interventions are needed to train companies in environmentally-friendly production, which typically means making more efficient the use of inputs, production operations and logistics. This reduces production costs (e.g. utility bills) and results into environmental compliance and increased productivity and competiveness of enterprises. In this context, the Uganda Cleaner Production Centre (UCPC) was established in 2001, as a joint project of GOU and UNIDO, to assists firms to implement Cleaner Production by addressing key issues of: (1) raw material optimization, (2) resource efficiency especially energy and water, (3) pollution prevention, especially emissions and effluent, (4) good housekeeping, (5) food safety and hygiene, and (6) occupational health and safety (see Chapter 2 for details).[38]

External trade

Widening trade gap calls for efforts to increase value of exports

Over the period 1985/86-2004/05, the share of exports in GDP rose slightly from 13.2% to 13.5%, while the share of imports increased significantly from 15.7% to 27.2%, thus *widening the trade gap*. The trade imbalance (good account) stands at 828mUS$, an increase of two-thirds within five years (from 483mUS$). There is need to increase both import-substituting production and the volume/value of exports, which highlights the importance of improved competitiveness and supply-side capacities, including HR. On the export side, within five years total exports (goods and services) almost doubled from 677mUS$ to 1,270mUS$ in 2004/05, after an earlier decline. Earnings from goods exports increased by about two-thirds, and more than doubled from services exports. About 62% of total export earnings are currently derived from goods, down from 68% in 2000/01. The positive development in services (increasing share in total export earnings) is due to the growth in earnings from travel (about half of service earnings) as well as financial and other business services (Table 11).

38 See also Oxfam (2008) on 'Climate change and poverty in Uganda'.

Table 11: Export earnings (US $m), 1995/96-2004/05

Export-earnings (US $m)/FY	1995/96	2000/01	2001/02	2002/03	2003/04	2004/05
Total export earnings	723.31	677.34	699.02	775.83	1037.15	1270.50
Goods export earnings	588.03	458.30	474.04	507.91	647.18	782.66
Service export earnings	135.28	219.04	224.99	267.91	389.97	487.84
Goods account (Trade balance)	-450.31	-483.00	-529.84	-622.76	-663.64	-827.54

Source: *MFPED (2006).*

Exports recover from late 1990s decline; non-traditional exports on rise

With respect to goods exports, Figure 5 indicates the declining share of the country's leading export commodity, coffee, and the considerable growth of other goods, including non-traditional exports. It also reveals the drop in exports from 1996/97 up to 2000/01 (due to the TOT shock in the coffee sector): Goods exports earnings in 2004/05 are about 100mUS$ higher than the amount in 1996/97.

Figure 5: Trends in goods export earnings (1992/93-2004/05)

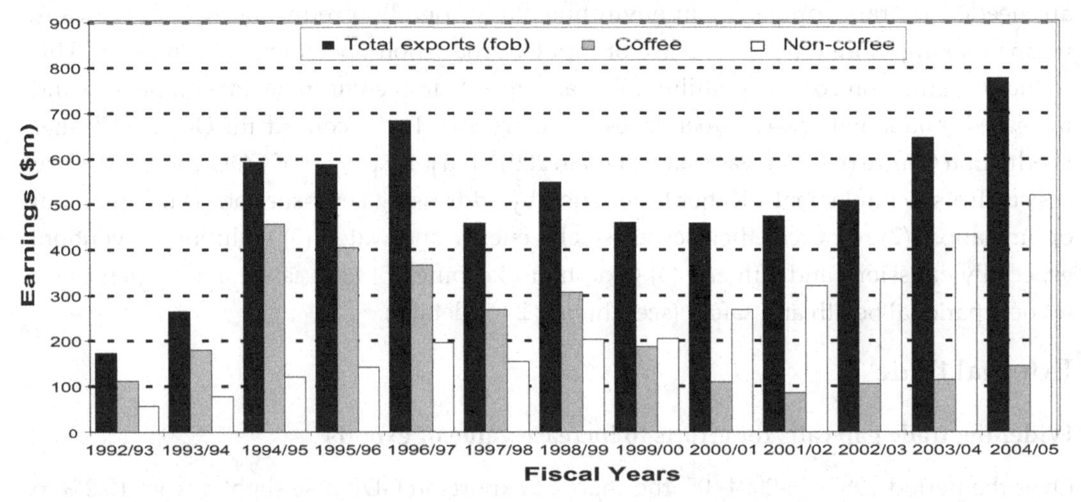

Source: *MFPED (2006).*

The main six top export earners of the Ugandan economy are: coffee and fish (above 100mUS$ each) as well as cotton, tobacco, tea and flowers (between about 30-40US$m each) (Figure 6). All sectors experienced growth in total earnings in the early 2000s. The growth record of the two non-traditional exports, fish and flowers, has been significant and is regarded as an example of non-traditional sub-sector development. Hides and skins have lost two-thirds in earnings (mainly due to unit price decline), and are at 6.4mUS$.[39]

39 Fish earnings have reduced in late 2000s due to depletion of fish resources (overfishing) in Lake Victoria, among other reasons.

Figure 6: Trends in goods export earnings (US$m), above 10US$m, 2000/01-2004/05

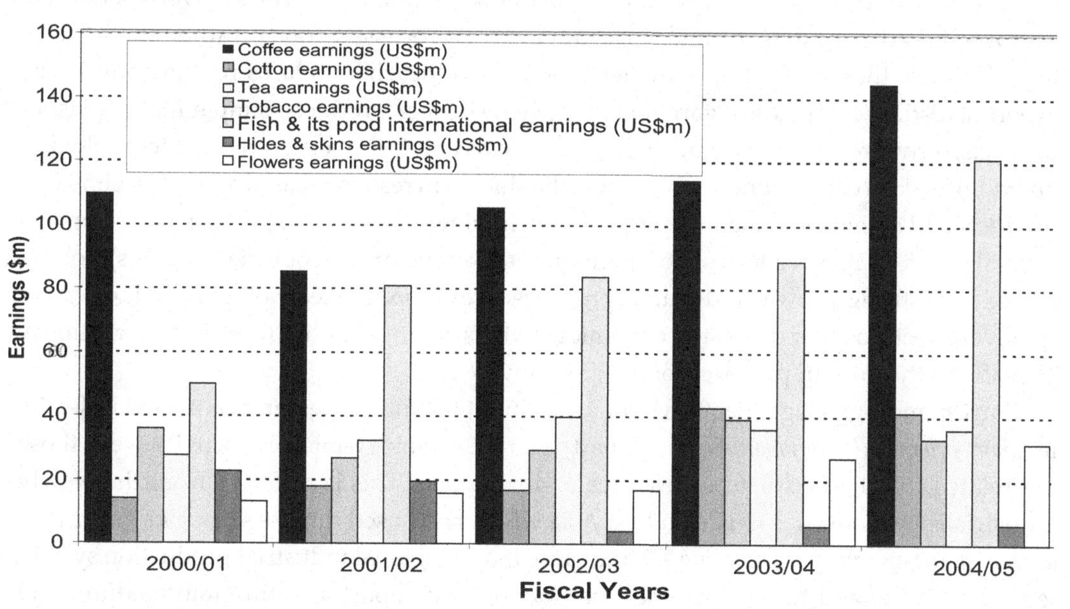

Source: *MFPED (2006).*

Figure 7 shows export goods that had annual earnings around/below 10mUS$ in 2000/01. Maize and beans doubled their earnings by 2004/05; simsim earnings increased fivefold (unit price increase).

Figure 7: Trends in goods export earnings (US$m), below/around 10US$m, 2000/01-2004/05

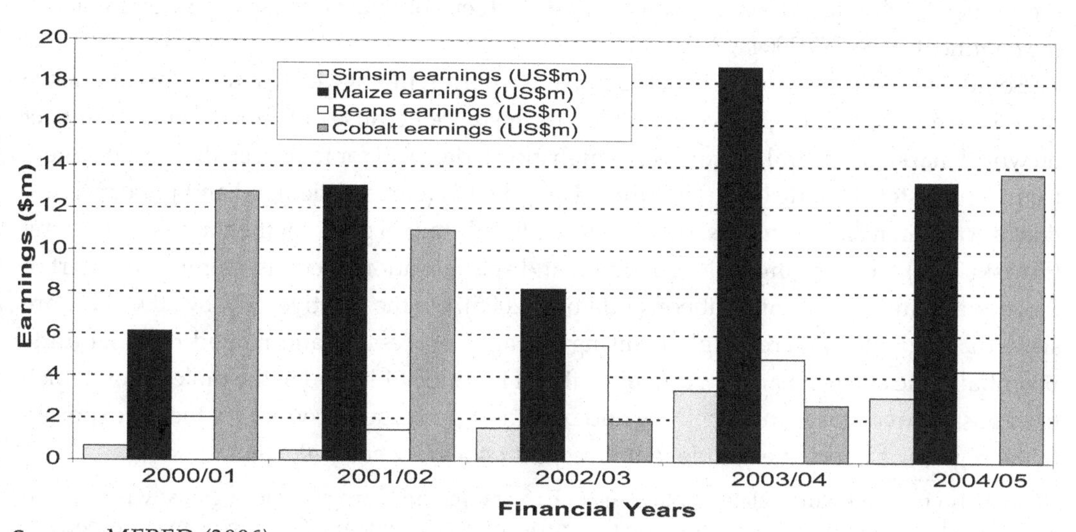

Source: *MFPED (2006).*

Composition of exports: overwhelmingly resource-based products

In terms of the technology composition of exports, Ugandan exports are overwhelmingly resource-based products (primary products and processed food), rather than 'pure' manufactures: there is no major low-technology product that features prominently in the export statistics (e.g. textiles, garments, footwear/leather products, simple metal/plastics products, furniture, glassware, and toys/games). This points to a relatively weak technological upgrading record of the economy, regarding the shift from resource-based and low-technology products and activities to medium and high-technology ones. The export structure appears generally and in relative terms (compared to other developing countries/regions) not yet geared very strongly towards dynamic products, use of modern technologies, and beneficial spillover effects to other domestic economic activities and institutions (positive externalities). This affects the growth prospects of the economy.

Correspondingly, Uganda, for various reasons at the time of research, attracted little FDI in *export-oriented ('pure') manufacturing*, particularly technology-intensive activities (e.g. those not related to inherited natural resource endowments). This is different from the Newly Industrialising Countries (NICs) in East Asia which have used diverse strategies - *some with a strong focus on capability building* - to integrate into the global industrial production system (e.g. into GVCs) and to improve their production and export structure into medium and high-tech products (Box 2 and Figure 8). It is not clear to what extent further dynamics will allow new entrants (from lower costs locations) obtain a stake in global manufacturing (Lall 2004a). This applies especially to firms from countries with low industrial capabilities, such as Uganda. The necessity of having policies and programmes that (a) support building of initial local capabilities and subsequent deepening, and (b) attract external forces to mobilise the internal potential, however, remain relevant to foster growth and upgrading in latecomer economies (ibid). The low level of manufacturing-oriented FDI is a characteristic of many economies in SSA, questioning to some extent the focus of PSD policies and programmes on the continent (UNIDO 2004a, 2004b, 2005d).

Some commodity sectors, in which Uganda is a player, might well (continue to) experience price increases, hence respective dynamics; for instance because of China's demand impact on world markets (natural resources), or high global demand for food. Yet, due to the largely (semi-) subsistence mode of agriculture in Uganda this (current) demand and price increase does not automatically or necessarily translate into substantial gains for the country's economy (Polaski 2006).[40] Enhancing scale economies and specialisation effects is an important part of the required improvements (Gibbon and Ponte 2005). On the positive side, by 2008 there are signs that Uganda is increasingly realising her agro-processing and related regional trade potentials. The entry of Sameer Agricultural and Livestock Limited in the milk sector, which has boosted investment in machinery and output of processed products (which is exported to the region), is a recent example in this respect (Wiegratz et al. 2007b).

40 See also relevant work related to the 'Asian Drivers' research programme; a globally networked research programme which focuses on the impact of newly dynamic Asian economies - especially large economies such as China and India - on low-income economies. The programme is coordinated by the Institute of Development Studies at the University of Sussex (Brighton, UK): http://www.ids.ac.uk/ids/global/asiandriversindex.html. See for instance Kaplinsky et al. (2006) as well as Kaplinsky and Morris (2006a, 2006b, 2008). See also Goldstein et al. (2006).

Box 2: Successful integration into the global production system and trends in export of manufacturers

The development of the NICs in East Asia is closely linked to the evolution in the technological structure (technology composition of products/activities) of global manufacturing and trade over the last 20 years. Specifically, the shift from resource-based (RB, e.g. processed foods and tobacco, simple wood products, refined petroleum products, leather, organic chemicals) and low-technology products/activities (LT, e.g. textiles, garments, footwear/leather products, toys/games, simple metal/plastics products, furniture and glassware) to medium and high-technology ones (MHT, automobiles, industrial chemicals, machinery, standard electrical, and electronic products; complex electrical and electronic products, aircraft, fine chemicals and pharmaceuticals). Notably, different technology groups have different growth trends/prospects (growth tends to rise with technological complexity), development implications and capability requirements (UNIDO 2004a, 135). "The technological structure of manufacturing in developing countries is upgrading in line with mature industrial countries. The share of MHT activities in MVA [manufacturing value added] in the developing world has risen from 41 percent in 1980 to 53 percent in 2000, while that of RB has fallen from 37 to 31 percent and of LT from 23 to 16 percent. These figures are strongly influenced by the evolution of East Asia, and the structure differs greatly from one region to another. The least advanced structure is that of SSA excluding South Africa" (ibid). Examples from the NICs in East Asia demonstrate that successful developing countries (DCs) have used different strategies to integrate into the global production system and improve their structural drivers of competitiveness. One can group them in three categories (Lall 2004a): (1) 'Autonomous' strategies, that mainly seek to build/deepen strong technological capabilities in local firms through decisive and selective industrial policies, including (a) restricting FDI in certain activities/(infant) sectors, and (b) targeting FDI for certain activities and functions they wish to enter (Republic of Korea, Taiwan Province of China; the first-tier-NICs), (2) Strong FDI-reliant strategies, that seek to plug into TNC production systems by supplying labour-intensive products and components, yet, that do not put strong emphasis on building local capabilities (Malaysia, Philippines, Thailand; second tier-NICs), (3) A mixture of the two: heavy reliance on TNCs combined with industrial policy that targets skills upgrading etc. within the TNC's global production structure (Singapore). It is clear that the global industry and the 'rules of the game' (e.g. trade, investment, and intellectual property policies under WTO) have changed since the rise of the NICs. Also, according to the literature, the spread of integrated production systems and the fact that certain technologies are increasingly available only through these systems make it more risky for latecomer countries to follow the autonomous path. As GVCs have so far found their way only to a few DCs, that now enjoy a first mover advantage, it is uncertain to what extent further fragmentation dynamics will allow new entrants (from countries with lower costs yet also low capabilities) to get their stake, e.g. firms from Uganda.

Besides, in terms of world exports of manufacturers, innovation-based activities/products are gaining at the expense of others. MT products are still the largest segment, with a stagnating share since the mid 1980s. Instead, "[h]igh technology products have raised their share of trade from the lowest to the second highest - they are now the main engines of growth in world trade. Primary and resource-based products have lost ground [and now account for 30% of world manufactured exports], and low technology products have stagnated since the mid-1990s. Good 'positioning' requires countries move into more innovative products [and activities]; the Asian Tigers, including China, have done just this; their recent export growth comes largely from [the shift from non-technology to] technology-intensive products" (Lall 2005, 7).

Notably, the value of exports from developing countries has increased in all technology groups in recent years, yet the increase was highest in the technology-intensive groups. However, it is not clear if/to which extent these trends will continue. Notably, in the period 1985-2000 all four categories of manufactured exports (by both developed and developing countries) grew faster than primary products (ibid, 8). The developing world's share in world MVA increased from 14% to 24% within two decades (1980-2000); East Asia including China (EA1) and SSA including South Africa (SSA1) account for 13.9% and 0.8% respectively (year 2000). South Africa accounts for 44% of SSA' MVA. Within the developing world's MVA, EA1 accounts for 58%, SSA1 for 3.4% (2000). In the same vein, the developing world's share in world manufactured exports doubled within the same period (1980-2000) to 27%; EA1 and SSA1 account for 18.4% and 0.6% respectively; within the developing world's manufactured exports, EA1 accounts for nearly 70%, SSA1 for 2.3% (2000). Export success in the developing world is highly concentrated, and increasingly so: The top 10 countries provided 81% (and the top 20, 90%) of developing country manufactured exports in 2000, up from 63% and 80% in 1981 (UNIDO 2004a, 183-6, Lall et al. 2004b, 18).

Figure 8: Share of high-tech products in a country's exports of manufactured products (%), March 2005

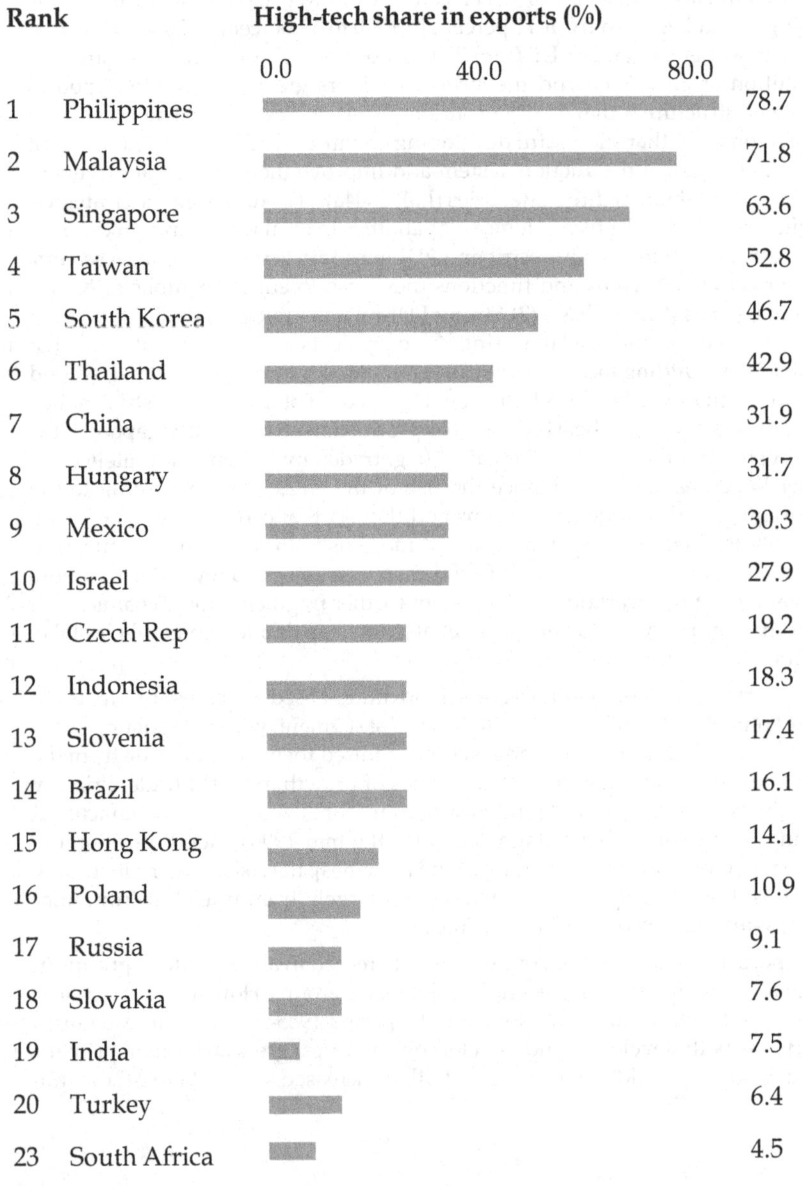

Rank	Country	High-tech share in exports (%)
1	Philippines	78.7
2	Malaysia	71.8
3	Singapore	63.6
4	Taiwan	52.8
5	South Korea	46.7
6	Thailand	42.9
7	China	31.9
8	Hungary	31.7
9	Mexico	30.3
10	Israel	27.9
11	Czech Rep	19.2
12	Indonesia	18.3
13	Slovenia	17.4
14	Brazil	16.1
15	Hong Kong	14.1
16	Poland	10.9
17	Russia	9.1
18	Slovakia	7.6
19	India	7.5
20	Turkey	6.4
23	South Africa	4.5

Source: *http://www.global-production.com/scoreboard/indicators/hitechexports.htm, (accesse 01/03/06).*

Interventions needed for new products and activities

One of the challenges for Uganda regarding the development of export-oriented capabilities is support of competitiveness and expansion strategies with regard to *new* export products, services and activities, as well as innovative solutions and models in the areas of business processes, organisation, logistics and new-market penetration. Research would suggest that some of the new Ugandan export products - including those arising out of fragmentation of production within GVCs - could likely have a relatively *high value-to-weight ratio* (light, high-value products, to overcome landlocked-status related transport disadvantages that increase transportation costs on import/export side) and *relatively low entry requirements*, such as low technology and/or very labour-intensive sectors and value chain segments (Lall et al. 2004a).[41] Relatively low entry barriers, however, also bear the risk of 'fallacy of composition': Due to the simultaneous market entry by several DCs pursuing the same diversification strategy, competition increases and prices/returns fall. Importantly, actors working in production and trade of *existing* export products need significant support as well, to improve their value chain operations, expand production and improve their products, respond to changing requirements (standards), or attract new buyers (Wiegratz et al. 2007a, 2007b).

Besides, Uganda "appears to also have a competitive advantage in some manufactured goods with respect to countries/regions that are even more landlocked than itself" (WB 2006a, ix).[42] Further, Uganda could become a *regional production and trading hub*. However, this (or the extent of it) is not an automatic outcome. Efforts will have to be increased in PSD issue areas such as HRD, support systems and incentives for diversification and expansion of production.

There is ample reason to emphasise Uganda's "natural advantage in agro-based products" (ibid). Crucially, again, this advantage needs to be combined with increased efforts in respective HRD and technology areas to allow *competitive* processing (value-addition) for export markets (Lall 2004a, 2005). "[T]he possession of natural resources gives an independent competitive advantage, but only for its extraction; subsequent processing ... needs competitive capabilities" (2004a, 24). HR and productivity need to be enhanced across the exporting manufacturing and (traditional/non-traditional) agro-export sectors. In this context, there seems need for an advanced debate on *how* to *create new competitive advantages* in the 'modern' endowments such as human capital (technological knowledge/capabilities, technical skills, social skills, knowledge) and SIs - in other words, those competitiveness factors that are *unrelated* to the country's natural resource endowments.[43] In the same vein, it is vital to strongly consider export diversification into products that are unrelated to the country's original (inherited) natural resource endowment and which could *coexist* with resource-based sectors. Efforts to attract call-centre operators to Uganda is an example in this direction. It is likely that competition between countries in the region to attract such investors will increase further.

41 Fish and flowers are examples in the Ugandan context of products with a high value-to-weight ratio. Mobile phone assembling would be another example which e.g. Rwanda seems to target (East African Business Week 2006). Further, in export services the landlocked-status and related transport costs seems of lower concern (WB 2006).

42 Examples include southern Sudan, eastern Democratic Republic of Congo, Rwanda, and Burundi.

43 See e.g. 'Building knowledge-based competitive advantages in China and India' (Altenburg et al. 2006).

Importantly for development, respective value chains (VCs) in *agro-business* (or other dynamic natural resource-based sectors) can be technologically dynamic and have technology/ knowledge-intensive activities, such as packaging, food preservation and safety, marketing and logistics, offering possibilities for increased learning, skills use, upgrading, value-adding and productivity.[44] Economic policies and programmes need to be 'in touch' and support such HR-related dynamics in the domestic industry. Take the example of the flower industry, which operates with state-of-the-art and fast-changing technologies to compete in global markets:

> "Ugandan floriculture demands technical focus: cutting-edge techniques associated with hydroponics (growing without soil), recycling, irrigation, filtration, and sterilisation are routinely practised. The number of hectares under hydroponics will increase to over 50% of production area under the sector's expansion plan. New techniques are constantly being introduced to reduce chemical usage in Ugandan floriculture. Access to trained staff is of paramount importance for operation of farms using *fast developing new technologies*" (Henderson 2005, slide 12, italic added).

It is crucial to consider that competitive firms from *China and India* are increasingly present in low-technology, labour-intensive segments/products in manufacturing and services respectively, raising supply capacity and competitive pressures and thus the need for responses from affected countries in SSA. Increased competition results from surplus capacity and surplus supply affecting competition for SSA producers in both domestic and (third country) export markets (Kaplinsky and Morris 2006b). China's economic expansion has also contributed to declining prices for some manufacturing goods/product lines in some sectors of the global industry (Kaplinsky 2006).

Recent findings of sub-sectoral studies (furniture, clothing/textiles) suggest that the impact of the Asian drivers of change in the global economy will generally make it *more difficult* for SSA economies to realise their industrialisation potential in a competitive and liberalising global economy and progress according to their economic and social aspirations, particularly if efforts that aim at increased competitiveness - via enhanced operating efficiency (firm level and VC efficiency), HR, hard/soft infrastructure - are not undertaken effectively. Indeed, the rise of China and India in the global economy impacts on possibilities for future trajectories of industrial development and diversification in SSA - and of course other developing regions, such as Latin America - in both export and home markets. The risk is exclusion or squeezing of SSA producers. Naturally, this discussion also touches upon the need for specific trade policies, e.g. preferences for SSA producers in external markets (Kaplinsky and Morris 2006a, viii-ix, 2006b, 2008, Kaplinsky et al. 2006, Goldstein et al. 2006).[45] Future impacts are likely

---

44 There is a blurring of boundaries between traditional and 'new' sectors/activities, for example between natural resource based activities and knowledge industries. ICT for example can help reducing coordination costs of local firms operating in agro-GVCs. See also the biotechnology example (Ferranti et al. 2002, 3).

45 Estimates of possible impacts of different Doha Round scenarios indicate that East African countries might well lose in any of the tested outcomes; among others, due to East Africa's large, uncompetitive and low-productivity subsistence agriculture (Polaski 2006). In particular, the poor countries/regions in the model, including East Africa, might lose unskilled jobs in the manufacturing industry due to intensified competition in several manufacturing sectors (including apparel and metal products) which might lead to slightly declining world prices. Some estimates suggest overall considerable world price changes (ibid): "World export and import prices for all agricultural products increase under the main scenarios. By contrast, liberalization of manufactured goods intensifies competition in several manufacturing sectors...and world prices decline slightly. These price trends are at odds with a longstanding historical pattern of

to affect level of jobs and poverty. Already, there are cases of severe job losses and firms that have to undertake backward moves towards the low end of VCs (downgrading: from furniture manufacturers to exporters of raw material). Importantly, these significant adverse impacts on certain sectors of SSA economies are recorded at a relatively *early* stage of China's expansion (ibid).[46]

There are a range of industries and market niches (e.g. the food industry) where prospects have not been adversely affected by the rise of China and India in global industry, for instance in complementary industries and products where there are chances of win-win-scenarios (ibid). Capital-intensive resource extraction industries (minerals, oil) are likely to be the main beneficiaries of recent global changes. Yet, patterns of ownership, income distribution, and poverty effects are different in these industries to those in labour-intensive industries (Kaplinsky and Morris 2006a, vi-vii).

Overall, the base line seems to be that "given the sheer size of these two countries and the enormous emerging supply of highly-skilled researchers, engineers, technicians and skilled workers, technological progress of China and India poses a ... [great] challenge for the [economic aspirations of the] rest of the world" (Altenburg et al. 2006, 4-5). Uganda's specialisation and diversification moves need to take these effects into account. The impression, however, is that Uganda's policy and support environment is to date still inadequate to respond opportunely to export competitiveness and HRD issues. Such inadequacies undermine processes of productivity catch-up (e.g. learning and innovation), and sector growth and hamper overcoming market and institutional failures in the development of skills and capabilities in the (new) export sectors. Box 3 illustrates the various dimensions of this argument for the flower sector; the case is an example of the difficulties that actors of a *new export sector* can face in Uganda, despite the expressed commitment of GOU to export growth and structural transformation. Furthermore, a study of the country's major export products and services to the European Union revealed the *persistent* challenge for exporting firms of developing appropriate HR (capabilities, skills, attitudes, and mind-set) among the workforce (Wiegratz et al. 2007a).

Indeed, the envisaged upgrading of the Ugandan production and trade structure and thus the "graduation to more complex transactions places greater demands upon the institutions and the professions needed for a market economy" (Collier and Reinikka 2001, 459). Developing adequate and permanent SIs - instead of over-reliance on short-term projects or on-off initiatives - for HRD in the private sector is one of the most important aspects in this regard. The described deficiencies are a competitiveness disadvantage for young exporting firms from Uganda in comparison to their competitors in other countries, who can utilise a more effective and focused support system, including a better education and training system (ETS). These disadvantages increase market entry costs and are a hindrance (disincentive) to export-oriented diversification, especially to more demanding markets.

---

declining prices for agricultural commodities relative to manufactured goods. Trade liberalization for manufactured goods increases demand for unskilled labor in most of the developing world. However, wages do not increase, due to the abundant supply of labor and the fact that liberalized trade in labor-intensive manufactures drives down world prices for such goods" (ibid, ix).

46 Note that China's manufacturing export sector has experienced severe problems since late 2008 due to the global financial crisis and its repercussions (e.g. decline in demand). Reportedly, thousands of exporting firms have closed.

Notably in this context: according to an enterprise survey, export growth in the mid 1990s (1995-1997) was almost entirely (95%) due to increased sales by incumbent exporters to European and other non-African countries. *Only a few new exporting firms entered the market;* they were relatively small and focused on regional markets only. This points to difficulties faced by newcomers entering (especially non-African) export markets (Gauthier 2001, 246-52), probably not only in terms of costs but also skills, knowledge, know-how, technology, and links to buyers.[47] If the status quo in terms of policy and support environment, including HR, cannot be improved, Uganda might fall short of or further delay exploiting her export potential, especially regarding processed products.[48]

Box 3: Competitiveness strategies, skills requirements and the state: The flower sector experience

The flower sector, now one of Uganda's largest export earners, transformed from infancy stage to a vibrant and competitive export business with a growth rate of about 14% and a total investment of estimated 60mUS$. Uganda is the fifth-largest African exporter of cut flowers, after Kenya, Zimbabwe, South Africa and Tanzania (2006). About 60% of Dutch chrysanthemum cuttings production comes from Uganda. The sector consists of 20 exporting companies with relatively strong management and technical expertise, and, in total, 205 hectares under production. Five companies are joint ventures between Ugandan and foreigners and six are 100% Ugandan-owned. The industry directly employs about 6,000 people, of whom approx. 80% are female workers (2004). The sector provided a stimulus for the supporting industries. The sector's annual export revenue was about 32mUS$ (2004); it also puts an estimated 20mUS$ p.a. back into the economy (wages, transport fees, packaging). Currently, 20% of exports are sold through Dutch auction houses and 80% are direct sales (some years ago auction sales were predominant). According to the floriculture competitiveness strategy for the period 2005-2010, the growers aim at export earnings/revenue of at least 50mUS$ per year, which would increase the level of direct jobs in the industry to 10,000 (benefitting up to 60,000 Ugandans). Half of this growth is expected to come from new investment, another 30% from expansion into new areas/products and *20% from productivity improvements (new technology)*. The strategy focuses on building a competitive industry which is able to exploit market opportunities through strategies for new market positioning and new, competitive products. To accomplish these investment and growth goals the sector will have to address the following issues in coming years:

- improve, differentiate and diversify products, including related services,
- penetrate new markets (e.g. Germany, Dubai, Russia, UK, US, Middle East and South Africa) which points to a need for strategies regarding products and access points, e.g. participate in bidding by e-mail auction, respond to demand for cut flowers in large retail markets/ supermarkets through operation of flower bouquet-houses, and build direct relationship with US industry,
- realise economies of scale through collective action: operation of joint procurement and marketing services and training and R&D programmes through the sector's association (Uganda Flower Exporters Association, UFEA),
- strengthen quality, compliance to industry-wide ecological and social standards as well as buyer-specific requirements, branding and labelling, reputation (professionalism, quality, services, and consistency) and marketing,
- find innovative and cost-effective solutions for transport, logistics, and distribution (e.g. establishment of own repacking/distribution facility in Europe),

47 The survey in 1998 covered 177 firms (mainly from manufacturing/agro-processing sub-sectors). See also Wiegratz et al. (2007a) regarding challenges that Ugandan exporters face when they try to enter and compete in GVCs.

48 Further noticeable in this context, a comparison of the WB's survey of 1998 and 2002/03 states: "The share of firms exporting remained almost the same over the period, at 14 percent. The share of total manufacturing output exported was also similar, at around 10 percent. But differences emerge across firm size classes. Larger firms reported exporting a significantly larger share of their output in 2002/03 (47.5 percent) than in 1998 (31.4 percent)" (WB 2004b, 53). See also Chapter 7 on discussion of market failures that hinder diversification (including into new export activities) and thus require a policy response.

- deepen linkages/collaboration with domestic suppliers and support industries (chemical supply, packaging, transport),
- increase productivity (technology use), R&D (industry-research nucleus) and skills training and improve the situation regarding finance, access to land and infrastructure.

Given this list of competitiveness challenges and opportunities, the related areas for specific state interventions as well as collaboration with the industry should be straightforward. Yet, up to the mid 2000s, the record of GOU's interaction with the sector is reported to have been quite poor, which is surprising given the potential and the need for a partnership during the sector's recent dynamic growth period. Inadequacies in skills development as well as innovation and learning are as follows (based on information and views of sector representatives and experts provided in early 2006):

(1) Inadequacies of SIs for skills development and training: The flower sector suffers from insufficient supply of a highly skilled Ugandan workforce in some relevant areas of expertise, e.g. farm management and supervision. Thus, the sector is still dependent to a certain extent on foreign experts, e.g. from Kenya and the Netherlands. Recently, the industry launched a training programme ('Applied Tropical Floriculture') in two agricultural institutions with the help of Dutch funding; Bukalasa College and Mountains of the Moon University. In the past, there was no agricultural training college in the country that had a good floriculture-oriented programme. Then, there is a newly opened horticulture course at Makerere University, and the institution plans to start a new course in flower farming. The current horticulture course appears to be too theoretical, with little concern for applied and industry issues; graduates and lecturers generally show little aspiration to engage with farm-level issues. Consequently, the industry rarely employs talented and committed graduates from the course. Therefore, UFEA has been active in developing programmes (often in collaboration with foreign training providers and support from donors) that incorporate the sector's technical training needs. UFEA has been involved in conducting practical Applied Tropical Floriculture Courses (ATFC) in the past years in conjunction with Makerere University and USAID. The focus was on training 20 farm supervisors each year in the theory and practice of floriculture, which included a trip to flower farms in Kenya as well as to auctions, buyers, and flower farms in Holland. Over the 10 years that the course has been in place, 196 supervisors in the Ugandan flower industry have been trained. At the moment the ATFC is presented as a short course training which runs for three consecutive days every month. A new course is supposed to focus on Human Resource Management (HRM) in particular sections of the farms.

Other HRD-related efforts include: training to improve the cooperation, learning and communication structures (e.g. between senior management and farm supervisors) within a flower farm and between farms and firms in the industry, and upgrading of training programmes, particularly at middle management and supervisor level (e.g. train the trainer) to get better results in terms of workers' training and subsequent performance. There are efforts at some farms to enable all staff levels to be well represented on the elected workers' committees. Many farms have various incentive programmes to enhance productivity where it is practical to do so. All UFEA flower exporters' farms follow the Horticultural Code of Conduct and are audited under MPS/Eurepgap for compliance with international health and safety requirements, traceability of product, and worker welfare. The farms have their own health clinics and some have built schools and sports facilities. According to international experts, Uganda apparently has the best trained middle management on flower farms in East Africa, mainly a result of the UFEA training programmes. A comprehensive horticulture training development centre is now in the planning process. Importantly, the industry has discovered direct links between HRM and the quality and uniformity of the flowers exported from the various farms.

(2) No significant links between the sector and research institutions exist. In the context of government's agenda of poverty eradication and subsequent focus on small-farmer support, the agricultural institutes mostly carry out research on traditional crops - seemingly assuming that is the major way forward. The Plan for Modernization (PMA), National Agricultural Advisory Services (NAADS), and National Agricultural Research Organisation (NARO) together do not offer significant research and extension services (technical knowledge etc.) to the sector, or undertake significant initiatives to transfer foreign technology. The growers try to carry out some in-house research activities, often with the help of foreign expertise, or hire the expensive services of laboratories abroad. For instance, rose varieties were tried and tested at a trial centre managed by UFEA. The existing laboratories in Uganda cannot carry out sophisticated analysis and testing of the flower crops, in part due to lack of applied and sector-specific knowledge and researchers who specialise in flowers. As a result, the loss of opportunities for industry focused research and learning for the local universities/laboratories has been substantial. For its expansion

(including product diversification) strategies, the sector needs a comprehensive and industry-wide R&D programme and a state-of-the-art facility for testing, demonstration and upgrading of products and production techniques; negotiations with stakeholders are under way in this respect.

(3) GOU did not undertake efforts to support or initiate linkage building and deepening between the sector and its supplier industries, e.g. through local sourcing programmes. The same holds with regard to supplier development initiatives (e.g. on product development and quality). The industry has worked with the existing players of the domestic supply chain autonomously from public institutions, e.g. in the area of standardisation, quality and design of packaging boxes which, despite some successes, remain a constant challenge and thus an area for constant interaction between the players. At current levels, the flower sector's business with the domestic packaging industry has an annual size of around 1.1mUS$. Yet, the flower sector still imports polythene and non-paper packaging inputs of around 0.5mUS$ because the items are not made and/or available in Uganda. Considering that other agro-industry clusters (e.g. fish processing industry) likely have similar packaging requirements, collective action among these clusters and the packaging business could lead to increased investment in related production. Again, a more hands-on government/bureaucracy would probably encourage and coordinate such important cross-sector activities in a timely manner.49 Further, there is no floriculture sector policy in place; there are still doubts in the industry if the Ministry of Agriculture, Animal Industries and Fisheries recognises floriculture as an agro product. Government programmes do not seem to target or reach the sector. However, the sector is looking for incentive-schemes to be put in place in the near future. The strategic support from the Uganda Export Promotion Board (e.g. regarding in market information, marketing) has been insufficient for many years, yet improved recently. There are also good or improving working relationships between the sector and public institutions such as the Revenue Authority, Civil Aviation Authority, Ministry of Finance, and National Environment Management Authority.

The described deficiencies have not only slowed down the process of expansion (volume, product diversification) and competitiveness improvement of the industry, but have also limited employment and skills growth and the spillover effects to related sectors and institutions. In the absence of active and coordinated support for the development of the industry from most public institutions, the sector (according to its own accounts) has done almost everything which could bring progress in the different competitiveness areas on its own, with financial and technical support from donor partners (especially USA, Netherlands). However, the donor support cannot be regarded as a sufficient and sustainable substitute for the state support. It is also regrettable that positive developments in the sector have not been sufficiently applied by GOU to build and strengthen the related domestic agro-business capabilities, administrative competencies and knowledge in both domestic supplier firms and SIs (for research, technical advice, technology transfer and improvement) so that the firms/SIs can fruitfully engage with the industry. One of the problematic issues with respect to developing stronger domestic suppliers and research institutions through linkage building with the industry is that the critical level of (technical, technological, managerial) capabilities and capacities needed for interaction with and inclusion in the sector's VC increases gradually over time due to technological progress, various upgrading activities of the existing players, or changes in VC organisation. Thus the above-mentioned failure to more vehemently engage other domestic players - with view to developing their capabilities - has already delayed the catch-up process and, consequently, lowered potential for growth dynamics, thus enlarging the gap between the existing and the required capabilities for any future engagement of those domestic firms and institutions currently outside the VC. The effects of industry agglomeration and path-dependency show the cumulative costs of this strategic failure in the medium and long term, more so if this situation remains unchanged.

In summary, the cooperation between the young and (for some time) dynamic flower sector and the public sector raises doubts about the level of current commitment and capacity among some decision makers and technocrats to consistently support the development of other upcoming, dynamic growth sectors that authorities, according to their public statements and policies, at least, wish to see established and growing.[50] Because attracting and keeping such industries in the country means exactly this: to understand their business and support their

49 Note that GOU has succeeded in attracting a large scale packaging manufacturer in the late 2000s.

50 Note for instance also that firms in the tourism sector complain regularly, according to local newspapers, about insufficient state support for the sector's expansion.

efforts in maintaining and improving their competitiveness, including in HRD areas. In the words of a former UFEA executive director: "Investment incentives are more than finance or infrastructure support or tax incentives; it is the responsiveness of the total package to industry needs and the quality of public-private sector partnerships and working relationships that 'sell' a country. All partnership areas represent critical aspects of the total incentives package" (Henderson 2005, slide 22). See also Wiegratz et al. (2007a) for information on the flower sector's efforts to survive and grow in the global industry.[51]

Uganda's exports are further characterised by fluctuating price structures (TOT shocks) which can undermine sub-sectoral developments, e.g. weaken incentives for market entry, or investment in equipment and technology, skills development, or productivity improvements (Figure 9). In fact, external (favourable/adverse) TOT changes were a major force of rapid output growth as well as slumps in Uganda in the 1990s. The TOT rose from an index of 100 in 1991 to 208 in 1994. It deteriorated thereafter to 163 in 1999 and even 68 in 2002, and stands now at 73 (Ssemogerere 2005, ix-x, 29).

Figure 9: Trends in export price changes (%), 2000/01-2004/05

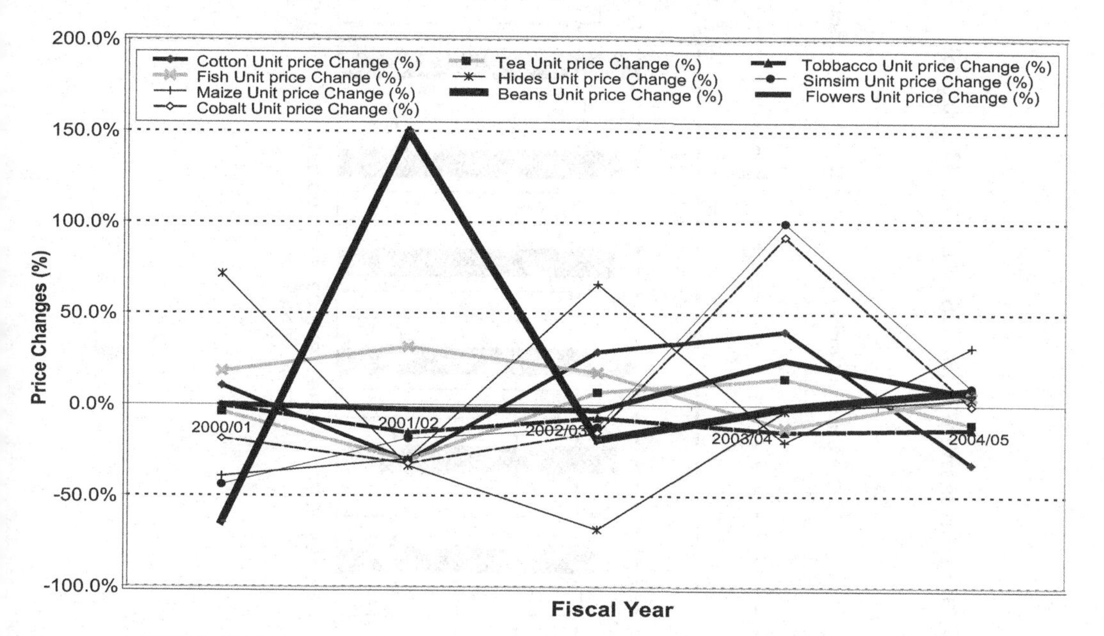

Source: *MFPED (2006)*

Finally, the growth in imports, particularly private sector imports, is considerable. Since 2000, the value of total imports increased by around two-thirds to 1.600mUS$. A significant portion of imported goods is for consumption purposes (Figure 10).

51 The political-economic aspects of the state-industry relationship are also relevant but are not included in this research.

Figure 10: Trends in imports (US$m), 1992/93-2004/05)

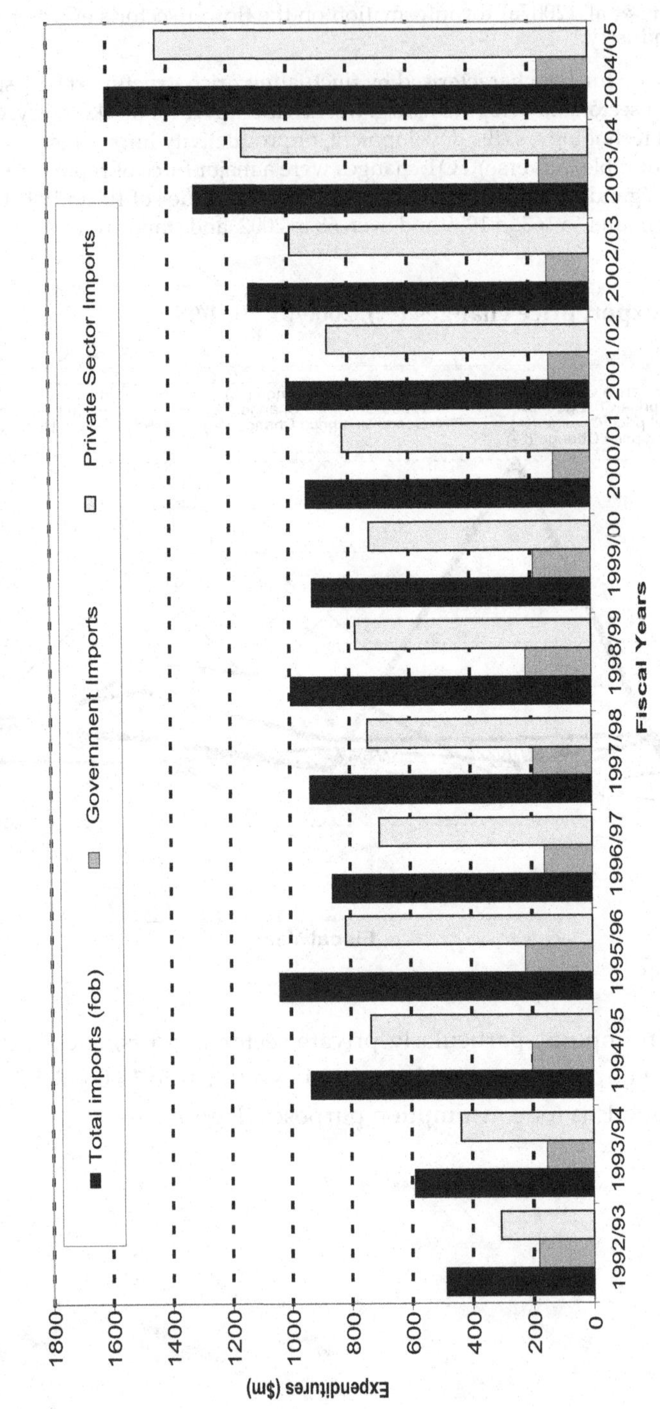

Source: *MFPED (2006).*

Other macroeconomic indicators

Concern: regional investment disparities, aid-dependency and low revenues

Inflation declined from 148.1% in 1985/86 to an annual average rate of 4.8% p.a. for the ten-year period up to 2003/04. Lately, inflation has risen more considerably. Total investment as percentage of GDP increased from 8.2% in 1985/86 to 19.1% in 1998/99 and 22.4% in 2004/05, which is encouraging, though it has slowed lately. There has been a continuous shift in the composition of investment towards private investment, which now accounts for around two-thirds of total investment. During the 1990s, (public/private) investments went mainly into construction: private construction accounted for half of annual investments, and another fifth was investment in public construction. Less than a third of total investment went into plants and equipment (machinery and vehicles) (MFPED 2006, MTCS Secretariat data provided to the author). The significant bias of the physical capital accumulation process towards construction (together with other reasons) limited the impact of the process on productivity outcomes (Ssemogerere 2005, xiii, 28).[52]

UIA figures regarding regional dispersion of investment projects (both local and foreign) illustrate the supremacy of actual investment and employment of the Central Region, the lower importance of the Eastern and Western Region and the marginalisation of the Northern Region (Table 12).

Table 12: Investment/employment by region (%, as of end of year 2001)

Region	Actual investment	Actual employment
Central	71.42	73.61
East	18.82	15.11
North	0.35	0.68
West	9.40	10.60
TOTAL	**100.00**	**100.00**

Source: *UIA (2004, 83).*

Government revenue as percentage of GDP grew from 8.6% to 12.6% (1993/94 -2004/05), well below the SSA average of about 20%. Credit to the private sector and gross domestic savings showed some positive developments, especially in recent years, and stand at 7.5% and 10.2% of GDP (2004/05). Aid flows have remained at high levels, with 12.9% vs. 12.7% of GDP for 1993/94 vs. 2003/04. Some of these indicators have shown no/little evidence of steady evolution. This signals economic difficulties also experienced by other LDCs/DCs in maintaining strong growth/transformation in the medium and long run after the experience of a rapid initial growth episode (MFPED 2006, Bevan et al. 2003).

52 According to Ssemogerere, "the capital accumulation process was erratic, inadequate in scale, biased towards construction rather than equipment and had a positive but weak impact on productivity" (2005, xiii). Accordingly, 77% of physical capital accumulation went into construction, 23% into equipment (ibid, 31). See the same study for a longer discussion of factors accounting for the bias towards construction: (i) the history of insecurity and economic mismanagement, (ii) the lending behaviour of FIs, and (iii) inadequate financial instruments to mobilise and formally channel remittances from working Ugandans in the diaspora through the banking system (ibid, 28).

Inward FDI record

Since the 1990s, Uganda has attracted increasing amounts of FDI. While the annual average for inward FDI in the period 1985-1995 was 30mUS$, the figures now stand at above 200mUS$ (e.g. 237mUS$ in 2004). It is estimated that the FDI inward stock has accumulated to 1,613mUSD (up to 2004). This is around 16.3% of gross fixed capital formation (Africa: 12.5%, East Africa: 14%), and 23.6% of the country's GDP (Africa: 27.8%, East Africa: 26.6%) (UNCTAD 2005d). Within Africa and SSA, or the LDC group in particular, the country's performance with respect to inward FDI and other investment-related indicators (e.g. investment climate) is *above average* and is sometimes ranked in the top category. In *proportion to the size* of the economy Uganda has attracted more FDI than most countries in the region, e.g. Kenya and Tanzania. According to UNCTAD, the inward FDI performance index, which ranks 140 countries by the amount of FDI they receive relative to their economic size,[53] Uganda is in 54th position worldwide and regarded as an 'above potential performer' (period 2002-2004) with a ratio that is clearly above the African average. Regarding the Inward FDI Potential Index, the country still ranks quite low (108th position, 2004) (ibid, UNCTAD 2004c, BOU et al. 2004).[54]

Four sectors accounted for around 90% of the Foreign Direct Equity Investment (FDEI) stocks in the economy: manufacturing (33%), wholesale (22%), financing (19%), and transport (16%). The secondary sector succeeded in attracting most of the FDI inflows during every year of the period 1992-2002, mainly in beverages, sugar, textiles, plastics, cement, footwear and packaging. Consequently, the secondary sector accounted for more than half (54%) of the total FDI stock (year 2000), ahead of the tertiary sector (42%) and the primary sector (4%). The composition of FDI inflows by type of investment is as follows (2001): 51% equity investment, 37% intra-company loans, and 12% reinvested earnings. Investors from developing countries (mainly Kenya, Mauritius, South Africa, Bermuda, India, Singapore) and developed countries (Belgium, France, Netherlands, Sweden, UK, Canada, US) accounted for 50% and 40% of the total FDI stock respectively (10% unspecified). Of the 23.6mUS$ that were remitted as profits or dividends to non-resident shareholders in 2001 (91% to UK, 6% to Mauritius), the financing sector accounted for 64%, wholesale 17%, construction 12%, and manufacturing 7%. The dominance of finance is notable (ibid).

Overall, the record of Uganda regarding inward FDI is regarded a significant success (UNCTAD 2004b, 2004c), given the size of the economy, its estimated potential for FDI, the level of economic development and infrastructure, the security situation in the region, the position as a land-locked country, or the competition regarding FDI attraction from Kenya. Box 4 offers some reflections on Uganda's inward FDI record: it is argued that stronger skills and capabilities are required to sustain and further advance the performance in the future.

53 This is calculated as the ratio of a country's share in global FDI inflows to its share in global GDP.

54 In comparison, according to UNCTAD categories, Kenya is an 'under performer' (low FDI potential, low FDI performance); the country attracted about 46mUS$ inward FDI in 2004 (a fifth of the Ugandan FDI inflows, per capita basis: 1.4US$ Kenya vs. 8.5US$ Uganda). Kenya's FDI inward stock is estimated to stand at 1,223mUS$ (2004) which is 2.3% of the country's gross fixed capital formation and 7.8% of GDP (UNCTAD 2005d, 2005b). "Kenya is now among the developing countries that have attracted the least FDI relative to their size over the past decade" (UNCTAD 2005b, 45).

Box 4: Remarks on Uganda's inward FDI record

The inward FDI record constitutes a very important accomplishment for Uganda, especially because it developed in a post-conflict context and from a low base. A few qualifications can be made. First, the positive inward FDI performance in comparative terms in the UNCTAD index needs to be seen in the light of a low GDP that impacts on the outcome. Other LDCs such as such as Angola (5th), Mozambique (23rd) or Sudan (29th) also rank high in the index. That notwithstanding, the index points to the fact that Uganda has been doing well against the background of its low GDP and an FDI potential that is considered to be low. UNCTAD thus groups Uganda in the category of 'above potential' performers (countries with low FDI potential but high FDI performance) and recognises the need to focus on further improvements of the FDI potential in order to sustain past FDI successes (UNCTAD 2004b, 16).

Second, FDI to Uganda has not accelerated significantly over the last years. This might point to difficulties in competing for FDI with Asian economies, for example, to attract sectors that require staff qualified and experienced in a specific field, and in promoting the development and exploitation of agglomeration economies in the relationship between foreign and local firms (clusters, capability formation and technology transfer). A stronger focus on agglomeration economies can set in motion a virtuous circle of growth, competitiveness, and investment in new capabilities (Lall 2004a) and thus increase the country's attractiveness to foreign investors. However, the results of FDI-related policies (enabling investment climate) which are part of the core economic policy package of GOU (macroeconomic stability etc.) are probably just beginning to emerge more strongly and play an increasing role as a driving force of rapid economic growth (Ssemogerere 2006, x).

Third, one needs to compare the absolute figures with data of other developing regions. In the context of the developing country group, Africa's FDI figures appear low: in 2003, Asia and the Pacific succeeded in attracting 107bUS$ FDI, Latin America and the Caribbean 50bUS$, and Africa 15bUS$ (mainly investment in natural resources). Only around 9% of total FDI inflows that are accounted for in the DC group (172bUS$) went to the African countries; that is 2.8% of inward FDI worldwide. It is the problem of the continent lagging behind as a whole with respect to global FDI flows that gives reason for caution about measuring Uganda's performance only within the continental or the LDC context. On country basis, Vietnam could attract 1,450mUS$ FDI, Thailand 1,802mUS$, and Malaysia 2,474mUS$ (2003) (UNCTAD 2004b). Africa receives little FDI-related to (advanced) inclusion of SSA economies/producers into (non-agro) global production networks (Santiso 2006).

Some reflections on efforts to achieve private sector development

What are key economic challenges for Uganda? Broadly speaking, they include:

- A renewed era of growth, fuelled by increased investment, competitiveness, market integration and productivity, improved local production and trade systems, more and higher-value-added exports (volume, quality, consistency), enhanced HR (besides education and health, focus on training, skills, capabilities, inter-firm networks and cooperation, local learning efforts, and HRM), as well as appropriate and effective institutional support structures, especially for firm/sector level capability formation and learning, and HRD generally.
- A broadened and improved formal sector (to foster learning and productivity, increase revenues, reduce aid dependence,) and export base (to counter the trade imbalances), and an enhanced informal sector.
- Transformation towards a higher level of industrialisation, commercial agriculture, and modern services, which can spur growth, employment, food security and reduce poverty.

Against the above, a few remarks on PSD-related efforts of GOU are appropriate. The purpose of these remarks is not to place the entire responsibility for described outcomes on the side of the state. The intention is to give the reader an initial overview regarding important deficits in the design and/or implementation of neoliberal PSD-related policies or programmes in Uganda. Such critical observations will be continued in the next chapters.

First, to date there is debate on government's side regarding the appropriate responsibilities of the private and public sectors regarding PSD. The book will discuss some of these matters. Overall, it is argued that there are some important areas where GOU appears to have failed to play its part sufficiently and/or successfully. In certain areas crucial for the economic, especially industrial, development of Uganda, it appears there was much discussion and analysis (though a few issue areas were also ignored, even at the analytical level), and yet subsequent implementation and thus real change on the ground was insufficient overall. *This concerns the following issue areas in particular*: productivity, innovation, technology, know-how transfer, linkage building, industrial, technological and social capability formation, and MSEs. In fact, the second generation of structural reforms - beyond security, macro stabilisation, recovery, and liberalization - seems overdue since the late 1990s. Some of the reforms and initiatives launched by GOU since the mid 2000s indicate that the authorities are now working on this second generation (see below).

With a broader reform agenda in the recent past, better state performance (e.g. implementation) in some issue areas and a different agenda setting by the donor community, Uganda could already have advanced further towards growth, transformation and competitiveness. Delays and deficits in the above areas have increased the present and future challenge of structural transformation and will make it more difficult in the coming years to achieve significant results regarding diversification, growth and catch-up (technology and productivity). The shortcomings will hardly change overnight, even if the neoliberal ideological stance of the donors and GOU can be 'softened', the economic policy focus broadened, the political and technocratic commitment and reform implementation records improved, and the performance record of both private sector and donors enhanced. Capability building is a *path dependent* and *cumulative* process (Lall 2004a). Even in a more positive domestic scenario, the catch-up process - building and deepening of capabilities, improving of productivity levels, upgrading of export structure etc. - will take much time.

The author's impression is that there are certain expertise deficiencies within the state on how deal to more successfully *on the ground* with some key PSD issues that go beyond the reform agenda of the 1990s. Overall, there seems to be insufficient recognition regarding actual and possible forms, mechanisms, and responsibilities for the envisaged private-public-sector-partnership (PPP) models - at least in areas such as productivity, technology, linkage building and value chain development. Also, the central administrative system seems too distanced from many PSD issues, e.g. in terms of information exchange, technical support, or joint and day-to-day learning about policy effects in various dimensions of PSD. For example, the overall appreciation and responses of the state to some present-day HRD issues in the (non-agro) private sector appears deficient. Of course, the authorities are aware of the need for a stronger, more competent administration; yet, there is still a considerable way to go to improve the status quo. As some authors argue, "[f]or too long the problem of incapability has been treated by removing the relevant responsibility rather than fixing the incapability. While this may work as a short-term fix it is unlikely to provide the foundation for lasting progress. However fixing the incapability will require real energy, resources, and political commitment" (Bevan et al. 2003, 34).[55] A competitiveness agenda implies complex

55 Furthermore, "[w]hile there is a core of bureaucrats in Uganda who are extraordinarily impressive in terms of their capabilities and dedication, this is far from true of the bureaucracy as a whole.

requirements for the public sector regarding its very own knowledge capacities, capabilities and institutions, as well as PSD-related strategies, policies and programmes: The requirements call for more interaction with relevant actors and specific support at sub-sectoral and firm level (meso and micro level). A policy menu of mainly cross-sectoral interventions (infrastructure etc.) will not do.

More to the point, the experiences of the flower sector (as described) and other sections of the economy (e.g. MSEs) of the state's limitations in organising vigorous support to boost competitiveness strategies, including HRD strategies, could indicate that some public institutions have not yet arrived at an effective mode of interaction with both domestic and foreign players from the private sector. For example, compared to some East Asian countries, Uganda has performed relatively poorly in the last two decades in establishing (or reviving) and running a number of *SIs and support mechanisms* for accelerated and sustainable expansion and upgrading of some of her economic sectors. Strikingly, the country had few effective strategies at firm and sub-sector level for systematically reaping the wider *development benefits and stimulations* of the operations of the more advanced, dynamic and upgrading domestic and foreign firms in the country, to ensure positive externalities and spillover effects, in areas of technology, knowledge,[56] know-how, capabilities and skills, management practices, supply industry, research-industry nucleus, or learning effects for administrative and technical SIs and their staff. For instance, the knowledge dimension includes the embodied knowledge inherent in intermediate inputs and FDI-related machines, equipment, and technical staff, and disembodied knowledge that comes with licenses or patents (Isaksson et al. 2005, 21-2).

Maybe this situation has partly to do with the dominance of the MFPED in the past reform era: its specific understanding of and approach towards PSD and its emphasis on macro-economic management, stability, tax revenues, etc. This focus has to some extent weakened a systematic acknowledgement of specific sub-sector and firm perspectives and the need for related (somewhat consistent, coordinated and predictable) government support; for support measures that fix market and institutional failures typical in the late-comer industrialisation process. Severe market failures in the economic catch-up process that need to be addressed include high externalities, risks and learning costs that deter the private sector from undertaking efforts towards technological learning, capability formation, innovation, risk-taking (entrepreneurial trial and error), collective action measures, and overall, diversification-oriented efforts (Lall 2004, Rodrik 2004).[57] These deterrents will be discussed in more detail below.

Current characteristics of parts of the bureaucratic apparatus responsible for economic development matters - in terms of organisational design, and the quality, capacity,

... Upgrading the quality of personnel in the public service has been a priority of government for some time, but it needs to be re-emphasised that the success of the whole strategy is vulnerable if this is not achieved" (Bevan et al. 2003, 32-3). Note that the problematic characteristics of the Ugandan bureaucracy at present are in part an outcome of the donor driven neoliberal public service reform policies of the past (downsizing etc., see on public sector reforms e.g. Harrison 2005a, 2005c, Williamson 2003, Kiiza 2000) and the post-1986 political-economic dynamics (job insecurity, corruption, nepotism, neopatrimonialism, donor agendas, etc.) in the country generally.

56 This includes the embodied knowledge inherent in intermediate inputs and FDI-related machines, equipment, and technical staff, and disembodied knowledge that comes with licenses or patents (Isaksson et al. 2005, 21-2).

57 See Chapter 7 for more detailed discussion of market failures.

commitment and management of staff - question *to which extent* the neoliberal Ugandan state can realistically be successful (1) in the efficient, flexible and, crucially, simultaneous coordination of the many overlapping growth and PDS strategies and initiatives, and (2) in carrying out or encouraging activities in the areas of capability building, know-how transfer linkage building, local sourcing by foreign firms, innovation, institutional improvements, R&D collaboration and related HRD. Of course, many issues cannot improve instantly, and some matters listed above seem to be rather new themes in the official policy and research debate on PSD in Uganda. Ssemogerere (2005) makes this observation ('newness') about the case of the productivity theme. It can be expected that policies and support interventions will increasingly reflect themes that were not on the forefront of reforms in the 1990s.

An observation on a related matter: seemingly, the state seldom shows strong interest (at least right away) in continuing innovative and useful donor programmes for PSD after their expiry. How much effort is spent on (a) constantly learning from the successes and failures of the dozens of donor programme activities in PSD,[58] and (b) subsequently including relevant experiences in the policy and programme development and adjustment process?[59] Of course, information and knowledge management has political, economic and cultural dimensions which cannot be discussed here.

In sum, meaningful PSD could be fostered if the PSD public policy and support systems worked towards: (i) a sufficiently broad and strategic account of economic development, competitiveness and HRD matters, (ii) a (more) coordinated design, implementation and adjustment of policies and programmes on various relevant issues, and (iii) appropriate and effective institutional structures to deliver the support.[60] In the end of course, one needs to examine in more depth the various political economy dimensions of the status of PSD reforms in Uganda - something which is beyond this book.[61]

---

58 Sometimes these are pioneering projects with all sorts of relevant 'lessons learnt'.

59 A related example: Hundreds of relevant PSD studies were carried out over the years by GOU, donors, NGOs, researchers, and companies. These studies are now scattered all over in offices in Kampala and elsewhere. It is unlikely that they are centrally collected, reviewed, archived and managed for future use (e.g. by students, economic actors and the interested public). It is the author's impression that findings of instructive studies carried out by researchers (from Uganda and abroad) are not as well used as they could be, e.g. the IDS Brighton/Makerere University tracer study of secondary school and university leavers by Kirumira and Bateganya (2003) was rarely referenced in any of the HRD related documents in Uganda by the time of writing. Positively, see the efforts by the MFPED (2008) with regards to an annotated inventory of poverty-related research studies in Uganda.

60 In the recent past, some of the major economic policies have been crosscutting (involving many ministries and stakeholders), which - in the absence of a strong central coordination and monitoring unit - increased the likelihood of non-implementation: "Numerous agencies are often identified as being jointly responsible for particular actions in the ubiquitous policy action matrices (PAMs). But joint responsibility can all too easily translate into no responsibility. ... [Moreover, one] role that the PAMs are presumably intended to fulfill is that of coordinating across these sometimes very complex policy domains. It is of course vital to identify policy interconnections, who has to do what and when for the ensemble to succeed. However, these coordination problems could be reduced if more care were taken to align the organizational structure with the policy mix" (Bevan et al. 2003, 38-39).

61 On political-economic aspects of Uganda's post-1986 reform path see especially the following: Kiiza et al. (2006), Kiiza (2004), Tangri and Mwenda (2006, 2003, 2001), Mwenda and Tangri (2005), Mwenda (2007), Barkan et al. (2004), Barkan (2005), Moncrieffe (2004), Harrison (2005a, 2005b, 2005c) and Robinson (2007).

The terms formal and informal sector

Before we proceed, let us clarify the terms *formal* and *informal sector*: UBOS defines informal sector firms by an employment level of less than five people (2006, 68). Consequently, formal sector firms are those with more than five employees. However, on the ground there are many firms with less than five workers that are in the formalised sector (read: registered), and there are many firms with more than five workers that are not registered. There may also be enterprises that are only partly in the informal sector (Becker 2004). Yet, the informal sector in Uganda constitutes many micro/small firms often with only two employees. See Box 5. In a labour market report, UBOS states:

> "Informal sector comprises ... small-scale businesses, usually with self-employed activities, with or without hired labour. They operate with low level of organization, low capital, low technology and often on temporary premises. Usually, they are not supported by formal financing institutions, and are not usually registered in government. A household enterprise is an economic unit owned by the household but without an identifiable location [and address]; the enterprise activity is carried out within the household. On the other hand, an establishment is a business activity carried out with an identifiable fixed location and address. Establishments having less than five paid employees irrespective of the number of working proprietors or unpaid family helpers were considered as small-scale establishments" (2006, 68, emphasis added).

Box 5: Estimated size of the formal and informal sector

The UBOS Business Register 2001/02 lists over 160,000 business establishments (with fixed premises), which employ about 444,000 people. Around 63% of these reported jobs are in the central region (42% in Kampala alone), 17% in the Western, 15% in the Eastern and 5% in the Northern region. Slightly more than *10,000 establishments* are reckoned to be in the *formal sector* (employment level of 5 or more people), with the remaining *150,000* in *the informal sector* (employing less than 5 people, often not more than two including the business owner). Accordingly, employment in the larger firms amounts to 210,000 jobs, almost half of total jobs reported in the Register. About 90% of the listed businesses are under sole proprietorship (rest: partnership or private limited companies) (2003a).

According to other sources, however, the actual informal sector size is larger (taking into account those without fixed premises and so on): There are an estimated *800,000* non-agro formal and informal *MSMEs* (Micro, Small and Medium Enterprises) operating in the country, most of them informal. These MSMEs are estimated to provide about 12% and 40% of employment in rural and urban areas respectively (MFPED 2004, 71). In the latest labour market report (based on UNHS data) UBOS gives estimates of about informal *300,000* ***rural*** *small-scale establishments* (less than five employees) - with around 480,000 people being engaged in these establishments. This was an increase of about 80% (establishments) and 43% (people) compared to an informal sector survey in the early 1990s. The Central region has the highest share of these rural establishments (29%), the Northern region the lowest (8%) (2006, 36). Furthermore, about *1.8 million households* are estimated to operate *'household enterprises'* (excluding crop farming enterprises; some households operate more than one enterprise) which is about 36% of the total number of households in Uganda, estimated to be around 4.9 million (ibid 18).[62] About *3.8 million households* are estimated to be *engaged in agricultural activities* (van Bussel 2005).

The next chapter analyses productivity matters in the young private sector in Uganda.

62 See below for more detailed characteristics of household enterprises.

2

Analysis of Productivity Indicators and Factors

Conceptual background

Structural change and productivity gains

In general, accelerated structural change is associated with *economy-wide productivity gains* through the movement of labour (and capital) into higher productivity, higher-value-added sectors; the gains are especially high where productivity differences across sectors were initially large, and the amount of transferred labour significant (UNIDO 2004c, 5). "Although structural change implies a shift of labor from agriculture to industry, in the long term industrial growth tends to contribute positively to agricultural productivity, as agriculture also becomes more capital- and skill-intensive" (ibid, 5).

Yet, significant productivity enhancement does *not* come *automatically* with structural change; it requires *constant local efforts* by the actors involved. Importantly, productivity improvements of a given firm are not sufficient if the (foreign) competitor is improving faster. Thus, structural transformation cannot stop at fostering the inter-sectoral shift from agriculture to industry and services: reform efforts need also to target the *intra-sectoral* and *firm* level to foster, in this case, continued productivity improvements. Industries, service operators, and farms have to be equipped to *become and remain productive at competitive levels* - against a moving target of improving competitors. That is why it is vital to understand that support is needed at essentially all levels of the economy: for cross-sectoral issues, and for actors (and their HRD efforts) in the modern, dynamic (export) sectors, in the traditional agricultural sectors as well as in the informal/semi-formal MSME-sector which tries to handle the adoption of technology.

Productivity: Driven by technological change and efficiency change

The level of productivity can be measured by the ratio of production inputs to outputs, or the value of what firms put into a production process compared to what they get out (Akella et al. 2003). In general, to increase productivity, a firm can work on output value (product-value) and/or input value (capital, labour, purchased goods/services). The level of productivity then reflects "the *ability* to transform inputs into outputs ... [or,] the state of our knowledge of production techniques" (Isaksson et al. 2005, 1, emphasis added). In this book it is assumed, following Isaksson et al. (2005), that productivity is driven by a combination of (a) *technological change/progress* and (b) *technical efficiency change* (economies of scale, capacity utilisation, learning-by-doing, work organisation, spillover, networks) (ibid, 1).

The HR dimension in this notion of productivity is evident. If *productivity enhancement* is mainly about the growth of technology - in other words about realising technological efficiency gains through better knowledge about and better application and handling of ever more efficient production techniques, then the main aspects of *human capital* (**education**, **training**, and **health**) and *R&D* are *paramount* (ibid, 6).[63] Training here includes formation of skills and capabilities of production workers, technicians, engineers, managers, field staff, farmers, etc. Importantly, the targets of human capital and R&D "are not mono-dimensional. Both R&D and human capital have several dimensions that policies may address. Nor are the targets independent from each other. There is solidarity between R&D and human capital in their influence on technology. Finally, the targets are not independent from other factors" (ibid, 46).[64]

Regarding R&D or innovation of industrial firms operating in the context of a LDC such as Uganda, this literature suggests that the *implementation (adoption and imitation) of already existing technology* (including second-hand technology) through local technological efforts, capability building and learning is *at present* the most relevant form of innovation; less than on-the frontier, 'radical' R&D (Isaksson et al. 2005, 51-2, Lall 2004a). The adoption of mobile phone technology in the Ugandan private sector is a straightforward and simple example of (the benefits of) an innovation based on the implementation of an existing technology that was developed elsewhere. The quote below and Box 41 (Appendix 2) clarify the important categorisation of different innovation forms:

> "When it comes to R&D, it is useful to differentiate innovation from the implementation of technologies innovated by others. Countries at high productivity levels will do relatively more innovation; *countries at low levels* will do relatively more *imitation* of simple *existing technologies*. Countries at intermediate levels will do more implementation of intermediate technologies. Clearly, policies will have to take into account the various facets of the technological effort. There will have to be policies for innovation, for implementation, and for imitation" (Isaksson et al. 2005, 46, emphasis added).

Note, of the gross domestic expenditure on R&D in Uganda, only 2.2% comes from the private sector, but 90% from external sources (donors), who mainly finance research in medical and veterinary sciences (UNESCO 2005, Muhumuza et al. 2005). The above considerations reveal: Uganda needs enhanced efforts to help firms and farms to adopt and imitate existing industrial technologies and improve existing products and processes. On-the-frontier research (e.g. regarding new or better local products) needs more attention as well, where appropriate.

In summary, in this view *pro-productivity actions are to a significant extent HR-oriented actions* (Isaksson et al. 2005): in the areas of *education, training* and *health*.[65] Given that (i) productivity is linked closely to HRD theme, and (ii) productivity (which is so relevant in the Ugandan catch-up and competitiveness context) has not been discussed in sufficient detail in relevant PSD policy circles in Uganda to date, Box 6 provides an overview of some

63 R&D can mean basic and applied research, product and process development.

64 Besides these two proximate factors, Isaksson et al. (2005) discuss what they call *more distant determinants* of productivity: business environment, macro-economic framework, investment, cost capital, savings, infrastructure, or institutions and markets. Politics, sociology and culture would come in here; though this book cannot address these dimensions it recognises the importance of studying these dimensions in future. See also Tangen (2002) for an introduction to the productivity theme. A source regarding the issue of measuring productivity (aggregate and industry-level) is the OECD Productivity Manual (OECD 2001).

65 Although training and health are not scope of the study (Isaksson et al. 2005), Isaksson emphasises the importance of all three factors for human capital in the productivity context (personal conversation May 2006).

fundamental considerations and assumptions related to the productivity theme. It highlights the considerable need for policies and programmes, and efforts in firms and farms and the institutions of the training and technology support system, which relate to productivity enhancement. Note, of course, education and health have received much attention by GOU and donors in Uganda. The argument here is that those circles involved in policy making for PSD have paid insufficient attention to the HR and productivity dimensions of economic transformation.

Box 6: Main source for productivity: Technology - the knowledge about available production techniques

- "Productivity comes [mainly] from technology ... Technology is knowledge about available techniques. From the point of economic analysis, a technique is fundamentally a combination of factors (for instance, a man with a bulldozer and a man with a shovel are two techniques) ... used to produce goods and services. The development of technology means that new techniques accrue to the set ... Productivity changes chiefly because, throughout time, the world set of available techniques (in short, world technology) is continuously changing in the direction of more productive techniques. More efficient techniques enter the set; less efficient techniques are discarded ...The new techniques allow the production of more per bundle of inputs (or they need less inputs to produce a unit of output). This gain - or saving - is the productivity gain resulting from the technological change.
- Access to this set is not, however, the same for every country ...To simplify ... the lower [technological] levels are accessible to emerging and other developing countries...
- World technology does not change in a homogeneous fashion: the top levels shift faster than the bottom ones. Consequently, countries on the bottom technology strata are doomed to become ever more distanced from the rest of the world as long as their domestic conditions will not permit them to climb the technological ladder. The position of a country on the ladder of *technology potential* is geared by the *current level* of productivity of that country, which itself is defined by *past levels* of accumulation and innovation.
- Given its position on the ladder, the technology potential of a country is defined by two proximate determinants: the apparatus of technology creation and diffusion (i.e., R&D), on the one hand, and the skills of the labour force manning this apparatus on the other ...The long-term development of the two proximate determinants is necessary, but not sufficient, for a country to climb the ladder of technological capability .... R&D and human capital are [rather] like the sails of the productivity ship. When the wind of opportunity blows, the sails propel the ship. Without wind a ship under sails does not move; actually, deploying the sails might even hamper using the currents of capital and labour accumulation to manoeuvre the ship. Within its endowment potential, any country can perform more or less well. Some will make full use of their potential; other - most countries - will only make partial use. A host of factors are at play in explaining the actual utilization of a country's productivity potential. Pursuing the previous metaphor, these factors would be the rigging with which the sails are optimally set to capture the wind
- To [utilise the technology potential and] make technical change a reality, technology must meet at least three prerequisites in the material world: an enterprise willing to take the risk and capable of operating a new technique; personnel with the required competence to work for the enterprise; and a market capable of remunerating the factors employed by the enterprise. Furthermore, the firms must find the right incentives, and form the property rights. Together, these prerequisites are almost coextensive with economic development itself. It is only exaggerating a little to say that technology brings about economic development, but it takes nothing short of economic development to bring about technology". Source: Isaksson et al. (2005, 6, 31, 49, bold added).

Uganda's productivity lags behind, also due to HR deficiencies

Overall, the Ugandan economy is known to have significant productivity problems, in particular in total factor productivity (TFP) and labour productivity (value-added output per worker) which, in turn, affects the sustainability and future growth prospects of the economy in general, and per capita growth and poverty reduction efforts in particular. Among the reasons for this status quo, this book argues, are deficiencies in the area of HR: education, knowledge, know-how, skills, competencies, LIS, and related efforts and attitudes (e.g. to explore, exploit and commercialise new technologies, organise commercial/professional networks, or share knowledge). In this regard, one can also refer to the relatively low pace, diffusion and limited application and improvement of technology and knowledge in the production process in Uganda.[66]

A number of deficiencies are closely linked to gaps in the system of SIs (for technology, business operations, and training). Other reasons for low productivity include: the sectoral composition of the economy (including level of product diversification) and labour force occupation (mainly subsistence agriculture, informal sector), the level of general and specialised infrastructure (including critical mass of ICT), and characteristics in terms of finance, firm size, international market exposure, utilisation of inputs (including information), firm organisation and staff performance incentive systems, business systems (production, logistics and marketing systems, or value chains), business practices (including business ethics), inter-firm specialisation and clustering. Some salient matters of productivity in Uganda will be discussed in the following sections of this chapter, and explored further throughout the book.

Average labour productivity trends and HR-related determinants of productivity levels[67]

Average labour productivity in the 1990s experienced no clear upward trend

An analysis of the trend in average labour productivity in the period 1961-2000 reveals the following features (Figure 11): Periods of rapid growth in average labour productivity (DLP) "were concentrated in the [immediate] years following independence ... propelled by the inherited health and education infrastructure, rated the best at the time. The more recent positive trend 1986/2000, although above zero, has yet to establish a sustained upward movement. Slump periods in ... [DLP] were less in the immediate post-independence period ... However, the civil wars of 1971-79 and 1981-86, together with economic mismanagement, led to a massive loss in overall labour quality accumulation [with negative consequences for subsequent DLP levels and thus the contribution of labour productivity to economic growth]" (Ssemogerere 2005, x-xi, 18). Relevant in the context of quality labour are the expulsion of skilled Asians in 1972 and the brain drain of local skilled personnel due to personal safety reasons in the period 1972-1986 (ibid, 15).[68]

---

66 Again, the political, sociological, and socio-economic dimensions of productivity and its HR underpinning are not discussed in this book.

67 The productivity chapter makes substantial reference to Germina Ssemogerere's (2005) pioneering study on productivity in Uganda.

68 Regarding the rating of Uganda's post-independence health and education infrastructure, Ssemogerere refers to WB (1982).

Figure 11: Trend in average labour productivity (DLP) in Uganda: period 1962-2000

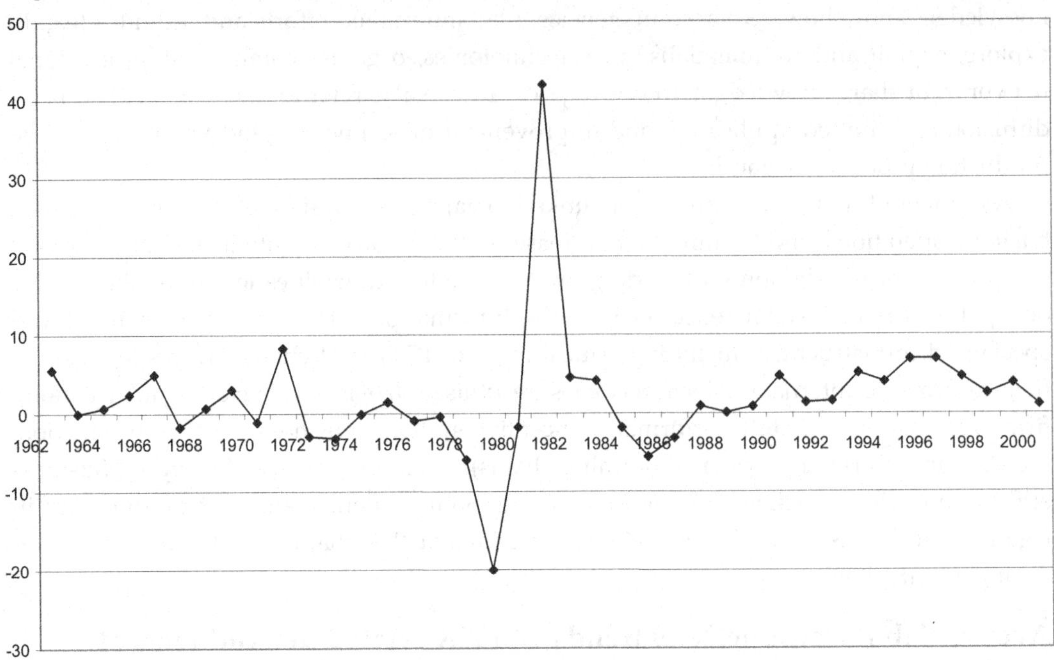

Source: *Ssemogerere (2005, 11) based on UNIDO Productivity Database.*

Apart from the early effects of the colonial inheritance of a (rather small) pool of skills, official development aid (ODA) was again the major driving force of *rapid growth in DLP* in the last four decades, including the growth incidences in the late 1980s/early1990s.[69] The economic policy package of the early 1990s (liberalisation etc.) - supported by ODA - also had a positive effect on DLP (ibid, 10). In particular, in the early 1990s, ODA and economic policies combined "led to a more efficient allocation of existing labour skills and the return of some exiles, which collectively boosted average labour productivity, independently of economic growth" (ibid). The country's reforms and efforts in the health and education sector since the mid 1990s "so far show [an] emerging but still weak contribution to DLP" (ibid). Notably, the magnitude of episodes of rapid growth in DLP has continuously decreased since the mid-1980s: from a score of 6.48% in the 1985/87 episode to a low 1.32% for 1998/99. Ssemogerere thus makes an important cautionary remark:

> "[The weaker result of the last phase] is cause for concern, given that investment in education and primary health care yield results, but only in the long-term, as does investment in measures to combat HIV/AIDS. [In other words, efforts related to] [l]ong term human capital investment ... have still to pay off" (ibid, 10, 12).

Moreover, the slumps in DLP in the 1990s have moved very closely with those in economic growth (ibid, 11-13).[70] Importantly, the trend curve for DLP has so far remained above zero.

69 Periods of rapid DLP were 1985/87, 1988/90, 1991/93 (productivity scores of about 6.5%, 4.6%, and 4.1 respectively). Growth periods later in the 1990s were 1994/95 and 1998/99 (2.9% and 1.3% respectively) (Ssemogerere 2005, 10).

70 The three episodes of slumps were: 1990/91, 1996/98 and 1999/2000 with negative DLP scores of about -3.4%, -4.4% and -2.8% respectively. Accordingly, the main forces behind these episodes are similar to those of economic growth slumps: decreased ODA and TOT. Ssemogerere interprets these slumps in DLP and economic growth to have been self-reinforcing (2005, 12-3).

"An improvement in economic growth will need to pay close attention to policies championing a related positive movement in growth of average labour productivity, particularly since the two variables have moved so closely, i.e. practically parallel to each other since 1991, with a firm upward trend yet to emerge" (ibid, 13). A related finding by UNIDO's Productivity Database is that the gap in average labour productivity between Uganda and the USA has *increased* in the last four decades. Despite the recovery success in the post-1986 period, Uganda experienced a relative average labour productivity drop of 0.45% points between 1961 and 2000 (3.29% to 2.84%) (ibid, xi).

Obviously, Uganda faces the challenge of conducting measures which enable significant labour productivity growth not only in the long-term but also and especially in the short to mid-term. Interventions are also needed to boost and sustain DLP independent of economic growth dynamics (its growth and slumps). A HRD focus that can actually have an impact on productivity outcomes at the ground is vital. In this context, increased general education levels are likely to have a stronger productivity impact if they are combined with efforts to develop and deepen productive and social capabilities for PSD, first, and improved HRM at firm level (to improve the application of knowledge and skills), including appropriate performance management systems,[71] second. This poses significant requirements for HRM capabilities and systems (firms), and the SIs that can boost productivity.

Further, growth and upgrading of private sector activities (including product innovation and differentiation or technology upgrading), and, related to this, improved labour market structures which set incentives for both the development and application of respective knowledge and skills, are needed in the future to translate improved HR levels into rapid and sustained growth episodes of DLP (Ssemogerere 2005). Also note in this context that "Uganda's manufacturing sector is still shallow and elementary, with limited opportunities for product innovation and differentiation to raise average labour productivity ... [G]rowth in manufacturing depth as a basis for labour to 'learn' productivity enhancing measures in Uganda is still far in the future" (ibid, 13).

HRD-related determinants of productivity levels

The creation, transmission and absorption of knowledge

In an analysis of determinants of productivity, Ssemogerere offers a *qualitative* account of the state and role of activities and systems for (1) the creation, transmission, and (2) absorption and adoption of knowledge.[72] With this she attempts to explain why, in the case of Uganda, the impact of (a) general knowledge/skills, (b) 'learning-by-doing' opportunities at work, and (c) investment in R&D did *not play a major role* in enhancing productivity in the period 1961/62-2000 (2005, 21).[73]

71 We will extent this argument on HRM systems further below in this chapter and in Chapter 12.

72 Other productivity determinants discussed by Ssemogerere (2005) include factor supply (including human capital, physical capital and physical infrastructure with focus on energy), factor/resource allocation, the financial system, business support institutions, invariants (size, location, shared resources), and aspects of (regional, international) integration. This writer will limit the discussion of the study to direct HRD aspects.

73 Note, however, the difficulty of an analysis of productivity determinants in Uganda due to limited availability of organised data. Ssemogerere notes: "To the best of our knowledge, there are no published studies on the determinants of productivity in Uganda, or any organized time-series to trace trends of these determinants. Therefore, this study, as the first venture into the subject, has

Concerning point (1), the study notes, among others, (i) the low level of R&D activities[74], (ii) the lack of protection and promotion of knowledge creation, (iii) the lack of an institutional mechanism which links producers (research institutions etc.) and potential users (firms etc.) of locally generated knowledge, as well as the respective policy-makers, (iv) a lack of private sector investment in respective plant and equipment to test and modify (laboratory) knowledge with a view to commercialisation, (v) insufficient operational HR (scientists, engineers, technicians in R&D)[75], and (vi) deficiencies in policies (including incentives) for promotion of joint ventures, sub-contracting and backward-linkages to FDI to capture knowledge and know-how from FDI.[76] Further, related policy and other efforts in more recent years by the UNCST (Uganda National Council for Science and Technology) have not yet impacted on productivity growth (ibid, xii-xiii, 24).

Regarding (2), Ssemogerere argues that the process of absorption of knowledge "requires local capacity to select, process and modify/develop technology into [an] appropriate form to locally impact on productivity. ... [However,] Uganda's stock of skills to absorb knowledge is very limited ... [, which makes it] difficult for the Ugandan workforce to readily pick up ... [required] skills to enhance productivity" (ibid, xii, 25). Reference is made to deficient educational attainment (including a small share of persons with S6+, and few with vocational training) and the patterns of occupation of the labour force (high level of semi-subsistence and informal sector activities) which limit the workforce's capabilities to absorb knowledge (ibid, 25-6).[77] In summary, it is therefore suggested that "Uganda's low participation in R&D activities and protection of intellectual property rights, the absence of incentives and institutional infrastructure to transfer both locally produced and foreign knowledge via FDI... together with the extremely scarce stock of human capital to absorb knowledge lead ...[to the conclusion] that knowledge acquisition, transmission and absorption have not been [an] important group of determinants in effecting productivity in this country" (ibid, 26).[78] The assessment reveals the importance of emphasising related HRD aspects to a greater extent in future.

The determinants of quality labour supply and their impact on productivity

Further, Ssemogerere discusses, in a *historical perspective*, selected determinants of quality labour supply in Uganda and their impact on average labour productivity for the period of concern. In particular, these are (1) the political insecurity and economic mismanagement during the 1970-1986 period, (2) the current functioning of the labour market, and (3), the HIV/AIDS epidemic[79]. Accordingly, relevant regarding (1) are the expulsion of skilled

to piece together scattered glimpses of possible evidence, based on different methodologies and time-span. Given this limitation of background information, the assessment of each determinant is qualitative" (2005, 21).

74 See also Hasunira (2004) or Muhumuza et al. (2005) and the discussion of R&D activities Chapter 8.

75 The arguments (iii) - (v) on deficiencies in transmission mechanisms for locally produced knowledge necessary to boost productivity are based on an analysis by Kakembo (2003).

76 See also discussion of the UIA incentive regime in Chapter 7.

77 We will analyse characteristics of the labour force in more detail in Chapter 3.

78 In fact, these determinants "were so weak that for practical purposes their contribution was near zero (or irrelevant)" (Ssemogerere 2005, 47).

79 Uganda has a HIV prevalence of 6.7%, about new 130,000 infections each year, and an estimated 1 million HIV/AIDS positive people (MFPED and UNDP 2008, UNDP Uganda 2008).

personnel of Asian origin in 1972 and the brain drain of local skilled/educated personnel due to personal safety reasons in the period 1972-1986[80] (2005, 31). "The impact [of this human capital decline] on productivity was extremely negative" (ibid).[81] Also, (a) educational institutions were malfunctioning, and (b) opportunities and conditions for on-the-job learning-by-doing efforts were limited overall in both the formal private and public sectors in this period, for various reasons. Replacing the lost HR presented significant difficulties (ibid, 32, 15 based on GOU 1992). Uganda continues to be affected by brain drain of skilled labour in present times (Docquier and Marfouk 2006, Kapur and McHale 2005a, 2005b).[82]

Regarding determinant (2) Ssemogerere's analysis points to the adverse effects of the weak labour market and the estimated high level of unemployment/under-employment in Uganda at present.[83] Accordingly, characteristics that limit the structures and mechanisms of quality HR formation, e.g. the money and time that affected workers can spend on meaningful formal and informal acquisition of knowledge and skills to raise productivity levels, include: low payment, casualisation of work, job insecurity, low use of employment benefits and incentives (e.g. bonus) systems[84], large share of (semi-) subsistence activities among the labour force which has lead to a neglect of labour market issues in the past), a large informal sector, and workers/employees holding several jobs (2005, 33). Finally, (3), the HIV/AIDS epidemic - as discussed below - is a more recent determinant of a labour productivity loss (ibid, xiii-xiv).

With respect to the intensity of the impact on productivity, Ssemogerere estimates that "historically the brain drain had the most important negative intensity especially given the environment of insecurity in which it occurred that made it impossible to train replacements due to the fact that training institutions and the workplaces also deteriorated with the exodus of skilled personnel" (ibid, 35). Further, the impact of the state of the labour market as well as the HIV/AIDS epidemic "is still being felt and the overall cumulative effects will only emerge over time as they are addressed" (ibid). In sum, Ssemogerere suggests: "Given the negative determinants, the available pieces of evidence indicate that Uganda's accumulation of quality labour is low, even by SSA standards ... [T]he net effect of the three [discussed] determinants of human capital accumulation is a massive loss of skilled personnel with a highly negative impact on productivity" (ibid, 35, xiv).

In a discussion of other determinants of productivity, Ssemogerere highlights the positive effect on productivity growth of the resource/factor allocation policy of GOU in the post-1986 period. The government's emphasis on (i) exports, and (ii) manufacturing contributed very positively to productivity growth; some evidence, though, points to exhausting trends of certain respective impulses by the late 1990s (ibid, 37-8).[85] Regarding the contribution to

80 "[T]he brain drain constituted a second prolonged and larger round of loss of quality labour" (Ssemogerere 2005, 32).

81 For instance, the phases of slump in DLP during that period were: -11.52% (1971/74), -20.44% (1975/79), and -47.52% (1981/85) (Ssemogerere 2005, 12). We referred earlier to the positive impact of the return of exiles in the post-1986 period on PSD/productivity.

82 See also information below in Chapter 3.

83 Ssemogerere refers to the Draft Employment Policy of the MGLSD (2004), which gives an estimated total level of unemployment and under-employment of over 60%. This is about three times the level given (20%) in a recent UBOS (2006) labour market report.

84 See WB (2004b), and discussions in other parts of the book (e.g. on casualisation of work in Chapters 2 and 3, and on performance incentives in Chapter 12).

85 For data on (a), see Gauthier (2001) and the discussion in the section in this chapter on 'Low labour productivity levels in manufacturing firms' (below). Regarding (b), the average output growth

enhancing productivity of key public sector business SIs, the study refers to insufficient funding and technical staffing of these institutions, which limited their programme implementation and thus their contribution to productivity growth (ibid, 42-4, xv-xvi).[86] Importantly, note again that Ssemogerere provides a historical account of productivity trends and determinants. Since the mid to end 1990s, the GOU undertook efforts to address some of the productivity-related weaknesses and challenges through a number of reforms and policies (education, health, and establishment of business SIs); yet mostly, as explained, they are too recent to show significant impact on productivity growth at the time of writing. Some of those reforms will be discussed in more detail in other chapters of the book.

The findings of the productivity analysis presented above clearly reveal the crucial role of more intensive *HRD for productivity advancement* in Uganda, and the level of the HRD challenge due to the decline of HR and related structures in the pre-1986 period. Overall, in the coming years the various HR determinants of productivity in Uganda need to be addressed more vehemently, so that their *contribution* to productivity growth can become and/or remain positive in *direction*, yet can also increase significantly in terms of *impact* (ibid, 47). This is vital to improve and sustain the envisaged beneficial impact of recent reform moves (including those in certain HRD areas) on productivity outcomes. Policy-makers need to take note that "productivity issues are central to the successful implementation of ...[the declared] paradigm ...of economic growth, via export-led industrialization" (ibid). The next section discusses issues of TFP growth in Uganda.

Total factor productivity: Low impact during post-1986 growth episode

Total factor productivity (TFP) can be defined as "the growth of output in excess of growth in inputs ... [or,] the productivity of the principals or of all (identified) factors combined" (Isaksson et al. 2005, 45, 1). Growth in TFP reveals improvement in the *efficiency* by which production factors/inputs (capital, labour/human capital, as well as information, technology, and organisation) are *used* (IMF 2005, 5). In other words, for the IMF: "TFP reflects *inherent advancements of* ***knowledge about the production process***, as well as *reallocation of resources* from low-productivity sectors (such as agriculture) *to high productivity sectors* (such as manufacturing). These are processes that gradually unfold over a longer period of time"

of 14.1% p.a. in the manufacturing sector (index of industrial production, 1987-2000) has already been mentioned. Notably, some of these effects were exhausted in late 1990s, e.g. aspects of the recovery impulse (e.g. improved capacity utilisation) in the manufacturing sector (Ssemogerere 2005, 17).

86 The functions of the Uganda Industrial Research Institute (UIRI), the Uganda National Bureau of Standards (UNBS), and the Uganda Export Promotion Board (UEPB) are discussed. The assessment corresponds with one put forward in this book. Finally, among the policy issues that were discussed from an ex-ante perspective (likely impact/effectiveness) are the moves towards regional integration. For various reasons (e.g. Uganda's market size, landlocked position, shared resource with neighbouring countries), regional integration arrangements with its East African Community (EAC) neighbours are estimated to have productivity enhancing effects in the medium term (lower costs, shared infrastructure). Although, in the short-term, the productivity impact is expected to be limited by static costs (efficiency loss) of trade diversion within the East African Community Customs Union (EACCU) arrangement due to changes in tariff structures, which will probably lead to Ugandan firms switching import sourcing from least- cost world producers to higher cost EAC-producers, because of the higher common EACCU external tariff (Ssemogerere 2005, xvi, 45).

(ibid, 6, emphasis added), because they are closely linked to structural changes. TFP growth is one major way to realise output growth; increase in inputs (more capital, more labour, higher factor quality) is the other, with a residual for short-term factors (fluctuating around long-term output). On the importance of TFP, a study by the IMF (2005) on the estimated role of TFP in the Ugandan economic recovery period states:

> "The main point is that a country's technology, including TFP, determines its long-term growth potential. Essentially, the importance of TFP growth is explained by the neoclassical growth model's assumption of diminishing returns to capital ... which implies that capital accumulation cannot sustain long-term growth while TFP can ... [P]ositive growth in output per capita could not be sustained, unless TFP growth is positive. Higher TFP growth allows for higher levels of sustainable investments, which in turn generates higher long-term growth in output per capita"(ibid, 6-7).

Disintegrating output growth for the Ugandan recovery period 1986-2003 into its main sources, as done in Table 13, reveals that the growth of capital and labour contributed 5.5% and 1.0% percent respectively, while the TFP growth added merely 0.1%. Accordingly, capital accumulation explained about 85% of output growth; *TFP had a very limited impact* (ibid, 8). The IMF comments on the relatively small contribution of TFP as follows: "This is surprising given the progress made in liberalizing markets and trade. However, this is probably attributable to the relatively small share of the tradable sector and slow growth of subsistence agriculture" (2006, 24). Overall, the notable results of TFP analysis (and productivity analysis generally) deserve more attention from GOU and other stakeholders of economic development in Uganda.

Table 13: Sources of growth (average annual growth rates, %)

	Total GDP	Sources			
		Capital	Labour	TFP	Short-term factors
1961-2003	3.9	2.5	1.0	0.3	0.1
1961-71	5.2	2.7	1.3	0.1	1.1
1972-85	-0.4	-1.4	0.8	0.5	-0.4
1986-2001	6.4	5.5	1.0	0.1	-0.2

Source: *IMF (2005, 8).*

Notably, as a result of the recent capital accumulation Uganda has, on average, a relatively young capital stock (WB 2004b). This should increase prospects of sections of the capital stock to be relatively up-to-date in terms of technology and thus also productivity-enhancing (TFP, efficiency). A recent investment climate survey by the WB among formal sector firms in Uganda confirms a young capital stock in the *manufacturing sector*: Over 40% of the capital stock in manufacturing firms is less than five years old, and another 35% is less than 10 years old; other SSA countries typically have a large share of capital stock older than 20 years. Capital productivity in this sector is high compared to other SSA countries, about twice as much as in neighbouring countries. Capacity utilisation is only at about 60% (WB 2004b,

6, 26-9).[87] Importantly, however, the various changes and policy reforms in the post-1986 period have resulted in overall improved capacity utilisation and technical efficiency levels in manufacturing firms (Ssemogerere 2005, 13-4).

Against the background of a young capital stock, especially in the manufacturing sector, the low TFP impact (in the economy as a whole) during the recovery period *could* imply cross-sectoral problems in the private sector (and of the system of SIs): to transform and upgrade methods of production, adopt and use new technology and equipment in an efficiency-enhancing way, tackle related requirements in capabilities and organisational techniques, and thus realise productivity gains. The productivity inadequacies in the (semi-) subsistence as well as more commercial part of the agricultural sector are also important in this context. Furthermore, it could point to challenges relating to moving faster into high-productivity activities/sub-sectors (including expanding the manufacturing sector), which would require developing the respective products, processes and HR. Importantly, related TFP growth potential has to be realised, not only in activities usually related to the realm of production, but also in design, quality, marketing, logistics, intra-firm organisation or value chain management across different firms (or actors). If such inadequacies can be addressed, the potential for productivity improvements seems considerable. Going back to the argument about the prime importance of knowledge to realize TFP growth, the role of HRD in this context cannot be overemphasised.

Notably, the IMF states, "addressing productivity and growth performance, while mitigating the impact of exogenous shocks, will be important tasks for the Ugandan government" (2006, 24). Yet, the policy and intervention cocktail suggested by the IMF (2005, 2006) falls short of the IMF's own definition of TFP growth which, as presented, stresses "inherent advancements of knowledge about the production process, as well as reallocation of resources from low-productivity sectors (such as agriculture) to high productivity sectors (such as manufacturing)" (2005, 6). The HRD dimension within the productivity agenda certainly needs more serious consideration by major policy players than it receives at present.

Strong growth in TFP needed to support Uganda's development agenda

Over-reliance on mere capital accumulation is of concern for growth sustainability

The IMF puts forward two concerns with the characteristics of capital-driven growth in Uganda:

> "First, the strong reliance on capital accumulation and near absence of TFP growth raise doubts about the sustainability of growth ...Without a significant contribution from TFP growth, more investment will increasingly be required to sustain GDP growth rates of 6-7 percent ...Second, the combination of low TFP growth and high population growth substantially constrain an increase in output per capita ... Clearly, with an annual population growth of 3.2 percent ... and virtually zero TFP growth, the stock of capital would need to grow by a similar rate to prevent output per capita from declining. Also, with a fairly low marginal product of labor ..., a failure to increase capital sufficiently would have devastating negative effects on output per capita" (2005, 8-9).

One of the consequences of the above scenario would be increased pressure to advance both national and external savings, beyond the current levels, which are already quite dependent

87 The survey covered 392 firms across four sectors, manufacturing, tourism, commercial agriculture and services, with 300 of the responding firms coming from the manufacturing sector.

on external sources (ibid). Notably, national savings are fuelled by significant inflows of external transfers. The sustainability of donor flows is a crucial aspect in the context of the TFP problem.

Another study on TFP offers a somewhat *more positive* view. According to estimates by Dunn (2002), TFP growth was an important growth component up to the mid-1990s - representing the scale of rehabilitation, removal of distortions and efficiency gains (or recovery from the earlier fall in TFP) - but it has since fallen to much lower levels (quoted in Bevan et al. 2003, 15).[88] A positive contribution of TFP growth to Uganda's economic development and growth episode during the 1990s is also emphasised in Collier and Reinikka (2001), Siggel and Ssemogerere (2004) and Ssemogerere (2005) with general reference to the gains due to improved utilisation of existing capacities (plant and equipment) in the recovery period, for instance in the manufacturing sector. The conclusions drawn by Dunn (2002) and the other studies are nevertheless similar to the one of the IMF: Further *productivity improvements* - including enhanced capacity utilisation/technical efficiency levels of the equipment installed by recent investments - are needed to support the country's economic and social agenda (e.g. growth, jobs, well-being).[89] It is difficult to see how this could be achieved without considerably greater efforts to build HR and improve HRM for PSD.

> "The key implication ...is that while the positive effects of improved security and the elimination of extreme macroeconomic distortions may not have fully run their course, the scope for continued improvements in TFP from these sources is much reduced. Sustained higher growth over the next five years can be achieved only with much higher investment rates. Dunn estimates the prospects for TFP growth to be no greater that 0.5% per annum, and that achieving the PEAP target of 7% growth to 2006/07 would require investment to jump to 27% of GDP" (Bevan et al. 2003, 15).[90]

Productivity divergence at the global level: Uganda falling behind

In this context, note the increasing divergence in TFP performance between Uganda and the strong(er) TFP performers in the world. According to UNIDO's productivity database, Uganda lost ground *relative* to the USA in terms of TFP[91] in the period 1960-2000.[92] Uganda's score decreased from 24 to 19 (1960 vs. 2000; change: -5) relative to the USA (score 100 in 1960 and 2000), which was the most productive country in 1960 but has now been bypassed by Luxembourg (139) and Ireland (112) (Isaksson et al. 2005, 62). The related TFP ranking of 112 countries in 1960 and in 2000 shows, however, that many other countries (43 of the 112) have performed worse: They have fallen behind more significantly, relative to their initial performance in 1960. Thus, Uganda has still moved upwards in the ranking from 92nd to 82nd position. The top five performers in terms of catching up (relative to their initial positions)

---

88 Dunn estimates that, in the period 1986-1992, TFP growth contributed less than 1% p.a. to overall growth. This rate rose to 3% p.a. for the period 1992-1997, and fell back to around 0.5% thereafter (quoted in Bevan et al. 2003, 15).

89 See Selassie (2008) for a recent viewpoint of the IMF country representative in Uganda, titled 'Beyond Macro-economic stability: the Quest for Industrialization in Uganda '.

90 Keefer (2000) is of the same view, that key growth gains from improvements in the macroeconomic environment have already been reaped, and expects institutional reforms - tackling property rights, contract enforcement, tax administration, procurement procedures, corruption - to be of high importance to ensure growth (Bevan et al. 2003, 17).

91 TFP is adjusted by purchasing power parity.

92 The respective productivity data in Isaksson et al. (2005) is based also on Isaksson (2005).

are Luxembourg, Taiwan, Ireland and Hong Kong; while Mauritius, Botswana and Gabon are among the top 15 catching-up performers. Most other SSA countries are in the 'falling behind' group (ibid, 64-5, see also Table 45, Appendix 4a). Further, noticeably, "although there is some indication of convergence, it occurs only at the top half of the ... [country ranking] In the bottom half we see clear signs of divergence, and it appears that a bipolar situation has developed during the four decades" (ibid, 53).

A UNIDO analysis of the positioning of LDCs in relation to the World Technology Frontier (WTF) points to a similar problem, of increasing divergence in the last four decades between the LDC group and the leading performers (1960 vs. 2000). The WTF indicates an international best practice level (benchmark frontier) in terms of maximum output achieved with a certain technique or, the output per worker at a certain level of capital intensity (capital/labour ratio, capital per worker), by the 112 countries represented in the sample in a given moment of time. A country's performance can be compared to the international best practice level (the WTF) *at its technological level* (capital/labour ratio)[93] (ibid, 50).

> Thus, the "benchmark frontier represents the potential technology level common to all countries that have arrived at a given stage of development. The efficiency of the country is its degree of utilization of the potential technology ... [The] individual productivity performance [is constructed] as the distance of a country from the worldwide best practice pertinent to the technological level of the country" (ibid, 50-1, emphasis added).

Changes in a country's productivity performance can be related to shifts of the WTF (better techniques, better best practices)[94] and changes in the distance between a country and the WTF as a result of decreasing/increasing efficiency levels of the country (*catching up*: distance decreases; *lagging behind*: distance increases)[95] (ibid, 51-2).

Table 14 indicates the distance of groups of countries to the WTF: the respective actual efficiency levels relative to respective potential technology levels (best practice: maximum output at a certain level of capital intensity) at a certain moment in time (1960 and 2000). The table shows the strong catching-up achievement of the so-called Dynamic Developers.[96] In 1960, and in the context of the less sophisticated technologies of the time, they produced at 48% of their potential.[97] This was an efficiency level in the neighbourhood of the LDCs, which produced at an average efficiency of 46% (ibid, 54, 66). The low figures indicate "considerable productivity gains were feasible by mere efficiency advances" (ibid, 54).

---

93 "The country's performance is measured in relation to the point of the borderline that is closest to its position, i.e., with the best performer who shares the same or the closest capital/labour ratio" (Isaksson et al. 2005, 50). See Figure 12 below for a general illustration.

94 The frontier shifts "either because better techniques are brought into existence, because existing techniques are brought to new records of productivity, or because less sophisticated techniques are discarded. It is noteworthy that a shift not only marks a change in the actual performance of the country that made the breakthrough but also in the potential performance of all other countries using the technique that recorded the productivity gain. In principle, the best practice can be transferred internationally. Hence, when the best practice changes, the productivity potential of all countries changes too" (Isaksson et al. 2005, 51).

95 An *immobile* country (no changes in techniques or productivity) can lose efficiency levels just because the WTF (potential technology level) shifts upwards (Isaksson et al. 2005, 52).

96 These are Botswana, Chile, China, Hong Kong, India, Indonesia, Korea, Malaysia, Mauritius, the Philippines, Singapore, Taiwan, and Thailand. Uganda is in the LDC group.

97 The potential is the maximum output their technology is capable of producing (achievement of the best performer with similar/closest capital/labour ratio) (Isaksson et al. 2005).

Table 14: Distance to the World Technology Frontier, 1960 and 2000

Country group	1960	2000
World	0.56	0.58
Industrialised	0.75	0.68
Dynamic Developers	0.48	0.62
LDCs	0.46	0.44

Source: *Isaksson et al. (2005, 66).*

By 2000, the Dynamic Developers had succeeded in achieving a considerable catch-up: They produced, on average, at 62% of their maximum[98], demonstrating that *catching up is possible.* The *LDCs, instead, experienced an average efficiency drop* to 44% (at their respective potential technology levels), which means that the average LDC in 2000 operated at further distance from the WTF (best practice) than in 1960: The average efficiency performance has lowered and remains at less than half the potential. Markedly, the average efficiency of the Industrialized Countries - at their level of technology - has dropped as well. The world average efficiency level, however, has improved to some extent (56%/58%) (ibid, 66).

> Indeed, the Dynamic Developers "have gone a fairly long way towards more efficiency, while the performance of the remaining developing countries, already fairly low in 1960, has fallen further. This is, of course, a rather dismaying observation. In four decades, the majority of developing countries have not managed to improve the efficiency of techniques that, for them, have practically not changed" (ibid, 55).

Positively, the data for Uganda indicates that the country is now *one of the most efficient countries in the LDC group*: Compared to 1960, by 2000 she had significantly closed in on the frontier and operates at higher technical efficiency levels; again, indicating that catching up is possible, in this case in terms of the level of resource use.[99] The point for Uganda, as for other LDCs, however, is that they remain at a low level of capital per worker (little technical change). They will have to increase their level of capital intensity (technology etc.) to increase output closer to the level of the advanced countries. One of the challenges in this context is that Uganda's firms will have to adopt the new technology and learn how to operate it efficiently. There is evidence that efficiency levels tend to drop in DCs in the initial phase of this process of technological upgrading (ibid, 60).

> "In developing countries, efficiency appears negatively correlated to technical change. This correlation is by no means intuitive, and research is on course to find an explanation. At this stage one may conjecture that it has to do with the adoption of techniques that are new to the host environment but mature in the original environment. When developing countries make technological progress, it is mostly by way of adopting techniques already in use in developing countries. In developed countries learning-by-doing had brought the industries released to the developing countries to maximum productivity. In developing countries, the adoption of these technologies is only the beginning of the learning curve. Therefore, the transfer of the technique means, ipso facto, regress in efficiency" (ibid, 60-1).

---

98 The maximum is the potential technology level at their stage of development in 2000.

99 The information on the Uganda-specific change in terms of distance to the WTF was provided by Anders Isaksson (UNIDO); it is not included in Isaksson et al. (2005). Isasksson also referred to the ODA impact.

Hence, in the context of need to adopt and master new technology *competitively* (in the context of FDI inflows), there will be need for increased efforts to support local firms in their learning processes - and *provide or upgrade respective skills and capabilities* - so that the efficiency level drops less severely and/or improves faster in the initial period of use. Further, it is plausible to argue that the level of adjustment (e.g. learning processes) required to handle new technology will also be related to the locational source of technology: Respective learning efforts and costs might be lower in the case of import of (e.g. intermediate) technology used in other developing countries which, vis-à-vis high technology from industrialised countries, could be more adaptable to the Ugandan development context. Reaping such learning and productivity benefits of more South-South trade and cooperation can be considered vital for Uganda (ibid, 60).[100]

Further related findings of the WTF analysis are: (i) a division into a cluster of relatively poor and relatively rich countries, and (ii) a widening income gap in absolute terms (output per worker) (ibid, 55). "[F]or the majority of developing countries, where the situation has hardly changed since 1960, the goal of closing the productivity gap seems more distant than ever" (ibid). They continue to operate at low capital intensities (they stay relatively close to the origin in Figure 12) and often at low technical efficiencies which affect their level of output per worker, relative to the rest of the world.

Also significant is that world technological progress,[101] characterised by a shift in the WFP, has been remarkable; yet, it is more intense among advanced technologies and has remained almost entirely connected to the top section of countries/WTF[102] (ibid, 55, 60). The other countries, including the LDCs, "still occupy the technological space already charted in 1960" (ibid, 55, Figure 20, Appendix 4b). This and other evidence and interpretations presented in the UNIDO study suggest rather limited effects of world technological progress for less advanced countries, with adverse consequences for real income levels and learning and thus HRD (ibid, 59).[103] For LDCs, including Uganda, the threat of further marginalisation (falling behind) in terms of technology (capital) intensity, productivity (value addition, e.g. MVA) - is evident. Figure 12 illustrates the situation for 2000; Figure 21 (Appendix 4c) for 1960.

100 The author is grateful to Anders Isaksson for related comments.

101 Shift of the WTF: Increase in top output per worker by conditions of increased capital intensity. We already mentioned the labour saving feature of technological progress in the last four decades (Isaksson et al. 2005, 55).

102 In this case, these are the Industrialised Countries as well as Hong Kong, Israel, South Korea, Singapore and Taiwan.

103 Note, for instance, the observation that countries behind the border "tend to gain more productivity by moving towards the border (progressing within a given technology) rather than by shifting towards more advanced technologies. This case suggests that learning-by-doing is easier than adopting a new technique. It also suggests that the attraction effect of innovation at the border will not be felt evenly by behind-the-border countries; instead, it will be more powerful in countries in the technological neighborhood of the innovative segment. Knowledge would then seem to be more technology-specific" (ibid, 60).

Figure 12: World Technology Frontier 2000

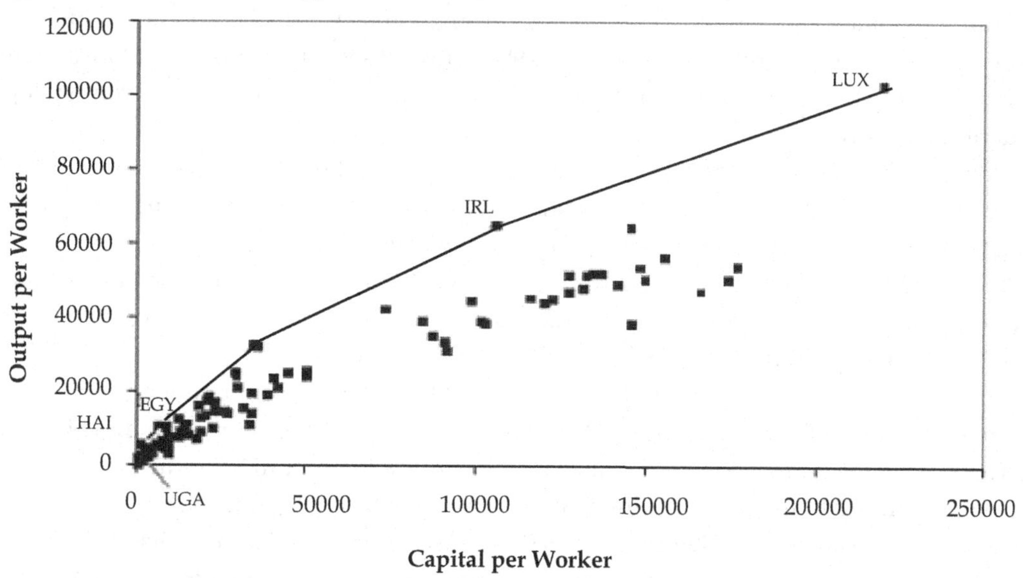

Source: *Isaksson et al (2005, 71).*

A number of vital implications can be drawn from this analysis[104]: One is that LDCs such as Uganda risk falling behind relative to non-LDCs in terms of both capital intensity (technology) and productivity. LDCs need to enhance their *absorptive capacity* to allow higher productivity levels (ibid, 57-8); certainly, Uganda is undertaking efforts in this direction. A key message in the quote below is that what matters is the application of knowledge - LDCs have significant deficits in this regard.

> "The basic reason for this stratification of countries [mentioned above] is that technology is not pure knowledge but *implementation of knowledge in the material world.* In order to absorb technology, an absorptive capacity is needed. To build up this capacity requires investment; to operate it requires expenditures. Only countries that have invested in building up an absorptive capacity and have taken care to maintain this capacity are able to implement technology developed elsewhere" (ibid, 57, emphasis added).

Besides, other possible reasons for divergence capacity differences are: random (positive and negative) shocks, features of the innovation process[105], and, of course, policy differences. With respect to shocks, it is important to note that the shift of the WTF

> "exerts a continuous pressure to keep up with the adaptation effort. Any accident that temporarily compels a country to seek some respite may have punishing consequences. The break acts like an opening scissor. On the one hand, the leading edge of technology becomes more and more difficult to absorb as the world shift goes on; on the other, the absorptive capacity becomes more and more eroded as the break lasts ... After years of fiscal austerity, the laboratories and the technical departments or universities are dilapidated and thee professors have moved abroad; after years of recession there is practically no industry left, no more private adaptation development, no incentive to do R&D, and no engineers or technicians to implement it" (ibid, 58).

---

104 See Isaksson et al. (2005) for details.

105 "[T]he absolute level of technological progress has been greater at higher income levels" (Isaksson et al. 2005, 59).

Against this background, post-1986 Uganda had to recover from a longer break (the years of turmoil), that significantly reduced her absorptive capacity. Further, under the changed internal and external conditions of the post-1986 period, it seems considerably more difficult for the country to ensure a (successful) process of absorptive capacity building and technology adaptation efforts.

Beyond this, to benefit (most) from a positive innovation shock, a country needs to be able to invest accordingly, and it must be economically active in the sector (industry/industry segment) where the opportunity occurs, because opportunities of new innovations are quite often specific and related to a certain sector or set of activities. This is a relevant qualification for Uganda given the stage of diversification and technology (capital intensity) from where she will have to progress (ibid, 58).

From the above, it seems vital that Uganda and her development partners consider the reasons for, as well as implications of, the trends presented above: the falling behind in terms of TFP, the limited benefits from worldwide technological progress, the (institutional, sectoral, firm and individual) requirements for absorbing technology, the relatively low level of technological and innovative efforts, and the consequences of related deficits for the future participation of the country in the world economy and corresponding issues such as real income levels and workers' productivity. The aspects of productivity and HRD discussed in this book - capabilities, HRM, technology and SIs (for matters of technology operation and training) - need to constitute a significant pillar in Uganda's response to the challenges and opportunities in today's world with regard to enhanced levels of productivity and innovation in the local economy. Isaksson et al. put forward a view that is essentially the same as other main arguments that are suggested in this book:

> "Countries that cannot innovate or imitate, stagnate in the inefficient use of unchanging technology. These countries seem to be too far away from the border to benefit from any demonstration effect. Compared to 1960, the distribution of countries in 2000 [regarding output per worker in order of increasing capital intensity] has assumed a much more bipolar shape, suggesting divergence in income per worker. In addition, the World Technology Frontier had moved outwards in a non-neutral fashion, which means that innovation basically occurs at high levels of capital intensity ... For all there is to be seen, the divergence will continue. If the countries lagging behind are to escape from falling further behind, a process of brisk imitation must be set in motion. The international community must help in the transfer of much more technology than was transferred in the past forty years, and the countries lagging behind must accumulate capital in order to, as Abramowitz (1986) has pointed out, increase social and technological capabilities" (2005, 61; see also Abramowitz 1986).

What do such productivity-related findings, interpretations, and recommendations tell us about HRD requirements in particular? Throughout the book, there are attempts to refer to related aspects.

Pro-productivity agenda: Linked to formation of local skills and capabilities

The productivity diagnosis clearly signals the requirement for Uganda's economy to boost TFP and labour productivity. This includes achieving related advancement of structural transformation and investment dynamics to ensure future growth of both total GDP and GDP per capita. Besides justifying continued efforts related to the quality of the education system, this builds a strong case for: the formation of (technical, social, etc.) skills and capabilities, better business management and process organisation, and (explicit and implicit) training practices to *improve productivity in general*, and the *use of technology* as well as the *efficiency of production processes* and *input use* in particular. Note, for instance, that there can also be sector-specific levels of productivity of learning-by-doing (Isaksson et al. 2005, 28-9). This implies the relevance of day-to-day learning on the ground and across the economy, the sub-sectors and the various activities therein (along the value chain).

A pro-productivity agenda calls for the development of the national Innovation and Learning System (ILS) (Isaksson et al. 2005), which includes a strong *local training system*. The latter is often referred to as BTVET system.[106] The analyses of data in the sections below confirm the importance of training, learning and experience[107] (besides health, education and larger and advanced markets) for firm performance. To be sure, education - which has been more in the focus of policy making in Uganda to date - is paramount for productivity; yet (formal) education will not be discussed explicitly in this book.[108]

Further, as argued before, most benefits of the stability and recovery period have been reaped. New dynamic sources of economic development and growth have to be realised. In this context, productivity enhancement has to be a top concern. Knowledge, skills and capabilities and the related support systems and SIs (for training and learning, technology and innovation) will have to be considered more robustly by economic policy-makers and private sector actors; especially as Uganda aims to become an industrial, services and knowledge economy: *All this requires higher levels of human capital.*

However, to date the private sector's own assessment of constraints to PSD (investment and growth) does not - according to surveys by the UIA and others - feature the categories skills, knowledge or business practices and norms very prominently (Table 15). For instance, a WB survey among manufacturing firms (year 1998) ranks 'lack of skilled labour' at 13th position among the main constraints to the sector; 'lack of business support services' was ranked at 11th position (2004, 47). In the WB Investment Climate Survey 2002/03, around 31% of firms indicated 'skills and education of available workers' to be a general constraint to their business operation, which gives it the 9th position in the 'constraints ranking' (ibid, 39). Other surveys, e.g. the Global Entrepreneurship Monitor (GEM) or EU/GOU surveys reveal a different picture: skills deficits are identified as a key problem (see below).

The low ranking of skills by some major surveys could be explained by: (i) skills indeed not being (perceived to be) a core constraint, (ii) firms are operating in low-skill sectors/markets that are not really driven by specific (e.g. technical, managerial, organisational) skills, (iii) the high impact level of issues which rank highly, and/or (iv) deficiencies in private sector awareness regarding skills' importance. A problem with such findings, based on perceptions of *existing* players in the private sector, is that if GOU (and donors, NGOs, researchers) base their PSD agenda mainly on this assessment, support interventions will likely not: (i) cover views of potential investors, for example (who shy away in the first place due to deficiencies

106 Isaksson et al. (2005) in their study discuss a policy focus on the following critical conditions for productivity: the NIS, the education system as well as the communication and energy infrastructure. Training, as said, is not scope of their study. See Box 42 (Appendix 3) for more details.

107 Exposure of managers to operations of foreign firms, or production of firms for export markets, for example.

108 The research focus for this book and the expertise of the author did not allow for substantial statements on formal education.

in skills and other non-listed problems), or (ii) address issues that are actually relevant (e.g. low capabilities, low trust, malpractices) yet do not appear in such lists because they have been 'discovered' as relevant only by a few entrepreneurs (e.g. in newly diversified sectors) or are more pronounced in the informal sector.

Table 15: Main constraints to private sector/investment according to investment surveys

1995	2000	2001	2003
1)Electricity 2)Tax policy 3)Tax administration 4)Cost of finance 5)Access to finance 6)Utilities 7)Bureaucracy/ corruption	1)Foreign exchange trends 2)Inflation 3)Interest rates 4)Tax administration 5) Bureaucracy/ corruption Bureaucracy/corruption 6)Access to credit 7)Tax policy 8)Incentives 9)Int. commodity prices 10) Domestic Competition	1)Foreign exchange trends 2)Interest rate 3)Corruption 4)Inflation 5)Smuggling 6)Size of government expenditure 7)VAT efficiency 8)Financial stability 9)Customs duty 10)Tax policy	1) Exchange rates 2) Inflation 3) Corruption 4) Interest rates 5) Tax policy 6) Income tax 7) VAT 8) Globalisation/ smuggling 9) Corporate tax 10) Customs duty

Source: *UIA (2004), BOU et al (2004).*

Low labour productivity levels in manufacturing firms: Exporting firms display better productivity performance

Despite the investment of the last 15 years, Uganda's manufacturing firms, especially smaller ones in the sample of the WB survey cited above, are estimated to have low capital-intensive operations with, on average, about 1,500US$ of *capital per worker*, with other African countries' ratios being about three to four times larger.

> "Large firms have the highest amount of capital per worker, more than four times the median value. Micro firms have very little capital, slightly more than half the median value. Not surprisingly, exporters have substantially more capital per worker than non-exporters ($3,277 versus $1,408), and firms with foreign equity have a median value of $3,930 worth of capital per worker compared with $1,408 for firms with no foreign equity ... [Further noteworthy is that] the largest firms in Uganda have higher capital intensity than firms of a similar size in India, but lower capital intensity than the largest firms in Sub-Saharan Africa. The largest firms in the region appear to be substituting capital for labor, perhaps because of labor laws or a lack of skilled labor" (WB 2004b, 43, 27-8).

Moreover, the *median of value added per worker*, a measure of labour productivity, is 1,085US$ p.a. (2002) in the Ugandan manufacturing sector. This is the lowest rate in the SSA survey group and fairly below regional competitors Tanzania (2,061US$), Zambia (2,680US$), Kenya (3,457US$) as well as India (3,432US$) and China (4,397US$) (see Figures 13 and 14). Labour productivity in Uganda is higher in exporting firms (2,901US$ vs. 1,117US$ for non-exporting firms), larger firms (3,338US$ vs. only 578US$ and 897US$ for the micro and small firms respectively[109]), and foreign firms (2,747US$ vs. 1,182US$ for domestic firms) (ibid, 29-31).[110]

109 Micro firms are defined as those with less than 10 employees, small firms by an employee level of 10-49. Medium-sized firms (50-99) in Uganda have a labour productivity of 1379US$ (WB 2004b, 31).

110 See earlier discussion of labour productivity figures for Uganda.

Figure 13: Median annual value added per worker in manufacturing, selected developing countries

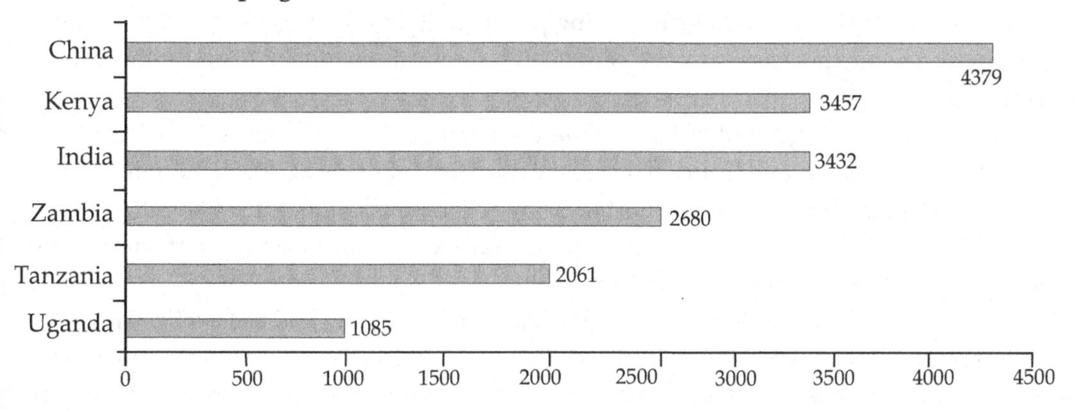

Source: *WB (2004b, 30).*

Figure 14: Labour productivity in manufacturing relative to that of India

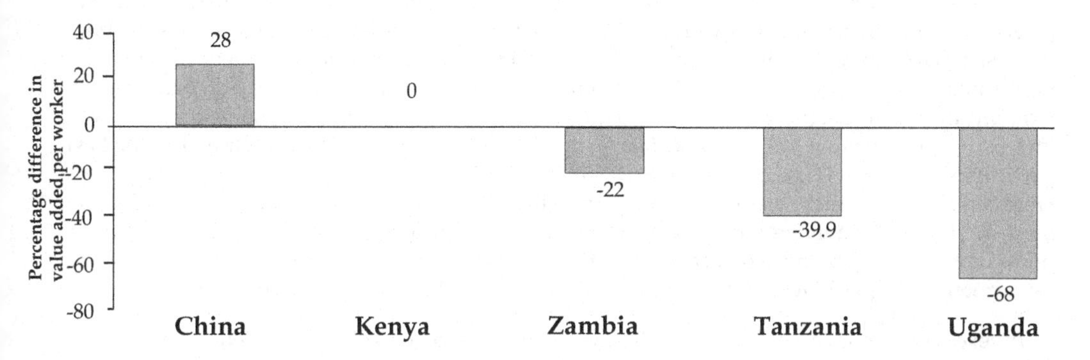

Source: *WB (2004b, 30).*[111]

One of the manufacturing firms' responses, to offset productivity disadvantages and keep production at competitive levels, seems to be a comparatively low level of monthly earnings for unskilled production workers, which is about 57US$ and reportedly lower than wages in Kenya and Nigeria (about 73US$-100US$ p.m.) and some of the Asian countries, but higher than in India (45US$), for example. In terms of *unit labour costs*, Uganda's manufacturers reportedly cannot compete with much more efficient Asian economies (0.39 vs. 0.27 and 0.32 for Indian and China respectively; Tanzania: 0.39, Kenya: 0.39). More specifically, the larger firms (100+ employees) in the Ugandan sample compare well with counterparts in India and China (0.25 vs. 0.24 and 0.29); while the small firms (10-49) demonstrate severe disadvantages in unit labour costs (0.56 vs. 0.30 and 0.38). Notably, within the Ugandan sample, large firms, exporters, foreign firms, and firms owned by non-indigenous entrepreneurs have lower unit

111 The base case is labour productivity in India (2002-03). Data are based on nominal exchange rates.

labour costs than their counterparts - the small, non-exporting, no foreign equity, indigenous entrepreneur firms; which is explained in the report by higher productivity levels (ibid, 22-35). Box 7 presents similar findings regarding productivity differences - especially between exporting and non-exporting firms in Uganda, with significantly higher levels for the former (Gauthier 2001).

Note, given their large pool of labour, there are apparently few prospects of *significant* labour shortages in India and China in the near future (Altenburg et al. 2006), though in some industries in China, forms of labour shortages have been reported recently. Overall, the unit costs of Chinese and Indian firms are likely to remain a long-term challenge for firms in SSA who face competition from these countries.

In summary, one can conclude that *productivity-related support* would be beneficial for both groups: for (a) exporters - to maximise benefits from learning opportunities, technology, and improvement pressures in relation to export market exposure, and (b) non-exporters - e.g. to allow learning from more productive domestic exporters (where appropriate), and reaching higher productivity levels which can help to finance subsequent entry into export markets (if desired) (Gauthier 2001).

Box 7: Better levels and growth of productivity for exporting firms vs. domestic market-oriented firms

An analysis of survey data (1995-97, liberalisation period) by Gauthier (2001) found that productivity levels (in all different productivity indexes112) were higher among exporting than non-exporting/domestic market-oriented firms. Foreign-owned or joint foreign and local ownership firms also performed better - especially in the labour productivity index - than domestically-owned firms.113 Notably, the technical efficiency levels of Ugandan firms (both exporters and non-exporters) were lowest in comparison to four other African sample countries: in total, it was half that of the best-performing country, Cameroon (0.19 vs. 0.38). The calculated indexes for productivity growth were better for exporting firms (vs. non-exporting firms) and for foreign-owned (vs. jointly/locally owned).114 For the average firm in the sample, though, efficiency levels dropped (-2.4%) in the period covered; the second-worst change in efficiency performance in country comparison (worst: Cameroon: -2.6%).115 Overall, the study findings suggest that "export orientation is associated

112 Indexes covered levels of labour productivity, total unit costs, TFP and efficiency.

113 Total sample: 139 firms. Exporting firms (vs. non-exporting firms) experienced: higher labour productivity (by 60%), higher TFP (by 12%), higher technical efficiency (by 28%), and lower total unit costs (by 46%). Further, locally owned firms have a slightly higher TFP level, a lower labour productivity (five times, compared to joint ownership firms), higher total unit costs (twice), and lower efficiency levels (almost half). Note *output growth* in the period was also stronger for export firms as well as foreign and jointly owned firms (Gauthier 2001, 239-41).

114 In exporting firms (vs. non-exporting firms) labour productivity grew about 10 times faster, unit costs grew 6 times slower, TFP increased twice as much, and efficiency improved by 7% (vs. -5% for non-exporters). Overall, labour productivity and TFP improved, while unit costs and efficiency levels worsened (average firm). Firms that relied strongly on imported inputs experienced higher productivity growth (labour productivity, total unit costs, TFP, not: efficiency) than firms relying on domestic inputs (Gauthier 2001, 242-4). Also note the study by Rasiah and Tamale (2004), which examines productivity, export-intensity, skills-intensity and technological differences between exporting foreign and local firms in several industrial sub-sectors in Uganda and found "[n]o clear statistically significant productivity ... differences exist between foreign and local firms in most industries. Foreign firms in food and beverages [though] enjoyed a substantially higher labour productivity" (ibid, 29).

115 This is not significantly explained or commented upon in the study. In the country comparison, two other countries also experienced overall drops in efficiency (two others: positive trend; for all five countries: survey in respective liberalisation period). In all countries, non-exporters/domestic market oriented firms performed worse than exporting firms (Gauthier 2001, 244).

with significantly greater output growth ...and with higher productivity levels and growth ...of productivity" (ibid, 246). In particular "the effect of exporting on technical efficiency is ...positive and significant, indicating an important learning effect associated with exporting activities among sample firms during that period" (ibid, 245). It is relevant to consider that this form of analysis cannot "answer the question of whether exporting leads to efficiency gains or if the relationship runs from efficiency to exporting" (ibid). Accordingly, results from other studies (e.g. Roberts and Tybout 1997) - not tested in this Ugandan study though - suggest, that "high productivity precedes [subsequent] entry into the export market ... [one reason probably being] that high-productivity producers can afford the cost of entering the export markets" (Gauthier 2001, 245).

Health, education, training and on-the-job learning relevant for better performance

The WB survey cited above (which sampled mostly manufacturing firms) reveals that, across all sectors, about every fourth worker interviewed reported having been ill within the previous 30 days. Over a 30-day period, illness led to an average loss of 3.2 days, which is about 15% of available workdays (around 37 days p.a.). In manufacturing, if the figures were in that range too, this would result in a production loss of 11%.[116] Compared to smaller firms, larger firms have a higher share of ill workers, but lower level of 'days lost' (WB 2004, 69).[117] In this context, it is suggested that 8-10% of the Ugandan workforce is infected with HIV/AIDS (Ssemogerere 2005, 34). HIV/AIDS - and the health status of the workforce generally - impacts substantially on productivity due to, among others, loss of time and skills, and lower concentration of workers (ibid).[118] According to estimates for Africa HIV/AIDS lowers GDP by around 1%, which calls for related responses from firms, workers, the state and others (WB 2004b, 68, Sachs and Blum 1998). "Improving the health status of the labor force as quickly as possible is therefore critical" (WB 2004b, 8).[119]

The WB survey results further indicate that relevant variables for explaining outcomes of TFP (value added) in the Ugandan sample are, besides labour and capital, the levels of: (a)

116 Assuming a constant rate of illness over the year and applying the study's TFP estimation.

117 Uganda's manufacturing sector operates with a working week of six days; Chinese firms can operate seven days.

118 Ssemogerere writes: "The loss of productivity arises from: [a] Morbidity from Aids and opportunistic infections which reduces concentration of the patient at work; [b] Frequent absence of the patient from work: to attend to clinics for medical care, counselling sessions from paramedical personnel, laboratory monitoring tests, pharmacy waiting lines to fill prescriptions; [c] Time lost from work by the healthy but next of kin: to care for the sick; attend funerals and resolve after funeral rites; care for the surviving dependents, which Deininger et al. (2002) note to have adverse effects on income, consumption and investment, which collectively reduced productivity; [d] Time lost by the employers, when labour turnover, due to death or incapacitation necessitates: search for a replacement, with more search time lost as seniority of the patient increases, requiring search for expatriates in some cases, orientation and training of newly hired replacement staff. ... [A] study of Uganda Railway Corporation workers estimated the labour turnover due to Aids to be about 15% p.a." (2005, 34).

119 For more information, see a study by the MFPED and UNDP (2008) on the macroeconomic impact of HIV/AIDS in Uganda. It estimates that HIV/AIDS is likely to slow down the GDP growth rate of the economy (on average 1.2% p.a. in period 2008-2016), reduce wage growth and per capita GDP, and increase household poverty levels (by 1.4% in the short term and 0.5% in the long term, taking into account income and expenditure effects) due to, among others, the impact of HIV/AIDS on the labour force, productivity, investment, and HIV/AIDS health-related costs (with the latter burdening especially rural households). The exact HIV/AIDS impact will also depend on the level of Antiretroviral Therapy provision (ibid).

capacity utilisation and (b) *education of the managers/entrepreneurs* (university and secondary education) as well as the (c) number *of years of experience of the manager at a foreign firm* (ibid, 33).[120] This finding underlines the importance of skills formation and related learning processes through education and training, including on-the-job training and learning-by-doing efforts in the workplace.[121] It also points out the strength of *combining foreign and local sources of competitiveness,* here in terms of skills, capabilities and know-how:[122]

> "The learning of entrepreneurs - whether through advanced education or work experience in a foreign firm - is among the most important factors in determining a firm's productivity and growth. ... This result shows the importance of general training received by employees at foreign enterprises; this training helps entrepreneurs start and manage more productive firms" (ibid, 6, 33).

Moreover, regarding average technical efficiency levels, the Ugandan score is 0.51 which indicates that, on average, firms are only about half as efficient as the most efficient firm ('best practice') within the sample. This, according to the study, is typically associated with uncompetitive, segmented markets (low competition pressures). Firms in competitive markets (economies) have average scores of up to 0.75-0.80 (ibid, 33-4). However, the efficiency disparities and thus performance variability in the Ugandan case could also serve as an indicator of (a) the low priority given to productivity issues by many firms, and/or (b) the different capacities and capabilities of firms to *understand* efficiency (productivity) issues and be *able* to address them. For instance, a firm (staff) might not have the required social skills needed to apply new knowledge in order to improve economic processes and activities. The efficiency disparities further indicate (c) the potential for catching up if Ugandan firms would be more aware of related issues *and* be in a position to address them. In this context, a higher level of inter-firm cooperation, learning and networks, as well as better in-house HRD (e.g. training and informal learning environment) could help in advancing the average efficiency level closer to the level of the 'best practice' within the domestic economy/sectors.

Further to the WB survey results: firm size and foreign/domestic ownership are not significant factors for efficiency outcomes. However, the larger firms in the sample and the exporting ones are more efficient than smaller, and non-exporting firms. Accordingly, the most significant explanatory factor in firm efficiency is the *education of the entrepreneur*. Here, those managers with college and technical education score second highest, after the university group. *Experience* in foreign firms also contributes to higher average efficiency scores than in the without case (ibid, Table 16).

---

120 Note the already presented finding of a significant link between exports a high productivity (Gauthier 2001).

121 Note that an analysis of manufacturing firms in Ghana, Kenya and Zimbabwe pointed to the significance of learning mechanisms in enhancing productivity. In particular, on-the-job training of workers had relatively the largest impact on productivity (Biggs et al. 1995); "[s]pecifically, an increase of 1% in the number of workers trained potentially increases the value added of the sampled firms by as much as 60%" (WB 1996, review of Biggs et al. 1995 study).

122 The WB report does not offer cross-country reference/analysis of TFP features, which would have been helpful.

Table 16: Average efficiency of manufacturing firms grouped by various characteristics, Uganda

Characteristic	Average efficiency
Entrepreneur's highest level of education achieved	
Primary	0.47
Secondary	0.51
Technical	0.53
University	0.60
Entrepreneur's prior experience	
Foreign firm experience	0.56
No foreign firm experience	0.51

Source: *WB (2004b, 34).*

Reflecting on these findings the authors conclude: "learning channels are the most significant driver of firm performance. Learning - whether through export experience, work in a foreign firm, or advanced education - helps boost firm performance. Government policies that help develop these learning channels will thus foster private sector growth in Uganda" (ibid, 34). This is a *strong confirmation of the relevance of broad-based HRD measures for the Ugandan case.* Table 17 gives an indication of the education and experience of Ugandan entrepreneurs in manufacturing. The share of entrepreneurs in China or India with university education is more than twice the level in Uganda (above 80% vs. 40%). The same holds for years of professional experience: 10 years vs. five years.

Table 17: Education/experience of manufacturing entrepreneurs, selected developing countries

	Uganda	Kenya	Mozambique	Nigeria	China	India
Entrepreneurs by highest level of education achieved (percent)						
None	3.4	0.0	0.0	3.1	0.0	0.4
Primary	8.1	4.0	17.8	5.21	0.1	0.6
Secondary	19.8	23.2	44.1	10.8	15.2	9.8
Vocational	29.2	13.4	23.5	-	-	-
University	39.6	59.4	14.7	70.8	84.7	89.2
Average years of experience	5.0	5.4	-	-	10.4	9.95
Share of Entrepre-neurs with experience in foreign firm (%)	21.6	22.9	-	-	-	-
* - Not available						

Source: *WB (2004b, 24).*

The importance of education and experience in explaining firm performance is confirmed by differences between ethnic groups in the Ugandan manufacturing sector (Table 18)[123]:

> "Indigenous African entrepreneurs have less education and experience than their Asian and European counterparts, and their firms grow significantly more slowly. And when entrepreneurs establish their own firms, more likely for African than for Asian entrepreneurs, the firms tend to grow more slowly. On the whole, Asian firms enjoy the benefits of inherited ownership and experience" (ibid, 26).

Further, regarding the wages of manufacturing workers, the human capital variables years of education, years of experience with the firm, and other work experience "all have a positive and statistically significant effect ... Thus the greater a worker's endowment of human capital, the higher his or her wages are. Formal training also has a positive and significant effect" (ibid, 73-4). These findings and related implications for HRD are critical. *Education, training and experience of managers/entrepreneurs (and staff more generally) are factors that explain differences in firms' performances.* On average, indigenous entrepreneurs/managers face a gap compared to their Asian competitors regarding education and experience. This indicates the need for more focus on and support for institutionalised education and training (E&T) as well as processes of on-the-job training of and learning (especially learning-by-doing) by the local Ugandan entrepreneurs and workers. Interestingly, against the significant HRD role in explaining firm performance, the authors of the investment climate analysis note in a footnote that "several investment climate variables were included in the production function to evaluate their impact on productivity. These specifications ... were not significant" (WB 2004b, 35).[124] Against the rising prominence of the investment climate focus in Uganda's policy circle, this critical observation should be noted by authorities and donors.

Table 18: Characteristics of manufacturing entrepreneurs and their firms by ethnicity

	African	*Asian*
Highest level of education achieved (%)		
None	4.4	0.0
Primary	11.5	0.0
Secondary	62.4	33.3
University	21.6	66.7
Entrepreneurs' prior experience		
Average years of experience	3.8	8.1
Share who worked in foreign firm (%)	15.9	47.9
Share who established own firm (%)	87.9	75.0

123 The emphasis on HR indicators is not to deny the relevance of financial capital and other factors for firm performance.

124 "Several factors probably account for this: the sample of firms includes relatively little variance; firms compensate for the poor investment climate (for example, electricity users facing high power costs purchase generators) and select activities that minimize its adverse impact (for example, avoiding continuous process manufacturing); and the characteristics of the investment climate may well be embodied in (and correlated with) the attributes of labor and capital" (WB 2004, 35).

Share of entrepreneurs obtaining start-up finance (%)		
Informal loans	6.4	9.6
Formal loans	7.0	17.3
Firm characteristics		
Firm size at start-up (employees)	14	39
Average firm age (years)	9.7	10.1
Current firm size (employees)	31	104
Average annual growth (%)	0.19	0.21

Source: *WB (2004b, 25).*

A final note: There have been dozens of studies in Uganda on specific sectors, on trade matters etc., while there is hardly any research available that addresses drivers of productivity in Uganda in detail, including respective political-economic, technological, organisational, as well as behavioural and socio-economic aspects such as social norms, cultural values and practices of inter-firm interactions. As mentioned, there is a handful of analyses with reference to productivity matters - these are mainly IMF (2005), WB (2004b), Rasiah and Tamale (2004), Dunn (2002) and Gauthier (2001) - and there is now a specific study available on productivity trends in Uganda for the period 1961-2000 (Ssemogerere 2005).[125]

More comprehensive productivity studies need to be undertaken in the aftermath of findings on Uganda's productivity difficulties. Future research should follow up, among other points: the reasons behind the low average technical efficiency level (including the big gap of many firms in relation to the most efficient firm), or sectoral differences of productivity advancement through learning-by-doing efforts and processes. It is also relevant to explore the link between *competition pressures or competitiveness dynamics* on the one hand and (b) *productivity enhancing efforts* (including technology upgrading, HR improvements) by different sectors/firms, depending on different target markets (domestic, regional or international)[126], or firm's sizes, on the other. Also, the links between competition pressures, business practices and norms (e.g. level of trust, honesty, and cooperation) and productivity levels needs to be analysed. Overall, quantitative studies need to be complemented by qualitative methods (e.g. case studies).

---

125 There might be productivity studies in agriculture, which the author has not searched for in particular.

126 Findings of a survey among industrial firms in Uganda revealed the statistical insignificance of export-intensity on *process technology*. This seems to suggest that firms, irrespective of ownership, do not seem to "specifically choose techniques, machinery and equipment on the basis of markets. This appears sensible since most firms only export to Tanzania, Rwanda, Burundi, Zambia and Kenya where demand conditions are similar" (WB 2004b, 25-6). However, in the case of foreign firms export intensity had a statistically significant relationship with the *overall technology index* (influence on choice of overall technology).

Knowledge, capabilities, learning and organisation relevant for productivity improvements

The findings discussed in the above sections illustrate that knowledge (absorptive capacity), know-how, skills, capabilities and learning are essential if an attempt is to be made to close the firm-level gaps in Uganda in terms of productivity, efficiency, and growth. The variable 'experience' points to the importance of on-the-job learning processes, including obtaining tacit knowledge. Moreover, organisational issues, such as incentive systems, business processes, organisational technique, and management practices have a strong impact on productivity (value of outputs and/or inputs); not just technological or product innovations (Akella et al. 2003). There is ample room for related improvements in Ugandan firms and farms; efforts need to include, where appropriate, interacting with SIs, and learning from foreign firms that operate in the country. Box 8 gives more background and examples of productivity-oriented measures; the agenda is complex and often rather long-term in character.

Box 8: Enterprise productivity

(1) New ways of organising and managing enterprises which impact on productivity

Opportunities

- Clustering, networking and specialisation increase efficiency and productivity.
- New managerial methods and production techniques also enhance efficiency and productivity.
- ICT provide access to new knowledge on management methods, production techniques, marketing and export opportunities (e-commerce).

Challenges

- Increased competition at all levels in both export and domestic markets due to trade liberalisation.
- New skills and capabilities are required to master IT, especially for new design, production and marketing systems.

Source: *UNIDO (2002, 17).*

(2) Making business more productive

(Source: Akella et al 2003)

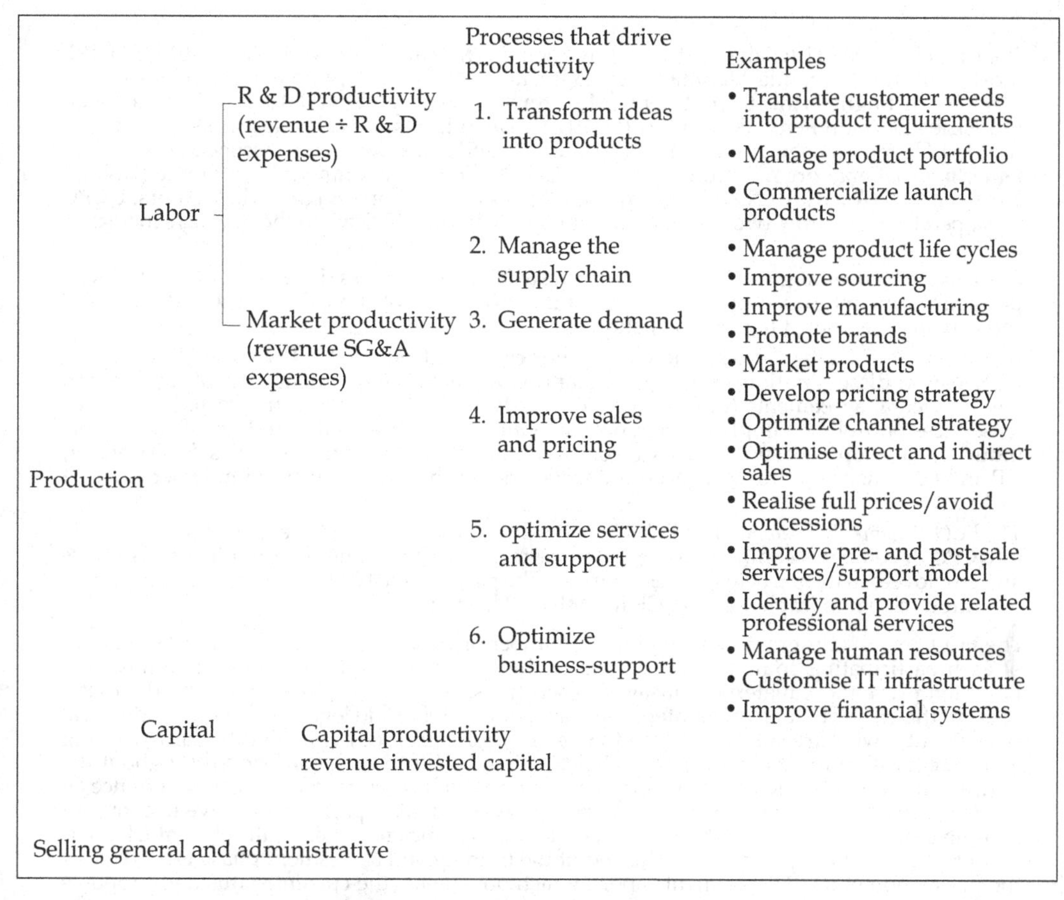

Against this background, the experience of the UCPC mentioned earlier, dealing with efficiencies (e.g. energy efficiency) and related aspects of productivity, demonstrates that the dual aims of economic growth and environmental protection can be met by improving the environmental efficiency of businesses. By reducing environmental impacts and cutting waste, firms can improve their productivity, save money and become/remain competitive, especially in global markets where growing consumer concern about the environment is already being reflected in purchases of goods. Box 9 provides more information on UCPC's work.

Box 9: Technological capability formation - the work of the Uganda Cleaner Production Centre

"*Definition of Cleaner Production (CP):* Cleaner Production is defined as the continuous application of an integrated, preventive strategy to processes, products and services to increase overall efficiency and reduce risks to humans and the environment.

"*Definition of Cleaner Production (CP):* CP is the continuous application of an integrated preventive strategy to processes, products and services to increase overall efficiency and reduce risks to humans and the environment.

Background: UCPC was established in 2001 as a joint effort between the GOU and UNIDO. UCPC is one of 35 National Cleaner Production Centres (twelve in Africa) which have been established worldwide since 1995. UCPC is a component of the Uganda Integrated Programme (UIP) of UNIDO and is currently hosted by Uganda Industrial Research Institute (UIRI, Nakawa Industrial Area, Kampala). UCPC operates under the guidance of an executive board and an advisory board, where the key national stakeholders such as the private sector, government, research institutions and industrial associations are represented. The members of the Executive

Board include: MTTI (chair), National Environment Management Authority (NEMA), UIRI (host institution), Uganda Manufacturers Association (UMA), Department of Chemistry and Mechanical Engineering Department (Makerere University), UNIDO UIP, Uganda Metal Industries Development Association (UMIDA), Uganda Small Scale Industries Association (USSIA), Uganda Gatsby Trust, and Uganda Leather and Allied Industries Association (ULAIA). Other international organisations such as United Nations Environment Programme (UNEP), Horizont3000 (Austria), GTZ (Germany), and Norsk Form (Norway) are collaborators. UCPC was operating with only two permanent technical staff until 2005 when the numbers increased to four.

Objectives: The overall goal is to contribute to 'sustainable business development and reduced pollution from enterprises in Uganda' through application of the CP concept and increased capacity in CP amongst national stakeholders.

Core Services and Programmes: The core activities carried out by UCPC since 2001 include information dissemination, training, in-plant assessments, implementation of multilateral environmental agreements (MEAs) and policy advice. In 2004, the centre started to enlarge its services portfolio by implementing new activities coherent with the strategy of sustainable industrial development such as working on environmentally sound technologies (EST) transfer, CP and EST financing projects, corporate social responsibility, and further implementation of ISO 14001.

The ECO-Benefits Programme: The ECO-Benefits Programme is one of the key CP programmes of UCPC. It combines comprehensive CP assessments with training of individual consultants and employees in the participating enterprises. The programme has proved to be a good engine for introducing and implementing CP in SMEs in Uganda.

The ECO-Benefits programme starts with a number of workshops where two representatives of each participating company are trained in the various CP-concepts: waste minimisation, pollution prevention, material utilisation, good housekeeping, record keeping, productivity, energy efficiency, preventive maintenance management, OHS and legal compliance. Individual participants, who are university graduates or (UCPC trained) consultants with working experience within industries in related fields, are attached to each company throughout the entire programme period of ten months, during which they gain practical experience in implementing CP-concepts. During this first phase, companies' participants have to carry out a number of tasks; this helps them to assess their companies in detail in all relevant CP areas and practise the concepts learned. The end of the training and assessment phase is marked by the production of a CP assessment report, which documents the current status and proposes a CP programme with a number of CP options to be implemented in the company during the next phase - the implementation phase. During the implementation phase companies start with the implementation of no-cost and low-cost options. This results in immediate economic and environmental benefits. These savings are then used for the implementation of more costly options. For high-cost options, which require capital investment, UCPC supports the companies in finding financing and preparing the necessary documents.

From the available case studies it is evident that all companies which have gone through the whole ten-month programme have achieved measurable and remarkable improvements in all areas addressed by the programme. These achievements are evaluated by an independent commission during the evaluation phase of the programme. Successful companies are then awarded a CP certificate, which is renewed every year. So far six ECO-Benefits programmes have been carried out and 50 large, medium and small-scale companies from different industrial sectors have participated and benefited from the implementation of the CP concepts. Seven out of these companies attained ISO14001 certification in 2004.

Success factors: For the implementation phase to be successful UCPC has to provide continued guidance and supervision of the participating companies. Also, the programme tries to involve the entire staff of the company - from the top management down to the shop-floor workers, which creates a sense of ownership. Success of the programme is based on commitment of top management and change of attitude amongst management and employees of participating companies.

Productivity/efficiency: There are many examples, such as significantly reduced water consumption in sugar, dairy or fish processing firms, improved energy efficiency in all firms, improved productivity, and reduced chemical consumption by textile companies. The Eco-Benefits Programme alone resulted in a total savings of 1.5mUSD p.a. from all the companies that participated in the first four Eco-Benefits programmes.

Participation in international programmes since 2006: UCPC - together with other Dan brew, the Directorate of Water Resources Management Uganda, the African Roundtable on Sustainable Consumption and Production (ARSCP), UNEP, and DANIDA - implemented CP under the African Brewery Sector Water Saving Initiative (ABREW) project in two breweries in Uganda

(Nile Breweries Ltd and Uganda Breweries Ltd) with a specific focus on water savings and pollution prevention. The study was extended to breweries in three other countries (Ethiopia, Ghana and Morocco); the in-plant assessments were only confined to the breweries in Uganda. A framework analysis and sector study reports were some of the key outputs along with a water use efficiency toolkit. A follow up project to ABREW, the African Beverage Sector Water Saving Initiative (ABWSI), will soon be rolled out under the auspices of UNEP, GTZ, ARSCP and UN Global Compact.

The e-waste project: A situational analysis of e-waste management and generation with special emphasis on personal computers was carried out with support of the Swiss Institute of Materials Science and Technology and the Uganda UCPC. This was done within the framework of the partnership agreement that was signed in July 2006 between UNIDO and Microsoft that plans to make secondary PCs available to SMEs in developing economies in a safe and sustainable way. The initiative intends to support the establishment of local sustainable e-waste recycling facilities. The study's objectives were to provide a situational analysis with respect to the generation and management of electronic waste in Uganda. UCPC also participated in an e-waste meeting in Durban (2008) which resulted in the Durban Declaration on e-waste management in Africa.

Institutionalization of ARSCP: UCPC made contribution to the development of SCP in the African Region under the Marrakech Process and in formulation of the African 10-Year Framework Programme on Sustainable Consumption and Production, a process initiated by UNEP and UNDESA in partnership with the ARSCP.

Finally, UCPC provided technical assistance (CP assessments) to ten enterprises in Rwanda in 2005 under the component of Enhancing Institutional Capacity for Industrial Environmental Management in Rwanda, initiated jointly by UNEP and UN-Habitat. The programme also attracted participants from government institutions.

Latest Developments:

UCPC has recognised HIV/AIDS as a cross-cutting issue and has integrated it in its Eco-Benefits Programme (unit 7 on occupational health and safety). UCPC not only helps companies to develop health and safety policies but also HIV/AIDS in the work place policies. In partnership with a social marketing NGO (Population Services International Uganda); a HIV/AIDS in the work place programme was established at Phenix Logistics (a leading textile manufacturer in Uganda). In cooperation with the Energy Advisory Project of GTZ and MEMD, UCPC has integrated energy efficiency in operations of small-scale enterprises that are owned by individuals and are located throughout the country. These companies are, however, too small to fit in the mainstream structure of the Eco-Benefits Programme. UCPC therefore developed a CP training methodology that was tailored to SMEs. The approach was used to conduct regional programmes in Kasese and Lira, which are in Western and Northern Uganda. In conjunction with Uganda Gatsby Trust, UCPC is to start similar programmes in Eastern Uganda (Mbale district) and other parts of Northern Uganda. The regional programme also included two technical training institutes. These institutes implemented CP concepts as organisations and were ready to integrate the CP concept in their curricula, which will not only give their graduates a competitive advantage on the labour market but also bring the national capacity building in CP to a higher level. Another effort to increase CP capacity in tertiary education is the development of a post-graduate diploma in CP at the Department of Chemistry, Makerere University (2006).

Future focus of the UCPC: UCPC is planning to launch a third phase (2009-2011) of activities focusing on the following issues: Strengthening management framework (institutional, resources and systems) of UCPC for sustainable implementation of CP activities in Uganda; mainstreaming CP activities and initiatives in key private and public sector investments and institutions; continuation of awareness raising and training in CP through the Eco-Benefits Programme as a continuous and core service of the UCPC, targeting, among others, industrial firms and associations, consultants, government, financial institutions, institutes of higher education, and NGOs; assisting enterprises in practical adoption of CP and other related concepts (including in-plant demonstrations showing the successful tangible application of CP options in various industrial situations); continuation of programmes in Environmental Management System and ISO 14001 certification for companies that have worked with UCPC through the Eco-Benefits Programme, in close cooperation with other institutions providing trainers to the process and assisting enterprises to implement such systems and other CP-related concepts; transfer technology and know-how to enterprises in Uganda especially in energy efficiency; provision of technical support to policy-makers in ensuring that the CP concept is duly taken into consideration when developing new policies and national development strategies; incorporating CP in the curriculum of higher institutions of learning especially universities and vocational training institutes; and continuation of technical support for implementation of MEAs. UCPC finally plans to roll out CP plus concepts that include: life cycle analysis, eco-labelling, eco-design and product innovation, occupational health and safety, and corporate social responsibility. It is envisaged that by the end of the third phase, UCPC will be an institution recognized as a centre of excellence for CP services. It is also expected that UCPC will have acquired internal capacity to be become a service facilitator or sub-contractor in the framework of larger programmes financed by the GOU, international finance institutions and development partners".

Source: *Uganda Cleaner Production Centre. Text produced for this research. See also UCPC (2008).*

The point is that UCPC programmes target the way in which firms - both larger and smaller ones - operate and use their inputs, and the way in which they apply technology. This focus on aspects of efficiency - or how firms produce (Ferranti et al. 2002, 7, 10) - and related use of resources and technology in production should be one of the main frontiers for efforts to improve productivity and competitiveness in Uganda. Note that the critical success factors which UCPC has noted are chiefly related to human beings - involvement of staff, commitment of top management, change of attitudes. Of course, money is needed to finance certain investments and hence succeed meaningfully in the implementation phase. Yet, the important point is to take account of the 'people-dimension' of productivity and efficiency growth.

Furthermore, UCPC also helps firms to analyse their productivity performance (e.g. calculating indicators). So far, UCPC runs at the project level. At the time of writing, there are plans to make it a national institution, which GOU seems to support to date. Helping firms to boost productivity and efficiency should be on the development agenda for environmental, economic and social sustainability reasons. The sustainability issue demands a gradual move in the medium to long-term from factor-driven growth (based on resources, low-cost skills) - via investment-driven (skilled labour, infrastructure, scale facilities, efficiencies) - to productivity-driven growth (upgrading, innovation and learning). Productivity advancements are further of relevance to the export agenda: the increase in profits can help firms to finance the penetration of and expansion in export markets. This should be considered important, especially in the light of findings that the number and impact of new exporting firms in Uganda has been, according to Gauthier (2001), rather low in the liberalising setting of the mid 1990s.

Better performance-oriented incentive structures needed

In the context of E&T on the one hand and productivity on the other, there is an important qualification to make. E&T (skills etc.) are necessary yet often insufficient for productivity: without incentives to perform (and disincentives for non-performance) skills and certificates, might remain of little consequence in relation to the increase of production. What do we know about the link between E&T, incentives and performance in the private and public sector in Uganda?[127]

One of the characteristics of incentive systems in Uganda is apparently a low wage premium for experience. Informative in this respect is a recent tracer study that analyses labour market outcomes of different cohorts (in the period 1980-1999) of secondary school leavers and university graduates in the country; the study project, financed by DFID, included

127 This section on incentive systems also draws from the work and insights of Victor Richardson (UNIDO consultant and HRD expert). The author is grateful for related comments. See also UNIDO (2007).

similar surveys in Malawi, Tanzania and Zimbabwe. Accordingly, in Uganda there is a relatively low financial experience premium, as indicated by a relatively small increase of salaries for university graduates over the years (Kirumira and Bateganya 2003). In other words, the incentive system might not sufficiently reward on-the-job performance and, possibly, increase in responsibility (assuming, for example, a senior engineer has more responsibilities and functions to carry out than his junior colleague). Table 19 shows that - comparing wages of 1999 graduates with 1980 graduates - the wage premium for 20 years of experience (and, likely, for most university-leaver job categories: a higher level of skills and productivity) is just about 33%, with not much difference between the private and public sector. In the tracer study for Tanzania, the premium was about 100%, three times the Ugandan premium (Myanuzi 2003).

Table 19: Monthly wage income by public and private sector for university graduates

	1980	1987	1994	1999	Total
Public	554,310	521,721	477,273	408,654	483,894
n	29	61	66	52	208
Private	558,333	585,714	576,724	428,205	512,637
n	9	14	29	39	91
Total	55,263	533,667	507,632	417,033	492,642
n	38	75	95	91	299

Source: *Kirumira and Bateganya (2003, 36).*

The WB survey mentioned earlier confirms the finding of limited performance incentives in Uganda:

> "In manufacturing, wages account for about 88 percent of cash earnings on average, cash allowances for about 10 percent, and performance bonuses for about 1.3 percent. Bonuses account for a relatively small part of earnings compared with the share in some other African countries; they were around 6 percent of cash earnings in Nigeria in 2000 and about 7.5 percent in Eritrea in 2001 ... Workers' earnings in manufacturing appear to be only weakly linked to their performance, as shown by the small share of bonuses in their pay and the insignificance of hours worked in explaining the level of earnings. Thus workers have little incentive to increase their level of effort. To increase incentives, earnings should be clearly linked to performance" (WB 2004b, 71-2, 78-9).

Low experience and productivity-performance differentials - but significant 'degree-differentials' - for secondary school teachers were also observed by Liang (Liang 2002, 39-40). In Chapter 12, we also discuss survey findings of deficiencies in Ugandan organisations and firms (public and private sector) in using competence-based approaches for their performance management (see FUE 2003, 2005a as well as Box 55, Appendix 31). According to these sources, local firms are more likely than those with multinational origin to operate on position-based management; many are reported to show significant deficiencies in managing (in-house) competencies and performance, including applying HRM tools and systems (FUE 2003, 16-22). In the same vein, results of a study on firms operating in the Ugandan industrial sector suggest "wages are more responsive to productivity changes within foreign firms than in local firms" (Rasiah and Tamale 2004, 23).

These findings point to significant problems in performance management in the Ugandan public and private sectors, and in particular in local firms: to operate, where appropriate (not only but especially at management level), with proper incentive/disincentive systems that reward on-the-job performance. Here, the argument is applied mainly to financial incentives, e.g. wage structure, but it can be extended to non-financial incentives. Significant performance management deficits in organisations can be observed at the level of an individual employee, or at the level of teams and the whole organisation; the write-up of the experience in this regard of an *Organization Development Specialist* in Uganda is indeed insightful (Box 55, Appendix 31). It points out that deficiency in performance management is a multifaceted problem of inadequate HRM competencies and practices, and is linked to a number of HRM issues, such as recruitment systems and practices, induction and appraisal systems, staff development, team leadership, communication management, organisational culture, salaries, and benefit structures. These are complex deficiencies; tackling them effectively and with a lasting impact is and will continue to be a tricky exercise (ibid).[128]

Most likely, these shortages have negative consequences for the level of work efforts/attitudes, and thus explain part of the productivity problems. The common surveys and report findings of widespread 'negative work attitudes', especially among the better educated and better trained workforce group (e.g. Nalumansi et al. 2003b, 2) and 'low labour productivity' might be related to discouraging effects of existing patterns of incentives, staff treatment, organisational culture, firm management, the high level of casualisation of employment, and other characteristics of the business culture and the economic and political environment in Uganda. The effect of high levels of corruption, for instance, should be considered in the debate on setting of incentives/disincentives to achieve increased performance-oriented efforts by firms and organisations in Uganda.

The argument for better incentive/disincentive systems and performance management is relevant for both management and professional employees, e.g. the top employees, heads of departments, and certain categories of workers (including technicians, and field workers), farmers who supply processors. Again, productivity and value creation have to be addressed, not only in the sphere of production, but - applying a value chain perspective - also in areas such as product design, quality, delivery or marketing and interactivity. More attention should be paid to incentives (motivation) for senior staff in particular so that they acquire and use new skills and improve work organisation and productivity in the firm. Related HRM competencies[129] of personnel managers and CEOs (in larger firms), as well as of owners and managers (in smaller firms), but also of the relevant professional staff (e.g. department heads who supervise people) need further upgrading through institutional and on-the-job training. Investment by firms in the further development of their employees, especially those who are just starting, should also become more relevant. Talent management and career planning will have to advance as well.

The described deficiencies in incentive setting and performance management - and related aspects of organisational techniques and HRM generally - are affecting the impetus

128 Related aspects will be discussed in Chapter 12.

129 In matters of design and implementation of incentive systems, or in issues of organisational culture.

for advanced productivity, competitiveness and upgrading negatively. It is surprising that the GOU and the influential donor community have not really commented on past findings regarding the deficiencies in incentive systems, casualisation of labour and 'negative work attitudes', or responded through support of targeted training efforts (e.g. in HRM matters) and designing incentive in the private (and public) sector, which could help to advance productivity, for instance. Positive results could be expected from targeting both the larger firms and the (progressive) SMEs, for a start. Further, the new labour laws could bring about some changes in this area; more systemic change is needed in HRM matters in the private sector, however.

One respondent noted that it is not easy to make production workers and employees in Uganda understand and handle *performance incentive* systems; also, workers and employees seem to prefer a high share of wages in total earnings (rather than insecurity within a payment system based on incentives). Another challenge of incentive systems is *performance assessment*. It needs to be assessed carefully where the introduction of incentive systems is appropriate. Generally, the mixed fate of public sector reforms in African countries reveals the difficulty of changing organisations and people working therein and of applying schemes such as performance incentives which might be foreign to specific cultures.[130]

A vital aspect in the context of this section is the finding that more than half of the university graduates surveyed in the tracer study were employed by the state (a few in local government).[131] The trend though is that the share of employment in the private sector is increasing, from 18% to 43% within eleven years (1988-1999) (Kirumira and Bateganya 2003, 23, Table 20).[132] When it comes to hiring and promoting people, the majority of graduates operate under the incentive structure of the public sector, which seems to give, in most sections, a premium to degrees obtained, rather than to job experience and achievements (past performance or track record), and thus relevant capabilities and skills displayed. It can be assumed that a similar structure is in place in parts of the private sector, which competes with the public sector for the same graduate cohorts.

The high level of effort and money invested by graduates to obtain additional E&T (by enrolling in post-graduate studies, other certificates and diplomas) is one outcome of this incentive system; about 40% of household incomes in Uganda are invested in education (PEVOT 2006). It is further noticeable that about 55% of graduates had secondary employment (wage employment/self-employment, part-time/weekend) besides their main jobs. Note, recruitment practices that are based on other considerations (personal connections etc.) than the competences of the applicants also have a negative impact on incentive systems and productivity outcomes (Box 55, Appendix 31).

---

130 Again, the political and socio-economic aspects of incentive systems cannot be discussed in this book.

131 The author is grateful to Victor Richardson; his views have shaped the writing of the following paragraphs.

132 According to analysis of the labour force, the public sector is indeed the major provider of the relatively few *permanent* wage/salary jobs in Uganda (55% of permanent jobs, rest private sector, UBOS 2003). See Chapter 3 below.

Table 20: University graduates' wage employment by employer (%)

	1980	1988	1994	1999	Male	Female	Total
Central government	53	53	48	30	42	54	45
Local government	5	8	7	9	8	7	8
Parastatal	18	21	14	17	18	13	17
Private	24	18	31	43	32	26	31
Total	100	100	100	100	100	100	100

Source: *Kirumira and Bateganya (2003, 23).*

Indeed, these Ugandans do respond to incentives (and necessities), e.g. to the opportunity to earn an extra income and the trend (or assumption) that employers hire and promote those with post-graduate degrees. However, do leaning efforts that aim chiefly at obtaining a formal qualification result in a significantly enhanced skills and knowledge-set and thus better job performance? In this context, an interesting observation was made by one of the informants for this research: The focus on (or culture of) formal qualifications lowers the impetus of an employee to actually develop his/her capacity to perform better in the job through training etc., especially in-house and on-the-job training (Box 55, Appendix 31). Correspondingly, firms and their managers, embedded in the same culture, appear to focus (too) little on on-the-job-training and learning. Such patterns in training efforts (of firms, employees, or trainees) limit 'learning-by-doing' effects, which are considered a significant part of the pro-productivity effort in other countries. One of the many relevant questions in this context is: Does this incentive system that operates in Uganda set an incentive pattern which results in a stronger focus on degree certificates than training content and job performance? Both the state and private sector need to shift their focus away from rewarding merely degrees and underplaying experience and performance - as discussed here for the case of the higher educated employees - so that greater efforts are undertaken by managers and employees to perform in the main job.[133]

Against the above findings and related discussions, it can be argued that in many cases, employees and managers and perhaps also employers/owners, might be educated but untrained (in BTVET); they lack the skills and capabilities required to operate enterprises (capacities) in an economically efficient manner (including applying performance incentives and disincentives): there are numerous training needs at the upper echelons of Ugandan manufacturing and other sectors, including many employers/owners; training can enable managers and staff to operate more efficiently and effectively (see also Dorgan et al. 2006).[134] The following seems necessary in the Ugandan case: (a) training for managers in basic HRD systems and frameworks (e.g. retention of quality staff and personal development to improve

133 The issue of 'work centrality' is applicable here as well.

134 A recent study suggests considerable links between organisational, managerial and skills deficiencies and low productivity in SSA clothing firms: "[S]cales are low in SSA plants, and many producers suffer from poor bureaucratic and physical infrastructure. But there is also pervasive evidence that many SSA clothing plants suffer from low levels of productivity arising out of poor organisational procedures, low levels of skill and inadequate management within plants" (Kaplinsky and Morris 2006a, vi).

their skills), (b) introduction of corporate and personal governance and value management at director/senior manager level, and (c) introduction of good procedures and practices from recruitment to termination and contract formation, based on best practices, but in local (cultural) context.[135] Further, managers need to reflect seriously about the other social incentives they can put in place to motivate their work forces; e.g. to respond to workers expectations of employer loyalty or to staff values (community, family, inclusion/common aspiration) (Jackson 2003).

Agricultural sector needs productivity advancements

Similar challenges regarding productivity improvements are reported for the agricultural sector in Uganda. Land degradation (soil erosion/soil fertility, mining), weather dependency[136], the low use of fertilizers, and a high level of (semi-)subsistence agriculture with related deficiencies in agricultural practices and land management result in low levels of product quality, productivity and incomes. Some crops experience declining productivity (IFPRI 2004, Deininger and Okidi 2001).[137] Problems of many farmers include a low level of general education and know-how, knowledge and skills; in particular deficits in terms of (i) agricultural practices and technology,[138] (ii) commercial, organisational, communication, negotiation and other interaction and collective action issues (Wiegratz et al. 2007b),[139] (iii) as well as social and health issues.[140] Many farmers 'end up' in the sector 'by default', not by choice, adversely affecting the reputation and HR features of the sector. However, there are also considerable improvements in the sector in the HR relevant areas; see for instance Wiegratz et al. (2007b) for some case studies of buyer-farmer cooperation on training matters (agricultural technology and practices). In these case studies, training and day-to-day learning have increased farmers' productivity (see for more details the chapter on value chains below).

According to WB/FAO figures, farmers' yields in Uganda increased in recent past for some crops. Also, in aggregate, agricultural labour productivity is higher in Uganda than in some neighbouring countries (Figures 15-17, WB 2005a). Some experts infer the improvements are due to productivity-enhancing efforts (including training) of Government and donor programmes (e.g. PMA, NAADS), which is encouraging. A number of notable training initiatives are further undertaken by the private sector itself (e.g. local/international buyers of agricultural produce), or NGOs. More intense buyer-farmer interactions and relations

135 The author is grateful to Geoffrey Burton, HRD expert, Manchester Business School, for related inputs at this point.

136 For instance, in the second half of 2005 there was a productivity drop due to a drought.

137 Around 95% of the total use of fertilizers is by a small number of large-scale farmers. Kenya used about 25 times more NPK fertilizer than Uganda in 2001 (IMF 2005, 10-1).

138 These include sustainable/environmentally sound production methods, integrated production systems, harvesting and post-harvest techniques, marketing (including traceability, certification if required), or management practices, relating to time, land, product quality or collective action in farmers' organisations.

139 Note that collective action and negotiation behaviour, similar to many other farmer-level issues, have a severe political-economic dimension (related to, for example, power imbalances between farmers, traders, and government officials). However, this will not be discussed here.

140 These include record keeping and decision making, as well as reproductive health, family planning, sanitation, hygiene and HIV/AIDS. The author is grateful to Ina Wengrzyk (Neumann Kaffee Gruppe, consultant for sustainable production in the coffee sector), for related comments.

in more explicitly governed agro value chains is a promising way to increase skills levels of farmers: they provide the base for day-to-day learning through repeated interactions by farmers and buyers who have an interest in more competent farmers. Such buyers provide incentives and support (e.g. training provision, motivation) for skills advancement of farmers and can be called 'developmental buyers'. An analysis by Wiegratz et al. (2007) of case studies of relations between farmers and developmental buyers concludes:[141]

> "The upgrading results of the interaction and cooperation between ... [developmental buyers which are also called lead firms, LFs, in the value chain literature] and farmers are usually significant: respective farmers (not all though) have increased their skills, operate with better processes, expand their fields, achieve higher productivity, increase quantity and improve quality (the latter resulting in lower rejects by the LFs), have better group organization, coherence and activities, or develop a more business oriented mind with incidences of long term thinking and planning. Farmers' upgrading also shows that farmers can improve their production practices and products yet face a more substantial challenge in terms of technological advancement" (ibid).

Moreover, productivity and income-enhancing measures must be balanced with environmental sustainability (trade-offs); the substantial knowledge and know-how links between these themes need to be reflected in E&T and skills development (IFPRI 2004).[142] This holds even more against the background of the *population increase* which is expected to lead to mounting pressures on the natural resource base, especially in rural areas where the vast majority of Ugandan live (about 86%), yet also due to trends such as urban unemployment, which might force unemployed urban workers to return to the villages in search of survival. UBOS points to related pressures on natural resources and possible consequences: "The large numbers of persons in the labour force in rural areas exert pressure on the natural resources which may lead to desertification, land fragmentation, deforestation and soil degradation" (2006, 5).

Overall, skills development and know-how transfer - and the related organisation of farmers groups - in the agricultural sector are all rather difficult and long-term-oriented

141 See Wiegratz et al. (2007b) for information and analysis of such training. For instance, Neumann Kaffee Gruppe (Germany), through its HRN Foundation (which aims at supporting sustainability in the coffee sector) currently implements five projects aiming at 15,000 smallholder coffee farmers in the districts of Luweero, Kamuli, Masaka and Mubende. The projects are incorporated in public-private partnerships: involvement of industry (International Coffee Partners, German Coffee Association, Ibero Ltd.), donors (EU, GTZ, DANIDA, USAID), NGOs (Solidaridad, PLAN International) and local government. The projects address components such as (a) strengthening productivity and promoting integrated coffee production systems (including environmentally sound practices), (b) quality improvement, (c) establishment/strengthening of farmer organisations, (d) coffee marketing including traceability and certification if required (linkage with commercial models is targeted where verification/certification with standard programmes can play a role), (e) credit/microfinance operations, or (f) social aspects in producer communities. See Wiegratz et al. (2007b) for a study of this case. See also UNDP (2007a) for a recent call to provide more support to the agricultural sector in Uganda.

142 A recent survey among 451 households in 107 communities revealed that: "Education significantly influenced households' income strategies, land management practices, and labor use in crop production. As expected, higher education contributed to significantly higher household income [especially when education beyond the secondary level is attained] and reduced soil nutrient depletion, but it also led to less labor intensity in crop production. ... Higher education promotes off-farm salary employment, nonfarm activities, and livestock production ... [Moreover] Agricultural extension and training increases productivity but also contributes to increased soil erosion and soil nutrient depletion, by promoting increased production of annual crops without sufficient promotion of soil fertility improvements or soil and water conservation measures" (IFPRI 2004, x).

activities due to: a high level of (semi-) subsistence practices, a low level of educational attainments and skills, a specific business culture and related issues of political economy and economic sociology in rural areas. Successful interventions require adequate farm-level interactions between farmers, technical experts, buyers, technocrats and politicians. This has been problematic for Uganda and remains a matter that requires improvement.

Figure 15: Agricultural labour productivity, country comparison

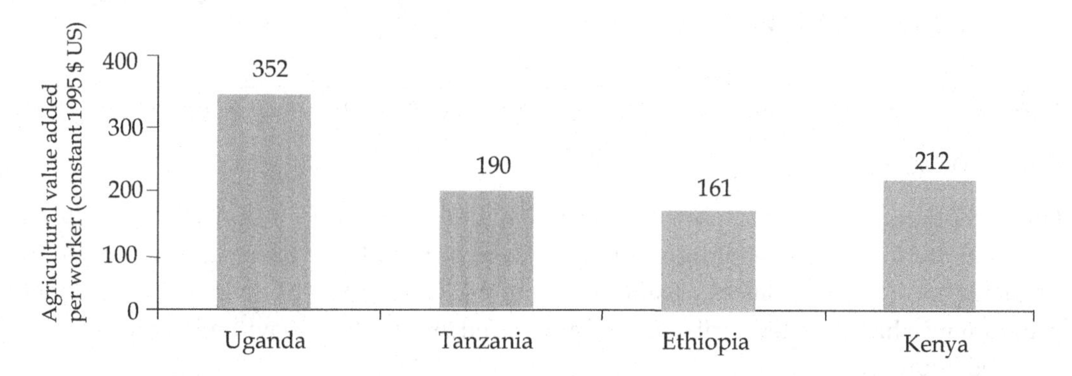

Source: *WB (2005a, slide 6).*

Figure 16: Productivity trends in selected major crops, country comparison

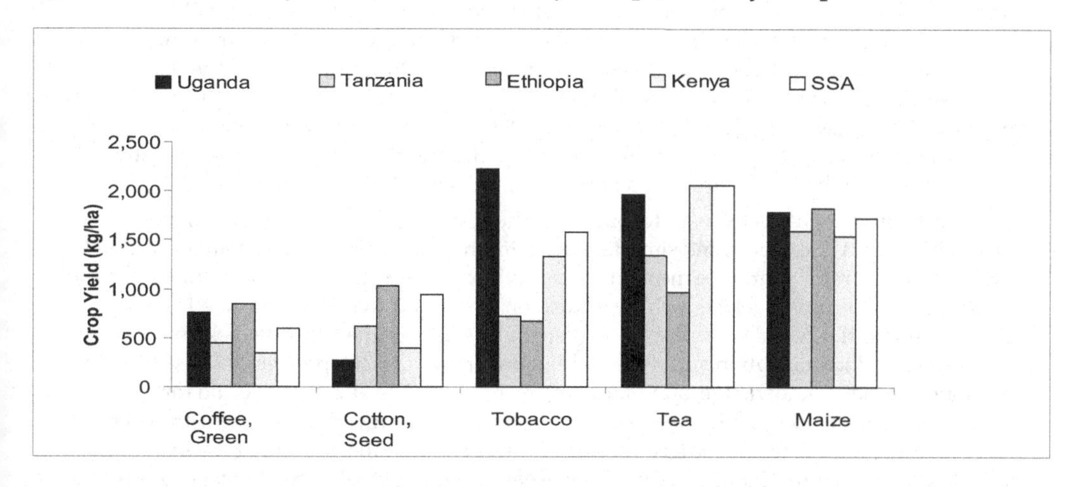

Source: *WB (2005a, slide 5).*

Figure 17: Productivity trends for selected major crops (1995-2003)

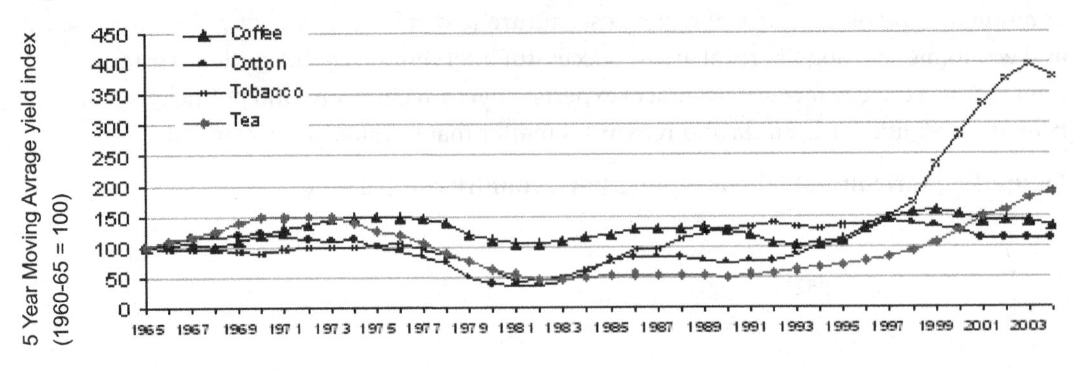

Source: *WB (2005a, slide 8).*

One of the donor programmes that focus on agricultural productivity is USAID's Agricultural Productivity Enhancement Program (APEP) which undertakes training in agricultural practices and farmer business organisation, among others. Box 10 reviews a forerunner programme which targeted agribusiness training and input networks within a supply-chain-oriented approach.

Box 10: The Agribusiness Training and Input Network (ATAIN) Programme

"ATAIN was developed in 1998 by Uganda's Investment in Developing Export Agriculture (IDEA) Project in response to the growing demand by smallholder farmers for agricultural inputs, and the need to make such inputs accessible and affordable at the village level. Although there were a good number of dealers in agricultural inputs prior to the ATAIN programme, most of them were urban-based largely due to cost considerations. On the other hand the users of the inputs were rural-based and a marginal number of them could afford to look for the inputs from any nearest town, again largely due to cost considerations. Inputs thus remained unavailable at the village level as agricultural input distributors did not have sufficient financial strength to afford the risk inherent in building a network of village-based stockists.

The idea behind the ATAIN was to build on the growing demand for improved inputs, particularly at the village level, and simultaneously improve the input supply chain. Accordingly, IDEA initiated a credit guarantee mechanism that allows wholesalers and distributors to extend credit facilities to rural stockists, which in turn enables them to carry adequate inventory of selected inputs. IDEA linked stockists to distributors and trained those stockists in record keeping, credit documentation and management, inventory control, product safe use handling and storage, product knowledge, and marketing techniques. The guarantee period for a stockist was four seasons beyond which the stockist was required to revert to standard trade credit. The ATAIN experience was leveraged through distributors training additional stockists outside the IDEA guarantee mechanism. A number of large international agro-chemical companies contributed to training sessions.

Programme Results and Impact:

Over a six-year period (1998 to 2003), the number of stockists under the ATAIN programme increased over five-fold, while the number of farmers served increased from 12,250 to over 116,b000. Total value of inputs sold under ATAIN increased from about 174,000US$ in 1998 to over 1,000,000US$ in 2000, before declining to about 890,000US$ in 2003. A sum of ATAIN performance is shown below.

The ATAIN programme impacted positively on distributors, stockists and farmers. For instance, Rakai Farm Supply joined the ATAIN programme in 1998. Two years later it was no longer a small shop conducting a negligible volume of business but a leading distributor of seeds, fertilizers and agro-chemicals in Rakai, Masaka and Ssembabule districts of south-western Uganda. Originally, supplying just eight stockists, Rakai Farm Supply, by 2000, was supplying 40 stockists directly linked to the ATAIN programme and a similar number of non-ATAIN stockists. Initially, the biggest barriers to business development were the lack of credit facilities and product knowledge. However, through the ATAIN programme, both these issues were tackled. A combination of linkages between distributors and suppliers on one hand and trained stockists on the other improved both the accessibility and affordability of inputs to the farmer. Improved inputs supply had a direct effect on agricultural productivity, which in turn resulted in improved rural incomes and food security. ATAIN's approach covering several aspects of business and product training, created a successful network of agricultural stockists with IDEA-supported stockists as their main suppliers."

Source: *Agricultural Productivity Enhancement Programme.* [143]

In the next section we shall look at labour market and labour force indicators, to better understand the employment structure of the Ugandan economy and the areas requiring HRD.

143 The author is grateful to APEP's managing director, Clive Drew, for his comments on productivity-oriented skills development in the agricultural sector in Uganda.

3

Labour Force and Labour Market

Overview: A non-urbanised, young population

Uganda is relatively un-urbanised, even by African standards: 86% of the population lives in rural areas; yet, a degree of urbanisation takes place. The *population* - estimated to be around 25 million (2002/03)[144] - is very young: 52% are in the 0-14 years age group; 37% are below the age of ten. The majority (52%) are women (UBOS 2003a, 7-8, Tables 21 and 22). The *population of working age* (14-64 years) is about 12.2 million and smaller than the group of those who are actually too young or old to work (13 million) (dependency ratio ›100).

Table 21: Regional and rural-urban distribution of the population (%)

Region/Area	Sex		
	Male	Female	Total
Central	29.5	29.7	29.6
Eastern	27.8	27.1	27.4
Northern	17.6	18.8	18.2
Western	25.0	24.4	24.7
Urban	13.4	14.0	13.7
Rural	86.6	86.0	86.3
Total Population	**100.0**	**100.0**	**100.0**

Source: *UBOS (2003a, 8).*

Table 22: Age distribution of the population (%)

Age group	Sex		
	Male	Female	Total
0-9	38.0	36.1	37.0
10+	62.0	63.9	63.0
0-14	53.3	51.4	52.4
15-64	44.3	46.6	45.5
65+	2.4	2.0	2.2
Total Population (million)	**12,2**	**13,0**	**25,2**

Source: *ibid (7).*

144 Data from Uganda National Household Survey 2002/03. By the late 2000s, the population is around 30 million people.

A challenge: Level of education and skills in the labour force

This section will mainly use the statistics provided in the latest UBOS labour market report, which combines the (partly revised) results of both the 2002 Population and Housing Census and 2002/03 Uganda National Household Survey (UNHS) and entails some adjusted concepts and definitions (UBOS 2006).[145] Reference will also be made in this section to the Labour Force Survey 2003 (UBOS 2003a), which uses 2002/03 UNHS data and provides additional and useful information.

According to the new labour market report, the *labour force* (LF) - defined as the currently economically active population - is composed of those of working age (14-64 years) who are either employed (formal, informal, subsistence or self employed) or unemployed.[146] Table 23 provides information on LF characteristics: The *LF* is estimated to include around *9.8 million people;* about 76% in the group are below 40 years (51% below 30 years). About 85% of the LF live in rural areas; roughly 53% are females. The Central (30%) and Eastern (27%) regions have the highest share of the LF. About two-thirds (70%) of the LF are literate. Regarding educational attainment, almost four-fifths (77%) have no formal education or primary education. A very small percentage (6%) has an educational level above secondary. Gender-differences exist: For instance, 24% of the females have no formal education vs. 9% of males (UBOS 2006, 5-6). There are also rural-urban-discrepancies: the LF in urban areas is considerably better educated (UBOS 2003a).[147] The UBOS authors summarise: The LF "is characterized by young, untrained and rural labour force" (2006, 5).

---

145 According to UBOS, most of the results of the census and household survey differ; due to different definitions and sample coverage, among other reasons. The UNHS seems more appropriate for labour market analysis. Note that in the new report, the age category of the labour force was changed from 10+ (UBOS LF Report 2003) to 14-64 years (2006, 4-5).

146 Reference period: the seven days preceding the date of survey enumeration. To be 'employed' requires working at least 1 hour in this period. 'Unemployment' is the 'total lack of work' (UBOS 2006, 66-7).

147 According to the LF Report 2003, about 75% of the LF *(definition 10+ years)* in rural areas has an education level lower than 'completed P7' (including no education), vs. 45% for urban areas. About 1.8% in rural areas completed S4 and above, vs. 11% in urban areas. The proportions are lower for females in both rural and urban areas; while urban-rural disparities exist. The literacy level for females in the rural North and East are at 40% and 52% respectively (UBOS 2003, 9-10). See Tables 46 and 47 (Appendices 5-6).

Table 23: Size of the labour force by sex, residence, literacy, education, age-Group (14-64 years) ('000)

Background Characteristics	Economically Active/Labour force Population		
	Male	*Female*	*Total*
Total labour force	**4,634.2**	**5,138.4**	**9,772.6**
%	47.4	52.6	100.0
Residence			
Rural	84.5	85.1	84.6
Urban	15.5	14.9	15.4
Total	**100**	**100**	**100**
Region			
Central	31.0	29.4	30.2
Eastern	26.3	26.8	26.6
Northern	16.9	19.5	18.2
Western	25.7	24.4	25.0
Total	**100**	**100**	**100**
Literacy status			
Literate	80.4	60.1	69.7
Illiterate	19.6.	39.9	30.3
Total	**100.0**	**100.0**	**100.0**
Educational attainment			
No schooling	9.2	24.4	17.2
Primary	61.5	57.8	59.6
Secondary	21.2	13.7	17.2
Above secondary	7.6	3.9	5.6
Do not know	0.5	0.3	0.4
Total	**100.0**	**100.0**	**100.0**
Age groups			
14-19	15.1	14.3	14.6
20-29	33.0	38.7	36.0
30-39	26.6	24.8	25.7
40-49	14.7	13.4	14.0
50-59	7.6	7.0	7.3
60-64	3.1	1.8	2.4
TOTAL	**100**	**100**	**100**

Source: *UBOS (2006, 6).*

The LF Report 2003 furthermore reveals that only about 10% of the population (10+) had vocational training; 12% of the males and 8% of the females respectively. More than half of the females were trained in arts and crafts (52%). Of the males, nearly two-thirds were trained in crafts, teaching, brick laying/construction or mechanics; the low share of training in agriculture, forestry and fisheries is notable (4%) (UBOS 2003a, 10-11, Tables 24 and 25). Overall, Uganda's capacity (general/specific education and skills) to absorb knowledge is severely limited, with adverse effects for technology operations and productivity (Ssemogerere 2005, xiii). Note, Uganda also experiences a significant brain drain (to OECD countries) in present days; the country's emigration rate for skilled labour (as proportion of the educated LF) is estimated to be above 30%; Uganda's rate is the 6th highest in a research sample group of countries with populations above five million people.[148] Africa as a whole is extensively affected by brain drain (Docquier and Marfouk 2006). For DCs in general, one "dilemma is that those most likely to be institution builders are those most likely to emigrate" (Kapur and McHale 2005a, 4).

Table 24: Population with Vocational Training (age group 10+, %)

	Sex		
	Male	*Female*	*Total*
Total	100	100	100
Vocational training	11.7	8.0	9.8
No vocational training	88.3	92.0	90.2

Source: *UBOS (2003a, 10).*

Table 25: Type of vocational training of household members (10+, %)

Type of vocational training	Male	Female	Total
Total	100	100	100
Crafts	15.5	52.4	31.0
Teaching	13.8	12.8	13.4
Brick laying/construction	18.8	0.5	11.1
Mechanics	15.5	0.5	9.2
Agriculture, forestry, fisheries	4.0	0.7	2.6
Metal-work	2.2	0.2	1.3
Hotel & tourism	0.6	2.0	1.2
Electricity	1.7	-	1.0
Police	1.0	10.0	0.6
Others	26.9	30.8	28.5

Source: *ibid (11).*

148 See Docquier and Marfouk (2006) for details. See also Kapur and McHale (2005b) for further brain drain estimates.

The *LF participation rate* - the ratio of economically active persons (aged 14-64 years) and the total number of persons in the working-age group - is about 80%. The participation rate - which indicates the level of labour market activity - is slightly higher in rural areas (vs. urban areas); it is highest in the North (Table 26). Persons with secondary education have the lowest rate (69.4%); those with 'no schooling' the highest (90.2%). The illiterate group has a higher rate than the literate one (UBOS 2006, 7-8, 69).

Table 26: Labour force participation rate by background characteristics (14-64 years, %)

	UNHS 2002/03		
	Male	*Female*	*Total*
National residence	**80.3**	**79.9**	**80.1**
Rural	80.7	81.8	81.3
Urban	78.4	70.4	74.1
Region			
Central	81.2	76	78.5
Eastern	80.2	82.3	81.3
Northern	80.9	85.4	83.4
Western	78.9	78.2	
Literacy rates			
Literate	79	74.5	76.9
Illiterate	86.2	89.7	88.6
Educational attainment			
No schooling	90	90.2	90.2
Primary	78.1	78.1	78.1
Secondary	73.3	64.5	69.4
Above secondary	91.6	86.9	89.8
Age Group			
14	30.4	25.6	28
15-19	47.1	52.4	49.8
20-24	83.6	85.6	84.8
25-29	97.4	90.7	93.7
30-34	98.5	94.5	96.4
35-39	98.2	94.3	96.2
40-44	97.2	97.1	97.2
45-49	97.2	93.5	95.3
50-54	94.6	92.3	93.4
55-59	93.6	87.1	90.4
60-64	91.4	80.5	86.8
Total	**80.3**	**79.9**	**80.1**

Source: *UBOS (2006, 8).*

Further, the *employment to population ratio* (rate of utilisation of labour) for the working-age group is at about 77%. Again, the group with secondary education has the lowest rate (66%) and 'no schooling' the highest (90%) (ibid, 9). The UBOS authors comment on this pattern as follows:

> "Persons with secondary education are less likely to get [or have] jobs compared to those either with no formal education, primary or above secondary. The probable reason is that those with secondary education consider themselves educated, so they end up despising elementary occupation and look for white-collar jobs, which do not come easily" (ibid, 9, 11).

The UBOS authors suggest further that these people desire white-collar work, but lack the necessary skills (ibid). Moreover, the educated group might struggle to respond to the dynamics of the level and pattern of skills demanded by the Ugandan economy, e.g. in the labour market that offers non-farm jobs for secondary level graduates. The level and mix of education and practical training (including soft skills) in this group might be wanting. Expressed differently, in a difficult economic environment, the market seems tiny for semi-educated, (relatively) un-skilled persons with deficiencies in soft and functional skills, and without the (informally) required 'connections' (who-knows-whom). Further adequate skills and capability formation is then needed to address the current 'mismatch'. The capacity of this group to realise income-generating economic opportunities needs to be enhanced; and (economic, cultural and political) conditions that generate economic and professional opportunities in the first place need to improve.

Unemployment and Underemployment

The official unemployment rate is 3.5% (around 330,000 people) and includes persons who are actively looking for a job but who are not in any type of formal or informal employment (total lack of work, without any income opportunity) (UBOS 2006, 42).[149] The about 0.3 million (actively) unemployed people and about 9.5 million employed people constitute the LF of 9.8 million people ('currently economically active population' during the survey period). Note that some labour market experts find the estimates for un- and underemployment rather low. Also, UBOS states: "The unemployment problem in Uganda is a very complex one and a great deal of controversy exists concerning the reliability of available data and therefore the real level of unemployment in Uganda" (2006, 42).

Particularly, unemployment is higher:[150]

- In urban than in rural areas (12.2% vs. 1.9%)
  - Overall, this is driven by high unemployment in Kampala,[151]
- Among females (4.2% vs. 2.6% for males), especially in urban areas (17% vs.7.6%)
  - Pattern holds for all educational categories, except for 'no schooling' group,
  - Female unemployment is driven by high female unemployment (above 20%) in Kampala,
- In the central region (6.9% vs. between 1%-2.4% in the other regions),
- Among the educated, and highest for persons with secondary education (7.4%),
- Among the youth (15-24 years: 6.3%) which constitute 58% of the total unemployed group (ibid, 42-3, 2003, 34).

For UBOS, "Uganda's unemployed consist mainly of young and unskilled workers" (ibid, 42); this could point to a low functional skill level of the educated groups and the general difficulties of getting into or creating employment in Uganda. The gender discrepancy in unemployment matters is notable as well. Further, non-poor households (80%; rest: poor households) and male-headed households (70%, rest: female-headed households) account for largest share of unemployed persons (2006, 43).

149 In the reference period: the seven days preceding the date of survey enumeration.

150 See also Table 48 (Appendix 7).

151 See Table 49 (Appendix 8) for geographical unemployment distribution with 'Kampala category' (UBOS, 2003).

Youth unemployment is almost twice the national average (6.3% vs. 3.5%). It is particularly high in urban areas, where the level is about five times higher than in rural areas (22.8% vs. 4.2%; Kampala: 32%). The Central region has youth unemployment of 13.4% (the Kampala effect), the other regions between 3.4% and 4%. Young people with secondary (12.9%) and above secondary education (20%) experience the highest level of unemployment (other education categories: 4.5%-4.9%, ibid, 45-6, 2003).[152]

There is also a high percentage of people who are *visibly underemployed* - those who worked involuntarily for less than 40 hours in a particular activity while being available and willing for more hours of work during the seven days prior to the survey - which UBOS puts at **17%** (or, 1.57 million people, time-related underemployment). Visible underemployment is higher in rural areas (17.9% vs. 10.7%), among men (18.9% vs. 15.1%), and the youth (20-29 years: 19.7%). Four out of five underemployed people have an educational level of primary (65%) and below (15.5%) (2006, 47-8).[153] Notably, the MGLSD Draft Employment Policy refers to an estimated total level of unemployment and under-employment of over 60% (2004); three times the level that UBOS reports.

Employment status: 85% are self-employed or unpaid family workers

Only 15% are employees: two-thirds of them as casual/temporary workers

One of the crucial tables for understanding economic and employment issues in Uganda is Table 27. Only around 15% of the about 9.5 million employed people are wage/salary workers (employees). About 57% are self-employed (own-account workers and employers with the latter accounting for less than 1%) and 27% are unpaid family workers (UBOS 2006, 10-11). UBOS suggests: "The high proportion ... of the labour force who worked as self-employed indicated a low growth in the formal sector and high rate of job creation in the informal economy. In addition, a high proportion of the labour force who worked as unpaid ... workers indicated poor development, little job growth, widespread poverty and a largely rural economy" (ibid, 17).

Table 27: Distribution of employed persons by employment status (%), UNHS 2002/03

	UNHS 2002/03		
	Male	**Female**	**Total**
Wage/salaried workers	22	8.5	15.2
Self employed	64	51.2	57.4
Unpaid family workers	14	40.3	27.4
Total	**100**	**100**	**100**

Source: *UBOS (2006, 11).*

152 See Table 50 (Appendix 9) for details on distribution of youth unemployment.

153 "Examples [of underemployment] are people who look for additional work but cannot find any, or who do not work because they say there is a lack of business. Lack of finance or lack of raw materials is another reason why people might not be able to work more hours. Other involuntary reasons may result from an industrial dispute or from a breakdown of equipment, or because it is currently the off-season" (UBOS 2006, 47).

Furthermore, the level of wage/salary employment in *non-agricultural* employment is small and stands at 27%. In addition, only about three out of ten employees in this group (wage/salary non-agricultural employment) are women (28%). This points to limited job opportunities, first, and gender inequalities, second (ibid, 11).

Importantly, Table 27 draws attention to the high number of people outside any form of wage/salary-based employment structures: Among the females, around nine out of ten were either self-employed or unpaid family workers (males: eight out of ten). Almost two-thirds of males are self-employed. "[M]en predominate in the formal sector and women in the informal, especially in the 'invisible' sector" (UN 2004, 25). Note that women own almost 40% of the individually owned enterprises (sole proprietorship, fixed premises) listed in the Uganda Business Register (year 2001/02) (UBOS 2003b, 10-1). Regarding this large group of people outside wage employment one might ask: what are the skills needs in their occupations and what could be measures to address them?[154] How can meaningful interventions reach people in informal structures and informal businesses? What about the unpaid house-workers? What is the role of rural development in this respect?

It is very possible that the mixture of skills needed is extensive: basic, technical, life skills, etc. Also, there are specific incentive structures at work that hamper systematic skills development in the informal sector in both the rural and urban areas, e.g. poor working conditions, fluctuation of trained workforce and related contract, payment and incentive matters for workers (Isaksson et al. 2005, 92). Further, there are a range of gender-based disparities and related (cultural) practices at play at the level of household, community, and work-place, e.g. intra-household dynamics and incentives, economic dependence, practices, norms and attitudes, which adversely affect females' prospects and pathways, not only in terms of E&T but also with respect to jobs and incomes (Ellis et al., 2006, 19-25, Mukasa et al. 2004).[155]

Current deficiencies in parts of Uganda's state structures - limited capacities and capabilities, both at central and district level, in matters of production and trade, public spending priorities as well as incentive systems and attitudes of the public service - are limiting the prospects for reasonable public measures for HRD in these disadvantaged sections of the LF.

Permanent wage/salary jobs ('paid employees') for less than 500,000 people

The LF Report (UBOS 2003a) gives important additional information on the *composition and characteristics of the employees group* (wage/salary workers) as summarised in Table 28.[156] The

154 The section on the GEM study below gives more information on this self-employed section of the LF.

155 See Mukasa et al. (2004) and Ellis (2006) on practices such as payment of bride wealth, domestic violence, widow inheritance, polygamy, female genital mutilation, or inheritance practices and their economic and socio-economic effects for women. See Box 43 (Appendix 10) for an overview of cultural influences that can impact on the socio-economic situation, including the knowledge and skills formation process of females in Uganda. See further discussions in Tikly et al. (2003) on 'gendered stereotyping barring women access to 'male' skills' for the cases of Rwanda and Tanzania. See also Snyder (2000) on business ventures and investment patterns of Ugandan women.

156 Table 28 gives additional information on the group 'wage/salary workers'; which the UBOS 2006 report puts at 15.2%. The LF 2003 puts it at 14.3% (also note: different age group: 10+). The data presented in Table 28 is not given in UBOS (2006). Although UBOS has adjusted the respective aggregated data slightly in its new report the implications as discussed in this book are nevertheless applicable. See UBOS (2007) for an updated version of labour market issues.

percentage level of employees is significantly higher in urban areas (with 39% of the total employed vs. 10% in rural areas); most in this group are in the private sector. Only about one out of twelve women is an employee (8%); for males the ratio is one out of five (20%) (ibid, 20).

Table 28: Composition of group of Paid employees (% of total employed), aged 10+, by residence and sex

Employment status	Rural			Urban			Total		
	M	F	T	M	F	T	M	F	T
Paid Employees	**16.0**	**5.0**	**9.7**	**45.9**	**31.3**	**39.0**	**20.3**	**8.2**	**14.3**
Government permanent	2.9	1.1	1.2	0.7	3.9	5.5	3.4	1.5	2.5
Government temporary	0.7	0.2	0.5	0.8	0.7	0.7	0.8	0.2	0.5
Government casual	0.0	0.1	0.1	0.2	0.0	0.1	0.1	0.1	0.1
Private permanent	1.0	0.5	1.0	9.2	7.1	8.2	2.7	1.3	2.0
Private permanent/ casual	10.8	3.1	6.9	28.7	19.6	24.5	13.3	5.1	9.2

Source: *UBOS (2003a, 20).*

Of those few paid employees (here 14% of total employed): Around one-fifth are in government, and four-fifths in the private sector. There is an astonishingly *high level of temporary and casual labour*, especially in the private sector category where, in aggregate - according to this survey - about four out of five paid employees/workers are not permanent (82%). Of government paid employees, about one-fifth are of the temporary/casual type. In other words, of the overall currently employed people (9.5 million), *less than 500,000 people* (about 430,000, 4.5%) are estimated to be in a structure of *permanent wage/salary employment*, about 190,000 (2%) of them in the private sector.[157] The majority of permanent jobs (55%) are in government/public service - which points to the signalling (or demonstration) effect of public sector HRM for the (especially formal) private sector. Note also the different level of 'permanent employee' in the private sector in the urban (8.2%) vs. rural (1%) area. Without the return of capital flight from the expelled Asian entrepreneurs (Africans of Asian origin) - and FDI from elsewhere - the level of paid employment in Uganda might have been even lower.[158]

Despite the successes in GDP, FDI, and exports and significant ODA in Uganda, the above data reveals problems of the recent PSD process in the country. It points to shortcomings and difficulties regarding: (a) the level and nature of private sector activities (including entrepreneurship, competitive entry into new, dynamic markets, patterns of 'jobless growth'), (b) the state of skills and capabilities, and (c) the possibilities of developing a formal sector in a latecomer SSA economy (in the context of the global economy). In short, these figures give an impression of the characteristics of the catch-up and diversification process and related outcomes to date regarding employment structures. It points to numerous challenges that

157 See also discussion of WB data below: The level of casual and part-time labour in the sample - the upper formal sector - is about 40%.

158 As the main source of permanent jobs, government's HRM practices, including recruitment, remuneration, incentives/performance systems, have an impact on various HRD dynamics, especially in the group of qualified persons.

need to be tackled to handle and improve this problematic status quo, for instance, through adequate support for advancement of current and new firms, including the large group of small-scale entrepreneurs in the informal economy.

This LF structure, especially the low level of permanent paid employment (and high level of own-account workers), affects (i) the HRD mechanisms (e.g. extent of on-the-job learning processes, use of performance incentives by employers), and (ii) dynamics of related markets (e.g. for demand and supply for E&T, 'rate of returns'), both short and mid/long-term. The adverse effects on HRD are also distressing the PSD agenda, e.g. prospects for enhanced productivity, growth, exports, employment creation, and taxation. Related HRD questions are: How does HRD work in such a LF context? What are forms of training that can target the 95.5% that are not permanent employees; besides those few who actually benefit from some government/donor-provided training programmes (e.g. PMA in agriculture)? What could be done to reduce the casualisation of work, and to address wanting working conditions in many companies? What are the implications of the difference between urban and rural levels of paid employment (including permanent job arrangements) for HRD dynamics but also for pro-poor development? Separate analyses of urban and rural dynamics are needed to undertake informed HRD efforts.

The situation of the low-level of wage/salary employment is - besides the pre-1986 causes - also linked to effects of the liberalisation and privatisation policies of the last two decades, where many people, especially public servants, fell out of formal structures while at the same time facing a small and slowly growing (advanced) private sector.[159] How many of those skilled workers and technicians, who lost their jobs in that period, are now working in regular jobs (which are to some extent related to their education, training and experience profile)? If the current activity (e.g. specific self-employment) is different from the initial profile, how did the people obtain the knowledge and skills needed to perform in this activity? What are the most pressing skills gaps for them as 'new entrants'?

Casualisation and informalisation of world-of-work challenge HRD aspirations

The casualisation of the world-of-work as characterised by the high rate of temporary labour usage (casual and part-time employment) is notable (UBOS 2003a). Further evidence is provided in the WB firm survey quoted earlier which targeted the upper part of the formal sector: In the survey sample, the average share of casual and part-time employment in total employment is about 40%, with a respectively lower level in tourism (20%) and commercial agriculture (24%) and a higher level in manufacturing and construction (44%, 66%) (Table 29).[160] The average share of casual/part-time labour in Uganda is considerably higher than in other countries in the sample, and has, overall, not changed much since a similar survey was done in the 1995-97 period (WB 2004b, 53). For instance, the level of permanent workers was low in the sample of manufacturing firms in Uganda (56%), and it was significantly higher for Eritrea (91%), Pakistan (87%) and China (85%) (ibid, 136). The study team comments on this finding as follows: "The incentive to hire casual workers is usually their lower cost. In countries

159 The number of public servants in Uganda has been reduced from 320,000 in 1993 to 150,000 in 2000 (Kiiza 2006, 15). The level of people in public service employment has increased slightly in the 2000s, due to recruitment of teachers, for example.

160 A recent survey from the Federation of Uganda Employers (FUE) among 100 organisations from nine sub-sectors, on employment terms and conditions puts the share of permanent employees at 54%. The remaining staff are on contractual (24%), casual (13%) or temporary (9%) terms (FUE 2005b, 11).

like Uganda, where the HIV/AIDS crisis is severe, hiring casual workers might be a way for firms to avoid high health benefit costs" (ibid, 53). For the authors, cost considerations in terms of wages/benefits seem to drive this trend, in addition to other reasons such as capacity underutilisation.[161] The author of this book could not investigate the reasons and dynamics of casualisation of work in Uganda further; this requires specific research. However, the author believes casualisation is related not only to outcomes of cost-benefit calculus of employers, but also to political-economic structures and dynamics in the country, e.g. the 'liberal' stand of the government regarding industrial relations matters, and the poor bargaining power and weak representation of workers vis-à-vis employers and government.

Table 29: Employment structure in selected sectors by firm size class (%)

Sector and employment category	Micro (<10 employees	Small (10-49 employees)	Medium-size (50-99 employees)	Large (100+ employees)	All firm size classes
Commercial agriculture					
Permanent full time	76.19	44.30	3.33	78.87	76.38
Casual full time	9.52	13.16	0.00	9.11	9.14
Part time	14.29	42.53	96.67	12.02	14.49
Construction					
Permanent full time	100.00	66.67	16.67	31.04	33.97
Casual full time	0.00	3.70	83.33	61.04	56.39
Part time	0.00	29.63	0.00	7.92	9.64
Manufacturing					
Permanent full time	63.82	62.04	56.81	55.42	56.10
Casual full time	25.66	31.46	31.16	26.41	27.10
Part time	10.53	6.51	12.03	18.17	16.80
Tourism					
Permanent full time	83.33	85.87	85.61	76.27	79.53
Casual full time	13.33	9.78	13.16	16.94	15.34
Part time	3.33	4.35	1.23	6.79	5.13
Full sample					
Permanent full time	67.19	61.70	58.74	59.35	59.54
Casual full time	22.57	26.82	27.35	24.68	24.97
Part time	10.24	11.49	13.90	15.97	15.48

Source: *WB (2004b, 76).*

Significantly, in manufacturing almost half of the employees are casual/part-time workers (year 2002/03); presumably this encompasses mainly production workers, skilled and unskilled. Casualisation in Uganda is much higher than, for instance, in Nigeria (2001) and Eritrea (2002), where about 89% and 85% respectively of manufacturing workers had permanent full-time contracts; Uganda (56%) and Kenya (58%, 2002-03) remain below 60%. There is also an almost inverse relationship between firm size and permanent employees' share: the smaller the size category, the larger the share of permanent employees. Manufacturing firms in the

161 Of a recent survey sample, about 60% of the formal sector enterprises utilise only up to 50% of the installed capacity; approximately every fifth firm uses between 76-100% of the installed capacity. Main reasons for low capacity utilisation were: lack of demand/market (21%), stiff competition (17%), insufficient working capital (17%) and inadequate supply of raw materials (12%) (BOU et al. 2004).

very small size class have a share of 64% of permanent workers, medium and large firms of only around 57% and 55% respectively (ibid, 75, 79).

Informants mentioned the presence of a high number of under-employed (casual) factory workers in some firms. This situation of notable presence of casual labour and underemployment in factories - which would, by the way, lower average productivity figures - could point to: (a) deficiencies in process and HR management, (b) the low skill level required by production activities in firms, the reason why firms can operate with a significant share of casual (low- or un-trained) workers in the first place, (c) the working of economic, political, and cultural structures and 'incentives' in the country for employers to opt for low-paid casual workers rather than employing qualified persons for certain activities/positions more permanently, and (d) other social and political dynamics.

Overall, the 'casualisation trend' in the Ugandan economy may go even further in the years to come and thereby adversely affect the employment and career prospects of the next generations of school leavers and graduates. *Casualisation* could also offer a major explanation for the low level of productivity in Uganda. Further, the casualisation and informalisation of labour in parts of the modern economy limits the prospects for skills and capability development - *and thus the agenda of productivity, technology transfer and adoption, innovation, and poverty reduction* - and poses a significant challenge for actors concerned about HRD. *Casualisation* of the workplace, low and unstable payment and job insecurity *undermines and limits* workers' motivation and commitment, meaningful on-the-job learning and experience accumulation (capability building and deepening), technology, knowledge and learning transfer and thus, as a result, productivity. The features of 'negative work attitudes' and 'low productivity' regarding the Ugandan LF have often been noted in public debate and in reports. The argument that the features might be in part linked to incentives and insecurity patterns that the 'casual labour' group is facing has rarely been put forward.[162]

Note that because of interlinkages with and 'spillover effects' of the casual economy, also (large) parts of the 'permanent' employee group who are under threat of losing their job, or who have to accept worse contract conditions, are affected by these insecurity patterns characteristic of a casualised economy. The persistent problem of low (and often falling) real wage levels (Jamal 1991) and the current nonexistence of a minimum wage in Uganda are important aspects in this context as well.[163]

Against this background, relevant questions are: What is the context and rationale underlying the high proportion of casual labour in a company (matters of costs, seasonal work, process management, and politics of business practices)? What are characteristics of the relationship between employer and this group of workers (e.g. responsibilities, commitments from *both* sides, conflicts)? What incentive structure does a casual worker face? Will a part-time worker (without social security) make an effort to contribute to the improvement of the firm's product and processes? Will this worker share his/her professional knowledge and expertise with colleagues? How many of the part-timers are enjoying planned HRD measures at firm level (e.g. on-the-job training) to upgrade their skills? How many of them can build, advance

162 The author is grateful to Victor Richardson for the observation.

163 Between 1972 and 1984, for instance, real wages for wage earners fell by 85% (Jamal 1991). In the late 2000s, rising inflation, among others, has lowered the purchasing power of Ugandan job occupants. For further studies on labour issues in Uganda see Mamdani (1996a), Asowa-Okwe (1999), Barya (2001), and Namara (2001).

and utilise special skills and capabilities over time, which would advance productivity? How does the 'casual labour status' affect workers' attitudes? How do different management styles practiced in the country impact on this scenario? In short, how are (deficiencies in) *management practices, including HR* and *process management* linked with the problem set of *productivity, incentives, work attitudes* andlevel of *casual work* and *underemployment* in some firms? What is the link to local politics? Again, the apparent relative silence of GOU and donors on these issues is costly; the status quo undermines their expressed agenda of economic transformation.

Other relevant questions would be related to the link between incentives, work attitudes and productivity of the better educated/trained group; those managers, key employees and production workers who are (maybe) less affected by casualisation of work but might have a relatively more negative work attitude (according to earlier quoted report finding).

The working poor

About 36% of the LF in Uganda is classified as 'working poor'. The approximately 3.5 million people in this group are part of the LF and are working. Yet their incomes are below the official poverty threshold (UBOS 2006, 38-9). The likelihood of working but being poor is significantly higher in rural areas (40.3%) and in the Northern (61.2%) and Eastern regions (43.6) (Table 30), and for those that are underemployed (43.6%). About every one in three (34.5%) full time workers earning is less than the poverty threshold (ibid). Furthermore, young and old workers experience higher incidences of poverty; as do people in the primary sector (Table 31).

Table 30: Working poor by sex, residence and regions

	Working population			**Number below poverty level**			**Rate (%)**		
	Male	*Female*	*Total*	*Male*	*Female*	*Total*	*Male*	*Female*	*Total*
Residence									
Rural	3,906	4,365	8,272	1,550	1,785	3,335	39.7	40.9	40.3
Urban	720	769	1,490	79	90	169	11.0	11.8	11.4
Region									
Central	1,445	1,514	2,959	276	285	561	19.1	18.8	19.0
Eastern	1,221	1,380	2,601	536	599	1,135	43.9	43.4	43.6
Northern	776	996	1,771	473	610	1,083	60.9	61.3	61.2
Western	1190	1,244	2,430	344	381	725	28.9	30.6	29.8
Total	**4,627**	**5,134**	**9,762**	**1,629**	**1,876**	**3,505**	**35.2**	**36.5**	**35.9**

Source: *UBOS (2006, 39).*

Table 31: Working poor by sex, age and sector of the economy

	Working population			Below poverty level			Rate		
	Male	Female	Total	Male	Female	Total	Male	Female	Total
Age group									
14	107	92	199	56	43	99	52.2	47.3	49.9
15-19	585	644	1,229	264	225	489	45.2	34.9	39.8
20-24	706	1,025	1,731	216	309	525	30.7	30.1	30.4
25-29	812	959	1,771	233	329	562	28.7	34.3	31.7
30-34	701	716	1,417	232	292	524	33.1	40.8	37.0
35-39	539	559	1,098	189	198	386	35.0	35.4	35.2
40-44	382	387	769	141	165	306	36.9	42.7	39.8
45-49	298	302	600	107	118	225	35.8	39.1	37.4
50-54	211	223	434	74	92	166	35.2	41.3	38.3
55-59	143	136	279	64	68	132	45.0	49.8	47.3
60-64	143	91	234	53	37	90	37.2	39.9	38.3
Sector of Economy									
Primary	2,456	3,193	5,649	1,110	1,373	2,482	45.2	43.0	43.9
Manufacturing	326	222	548	84	69	16	25.8	31.1	29.0
Service	1,843	1,717	3,560	436	434	870	23.6	25.3	24.4
Total	**4,627**	**5,134**	**9,762**	**1,629**	**1,876**	**3,502**	**35.2**	**36.5**	**35.9**

Source: *Ibid (40).*

Workers with low or no formal education are more likely to be poor than those with higher levels of education. Notably, workers with 'primary/specialised training' experience the lowest incidence of poverty (Table 32). Persons employed in agricultural, elementary, crafts-related occupations have relatively high poverty incidences (Table 51, Appendix 11).

Table 32: Working poor by sex and educational attainment

	Working population			Below poverty level			Rate		
	Male	Female	Total	Male	Female	Total	Male	Female	Total
Educational attainment									
No formal education	423	1,243	1,666	233	685	919	55.2	55.1	55.1
Primary	2,835	2,954	5,789	1,160	1,095	2,255	40.9	37.1	38.9
Primary/specialised training	390	228	617	37	15	53	9.6	6.8	8.6
Secondary	977	707	1,684	198	80	278	20.3	11.3	16.5

Source: *ibid (40).*

The informal sector as a permanent characteristic of the economy

With regard to the above characteristics, especially of a large informal sector, Chen (2004) reminds us that there is increasing recognition in many DCs around the world that the informal sector is a permanent pillar of an economy. A context-specific response from GOU and key actors is needed to tackle informal sector matters as a key area of poverty reduction:

> "[T]he informal economy is growing and is not a short-term but a permanent phenomenon [; ...] it is not just a traditional or residual phenomenon but a feature of modern capitalist development, associated with both growth and global integration. For this reason, the informal economy needs to be seen not as a marginal or peripheral sector but as a basic component - the base, if you will - of the total economy. ... [P]roduction, distribution and employment relations tend to fall at some point on a continuum between pure 'formal' relations (i.e., regulated and protected) at one pole and pure 'informal' relations (i.e., unregulated and unprotected) at the other, with many categories in between. ... Moreover, the formal and the informal ends of the economic continuum are often dynamically linked. ...Also, many formal enterprises hire wage workers under informal employment relations. ... [I]improving the conditions of work in the informal economy is an essential pathway to reducing poverty. This requires an informed understanding of the composition and characteristics of the informal economy in given sectors of the economy. ... [Further,] working conditions in the informal economy need to be addressed through economic policies as well as social policies - not just by social policies. This requires an informed understanding of how existing policies - both economic and social - impact on different segments of the informal economy. ...What is needed is an informed and comprehensive policy approach that can be used to formulate *context-specific responses* by governments and other key actors" (4-5, 16, emphasis in original).

Table 33 summarises old and new views on the informal sector and points out that the informal sector is likely 'here to stay' and should therefore be nurtured better to promote its contribution to GDP, development, HRD and job creation (Chen 2004).

Table 33: Old and new views of the informal economy

The old view	The new view
The informal sector is the traditional economy that will wither away and die with modern, industrial growth.	The informal economy is 'here to stay' and expanding with modern, industrial growth.
It is only marginally productive.	It is a major provider of employment, goods and services for lower-income groups. It contributes a significant share of GDP.
It exists separately from the formal economy.	It is linked to the formal economy -it produces for, trades with, distributes for and provides services to formal firms.
It represents a reserve pool of surplus labour.	Much of the recent rise in informal employment is due to the decline in formal employment or to the informalisation of previously formal employment relationships.
It comprises mostly street traders and very small-scale producers.	It is made up of a wide range of informal occupations - both 'resilient old forms' such as casual day labour in construction and agriculture as well as 'emerging new ones' such as temporary and part-time jobs plus homework for high tech industries.

Most of those in the sector are entrepreneurs who run illegal and unregistered enterprises in order to avoid regulation and taxation.	It is made up of non-standard wage workers as well as entrepreneurs and self-employed persons producing legal goods and services, albeit through irregular or unregulated means. Most entrepreneurs and the self-employed are amendable to and would welcome efforts to reduce barriers to registration and related transaction costs and to increase benefits from regulation; and most non-standard wage workers would welcome more stable jobs and workers' rights.

Source: *Chen (2004, 7-8).*

Industry occupation: Two-thirds of workforce is in subsistence agriculture

The *sectoral shares* in employment manifest the dominance of the primary sector: About 67.5% of the labour workforce is engaged in primary activities; almost entirely at subsistence level.[164] About 97 out of 100 workers in this sector operate in a subsistence mode; only the small remaining part is engaged in non-subsistence, market-oriented/commercial production. UBOS comments: "The large share of primary sector reflects a stagnant share of wage employment and a high proportion of contributing family workers who are widespread in the rural area in Uganda" (2006, 17). Further, the very high share of women in agriculture is notable. "Estimates show that women contribute approximately 80% of the labour force for food production, 60% for planting, 70% for weeding, 60% for harvesting and 90% for processing/preparation. The women's efforts are mainly concentrated on food crops for non-monetary family consumption whereas the men concentrate on the production of cash crops" (UN 2004, 25 based on NAADS Secretariat 2003).[165] Besides the primary sector, the other two sectors have employment shares of 6.1% for industry (mostly mining and manufacturing) and 25.2% for services (about half of it: sales, maintenance and repair) (UBOS 2006, 12, 2003).[166]

Given this very low level of commercial agriculture, Uganda still has a long way to go to achieve a significant agro-based, employment-intensive, export-led industrialisation. It has been difficult to implement the country's value-addition agenda and to foster competitive, large-scale production due to, among others, the predominance of subsistence agriculture with a low number of large-scale commercial farming enterprises (compared to Kenya). Some development projects targeting agro export sectors were not very successful (at least in first attempts) (WB 2006b). The high level of subsistence farming indicates the need for measures that improve skills, capabilities and the organisation of farmers as well as the interlinkages

164 The primary sector includes agriculture, fishing, forestry, hunting, mining and quarrying.

165 See also the report on 'Gender and Economic Growth in Uganda' (Ellis et al. 2006).

166 The Labour Market report 2006 provides this aggregated version only, without giving further details on shares of specific sub-sectors. The LF report 2003, however, provides this information, including details on residence (rural/urban) and sex (male/female). See Table 52 (Appendix 12). Comparing the versions (2003/2006), the sub-sectoral proportions *generally hold*, yet there might be very small percentage differences at times. Note the 2006 version has about 9.5m people in the employed group, the 2003 version about 9.3m people.

between farmers and buyers to allow for more successful and expanded commercial agriculture. In general, GOU programmes had mixed results to date in commercialising and improving the sector.[167]

Note also the proportional GDP contribution of respective sectors: While industry employs 6% of the LF, it counts for 21% of GDP. For the services sector: 25% of the LF produces 43% of GDP. Agriculture employs two-thirds of the LF yet produces about one-third of GDP. This gives an idea of the necessity to not only make agriculture more productive (and stable), but also to facilitate the expansion of the industry and service sectors (and the movement of parts of the LF into the latter two), which contribute to growth, upgrading of the economy, as well as income and employment generation.[168] The author's assessment is that GOU has not yet succeeded in fostering sufficiently important competitiveness and development aspects of the service and industry sectors, apart from some notable success in the stability, investment climate and enabling business environment agenda.

Finally, Table 34 gives information on the *main occupation* of the LF. Agriculture and fisheries workers are dominant (two-thirds); service and sales workers as well as elementary occupations are also significant.[169] The share of associate professionals and technicians is small (UBOS 2006, 13).[170] About every fourth person in the LF undertakes a secondary activity, especially service/sales and crafts workers and managers/administrators (UBOS 2003a, 23).

Table 34: Distribution of persons currently employed by occupation and sex (%), 14-64 years, 2002/03 UNHS

Occupation (ISCO 1988)	Male	Female	Total
Agricultural and fisheries workers	57.8	74.2	66.1
Service workers, shop/market sales workers	14.8	14.4	14.6
Crafts and related trade workers	6.9	4.1	5.0
Elementary occupations	13.0	4.8	8.9
Associate professional and technicians	3.6	2.0	2.8
Others	3.5	1.4	2.4

Source: *UBOS 2006, 13. (ISCO: International Standard Classification of Occupation).*

Box 44 (Appendix 15) gives information on earning/wage structures according to education, industry and occupation. Those with specialised training/above secondary education and

167 However, about 44% of household expenditure was spent on food and beverages in 2002/03, showing the importance of the agricultural and agro-industry sector for domestic consumption (UBOS 2005, 20).

168 The author is grateful to Joseph Kitamirike, who made this argument in a personal discussion.

169 Service and sales workers include barbers, waiters, persons selling goods in kiosks, shops, etc. Elementary occupations include house personnel, drivers, car washers, street vendors, etc. (UBOS 2006, 13).

170 See Table 53 (Appendix 13) for an alternative overview on occupations including regional break-down. Table 54 (Appendix 14) also provides information on absolute numbers of main occupations and information on proportion additionally engaging in secondary occupations (all from UBOS 2003).

those in financial intermediation, electricity-gas-water supply, and public administration, for example, earn relatively better on average. On the other hand, those in services, manufacturing, construction and especially agriculture, receive (very) low monthly earnings (UBOS 2006, 15-7).[171] Finally, a UBOS analysis of job advertisements in main newspapers (2002-2004) revealed that in the three years, most vacancies advertised were in the major groups of professionals, technicians and associate professionals. No vacancy was advertised in the group of skilled agriculture and fishery workers (ibid, 62-3).[172]

Outlook: Labour market pressures to continue

Many of the characteristics of the labour market and LF in Uganda presented above can be expected to have limiting effects on prospects for accelerated, significant and meaningful HRD (and thus enhanced productivity, competitiveness and economic development). Moreover, in the coming decades, Uganda faces a significant challenge with respect to integrating new generations of young people into the labour market, given that if the country's population growth rate remains at the high level of 3.3% (1991-2002) - the highest in East Africa, and one of the highest in the world (Uganda has the third highest fertility rate in the world) - Uganda's population is estimated to double from 25 million to about 50 million people by 2025 and to 100 million by 2050. Currently, more than half (52%) of the population is under 14 years of age, and will demand chances for employment, income generation and economic and social development. There are estimates that around 390,000 people enter the labour market each year. Accordingly, about 40% of the new entrants (employment seekers) are absorbed in the informal sector, mostly in agriculture; a few are absorbed in the formal sector, while half of the new entrants do not find employment (MGLSD 2004, NV 2008c).[173]

Graduates from all educational backgrounds face the situation of a small formal sector and a large (mostly survival-oriented) informal sector. Actual unemployment levels in Kampala - especially among females and the youth - are considerable. After advancing through the school system and investing much effort and money in education along the way, graduates from universities and other tertiary schools struggle to find meaningful employment in a highly casualised labour market. Another challenge is that sections of mainly secondary but also tertiary level graduates seem educated but insufficiently skilled (trained and experienced) to find formal employment or undertake an entrepreneurial activity. The UBOS experts point to one of the many important concerns regarding the mid to long-term effects of this youth unemployment: "Because these people cannot get the benefit of rapid acquisition of skills, experience and the habits of work, which young people normally learn before the age of thirty, they will be virtually unemployable in future. Most of these young people abandon all hope of finding employment opportunities, becoming the so-called 'discouraged workers' (2006, 44).

171 This analysis comprises informal and formal sector activities.

172 The newspapers were New Vision, Daily Monitor and East African. See Box 45 (Appendix 16) for more details.

173 See also Appleton and Ssewanyana (2003) on the low absorption capacity of the wage employment sector in Uganda. The author's PhD research in and around the town Mbale in Eastern Uganda in late 2008 reveals social, cultural and economic problems in various localities (theft, drug use, desperation, tensions between youth and other community members) related to the high levels of unemployment- and underemployment among youths.

4

Sectoral Dynamics and their Impact on Poverty Incidence

Income diversification into (often informal) non-agricultural activities

Despite the structural transformation that Uganda has undergone since the mid 1980s, the country remains based largely on agriculture and a considerable share of trade and manufacturing is based on products of the agricultural sector. The relevance of agricultural dynamics for poverty outcomes in the country is significant. Yet, increasingly, Ugandan households diversify their income activities towards off-farm earnings, a tendency which has helped some households to work themselves out of poverty. In this context, the following dynamics are important to note: First, since the late 1980s, there has been a general trend among households to diversify their income sources: Almost every second household, and about one-third in the rural areas, started a non-agricultural enterprise within five years (1988-1992/93), in particular in the Central and Western region and mostly in the trade sector. Notably, poor households now rely on different activities, including farming, farm work on larger farms, and trade activities (Deininger and Okidi 2002).

UBOS household surveys in 2002/03 (classified by main occupation of household head) confirm a shift into non-agricultural activities, e.g. into informal trade and manufacturing (Kappel et al. 2004). As a result, almost half of the households surveyed have now a non-agricultural enterprise. The largest part of these non-agricultural enterprises relies on family labour to run a business and should therefore be expected to be fairly small. Less than 15% of them employ any labour (Okidi et al. 2004).[174] Possibly, the latter feature will change over time; and semi-professional structures in family businesses (less family labour) will play a role even at the lower end of enterprises.

In particular, there is an inter-sectoral shift in *rural areas* regarding the occupation of the household head towards trade and manufacturing; both sectors have more than doubled their population shares in the period 1999/2000-2002/03 (classified by occupation of the household head): manufacturing from 3% to 7%, trade from 5% to 12% (Table 35, *column Pop. share*). Presumably, most of these non-agricultural activities in rural areas are informal, e.g. petty traders. As a result of these dynamics about one-fifth of the rural population are now experiencing the business requirements in the (mainly small-scale) manufacturing and services sectors. In one way or another, the rural working population is confronted with and has to respond to new business models and forms of competition. Government services also increased its share significantly, from 1% to 6%. Correspondingly, the share of agriculture (crop/non-crop) in the total economy fell by 12% to about 68% (all for rural areas).[175]

174 According to UBOS' household enterprise analysis (excluding crop farming enterprises), only about 10% of total people engaged in these enterprises are employees (causal/permanent) (2006, 26).

175 In Tables 35-37, the column *PO* stands for poverty headcount in the respective sector (based on

Table 35: Sectoral poverty profile (%), decomposition of poverty changes, rural areas, 1999/00-2002/03

	1999/00			2002/03					
	Pop. share	PO	Contr. to PO	Pop. share	PO	Contr to PO	Intra-sectoral	Inter-sectoral	Inter-action
All sectors		37.97			41.94				
Crop agriculture	77.11	40.43	82.11	62.55	51.04	76.12	8.18	-5.89	-1.55
Non-crop agriculture	3.10	45.77	3.73	5.70	36.75	5.00	-0.28	1.19	-0.24
Fising and hunting	1.03	34.86	0.95	0.34	39.32	0.32	0.05	-0.24	-0.03
Mining	0.50	44.77	0.59	0.22	25.28	0.13	-0.10	-0.13	0.06
Manufacturing	2.94	37.78	2.93	6.52	32.67	5.08	-0.15	1.35	-0.18
Public utilities	0.13	0.00	0.00	0.05	28.21	0.04	0.04	0.00	-0.02
Construction	1.28	33.78	1.13	1.57	26.65	1.00	-0.09	0.10	-0.02
Trade	5.42	18.68	2.67	11.86	21.54	6.09	0.15	1.20	0.18
Hotels	0.61	0.61	0.32	2.08	24.06	1.19	0.03	0.29	0.06
Transport/ comm.	1.08	1.08	0.72	1.85	27.89	1.23	0.03	0.19	0.02
Misc. services	5.46	5.46	3.74	1.64	45.01	1.76	1.04	-0.99	-0.73
Gov. services	1.35	1.35	1.12	5.62	15.30	1.05	-0.22	1.34	-0.69
Total effect							8.68	-1.57	-3.13

Source: *Kappel et al. (2004, 39).*[176]

In urban areas, *manufacturing* and *trade* activities of the household head represented about half of the urban population in 2002/03: Within three years, manufacturing increased its share to 15% (up from 9% in 1999/2000), trade to 35% (30%). Another third of the population lives in households related to *other services* sub-sectors. Rather significant/small increases in shares are also reported for government services (now 12%) and hotels (5%) respectively, while crop agriculture, construction, transport/communications and miscellaneous services all lost shares, although some only in small ranges (Table 36, *column Pop.share*).

main industry of household head's work), 'Contr. to PO' stands for sectoral contribution to overall PO change. Further (a) 'Intra-sectoral' and (b)'Inter-sectoral' stand for contribution to overall PO changes due to in the case of (a) moves/changes within the sector, and (b) moves of people in-between sectors. For the latter, '-' can indicate that people move out (lower Pop.share) of a sector with a high PO, so that the inter-sectoral contribution actually *reduces* poverty ('-'). A '-' for the *interaction component* would then indicate that people move out of a sector with rising poverty (see Kappel et al. 2004, 37).

176 Kappel et al. note that: "these results are of a preliminary character ... We stress this point here, as the sectoral shifts that seem to have occurred since 2000 are very large, which casts doubt on the reliability of the data. Furthermore, changes in the sector classification may have contributed to some of the sectoral shifts, in particular in the service sector" (2004, 37).

Table 36: Sectoral poverty profile (%), decomposition of poverty changes, urban areas, 1999/00-2002/03

	1999/00			2002/03					
	Pop. share	PO	Contr to PO	Pop share	PO	Contr to PO	Intra-sectoral	Intra-sectoral	Intra-action
All sectors		9.84			12.58				
Crop agriculture	13.80	23.74	33.27	10.99	38.65	33.77	2.06	-0.67	-0.42
Non-crop agric.	1.49	1.95	0.30	2.00	9.73	1.54	0.12	0.01	0.04
Fishing and hunting	0.68	1.42	0.10	0.27	11.71	0.25	0.07	-0.01	-0.04
Mining	0.59	4.84	0.29	0.30	48.77	1.18	0.26	-0.01	-0.13
Manufacturing	9.05	6.17	5.67	14.57	15.87	18.37	0.88	0.34	0.54
Public utilities	0.72	0.00	0.00	0.70	0.75	0.04	0.01	0.00	0.00
Construction	4.30	14.91	6.51	3.97	13.42	4.24	-0.06	-0.05	0.00
Trade	29.51	8.11	24.31	34.71	8.67	23.91	0.17	0.42	0.03
Hotels	4.71	9.45	4.52	4.83	9.56	3.67	0.01	0.01	0.00
Transport/ comm.	9.98	7.68	7.79	7.62	8.94	5.42	0.13	-0.18	-0.03
Misc. services	20.69	6.48	13.63	8.27	7.15	4.70	0.14	-0.81	-0.08
Gov. services	4.50	7.93	3.62	11.78	3.11	2.91	-0.22	0.58	-0.35
Total							**3.54**	**-0.36**	**-0.44**

Source: *Ibid (40).*

In summary, there is a shift at national level signalling that *non-agricultural/off-farm activities are gaining in importance* (if household head's main occupation is considered). The proportion of Ugandans living in households with crop-agriculture as the main activity declined from around 69% to 56% between 1999/2000 and 2002/03 (non-crop agriculture: 3% to 5%). Instead, manufacturing (from 4% to 8%) and trade (9%-15%) doubled their respective shares; government services' share increased from 2% to 6% (Table 37, column: Pop. share). Manufacturing and trade now employ household heads that represent more than a fifth of the population. Other non-agricultural sectors showed little positive dynamics regarding their population share (Kappel et al. 2004, 36-41). Many of the non-farming activities (outside the government service realm) are likely to take place in the informal sector. There is evidence that many people, pressed by the low returns of agriculture to start other activities, shifted from agriculture to non-agriculture self-employment because the wage employment sector could not absorb people released from agriculture (Okidi et al. 2004, 11).

Table 37: Sectoral poverty profile, decomposition of poverty changes, national level, 1999/00-2002/03

	1999/00			2002/03					
	Pop. share	PO	Contr to PO	Pop share	PO	Contr to PO	Intra-sectoral	Intra-sectoral	Intra-action
All sectors		34.30			38.07				
Crop agriculture	68.85	39.99	80.29	55.75	50.72	74.28	7.39	-5.24	-1.41
Non-crop agric.	2.89	42.83	3.61	5.21	35.39	4.85	-0.21	0.00	0.17
Fishing and hunting	0.98	31.83	0.91	0.33	36.33	0.32	0.04	-0.21	-0.03
Mining	0.51	38.78	0.58	0.23	29.41	0.18	-0.05	-0.11	-0.03
Manufacturing	3.74	27.81	3.03	7.58	28.41	5.66	0.02	0.07	0.02
Public utilities	0.21	0.00	0.00	0.14	9.91	0.04	0.02	0.00	0.01
Construction	1.67	27.40	1.34	1.89	22.98	1.14	-0.07	-0.06	0.01
Trade	8.56	13.92	3.48	14.87	17.57	6.86	0.31	0.88	0.23
Hotels	1.14	14.18	0.47	2.44	20.28	1.30	0.07	0.18	0.08
Transport/ comm.	2.24	15.06	0.98	2.61	20.59	1.41	0.12	0.06	-0.02
Misc. services	7.45	18.93	4.11	2.52	28.60	1.89	0.72	-0.93	-0.48
Gov. services	1.76	23.64	1.21	6.43	12.36	2.09	-0.20	1.10	-0.53
Total							**8.16**	**-2.14**	**-2.25**

Source: *Ibid (38).*

It is relevant for HRD to support this chapter of the evolution of the Ugandan economy: the shift into non-agricultural activities, the shift from subsistence to commercially oriented work, and the instances of formalisation and increased professionalism, in the urban but especially rural areas where extension services and training provision, be it from GOU or other organisations, have been too thinly spread over the sub-sectors. Actors concerned with HRD need to look at young micro and small enterprises and their growth strategies and skills needs and help to assess and develop them and make an attempt to offer relevant training (see training needs study by EU and GOU 2003 below).

Move into non-agriculture limits poverty rise; uneven poverty dynamics

Recent analysis on the relation between growth and consumption expenditures (headcount income poverty levels) in Uganda for the period 1992/93-2002/03 highlight a significant pro-poor outcome, especially during the years 1992-2000, when growth in consumption was robust across percentiles and poverty headcount fell considerably (based on household survey evidence). The growth pattern over the entire period can be characterised as overall *pro-poor*; using broad and aggregate indicators. This outcome is linked to the economic recovery and growth strategies of GOU. Today, empirical disparities between rural and urban areas and between different regions in Uganda, especially the North (with current headcount poverty at 64%) and the rest of the country, are growing at the time of writing. Gender inequality remains a major challenge and the situation of women, according to reports, has not improved significantly. Together, this points to an unequal process of poverty reduction, in geographical, ethnic and gender terms (Kappel et al. 2004, Okidi et al. 2004).

Despite overall economic growth, the early 2000s saw a setback in national headcount poverty, which rose from 35% to 38% (corresponding to an increase in the number of poor people, from 6 to 9 million)[177] due to rising poverty, especially among agricultural households (ibid). In more recent statistics, poverty levels have fallen again, to 31%, yet the number of poor people has remained around 9 million.[178] About one-fifth of households experience chronic poverty (poor in successive surveys). Overall, *poverty is still a predominantly rural phenomenon*, manifest especially among crop farmers. Rural poverty headcount decreased from 60% in 1992 to 37% in 2000 and rose to 42% in 2003. The related figures for urban areas are 28%, 10% and 12%. The contribution of rural areas to national poverty remained at about 96% (Okidi et al. 2004, 10), pointing to the effects of subsistence agricultural rural economy, with its problems of transformation (in a neoliberal policy setting), dependency on urban economic dynamics, and hurdles to exploiting the opportunities of (regional and international) export markets.

More to the point, the period 2000-2003 revealed rising welfare inequality (especially in the urban areas). While the richest 20% experienced a 9% increase in consumption expenditure, the rest of the population faced a decline in this respect (Gini index increased from 0.4 to 0.43). Notably, while the *distributional* pattern of growth in household consumption expenditure for the whole period (1992-2003) disfavoured the poor, some parts of that period, especially the years 1992-1997 (with substantial growth rate in agriculture) favoured the poorest 20% disproportionably (above-average growth in consumption expenditures for this group) (Kappel et al. 2004, Okidi et al. 2004). Tables 38 and 39 present changes in monthly household and per capita consumption expenditure respectively (1999/00-2002/03). In total, within three years, real increase was 4% (household) and 6% (per capita) respectively. Importantly, while the Central region experienced improvements in both indicators, other regions had a mixed record. The imbalances between Kampala/Central region and the rest of the country are significant, e.g. the average household expenditure (and per capita expenditure) in Kampala is almost three times (four times) higher than in the East. The discrepancies in comparison to the North are more severe. Research indicates that, over the last two decades, feelings of exclusion and marginalisation from the economic dynamics have existed among the population in both the Northern and Eastern parts of the country (International Alert 2006, 2008, PhD research of the author).

---

177 As explained earlier, there are about 3.5 million 'working poor'. The remaining 5.5 million people below the official poverty line are children and adults who are not part of the LF (UBOS 2006, 38).

178 The recent statistics will not be analysed due to time limitations that come with every research project.

Table 38: Monthly consumption expenditure per household ('000 Shillings)

	1999/00			2002/03		
	Rural	Urban	Total	Rural	Urban	Total
Uganda	109	266	134	113	266	139
Central*	138	221	150	151	249	165
Kampala	-	335	335	-	328	328
Eastern	104	201	113	103	184	112
Northern	65	132	68	65	152	69
Western	122	269	133	117	224	126

***Note:** The Central region excludes Kampala district

Source: *UBOS (2005, 19).*

Table 39: Monthly real mean per capita expenditure ('000 Shillings)

	1999/00			2002/03		
	Rural	Urban	Total	Rural	Urban	Total
Uganda	20	61	25	21	65	27
Central*	27	52	30	28	60	32
Kampala	-	79	79	-	88	88
Eastern	19	44	21	18	44	20
Northern	12	27	13	13	30	13
Western	21	58	23	22	47	24

***Note:** The Central region excludes Kampala district

Source: *Ibid (20).*

To continue, one of the key findings supporting a call for accelerated growth in Uganda is probably that "growth (much more than redistribution) has driven the poverty reduction in Uganda during the 1990s" (Okidi et al. 2004, 10). Similarly relevant is the following: "Especially in urban areas, the worsening income distribution has prevented growth from reducing poverty more effectively. For the future, higher inequality levels imply that higher growth is needed to achieve a specific poverty reduction target" (Kappel et al. 2004, 32-3). A growth focus therefore seems valid; however, it is important to clarify the nature of growth and development one has in mind, including implicit requirements and implications for justice, inclusion, equity and thus the moral economy (Thompson 1971, 1980, Scott 1979, 1985) in the country. Uganda needs to take advantage of opportunities to set in motion inclusive and structural dynamics in production, trade and employment, and develop social and economic policies and programmes which take into account "the interests of the vast majority in society" (Mamdani 1995, 78). Maybe, the future - more specifically, the political and economic dynamics of the next years - will bring a more pro-poor and equitable development, which will reduce pressure on growth rates. Perhaps the inequality trends will continue, which could increase economic, social and political tensions and (further) question the appropriateness and legitimacy of parts of the liberal economic paradigm which has been applied by the GOU and the donors since the 1990s.

Another relevant finding can be taken from a livelihood analysis for households in the production of tradable goods (Morrissey et al. 2003). It reveals the importance of developing skills and capabilities around matters of value chains and producer organisation as well as social norms and practices that shape economic activities.[179]

> "Tangible benefits to the poor people involved in the production of these tradable products are limited. The most important explanatory factors for why the poorest did not benefit are the absence of effective organisation of producers (especially if they have little or no choice in who to sell to) and exploitative employment practices (especially where there is only one employer). Unequal gender relations often mean that although household income may increase, this is under the control of males and women derive limited benefit" (ibid, 4).

Regarding poverty incidences, another message of the above analysis is important: During the 1990s the key contributors to overall poverty reduction were *intra*-sectoral improvements, (a) foremost within agriculture - for food-crop and cash-crop households especially in the Central and Western (coffee) regions[180], but (b) also (although to a lesser extent) within the most important non-agricultural activities - for households whose heads worked in manufacturing, trade and government services. For the immediate period after the year 2000, when overall poverty rose from 35% to 38%, *inter*-sectoral shifts, instead, played a more significant role in determining final poverty outcomes (Tables 35-37 above, *columns:* intra-sectoral, inter-sectoral changes, inter-action). In particular, the move from agricultural to non-agricultural activities (measured by household head's main occupation) limited the increase in poverty.[181] Among manufacturing and trade households, poverty incidence at national level remained almost constant (case of manufacturing) or rose only slightly (trade) during this period (Kappel et al. 2004, 36-41, Morrissey et al. 2003). In other words, "people have been moving out of sectors with relatively high poverty incidence, and out of sectors where poverty was rising. This finding might be interpreted in the way that poverty outcomes would have been a lot worse, if people had stayed in agriculture" (Kappel et al. 2004, 40). The evolution of poverty dynamics illustrates the dynamic and volatile environment poor households operate in, and the level of change and related new challenges and opportunities they have to deal with.

The shift into non-agricultural (often informal) activities highlights the need for HRD-related policies and strategies to include the non-farm informal sector and to increase formal sector employment opportunities, in both SMEs and larger firms. More so, since poverty levels are lately also fairly high (although lower than in agriculture), and in part slightly increasing among urban households, where the main occupation of the household head is a (informal) non-agriculture activity, e.g. services, trade and manufacturing (ibid, 38).[182]

---

179 See also Wiegratz et al. (2007b) on these issues.

180 Relative price changes motivated farmers to change from less profitable crops (e.g. cotton and millet) to more profitable crops (e.g. coffee and maize).

181 Note that the analysis "suffers from the possibly important drawback that it does not take into account the composition of household income. Households are classified according to the industry of the main occupation of the household head. Had poverty been reduced due to intersectoral changes of other household members, including possible increased labour market participation by women, it would not be taken into account" (Kappel et al. 2004, 40)

182 For further studies on (chronic) poverty in Uganda see the following: Bird and Shinyekwa (2003), CPRC-Uganda (2005), Ellis and Bahigwa (2003), Hickey (2005, 2003), Lawson et al. (2003), Okidi et al. (2003), Okidi and Kempaka (2002), OPM (2008), UBOS (2007, 2004), MFPED and CBR (2007). See also Bush (2007) on poverty and neoliberalism.

"A possible policy implication for the period of the 1990s alone might have been the following: Concentrate on agriculture, as this is where the poor are and where poverty reduction efforts will be most effective. In light of the ... results from the recent household survey together with what we have learnt from the UPPAP [Uganda Participatory Poverty Assessment Process], this conclusion does not hold any more for current and future years ... [A]griculture is still by far the most important sector and thus it will have to be the major focus of policy interventions directed towards the productive sectors. However, the poor are increasingly found in trade and manufacturing activities. The Ugandan economy appears to experience a major transformation in its employment structure with an important impact on poverty. Therefore, policies have to prevent that switching from agricultural into other activities does not result in a switch from one type of subsistence activity into another" (ibid, 40-1).

Diversification processes need a stronger HRD response

HRD policies and strategies have to make an attempt to support this process of change, especially the growth in non-agricultural activities, while trying to also improve the agricultural sector and reduce poverty incidence therein. Note that the process seems highly dynamic, with a high rate of business closures which makes a decisive HRD reaction even more desirable, to allow entrepreneurs to catch up in their new activity (sectoral occupation) and realise income-earning opportunities. Skill formation for market and product development and productivity improvement in the wide sense (for simple 'survival' in most cases) is thus vital for the transformative (yet partly volatile) Ugandan economy, where many economic actors operate with little or no training. Overall growth of the economy alone will not put the smallholder farmer or the micro entrepreneur in a position to participate favourably in competitive markets and make a living. Market-oriented training and skills development needs to put him/her individually and collectively in a position to initiate a supply-side response within the current competitive context and to learn about business opportunities, market transactions and negotiations, and technology. Measures that target market integration, linkages, extension services, the development of market and other infrastructure and value chains, and the protection of certain sectors or activities (from outright competition) are complementary. The agenda has to include improved handling of technology.

Key findings of experiences in 14 developing countries (including Uganda) with the growth-poverty nexus (pro-poor growth) in the 1990s generally support this suggested focus. Since the related empirical study is rather authoritative and can be expected to somehow shape the common sense and rhetoric of the main development agencies involved (WB, DFID, GTZ and Agence Française de Développement) and concerned partner agencies, it is given a lengthy quotation:

"Greater poverty reduction was observed where policies were in place to enhance the capacity of poor people to participate in growth ... [which, in other words] increase the quantity and quality of poor people's productive assets and their ability to participate on an equal footing in product and factor markets. ... The country studies also illustrate the value of viewing growth through a pro-poor lens for analyzing and addressing the constraints that poor households face in participating in growth ... [In particular, five policy interventions were important in helping to raise the agricultural earnings of poor households in the 1990s].

- Improving market access and lowering transaction costs.
- Strengthening property rights for land.
- Creating an incentive framework that benefits all farmers.

- Expanding the technology available to smallholder producers.
- Helping poorer and smaller producers deal with risk" (WB 2005b, 3-5).

The report also notices, "in Uganda where 90 percent of poor households are in rural areas and 80 percent of the workforce is engaged in agriculture, promoting sectoral growth for smallholders and sectoral mobility will be central to the country's pro-poor growth strategy" (ibid, 11). Three research areas are suggested with a view to increasing participation of the poor in growth and to accelerate poverty reduction:

> "First, movement from agricultural to nonagricultural employment was important in raising the incomes of poor households in many countries, but there is also evidence that the more educated, better connected workers were more successful in this regard. Understanding how sectoral mobility might be enhanced is an important area for further research. Second, the impact of growth was uneven across regions within countries. Understanding how to craft public investment strategies that can address subregional growth and poverty is another important area for further analysis ... Third, political economy considerations often affect the distributional outcomes of structural and investment policies, at times at the expense of poor households. Understanding how to make public policy to enhance the ability of the poor to participate in and influence government processes is also an area for further exploration" (ibid, 11).

Part of these findings can be interpreted as underlining - directly and indirectly - the role of capabilities in allowing the poor to advance personally while their country experiences economic growth. For instance, the following terms mentioned in the study justify and demand a concern for a comprehensive, enduring HRD agenda: technology, transaction costs, sectoral factor and labour mobility (which can enhance responsiveness and adjustment capacity of the economy), (responding to) market access, dealing with risk, and the respective collective actions implications. The question is if and how donors will follow up such findings of their own studies.

Some implications for formal sector development, especially industrial development

Against this background, the fact that most people live in rural areas and almost all of them are poor commonly leads to the argument that - to ensure improvements in the poverty reduction agenda - priority has to be given to rural development targeting the poor, the sector where the poor engage in and earn incomes from (agriculture, informal sector). While this is intuitive and in large parts correct and sensible, it would be misleading to believe that this strategy is sufficient as a national development strategy for Uganda. If the small formal sector - which is currently located around the urban centres, especially Kampala - is not supported in constant skills development, learning, and productivity advancement it is likely that: potential business opportunities remain untapped, advancements in business practices and performance outcomes are not achieved, sectoral growth, including export growth, which can lead to certain spillover effects, is not sufficient, intra- and inter-sectoral linkages remain narrow, external shocks hit the economy severely (see electricity crisis), government revenues remain limited and graduates of advanced courses (e.g. ICT) cannot apply their knowledge productively or/and try to leave the country (brain drain). Anecdotal evidence suggests that brain drain has been a significant trend in Uganda.[183]

183 Further, many of the well-trained and experienced professionals work for the international organisations, NGOs and international companies in the country.

Moreover, some businesses, both established and new ones, will not grow but will collapse against the background of more competitive businesses from neighbouring countries such as Kenya, and South Africa, or import competition from Europe and East Asia. In sum, without enhanced support for non-farming activities we might have to deal with a scenario that Lall calls 'destruction of capacity and the dispersal of existing capabilities' (2005, 36).

Further, certain forms of FDI - for instance, participation in Global Value Chains (GVCs) in modern manufacturing or agro-processing - might not be attracted to Uganda without a better set of support measures. Such a setback would impact on those poor people who are in agriculture or/and have lately diversified into non-farm activities. Another point related to urban development is that theories of local innovation and accumulation dynamics make a case for supporting the economic evolution in the urban and semi-urban centres. It is there where a critical mass of firms, SIs, and people with skills and capabilities can exploit (i) economies of scale, (ii) lower transaction costs and (iii) the advantage of location and proximity in terms of spillover effects, including exchange of ideas and knowledge (firms cooperating and innovating together).

In this context, HRD-related measures could help to avoid Lall's destruction scenario and speed up the development and expansion of non-primary sectors (e.g. agro- and non-agro industrial sectors), which might then improve capacities to absorb and integrate the labour released or escaping from agriculture further. Such non-agriculture growth is vital to enable a move into expanding sectors, to participate in higher-value activities and pursue the HRD agenda that - as this book argues - is vital for Uganda's economic development.

Moreover, implications of the described poverty dynamics for the realm of industrial development are likely to be follows: There is an imperative: (1) to strengthen the agriculture-industry link (agro-industry) so that a more dynamic, sustainable and valuable agricultural development can take place (in the rural areas, where most of the poor live at present)[184], (2) develop the agro supply side to achieve volumes, quality and consistency (commercial farming), (3) speed up the growth of agro- and non-agro industrial sectors so that more labour can be integrated into expanding industries and participate in productive and higher-value activities, (4) support the MSME sector and (5) focus on related capability formation. As far as a more widespread agro-industrial development and thus a linking between urban and rural areas are concerned, the pattern of industrial development policies and measures will have to change considerably. This includes paying more attention to the following: informal sector issues, productivity and innovation, spillover effects, technology transfer, skills and capability formation, value chain formation and strengthening, inter-firm linkages, clusters, SIs, supplier industry, and business practices and norms (business culture).[185]

The evidence which will be reviewed in the next chapter gives additional empirical information on the recent evolution of small business operations in Uganda.

---

184 See in this regard Wiegratz et al. (2007b), on buyer-farmers relations in agricultural value chains in Uganda.

185 See also Fukunishi et al. (2006) on pro-poor industrialisation strategies.

5

Skills Requirements in the MSME Sector

Survey on MSE skills needs

Most firms have never received training

A relevant EU/GOU survey on training needs among 913 micro and small entrepreneurs and enterprises in the districts Kampala, Mpigi and Wakiso revealed that only 43% of the surveyed firms had participated in any formal training related to their businesses; and a quarter of this group had received the training more than five years prior to the survey.[186] Table 40 shows that formal training was mainly related to book-keeping, financial management, customer care and marketing. Fewer enterprises received training in business planning (10%), entrepreneurship (9%) and taxation (7%). The report notes: "It appears that training programmes having been provided did not target new or potential MSEs, nor emphasized strategic aspects of business management" (EU and GOU 2003, 17).

Table 40: Trained MSEs' attendance of specific formal training courses

Topic of formal trainings ever attended	Exposure by sub-sample MSEs to training topics*	% of exposed sub-sample MSEs having attended topic (n=849)	% of exposed sub-sample having attended training in topic (n=390)
Book Keeping	229	27	59
How To Save from an Enterprise	190	22	49
Customer Care	151	18	39
Marketing of Products	119	14	30
Starting a Business	58	7	15
Business Planning	41	5	10
Entrepreneurship	35	4	9
Taxation	26	3	7
Total responses	**849**	**100**	

**A total of 390 respondents had received formal training, and most had received training in more than one topic, giving a total of 849 positive responses by the 390 MSEs to topics in which training had been attended.*

Source: *EU and GOU (2003, 18).*

186 56% of those interviewed had businesses that had existed for 1-6 years while another 28% for less than a year.

Tables 41 and 42 give an indication of the variety of training that the surveyed MSEs have 'heard about'. Notably, (a) firms with formal training show considerably higher awareness of training topics, (b) only about one out of ten firms had heard about 'starting a business' training, (c) technical skills awareness was highest with respect to agricultural skills, (d) about half of the firms had heard about food and beverage processing, one out of 14 firms had heard about computer training, and (e) peri-urban and urban respondents had more training awareness than those in the rural areas. The poor awareness about certain training topics is significant in the 'no formal training' group where, for instance, only about 2% had heard about training in marketing or business planning or about formal training in general.

Table 41: Business management training topics heard about

Topics heard about	By groups of MSEs without formal training (n=506)	By groups of MSEs with formal training (n=383)	By MSEs interviewed individually (n = 24)	Total frequency (n = 913)
Informal training	357	342	24	723
Book-keeping	252	381	24	657
Profitability and costing	50	383	13	546
Business management	121	383	17	521
Customer care	94	383	20	497
Savings for an enterprise	160	308	22	490
Formal training	11	383	24	418
Marketing of products	10	383	24	417
Business planning	10	300	5	315
Starting a business	0	100	6	106
No response	11	0	0	11

Source: *Ibid (19).*

Table 42: Skills training topics heard about

Topics heard about	By groups of MSEs without formal training	By groups of MSEs with formal training	By MSEs interviewed individually	Total frequency
Poultry/cattle/ animal keeping	409	380	19	808
Intensive agric/crop farming	402	367	22	791
Tailoring and designing	384	250	2	636
Food/beverage processing	250	209	17	476
Metal-work	89	150	3	242
Entertainment	91	23	0	114
Leather work/shoe accessories	54	51	0	105
Computer packages	58	3	5	66

Source: *Ibid (19).*

In high demand: Production and business-enhancing skills

Asked about which kind of business management training firms would like to receive, 95% of all respondents highlighted skills related to internal business matters, e.g. book-keeping, sales and marketing, credit, savings and banking, how to start a business, improving a business, and marketing information. Respondents with no formal training further stressed a need for interactive business skills including: entrepreneurship development, how to make good business choices, and information on accessing markets. Regarding skills training, two-thirds of the respondents highlighted agro-based skills including: improved farming methods, knowledge about varieties of livestock and crops, and processing expertise. Location - rural vs. semi-urban - had a significant impact on the skills needs. Other skills required, mainly from the group who had not received any training , include more vocational trade skills: knitting, tailoring, and clothes designing, hairdressing, catering and confectionery, adult literacy, home management and childcare. Leadership training was mentioned by 1% of the sample as a training need (ibid, 20).

The survey gives other important insights for policy-makers and HRD practitioners: about 89% of respondents preferred training sessions of 1-2 hours at a time, once or twice a week, since they wish to continue their businesses. About 79% of the sample of formally-trained respondents accessed information about training opportunities from political, community and group mobilisers, including LC1s, secretaries for mobilization at the Sub-Counties, group chairpersons and members of parliament; 15% of the sample have been informed by graduates of training institutions (ibid, 24-5). Regarding the desired outcomes of training, 61% of the respondents indicated that training should result in *higher productivity* and *increased profits* as "a result of *employing improved production techniques* and *diversification* of *business products* and *services*. Another desired outcome was the *adoption* of *better management skills* or tools to help MSEs monitor their business progress" (ibid, 27, emphasis added). Note, training is expected to result in increased productivity and profits. Factors that hindered applying new knowledge and skills include: access to finance, poor attitudes, insufficient information on market conditions (e.g. on input sourcing and market players along the VC), insufficient learning capabilities as well as challenges in recognising and pursuing business opportunities, including related collective actions (ibid, 28).

Consider also the finding of a pre-assessment study on the need for a modern BTVET in Uganda: It was found that smaller firms and/or entrepreneurs value work-related, practical skills and experience more than mere paper qualifications: "Entrepreneurs and self-employers value practical hands-on training and all kinds of work experiences higher than formal education & training and certificates" (Nalumansi et al. 2003, 2). Regarding adequate training formats, the report states, "[m]odules (short training courses of one week or more duration, which can be combined flexibly to build required competence profiles) are perhaps the single most important advantages of BTVET" (ibid).

Processing SSEs' survey: Technology and capabilities needed

Let us also look at the findings of a study - commissioned by UNESCO - on 150 small-scale enterprises (SSEs) (from Kampala/Central, Mbale/East, Lira/North, Masindi/North West and Mbarara/South West) that use technology to process raw materials and add value to their business processes (Byaruhanga 2005b). One of the purposes of the study was to assess policies and programmes that are likely to promote the adoption of technology (skills, knowledge, hardware) and growth of SSEs, thus facilitating the transformation process. The findings indicate clearly that many key constraints for SSEs (adversely affecting growth, productivity, and product quality) are closely related to HRD issues, including severe inadequacies in (i) technological, innovative, managerial and entrepreneurial capabilities and (ii) related training efforts and structures. The study points to the poor record of GOU regarding support to the sector in terms of policies and programmes. Importantly, the related case studies demonstrate that with an *injection of production technology and related skills training*, subsistence operators can transform into small enterprises that can grow and create employment and incomes (ibid).

Box 11 reveals the many inadequacies regarding business and technical skills of the vast majority of SSEs. These deficits - coupled with the various gaps in GOU support to this sector and the import competition – add up to a pressing issue for SSEs. The critical assessment of government's track record in SSE support is significant. The *country lacks appropriate policies to facilitate the acquisition of technology and thus enhance technological capacities and capabilities.* Almost all firms indicated a need for technology and long-term investment, especially machinery and equipment and related skills to create increased production capacity, quality, and innovation (ibid). The problem of adequate finance with respect to the acquisition of technology is also highlighted: it limits firms' upgrading and productivity (ibid). Indeed, the insufficient inclusion (or, in fact exclusion) of SSEs/SMEs by the modern commercial credit system in the country "reduces the effectiveness of the financial system as a determinant of productivity by facilitating resource allocation across economic agents" (Ssemogerere 2005, xv). It thus limits respective HRD dynamics in the SSE/SME sector.

Box 11: Selected key findings - SSE survey on technology adoption, business growth, and microfinance

- Types of businesses: The majority of SSEs surveyed were sole proprietorships.
- Sources of start-up capital: Majority started with own savings and accumulated family funds.
- Gender: On average 77% of the businesses were male owned, 23% female owned.
- Capitalisation: Mostly capitalisation levels of less than 50mUsh with the largest percentage in 1-5mUsh.
- Machinery: Most SSEs had machinery valued below 20mUsh. The tools, equipment and machinery in use were outdated, inefficient, of low capacity and in some cases inappropriate.
- Employees: Most SSEs employed 3-10 employees who were mostly unskilled.
- ICT use: Although 94% had mobile phones they lacked access to and use of computer, email, fax and Internet for business.
- Sources of Credit: The largest percentage (64%) borrowed from microfinance institutions (MFIs). Some SSEs (16.6%) were able to get loans from banks like DFCU, Stanbic and Centenary, all for working capital. There was a complaint that MFI loans were unsustainable because the interest rates were high (28%-48%), there was no grace period, but a short payback periods usually not more than six months.
- Perception of government service delivery
  - o 84% of respondents felt that GOU was not creating an enabling environment for their growth.
  - o Connections to the electricity grid were expensive and the tariffs charged very high.
  - o Government technocrats did not provide advice to SSEs and service delivery was generally poor.
  - o There was little access to information to facilitate the growth of SSEs.
  - o The policy of liberalization posed a serious risk of big companies swallowing up small SSEs.
  - o Although SSEs had access to tenders, the system was susceptible to corruption.
- Market penetration: 93% were producing for a local market.
- Management and organisation: Only 20% of SSEs had good management and organisational set ups. These contracted professionals to plan their business, audit accounts and give taxation advice. The majority operated without clear plans, had poor records and generally poor management (e.g. management of multiple micro enterprises).
- Expansion and technology needs: 94% needed technology and long-term investment. They had visions and ideas for new products, or improvement of existing products. They needed skills, bigger working space, machinery and equipment for increasing production capacity quality, and innovation. MFIs cannot really go into long-term-oriented technology funding since the Micro Deposit Taking Act 2003 restricts loans beyond 24 months and defines a MFI as an institution giving loans that are of not more than 24 months duration.

SMEs reported the following as their key constraints:

- Lack of access to long-term finance for asset acquisition, thereby obsolete equipment and machinery affects quality and production.
- Lack of design and innovation capability - leading in most cases to 'copycat business', lack of R&D/innovation in 90% of surveyed firms - because of low skills and lack of specialisation, low entrepreneurial capacity, poor managerial skills and unskilled employees - while having no/little training in place in many enterprises, also due to fear that trained employees will leave for better jobs or start up competing businesses.
- Hardly any use of ICT except mobile phones.

- Competition from cheap imported products (coupled with significant levels of tax evasion).

The study found that GOU was not deliberately promoting the growth of the SSE sector on the ground (implementation level); accordingly, there was:

- No clear and deliberate policy on SSE development is in place, no skills development policy is being implemented (including lack of specific emphasis on formal education for specialisation and skills development in technical areas), no development finance agency/bank from which SSEs can access long-term finance for technology acquisition,
- Inadequate funding for science and technology institutions such as the National Council of Science and Technology and iniversities,
- Further, the MTTI, the UIRI and the UNBS, all of which are important for SSE development, have been under-funded and have not contributed as much as they could,
- Policies/programmes with positive impacts on sections of SSEs included: Liberalisation of the economy especially the financial, telecommunication, and transport sectors, some poverty alleviation programmes, universal primary education, infrastructure Development, health infrastructure, support to private sector through the Private Sector Foundation Uganda (PSFU) (e.g. BUDS-EDS Scheme).

Some SSEs indicated the following as reasons for their stagnation:

- Insufficient capitalisation, diversion of funds from business, excessive withdrawals from the business because of high personal or family demands, and poor saving and loan repayment culture.
- Further, not following the business plan, lack of discipline, insufficient supervision of workers, low productivity, poor quality of products and services, and poor marketing.
- Excessive competition.

Source: Byaruhanga (2005b, 3-12, 2005a).

Byaruhanga concludes: "The case studies given in the study showed that if technology is injected into their operations, SSEs can be transformed from subsistence activities into small and medium scale enterprises which create wealth and employment. The SSEs can be facilitated to acquire technology if there are deliberate policies by Government and MFIs to promote development of the SSE sector" (2005b, 12).

Implications of findings on HR dynamics in MSME sector

Training needs to reach the ground and upgrade entrepreneurial activities

The survey findings presented in Chapters 4 and 5 highlight the need to conduct affordable and well-designed (regarding theoretical and practical parts, level, and length) skills training in a comprehensive and constant manner (follow-up, post-training support and mentoring, linkages to other business and technology SIs, training in day-to-day business context) for both start-ups *and* established enterprises. Besides business and management capabilities (with focus on time-management, multitasking, change management, incentive setting, worker motivation, market and customer development, marketing, and teamwork) as well as technical skills, there is need to build and deepen the following: social and life skills, productive, entrepreneurial, creative and learning as well as problem analysis skills, and networking, organisational and trust-building skills. The findings showed that firms expect training to help them improve their production and business operations and thus increase productivity and profits.

In particular, the observation that many entrepreneurs start a new business after a previous failure points to the importance for skills pooling, learning and reflection exercises, and learning networks in order to *link* systematic, work-oriented learning with the practical, daily (working and learning) experiences and knowledge accumulated by entrepreneurs and workers. Emphasis needs to be put on creating a 'learning culture'. Notably, training is placed within a structure where entrepreneurs (and workers engaged in the firms) have at times several jobs (income-generating activities) to perform; this may decrease their ability to specialise, train and increase productivity in each of the jobs. Also noticeable are gender dimensions and disparities - such as intra-household dynamics, economic dependence, traditional practices and attitudes and lower level of E&T - that affect levels of business activities and prospects of many female entrepreneurs.

Further, it can be expected that flexible, relevant and affordable skills provision (for production, quality management, market research, marketing, network building and so on) is appreciated by the inexperienced, struggling, motivated entrepreneurs and workers. In the context of change, there is also a case for making structures flexible enough to allow career shifts through modular BTVET system and adjusting the training provision to realities on the ground, especially for the MSMEs.[187]

HRD-oriented policies and programmes need to consider and tackle these complex issues in order to allow entrepreneurial dynamics to have a significantly positive impact on growth, development and poverty levels. Entrepreneurship training and related interventions that acknowledge and deal with the entrepreneurial realities in the informal sector - including the dynamics of household enterprises - are required. This often includes neglected dimensions such as improving soft market infrastructural issues, e.g. sanitary conditions at outdoor markets and related training.

It is not clear which agency could establish and facilitate such diverse and comprehensive training and learning structures at broader level. *Overall*, the public service seems to have a rather poor track record of interactions with the private sector in terms of training: a number of programmes have failed to link with the economic realities on the ground in an adequate manner. The same holds for some of the donor and NGO financed/organised training programmes. It is further uncertain to which extent the technocrats in the Ministries (say MOES) can, for the time being, keep track of the dynamics and HRD implications in the informal and formal private sector (literally - seen from 1986 - the 'new thing': this liberalising economy with investment and de-investment flows, new 'rules of the game', new export links and a huge informal sector), and develop appropriate, effective and timely responses of the E&T-systems that they are in charge of.

In this context, one of the relatively successful interventions has been the offering of entrepreneurship education (EE) in pilot schools (up to end of 2004) with GOU and donor money going into the programme for some time. Additional support to enable continuation

187 Regarding affordability: The FUE - in cooperation with the Management Training and Advisory Centre (MTAC) - offers three-days courses (at the level of management, professional, and support staff) that cost around 180,000Ush (according to e-mails the author receives from FUE from time to time). Is this a price many SMEs can afford to pay?

of this key intervention had not materialised by the time of research (2006); the roll-out phase is now driven by the limited capacities of schools to finance EE themselves. Feedback from pupils and teachers of the pilot schools (e.g. essay competition on EE) demonstrate the impact of the programme. In particular, it is reported to trigger a mindset change, even among parents who, at times, were against the 'teaching of money making'. The latter case signals a cultural and thus political conflict at work regarding the nature, realm and limits of teaching and practicing 'money making' in Uganda. See Box 12 for details on the pilot EE programme. Importantly, "Uganda's EE includes important topics on dignity of work, business ethics, environmental concerns in business and many others geared to addressing the moral aspects of doing business in Uganda". Research should follow-up on the effects of teaching moral aspects of doing business in the context of EE. Overall, EE seems a valid intervention; given that many pupils are confronted with the world-of-work in the informal sector at early age (they earn money for school fees, leave school early without degrees), and many school-leavers will have to earn their livings in informal economic activities throughout their lives.

Box 12: Entrepreneurship education in secondary schools in Uganda

"EE was introduced into secondary schools (on a pilot basis) in 2002. The piloting ended in 2004. UNIDO supported the National Curriculum Development Centre (NCDC) to develop and introduce EE into secondary schools. However, due to demand by schools, EE was rolled out before the piloting exercise could end and was by 2006 being taught in about 150 schools to students in S1-6. Further, S4 and 6 candidates are examined by Uganda National Examination Board (UNEB) (since 2003 for S6, and 2004 for S4). The piloting exercise resulted in proposals for revising the curriculum. The first draft of the revised syllabus was produced in January 2005. The process of revising and completing the curriculum and formally rolling it out however stalled, for financial reasons. Presently schools are being encouraged to privately sponsor their teachers for induction training after which they purchase the syllabus and the teaching materials and commence teaching the subject. The NCDC has completed integrating EE with Home Economics and Art and Crafts to produce the Integrated Productive Skills (IPS) syllabus for primary education (with UNDP and UNIDO support). It was recently revised and redesigned for roll out (AfDB support). EE was also introduced at Nakawa Vocational Training Institute (NVTI). The Institute sought to link vocational training with entrepreneurship training hoping that this would motivate and help some students to start their own businesses later in their careers, after some years of employment. The entrepreneurship training curriculum for NVTI was developed and instructors were trained (UNIDO support). The teaching of EE commenced in 2002 and it is doing well so far. NVTI has approved the curriculum and has established a specialised department for the entrepreneurship training programme.

Many developing countries learned from Uganda's experience regarding the teaching of EE. So far, Timor-Leste, Mozambique and Namibia have used Uganda's experience to develop their own EE curriculum. Rwanda, Tanzania and Cameroon are finalising their project documents on developing and introducing EE into their education systems. Uganda's EE includes topics on the dignity of work, business ethics, and environmental concerns in business geared to addressing the moral aspects of doing business."

Source: *Billy Butamanya, UNIDO Consultant for entrepreneurship education. Text produced for this research. See also: UNIDO (2003b).*

HRD response to the dynamics of a changing economy: Equip 'new entrants' for a transformational and catch-up economy

At a general level, the last 15 years have opened up economic opportunities in Uganda in a partly new, liberalised economic context. Many people tried to respond to this situation by opening up new businesses or diversifying their income sources; hence the entrepreneurship trend in the country. The latter is, to a significant extent, driven by poverty and un- and underemployment. Post liberalisation, a significant fraction of Ugandan entrepreneurs are 'newcomers' or 'new entrants' (often on a small scale) in the sector or position they work in now. They have not worked in this occupation for long. They are often in need of additional skills to help them to catch up and adjust in terms of performance and efficiency, including mastering and upgrading of their business operations.

Box 46 (Appendix 19) illustrates this argument for the tourism sector. Accordingly, a number of tour operators and other companies in the domestic tourism sector experience (or have experienced) severe deficits in the very basic skills they need to operate and perform adequately. After Uganda's re-entry into tourism in the mid-1990s, many players entered the industry in response to market opportunities, without necessarily having a tourism-related E&T. Ten years after the kick-off, overall (a) local entrepreneurship and managerial skills remain inadequate in many companies, and (b) the local skills pool in the sector is still weak in many aspects. Thus, skills in basic marketing and sales, customer relations, food preparation as well as health, hygiene and safety must be strengthened (WB 2006b, 115-22).

The experiences of an entrepreneur who runs a small business in the upmarket hospitality industry regarding skills development of staff illustrate various challenges (Box 47, Appendix 20), especially those in relation to skills shortages which make it difficult to carry out and implement advanced activities and business models. This entrepreneur identifies: (i) the weak output of the ETS regarding not only productive capabilities but also social and attitudinal[188] skills of graduates, (ii) the stigma of such service jobs caused by cultures (e.g. attitudes) in society, and (iii) deficiencies and gaps on the training supply side. There is also considerable competition for personnel from newly-constructed international hotels; the latter try to attract the trained staff of the entrepreneur's firm, which is one of the pioneers of staff training for this section of the industry. Generally, the status quo in local HR as well as training structures hampers the expansion and upgrading ambitions of promising sectors such as this one. [189] However, the industry itself also needs to engage in improving sector-wide training structures.[190]

Moreover, the mushrooming micro and small enterprises, which were started in a self-entrepreneurial fashion in the last few years by people keen to move out of agricultural activities, need an injection of relevant skills, which will enable those survival and subsistence-oriented economic actors to work themselves out of poverty, or successful entrepreneurs to grow more, link up with new buyers and markets, and create meaningful employment and spillover effects at local levels. Training can also help to counter the problem of the high level of business closure within a short period after business start-up: In Uganda, "for every 10

188 For instance, skills related to customer care and services.

189 For similar arguments see also the article by the president of the Uganda Tourism Association (Appendix 21).

190 This is a general point for the Ugandan private sector. This research did not look into the empirical situation for the tourism sector in this regard.

new businesses started every year, only three survive up to the second anniversary and only one may see the light of day in a decade" (Masiga 2008).[191]

From a HRD perspective, the problem of rapid business closure is related to the interruption of the capability accumulation process of the company and its managers and staff. It is therefore important that 'learning businesses' that supply domestic and foreign markets stay in business over a longer period (rather than collapse) because of the considerable time dimension of the underlying processes of: (i) building up the HR (experience, learning on the job, formal training) and (ii) setting up and improving relationships between the actors in the value chain and 'getting it right' in terms of business operations and relationships (Wiegratz 2008, 8). Publically (co-)funded training support can help rin this respect. Another example of skills requirements in present day Uganda is cooperative members, who are trying to expand (scope and/or scale of their) operations, with their own members in positions where they have to undertake new activities. Skill and capability development will help in all these cases to improve business development and reduce the risk and rate of business failure. Many professionals in salary/wage jobs are 'newcomers' in their fields as well and sometimes lack experience and skills, e.g. in management, HRD, or marketing.

There are many new[192], pioneering forms of business, products, and organisations evolving in the Ugandan context. Certain sub-sectors are still in an emerging phase (e.g. agro-processing sub-sectors, tourism). Moving into new markets, products and organisational forms (e.g. inter-business relationships) will be required by most more advanced enterprises if they are to gain and sustain their growth dynamic. They have to be able to manoeuvre their way through and *utilise skills that allow them to respond to change. Structural transformation of a young (post-civil war) private sector means constant change at all levels - that is the situation the HRD (education, skills, capabilities development and learning) community faces.*

For these reasons, local skills and capability development at both enterprise (in the formal and informal sector) and institutional (the meso level support system, including the BTVET system) level are vital to allow the private sector to be able to respond to competitiveness challenges and business opportunities and accomplish survival and growth. Further, well-developed HR for improved enterprise-level competitiveness and practices is crucial for an economy that has disadvantages in terms of transaction costs (due to landlocked-country status, and a high level of opportunistic, short-term-oriented business behaviour and mostly on-off, low-trust business relationships),[193] infrastructure availability (power, roads, and railway) and related costs of production.

Skills development for local farmers, workers, managers, and entrepreneurs is essential: The Ugandan economy is dynamic (to a certain extent), offering, in one way or another, opportunities for income diversification to her people, including poor people. That means people will continue establishing or changing businesses as well as introducing new technologies and processes which would lead to a high level of *experimentation* among new market entrants.

This translates into a permanently high level of a range of HR needs, which can change regularly. For instance, the GEM report 2003 notes that, of the approximately 200 start-up

191 This figure was also circulated by the public SI Enterprise Uganda (see below for more information on Enterprise Uganda).

192 As said, typically new with respect to the local market.

193 See Chapters below on social capital and on value chains.

firms interviewed, 14% stated they had a new product ('new to all their customers'), and 19% that they utilised technologies or procedures for production or service delivery which were not available more than one year before (Walter et al. 2004, 24). HRD-oriented policies and programmes of GOU, donors, NGOs, and other development agencies and the private sector itself need to understand and respond to this situation and related dynamics. Structures for education and (further, non-formal, informal) training as well as knowledge transfer, inter-firm cooperation and learning need to be improved accordingly. This requires flexible responses from the formal ETS but also from other agencies providing additional training to complement and support firms' in-house, on-the-job training and practical learning. Yet, a significant share of staff in development agencies, respective government departments, NGOs or training institutions which are actually responsible for PSD, it seems, is also among the group of 'new entrants' with limited actual business or economic knowledge and experience. For instance, van Bussel observes that:

> "[m]ost staff at development agencies has no experience in running a business of any size and they operate as civil servants. They apparently have not realised the [relevant] constraints [in relation to, for instance, functioning local BDS markets] ... and seem unable to put themselves in the position of a businessperson who owns a micro or small business" (2005, 16).

Reaching the local, especially rural, level (firms, farms and SIs) with the appropriate training package (formal, non-formal and informal skills training) and having a broader, effective impact will thus be very difficult for training proponents, yet at the same time very necessary. Note in this context the lower literacy rate in the rural areas; around 67% vs. 86% in urban areas (UBOS 2003a, 10). However, consider Prahalad's argument that those at the bottom of the economic system, the poor and informal sector workers, are a source of considerable capabilities, innovation, and entrepreneurship (and buying power/commercial opportunities) which can be tapped for economic development, poverty reduction and social improvement (2004). Generally, the following forms of skills development can be differentiated:

> "*Formal skills development* which is the structured, qualification and certification-oriented education and training system and encompasses formal schooling, training colleges and universities ... *Non-formal* skills development which is a more flexible mode of skills training, focused on specific vocational skills, often taught in a modular fashion, with shorter, self-contained modules which together add up to some form of certification. While there is usually some flexibility on entry requirements, they can still be prohibitive to many people and curricula tend to be pre-determined rather than negotiated. This ...form of skills development ... can be used as a bridge between formal and informal skills development ... However, some of the current approaches [in this category] fall into the same trap as formal providers of vocational skills, offering two and three year courses that are not competency-based or market-driven, do not fit with the UVQF, and leave graduates unemployed and unqualified for self-employment ... *Informal* skills development is the way in which most people in developing countries get their skills. It includes practices such as traditional apprenticeship and family members teaching one another. It also includes informal learning of skills by motivated groups which recognise shared needs. It is cost-effective, accessible and workplace-based. This kind of learning takes place in any case. The impact of the learning can, it has been shown, be exponentially extended by linking it to [adequate] non-formal skills development" (PEVOT 2006, 2-3, emphasis added).

Box 13 summarises aspects of the above discussions: It argues for an informed policy approach towards the informal sector.

Box 13: A comprehensive policy perspective on the informal sector

According to Chen, an informed policy approach to the informal sector (IS) should be premised on the understanding that the IS:

- is diverse, including:
  - o survival activities and dynamic enterprises;
  - o unprotected workers as well as risk-taking entrepreneurs;
- contributes to both economic growth and poverty reduction;
- needs to be the target of both economic and social policies;
- is caused variously by jobless growth, economic crises, global competition, corporate business strategies, changes in investment patterns, lack of unemployment insurance and safety nets, cutbacks in social spending, increased costs of living, retrenchment of formal workers and privatisation of public enterprises - not only by decisions taken by informal workers;
- is affected by all policies, both general and targeted; and
- is affected in different ways by policies than formal enterprises and formal workers are.

A comprehensive policy approach needs to take into account the different dimensions of the IS:

- its component segments and their specific needs and constraints:
  - o the self-employed and their enterprises/economic activities;
  - o informal wage workers and their employers;
  - o disguised wage workers, such as home workers, and their employers;
  - o women and men within each of these categories;
- the informal workforce as a whole and its common needs and constraints; and
- organisations of informal workers and their lack of recognition/voice.

Source: *Chen (2004, 17).*

Deficits in the policy and support interventions in the areas of PSD and economic growth

Uganda, to a certain extent, captured the development and growth benefits of stabilisation, macro-economic focus, rehabilitation, privatisation, FDI, investment in infrastructure, education and financial market development, as well as donor support during the 1990s. While, in part, this package had been critical (in terms of laying a basic foundation for economic development), it will not be a sufficient policy mix for another era of growth, especially not for the dynamic growth that accompanies transformational changes (inter and intra-sectoral changes, in the urban and rural areas).

Importantly, there are some crucial policy areas that the neoliberal agenda of the 1990s has underplayed: technology transfer and use, productivity, innovation, R&D, MSMEs,

SIs (including university-private sector linkages, national LIS), clustering, networking and development of value chains, spillovers from advanced/foreign firms, and stronger specialisation and growth of the export sector. It has also underplayed those aspects of HRD that go beyond UPE and formal (academic) education and include BTVET, and the building and deepening of, for instance, industrial and technological capabilities as well as interactive skills and cooperative business norms in the private sector. In the past, there were too few programmes that worked along those dimensions.

Nevertheless, the BUDS-EDS scheme for instance, had some programme items for companies and entrepreneurs, including smaller firms that wished to improve their competitiveness through skills upgrading with the help of external expertise (market, technical or financial assistance, through 'hand-holding' services, and service providers) in areas such as business diagnostics and management, market promotion, or compliance with regulations.[194]

Also, the entrepreneurship training and business counselling provided by Enterprise Uganda (EUg) has helped to boost business operations of progressive SMEs in particular.[195] The impression is that a *larger, institutionalised* (and in part publically funded) EUg could function well as a core organisation that can deal with significant aspects of entrepreneurial training and advisory support; not only in Kampala but also upcountry.[196] Note however, EUg has no expertise in certain crucial areas such as technology (and related matters of productivity); these topic could be covered by other SIs.

However, of concern is the inadequate level of effectiveness and speed of response of sections of the public service system and public and private SIs regarding new requirements, challenges and opportunities for fostering economic transformation and growth. GOU faces challenges to design and, more importantly, implement support measures (e.g. for in-house and institutional training) at firm and sub-sectoral (e.g. cluster or value chain) level. Indicators for this situation are the inadequacies in the implementation of various strategies (for growth, export and competitiveness, see below), or insufficient support for the large informal but also formal sector in matters of productivity, technology acquisition and application, or skills development.

This status quo has probably contributed to: (1) limited advancement in structural transformation and thus growth prospects, (2) continued problems of entering and competing in higher-value-added sectors and activities, (3) a low level of (a) clustering of firms, (b) linkages between the industries and the university/research system, (c) systematically tapped spillovers from operations of advanced/foreign firms and (d) formation of a national LIS, and

194 The BUDS-EDS programme (matching grant scheme) has been managed by PSFU as part of the World Bank Private Sector Competitiveness Programme I: 1995-2000, and was also supported for some time by the EU.

195 EUg is a one-stop enterprise development centre providing support to SMEs to improve their business operations, competitiveness, productivity and growth. It was established under a framework of the UNDP Enterprise Africa regional initiative, and offers business and entrepreneurship training, linkage building, and mentoring, among others. A consortium of local and international donors including UNDP, Enterprise Africa, UNCTAD, NORAG, SIDA and the GOU is promoting it. Its concept is based on UNCTAD's Empretec Programme Model, which is a one-stop programme providing an integrated and comprehensive range of business support services for SMEs while using a hands-on approach. According to some entrepreneurs interviewed in Kampala, EUg has a good activity record and provides useful training and mentoring in business matters, *not in technical and technological aspects, however.*

196 The Uganda Women Entrepreneurs Association (UWEAL) also undertakes similar training.

(4) continued problems of the ETS to produce relevant capabilities and competencies.

Note that the GOU, like other governments in SSA, ascribed to the neoliberal policy prescription of the 1990s, in part, for political-economic reasons. It is argued in this book that it would (continue to) be costly for Uganda to maintain a mere neoliberal policy stand which 'plays down' vital aspects of PSD in a LDC context. GOU, public service and donors - for quite some time committed to a neoliberal policy mix including the 'enabling environment' view - struggle to provide the kind of support and public goods for productive sectors discussed in this book. This includes *continuous, institutionalised* (not just programme-based) support for HRD-for-PSD which would be vital to develop functioning and growing sectors in a liberalising economic environment that creates competitiveness pressures for domestic firms and farms. Certainly, as Lall notes, to promote competitiveness,

> "Africa will need investment - for additions to physical capacity in the form of factories, equipment and so on - but just building capacity is not the answer to African industrial problems. More important is to build capabilities [at least, at critical mass/minimum threshold level] to operate plants at competitive levels, raise quality, introduce new products [and efficiently apply new technology, realize collective efficiency and learning gains, develop clusters and networks, comply to various product and process standards, upgrade business processes, organization and practices] and diversify into higher value-added activities and to attract FDI into such activities. This needs a more precious resource than money - skills [, experience], organisation, knowledge, effort and institutions ... Throwing money at the problem will not resolve the fundamental issues of competitiveness - it may make it worse" (2005, 37).[197]

Against this background, *capabilities are needed to innovate (improve)* and *learn*, including dynamic capabilities to manage emerging needs. This can mean building and improving capabilities in and outside the production sphere, diversifying customers and markets, or developing the ability to introduce new products (UNIDO 2004a, 2004b, Lall 2005, 2001b). Box 14 reflects on the issue of *local technological efforts* at firm level; it calls for *constant* efforts and interactions.[198] Importantly, these improvement efforts are different from formalized 'pure' ('on the frontier') R&D and thus need a different support approach.

In sum, local technological learning - including capability building in related SIs (e.g. the training system) - presents one of Uganda's main challenges (or opportunities), to advance HRD and thus economic performance and the catch-up process. This argument points to the need for business incubation centres or a productivity centre, which can support firms' technological learning and upgrading efforts through localised technical assistance, e.g. mentoring. The level of (inter-personal and inter-institutional) interaction needed for this *cumulative* learning and upgrading process is considerable, making it ever more essential to address respective *interaction deficits* between the actors and institutions, in firms, SIs and the establishments of the ETS. In the context of a national Learning and Innovation System (LIS), for instance, "[s]trong user-producer interaction triggers learning-by-doing and thus reinforces technological capabilities" (Altenburg et al. 2006, 7). The next chapter reviews training interventions in the SME sector.

---

197 See Lall and Pietrobelli (2002) for an analysis of technology development and systems in African economies.

198 See also Box 48 (Appendix 22) for key features of technological learning in developing countries.

Box 14: Local technological effort and learning

Key for (industrial) competitiveness in a global economy driven by constant and rapid technological change is local technological effort and learning at firm level to access, use and keep up with new technologies efficiently and thus be able to respond technologically to new business challenges. Lall writes in this context: "Absorbing technologies is not a trivial or costless task, and industrial success depends on how well the process is managed. Since all countries have access to the same international technical knowledge, a critical determinant of industrial performance is technological 'learning' by different countries. ...While technological hardware (equipment, designs, patents and so on) is available to all countries, just importing the hardware does not ensure that it is used efficiently. This is because the disembodied elements of technology ('tacit' knowledge) cannot be transferred like physical products. ... Unlike the sale of a good, where the transaction is complete when physical delivery has taken place, the successful transfer of technology is a prolonged process, involving local learning to complete the transaction. ...

Learning calls for conscious, purposive efforts - to collect new information, 'try things out', create new skills and routines and strike new external relationships. This process is located in the production facility and embodied in the institutional setting of the enterprise. ...Enterprise technological learning does not take place in isolation: it is rife with externalities and inter-linkages. The most important interactions are those with suppliers of inputs or capital goods, competitors, customers, consultants and technology suppliers. Linkages also occur with firms in unrelated industries, technology institutes, extension services and universities, industry associations and training institutions. ...The ability of a country to undertake effective technological effort depends on a complex interaction between its incentive system, factor markets and institutions. The interaction ...reflects national policies, resources, support institutions, infrastructure, skills, business practices and history" (2005, 11, emphasis added).

Further, in the context of technology transfer and local technological learning, "all these processes (e.g. mastering, adapting, diffusing) to some extent vary according to firm, sectoral and technological idiosyncrasies. Thus, the properties of knowledge (e.g. complexity, cumulativeness, appropriability), the channels of technology transmission (e.g. technical assistance, labor mobility; licenses; turn-key plants) and the firms' differences in absorptive capacity influence the path, speed and direction of learning and innovation" (Morrison et al. 2006, 5).

Finally, note also the following relevant observations: According to a review by Ssemogerere, Biggs et al. (1995) argue "that R&D activities in LDCs such as those of SSA substantially differ from those in MDCs. They lack formalized procedures for innovation, specialized budgets and sophisticated laboratories. A practical approach to identify and foster R&D in these countries has to take into account and use concepts that cover a broad range of technological initiatives: modification of imported equipment and processes for practical application, differentiation or re-design of local products, copying, re-engineering or experimenting with foreign machinery in a 'learning' process and fabrication of spare parts" (Ssemogerere 2005, 63). These characteristics of many local innovative activities in firms in LDCs have been mentioned earlier in this book.

6
Training Interventions in the MSME Sector

The following sections examine a few training interventions in the MSME sector. The aim is to provide information and insights, illustrate some points made earlier and underline the usefulness of enhanced training efforts in the Ugandan context. Indeed, training can yield good results in some (not all) issue areas; the training process itself brings about improved understanding of vital aspects of PSD (actual status quo capacity of entrepreneurs and workers, HR and training needs) that might not be recognised as such in a 'no/low-training' context. Related to this, training can lead to other dynamics and synergies: enhanced entrepreneurship, teamwork, networks, trust and sector-specific collective action, for example. It is vital for PSD proponents to understand the difficulties, best practices and outcomes of vital training initiatives in Uganda.[199]

The Uganda Gatsby Trust model: Combine training with other services

The Uganda Gatsby Trust (UGT), a NGO located at Makerere University, Faculty of Technology, and affiliated to the Gatsby Foundation UK, sets an important example of firm-level support. UGT works with the more advanced sections of processing SMEs, helping them in terms of credit and technical assistance such as extension services (BDS).[200] Loans are used mainly for working capital and the purchase of machinery and vehicles. UGT operates through more than a dozen clubs (together more than 1,000 members) in various districts of the country, has invested in a few small industrial parks, and supported student training in firms. Its technical assistance includes business plan preparation, training courses, local showrooms, sponsorships to attend trade fairs, assistance with producer technology development and business management training.

The importance of UGT as an example for a SI that contributes to HRD and PSD is based on: (1) its focus on informal and formal sector firms, in particular SMEs that use technology in production to process and add value to inputs, with an emphasis on the upgrading and formalisation of businesses; (2) the package of combined finance and BDS services, including technological and business training for enterprise growth; and (3) its network or club approach

199 The following examples are by no means exhaustive; they are illustrative cases that the author is aware of and/or cases where information was provided, or could be obtained in the course of the research. In an attempt to provide relevant information on intervention models and lessons learnt regarding skills development, there will be again reference to some projects from the UNIDO Uganda Integrated Programme. Note that the author did not undertake field research to verify the information provided by training institutions and other contributors whose information appears in the various sections and text boxes throughout this book.

200 Joseph Byaruhanga is working at Makerere University, Faculty of Technology, and with the UGT. Part of the UGT section draws from the work of Victor Richardson.

which has brought some important results (e.g. improved trust among members). Similar to the example of UCPC, UGT helps firms to improve their production and business processes and deal better with technology, thus increasing their efficiency/productivity and product quality. The joint delivery financial resource provision and BDS/training (and here: a package of skills from technical to business and social skills) is a model which could be considered for replication by other agencies, including for training in HRD matters.

As mentioned earlier, UCPC embarked on combining technical, financial or health-related services in a package. UCPC has joined forces with a HIV/AIDS training agency to educate industrial workers on this topic ('life management') within the UCPC training framework; this makes the training more sustainable within a context in which trained workers have died of HIV/AIDS. EUg has apparently linked their training provision to the radar system and services of financial agents. Such an approach helps firms that have undergone training as well as assessment and advice to implement the resulting ideas sustainably. For instance, firms that have undergone UCPC training and assessment often need money to buy the required CP technology or change processes which, in the end, can make their businesses more productive and environmentally friendly. Securing finance for CP 'high-cost options' (e.g. to purchase technology and equipment to replace a whole outdated production line) is a hurdle, especially for SMEs. UCPC helping banks to assess firms' plans to invest in CP is one of the options which would lower risk for banks and firms and thus facilitate the transactions.

The Master Craftsman Programme

Box 15 provides an introduction to the Master Craftsman Programme (MCP, UNIDO support) that works on issue areas that are also related to those of the UGT. The Programme provides hands-on technical advisory and training services to SMEs in rural areas through experienced entrepreneurs who work as MCP advisors. Importantly, the training is embedded locally, practical in its focus, builds on existing experiences and skills sets as well as local institutional structures, and tries to enhance training and business network formation as well as exchange of information, know-how, ideas and expertise (role models) in an entrepreneurial and communal spirit.

Box 15: The Master Craftsman Programme

"Background: The MCP provides hands-on technical advisory and training services to SMEs in rural areas at affordable costs. Selected entrepreneurs, so-called MCP Advisors, from particular industry sectors (such as, metal work/fabrication, mechanical/electrical production, leather, garments, carpentry, electronics, and food processing) participate in an intensive six-month training programme to provide fee-based services to other micro- and small-scale entrepreneurs in their districts. During the first phase, the programme covered six districts throughout Uganda - Masaka, Mbarara, Kabarole, Mubende, Mbale and Lira. The MCP Advisors are themselves entrepreneurs. Hence, they often understand better the problems that SMEs encounter than someone from outside. In addition, entrepreneurs do not have to travel long distances for advice and training services. MCP Advisors are on the ground and can be approached within the districts where entrepreneurs are operating. The purpose of MCP is to improve the competitiveness, profitability and productivity of small-scale entrepreneurs. The MCP offers the following services to the small-scale industries: Industrial Extension/Advisory Services;

Facilitate self-help sub-sector groupings; Information and secretarial services; Business and Technical Skills Upgrading training

MCP Guiding P*rinciples: Cornerstones of the Programme*

*(1) Fee for serv*ices approach: The MCP is a demand-driven, private sector-led assistance programme, coordinated by local SME Associations. It is entirely self-sustainable by providing fee-based services to local entrepreneurs. UNIDO does not give the MCP any financial incentives or subsidies. UNIDO's role is to assist in the conceptual development and preparation of methodologies and manuals, and the training of MCP Advisors.

(2) Hands-on training: The MCP provides practical assistance to beneficiaries rather than general, theoretical methodologies. Rural entrepreneurs are not accustomed to classical classroom training and often do not have the time or capacity to refer to handwritten notes. MCP is based on a hands-on approach, through which entrepreneurs can apply the acquired know-how directly to a specific problem in their own company and witness the immediate impact of the change they introduced.

(3) Sector-specific approach: The MCP programme is based on modules that provide training in specific industry sectors, rather than general assistance. The programme consists of: 'training of trainers', technical skills training, industrial extension (tools to analyse the situation in an enterprise in order to deliver quality problem-solving solutions), or essentials in managing an association (EMA).

(4) Build upon existing know-how: MCP understands that entrepreneurs possess a wealth of know-how. Instead of imposing new methodologies, MCP builds on existing experiences, which gives beneficiaries the assurance of 'staying in control' of their own activities.

(5) Local capacity building: A key element of MCP is its grass-roots approach. Rather than parachuting external advisors into a rural setting for a limited period of time, the MCP Advisors are entrepreneurs who, upon completion of the training, return to their districts to provide advisory services to entrepreneurs within their own communities as well as clients in other districts.

(6) Role model - communal obligations: MCP Advisors often have substantial impacts on the communities. MCP Advisors often take up leadership positions in their local and serve as role models within their village. After graduation from MCP, many of them engage in training of the youth or support to orphans.

(7) Countrywide know-how exchange and networking: MCP actively supports the transfer of know-how and expertise on a countrywide basis by organising excursions of MCP Advisors to other districts. This exchange of ideas and expertise often proves to be beneficial to the participants, as entrepreneurs are able to learn from each other and realise that they encounter similar problems and challenges. In addition, these exchanges enable entrepreneurs to build up their own networks of business contacts throughout the country.

(8) Reliance on existing local support structure: The MCP takes advantage of district-level SME support institutions to raise awareness of the programme and disseminate information. Once the local SME associations buy into the programme, they advertise it among their members. This approach helps to save time in the implementation process and builds trust among beneficiaries. In addition, the MCP assists in strengthening SME associations at the local level, which often leads to an increase in membership.

(9) Self-help groups: Essential in the MCP strategy is the system of self-help groups. Business people in the same business community help and support each other, exchange know-how and co-finance material costs. Rather than working individually in an atmosphere of mistrust,

MCP introduces the concept of information sharing, which impacts peoples' way of working together and helps them to all benefit from increased sales and business opportunities.

(10) Low-key UNIDO image at the rural level-local rooting: MCP is a programme firmly rooted within the beneficiary communities, led and coordinated by local SME support associations. UNIDO intentionally plays a low-key role in the development of the programme at the local level to prevent the frequently encountered 'donor dependency syndrome' of beneficiaries.

(11) District administration support: Local government often used to outsource local tenders from larger enterprises in the capital since small-scale entrepreneurs were unable to cope with the required quantity or quality. By organising themselves into self-help groups and improving their quality, small-scale entrepreneurs in rural areas are now able to take up larger-scale orders and participate in local government tenders."

Source: *UNIDO.*

The work and experience of 'integrated experts' in local skills development

Butcher in the meat sector: Working towards quality products

The approach of supporting firms' competitiveness and IIRD efforts through the work of highly skilled integrated (foreign) experts is also promising for the Ugandan context. Box 16 reflects on the experience of a German butcher who is supported by CIM[201] - the HR placement organisation of the German Development Corporation - to build capacity in firms in the meat industry through transfer of related know-how and formation of capabilities over a period of several years (since 2001). Particularly, the expert works as a production manager for the local firm Top Cuts in Kampala. When he started, there were a handful of (both locally and foreign owned/run) butcheries in Uganda; most meat firms were slaughterhouses.[202] Top cuts - which used to be in state hands - was owned by Ugandan/Asian entrepreneurs and had started meat processing on a small scale. There was no in-house training; skills development and upgrading of staff were done at the Meat Technology Centre of the Uganda Industrial Research Institute (UIRI).[203]

To date, the integrated expert at Top Cuts has helped to strengthen and improve the firm's process and product standards, e.g. in terms of uniformity and quality of products or implementation of HACCP and ISO standards. Upgrading efforts also targeted product range or organisational aspects such as worker task profiles, performance management and teamwork (sense of responsibility, trust). Thus, the set of capabilities and skills improved and know-how transferred encompasses *not only technical but also vital managerial, organisational and social aspects*. This is done in day-to-day firm-level (on-the-job and hands-on) training,

201 CIM, the Centrum for International Migration and Development, arranges the recruitment and placement of technical and managerial experts in Asia, Africa, Latin America, and Eastern/South Eastern Europe and supports them with services and with subsidies to top up their local salaries. Partners are employers within the partner countries' civil service, private sector and civil society. CIM is a joint initiative of the GTZ and the Federal German Employment Agency, and is largely financed by the German Federal Ministry for Economic Cooperation and Development (BMZ); http://www.cimonline.de/en/.

202 The following paragraphs are based mainly on an interview by the author with Top Cuts management in May 2006. Information from GTZ (2005b, see Box 16) is also used.

203 With support of an international meat technologist who worked at UIRI for several years.

supervisory, interaction, and learning efforts. It requires commitment from the management level. Importantly, the firm now has a streamlined and comprehensive in-house training mechanism (cycle) in place that workers and trainees go through to acquire the required skills; the firm thus has a team of skilled workers.

Importantly, the expert not only trains the firm's workers, but - with agreement of the firm's management - also undertakes skills development for trainees from outside: vocational schools, interns (from hotels and restaurants), or university students. Further, he works as a trainer at UIRI's Meat Technology Centre. Other firms seek his advice over production and product matters as well. Together, this has very likely strengthened the overall meat industry and forms of cooperation in HRD. There seem to be some prospects for related collective action or even emerging pillars of clustering (comprising different firms and SIs) in the sector.

Box 16: The work of an integrated expert I: Local skill/capability formation in the meat industry

"**Trying** to be useless! The German butcher, Karl Reindl, was placed by CIM to train his own successor

One of the best places to get meat in Kampala is the Top Cuts butchery. This has a lot to do with the production manager, Karl Reindl from Munich. Sitting in a large and simple office - one door leads directly to the production floor, another straight into the front shop - Karl reveals both a passion for his trade and dedication to the training of the Top Cuts staff. He is [at the time of the interview in 2005] the only butcher in Uganda contractually bound to train his employees, and he should spend 40% of his time doing so. He is happy with that; as he says himself: training is inseparable from production. Since he arrived, three years ago, it has always been the key to improving quality. One of Karl's main targets is to train a fully qualified production manager to replace himself. 'The target is to make myself useless!' he laughs. Is he succeeding in this? 'Slowly,' he says. To give someone the same level of experience as himself is simply not possible in Uganda. 'The variety of firms and industrial experience is lacking.' There are other hurdles too. On the bright side, good trainees often leave to join other firms, or to start their own businesses. This is a sign of success for the Bavarian. More disturbing have been the effects of HIV/AIDS. 'We've already lost two very good men to the disease,' Karl explains. This has so far been the main obstacle to reaching the target of a qualified successor. Currently the best candidate for Karl to 'make himself useless' is a woman. In another two or three years, he says, she could perhaps take over the production. For now, Karl himself is still involved with hands-on butchery for up to five hours a day.

It is not only Top Cuts' own staff who benefit from the training. The factory has become a kind of vocational institute. Karl's first six months were spent building up the competence of his own team. Now, however, he is often busy training outsiders. About 15 trainees a year, mostly from hotels and restaurants, spend time at Top Cuts. This number is set to double soon, with the opening of a new training room funded by KfW[204]. Karl also has university students in his care. Makerere undergraduates studying food technology, and others from the Department of Wildlife and Animal Resource Management, visit Top Cuts for industrial training. The latter do a week's training with Karl, to learn how to butcher and process the meat from culled warthogs, waterbuck and impala. Karl recalls training these students in the field: 'A great party, and some good sausages at Lake Mburu!' As a trainer, Karl also works at the Meat Technology Centre of the Uganda Industrial Research Institute (UIRI).

When he began working, there were some differences of opinion between Karl and the Top Cuts management. 'There was too much secrecy,' he says, 'they were always thinking in terms of the competition.' Karl's idea of his mission was more inclusive. He shared recipes with employees and trainees, though he knew this caused some mistrust. 'It took about a year for this attitude to

204 This was supported by the project 'promotion of private training providers' of the KfW, the German Bank for Reconstruction.

change, but now they understand why I am open.' He is determined to spread his knowledge and do all he can for Ugandan butchery. To develop the meat industry in the whole country would benefit everyone. Supporting the trade nationwide is certainly on Karl's mind. He is particularly happy to meet ex-trainees who come to him for advice in starting their own businesses. In Mbarara, Mukono and Hoima, ex-students are putting their skills into practice. The German is proud of this. They are real butchers, the proof of his own success."

Source: *GTZ (2005b).*

The above reported mix of formal and informal training, different levels of actors (firms, training and other SIs) and collective action to expand and improve the pool of skilled labour is notable. Also significant is the effect of HIV/AIDS on the local skills development process in this example. Top Cut has now expanded: It is a larger and more competitive butchery, it offers different and better products, sales have tripled, and the firm is known for its quality products and for being among the best butcheries in the capital and country at large. Higher overall sales also boost meat production. For instance, the firm now sources animals from five farmers instead of one. Longer-term-oriented business relationships with these farmers have been developed and subsequently strengthened to ensure reliable and quality supply of animals, especially against the background of increased quality awareness among consumers, first, and animal diseases that are of public health concern, second.[205] About 20 jobs have been created at Top Cuts; workers who have gone though the training support both the firm and the meat and food sector. Ex-trainees work for other butcheries or hotels and restaurants and catering firms, or have opened their own businesses in other towns (three cases); there are continuous training and business relationships between some players.[206]

The firm level know-how transfer and formation of capabilities and skills of the integrated expert has helped boost sections of the local meat industry - but also related sections in the services industry - and thus the diversification of the country. The successful experience points to the value of the placement of experts in other industries to strengthen the local HR pool, especially in the food industry.[207] This type of intervention is crucial for Uganda's economic development aspirations; it is difficult to think of reasons why the integrated expert model is relatively little used by donors to accelerate practical HRD for the economic development of industries.[208]

Technical advisor in an institution of the learning and innovation system (LIS)

Another example of the work of an 'integrated expert' is related to an institution of the LIS (Box 17). From 2001-2005, a German expert worked as a technical advisor for UIRI.[209] A major

205 The upgrading of this part of the value chain (farm level) will be vital to enable further expansion of qualitative processing industry. MAAIF and other stakeholders have a strong role to play regarding training of farmers.

206 This write-up covers the firm's development until mid 2006 only.

207 A textile consultant interviewed recommended such integrated technical expert placements for the textile industry, for instance.

208 Of course, there are always political-economic reasons for development aid objectives and spending patterns. One interviewee was of the view that this could be related to donors' spending preferences. Topping up the local salary of the integrated international expert does not add up to the large sums that are spent in education, health or infrastructure programmes.

209 The UIRI is a statutory institution under the MTTI. Its main functions are (1) to conduct HRD programs, (2) to undertake applied research, and (3) to develop appropriate technology for the

focus of his work was to develop and strengthen 'e-learning' methods and related ICT-tools that support the formation of technical and business skills in several partner centres. UIRI works mostly with SMEs.

Box 17: Integrated expert II: Strengthening use of appropriate ICT tools for e-learning

"Sparking Innovation: Since 2001, Olaf Erz has been an integrated expert with the Uganda Industrial Research Institute (UIRI), placed as technical advisor through ... [CIM]. The remit of UIRI is to lead Uganda's industrialisation by identifying affordable technologies to enhance the value of local products. For this, the Institute adapts and adopts existing technologies and trains entrepreneurs in its pilot plants and through other initiatives. Much of the technology concentrates on food processing, to fit Uganda's largely agricultural economy. Olaf Erz' role is to help in the development of new pilot plants and business incubators, and to study the feasibility of deploying technologies in Uganda ... Particularly important for the Institute is now 'e-learning', used for the wider dissemination, through partner centres around the country, of the UIRI skills and business training, Such centres are currently operating in Mubende, Kabale and Mbale; and a fourth is being planned for northern Uganda. In Mbale, the partner is the community polytechnic where, next to the numerous artisans' workshops, a computer lab is now open. Over the last two years Olaf Erz has spent much of his time developing the ICT tools for use in these centres. These include educational films providing the Institute's courses in food processing techniques, with technologies for bakeries, dairies, fruit and vegetable processing and the meat industry. Next to the technical skills, business skills training is available in the same format. These e-learning products have already won the distinction of 'Best Ugandan E-Business Product', awarded by the World Summit Global Contest ... A further example is JoBoYo, the interactive careers guidance tool produced in collaboration between PCY, PEVOT and UIRI ...

A mechanical engineer and business manager by training, Erz has taken on an assignment through CIM before, in Ethiopia. His current post at UIRI was Erz' first experience of working in the public sector, and that itself presented challenges. 'For the development of Uganda, an institution such as UIRI which supports business incubation is vital for closing the entrepreneurial gap,' explains Erz. Related to this, it would be important to set up youth enterprise agencies, or employment agencies, giving information on where to gain skills, or where to find work. Currently, [apparently] young people mostly find work through their parents' connections. This is not good for their self-motivation. 'Entrepreneurship means innovation,' says Erz, 'but where do you get the innovation? School textbooks do not have the answers.' This, he says, explains the importance for him that UIRI is part of the new youth employment policy ... [being developed in 2005/06 by the MGLSD among others]".

Source: *GTZ (2005c)*

Supporting training institutions - improving human resources

The Textile Development Agency

The Textile Development Agency (TEXDA), a training institution supported by UNIDO, has undertaken efforts to develop the textile and garment sector through demand-driven training, technology transfer and enterprise development. A recent tracer study (UNIDO 2005b, sample of 79 ex-trainees) revealed the impact of the technical and business skills as well

rapid industrialisation of Uganda. The mission statement refers to the following: (a) To improve capacity and competence of indigenous entrepreneurs in undertaking viable industrial production processes and their ability to produce high quality marketable products, (b) To provide demand-driven scientific and industrial R&D, and internationally competitive technical services that will lead to rapid industrialisation, and (c) To be a model institution and a centre of excellence for the incubation of industry, and a pioneer of self-financing R&D to elevate the level of technology in Uganda and the region; http://www.uiri.org.

as entrepreneurial knowledge acquired on the trainees' development, their entrepreneurial ability and their businesses.

> "The advancement of technical skills, selected by 82% of all trainees, was the most important they learnt ... Yet only 44% felt that the acquired business knowledge was important. Creative skills, such as product development and innovation, marketing or adding value to products and services, was rated ... [as important as general management skills by] nearly 25%. It is positive to note that trainees rated skills such as time-management, multi-tasking, team work, persistence and neatness as important, at 4% each ... [T]echnical skills rated at 68% ... [, which included] surface design, product development, garment construction and weaving, to name a few, have had the most impact on their business activity. While general business management skills and costing impacted ... [the business activities of 37% of the ex-trainees. Apparently,] TEXDA's training predominantly advanced trainees' technical skills and only introduces them to entrepreneurial skills. Yet predominantly these technical skills have impacted their ability to see business potentials [18%], improvement of quality [16%[and development of a more efficient business activity [14%]. Through the introduction of new techniques, stimulation of their creativity and exposure to product innovation and differentiation, all rated at 10%, trainees feel equipped to develop their businesses further ... [R]ecord keeping, assessment of competition and skills to satisfy the customer, have been rated ... only 4%. It is also important to note that 8% of ... [trainees] claimed that TEXDA courses have opened their minds to new opportunities ... [Furthermore:] Ex-trainees offer training to others more readily than employment. 68% have trained an average of 11 trainees ... [who] benefit through a trickle-down effect of knowledge. Prior to training nearly three quarters of all ex-trainees had not employed anyone to assist them with production, and ... [after training] only 53% work alone. Ex-trainees employ on average 7 people" (ibid, 12, 14).

In a survey conducted in 2007, 20% of ex-trainees responded with similar emphasis, stating that the course helped with their employability and in setting up their new business ventures, while 15% recorded higher sales and 14% improved on their techniques and management skills. This survey, however, also showed that average income rose by 4.5% for only 21% of respondents, and the majority experienced a slight decline (Nkata 2007).

The above findings indicate the prime importance of technical skills and give good indications of the range of positive training effects. However, the tracer study results in 2005 also pointed to limited entrepreneurial skills among respondents, e.g. (i) unclear understanding of many marketing concepts, (ii) rapid change of business focus, or (iii) little reliance of business model on a specific product group and little development of products over the years (UNIDO 2005b, 15-6). Therefore, provision of technical skills training needs to be accompanied by constant upgrading of business and other skills, otherwise small entrepreneurs stay more or less at survival and/or neighbourhood-oriented type of business (e.g. selling most products to immediate family and friends). Note that only 3% of ex-trainees in the sample share their sales-point/shop (ibid, 14), which could serve as an indication that the issue of cooperative/networking capabilities must be included in training.

Box 18 gives more insights on the TEXDA training experience. It reveals that however difficult the process, it is worth investing in building (where appropriate, sector-specific) training institutions. Institution building has certain advantages over unconnected, on-off skills development projects run by teams which disappear when the project ends and often leave little in terms of institutional memory, knowledge and experience, and focal point for industry players.[210] As the UNIDO TEXDA consultant put it,

210 Of course certain HRD 'projects' (even if they do not build institutional capacity) are helpful.

> "Most training institutions in the world are supported financially, either by a Government, through direct ownership or grants, and/or the private sector, via industrial association contributions or tax-exemptible donations. The alternative is that the services a training institution offers are highly fee-based and the centre is self-sustainable through other means ... Since the textile sector in Uganda is weak, the private sector cannot carry this at all. The Government has to step in, if it is interested in developing the sector. This is a vicious circle - which only GOV can resolve if it wants to" (Box 18).

Another important issue that is highlighted is the issue of market-pull dynamics for HRD; it is indicated that Uganda's liberal import policy regarding second-hand clothes has adversely impacted on (the incentive for) skills development in the indigenous textile sector. The general argument is - as mentioned elsewhere in this book - that outright market liberalisation makes it more difficult to develop a young industry (including related HR), especially if public support for the industry's development is inadequate. In this sense, there are certain tensions ('trade-offs') between HRD and other government priorities. See also Box 49 and 50 (Appendices 23a and 23b) for detailed information on the Training and Common Facility Centre (TCFC) for the leather manufacturers' sector: The TCFC supports mostly MSMEs with skills development and deepening, provision of material and equipment, product development and interaction in the sector.

Box 18: The TEXDA training experience

"Overview: Started in 1999, TEXDA aims to 'promote growth and development in the textile and garment sector through demand-driven training, technology transfer and enterprise development for competitiveness, creation of employment and poverty eradication' (mission statement). Up to mid 2008, the agency has trained over 1,050 people, 85% of them women. Men who are drawn to this programme tend to concentrate on weaving, the more labour-intensive of the fields. Other subjects are (a) garment construction and product development, (b) surface design, basic dyeing and printing, (c) handloom weaving, and (d) business management. The courses are offered at a moderate fee. TEXDA's educational model is founded on the vocational school principle. While it offers practical training in the field of textiles it also offers business course modules which ought to boost development of an entrepreneurial spirit. This model was strengthened through linkages to industry by offering internships and future employment possibilities. The industry can profit equally from cooperating with TEXDA in hiring trainees, through the injection of creative ideas (products and design) and gain a motivated workforce which is more knowledgeable in many aspects of textiles.

Currently, once trainees have concluded any technical training, they assume - having obtained the pinnacle of knowledge (without much practice or outside certification) - they are masters; however, in the real world they struggle to respond to market challenges. Therefore, 'industrial extension' programme offering practical experience in textiles to university students rounds off their education, brings add-on project experience and exposes students to practical tools. Since the TEXDA facility is equipped with a variety of up-to-date machinery, a design library and recent publications, it offers a wide range of resources. Access to raw materials at cost and equipment is offered to all members post training. The training portfolio TEXDA offers is modular, so trainees can focus on one textile-related area. This is supported by business training, for example record keeping, product costing and financial management. Initially, a programme of four months allowed trainees to acquire basic techniques.

Post training, 53% start an unofficial business activity in which they produce products out of their homes and sell mostly to immediate friends and family. While 25% formalise and register their businesses after TEXDA training, 20% have gained employment and are now able to earn an income. Those who have come to TEXDA to upgrade their existing skills and who were active in any form of textile activity, experience more than 50% sales increase in their existing business.

Geographical scope: At the beginning, TEXDA was exclusively focused in Kampala, but in 2006 it expanded its field operations via UNIDO's Master Crafts Programme (MCP) which trains entrepreneurs cum trainers from various districts. While institutional capacity building evolved in cooperation with local training centers such as Nile Vocational Institute, YMCA and St. Matiya Mulumba Vocational in Jinja, St. Martin Pakoto in Mityana and Kachumbala Rural Garment Construction estate in Kumi; and selective training was also provided to programmes in Pader and Kasese district. More potential in institutional upgrading exists as NGOs expand beyond their initial food and security objectives, and are currently expanding towards the development of economic activity in these regions. Working relationships with UWEAL (Uganda Women Entrepreneurs Association), USSIA (Uganda Small Scale Industry Association), and UGAPRIVI (Uganda Association of Private Vocational Institutions) are expected to strengthen the outreach and thus the transfer of skills and knowledge.

Institutional challenges and dynamics: In the past years, TEXDA was constantly fighting high dropout rates, often due to trainees' inability to pay fees. The dropout rate could be closely ascribed to the lack of personal objectives, lack of entrepreneurial mind-set (ambition, persistence, diligence) and lack of vision. One solution to this phenomenon was to develop a more structured programme and introduce a one-year certificate course, which is concluded by a formal examination. In partnership with Kyambogo University, an accredited certificate is being developed and will be offered jointly in August 2009. However, in future, TEXDA needs to improve on the trainee intake, and stick to a profile that can guarantee future activity in the field. This would mean that some applicants may have to be turned away and advised to visit other training instructions, which offer a basic introduction to textile training. TEXDA has to focus on upgrading skills rather than developing them from the ground up.

Currently many applicants do not possess a concept of their personal career development, and are unaware of the industry, and their potential as an employee in such an industry. Therefore they have to be exposed to local markets and the portfolio of retail points, local trends in products and pricing structures. That is why TEXDA, with more effort, should conduct study tours, and increase participation in local fashion shows, so that entrepreneurs can be exposed to the commercial world around them. Such a hand-holding approach is resource intensive, but the benefit of providing exposure and opening of these creative minds is worthwhile.

Continuous strengthening of TEXDA with technology has positioned it as a leader in the field. Yet entrepreneurs and ex-trainees still rarely use this facility to reap the full benefit, therefore in the near future more activities are planned to attract them back. By introducing short workshops that focus on the development of one technique or product TEXDA plans to draw a larger audience and create a target-oriented design culture. In the future the challenge will be to develop productive links with a variety of niche markets. TEXDA currently runs a sales point and participates in regional exhibitions and trade shows, where entrepreneurs can exhibit and sell their work.

Recently, TEXDA has re-evaluated its positioning on the Ugandan training market and understood that to remain relevant it has to formalise its course portfolio with institutional partners such as Kyambogo University, introduce practical short courses and workshops to draw the attention of entrepreneurs and make resources available to a larger audience. Determining whether the training it offers should be closely linked to a university or follow a vocational training formula is not yet concluded. In fact, the market demand will force its readjustment as it has done for TEXDA in the past. Without doubt, on its own and without the support and supervision of the GOU and the industry TEXDA may not be able to sustain its operations.

Most training institutions in the world are supported financially, either by a government, through direct ownership or grants, and/or the private sector, via industrial association contributions or tax-exemptible donations. The alternative is that the services a training institution offers are highly fee-based and the centre is self-sustainable through other means, such as consultancy services or production, as it is (should be) with TEXDA. Since the textile sector in Uganda is weak, the private sector cannot carry this at all. The Government has to step in, if it is interested in developing the sector. This is a vicious circle - which only GOV can resolve if it wants to.

In view of the development of sector policies the ministry responsible for the development of the industry (MTTI) has commenced to formalise the Textile Policy, according to which TEXDA remains within its focal point as a Centre of Excellence, providing services to entrepreneurs in textiles as well as the industry. The future Textile Development Institute, as it may be named, shall take over the services TEXDA developed, and expand them so that it can foster the development of the sector. The question, however, remains: how can such training alone help and improve product quality; against market conditions with low purchasing power, where strong competition from second-hand clothing exists, thus leaving no room for market-pull effects in skills development. Nevertheless it is obvious that any skill-focused training without entrepreneurial savvy remains just a training product-push principle."

Carpentry training: Skills for a successful response to new market trends

The example in Box 19 (related to an Austrian project) describes support measures for vocational training institutes with carpentry production units on the side: the training focus is on skills upgrading of woodworkers and the improvement of related production techniques. Related efforts include improvements in product quality and diversification, processes, productivity, innovation and market links. The crucial importance of adequate training is revealed. Comprehensive training which responds to the *educational level of workers* and *their specific motivations* as well as to *market trends and requirements* can lead to vital results: new products and production techniques, increased interaction between training institutions, including knowledge exchange through worker exchange, more efficient use of material and overall, increased ability to react competitively to market changes.

Box 19: Training for sustainable timber-based batch production in Uganda

"Background: The project focuses on value-adding methods, marketing and wood utilisation in the area of carpentry. It is funded by the Austrian government, through the Austrian Development Co-operation and Horizont3000. The project targets upgrading of technical skills of woodworkers and related production techniques in three carpentry workshops located in Soroti, Kamwenge and Fort Portal districts in Uganda. Further major activities include strengthening of market links and undertaking product diversification and process upgrading to penetrate and exploit new or larger markets, e.g. in small wooden products or semi-serial production techniques (batch production). Training activities (mainly on-the-job training) aim at increased innovation, product quality and productivity, thus making the workshops more productive and sustainable. The existing project partners are vocational training institutes, with production units on the side. The project is now extending its operation towards new project partners who are fully involved in the private sector.

A major difficulty for Ugandan industry is the low level of education in technical occupations, particularly in carpentry. Apparently, this is because academic education is still more popular than technical education. Many people only embark on carpentry as a career when they have failed to be admitted on an academic level to other tertiary institutions. Importantly, however, people who are not very strong in abstract theories or formal education are not automatically inferior in terms of practical/functional or common knowledge. In fact, many people in the former category have a great sense of common knowledge and prove to be very good in practice (manual work) when given suitable training. Some time ago, academic education was more popular than technical education, even in Europe. But nowadays, developed countries know that highly qualified technicians contribute significantly towards economic success; this is why academic and technical education goes hand in hand in many of these countries. Academics have resorted to acquiring additional training from successful industrial institutions. Entrepreneurs, who combine academic and vocational training, have good job and income prospects.

Training: The project develops modern training modules focusing on the needed production skills. The modules are designed in a simple manner, using simple textual and pictorial training approaches. This is envisaged to reach a wide range of people, especially in the main target group: workers with limited educational backgrounds. Little use of text combined with a lot of pictures work best to deliver the message to the trainees and interested reader; e.g. two cartoon characters are used to transfer information, approaches, ideas, or experience. The modules are self-explanatory and need very little facilitation, if any. They are in a range of small independent leaflets that can be combined to make a booklet of guidelines for better carpentry. Efforts are under way to expand the scope of training material to encompass other relevant carpentry skills. Another training approach is the use of small-scale models for various products e.g. office desks and wooden houses. This is because the target group is not trained to read technical drawings or sketches but is very successful at copying models. In this context, scale models help to visualise the expected end product. Such methods are also used in advanced economies, especially in serial production facilities where batch and flow line productions are applied.

Product development: The project also enhances product development, use of environmentally friendly timber species and maximum material utilisation (off-cuts). The availability of wood and wooden products in Uganda is quite predictable: Wooden products (furniture) are used in people's homes to meet basic needs. Most products on the local market are primarily a response to functional criteria only: tables are produced and purchased for dining, chairs for sitting, beds for sleeping, or cooking utensils for cooking. There is a trend, however, to increasingly purchase wooden products on the basis of fashion and design criteria. Furniture and particularly wooden products are increasingly used as beauty accessories in homes and other living spaces. Probably, this can be attributed to the increase in the general standard of living among sections of Ugandan consumers. In short, the purpose(s) of 'using' wooden products change constantly in the domestic market. As a result of this, Ugandan carpenters now face a new, significant challenge to rise to this level of expectations: Products need to be finished in a way that they are not only strong and practical but also fine-looking and well proportioned (aesthetic aspects). This requires developing the required technical and other skills. If the supply response can be managed successfully, these new trends in customer preferences offer significant opportunities for income and job expansion and related training and learning effects. In this context, by producing small wooden products, the project has not only opened a new product range that mainly consumes off cuts and is very marketable but also achieved a significant training effect: Small items usually need specific and accurate workmanship, which, in turn, contributes to the quality of the general production.

Key outcomes include: (1) There is exchange of workforce amongst project partners leading to knowledge exchange and thus upgrading of workshop facilities. (2) Materials are more efficiently used as a result of new products which utilise off cuts. (3) Finishing techniques have been upgraded through introducing natural finishing materials e.g. oils, polishes and wax. (4) The introduction of serial production techniques has enhanced the production flow in all the project partners' facilities. (5) New product designs for various market segments were developed and implemented; through this, the skills of the craftsmen were upgraded.

Further experience: The exchange of ideas and experience between tree growers, converters, timber dealers, forest authorities, producers, the media and consumers as well as other market players is a key to success. Also significant is a shared desire among concerned woodworkers to cope with challenges that arise from market changes: Indeed, to give their products a finishing that can compete with any given standard; e.g. long-lasting and strong surface sealants, straight and proportionate, uniform colours, smooth to the touch, environmentally-friendly varnishing precautions like minimal use of chemical wood preservatives or efficient use of input materials."

Source: *Austrian Development Co-operation and Horizont3000. Text produced for this research.*

7

Further Justification for a Stronger Focus on Local HRD

Globalisation, technical change and rising 'entry-requirements'

Globalisation increases the need for stronger local capabilities, a vibrant domestic sector (e.g. critical mass of suppliers, linkages, and SIs) and flexible policies. Activating mobile external factors for domestic transformation and growth increases the need for *matching local capabilities* that are *competitive* (Lall 2004a). "FDI is not ... a replacement for local enterprises or capabilities - after a certain level of development the two are complementary" (ibid, 26). Put differently, without strong local competencies, foreign firms can hardly run efficient operations: A country with a strong local capabilities base and a reasonable, dynamic domestic industrial sector is better able and more likely *to attract* (higher value) production and export-oriented FDI and *capture externalities/spillovers* such as skills, technology, organisational techniques, and best practices from them (ibid).

As Lall notes, "FDI provides additional resources and/or missing factors but cannot substitute for a weak and inefficient productive base.... It is difficult to see ...how FDI can drive industrial growth in many parts of the developing world without the development of local capabilities [and enhanced value adding activities of local enterprises, value chains and clusters]" (2004b, 81, 2004a, 25).

Note, generally the fragmentation of global production "allows countries to develop competitive activities in niches - one component or process - and reach huge markets in ways not possible some years ago. The capability needs are narrower and more specialized than those in traditional forms of industrial specialization. TNCs can transfer the 'missing elements' of technology, skills and capital needed to complement local capabilities[,] if they see a competitive product at the end of the investment. In the process, they develop new capabilities - mainly production skills - in the affiliates to the extent needed for efficient production" (2004a, 25). Overall, even entry-level activities in agro-industry require significant - though, in comparison to medium and high-technology sectors, lower (thus more attainable for new-entrants) - technological, operational, and organisational capabilities to allow competitive production and delivery, including competitive responses to competition dynamics and attraction of related FDI types (2005, 36). Africa's industrialisation vision therefore requires the *formation of competitive local capabilities*:

> "Globalization ...leads to greater transfer of productive factors across economies. However, though capital, technology, information and skills are more mobile they do not spread evenly over low wage locations. They go only to places where competitive production is possible, to locations that can supply the inputs and institutions needed to complement the mobile factors ... Cheap unskilled labour or raw natural resources are no longer sufficient to sustain industrial growth: ... Even 'simple' entry-level industrial activities like clothing, footwear or

food processing require sophisticated capabilities if they are to face global competition...Low wages matter, but over time they matter less in most activities, particularly for unskilled labour. Only the possession of natural resources gives an independent competitive advantage, but only for its extraction; subsequent processing also needs competitive capabilities" (2004a, 4, 24). In other words, "progress in resource-based manufacturing may be an industrialization option for countries that have resources, but having raw materials does not guarantee a competitive edge in processing it. The leading resource-based exporters in the developing world are countries like Singapore and the Republic of Korea that do not have their own resources but are able to efficiently process imported primary materials. In the industrial world, countries with large resource bases (Canada, Australia or Finland) do export processed resources, but their success rests on having strong technological capabilities in these activities. Many processing activities need advanced capital- and skill-intensive technologies to meet the rigorous standards of export markets; food products are particularly demanding because of sanitary requirements. Africa cannot industrialise using its ample resources unless it develops the capabilities to handle such complex technologies efficiently" (2005, 36).

Moreover, a strategy of tapping into the global pool of mobile resources, e.g. knowledge and technology - as required and partly practiced in the case of Uganda - goes hand in hand with building *systems for domestic capability building and learning*. One of Lall's core messages is: Liberalising the economy and opening up to the dynamics of international trade, capital and technology flows is insufficient in the absence of strong local capabilities and SIs. This is especially the case against the background of fast technical change and a (slowly but steadily) rising level of minimum threshold skills and capabilities (basic and specialised) required to take advantage of latecomer status. The minimum threshold is rising due to increasingly science-based technologies used by advanced countries, and more stringent technical standards. Government thus needs to support more strongly - with the right mix of incentives, factors and SIs - firms' efforts to learn and foster appropriate capabilities to allow a vital supply response (2004a, 23-5, 2005, 36, UNIDO 2005c, 3-4, 8).

Lall's view is informative in this regard: "[T]he basic problem of African industry [its weak performance, and marginalization from technological dynamics in the global economy] lies not in the investment climate (which can certainly be improved) or in gaining market access to rich countries (which is already very good for manufactures, and has improved with initiatives like AGOA) but in the *low level of its industrial capabilities*" (2005, 1, emphasis added).[211] A similar view is expressed by UNCTAD: "In order to realize the potential for increased FDI and to derive greater benefits from it, African countries generally need to develop stronger industrial and technological capabilities [and upgrade them over time]" (2005a, 14).[212] In this context - and against the background of the accelerating dynamics of the global economy such as China's growth - it is also plausible to consider the following capability set: "The key

211 It would be interesting to see how many PSD experts in Uganda, including those from donor agencies, would, first, agree to this statement but more importantly, second, would start spending time, effort and money on the implications of this agenda.

212 See for instance Biggs et al. (1995) for an analysis of technological capabilities and learning in African enterprises. See also discussions on technological capabilities and export success in economies in East Asia in Ernst et al. (1998) and Lall (2004a). Examples of international organisations that work in the area of PSD and analyse the capability building approach are, as presented, UNIDO and UNCTAD. The UNIDO Industrial Development Report 2005 - titled 'Capability building for catching-up: Historical, empirical and policy dimensions' is dedicated to issues around capability building (2005c). Lall's paper on 'Reinventing Industrial Strategy: The Role of Government Policy in Building Industrial Competitiveness' refers substantially to capability building (published as a UNCTAD Discussion Paper, see Lall 2004a). UNCTAD has recently published a new index - the UNCTAD Innovation Capability Index (2005b).

capability which SSA economies require is the development of dynamic capabilities to scan changing environments, to develop appropriate strategic responses and to implement these strategies effectively. Unless these capabilities are built - in government, in the corporate and farming sectors, and in civil society - the opportunities offered by Chinese growth [or other potentially beneficial dynamics/trends in the global economy] may be overwhelmed by the threats which are raised" (Kaplinsky et al. 2006, iii).[213]

It is interesting to note that the importance of support for the formation of technological capabilities was pointed out more than a decade ago in research done by the World Bank, Africa Department (see e.g. Biggs et al. 1995, WB 1996). "Technological capabilities are at the center of the new theories of economic growth which focus on technology and human capital as engines of growth. Recent developments in this literature suggest that long-run economic growth, as seen most recently in East Asia, reflects sustained increases in firm productivity stemming from the continuous accumulation of technological capabilities. In this view, therefore, a liberal economic setting and policies to increase technological capabilities are the two blades of the scissors necessary to achieve increases in productivity and economic growth. One without the other is likely to be considerably less effective" (WB 1996). During the liberalisation period in Uganda in the 1990s (and in fact until very recently), the aspect of technological capability formation, it seems, has been somewhat overlooked, or sidelined - also by the WB.

The need for an enhanced focus on local capabilities (HR), as expressed in the various statements above, also applies to the Ugandan economy; the latter often lacks the critical level of various capabilities, skills and relevant SIs (including administrative competencies) that would make her firms (more) competitive in domestic and foreign markets.[214] This affects firm and value chain efficiency, business practices, or levels of technology use and technological learning.

Note the *UNCTAD Innovation Capability Index* (ICI) ranks Uganda in the low capability group. Accordingly, the country is also in the low group for the related *Technological Activity Index* (TAI) and *Human Capital Index* (HCI) (2005b, 114, 290-1).[215] Significantly, in all three indices Uganda has *improved* scores and positions in the period 1995-2001.[216] In the ICI, Uganda scores 0.14 in 2001 (vs. 0.081 in 1995). Her ranking improved from 107 to 99 (out of 117 countries listed). In the TAI, Uganda improved from 0.079 to 0.185 (position 107 to 90). And, the country's HCI improved from 0.083 to 0.095 (position 111 to 108) (2005b, 290-91).

Further, a study that applied the technological capability framework to Ugandan industry pointed to significant capability advantages of foreign vis-à-vis local firms in the metal-

213 The implementation aspect seems crucial in Uganda's Government/public service context.

214 See also the discussion on skills deficiencies in other sections of this book, e.g. Chapter 2 (Ssemogerere 2005 and others), Chapter 3, or Chapter 10 (van Bussel 2005, and others).

215 The ICI is an unweighted average of the TAI and the HCI. Each component of the Index has equal weights. The TAI value is the simple average of the normalised value of the three variables: R&D manpower, patents in the USA and scientific journal articles. The HCI is calculated from the literacy rate (weight of 1), secondary enrolments (weight of 2) and tertiary enrolments in all subjects (weight of 3) (UNCTAD 2005b, 290-91).

216 In the ICI, the leading country, Sweden, scores 0.979, South Africa on position 48 scores 0.548 (2001, see UNCTAD 2005b, 114). See Table 57 for Uganda's listing of the Human Capital Index (Low Index group, Appendix 24).

engineering sector (higher overall and process technology, HR, R&D capabilities). For other sub-sectors results were mixed; local firms enjoyed higher skills-intensity and wages in textiles and garments, or higher export orientation in metal engineering (Rasiah and Tamale 2004).

With regard to Lall's view on Africa's 'investment climate' and its relatively lower relevance in explaining the continent's industrial performance and development deficiencies, it is interesting to note the following: Uganda already ranks relatively well in the World Bank's 'Ease of Doing Business Index'. She holds a commendable 72nd position (year 2006, 155 countries) with economies such as China, India, Vietnam, Brazil, Rwanda, or Egypt firmly *behind* her (WB 2006c, 92).[217] The same picture holds for the Economic Freedom Index (year 2006, 155 countries) where Uganda ranks 66th (category 'mostly free') with economies such as Malaysia, Thailand, China, or India all *behind* her.[218] Uganda's position can be considered a reflection of the country's efforts to improve her investment climate and business environment in the recent past. Considering such rankings, however, one also needs to take into account the following comment:

> "Neither China nor India offer what liberal economists consider to be a conducive investment climate. China only ranks 112th ...in the Economic Freedom Index, and India ranks even lower (118th). On the World Bank's 'Ease of Doing Business Index' ...China ranks 91st and India 116th. Both countries nevertheless attract considerable FDI (with China being by far the leading destination of global FDI) and successfully induce spillovers. Future research will need to shed light on the links between business climate and investment" (Altenburg et al. 2006, 31).

From the above, indeed, Uganda's PSD agenda can and should be broadened beyond the already relatively well-developed investment climate. The gaps seem to be larger or in some cases even widening in other important areas, for instance in terms of productivity or industrial and technological capabilities. Following others cited above, it is suggested throughout this book that a longer period of efforts focused on vigorous HRD (including a focus on formation of a range of capabilities and strengthening of respective SIs) for private sector activities is needed to enhance not only chances of increased investment but especially for improved performance by firms and farms.

Incentives, factors and SIs for local capability formation, learning and upgrading

Important in the context of capability formation is Lall's notion of a *'national industrial learning system'* which comprises the *incentive framework, factor markets* (e.g. education and skills) and *SIs,* as well as *firms* that interact with these variables (2001, 2002).[219] The reference to learning highlights that firms in DCs are concerned "with mastering and using existing technologies rather than with innovating on the frontier" (2002, 7). "A good learning system stimulates investments in competitive capabilities by firms, embedding them in a rich information environment and providing them with the factors and institutional support they need. A

217 See Box 51 (Appendix 25) for the country ranking. The index covers issues around starting a business, dealing with licenses, hiring and firing of workers, registering property, getting credit, protecting investors, paying taxes, trading across borders, enforcing contracts, or closing a business.

218 See http://www.heritage.org/research/features/index/countries.cfm. (accessed 24/05/2006).

219 The learning system concept is not limited to the industrial sector; it can also be used for the analysis of other sectors.

weak learning system leads, by contrast, to poor capabilities that do not equip firms to face the competitive challenges of a globalizing economy" (ibid). The relevance of a functioning learning system, including a relevant BTVET system for Uganda, is evident. The capability formation and learning agenda is ever more vital for supplying liberalising and thus increasingly competitive markets (including export-oriented value chains with their increasing demands for capabilities, suppliers, and business operations), while trying - in the case of most Ugandan firms - to overcome the competitors' first-mover advantage (see below).

Incentives, factor provision and **SIs** need to be in place to help the private sector to develop and deepen capabilities. Sustainable competitiveness might not arise from an agenda that merely stresses liberalisation and business environment policies (Lall 2004a). This view overlooks the technological basis of competitiveness and underplays the role of government in LDCs/DCs in the complex, cumulative and systemic learning and capability building process of firms which are facing a list of problematic issues, like risk, externalities and high learning costs, as well as deficiencies in related skills, finance, technical and market information, export marketing and infrastructure, or managerial practices (ibid). As the UNIDO Industrial Development Report 2004 puts it:

> "The incipient private sector of an LDC can hardly be expected to engage in productivity catching-up and international competition in a policy environment that does not go beyond good macro-economic management, improved governance and a healthy investment climate. Functional capability-building policies are also required; that is, those relating to the technological infrastructure; extension services for the SMEs; enabling mechanisms for firms to master tacit knowledge, skills and experience; and training and assistance to speed up managerial, organizational and technical learning and to build up the ability to conform to standards and technical regulations in foreign markets. The provision of this kind of public goods is taken for granted in advanced industrial countries, but it still needs to become part of PSD policies in the LDCs" (2004a, xvii).

In other words, there is a need for a *more comprehensive view* of the determinants of *competitiveness*, including a particular focus on functioning and interactive meso level SIs (UNCTAD 2005c, 4). This discussion can be linked to what is regarded as *systemic competitiveness*. One major insight from this view is that competitiveness efforts have to address determinants at various levels, and ensure sufficient *connectivity* between the respective actors. "The *importance of efficient and interactive meso level SIs* is highlighted. The concept of systemic competitiveness is characterised by two distinguishing features. First, it emphasizes the significance of the meso level in addition to the micro and macro levels. The meso level includes local systems, ... [including] supporting institutions. Second, the most important aspect of systemic competitiveness is the interaction or connectivity among the various actors at the various levels and their collaboration in the design and implementation of policies and support institutions and programmes" (ibid, 4, emphasis added). Accordingly, related initiatives should include a focus on "increasing efficiency and interaction of meso-level institutions" (ibid).[220]

220 See also Esser et al. (1996) on systemic competitiveness. Note as well M. Porter's view of enterprise level competitiveness which he links to a firm's productivity level and its respective determinants (1990, 2000). Accordingly, the competitiveness and productivity of firms depends on a range of determinants that are summed up in the notion of a competitive platform that enables firms and sectors to compete favourably. The four parts of the platform, or 'diamond', are: (i) factor conditions (including HR), (ii) demand conditions, (iii) related and supporting industries/ institutions, and (iv) firm strategy, structure and rivalry (e.g. inter-firm cooperation, clustering), with (v) government (policies, programmes, laws) as an extra variable. See also the perspectives

Indeed, Uganda needs to build and strengthen SIs that can foster the development of a competitive, advanced, formal private sector as well as the upgrading of the informal sector. Further, networks and interactions are important for pooling scarce resources and capabilities, or to share experiences in upgrading or interaction with foreign clients; they are supposed to encourage collective action and learning. Also relevant is improvement of value chain management, which includes supporting the identification of core competencies of local firms with a view to finding ways of increasing specialisation, upgrading, outsourcing, or linking. For most of this, effective industry-university linkages are essential (UNIDO 2001, Kaplinsky and Readman 2001).

In Uganda, related SIs are often either not in place, not effective, not sufficiently funded, or not well equipped with capacities and capabilities to support improvement of local firms, products and competencies, to the level required for substantial and sustainable participation in domestic and foreign markets that Uganda is, or wants to be part of. Yet, without proper factor inputs and related support (e.g. in HR areas), firms cannot reach and sustain competitive performance levels that would enable them to engage in high-value-added activities (Lall 2004a).[221] Can the public sector help in meeting respective factor requirements, e.g. capabilities needed by a firm to perform a new activity in a VC, or facilitate the provision of technical support? Firms need new inputs to learn and compete, including new skills. Different firms at different technological and/or organisational levels have diverse needs that are often not anticipated by factor markets. GOU has a role to play in coordinating the firms' needs with the outputs of the respective factor markets, such as the ETS (ibid).

There is also a list of relevant support services - preferably, bundled and localised in information/expert solution centres for productivity and technology matters, science and technology (S&T) or industrial parks - that are essential for capability building. Further, GOU needs to find ways to foster research awareness in industry (and mobilize industry sponsored research), and build a research culture in laboratories and research centres that is more open and capable of engaging with the private sector (ibid, Kaplinsky and Readman 2001).

> "A crucial determinant of an effective relationship between university and industry is the degree of responsiveness of educational curricula and activities to the emergence of new areas of industrial technology or specialized sectors. This often entails establishing effective networks between institutions of higher education, technical and vocational training, research units, technical associations and industry. ... The scope of the contributions of universities and public research institutes to capability building in a sector must evolve in tune with technological activities carried out by national firms, their access to other sources of technological knowledge, and the structural characteristics of the evolving industry" (UNIDO 2005c, 6).

All this is, as always, easier said than done, also in the Ugandan context. Yet, in an overall weak inter-linkage system, there are encouraging examples: UCPC, UFEA, EUg and the NGO UGT are reaching out to the education system. Overall, it is essential that interventions keep

---

on competitiveness in UNIDO (2000) and in the journal issue *Developing Alternatives* 9 (1). See Cammack (2006) for an important political-economic critique of the concept of competitiveness and its use by mainstream aid actors such as the WB and the UN. See further http://www.politicsofglobalcompetitiveness.net/.

221 See the discussion of the Ugandan case in 'Africa's technology gap' (UNCTAD 2003). See Biggs et al. (1995) for analysis of the cases Ghana, Kenya and Zimbabwe regarding support services structure for technical learning, pointing to poor external learning sources available to firms in these countries.

pace with each other and with related policies. Creating basic and specialised infrastructure for agro-processing is not sufficient for competitive production, unless, among others, efficient and effective support industries and institutions as well as related competitive skills, capabilities, and procedures (e.g. for trade and investment) are in place. Also problematic are mismatches (instead of a co-evolution) in the pace of advance of capability building in the different sections of the national LIS (UNIDO 2005c).

The views point to growing demands on Uganda's National Innovation System (NIS) (UNIDO 2005c). This holds especially for the knowledge subsystem and its effectiveness and interactions with - to refer to a UNIDO discussion of a NIS - the domestic business innovation and policy/governance subsystems[222] with a view to ensuring, among others, a simultaneous development in the domestic supply and demand of innovative resources. Accordingly, the first step of the NIS evolution would be (a) to create the *threshold conditions for its emergence.* However, later phases of the NIS would be to promote (b) innovation-based growth, and (c) growth of specialised functions to generate systemic innovative responses to emerging opportunities (ibid). Currently, Uganda's NIS is considered underdeveloped (Rasiah and Tamale 2004, 8), with the economy being "at the bottom of the technology ladder" (ibid). Importantly, an effective NIS can help to foster technical learning mechanisms through three important international transfer channels: technology transfer through *external trade,* technological learning through *FDI* and transfer of knowledge through *return migration* (Altenburg et al. 2006, 7-8).

Uganda's S&T system, a study for the WB notes, has in the past "relied on ad hoc measures made possible by sporadic donor largesse ... In this situation, science and technology have developed in an ad hoc way, without much public debate or guidance from the S&T community. Discussions of connections between science education at different levels, or connection between tertiary education training and labour market needs, have been scarce" (Muhumuza et al. 2005, iv, 47).[223]

Dealing with Uganda's latecomer and catch-up position requires a specific HRD response

Latecomer advantages and disadvantages

Uganda, which strives to industrialise, finds herself having to deal with the special conditions of a late or late-latecomer industrialisation and economic catch-up process in a liberalising, competitive global economy: Her firms have to catch up with the *established competitors* (first-movers) from elsewhere in the (developing and developed) world in terms of technology, productivity, know-how, capabilities, learning systems or business networks. These first-movers benefit from accumulated capabilities and learning effects due to their earlier entry into the global economy. Also, they often find an advanced level of education, capabilities and support institutions in their host economies. This allows them to improve their capabilities relatively fast. Uganda's latecomer firms then have to catch up against a *moving target* (Lall 2004, Lall et al. 2004a, 2004b). Besides, the catch-up process of the latecomer is characterised

222 The three sub-systems together form the NIS in the UNIDO model.

223 There are some efforts under way - by government and donors - to strengthen the S&T system. See below.

by market failures in the learning process and in technology markets. Thus, while latecomer firms from Uganda can benefit from her latecomer status (e.g. by importing existing technology from elsewhere), they also face severe challenges in catching up to advanced competitors and developing the requisite skills and capabilities (including 'tacit' knowledge) at the level of enterprises and SIs to identify, adapt, and use this technology in the local economic context at *competitive levels* (UNIDO 2005c, 2005d).

> "[T]he situation facing firms that arrive late on the industrial scene, is one which combines apparently hopeless drawbacks, difficulties and inadequacies, with advantages that flow precisely from being 'late'. The latecomer has a world of knowledge on which to draw and a 'roadmap' of the future in terms of products and technologies to be mastered. It is the distinctive strategies pursued by such latecomer firms that are of interest. From a strategic perspective, the task of the latecomer is to devise ways of catching up by securing access to the knowledge and technology controlled by advanced firms in advanced countries. This requires them [the latecomers] to understand the character and driving forces behind the industrial dynamics that govern the spread and diffusion of industrial processes and technologies around the world...Latecomer firms can be effective in overcoming their disadvantages and exploiting their potential advantages (for example, of technological leapfrogging) only if the country in which they are located builds a set of supporting institutions that guide, shape and channel the linkage and leverage processes. This is a system of industrial learning, and one which itself adapts and improves over time in a process of institutional learning" (Mathews 2006, 8).

> "Latecomer firms from developing countries can exploit the advantage of their late arrival to tap into new technologies, rather than having to reproduce the entire previous technological trajectory. They can accelerate their uptake and learning efforts, engaging in collective, purposive and directed efforts to use the relationships with foreign partners ... to get the right technology and knowledge, and to learn and create new capabilities, capturing the externalities of collective learning" (UNIDO 2004b, 1-2).

Deficits (incentives, SIs, etc.) in Uganda in the area of capability formation undermine the ability of firms to catch up and handle rising entry requirements (e.g. technical standards) and competitiveness dynamics in markets. Importantly, these deficits also lower firms' abilities to *take advantage* of the latecomer status and accelerate their upgrading and learning through tapping into the global pool of resources, knowledge, good practices and technology, for instance, via harnessing the *linkages* with foreign buyers from advanced economies and fully utilising the *leveraging* (resources and knowledge) and *learning* opportunities in these business arrangements. This has been summarised under the LLL-approach (UNIDO 2002). [224]

The LLL-strategy materializes in different linkages with foreign partners with different skills implications: However, local capability formation needs to be undertaken, in part autonomously, to the constantly increasing minimum entry level of competencies needed to participate in today's production systems. Again, functioning SIs that boost learning and upgrading, or that help firms have better access to buyers, information, skills, and know-how are essential; in short, the provision of the right kind of incentives and public goods for productive sectors (2004b, 15-18).

It is vital for Uganda's economic-catch up process to establish a minimum threshold level of domestic capabilities and related operational, absorptive, adaptive, social and innovative skills in local firms that can then engage in LLL-strategies and benefit more from external

224 The LLL-approach states that to enhance their catch-up processes, firms from latecomer countries should follow a strategy of linking with global partners (buyers etc.) and continuously undertaking leveraging (knowledge, technology) and learning efforts (UNIDO 2002).

competitiveness factors. Indeed, firms in non-traditional export sub-sectors such as flowers, fish, fruits/vegetables, and tourism had to face a latecomer situation at their time of entry into the global economy and catch up with competitors on all fronts, particularly in the HR dimension (Wiegratz et al. 2007b, Wiegratz 2008). By the time of writing, however, hardly any substantial export-related policy or programme exists that tries to enhance leveraging and learning strategies of local firms in business arrangements with their international buyers.

Notably, there is little research about how Ugandan firms explicitly engage in and benefit from business relationship with their foreign partners (in terms of knowledge, information, technology, technical assistance) (see however Wiegratz et al. 2007a). We also know little about incidences of local knowledge and technology diffusion (and other demonstration effects) as a result of the presence of foreign firms (FDI) in the Ugandan economy. Owing to characteristics of FDI the diffusion effects in the case of sophisticated technology seem to be low for industry (Rasia and Tamale 2004, 30). Accordingly, there is a "dominance of stand-alone owner managed firms among foreign firms" (ibid, 30). The firms are rarely subsidiaries of a parent plant ('home site') with superior operations in a developed economy. It is suggested that this characteristic allows more space for growth of local firms (ibid, 10, 30).

Overall, insufficient existing analysis lowers the actual exploitation of potential benefits of the Ugandan latecomer status. In particular, this is the case if SIs do not carry out their function adequately in this context. In order to *take better advantage of LLL-opportunities in the global economy*, advanced efforts, entrepreneurship, knowledge, capabilities, networks, interactivity and collaboration (and related business norms and practices) in the PSD system will be required; in particular, against the background that the Ugandan private sector faces (1) prospects for South-South Cooperation in PSD areas and (2) the rise of TNCs and/or FDI at the global stage from developing countries such as China and India. This creates opportunities for inclusion in evolving global production arrangements, for South-South trade as well as related technology and knowledge flows and skills formation.

With regard to South-South interactions, it should be noted that the technological level (intermediate technological level/capital intensity) and respective forms of technological innovations in such economies *can* be more appropriate and relevant (vis-à-vis highly capital intensive technology from developed countries) for the Ugandan context of economic, technological and HR development (Isaksson et al. 2005, 60). Overall, the need for increased local capabilities and efforts in the context of globalisation does not only hold for firms but also the relevant SI of the national LIS which need to carry out LLL-strategies to take better advantage of the global base of knowledge and technology.

Box 20 discusses the first-mover advantage of advanced and capable TNC' suppliers in a few successful DCs that entered the global production stage earlier and developed their capability base in a *path-dependent* and *cumulative process*. Other advantages early entrants enjoy include agglomeration and clustering effects or economies of scale that allow them to produce knowledge and technology-intensive products successfully. This consolidation process (or 'rooting') gives them a competitive lead over especially late-latecomer, low-capability countries (Lall et al. 2004a, 2004b). "The cumulative nature of capabilities means that once FDI takes root in particular locations and global sourcing systems become established, it becomes more difficult to newcomers to break in, particularly in the more complex activities and functions. First mover advantages, in other words, mean that late-latecomers face *increasing* entry costs - without strong local capabilities they will find it difficult to overcome these costs" (2004a, 25, emphasis added).[225]

Note in this context that a certain growth of innovative capabilities in developing countries - some of them latecomers themselves - is beginning to emerge (Schmitz 2004, 2005). Although overall, innovative activities and capabilities (and related value-addition/profits) continues to be concentrated in developed countries (EU, US, Japan); "[w]e observe the build of innovation capabilities in China, India and other Asian countries, particularly in rapidly growing sectors such as electronics and software. The extent of this build up ... is not yet clear" (2005, 4). Yet, it is evident that TNCs

> "increasingly relocate knowledge-intensive, and even R&D, functions to these countries. An UNCTAD survey of the largest R&D investors among TNCs shows the mounting role of developing countries as recipients of corporate R&D. According to the survey, China is now the 3rd global destination for investments in R&D and India the 6th. What is more, their importance will increase substantially in the near future. In the UNCTAD survey, TNCs mentioned China as the most attractive location for future R&D investment, far ahead of the United States, with India ranking 3rd. This increasing interest by TNCs is matched by rapidly growing national R&D expenditure. Having quintupled its budget since the mid 1990s (!), China now invests more in R&D than any European country (84.6 billion US$) while India's expenditure mounts up to 20.7 billion, exceeding the levels of Canada and Russia" (Altenburg et al. 2006, 4 based on data from UNCTAD 2005b and OECD 2005).

Finally, consider Uganda's position in the Global Competitiveness Index (GCI) country ranking of the Global Competitiveness Report (World Economic Forum): Uganda ranked 80th, 79th and 87th (out of more than 100 countries) in the years 2003-05; in the African ranking she took 14th position in the 2003/04 ranking (25 countries); accordingly, 'low-quality public institutions' and its characteristics of corruption and bureaucracy adversely impact on Uganda's ranking (MTCS Secretariat 2006). In the late 2000s, Uganda's GCI ranking slipped from 108th (2006-2007, out of 122 countries) to 120th (2007-2008, 131 countries) and 128th position (2008-2009, 134 countries). More specifically, in the GCI 2008/09, Uganda ranked 133rd in health and primary education, 120th in higher education and training, 121st in technological readiness, 97th in business sophistication, 72nd in innovation, 113th in institutions, 92nd in macroeconomic stability, and 115th in infrastructure (CICS Secretariat 2008).

Box 20: The (late-)latecomer position - or, the relevance of the first-mover advantage of others

In the 1990s, a number of developing countries and transition economies (mainly in East/South-East Asia and Eastern Europe) consolidated their position as capable, reliable and specialised global suppliers for TNCs which had earlier outsourced certain non-core functions (unrelated to core competencies, e.g. generic services, logistics, volume production) to offshore factories in the developing world. This was done by TNCs with a view to be able to focus more narrowly on their core functions (design, technology, branding, logistics, marketing, after-sales service). Over time these TNCs' strategies led to the consolidation of a competitive global supply base with strong technical competencies (which offer, in turn, improved local sourcing potentials for TNCs) in different industries in a number of developing countries, and significant domestic industrial capability formation in a few. Beneficiary countries which joined this integrated global production system, governed in many cases by TNCs in developed countries, in the 1990s now enjoy the path dependence and cumulative character of this process (fragmentation/outsourcing process, integrated production systems' growth): they increase their lead over others. In other words, the

225 See also Box 52 (Appendix 26) on tendencies of rising entry barriers for newcomers in global industry.

first-movers are reaping the rewards of their early entry in terms of capability building and learning (itself a path-dependent, cumulative process), agglomeration and clustering effects and economies of scale. To a certain degree, these dynamics could likely lead to a consolidation of production in only a few major production sites worldwide/in each region ('rooting') - placed in established locations with advanced capabilities (especially in the more complex activities/functions) and infrastructure - which would get onto a virtuous circle of growth and development (Lall et al. 2004a, 410). This would build into a 'path-dependent' competitiveness and export success scenario (Lall et al. 2004b, 16-8).

It is uncertain to what extent further fragmentation dynamics will allow new entrants (from lower-cost locations) to claim their stake. This applies especially to firms from low capability countries that might wish to enter global markets through the 'old model' of wholly foreign-owned subsidiaries. The trend of the development of independent and capable specialised local producers and intermediate agents with strong technical competencies in a few countries (outside SSA) poses questions for conventional investment promotion policies as well as latecomer firms from Uganda that wish to enter global markets through the 'old way' (following formerly successful development trajectories which might now be foreclosed). That aside, with a strong developing countries' supply base, even developed countries' SMEs with no offshore investment can start global outsourcing strategies, opening opportunities for capable firms in developing countries. This could bring about opportunities for Uganda, assuming investment promotion strategies can be carried in a more targeted, informed (according to investment decision criteria) manner. The imperative of having (cross-sector/sector-specific) policies that support local capability building/deepening, and attract external forces to mobilise the internal potential for competitiveness and economic development remain highly relevant for fostering growth and upgrading. This can result in an increased level of local innovation or lower dependence on foreign technology (Lall 2004a, Gereffi and Sturgeon 2004, Ferranti et al. 2002).

Market/institutional failures that hamper the accumulation of capabilities and technology

As said above, functioning systems of SIs that help firms overcome *pervasive market and institutional failures* in the context of the catch-up and learning process are vital. Firms are facing a range of such failures that are particularly severe in LDC and late-comer economic catch-up and industrialisation context. Domestic capability formation is not an automatic or risk-free process, but requires deliberate efforts by government, to intervene in this process to support firms' upgrading efforts by overcoming such failures (Lall et al. 2004b). *Key failures* in DC/LDC economies that hinder competitive development and the supply response in general, and technical learning and capability building and deepening in particular are: imperfect competition, market incompleteness, scale economies, path dependence, risk, uncertainty, (widespread technological, informational and coordination) externalities, (high, unpredictable) learning costs, as well as information failures, asymmetries and complementarities (ibid): "As long as ...[such failures] exist, resources might not flow to the most productive industries because firms are not big enough, cannot get enough financing, do not have enough information or do not invest enough in human capital and technology" (ibid, 52). Consequently, the substantial and rising dispersion in economic performances between developed and developing countries and within the developing world, continues (Lall 2002, 2-3, Stiglitz 1996, 1998).

For these reasons, there is a case for a policy response from GOU (and support from other HRD proponents) to help firms overcome market and institutional failures in capability formation. There are, for instance, market failures at three levels that policies and programmes could address - the HRD dimension is inherent in all three:

> "The essential policy needs of capability building ... are *direct* - the infant industry case to provide space for enterprises to master new technologies and skills without incurring enormous and unpredictable losses - and *indirect*, to ensure that skill, capital, technology and infrastructure markets meet their needs. There is also a need to *coordinate learning* across enterprises and activities, when these are linked in the production chain and imports cannot substitute effectively for local inputs .... [L]eaving capability development to free market forces is hardly more promising. It can result in slow and truncated technological development, with gaps between countries rising. Some upgrading does take place over time, but it is likely to be slower and more limited than without promotion. Given the speed at which technologies are changing and path-dependence and cumulativeness in capability building, it can lead to latecomers being mired in low growth traps from which market forces cannot extract them" (Lall 2004a, 24-5, emphasis in original).[226]

The process of accumulation of *technology* - especially, due to the knowledge aspect of it - faces externalities and imperfect competition as well. A *free-market scenario is likely to lead to undersupply of technology below the socially optimal level.* This argument gives a role to economic policy to foster technology accumulation in the economy (Isaksson et al. 2005, 45).[227]

> "Given the public good character ingrained in the knowledge dimension of technology, the topic of economic policy enters the scene to take charge of the externalities that are at work. Market forces ignore the growth-enhancing potential of externalities. ...Thus, the market-geared rate of capital accumulation is inferior to the socially optimal rate. In such a case it might be useful to have policies to stimulate accumulation to the point where it becomes optimally supplied" (ibid, 45).

The above views are strongly in support of a *more focused response to the problems of capability and technology accumulation in developing countries*: In the recent past, Uganda's economic policy mix has not really targeted these aspects - probably with adverse effects for HRD and competitiveness. The long-term effects of such an inadequate focus in particular, can be severe in a path-dependent and cumulative learning and capability building context:

> "[Technological] learning processes are highly context-specific and cumulative. Initial investment decisions thus determine the available options at later stages of development. In other words, knowledge creation is path dependent, and economic development follows certain trajectories" (Altenburg et al. 2006, 6).

In the next section, we shall reflect on important policy considerations for the Ugandan economy, which is characterised by economic transformation, restructuring and experimentation, and thus by a search for new, profitable diversification opportunities and activities in a liberalising domestic and global economy. The section rounds up the points made above on market failures: it explores conditions of HRD in the context of structural transformation.

---

226 The three policy needs for capability building, put in more technical wording, read as follows: "The first is within the firm, in terms of promoting investment in complex new technologies when faced with costly and risky learning costs (infant industry promotion). The second is between firms and industries (coordination of investments in activities linked by externalities, needing the promotion of value chains or geographical clusters). The third is between firms and factor markets and institutions (coordination at the higher level)" (UNIDO 2004a, 6, based on Lall 2001).

227 See also Chapter 2 in Altenburg et al. (2006) for an overview of the academic debate on technological latecomer development.

Support the 'new': Experimentation and diversification and HRD

Dani Rodrik, in his writing on an industrial policy, has put particular emphasis on preconditions for successful diversification and restructuring of an economy, in particular in developing countries (2004). He outlines a vital rationale for policies in support of a *discovery* and *coordination process* in which firms and governments: (1) learn about underlying costs and profit opportunities linked to new economic activities and technologies, (2) assess possible externalities related to investment projects, and (3) push towards a more diversified and higher-value-added economy. In his view - similar to Lall's argument of market failures in the catch-up process - related policies have to address relevant *information and coordination externalities* that hamper experimentation and innovation:

> "Will the type of entrepreneurship that is required to build up nontraditional activities be amply supplied? There are good reasons to believe that the answer is no. Most fundamentally, market prices cannot reveal the profitability of resource allocations that do not yet exist. ...The returns from investing in non-traditional activities are therefore hazy at best. ...[There are] two key 'externalities' that blunt incentives for productive diversification: information externalities [entailed in discovering the cost structure of an economy] and coordination externalities [in the presence of scale economies etc. linked to certain investments]. Both are reasons to believe that diversification is unlikely to take place without directed government action" (Rodrik 2004, 7-8).

Externalities that hamper diversification of the economy

In this context, *information externalities* are relevant in the diversification/discovery process:

> "Diversification of the productive structure requires 'discovery' of an economy's cost structure - i.e., discovery of which new activities can be produced at low enough cost to be profitable ... [discovery] that a certain good, already well established in world markets, can be produced at home at low cost. ... [However,] what constrains productive restructuring is a ... fundamental feature of low-income environments: entrepreneurship in new activities has high social returns but low private returns ... The entrepreneurs who figured out that Colombia [or Uganda, one can add] was good terrain for cut flowers, Bangladesh for t-shirts, Pakistan for soccer balls, and India for software generated large social gains for their economies, but could keep very few of these gains to themselves" (Rodrik 2004, 8-9, 38).

Related information externalities, further exaggerated by a weak intellectual property system and high learning and capability building costs, limit experimental and innovative entrepreneurship to restructure and diversify low-income economies. Due to these information externalities and knowledge spillover effects, firms (and 'markets') alone will be *unlikely to push diversification to the socially optimal level.* Governments have thus reason to support entrepreneurial efforts to discover the productive potential of a country: the investments in new, non-traditional sectors and related production and trade systems. Accordingly, *support* can be given for subsidy in kind, feasibility reports, training of specific new activities, adaptation of foreign technology to local circumstances, risk/venture capital, or by the creation of certain market entry barriers which limit the level of imitation that would undercut returns to entrepreneurs in the self-discovery process. Rodrik suggests such rents/support should: (a) only be provided to the initial investor, not to an imitator - an important qualification in the context of widespread 'copycat' practices in Uganda; and (b) be linked to monitoring of use of money, and performance requirements (ibid, see also Ferranti et al. 2002, 3).

Regarding *investment-related coordination failures* in the context of the establishment of new industries which exhibit scale economies, have inputs that are non-tradable (e.g. specific technology) or require geographic proximity (e.g. clustering), the crucial point is that:

> "Many projects require simultaneous, large-scale investments to be made in order to become profitable ... Profitable new industries can fail to develop unless upstream and downstream investments are coaxed simultaneously ... [Thus,] the coordination failure model places a premium on the ability to coordinate the investment and production decisions of different entrepreneurs ... [Importantly,] what needs support is not specific sectors per se, but the type of technologies that have scale or agglomeration economies and would fail to catch on in the absence of support. The appropriate policy intervention is focused not on industries or sectors, but on the *activity* or *technology* that produces the characteristics of a coordination failure ... [Further, s]ometimes, when the industry in question is highly organized and the benefits of the needed investments can be localized, this coordination can be achieved within the private sector, without the government playing a specific role. But more commonly, with a nascent industry and a private sector that has yet to be organized, a government role will be required ... It is the logic of coordination failures that once the simultaneous investments are made all of them end up profitable ... The trick is to get these investments made in the first place" (Rodrik 2004, 12-4).

This form of support - different from overcoming information externalities - does not need to be costly for government. Further, note that policies designed to overcome information and coordination failures share a key characteristic: "Both sets of interventions need to be targeted on *activities (a new technology, a particular kind of training, a new good or service)*, rather than on sectors per se. It is activities that are new to the economy [and produce externalities] that need support, not those that are already established" (ibid, 14, emphasis added). In other words, support as a corrective measure for specific market failures across sectors has to be directed to, first, *'new'/innovative activities* (including related new skills and capabilities) which have potential for: (a) information/technological and learning *spillovers* (to subsequent entrants and rivals), and (b) *demonstration effects* (crowd in complementary investments), and, second, investment that has potential to *initiate new areas of specialisation* (ibid, 22-3). Rodrik explains the difficulties and flexibility requirements of such a policy approach and the vital role of social learning which materialises in:

> "discovering where the information and coordination externalities lie and therefore what the objectives of industrial policy ought to be and how it is to be targeted ... Just as discovering underlying costs require entrepreneurial experimentation, discovering the appropriate ways in which restructuring bottlenecks can be overcome needs a trial-and-error approach to policymaking ... [Such p]ublic strategies ... are often derided because they may lead to picking the losers rather than the winners. It is important of course to build safeguards against this ... But an optimal strategy of discovering the productive potential of a country will necessarily entail some mistakes of this type. Some promoted activities will fail. The objective should be not to minimize the chances that mistakes will occur, which would result in no self-discovery at all, but to minimize the costs of the mistakes when they do occur" (ibid, 18, 21, 25).

Relevance of the externality argument for Uganda's diversification and growth agenda

The statements made by Rodrik are relevant with respect to Uganda's economic agenda and reality. He suggests that support should be channelled to *activities*, including *specific skills, capabilities* and *technologies* that are *new* to a country, that is activities that can bring about spillover and demonstration effects and thus economic growth and transformation in the context of entrepreneurial experimentation and investment in diversification and improved (new) business strategies, solutions and models. Hence, support should be given to efforts that can lead to innovations as understood in this book: new or improved products, processes, organisational techniques or markets and development of VCs and range of related capabilities. The suggestion is: (i) to generate - for a certain period - economic rents and/or offer support (including, for example, sector specific training modules and institutions) for such pioneering entrepreneurs, (ii) identify coordination opportunities while constraining rent-seeking, and (iii) discover types of action that can cause the greatest response.[228] Closely related to Rodrik's concerns is Lall's argument of learning processes and related costs as well as widespread externalities of using new technologies or undertaking complex new activities (Lall 2004a, 11-3).

All this might sound rather abstract or academic, yet actually it is related to practical issues of supporting transformation in a LDC such as Uganda: for instance, in the context of global value chains (GVCs), a part of local value addition strategies can have at its core the embracing of new functions that foreign lead firms (such as agro-processors) wish to outsource to their local suppliers (traders, farmers). Or, foreign lead firms (global buyers) demand new products, services or advanced production methods from their suppliers. All this comes with the challenge for the local firm to develop the newly demanded functional attributes or capabilities (Gibbon 2003, Wiegratz et al. 2007a). The firms' achievements in this learning and capability formation process will determine their integration, continued participation and successful upgrading within GVCs. The point is that few local firms can perform the 'new' functions right away. If they succeed eventually, new diversification and growth prospects (including spillovers) could emerge - which was one of Rodrik's points. Earlier, we referred to findings that in Uganda, few new producers succeed in entering (especially non-African) export markets; newcomers are rather small in size and focused on regional markets (period: 1995-1997, Gauthier 2001). Part of this outcome can be explained by the above-mentioned externalities and coordination failures at play in the export-oriented diversification process.

Certainly, some of the above insights have become part of the agenda of the GOU, donors and NGOs in recent years (see PEAP, MTCS, Industrialization and Innovation fund, or the new BUDS-Technology Acquisition Fund), yet implementation and coordination of some of these activities has remained inadequate. The 'restructuring agenda', as Rodrik reminds us, sets high demands of policy making and implementation as well as public sector performance; but also, this book argues, on inter-firm business practices, cooperation and trust. Uganda's private and public sectors, some exceptions aside, have so far experienced difficulties in deliberately maximising spillover and demonstration effects of 'new' activities in the economy. Could GOU and donor partners design and implement fine-tuned policy measures and support programmes that better target the 'new' in the Ugandan economy?

A case in point is the plan of some flower sector players to move to the mountains to grow new species for export, e.g. larger-headed roses that grow under colder climate conditions at high altitude.[229] The first firm(s) that make this move and demonstrate that this business

228 Such a support mix is linked to the types of design and implementation of some form of competition policy (misuse of market power, copyrights, etc.) which can impact on the level of profit-making and investment levels in technology and skills, and thus on the level and nature of 'high-expectation' entrepreneurship.

229 Presently most flower farms are located in Wakiso district near Lake Victoria with a few farms located in Mukono and Mpigi districts.

is possible in Uganda can bring significant benefits to the economy, in terms of information spillovers to other investors, further diversification etc.: Among the issues that arise with this up-country investment is the recruitment of an untrained local workforce (other challenges are: refrigerated transport and infrastructure development, see Henderson 2005, slide 21). According to UFEA, by the time of research (2006), one grower had already opened a new farm at Ntungamo in South-West Uganda, to produce larger-headed roses. The new farm is a 25 hectare project which will employ 800 Ugandans in an area of high unemployment.

A GOU incentive for local skills development (LSD) could be considered to support such growth and diversification-oriented investment in new products and business solutions. Support has to be directed to 'new' (innovative) activities (including related new skills and capabilities) which have the *potential* to *kick off new areas* of *specialisation* and *create spillovers* (to subsequent entrants and rivals) and *demonstration effects* (crowd in more investments). Other examples are efforts undertaken by the private sector, GOU, and donors to export certified honey to the EU, or to establish call-centres that attract outsourcing contracts from abroad (e.g. training of staff who can work in the centres).

Importantly, certain investment-related incentives established by the Income Tax Act in 1997, the year the former tax holiday scheme was abolished (Box 21). There are sector-specific incentives (e.g. for horticulture: horticultural plant, or construction of green houses), and there are actually incentives for investors' training expenditures and for scientific research expenditure (100%) meaning that related expenditure can be deducted from taxable income. This is actually an *important incentive*. However, the training and research incentive is hardly mentioned by public or private sector players in relevant economic policy circles. Is it not relevant or not used? How much is UIA doing to raise awareness and promote this incentive more actively or to foster related relationship building with the support system that would be a partner in both: training and R&D? Is there sufficient monitoring: for instance, what is the impact of the incentives on firm decisions? How do firms utilise the training incentive? What are firms' views on the structure of the scheme? Do agents of the BTVET systems, including state and development agencies that are engaged in the field of training, promote this incentive among their partners and clients, especially from the SME sector?

It is important to determine the impact of the training and research incentives, and possibly to revise the design of the scheme. Regarding the level of utilisation of the training incentive by firms, a UIA official contacted referred the author to the Uganda Revenue Authority to obtain the relevant data. The UIA official also mentioned that not all firms are enthusiastic about training; the attitude is that expenditure on training reduces profits.

A further issue is that of the threshold level of the Investment Code: foreign investors require a minimum of 100,000US$ in planned investment in order to secure an investment license from the UIA; local investors need 50,000US$.[230] At this threshold level, according to Byaruhanga, many local SMEs are not covered by the investment code that provides the mentioned set of incentives and support. This discourages technology acquisition, R&D, and skills development in this significant section of the economy (2005a). At the time of research (2006), there was a UIA proposal before Parliament seeking to reduce the threshold level to

---

230 Apparently, local investors can also proceed with the investment without licensing from UIA.

25.000US$.[231] The deficient incentive regime for promotion of joint ventures and backward-linkages in the context of FDI has already been mentioned, including its limiting effect regarding knowledge transmission from FDI and related productivity boosts (Ssemogerere 2005, 24).

Box 21: Investment-related incentive structure

1) *Category 1:* Capital allowances/expenses (deductible once from a company's income)	
• Initial Allowance on plant and machinery located in	
- Kampala, Entebbe, Namanve, Jinja and Njeru	50%
- Outside Kampala, Entebbe, Namanve and Jinja area	75%
• Start-up cost spread over 4 years	25% p.a.
• Scientific research expenditure	100%
• Training expenditure	100%
• Mineral exploration expenditure	100%
• Initial allowance on hotel and industrial buildings	20%
2) *Category 2:* Deductible annual allowances, depreciable assets specified in 4 classes under the declining balance method	
• **Class 1:** Computers and data-handling equipment	40%
• **Class 2:** Automobiles (up to 7 t), construction and earth-moving equipment	35%
• **Class 3:** Buses, goods vehicles, tractors, trailers, plant and machinery for farming, manufacturing and mining	30%
• **Class 4:** Railroad cars, locomotives, vessels, office furniture, fixtures etc.	20%
3) *Category 3:* Other annual depreciation allowances	
• Industrial buildings, hotels and hospitals (using the straight-line method)	5%
• New commercial buildings (constructed after 1 July 2000 (straight line)	5%
• Farming - general farm works (declining balance depreciation)	20%
• Horticulture (horticultural plant/construction of greenhouses) (straight line)	20%

Source: *Investment Code, Uganda Investment Authority, analysed in 2006.*

Incentive and awareness issues related to local capability building, productivity, technology adaptation and innovation should be considered in relation to the running of the new industrial parks in the country. The geographical proximity between various actors in the parks builds a case for stimulating strong linkages between firms and support businesses and institutions (including training or testing centres, and research laboratories); related

231 On a related matter: It could also be useful to consider specific tax or other incentive for firms to acquire efficient and environmentally sound technologies.

investment and other incentives as well as coordination efforts should foster this linkage building process. A general comment on the incentive system in Uganda is that, seemingly, it does not discriminate between activities of (1) initial investors that have potential to expand and upgrade the production profile of the country into new (product) areas and create spillover and demonstration effects and (2) those investors (a) who are merely subsequent copycats, and/or (b) who enter into established sectors where risk is lower, and skills, information, and other prerequisites available. Importantly, special support and incentives have to be created especially for the first group. In the following chapter we will analyse characteristics of the private sector which affect prospects for HRD in the country.

8
Other Selected Matters which Impact on HRD

Relevant firm characteristics

Many firms in Uganda, especially family-owned SMEs, operate in a day-to-day 'survival mode', and are barely engaged in issues such as process and product improvement, organisational restructuring (including subcontracting), or new market penetration. In general, strategic planning, productivity improvements, and capability building are rarely undertaken; firms are reactive rather than proactive, operate on the short-term and can be reluctant to cooperate with each other. Competition of firms is often based on price, less on quality, product improvements, differentiation or technology, and customer service. Few formal private sector firms apply a mode of technology- or knowledge-based growth driven by innovation and learning (improved products, technology, business operations, organisational techniques) - and thus 'created' competitive advantage. Also, proper selection, use and maintenance of appropriate (foreign) productivity-enhancing technology and dealing with related know-how aspects remains a challenge for many firms, due to skill inadequacies of both management and staff (Muhumuza et al. 2005).

In the future, more firms will have to focus on branding and marketing coupled with quality improvements if they are to compete with imports, which are often preferred by customers due to (perceptions of) superior packaging. This challenge changes and increases the skills needs of firms. Notably the effects of the liberalisation policies of the 1990s in the commodity trading and telecommunication market have brought changes in the pattern and culture of competition in Uganda. Some sections of the food processing industry, for instance, have progressed in some of the above matters.

Overall, the majority of firms seem to lack a strategy and vision for business operations and growth; rather, they undertake a relatively unplanned and short-term-oriented entrepreneurial activity. This strategy is inappropriate for skills development and competitiveness prospects. But so is the opportunistic and solitary mode of operation which is also widespread among businesses and geared towards making short-term and quick profits through responding to arising opportunities that provide direct benefits; not to long-term business development (markets, customer base, HRD, or inter-firm partnerships). Regional export market links are developed and exploited systematically only by a few (larger) formal-sector firms, SMEs struggle even more in this regard. 'Pure' R&D by Ugandan firms is almost absent; as are applications for new patent, trade mark, or industrial designs (WIPO 2005, 2003).

Correspondingly, there is little locally-sourced R&D expenditure on matters relevant to industrial production. UNESCO statistics (year 2000) indicate that 90% of the gross domestic expenditure on R&D comes from external funds/sources (donors etc.). Business had a share of 2.2%. The rest was as follows: 6.6% government, 0.6% higher education, 0.3% private non-profit (NGOs). The distribution remained largely unchanged over the period 1996-2001 (UNESCO 2005). More than half (55%) of the established funding was on medical and veterinary sciences, especially for clinical trials (Muhumuza et al. 2005). Overall, the expenditure on R&D is estimated to be about 0.8% of the GDP. During the 1990s, planned government expenditure (according to budget allocation) on R&D fluctuated between 0.4% and 0.8% of total government expenditure. However, actual expenditure may have been far less due to 'budget cuts' (ibid, UNESCO 2005).

The survey among SSEs mentioned earlier pointed to the low level of innovative activities in the smaller processing firms; accordingly, R&D or innovation was not practiced by 90% of the 150 firms surveyed, one of the reasons was lack of capabilities (Byaruhanga 2005b). Another survey among industrial firms (most of them with export experience) notes: "Although the incidence of participation in R&D activities was fairly high for an underdeveloped economy [54% involving foreign firms and 44% involving local firms] ... the levels were extremely low" (Rasiah and Tamale 2004, 21). Other data suggests a low level of formal R&D in sections of the manufacturing sector, "revolving around minor alterations to imported machinery and fabrication of spare parts" (Ssemogerere 2005, xii, based on findings by Hasunira 2004[232]).

In part, the low engagement of the private sector in innovative activities might be due to sections of the private sector being preoccupied, for almost two decades, with the rehabilitation of capacities that were underutilised during the years of turmoil. While underutilisation is still a major issue nowadays (clearly limiting learning and skills development), the present challenges for firms (product differentiation, supply management, packaging) are somewhat different.

In addition, the heritage of the trading culture that emerged in the 1970s and 1980s (and earlier periods) - with profits made through (informal, partly illicit) buying and selling without additional value added - is relevant in this context. The country is slowly starting to move beyond this culture, towards an appreciation of more productive and 'value added', innovative activities. Yet, structural impediments in terms of available know-how, skills and technology, political economy, or financing of SMEs slow down the pace of change. GOU needs to foster the development of a culture of continuous improvements and learning effort in firms, with a view to value creation, especially regarding issues of production operations (including VC organisation), productivity (including maintenance culture) and product development. Local learning efforts in firms are insufficiently and inconsistently supported at the present time. Yet, given the prevailing corruption in the country, what kind of business culture are the state and its representatives actually promoting, explicitly and implicitly?

Risk behaviour also plays a role in this context; e.g. there is a common understanding that the experience of poverty is a lesson that leads people to favour a risk-adverse business approach. While, as discussed earlier, short-term-oriented entrepreneurial spirit certainly exists in the country,[233] Uganda lacks a larger group of indigenous entrepreneurs who engage in growth and performance-oriented, mid to long-term activities in agro-processing, despite

232 See Hasunira (2004, MA dissertation Makerere University), for the survey among 21 firms.

233 It is beyond the scope of the book to explore the links between short-term business action (or, business culture generally) and matters of history, politics, poverty, and shortage of finance in Uganda.

existing and ever-changing production and market risks. This absence creates a serious challenge for the country's export-led growth, industrialisation and competitiveness agenda, which is a *long-term project*. The development of growth-oriented indigenous processing firms should therefore be of high priority. At times, this will require partnerships with foreign firms with respect to supplier development, technology transfer, and learning networks, which points to the importance of interactive skills and practices.

Some figures illustrate the matter further: Among the top 200 taxpayers a very small fraction is owned by indigenous Ugandans. A handful of medium-sized indigenous firms have been operating for more than two decades. In the coffee sector, around 90 indigenous firms replaced the state monopoly after liberalisation in 1993. Today, very few indigenous firms exist in the sector, despite the fact that it is a multimillion-dollar export business (the economic and political-economic reasons of this outcome cannot be discussed here). A high failure rate among local firms during the 1990s was been observed in the fish and flower export sectors. Market-opening initiatives such as AGOA and preferential schemes for markets in Japan, Canada and Australia have rarely or only slowly been exploited by local entrepreneurs. Industry joint ventures, between foreign and local players, are not very common. Lall's note offers the background concern about this very crucial agenda: "Capturing the beneficial externalities of foreign presence [of investors] essentially requires entrepreneurial development, and this has proved an extremely difficult task in much of Africa, at least as far as modern manufacturing is concerned" (2003, 16). Finally, of the 118 public enterprises privatised as of July 2004, 71 (60%) were bought by indigenous Ugandans, yet less than a handful fulfilled the objective of the privatisation programme (higher productivity and return on investment, ROI, than under public management) while many others were abandoned, ruined and/or sold off (MTCS 2005, 58-59). This reveals severe entrepreneurial weaknesses *but also*, as Kiiza et al. (2006) and Tangri and Mwenda (2001) explain, the political-economic dynamics of privatisation (political 'sales' to politically connected actors) and other economic reforms in Uganda in general.

Furthermore, there is a certain aversion in the world-of-work in Uganda to (a) pooling expertise, information and financial resources at a higher scale and (b) sharing management and control functions amongst professionals, something which many Ugandans (notably, also the younger generation) don't seem ready to do, apparently due norms and practices of professional collaboration, (mis-) trust and past experiences in network affairs.

Elements of firm characteristics that are problematic - deficits in strategy, vision and professionalism - might be related to the ownership structure, the (typically small) family-owned company. Usually, the management style is hierarchical, and the firm is structured entirely towards the owner, who is often the head of the family and the manager of the firm. Business is personalised, with personal and business affairs and finances highly intertwined. A common problem associated to this mode of operation is the firm's failure to attract talent, or rather, the aversion to hiring a professional and trained person who is not from the family, not from the same clan, village or region and so on. There is anecdotal evidence that such informal 'hiring policies' along family and kinship ties (according to the 'who you know' principle) are widespread in the country. This undermines career prospects of those outside such boundaries and can affect the education, training and labour market significantly.

The limited companies, often also family owned, exhibit, to some extent, a higher degree of professionalism, yet mostly this does not reach a level which allows them to be competitive beyond the local market. Some firms employ professional managers and skilled labour, sometimes though only part-time because of limited finance. The directors' impact usually remains quite large; they are involved in day-to-day affairs. There is rarely a differentiated management structure (e.g. middle management, functional departments), and decision-making remains centralised. In summary, a large part of the private sector is characterised by poor management style and professionalism, which undermines prospects for firms to penetrate and succeed in demanding export markets. There is a 'missing middle' between the small family-owned companies and the few large corporate firms, such as Mukwano. Corporate governance and HRM practices need improvement. Nevertheless, there has been professionalissation of pockets of the private sector; it remains to be seen how this process continues, if it gets support from GOU and if it spreads to other sections of the economy.

Management-staff relations

Treatment of staff, working contracts as well as health-care provison seem poor in many firms. A small share of firms has HRD strategies in place but only few implement them. Systematic training and skills creation beyond on-the-job training in handling basic production requirements is apparently rare in some economic sectors, against the background of a high level of casual labour (about half of employees in manufacturing). However, the success and growth of firms in the tertiary sector[234] has probably brought increased competition for talent and competencies which might have triggered some improvements in contracts, payment, and HR concerns in general. HRD practices - with HR being a relatively new topic in the country (beyond what was former done by the 'personnel' section) - seem to be improving, especially in sections of the more advanced formal sector, in both foreign and domestic firms and organisations, with a more 'people centered' HRM approach and culture on the rise (FUE 2005a). HRM practices will be explored in more detail in Chapter 12.

Local cadre development

Some firms seem to apply a business approach that relies overly on the *import of expatriates* for technical, supervisory and management jobs, with a corresponding relatively low systematic effort to transfer and develop critical expertise to create a *local cadre* with more advanced supervisory, technical and managerial skills and capabilities. Officially (see investment code), expatriates are permitted to work in the country if Ugandans with similar qualifications, skills and experience are not available, and if the employer can prove that the foreign expert is needed. However, in cases of sensitivity the UIA seems relatively flexible in allowing foreign experts to work in Uganda, even if local skills are available. For instance, some foreign firms wish to bring in their own accountants (due to issues of trust). The deficits in terms of trust (e.g. between workforce and management), and other components of business culture and political economy intensify such industrial relations problems.

This has a negative impact on local capability building and deepening. It appears that certain management practices are not conducive to a process of strategic and comprehensive

234 This includes the telecommunications, banking, and insurance sub-sectors which have a notable presence of foreign firms.

local skill creation, including local staff participation in higher levels or technical tasks. The adverse effect of these firms' characteristics worsens in the context of a shortage of effective SIs (e.g. in technical training), or poor relationships between firms and training providers. According to statements from some informants, this description applies to a number of firms. Only a few skills development programmes in Uganda acknowledge or tackle these deficiencies in local workforce development.

There is need to recognise some of these practices and take them into consideration in programmes geared towards HRD. GOU will certainly not succeed in changing these practices across all sectors; but it could start working with those businessmen who are willing to encourage LSD more vigorously - against the background that there seem to be positive changes in some sub-sectors/firms regarding local cadre development, which need further encouragement. GOU could (1) offer to share costs of employing young, local, technical professionals who will help in implementing a productivity improvement programme, or (2) support apprenticeship programmes, (3) establish effective sector-specific training institutions (not 'white elephants'), or (4) give other forms of support and incentives for skills transfer (from trained expatriates to local staff). The point is that GOU and concerned parties need to be more frank on this front. Currently, there is not a particularly vibrant interaction between GOU and formal-sector firms (both local and foreign) on LSD; a hands-off approach dominates. Governments in East Asia had a more determined approach in this regard. The political-economic question is whether GOU wants to and can 'interfere' in the in-house HRM practices of, for instance, foreign-owned companies, on whom the government depends on other fronts. Crucially, very little research has been done about relevant aspects of the political economy of state-industry interactions in Uganda; such research could help to explain the action pattern of GOU in the above matters.

Key results of the study on 'Management and Change in Africa'

An empirical study on 'Management and Change in Africa' explored the nature of management and organisation across 15 SSA countries (Uganda not included). The study surveyed over 3,000 managers, and carried out an in-depth analysis of organisations in key economic sectors in SA, Kenya, Cameroon and Nigeria (interviews with managers, and management and employees surveys) (Jackson 2003, 2004). Key results with links to the above discussion are presented in Box 22.

Box 22: Key results of the study project 'Management and Change in Africa'

Using appropriate leadership and management styles

- A variety of hybrid management systems operate in Africa, some highly adaptive to the operating environment, and successful, some maladaptive.
- These can be described by reference to three 'ideal type' management systems: post-colonial (based on coercive leadership and alienative involvement); post-instrumental (based on remunerative reward and contractual involvement); and African renaissance (based on normative leadership and moral involvement).
- African management systems currently appear to be predominantly results and control-oriented (post-instrumental and post-colonial) with some country differences (control/people-oriented).

- There is a general desire among managers to be more people and results-oriented; but people orientation is not reflected in managers' projections of the future of their organisations, yet a higher emphasis on results is.

Gaining employee commitment: Work attitudes and organisational climate

- Humanistic and communalistic attitudes are prominent.
- Need for stability; employees have expectations of loyalty from their employers.
- Employees report a moderately high loyalty to the organisation, yet show a moderately low work-centrality.
- There is a separation between home/community life and work life.
- Reported levels of coercive control (post-colonial management systems) seem to be too high.
- Employees appear to be team workers.

Source: *Jackson (2003, 1-2).*

> Other apparently related findings include: On (1) *Managing complexity and uncertainty in the African environment*: "An ability to 'capture' the wider societal collectivism, humanism and entrepreneurial flair in Africa may all be key to organizational success. The capability to develop cultural synergies, and include different and wider stakeholders[,] is a prerequisite to making appropriate decisions, through a more thorough understanding of the operating environment: helping to reduce uncertainty, and including multiple stakeholders" (ibid, 1). On (2) *Managing decision-making*: "Understanding the influences of cultural differences on decision-making and managing different value systems is important in developing decision processes, and in transferring knowledge and decision systems from other cultures" (ibid). On (3) *Motivating and Rewarding Managers*: "Managers generally report a preference to work as part of team, but see this tendency as being lower in others. Work centrality is generally low: family and outside work life is more important" (ibid, 2). On (4) *Managing multiculturalism*: developing managers: "[Differences] in learning styles may suggest that Anglo-Saxon teaching methods with a focus on process may be inappropriate. Also questioned is the appropriateness of the 'Organizational Learning' concept that is being introduced into organizations in Africa, with very little thought" (ibid).

From these and other key findings, it is concluded: "management development, and organisational capacity building [in Africa], should include the following areas: understanding constraints and uncertainty; accommodating interests of multiple stakeholders; developing decision processes that give voice to those interests; motivating and gaining commitment by reconciling home/community and work life; assessing appropriateness of management principles and practices; managing multiculturalism and cross-cultural development" (Jackson 2003, 3). Accordingly, one of the key challenges for managers operating in Africa is the management of cross-cultural differences and dynamics as well as uncertainty and the worlds of work and life; these are also present challenges in the Ugandan context. The study's finding of high level of (coercive) control in management styles is noteworthy.[235]

Level and pattern of firm specialisation

Characteristic for the production structure in Uganda is further a low level of specialisation, exemplified by a low level of supplier industry, outsourcing, horizontal and vertical inter-

235 See also Shonhiwa (2006).

firm partnerships, and joint ventures. The small market size seems to induce firms to be quite protectionist in their business operations ('do everything yourself'). Concentrating on core competencies and sharing business (orders) between firms according to specialisation in the VC is not common. Rather, firms try to integrate vertically. Beside the protectionist argument there is a list of other reasons; deficiencies in awareness, trust, reliability, supplier capacity, cooperation culture, complementary competencies, and financial matters. Larger firms seem to perceive potential suppliers (say, smaller firms) as unreliable, inefficient, incompetent or just not trustworthy. Instead of engaging in perhaps difficult supplier-development partnerships (capability building, technical assistance), many seek vertical integration, or rely on business conglomerates.[236]

Such a pattern might work well for a company, but at the end it can also hinder specialisation and productivity advancement in and across sectors, with implications for skills development and learning curves. A high level of vertical integration in larger firms is partly related to the early stage of industrial development in the country, where suppliers and specialised firms often do not exist or are not yet sufficiently competitive in their capacities and capabilities. This should change over time, although the process is not automatic. Development of specialisation patterns and business linkages might well increase not only Uganda's productivity and competitiveness but also her attractiveness to potential investors. Notably, GOU has no particular policy that would favour sourcing from local firms, especially SMEs, with a view to developing their capabilities throughout the process.

236 However, see Wiegratz et al. (2007b) for case studies of agro-processing and trading companies in Uganda which engage in active supplier development (called 'developmental buyers' in the study). The supplying farmers in these cases reported improved skills and know-how.

9
The Relevance of Trust, Cooperation, Related Business Practices and Ethics

Social, cultural capital and economic development in Uganda

Social capital (SoC) is a relatively new concept in the economic development literature in SSA. It is thus important to consider both the merits and shortcomings of the concept and related debates about its relevance for economic development. Although the author shares some of the criticisms of the SoC concept and has reservations, in this book the term is used to make a number of fairly introductory points about issues relating to social and economic norms, practices, behaviours and networks as well as matters such as (high/low) trust, distrust, cooperation and related skills (e.g. social, or interactive).[237] In this sense, in this book and at this stage of the author's research of these matters in Uganda the term SoC is used more as a kind of proxy. Future in-depth research is required to study the topics mentioned below in a less catch-all fashion, in more specific ways using various other concepts, e.g. the notion of the cultural, social and political *embeddedness* (or *constitution*) of the economy and specific markets (Polanyi 1957, Granovetter 1985, Krippner and Alvarez 2007, Beckert 2007a).

SoC can be understood in the form of: (a) *systems* based on social norms, networks and relationships (informal institutions), (b) the *ability* to form, integrate into, interact in and sustain networks or, more generally, to form relationships of trust, cooperation/mutual support and common purpose (Lall 2002, 3-4), or (c) the *accumulation* of exchanges, obligations and shared norms and identities which provide actual or potential support and access to valued resources (Bourdieu 1984). It is useful to note the system and ability dimension - that mirrors structure-and-agency notions - in the definition suggested above. Lall confines SoC to "the norms that permit groups and networks (in civic society, enterprises, institutions and governments) to cooperate, share information and formulate and act towards common objectives" (2002, 5). Consider also the following description:

237 On social capital see for instance Durlauf (2002), Durlauf and Fafchamps (2004), Fafchamps (2002), Fine (2003, 2002, 2001), Franklin (2004), Harriss (1997), Knorringa and van Staveren (2006), Lall (2002), and Meagher (2007, 2005a, 2005b). On the shortcomings of the conventional SoC concept note for instance that the mainstream debate on SoC tends to gloss over some important aspects of political and economic structure, including various structural conflicts, and inter-actor power imbalanced in the economy that have an impact on the very issues (norms, networks, practices) that are in the focus of the SoC concept. SoC scholars rarely include in their analysis relevant aspects of the political economy of capitalism (Fine 2001), including conflict and violence in the context of economic transformation (Cramer 2007). The author's PhD research in 2008 confirms the view that inter-actor trade relationships and practices in a specific place have a substantial grounding in the locality's (cultural) political economy (e.g. inter-actor power imbalances, impacting broader political trends). It is beyond the scope of the book to reflect more deeply on these points; however, see especially Meagher's work for an informative discussion of the 'usefulness' of SoC and related concepts in the African context.

"Social capital consists of the *stock of active connections among people*: the trust, mutual understanding, and shared values and behaviors that bind the members of human networks and communities and *make cooperative action possible*. The basic premise is that interaction enables people to build communities, to commit themselves to each other, and to knit the social fabric. A sense of belonging and the concrete experience of social networks (and the relationships of trust and tolerance that can be involved) strengthen economies" (PEVOT 2006).

According to the literature, the existence and/or use of SoC in the economic context makes the following contributions:

- Contributes to functioning micro and meso-level institutions which play a role in economic development.
- Improves information flow, and allows production factors to be used more effectively (which could boost productivity).
- Enhances group-oriented, high-trust workplaces that consist of interactive and informal learning and cooperation networks (with colleagues, firms, customers).[238]
- Is vital to have trust-based VCs and clusters where different firms and actors address problems collectively and realise economic opportunities. Generally, it allows collective action and thus targeting of collective efficiency gains, positive externalities and knowledge transfer (e.g. innovation partnerships that enhance flows of new ideas and practices). For instance, it allows groups and individuals to share business risks, target markets, address challenges they face, and thus cope better with economic and political transformation and related stress, including technological change and liberalisation.
- It can reduce costs and risks of economic transaction and coordination (Lall 2002, Knorringa and van Staveren 2006, Fukuyama 2003, Johnson et al. 2005, Beardsley et al. 2006).

In summary, SoC can help boost market transactions, supply-side structure, productivity, HRD, value chain development (VCD), competitiveness, and PSD in general. SoC problems in Uganda would thus be a serious challenge for PSD and HRD.[239] For instance, with regard to (1) deficiencies in utilising SoC for improved organisational structures which allow higher productivity levels, (2) inter-firm cooperation which allows capturing of *relational gains* (Kaplinsky and Morris 2003, 12), (3) establishment of stable, long-term-oriented, high-trust VC arrangements that can compete successfully in complex and advanced market segments, and (4) on-the-job training and learning, and learning mechanisms in general (inter-firm, cluster, industry, and support system).

In particular, SoC deficits undermine learning and training processes at the workplace: continuous learning and skills development in day-to-day business activities and interactions are severely constrained by opportunistic and short-term business perspectives and systems (e.g. low-trust VCs) that dominate large sections of the world-of-work in Uganda.[240] Of course, the theme of business practices and behaviour (including trust/mistrust) in a transforming economy such as Uganda is linked to the larger (political-economic, cultural and social) context of the state of the macro, meso and micro-level (institutional) foundations or mechanisms that,

---

238 With a view to trends in the global economy, Fukuyama notes for instance: "Many recent productivity-enhancing managerial innovations have exploited the informational advantages and incentive structures accruing to group-oriented, high-trust workplaces. The flattening of formerly hierarchical organizations in effect substitutes informal social capital for formal organization ... [Also, just-in-time or lean production] rests on the delegation of responsibility to groups of workers who build horizontal relationships and learn to trust one another. This type of organization produces huge gains in worker productivity because it makes use of social capital" (2003, 12).

239 As said earlier, the author uses SoC as a proxy. Concrete terms should be used in further research, e.g. institutions, values, norms, practices, business ethics, or power.

240 See Chapter 10 below for more details on this matter.

for instance, facilitate trust between economic actors in a country (Humphrey and Schmitz 1998). Again, for future research and debates, it is important to break down SoC into more detail and investigate different concepts when talking about 'high'/'low' SoC, 'SoC deficits', etc.

Further, it is important to realise that trust and cooperation involve a capability component. For instance, Möllering defines trust as the ability to suspend uncertainty, accept vulnerability, and develop positive expectations regarding the intentions and the actions of the other actor in a business interaction/transaction context (2006, 2005). For him, "trust is an ongoing process of building on reason, routine and reflexivity, suspending irreducible social vulnerability and uncertainty *as if* they were favourably resolved, and maintaining thereby a state of favourable expectation towards the actions and intentions of more or less specific others ... [In short, trust is] a favourable state of expectation towards others in the face of ... vulnerability and uncertainty" (2006, 111, 6, emphasis in original).[241] The (level of) ability to suspend uncertainty is related among others to early childhood experience and learning (2005, 2006).[242] If biographical issues (and matters such as expectations regarding the behaviour of others) affect the economic actors' present-day trust behaviour, then the history of Uganda, the institutional environment, the trust culture of the country, the behaviour of role models, and the socio-economic and political-economic conditions play an important role in shaping the ability of Ugandan economic actors to develop and sustain inter-personal trust, with both domestic and foreign actors (Wiegratz 2008). GOU and other domestic and foreign (political, economic, social) actors need to consider their role in the current state of trust affairs (and other aspects of business culture) in Uganda (ibid).

In other words, the overall argument of this chapter is that Uganda's development aspirations - commercial agriculture, agro-industry, knowledge and service economy - require (1) a certain level of business ethics, codes of conduct, values and norms (including moral norms), trust, cooperative behaviour, social skills, productive networks, legitimacy, 'stable worlds' and 'skilful entrepreneurs' (Fligstein 2001a, 2001b)[243]; and (2) an environment (including politics) that fosters the formation and strengthening of these characteristics at different levels (family, school, private sector, and public institutions). Improving productivity and competitiveness thus *also* means (a) *raising* and *managing* workers' *ability to interact*: with management, colleagues, firms, and customers (Johnson et al. 2005, Beardsley et al. 2006) and (b) improving the (political, social, cultural and economic) *environment* in which relationships (including industrial relations) for meaningful PSD can develop. Regarding the role of SoC in industrialisation, Lall notes:

> "Social and behavioural factors that may affect the process and nature of the (massive) adjustment required of developing economies are rarely taken into account [by the dominant view which

241 'Suspending' uncertainty then refers to a situation of not totally neglecting uncertainty but acting as if it does not exist for the moment; *as if* the reasons for uncertainty (regarding an interaction/ a person) were resolved. However, the uncertainty-suspending actor knows that doubts and uncertainty remain in the background of the relationship.

242 In his discussion on this point, Möllering (2005, 24-5) refers to Giddens' (1990) work.

243 Sociological institutionalists such as Fligstein or DiMaggio (1988) refer to 'institutional entrepreneurs' who create or reshape new/old institutions, and are "able to work within and around institutions and ideas" (Hay and Wincott 1998, 952).

focuses on the business environment]. There is again an implicit assumption that these factors do not matter, or that, if they do, exposure to globalisation and the adoption of market friendly policies will ensure that social norms and patterns of group behaviour will automatically adapt to economic needs. There is growing evidence that this view is over-simplified and possibly harmful. ... [*S*]*ocial capacities* ... allow economic capabilities to be developed and efficient policies to be designed and implemented[;] ... social capital ... provides the basic precondition for structural change and policy" (Lall 2002, 2-3, emphasis in original).

Furthermore, Swedberg notes in a discussion of the labour factor in the production process:

> "Two institutions which are central to labour, before it enters into production, are the home and the school. In the home children learn values, discipline and how to interact (what some analysts refer to as social capital, or cultural capital). They also get to live in a household economy and become influenced by its values. In school, labor is taught various skills, some of which are of value in production" (2003, 20-1).

For the reasons discussed above, the dimensions of the SoC definitions presented at the beginning of this chapter can be considered main variables for determining the level of collective efficiency gains which are realised through collective action, e.g. joint innovation and information sharing. In this respect, the level of success or failure (or pace) in industrial development and related public and private sector activities often has a considerable link to SoC characteristics and patterns of social interactions in a country (Lall 2002, 2-3). Figure 18 indicates the ample requirements for SoC in the various relationships and networks that underpin industrial and economic development.

Figure 18: Social capital needed for industrial development

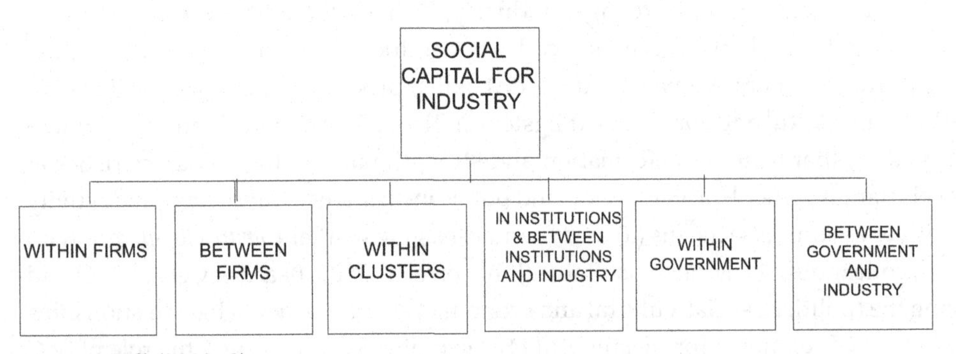

Source: *Lall (2002, 8).*

Overall, Uganda would probably have a mixed record in SoC categories for PSD. To mention a few examples from the public service side: In general, there is, for instance (a) a weak intra and inter-ministerial cooperation and exchange of knowledge and information, or (b) at times, rather ineffective and little result-oriented interaction with the private sector on certain issues in terms of policy, strategy and implementation. The relations between GOU and most private sector players still seem to be quite far from being robust, genuine, inclusive, trust-based, open, transparent and result-oriented; even so, a number of exceptions do exist. As described in the example of the flower industry in Box 23, the overall pattern of (formal) private sector working with the public sector seems to be that relationships are often only based on highly individual contacts, a mode which comes with certain flaws. However, note the recent efforts of GOU to consult and interact more consistently with the private sector on matters of PSD.[244] The private sector has a range of SoC problems as well, e.g. regarding collective action, interaction with the state, trust-based economic interactions, honesty, or value chain and cluster development (Wiegratz 2008, Wiegratz et al. 2007b). The decline in fish stocks in Lake Victoria in 2007-08 due to continuous deficits in both fishing practices (overfishing, fishing of immature fish) and state regulation of the sector is a painful example of the likely consequences of unresolved issues in the context of a neoliberal policy framework and business culture.

Box 23: Patterns of private and public sector interactions, the example of the floriculture sector

Based on discussion with a few industry representatives and PSD experts, the overall problem of working with the public sector seems to be that relationships are mostly based on individual contacts. In the views of the informants, the interaction is often highly personalised and thus not founded on, or guided, by functions, policies or departmental responsibilities. This makes the characteristics and success of private-public interaction patterns often a matter of luck, in the sense of whether or not the respective officer or commissioner is sufficiently informed, competent, committed, enthusiastic, and influential. The common problem of weak as well as overly hierarchical intra-ministerial information and communication flows comes into play here: In situations where a ministry's junior officer attends the sector's stakeholder meetings because his/her supervisor is not sufficiently interested in or conversant with the topic of concern, the result is most likely an unpredictable and incoherent response pattern and thus a slowing down of decision making and implementation on the ministerial side.

Another common risk of such an individualised mode of interaction is the interruption or breakdown of the public-private sector collaboration if a public servant who has worked with the sector moves to another position. In addition, such relationships tend to be non-transparent, with negative effects for consistent policy implementation, level playing field, and expectations of economic actors. For instance, in order to get things moving in such an administrative environment, the flower sector's representatives tend to try accessing the highest political level possible where authority and decision making power is assumed to be (principle for success: know the right people, have the right political connections). This, of course, further undermines departmental functions and competence building. However, a recent example of this strategy is the commitment expressed by GOU to support the expansion of the present dedicated cool chain facilities at Entebbe airport. This step forward in 2005 was mainly the outcome of the good relationship between the sector and the minister for Investment. Since then, however, the government promise has not actually materialised in practice (by 2006) - to the disappointment of the sector.[245] Taken to the general level of argument, the characteristic described above, of

244 See, for instance, the recent establishment of the Presidential Investors Roundtable (PIRT), a forum to promote high-level discussions between (local and foreign) firms and investors, the president, ministers and public service representatives. Supposedly, the actions agreed in the forum should be followed up by ministries. Also note the following view which compares Ugandan policy reforms with that in Kenya: "Uganda's manufacturing firms ... are not facing as many impediments in the policy environment as Kenyan firms do. Uganda's government seems to be more responsive and flexible in dealing with their problems" (Siggel and Ssemogerere 2001, 32).

245 Note also the following observations: "Although Uganda appears to have a strong and well-established national commitment to encouraging the private sector, and certainly the impressive growth over the last decade or so is driven by the private sector, there is scope for much more effective communication and coordination between the government and the private sector. With the exception of a few lead players in the private sector that lobby at the highest political level on specific interests, there is [overall] no effective consultative mechanism or forum for which wider private sector concerns are discussed with GOU. There are a few examples of private sector organizations that effectively represent their members' interest but there is not a strong private sector organization that represents across-the-board private sector interests. To some extent, this may reflect the stage of development of the Ugandan private sector - a more mature private sector may be able to organize itself and represent its own interests better. But it also reflects the fact that the private sector does not have an effective GOU counterpart with which to interact on

one example of government's dealing with the private sector, can send "a signal that political lobbying and the acquisition of contacts has [potentially] a high pay-off … [T]his will induce some entrepreneurs to redirect their efforts away from more socially productive activities, with potentially serious implications for investment, sustainable exports and growth" (Bevan et al. 2003, 45). However, the issue of state-private sector relations requires more research.

Understanding of the political, social and cultural embeddedness of the economy needed

Thinking about SoC raises a number of important questions, for instance: Where and how is SoC created and reshaped in Uganda? What have Uganda's social organisation (strata, classes, religious groups) and practices as well as the post-conflict situation or the high levels of poverty and casual labour, or the informal sector or gender-linked characteristics to do with it? What is the colonial legacy in this regard (e.g. on social cohesion and divisions, culture and politics)?[246] To which extent and how do families, communities, education and training institutions, public authorities and commercial actors develop the social and cultural (including moral) resources and character of the young generation? What is the impact on SoC formation of the following: the level and nature of corruption, patronage, clientelism, tribalism, brain drain, urban-rural and 'North-rest of the country' gaps, public-and-private-sector interaction patterns, behavioural patterns of the local elite, or donor dependency of sections of the economy, state and NGO-community? Does SoC relate to the finding of 'negative work attitudes', especially among the more educated and trained people in the LF? Does SoC play a role in explaining the level of interaction between the private sector and training institutions as well as interaction between actors within the BTVET system? What are the characteristics of interaction between the local and foreign elite? What is the impact of SoC on the formation of knowledge sharing and mentoring relationships in the private sector? What has been the impact of liberalisation and the political-economic trends since the 1990s on norms and practices of economic and social interaction between people in the country? In other words, what is the link between actors' practices (e.g., cultural and economic) and the changing political-economic situation of a locality (Ferguson 1999).

Furthermore, what are the different features of indigenous Ugandan vs. Ugandan-Asian[247] business networks? Are some of the reasons for the dominance of Ugandan-Asian managed supermarkets and factories also related to their efficient domestic and international economic networks and lower transaction costs due to trust-based trading, financing and information systems? Is the presence of Kenyans in sections of the local labour market not only a sign of certain advantages in technical but also in social skills? How do characteristics identified by the above questions impact and interrelate with each other, and how do they accelerate or impede the emergence of SoC, and, subsequently, specialisation, networks, clustering, innovation, technology use, business practices, entrepreneurship and productivity improvement in the private sector? To which extent are adverse features of business behaviour and systems (e.g. low-trust VCs) related to the loss of business opportunities, or the decline and closure of businesses?[248] Finally, what is the politics and economics of: *who* accumulates wealth in

private sector development issues. As a result, the private sector cannot be confident that GOU will address their interests" (WB 2006a, xxi-ii).

246 See e.g. Mamdani (1996b), Thompson (2003), or Tiberondwa (1998).

247 Ugandan/African businessmen of Asian background.

248 The analysis by van Bussel (2005) suggests a strong link between low-trust business practices (VCs)

Uganda and *how* (Cramer 2008)? Which modes of economic relations, norms and behaviour are promoted (directly and indirectly) by the dominant economic, political and technocratic actors, and how do these factors impact on HRD?[249]

Impact of the ETS on relevant norms, values, skills and practices

It is with respect to SoC formation that the following characteristics of parts of the E(T)S might well have their impact, in one way or another: The apparently relatively low level, in the 'average school', of encouraging pupils and students towards: analytical, problem-solving and innovative thinking and acting, contextualising and questioning presented facts, communication, exchange of ideas, teamwork and trust-building, or self-initiative and more autonomous decision-making. One could also consider the impact of teachers, who are positioned as authorities with various means of punishment at their disposal (including corporal punishment), and an extreme insistence on discipline (narrowly defined) and compliance to hierarchy. Also, an examination-oriented system, favouring rote memorisation and theoretical knowledge (vs. creative and critical application of that knowledge to practical issues), boarding schools with, in certain cases, very long hours of classroom-work[250] and the practical absence of love and care of the family home during school time, rigid marking schemes and selection channels (to the better schools and universities), little participatory or truly interactive teaching methods[251]: they all have their share, in one way or another, in the formation of SoC and related skills of the future members of society and the economy. The author recognises the difficulties of establishing enhanced methods in the Ugandan school system,[252] including financial constraints, and also notes improvements in many schools in this respect.

Likewise, most universities, it seems, do not encourage or demand in a notable and systematic sense teamwork and team projects, and are not at a sufficient level of deliberately developing the needed social, interactive, and innovative competencies among their students. Often, those graduates, who (i) (also) obtain a degree from a foreign university that encourages such forms of skills development or (ii) work for those companies and public service institutions in Uganda which apply HRD methods (e.g. for team and trust building) manage to gain such competencies later in their career. However, the impression is that opportunities are not sufficiently tapped by the ETS and the private sector, to spread such competencies more widely (e.g. through learning networks). The effect of the structures and incentives of the ETS is complemented by a cultural system that, to some extent, favours tradition, hierarchy, and authority (sex, age and, lately, money). Related norms and practices impact on ways of thinking and acting (details of which need further research). In urban areas (especially Kampala) 'alternative' sources and structures of knowledge and social practices, available to, for instance, the younger generation (e.g. peer culture, Internet), have started

and the growth problems of Ugandan businesses. See also Zak and Knack (2001) on equality, trust and economic growth.

249 See also Ssemogerere and Wiegratz (2006).

250 At the expense of extra-curricular, recreational activities which help in character formation and can form creative or social skills.

251 Teachers are over-reliant on writing on the blackboard or reading from books or notes and pupils taking notes.

252 For instance, participatory and more child-friendly teaching methods in primary school, with classrooms of up to 100 pupils.

to impact on patterns of knowledge and information flows, interpersonal interactions and thus culture.[253]

Characteristics of (changing) culture in Uganda are likely to be highly relevant for the future of economic development in the country - yet this was not researched for this book. For instance, moral codes play a role in shaping business culture. What is, in a particular location and period of time, perceived to be acceptable or inacceptable, responsible or irresponsible, praiseworthy or blameworthy, allowed or prohibited behaviour and trade practices in the light of the moral principles of fairness, justice, care, solidarity, decency and propriety (standards of interaction concerning others' welfare), will shape the sentiments, motivations and actions of economic actors (Watson 2005a, 2005b, Sayer 2007, Keller 2006, Nunner-Winkler 2007). In this context, Watson refers to the neoliberal political project of the cultural conditioning of individuals according to imperatives of capitalist accumulation: the shaping of actors' cognition and behaviour (habits of thought and habits of action) through specific socialisation (Watson 2005a, 160, 181-97). He notes that

> "patterns of behaviour within market arenas are shaped by prevailing social institutions, which in turn reflect the dominant political orientation of society ... What counts as acceptable behaviour is related to political decisions about dominant social institutions in a society in which the market is embedded ... [Crucially, a]ccumulation imperatives [or, ensuring a structure of society that allows business to take profits out of society[254]] require the state to intervene within society, in order to promote a specific rationality amongst members of that society, a specific cognition and a specific set of instincts, all of which complement the attempt to satisfy the accumulation function" (2005a, 179ff.).

The major point is to be aware that a prevailing business culture (and contemporary common-sense assumptions about economic actors' motivation, e.g. self-interest, instrumental rationality) is the result of a long-term and conflictual political-economic, cultural, social and cognitive process (e.g. conflict over competing ideas about 'the economy' and 'development') (Carrier 1997, Callon 1998, Watson 2005a, 2005b, Beckert 2007b).[255] Thus, business culture is not fixed, an actor's motivation is not immanent, natural or permanent, and the overall purpose and organising principles of an economy not self-evident or predetermined, but

---

253 The author has tried to avoid making undue value judgements about cultural elements in Uganda. Instead of saying a certain practice is right or wrong, his intention has been to identify different cultural (and related political-economic) characteristics and processes that are likely to have different implications for and effects on economic, cultural, social and political development (including HRD) in Uganda, which should be explored and, indeed, further assessed (e.g. against the background of Uganda's development aspirations) in future empirical research. Only when this has been done can the question, 'What would realistically be the constituting elements of a (more) developmental business culture in the Ugandan context', maybe be answered. The meaning of the term 'developmental' has to be clarified, of course, as the meaning would depend on the researcher's or reader's (normative) point of departure. Further, the author does not wish to give the impression that there is one essential, homogenous Ugandan culture; rather, like in any other country, a (changing) diversity of (partly contradictory) norms, values, beliefs, attitudes, habits, and practices exists among the population (Olivier de Sardan 2008).

254 In contrast, the legitimation imperative is related to ensuring a sufficient flow of material benefits into society, by socialising parts of society's wealth creation through redistribution of rewards away from owners of means of production (Watson 2005a, 184-5).

255 For instance, Adam Smith - whose 'invisible hand' analogy has been (mis) used by neoliberal free-market economists to argue for (and try to establish) self-interest as the sole market coordination mechanism - held strong views on the role of both, self-interest *and* moral behaviour (e.g. propriety and fellow-feeling) in an economy. However, modern mainstream economics sidelined Smith's moral writings in favour of abstract modelling (e.g. Watson 2005a, 2005b).

shaped in various ways (e.g. politically), and therefore debatable, contestable and subject to change (no matter what hard-line economists preach on the basis of their abstract, flawed and esoteric mathematical models of demand, supply, prices and equilibrium). For instance, individuals can not only acquire certain patterns of rationality, cognition, and instinct with view to economic action, but also unlearn or rework (some of) them again (ibid).

The author's ongoing PhD research suggests that liberalisation and other economic, social and political reforms in Uganda since the 1990s have had a substantial cultural impact on society. There are a range of problems and tensions related to cultural change (especially moral change) in neoliberal Uganda which, in turn, has an effect on prevailing business practices and thus economic development in the country. To date, this aspect has hardly been discussed in policy circles and public debate arenas; also, it is yet to be researched extensively.

Insufficient debate on links between political economy, (business) culture and economic development

The discussion in Uganda of the matters raised above is at a surprisingly low level. To the best knowledge of the author, there are hardly any authoritative research studies that analyse the role and state of SoC aspects in PSD. Usually SoC (or normative/moral and behavioural dimensions) are discussed in Uganda mainly in the context of corruption and public service performance delivery (New Vision 2006a, 2006b, Collier and Reinikka 2001); and sometimes also in relation to working ethics (NV 2006c) or poverty (Munene et al. 2005).[256] Only very few PSD programmes seem to deal with key SoC issues and related themes of (cultural) political economy, sociology, and anthropology.[257]

Reports of the anti-corruption agencies or the UN, refer to what can be called SoC problems in the public service and the state-public relationship. They typically discuss the adverse effects of the pre-1986 years of political turmoil and war with respect to: (1) undermining public institutions and leadership, administrative effectiveness and efficiency, transparent management of public resources, legitimacy of the state, politicians, and civil servants, integrity of the public service, or ethical standards, and (2) a corresponding rise in patronage, nepotism, distrust (both between the people and the state as well as within administrative structures) and corruption during this era to an unprecedented level; and related mid and long-term consequences for the business culture in the country (DEI 2004a, DEI 2004b, Matembe 2003, UN 2001, Flanary and Watt 1999).[258] By the late 2000s, levels of corruption are

256 See furthermore Munene and Schwartz (2000) and Kinyanjui et al. (2005).

257 However see International Alert (2008, 2006) for a political-economic analysis of the economic recovery process in Northern Uganda. See also the study 'Bad surroundings' by Finnström (2008) on the anthropology and political economy of war in Ancholiland. See further Dolan (2009, 'Social torture') who describes how individuals, and society in te North as a whole, came to exhibit symptoms typical of torture. See also Dolan (2007). The point in the context of our analysis is that technocratic measures to enhance HRD and economic development in the North (and, actually, elsewhere in the country as well) have to take into account and be sensitive, among others, to the history, patterns and consequences of past and present conflict(s), and the world views, perceptions, moral sentiments, and motives of actors involved. Whether policy makers and programme implementers actually want to be more considerate is another matter altogether.

258 Two other exemplary observations about that time of economic and political collapse link to the deliberations on the SoC theme: First, "[t]he two decades of state inspired terror produced a culture of silence in face of all wrongdoing [namely bad governance] including corruption" (Matembe 2003, 2). Second, "[t]he sense of national[ism] had been replaced by extreme individualism and

high and increasing; corruption is considered normalised, endemic and a way of life (IGG 2008, Tangri and Mwenda 2006).

Anti-corruption experts, mainly, undertake efforts to stimulate a discussion on integrating aspects of SoC and ethics training into the primary schools curriculum, to promote values of honesty, respect and fairness (and thus, in this case, to fight corruption). According to the plans this could be done in the context of religious education and in alliance with religious groups and leaders (NV 2006a, 2006b, Appendix 27).[259] Notably, from the anti-corruption literature is slowly emerging a literature on business ethics in Africa (see e.g. Gichure 2006, Kanyandago 2003, 2000, 1999, 1994).

Interestingly, some years ago, leading PSD-in-Uganda experts of the WB called for behavioural change as a major reform pillar for growth and PSD yet limited their discussion mainly to corruption and public service delivery, instead of broadening the debate by including norms and practices that are predominant in production and trade in Uganda. The book edited by Reinikka and Collier (2001), on Uganda's economic and social recovery, of which about half of the contributing authors, including the editors, were related to WB/IMF (staff) at the time of publication, made a strong statement about the need for behavioural change. In fact, behavioural change was one of the two main pillars ('investment and behavioural change') suggested to constitute the forthcoming reform agenda for stronger economic development 'beyond recovery' and its agenda of 'peace and prices' (see ibid, 455 and final chapter in general). The authors mainly referred to "inherited pattern of opportunistic behavior that spanned the public-private divide" (ibid, 454) that undermined public service delivery in the 1990s. It is further noted that "[in] the private sector, the inherited norm of opportunism was most debilitating for the banking system" (ibid), negatively affecting reliability of profit statements and loan default rates (ibid). Yet, overall the call for behavioural change in this book refers primarily to reducing corruption and improving service delivery (ibid, 454-6).

The behavioural and normative and inherently political aspects of PSD are considerably broader, as this book suggests (see also Cramer 2008, 2007). It is in part astonishing that the WB and related groups did not increase their efforts to explore the vital behavioural and normative theme more adequately. On the other hand, this situation is to be expected considering (i) the shortcomings of the neoliberal frame of mind applied in WB writings, (ii) the tensions between neoliberal assumptions (regarding actors, groups, and societies, for

---

opportunism ... There was a tendency of those in power to enrich themselves as quickly as possible, knowing that they may not be in power the following day. Job insecurity and excess ambition to get rich quickly has also proven to be one of the contributing factors to corruption" (UN 2001, 97, 99). These shifts and changes in structures, institutions, ethics, and attitudes fuelled the rise of corruption (and related patterns of moral codes and moral behaviour) in Uganda, and are relevant - as they have had mid to long-term effects up to now - in explaining some of its character and roots as well as the broader socio-economic environment of the pre-1986 happenings. For instance, the lasting patronage system (which existed in the Ugandan society before its significant rise after independence) affects the public position towards corruption and "continues to be reflected in ambivalent public attitudes to the misuse of public funds and in some cases admiration for those who enrich themselves from the public coffers" (DEI 2004a, 8). Also note the remarks about the state-citizen relationship in general, and Uganda-specific studies in Brock et al. (2004). Reference is made therein to pre-, colonial and post-colonial dynamics and inter-linkages.

259 There was reference to moral, ethical and spiritual values in the 1992 Government White Paper on Education and the current Education Sector Strategic Plan refers to the White Paper as the main guidance for the sector (see GOU 1992 and MOES 2005).

instance) and realities on the ground, and (iii) the politics of neoliberal PSD and social change in Africa (Harrison 2005b).[260]

Astonishing or not, the low level of discussion about SoC aspects in PSD is harmful because the country's agenda items - growth, innovation, productivity, competitiveness (including costs of production, e.g. coordination costs), skilled workforce, producer organisations, knowledge based economy - are all closely related to aspects of collaboration and related political, normative and behavioural aspects. For instance, studies in the context of VCD have highlighted that SoC, in the form of high level of mutual trust and commitment between VC partners, e.g. out-grower farmers and the key firm in the domestic VC (the exporters/ processors), is a vital success factor in domestic VCD in Uganda (Ribbink et al. 2005, Wiegratz et al. 2007b). The importance of inter-actor trust, cooperation, and reliability for competitive VCD is confirmed by a study on relations between exporters in Uganda and their buyers in Europe (Wiegratz et al. 2007a).

Further, the silence is harmful because the Ugandan business culture suffers from a range of weaknesses. Several VC studies have pointed to problems in relation to trust, honesty, reliability and other matters of business behaviour and practices (van Bussel 2005, AT Uganda et al. 2005, Ribbink et al. 2005, McGuigan et al. 2005, BSMD 2005, Wiegratz et al. 2007b, see discussion below). Also, SoC issues might in fact deserve extra attention due to the country's situation as a post-conflict and liberalising economy, with a difficult historical record of collective action in the economy in the pre-1986 period[261], and a high level of constant and often externally induced socio-economic and cultural change (e.g. colonialism, westernisation, TOT shocks, and structural adjustment programmes).

In addition, take into account that the agricultural background and level of development of the country (e.g. poverty, socio-economic processes at household level), also have an impact on personality and thus normative and behavioural aspects of sections of the LF. Though this book cannot provide a more in-depth analysis of this and other points listed above, it is argued here that such aspects have to be considered in the diversification process towards non-agro sectors, e.g. in training (including awareness and reflection exercises). Especially, for graduates from lower educational and/or poverty backgrounds to have a realistic chance to gain and retain meaningful wage jobs or self employment and be productive therein, they may need training to cope with the (changing) requirements of the corporate world; the expected urbanisation trend of the LF - and thus (re-) training needs - plays a role in this context. An entrepreneur from the restaurant industry in Kampala, for instance, pointed to the problem of gaps between requirements of the (partly tourism-based) service industry and level of sets of skills of young employees based on family upbringing, exposure and household level backgrounds.[262]

260 Note that, due to its specific research focus on HRD, this book will not examine the neoliberal economic development approach at a general level (e.g. the ideology, the political economy, the role of the state, or the overall economic policy mix). In this book, the author works generally within the boundaries of the economic development approach adopted by the GOU since the 1990s (e.g., PSD, growth, competitiveness, private sector-led industrial development). However, on neoliberalism see Williams and Young (1994), Harrison (2005b), Robison (2006, 2005), or Bush (2007). Neoliberalism can be seen as a project or as acts to deepen market-like (or capitalist) social relations, foster marketisation of society and thus change the state-society relationship, among others (ibid).

261 Consider the problems of cooperatives (Asiimwe and Nahamya 2006).

262 Naturally, a certain level of deficiencies in professionalism regarding requirements of the world-

Finally, note that in the last two Ugandan surveys for the Global Competitiveness Report (GCR) of the World Economic Forum, *poor work ethics* in the national LF was ranked as the fifth top business constraint (MTCS Secretariat 2006, NV 2006c) which is - given that HR issues have typically been ranked lower in the past - a significant position. If one interprets the term 'work ethics' more broadly and tries to map underlying forces, one can see the relevance of the discussions in this book.[263] Indeed, one wonders (i) if/how GOU, donors and experts of the ETS and of PSD will respond to this finding of problematic LF work ethics and (ii) whether or not a wider approach (e.g. political economy and economic sociology) will be applied by GOU and donors to track the reasons of this status quo.

The general point, however, is: although the concerned public, government officials and firms all complain about various related skill, behavioural and (sometimes) normative 'deficits' or 'gaps', to date they have apparently failed to change the structures, incentives and practices that systematically hinder or even rule out the creation and development of a set of societal conditions, social skills and norms, and economic practices which would allow the strong emergence of more cooperative patterns, collective efficiency gains, fair business practices and work conditions, skilful capitalists, and a competent workforce. Moreover, the family, school and BTVET system need to play their part in the development of these aspects of the LF (and industrial relations); merely letting the private sector 'fix it' (at the last stage of E&T) will not be sufficient, given the process of character formation, the intensity of the challenge and the deficiencies in management, training and business practices and ethics in the private sector itself. Indeed, the ETS system and the state agencies dealing with E&T, PSD and justice, as well as the private sector, need to find appropriate roles in this skills and norms formation process. As mentioned earlier, the public and the private sectors need to reflect on their roles in the formation of SoC aspects, such as the state of trust, fairness, and (business) culture in the economy and the country at large (Wiegratz 2008).

To mention only a few possible improvements, and to link the argument to the prevailing 'cost of production'-discussion in Uganda: Advancement in productive networks, trust, business and work-related norms and practices - in short business culture - can reduce costs and risks of economic transaction and coordination, allow collective action (which comes with positive externalities), boost knowledge transfer and training and thus facilitate market transactions and supply-side structures. Moreover, certain SoC forms - not all SoC is 'positive' (e.g. excluding/corrupt networks, Lall 2002) - are desirable in the Ugandan context as they would allow communities, cooperatives and individuals to jointly target collective market opportunities, address challenges (including injustices) and risks, and thus cope better with the difficult economic and political transformation and related stress, including technological change, and liberalisation. Such advancement would also help in making the implementation of government strategies more effective. Government interventions that deal with market failures require an especially high level of SoC (ibid, 4).

Some donor programmes touch upon social skills and SoC in the context of PSD (without analysing the relevant issues directly or in more depth). For instance, the - now closed - Business Services Market Development (BSMD) programme (DFID/ILO) which focused on VCD in agro-sectors, had to tackle economic behavioural factors to achieve cooperation of actors in the chain. In the later project phase, the BSMD team tried to promote trading

of-work is common among young workers and professionals worldwide.

263 See GCR for 2004/05 and 2005/06.

and business principles and ethics to minimise conflict in business transactions. A body of work around templates for codes of conduct, agro trading principles, contract guidelines and a model contract ('sale agreement') were developed. The trading principles and sale agreement were translated into several Ugandan languages; and awareness was raised among stakeholders. These tools can now be adopted and adjusted by practitioners for VCD. Undertaking these specific efforts was a reflection of the identified need for improved business principles and ethics as well as attitudes.[264] Improvements along these lines was considered vital to allow the emergence and expansion of better coordinated and functioning agro production and trading systems which have an enhanced capacity for self-regulation (lower transaction costs) (van Bussel 2005, AT Uganda et al. 2005, Ribbink et al. 2005, McGuigan et al. 2005, BSMD 2005).[265]

> "[T]here was a growing consensus within the agro industry that the business culture and current trading practices are unsustainable and costly for all players and; there was widespread interest in creating a set of business-to-business 'trading principles' around which to build greater trust between businesses in the sector. Based on the [grounding study for Agro-Trading Principles] ... and subsequent consultative meetings with many representatives of business and support agency, a framework of agro trading principles was developed by BSMD and its partners" (van Bussel 2005, 13).

Another example: The PEVOT Local Skills Development Project (LearnNet Uganda) which is working with local learning groups is also addressing SoC issues; with some success. An interesting observation on dynamics in such groups was made in a recent project evaluation report:

> "[S]uccessful groups are those that have clear and realistic objectives uniting its members. Furthermore, they have a good capacity of communication and decision making, an elected leadership and clear rules and regulations. 'We learnt working together' is something that training participants mentioned again and again as one of the real benefits of their work. It seems that performance in groups is something that can be learnt and enhanced by good facilitation. Smooth functioning of groups seems to be a key to successful planning and implementation of trainings. Strong groups had fewer difficulties to raise funds for their training, where as in weak groups it happened that contributions disappeared and members found it increasingly difficult to raise money for the training. It would be interesting to study the different modes along which groups operate and identify those modes that prove to be successful" (PEVOT 2005, 29).

GOU and the NGO and mainstream donors have so far not shown significant and systematic interest (at least, if judged from the focus of their reports and projects) in most of the issues discussed in this chapter; also probably because 'fixing' them is an uncertain, difficult, long-term and 'tricky to measure' undertaking (van Bussel 2005).[266] The reality in present-day

264 Included are trust, honesty, transparency, reliability, efficient communication, coordination and negotiation, joint planning, investment, production, logistics, management and payment issues in VCs, or willingness to cooperate.

265 See also the in-depth discussion of the BSMD studies in the value chain chapter below. See Gibbon's remarks on the certified organic export sector in Uganda as well: "Observers of the sector note that, partly for the historical reasons alluded to above, but mainly for reasons common to business life in Africa generally [including, according to Gibbon, the short-term and highly risk adverse orientation of many African businesses, as well as the lack of enforceability of contracts], overall levels of trust and cooperation between enterprises in the sector are low. This was seen as having negative implications for alleviation of problems concerning diseconomies of scale" (2006, 9).

266 As said, the call by leading WB researchers for behavioural change as a core reform pillar for the post-recovery transformation and economic diversification process (Collier and Reinikka 2001) seems not to have been expanded beyond the themes of corruption and public service delivery,

Uganda, however, would suggest that understanding and improving norms, values and practices that constitute the prevailing business culture and thus business behaviour and ethics - including related sociological, economic, political and historical causes - is relevant for the country's economic development.[267]

The private sector and the SIs for PSD as well as institutions of the ETS, the family system and the legal and political system need to play a stronger role in the development of the norms, values, practices, behaviours, attitudes, capabilities, skills and relationships that help in forming systems of trust, cooperation, morality, learning, information sharing, mutual support, or common purpose. Policies and programmes for PSD have to tackle the challenges and opportunities highlighted above, e.g. in helping (1) to foster inter-firm cooperation, (2) developing trust-based and sustainable VCs (between producers, exporters, and importers), (3) regulating contentious business practices (e.g. cheating of business partners), and (4) enhancing productivity of all VC actors. Of course, against the above, a major issue is the political economy of capitalist business culture in neoliberal Uganda, e.g. who has interests in the prevailing business structures, practices, principles and distribution outcomes (and why), and who has interests in a different organisation and operation of the economy, and thus a different accumulation regime and moral economy (and why); and, what are underlying power structures of the status quo and the possibilities for change (Watson 2005a)?

However, research efforts have to address the dimensions highlighted above and to analyse, for instance, relevant trends in the country as well as examples of firms, farmers, traders, communities, SIs and the state addressing related challenges and opportunities. As indicated, the SoC concept might need to be replaced by other (more specific) concepts to study and communicate about particular topics in future.[268] An uncritical adoption of the SoC concept in both research and practice (development interventions, including E&T) as it is used in the mainstream development debate is likely to be academically, economically and socially unhelpful and even hazardous.

---

towards other PSD aspects, e.g. trust and cooperation.

267 The chapter on value chains below illustrates this argument further.

268 The author is grateful to Kate Meagher for a related comment. See also the concluding part in Wiegratz (2008).

10

Clusters and Value Chains in Uganda: Implications for HRD

Against the background of the discussed competitiveness challenges and the characteristics of sections of the private sector (relatively young and of small size with various capability deficits), this author argues that more attention needs to be given to matters such as clusters, (vertical/horizontal) business networks, inter-firm linkage building and cooperation, VCD and supplier development, as well as learning networks and SIs. The objective of such a focus is to stimulate and facilitate a more complex and competitive private sector with (a) stronger firms and an enhanced mix of inter-firm cooperation and competition, (b) inter-firm networks with improved capabilities, capacities, products, as well as interactions and learning patterns which are able to exploit market opportunities; and thus a more beneficial integration of the Ugandan economy into the domestic, regional and global economy. The set of policies addresses a medium to long-term agenda. A common characteristic of the above approaches is that they are based on collective action, collective efficiency (linking, or pooling of resources and skills), specialisation, interdependency, *collective competitive advantage* and thus matters of related norms, values and capabilities. Below, the terms are clarified.

Conceptual and policy background I: Clusters and networks

A cluster can be described as a sectoral and geographical agglomeration (concentration) of firms that produce and sell a range of related or complementary products and, thus, face common challenges and opportunities (UNIDO 2001, 9, 2003a). The cluster actors can include: the lead firms (Lf) and their suppliers, buyers/customers, trading organisations, and sector-relevant SIs with specialised competencies and capacities (e.g. in technical support services, entrepreneurship development, mentoring, training and technology centres, marketing bodies, laboratories, or business associations). The key firms operate in proximity and share business interests, e.g. product markets, or infrastructure and capability needs.

The competitiveness as well as the dynamics of upgrading and innovation of a cluster is related to (1) the capabilities of producers, suppliers, and SIs, and the pattern of competition and cooperation (interaction/joint action) between them - thus to the degree of effective specialisation and division of labour within a cluster - and (2) the characteristic of linkages to external actors and forces, including markets. Typically, the Lfs, with partners, develop and implement cluster strategies that respond to the competitiveness challenges and opportunities that the group faces. Note that competition is still existent in a cluster, but cooperation plays an important role in certain areas of joint interest - such as joint innovation and learning, upgrading, productivity initiatives, training, marketing, and standardisation - to tackle shared challenges and/or opportunities (UNIDO 2001, 2002, 2003a).

Clusters are known to give rise to economies of scale but also external economies: e.g. to the emergence and growth of specialised suppliers of raw material or equipment, as well as sector-specific skills and technical or managerial services. Another key advantage is the fast spread of ideas, practices, information and knowledge (inputs, technological solutions, markets) through proximity (face-to-face contact, joint projects); a characteristic that tends to benefit all cluster firms. Further, clusters are nodes for collective action, resulting in collective efficiency and collective competitive advantage (collective identity, sharing risks and costs in innovation, skill formation, and upgrading). Networks and institutions for different purposes can be established more effectively and cost efficiently. The same is generally true for the provision of government services that target clusters (UNIDO 2001, 2002, 2003a, Pietrobelli and Rabellotti 2004, Meyer-Stamer 2003, Schmitz and Nadvi 1999).

The cluster approach has been applied increasingly in both developed and developing countries, to enhance competitiveness of enterprises, subs-sectors and cities/regions through exploiting the dynamic processes of cumulative growth in a particular location. This interest in the *locational sources* of competitiveness and competitive advantage, partly caused by new insights regarding the network and proximity characteristic of the innovation process, has given rise to new prominence of regional and local development policies (ibid). The cluster approach is closely interlinked with other concepts e.g. network and linkage building, or VCD, which can be applied within or independently of clusters. The practical synergies between them - in terms of policies and programmes for PSD - are manifold, which can lead to an important boost for Uganda's economy.

For instance, *networks* are groups of firms that cooperate in a joint project, complementing each other and specialising in order to overcome common problems, achieve collective efficiency and penetrate markets beyond their individual reach. Networks can be horizontal (e.g. common business initiative formed by SMEs), or vertical (e.g. between larger-scale enterprises, or a larger and small enterprises) (UNIDO 2001, 9). Learning networks, where entrepreneurs can, for instance, share their experiences and practices, are vital in this context.

Also important are *businesses linkages and related promotion programmes*. From the policy perspective, the latter are developed with a view to increasing and deepening linkages between larger and smaller firms, or foreign affiliates and domestic firms, thus upgrading local competencies to engage in higher value activities in a competitive environment. They are assumed to lend support where there is (1) an 'information gap' on the part of both buyers and suppliers about linkage opportunities, and (2) a 'capability gap' between the requirements of buyers and the supply capacity of suppliers and where the costs and risks for setting up and deepening linkages can be reduced (UNCTAD 2001). In this respect, one can more broadly improve the enabling framework for linkage formation, on the one hand (e.g. improve the underlying issues of political economy and business culture), and/or have specific focus on a selected number of industries and firms on the other. Generally, according to the literature, several components are central to any of this: Market and business information, matchmaking, and managerial or technical assistance, training, and financial support and incentives. FDI promotion to attract investors in targeted activities, and to encourage them to increase domestic sourcing over time can be part of this agenda as well (ibid).

Inevitably, linkage promotion is closely intertwined with sub-contracting, supplier development and related programmes. Larger firms or foreign affiliates are typically encouraged to participate in such initiatives, including coaching and mentoring arrangements aimed at upgrading local suppliers' technological capabilities. More specifically, supplier-upgrading programmes are initiated to support SMEs moving through the stages of upgrading, especially process upgrading (Kaplinsky and Readman 2001). The specific involvement of global buyers and TNCs in the upgrading of local suppliers is generally a promising tool to undertake targeted and market-oriented improvements. GOU needs to encourage such activities far more in future; set incentives and respond to upcoming capability gaps that hinder linkage building and deepening with foreign buyers, e.g. raise producers' capabilities to produce according to new technical requirements and standards. GOU could further promote (a) the organization of supplier associations (clubs), (b) a linkage forum (public-private partnership), linkage workshops, or a linkage centre, (c) find other ways to support linkage building (complementary to the activities in the private sector), or (d) collect relevant information and lessons learnt and support related research.

Conceptual background and policy background II: Value chains

The following is adopted from Wiegratz et al. (2007a, 2007b) and Wiegratz (2008); see ibid for more details. A VC describes the full range of discrete value-added economic activities needed to bring a specific product or service from its conception through the different stages of production to its use and final disposal after use. This includes activities such as market research, input sourcing, product development, design, production (manufacturing), quality control, marketing, distribution, customer support and recycling; with production being only one of several value-added links in the chain. Value addition takes place at every stage of the chain. The activities that comprise a VC can be contained in a single firm, or can be divided strategically among several firms (or economic actors) (UNIDO 2004b).

In Global Value Chains (GVCs), for instance, activities are divided among multiple firms and spread across wide geographic spaces. A domestic value chain (DVC) can be part of a GVC (e.g. fruits for export). Most of what is written about GVCs is applicable to the DVC context.[269] Figure 19 shows a simple VC. In many product categories, it is different VCs - not individual VC actors only - that compete against each other. The systemic efficiency of the entire VC becomes important then; competitiveness (and productivity) improvements in advanced VCs are often based on flexibility, specialisation, use of new knowledge and technology (in products, processes as well as in organising firms and coordinating inter-firm supply relations), advanced inter-actor coordination and interaction, as well as accelerated learning of all VC actors involved (ibid, see also Humphrey and Schmitz 2002, Humphrey 2005, Schmitz 2005a, Ponte and Gibbon 2005, Gibbon and Ponte 2005, Gereffi 2005, Gereffi et al. 2005, Kaplinsky and Morris 2003, Wiegratz et al. 2007a, 2007b).

269 In what follows below, the author cannot always make these similarities explicit due to limited space.

Figure 19: A simple value chain

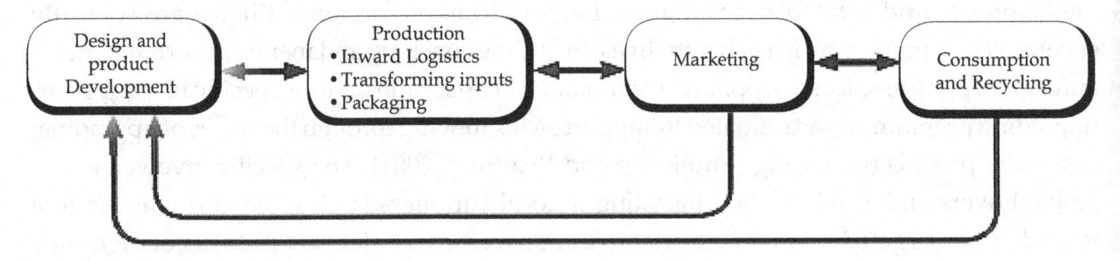

Source: *Kaplinsky and Morris (2003, 12).*

The *nature of relations and links* among VC actors and their governance by so-called key or *lead firms* (Lfs) has implications for upgrading prospects of actors in the upstream chain end (towards the producer), for instance, Ugandan exporters and farmers; this in turn has consequences for the latter's level and prospect of value-creation/capture, incomes and skills.

To date, the analysis of GVCs focuses on (1) the strategic global dispersion of different value-added activities in product specific VCs and the related organisational fragmentation and change in various sub-sectors, and (2) the related upgrading possibilities - improvements in terms of products, processes, functions and sectors - for local firms. A main concern of research is (3) the analysis of inter-firm relationships and interactions in GVCs; in particular, the way in which the lead firm (Lf) of a GVC governs - that is organises, coordinates, and controls - the dispersed activities and inputs of the firms participating at different functional positions in the upstream GVC part (e.g. up to exporters and farmers in producer countries such as Uganda). Research areas are further: (4) value creation/capture along the VC, and (5) the institutional embeddedness of VCs in terms of related policies, regulations, and standards (UNIDO 2004b, Humphrey and Schmitz 2002, Gereffi 2005).

Lead firms (Lfs)

Lfs in product-specific GVCs or DVCs can be powerful buyers, traders, marketers, or processors. These Lfs carry out the functional integration and coordination of dispersed VC activities and are key actors ('chain drivers') in setting up, managing and controlling the production and trade networks (Gereffi 1999, Humphrey and Schmitz 2002). "When a group of firms in a particular functional position (or positions) in a value chain is able to shape who does what (and at what price, on the basis of which standards, to which specifications, and on the basis of which delivery schedules) along the chain, they are said to be in a lead firm position" (Gibbon and Ponte 2005, 81). Lfs (and other VC 'governors') can influence or even control the market access and upgrading prospects of participating firms. Even more so, as the global economy is more and more concentrated at the top (e.g. retail concentration) and fragmented at the bottom (both with respect to countries and firms), often leading to squeezed profit margins and incomes as well as increased risk and uncertainty for those at the bottom (e.g. farmers in DCs), and those that do not manage to advance into the higher-value-added product range. The strategies and capabilities of Lfs in organising and coordinating VCs and thus the activities of different actors therein are a determining factor for success of VCs, first, and of participating VC actors, second (UNIDO 2004b, Humphrey 2005).

Lfs often have the necessary markets, information, capabilities and networks that not only Ugandan exporters and/or farmers (in GVCs/DVCs) need to advance but also development workers and government officials need to assist the respective Ugandan economic actors. Exporters, for instance, acting as Lfs in the DVC, can operate as strategic blocks linking farmers and foreign importers. This linkage is vital for creating a gradient along which farm produce can flow, stimulating improved production, exchange of information, thus income generation. The terms governance and upgrading become important in this context.

Value chain governance

Governance of VCs can be defined as the way in which the Lf of a specific VC *organises, coordinates,* and *monitors*[270] the activities and inputs of the participating firms or farms - thus, the functional division of labour in the VC. Governance entails defining the barriers of VC entry and coordinating, and thus often controlling, *along the VC* the spread of skills, technology, information, knowledge, production techniques, advice and other support, means for marketing, finance, profits ***and*** upgrading opportunities and capacities. *Governance activities* by the Lfs or other 'governors' in the VC can involve the following: (1) setting rules and conditions for VC participation (e.g. specifications in terms of product, process and logistics), (2) incorporating/excluding other VC actors accordingly, and allocating to them value-adding activities that Lfs do not wish to perform, (3) monitoring and auditing actors' performance and compliance with rules (enforcement), and (iv) assisting them in meeting these rules (Ponte and Gibbon 2005, Humphrey and Schmitz 2002, Kaplinsky and Morris 2003). Governance is about how "some firms in the chain set and/or enforce the parameters under which others in the chain operate" (Humphrey and Schmitz 2002, 4). The use of formal/informal rules, conditions, standards, as well as sanctions and rewards for non-performance and performance is relevant for VC governance.

Research refers to a few major reasons for buyers undertaking deliberate VC governance efforts (including supplier development) rather than relying on the general market and its output: (a) reduce the *risk of supplier failure*[271], (b) strengthen the efficiency of each chain element and linkages between them, and thus improve the VC's *systemic competitiveness* and *reduce VC governance costs,* and (c) implement strategies of *product differentiation.*[272] The economic benefits for the Lf's investment in the supplier' capabilities have to *outweigh* related coordination costs (including technical assistance costs) and risks (UNIDO 2004b, Gereffi et al. 2005, Humphrey 2005).

Importantly, there can be *different actors involved in the governance* of one VC leading to 'multiple points of governance' and different forms of governance in the different links of a VC. In certain VCs, major governance work is not done by the Lf, but by intermediaries,

270 There is an element of control in all three governance aspects.

271 "[Buyers fear] not having the product to the right specification, at the right time in the right place" (Schmitz 2005b, 36). The rationale here is as follows: "the increasing importance of non-price competition based on factors such as quality, response time and reliability of delivery, together with increasing concerns about safety and standards, means that buyers have become more vulnerable to shortcomings in the performance of suppliers" (Schmitz 2005c, 5). Governance-related efforts ought to reduce this risk.

272 "The more the buyers pursue a strategy of product differentiation ... through design and branding, the greater the need to provide suppliers with precise product specification and to ensure that these specifications are met" (Schmitz 2005c, 5).

specialist producers or suppliers, buying agents, state actors, consulting firms, or NGOs. Furthermore, trust between VC actors and legitimacy of the Lf play a significant role in modern, flexible VCs (ibid, Ponte and Gibbon 2005, UNIDO 2004b). Kaplinsky and Morris (2003, 14-5) refer to *high-trust and low-trust VCs* and link each of them to a set of particular business relationships, procedures, and practices between VC agents.

> "In the low-trust chain, suppliers are frequently changed to pursue short-term price advantages, and failure to conform with the wishes of the governor [the LF] leads to the rapid sanction of exclusion from the chain. By contrast, in modern, flexible production systems, trust becomes increasingly important, and failure to reach the required level of standards does not automatically result in the sanction of exclusion; instead, executive governance is exercised to assist the transgressing party in achieving the required levels of performance. Such high-trust relationships ...tend to be long lived" (ibid, 14).

Finally, VC research has developed the following **classification of VC governance types** and thus inter-firm relationships within a spectrum, from pure market relations to hierarchy: (a) *arm's-length/spot market type*, (b) *network-type* (with its three types: modular, relational and captive relations) and (c) *hierarchical type* (vertical integration) (Gereffi et al. 2005). Reasons for different governance types can be related to market/product characteristics including transaction complexity levels, information/standards requirements (codification of knowledge flows along the chain), production techniques, technology, supplier capabilities, trust levels, and relevant trade policies. Changes in these characteristics in a specific VC can lead to changes in the governance type, e.g. (i) from market to network governance due to increased complexity of the transaction, or (ii) from hierarchy to network type due to increased supplier competency (ibid, 85-90).

VC research is particularly interested in the explicit (or non-spot market) type of coordination of inter-actor relations in production and trade (that is b and c above). Depending on the governance type, one can find different forms of inter-actor relationships with different degrees of: cooperation (knowledge/technology sharing, support for upgrading), power asymmetries (monopoly, oligopoly) and thus VC actors' equality and autonomy, as well as capability requirements for VC participation. Production and trade dynamics at firm and inter-firm level (sales, profits, and upgrading) are related to VC governance forms and trends (Humphrey 2005, Humphrey and Schmitz 2002, Gereffi and Sturgeon 2004, Kaplinsky and Morris 2003, Ponte and Gibbon 2005, UNIDO 2004b). Mathews (2006) discusses GVCs in the context of latecomer strategies and points to GVCs as new 'institutional expressions' of well-known underlying forces of economic dynamics and restructuring in the global economy: efficiency search, cost and logistics advantages.[273]

273 "The issue is: who is strategically driving these production networks? From the perspective of the advanced firms, such as production houses (like Nike in athletic footwear) or buyers or retail chains (like The Gap or Tommy Hilfiger), the strategic initiative lies in seeking greater efficiencies and lower costs. From the perspective of the latecomers [countries in the global industrial scene, such as Uganda], the strategic issue is how to become inserted in such value chains. Thus the strategic options expand, for both advanced firms and latecomers. However, the underlying latecomer industrial dynamics, of shifting production and, more recently, research and development (R&D) activities according to competitive cost and logistics advantages, remain in force. It is just their institutional expression that has changed" (Matthews 2006, 322). See also Smith (2007).

Upgrading in value chain structures

The notion of *upgrading* (or improvements) is also relevant, for instance upgrading of local firms in GVCs. Different governance modes offer different upgrading conditions for participating VC actors. In research terms, "upgrading means enhancing the relative competitive position of a firm [or actor]" (Schmitz and Knorringa 2000, 181). The literature distinguishes upgrading in terms of: (a) products (improving existing products and/or developing new products), (b) processes (improving issues of process efficiency within a firm/between firms in a VC, process technology as well as product development), (c) functions (new mix of activities conducted in a firm with a higher skills content) and (d) sectors (inter-sectoral upgrading: moving to a more profitable VC in another sector) (UNIDO 2004b, Humphrey and Schmitz 2002, Gereffi et al. 2005).

> "One of the ways that developing economies can increase returns to involvement in global value chains is to take on new activities. The way in which successive activities are bundled together or split apart affects the opportunities for adding value to exports. Lead firms play an important role in determining this. The dangers of developing country producers [are] being trapped in narrowly-confined value chain activities with low skills and low returns..... However, value chain analysis also points to the real opportunities for upgrading arising from the outsourcing of activities by enterprises in developed countries. One clear example of this is the transfer of post-harvest processing of fresh vegetables to producer countries" (Humphrey 2005, 26).

Further, the literature categorizes two types of GVCs: *buyer-driven chains* and *producer-driven chains*. Generally, the fragmentation into GVCs is primarily driven and coordinated by international firms (TNCs) who foster the spread of these production sharing systems in developing countries. Such increasingly powerful TNCs can be global producers who source inputs globally from suppliers (producer-driven chains), or, increasingly, global buyers such as retailers, branded marketers, wholesalers and supermarkets who do not produce goods but play a main role in organising production and trade globally at different locations, e.g. with producers in developing countries (buyer-driven chains) (UNIDO 2004b). "Buyer-led chains are actively 'driven' in the sense that large retailers and branded marketers use them not merely to source products, but increasingly also to reshape their own portfolios of functional activities and to achieve higher levels of flexibility" (Gibbon 2003b, 616, Gereffi 1994). Furthermore, "[i]n order to understand how [for instance] 'buyer-driven' governance arises, what forms it takes and how it changes, we need to clarify how 'lead firms' achieve flexibility and externalize functions (to the extent that they wish to) and, at the same time, how they keep control over ('drive') the value chain (Ponte and Gibbon 2005, 22).

Relevance of VC approach for promotion of Ugandan firms and farms

Against this background, the *VC perspective* is recognised to be helpful for purposes of **strategizing for economic development** as it: (1) *moves from a focus on production* to other (bundles of) activities that are relevant in the process of bringing a product to the market (value adding stages), (2) captures *flows* of information, resources and goods between the stages of activity in the chain, and therefore reveals the variety of inter-firm linkages and their implications for the *mode of* transfer of resources, technology, knowledge, information, and skills in a particular chain, and (3) helps in identifying *high-return activities*, or anticipating new sources of *dynamic economic rents* (or new ways to avoid their erosion) along the chain, which is key for understanding the structures and distribution of the returns of production and trade. By focusing on all activities in each link of a VC, it becomes easier to distinguish activities subject to rising or decreasing returns and competitive pressures and to understand the nature and dynamics of innovation, competition, cooperation and profits. This reveals a range of possibilities and requirements for value creation, capability formation and upgrading as well as explaining what hinders value creation. For instance, specific skills and capabilities, e.g. organisational or communicative capabilities, are vital for realising new sources of competitive advantage, and thus dynamic economic rents (UNIDO 2004b, Pietrobelli and Rabellotti 2004, Humphrey 2005, Humphrey and Schmitz 2002, 2000, Schmitz 2005c, Kaplinsky 2000, Kaplinsky and Morris 2003, Gereffi 2005).

Furthermore, the approach stresses that the effectiveness of *linkages* between actors in VCs is relevant. It is sensitive to actors (buyers and smallholder farmers/SHFs) and their *relationships* in the VC. The VC approach can therefore provide insights on a range of vital PSD issues, including local firms/farms' *market entry strategies* through linkage building with buyers. Understanding VC aspects helps to analyse the nature and determinants of competitiveness drivers and related challenges and opportunities for PSD (ibid). It also helps in identifying, prioritising, and pursuing *strategies for increasing and sustaining competitiveness* (Kaplinsky and Morris 2003).

"One of the key findings of value chain studies is that access to developed country markets has become increasingly dependent on participating in global production networks led by firms based in developed countries. Therefore, how value chains function is essential for understanding how firms in developing countries can gain access to global markets, what the benefits from such access might be, and how these benefits might be increased" (Gereffi 2005, 178, fn 20).

VC analysis as a **management tool** for Lfs points to the importance of: (1) binding different activities (e.g. planning, producing, and selling) and connecting them to inter-actor relationships that enable buyers to target large and more beneficial markets, (2) synchronising information, production, logistics and cash flows, and (3) creating trust-based relations between different VC actors, for instance between SHFs, LFs, input suppliers, distributors, retailers and customers (UNIDO 2004b).

A commonly-mentioned advantage of VCs is that producers can gain from the *changing division of labour within a chain*. They can seek involvement and specialisation in these systems at their level of competence (and where they have a competitive costs-capabilities mix) carrying out *only selected* segments and functions of the value creation process. Integrated producers can strategically lever their participation to reach higher capabilities, expand their markets, and take over different value-added activities (e.g. quality control, sorting, processing) in the system through upgrading efforts (UNIDO 2004b). Further, a useful perspective on the importance of linking producers with buyers is the previously mentioned *LLL-approach* (UNIDO 2002). SIs are needed to enhance efforts of local firms/farms to carry out the LLL-approach (ibid, Mathews 2006). The message is that inter-firm relationships have to be understood, not just from the point of business volume/profits but also from the perspective of leveraging, learning and upgrading.

Research shows that *governance* - the features of the relationships and links among various VC actors and their coordination by the Lf or its partners (other 'governors'), such as first tier suppliers, buying agents, consultants, as well as public and private SIs - has *implications for the nature and prospects of upgrading* of local firms in developing countries (such as Ugandan firms/farms). In this context, participating in explicitly-governed VCs is seen as an *effective* and *fast-track strategy* for local firms/farms to gain access - via links with Lfs - to: markets, marketing channels, credit, technologies, information, knowledge[274], skills and management practices of the LFs (and its partners). These factors can foster learning and productivity of the local firms/farms and thus mobilise the local growth potential. Specifically, VC participation can help SHFs to obtain information and knowledge about the upgrading necessary to supply markets and how to meet these requirements (UNIDO 2004b, Humphrey 2005). "The value of technical assistance [from a buyer] lies not [only] in the transfer of knowledge about market requirements, but rather in the transfer of knowledge about how to meet these requirements" (Humphrey 2005, 40). The deficit in capacities/capabilities to respond to product/process requirements of the developed countries' markets is a common feature in developing countries, particularly LDCs - that's why such assistance and learning relationships are deemed to be so important (UNIDO 2005b, 6). Crucially, every new requirement (e.g. imposed by a new standard) brings about new incompetencies of suppliers and creates a need for respective adjustment and catch-up efforts (Humphrey 2005, 34, 2004).

Integration into GVCs has been associated with the growth of a strong supplier base in a few developing countries (especially in Asia) in the past 15 years. It is suggested that a major explanation for the rapid upgrading of some local firms (e.g. newcomer suppliers) is a mix of pressure and (formal/informal) assistance from global buyers (UNIDO 2004b, Schmitz 2005b, Humphrey and Schmitz 2002, Gereffi et al. 2005). Schmitz' comment below is made with respect to GVCs but can be read in the same spirit for DVCs, e.g. exporter-farmer relations in Uganda:

> "[A]ccepting foster parents offers a fast track to product and process upgrading. Captive local firms producing for global buyers can expect to progress fast. This applies in particular to newcomers - when certain conditions are met. The fast upgrading of the suppliers results from the dual role of the buyers: they are extremely demanding but they also need to provide assistance so that these demands are met. Much of this assistance takes place in the context of detailed monitoring, i.e. not just exposing failures but also showing how these failures can be overcome. It is this combination of high challenge and [often incidental] support which propels the supplier forward and leads to fast improvement in processes and products. ... [S]upplier learning, where it occurs, is not necessarily due to an explicit and elaborate support policy of the buyer. Much learning occurs in the context of constructive monitoring, that is identifying failure and indicating ways to overcome them" (2005b, 27-8).

Further, the GVC approach brings the discussion on trade competitiveness and prospects from the macro/meso level (investment climate, interest rates, infrastructure, trade tariffs) to the *meso/micro level* of the evolution of industries (GVCs) and related firms' strategies, interactions and the like. It offers insights, not only of global buyers' governance strategies and their consequences for local firms, but also local firms' efforts to improve their performance in VCs, enhance coordination, communication and trust (e.g. with buyers, SIs and other actors), switch to more promising business partners or VCs and so on.

The *organisational* perspective of VC research is distinctive and differs from the open market approach of emphasising (abstract) market forces as the only key determinant of producing and trading agro-products. Being sensitive to actors (their motives, strategies,

274 This includes knowledge about trends in markets, standards, customer taste, organisational methods, or chain management.

embeddedness) and the links between them is also a main difference between VC analysis and conventional sector analysis. Overall, the analysis of the underlying structures and processes of the global fragmentation, relocation, and coordination of economic activities in GVCs becomes vital for entrepreneurs and policy-makers in developing countries who face challenges and opportunities in their efforts to *integrate local firms into the global economy in a competitive and beneficial manner*. GVC researchers believe it is vital for actors and stakeholders of global trade to understand: (1) the GVC structures and functioning, including (especially non-market) governance modes and dynamics in different sections along a GVC, (2) ways in which a Lf might intend to incorporate and support a local firm and allocate new tasks to it, and the (3) requirements for the latter's integration and upgrading (UNIDO 2004b, Schmitz 2005b, Humphrey and Schmitz 2002, Gereffi et al. 2005).

In summary: The characteristics of (global, regional and domestic) production and trade systems, the strategies and demands of Lfs and the features of relationships between actors along the VC are all relevant variables for the design of strategies for promotion of local firms/farms. These include strategies for relationship building and deepening with the Lf, upgrading of technology, knowledge transfer, and training (UNIDO 2004b). Insights into governance and upgrading can help to examine: (a) issues of market access for Ugandan firms and farms via better links and interactions with Lfs, and (b) related benefits and costs of VC integration, as well as requirements for the VC participation and performance of the firms/farms. It can further help (c) Ugandan firms/farms in undertaking upgrading efforts more selectively to meet specific buyer requirements, and (d) GOU in building institutional support structures, carrying out training and enhancing cooperation and learning between VC partners. It is thus essential to recognise the modes of coordination, control and cooperation in all the phases of value creation/capture: product development, production, marketing, and logistics. Each VC has its own complex reality (including power asymmetries) that favours or hinders insertion and upgrading of new local actors (ibid, Pietrobelli and Rabellotti 2004, Humphrey and Schmitz 2000, Gereffi 2005, Stamm 2004, Kaplinsky and Morris 2003).

Generally, the implications of forms of VC participation and Lf governance for upgrading of Ugandan firms/farms are manifold. There can be differences across VCs regarding upgrading possibilities, or efforts by Lfs to support the upgrading strategies of local firms/farms with knowledge, technology, technical, financial and logistical assistance, or training, advice and supervision. Hence, depending on the power asymmetries as well as different possibilities, incentives and requirements for upgrading in different VC, one can expect different prospects for firms/farms' learning, innovation and capability building.

Since interacting, learning and innovating within VCs is crucial for enhanced performance of Ugandan firms/farms, it is vital to understand VCs and the governance of relations in them, the way in which exporters benefit from links with foreign Lfs (or farmers from relations with local processors), and the related constraints. "In a nutshell, relationships matter. If policy-makers want [Ugandan actors] ...to learn fast from participating in the ... economy, they need to know whether [they] ... engage merely in transaction (buying or selling) or interaction (which involves also intensive exchange of information and the transfer of ideas)" (Schmitz 2005b, 6). In this context, "[t]he quality of relationships with global lead firms is ... particularly important for latecomer development" (Altenburg et al. 2006, 8).

There is, finally, another important point to make: the strict term 'value addition' somewhat conceals the fact that the share each VC actor gets of the final value of the product also has to do with issues of power asymmetries and bargaining power between actors in the chain, and thus in the global and regional economy at large (Hess 2008, Gibbon and Ponte 2005, Smith 2007) and related matters such as market dynamics, organisational changes in the VC, trade policies, technology effects, and political economy. The term 'value capture' might bring out this dimension more clearly (Smith 2007). This approach argues that the value of a finished commodity is divided between firms participating in the VC *according to their ability to exert different forms of monopoly power*, and not at all according to their actual contribution to its final value. Thus "values created in one link condense as prices received elsewhere, by other links in the chain, even though these separate 'links' are in fact different firms in different continents" (ibid, 27). In this view, the concept of 'value-added' should therefore be replaced by a concept of 'value-captured'. Emphasising the fact that those firms in GVCs that succeed in capturing the largest slices of final value are overwhelmingly located in Europe, Japan and North America, it argues that the most important force motivating their proliferation is the efforts of these northern hemisphere firms to support sagging profits by expanding their direct or indirect exploitation of low-waged labour in the global south.[275]

In short, Ugandan exporters might be able to capture a higher price (or portion of final price) for reasons other than technical changes in the product (e.g. going from unprocessed to processed stage, improving quality). A higher value capture might be the outcome of changes in power asymmetries in the GVC configuration that the exporters face, e.g. an increase in bargaining power on the Ugandan side. To give just two simple examples from Wiegratz et al. (2007a): the use of mobile phones and other communication channels (and the entry of ever more new Ugandan exporters) has enhanced price transparency and competition in the fruits and vegetables export business (for both the exporters and importers) and thus impacted on value capture-dynamics in this VC segment. One of the several effects has been that margins for Ugandan exporters in this industry have been *narrowed*. On the other hand, exporters could *limit* the downward price pressures from European importers to a certain extent by network-like sharing of price information: Via the phone, an exporter could get information on market export prices on a given day from their Ugandan competitors. Hence, importers' claims regarding even lower offers being made by other Ugandan exporters could be confronted. Or, as mentioned earlier, some exporters in the same sector are suffering from malpractices by their European buyers (e.g. only part or no payment is being made after delivery of the goods, or quality defects are invented); yet these practices are not regulated (e.g. sanctioned in the export destination country) in any meaningful way. Hence, Ugandan firms' *value capture* is lower than necessary due to power asymmetries. Other exporting firms (in different sectors) have reported that their value capture depends on the nature of the business relationship (e.g. arms-length or close) with the importers and of course the pattern of competition and inter-actor power imbalances in the GVC (ibid).[276] The point is

275 The author is grateful to John Smith for related clarifications. See also Taylor (2008, 2008) on power and conflict in the global economy in the context of debates about the limits of the GVC approach to capture such dimensions. See also Bair (2009) and Fold and Nylandsted Larsen (2008) for a collection of recent research on GVC matters.

276 In this industry, there are also examples of malpractices by Ugandan exporters (Wiegratz et al. 2007a, Wiegratz 2008).

that the dominant value-addition debate in Uganda (aiming at processing of raw materials) underplays dimensions of value capture in GVCs.[277]

General questions regarding GVCs in the Ugandan context include: how systematically do the private and public sectors, including the SIs, currently contextualise their work in terms of VC related dynamics and strategies? Will VC approaches become more relevant in Uganda, in informing both the private and public sectors? In the following sections the author tries to identify more specific implications of applying the VC approach to the Ugandan HRD context. Note in this regard that the studies by Wiegratz et al. (2007a, 2007b) have applied the VC approach to the context of VC governance between (a) Ugandan exporters and their European buyers, and (b) processors/traders in Uganda and their supplying farmer. The studies confirm the points and statements made above about GVCs for the Ugandan case. Below, the author draws on related findings where appropriate; however, the emphasis is first of all on the findings of other authors.[278] The two studies by Wiegratz et al. comprise a volume of over 1,000 pages; in this book the author can only point to a handful of findings which are relevant for our HRD discussion.

Clusters and value chains in Uganda: General observations and remarks

Clustering: Underexploited opportunity for stronger PSD

Clustering and value chain development are issues that need more attention in the context of Uganda's economic agenda. With a few exceptions (e.g. the flower sector), by the mid 2000s, the approaches and methodologies discussed above had not been applied on a significant scale or in a coordinated, proactive and comprehensive manner, with focus on commercial agriculture, agro-processing and the manufacturing industry. The few important interventions in this direction - by GOU, NGOs, donors and SIs - remained fragmented. A weak support system and little interaction between SIs and the industries also characterised that period. Yet, more recently, things began to change, and we see increasing concern and application of related concepts and strategies for PSD (see below).

The successes of the improvement and changes within the fish sector following the externally-induced crisis – which involved a ban of Ugandan exports to the EU due to deficiencies in production standards and quality of Nile perch in the late 1990s - should have been a stimulus for GOU and the private sector to decisively replicate the concepts applied at the time (e.g. the cluster and PPP approach) and the lessons learnt (especially, collective action to solve sectoral problems) in other sub-sectors: the stakeholder response during the fish sector crisis was significant and thus potentially instructive for the whole economy. As Ponte notes, in general "there has been a much more concerted effort to solve problems at the industry level in Uganda (and Tanzania) than has been the case in Kenya" (2005, 71-2, based on Henson and Mitullah 2004). Between 2005 and 2008, however, the fish industry experienced problems again, this time related to collectively (1) close the gaps along the chain related to compliance with EU food safety regulations and (2) address improper fishing practices which have resulted in a decline in fish stock.

277 The debate is also not very explicit at times on how to avoid the diminishing or losing of value in the chain; the post-harvest related measures to help farmers handle and store their produce better are a step in this direction, however.

278 Wiegratz et al. (2007a, 2007b) might be published as books in the near future.

The advances of collective action in the flower sector and the experience of the fish sector in the late 1990s/early 2000s demonstrated the benefits, and, in fact, necessity, of joint action and comprehensive cooperation by all stakeholders in specific sub-sectors in order to ensure vigorous and successful responses to various competitiveness challenges. It proved the benefits of the methodology, including organisational and technical recipes to foster, for instance (a) interactivity between cluster players, and (b) upgrading (production, quality and logistics) at both firm and cluster levels and thus along the VC. The experience also revealed the importance of a national LIS sensitive to the needs of export sectors. Some of the deficiencies in Uganda's fish sector prior to the crisis in the 1990s have subsequently been addressed through the adjustments and learning experiences of the restructuring process (Kiggundu 2004). Kiggundu concludes in an analysis of the case:

> "Learning to close deficiencies in local innovation system is not easy ... [I]t is simply not a matter of building organizations and having occasional interactive events to diffuse research results and information to would be users. Instead, continuous competence building programs to support firms to assimilate, accumulate tacit knowledge, interact more with suppliers, foreign firms, buyers and other actors transform all this into new and better products and processes is likely to be more effective ... Overall, [through the process of adjustment] firms learnt to seek greater knowledge inputs while support agencies learnt to diffuse this knowledge[,] better closing some of the knowledge deficiencies that existed prior to the ... ban" (ibid, 473-4).

These are important findings relevant to future interventions for the development for other agro-industrial (export) sectors. The flower and fish sector examples might be specific to the Ugandan context: *at industry (processing) level*, the two sectors have a limited number of commercial actors who operate on a relatively large scale and with state-of-the-art technology. These actors also face fairly similar market conditions and industry issues (challenges/ opportunities) and related benefits of collective action, especially given the export stimulus that binds actors together in their determination to overcome problems. Further, both sectors' business associations seem to operate quite independently from direct external influence in running the associations' affairs.[279]

Since the early 2000s, GOU has undertaken sub-sectoral interventions that are part of a cluster development or VCD menu, e.g. sub-sector-specific training and marketing initiatives. There are also initiatives to revive (formerly failed) cooperative structures, strengthen smallholder agricultural producer organisations and link them with (state supported) microfinance schemes and/or other services. Notable is a *linkage programme* currently implemented by EUg, which has so far supported training of farmers in the context of supplier development/outgrower schemes of a large brewery and sugar factory; such efforts should be continued and scaled up. EUg should undertake efforts to share their experience and 'lessons learnt' in these vital interventions as soon as possible. Also NAADS, activities have characteristics of clustering and VCD (see Box 24).

---

279 The author is grateful to Clive Drew (APEP) for the observation.

Box 24: Clustering/VCD: NAADS partnerships with lead firms, NGOs and development agencies

"*1. Agribusiness Development Component (ABDC)*

ABDC is one of the components of DANIDA's Agricultural Sector Support Programme. ABDC's activities include, among others, SME agribusiness development; strengthening capacity of producer organizations to improve business support services to smallholder farmers and to develop policy and advocacy capacities; and supporting small scale entrepreneurs through micro leasing schemes. Partnership with ABDC provides market-oriented farmers and small-scale agro-processors easy access to investment capital covering enterprises such as dairy, livestock, fruits and vegetables, maize, poultry, tea, coffee, fish, apiculture and cotton. The partnership with ABDC is enabling processors and other value chain partners access capital. For example, Jakana Fresh Fruits Company Ltd a fruit processing company with handling capacity of 3,000 kg of fruits is currently benefiting from ABDC support to increase capacity [so as] to provide a vital market linkage. The partnership has enabled Jakana to access a bank guarantee ... [to improve] on packaging fruit. The factory mainly processes citrus, mangoes and banana fruit. The company is currently buying 3 tonnes of oranges from farmers under Teso Tropical Fruit Growers Association, in Soroti district, per week.

2. Agricultural Productivity Enhancement Program (APEP)

The USAID's APEP aims to expand rural economic opportunities in the agricultural sector by increasing food and cash crop productivity and marketing. APEP addresses targeted commodities and related systems; production-to-market transactions; improvements in input distribution, technology transfer, and farmer organisations; and the development of competitive agricultural and rural enterprises such as grains. NAADS' partnership with APEP enables farmers to access vital advisory and technology development services. NAADS is partnering with APEP to enhance technology development in Upland rice production and farmer linkage to markets in Bugiri, Kumi and Luweero districts and also enhance the efficiencies of cotton production at smallholder level in the districts of Hoima, Kamuli, Iganga, Bugiri, Kaliro, Mbale, Bukedi, Kasese, Bushenyi, Tororo, Butaleja, Busia, [and] Nakasongola. Under these partnerships, farmers have been able to access improved technologies and also ... [develop] their capacity to improve marketability and quality of produce.

3. Bee Natural Products (BNP)

BNP is a private company which has installed a honey and other by-products processing plant with an annual capacity of 600 tonnes in Arua district. This has provided an opportunity and incentive for the beekeepers in the entire West Nile sub-region to intensify their production of quality honey as it provides a non-exploited market opportunity. It also enables farmers to access national, regional and international markets. Currently, a total of 120 farmer groups in the West Nile region are accessing advisory services, modern beehives (KTB and Langstroth), harvesting gear, and honey extraction equipment from BNP under this partnership. The farmers are also benefiting from a revolving fund and BNP provided the market for the honey. This has increased honey production and farmers' incomes in the region.

4. Mukwano (A.K Oils)

The Mukwano Group of Companies, a private company involved in the development and promotion of oil seeds, has a crushing capacity for 300 MT of sunflower per day. The company provides a clear opportunity for increased farmer access to improved technology; advisory services and linkage to the established agro-processing facility and market. The main objective of this partnership is to increase productivity and profitability of sunflower production through farmer organisation, and by linking farmers to markets. The partnership covers 6 subcounties of Lira, Amac, Adekwok (in Lira district) and the subcounties of Ayer, Acaba, Iceme (in Apac district). 250 lead farmers have accessed technology kits for demonstration and training.

5. The National Union of Coffee Agribusinesses and Farm Enterprises (NUCAFE)

NUCAFE is the hub of affiliation of more than one hundred associations representing more than 100,000 farmers located throughout the major coffee-producing districts of Uganda. NUCAFE is responsible for establishment of a sustainable and profitable farmer-operated organisation for the benefit of coffee farmers. It is envisaged to support the promotion of speciality coffee through technology promotion and advisory services provision including quality control. NUCAFE is supporting farmer groups and associations for organized coffee production, value addition and marketing, under this partnership.

6. Sasakawa Global 2000 (SG 2000)

SG 2000 is an NGO whose objective is to empower smallholder farmers to access services; mobilise resources for production, agro-processing and marketing; and increase farmer productivity using proven profitable technologies for production, agro-processing and marketing. Other activities include improving approaches and best practices that will scale out and sustain diversified value chains in the areas of comparative advantage through comprehensive service delivery. NAADS developed a partnership with SG 2000 for the empowerment of farmers and scaling out technology transfer and marketing through Higher Level Farmers' Organisations using the One Stop Centre Association (OSCA) approach. In partnership with SG 200, NAADS is supporting farmers in Zirobwe under Zirobwe Agaliawamu Agri-business Training Association (ZAABTA), a farmers association to access advisory services in production, post-harvest handling and marketing, and better technologies. The Association has built a one-stop-centre which includes a training hall, stockist shop, warehouse and rice mill."

Source: *Daily Monitor, 'NAADS: Transforming lives through partnerships', 18/05/2007, p. 22.*

Overall, in the last years efforts to build on and replicate the cluster approach across the economy have been mixed, but seem to be improving of late. Some of the support activities have yet to be geared, where appropriate, towards the broader and more long-term clustering perspective, which is based on the notion of joint industry action and industry-SIs interaction. The learning processes of cadres from the public and private sectors need to be fostered. The expressed commitment of GOU to engage in PPPs has, at times, been difficult to translate into practice. An example is the attempt to use the AGOA initiative stimulus to develop a textile cluster; there are various (especially political-economic) reasons why, overall, the outcome has been rather wanting.[280] Phenix Logistics, however, appears to be a company which could be a leading player in a future textile cluster. It seems to be interested in building relationships with training institutions, farmers, and government.

In general, the flower cluster can be seen as a role model in some aspects. It offers important lessons for the development of other potential clusters in areas such as: shared cluster diagnosis, vision and strategy, and projects that have a pilot character at the beginning (often short-term) and more strategic nature later in the process (rather long-term). The flower cluster case reveals the importance of training local staff, of PPPs, of interaction with foreign Lfs and other partners, the export stimulus (strong market opportunities), and the role of SIs, donors and supplier industries as well as a business association that provides complementary specialised services. The experience of this industry also demonstrates the difficulties of cluster development caused by deficits in the public sector (e.g. the electricity crisis in 2006/07, which was one reason why some companies went bankrupt and/or left the country for Ethiopia).[281]

280 In one way or another, political-economic dynamics can be expected in PPPs for VCD in Uganda; e.g. local politicians/technocrat-cum-businessmen are known for their 'interference' in local agricultural projects through tendering (author's PhD research interviews 2008).

281 See Wiegratz et al. (2007a) for details on the flower cluster activities.

Notably, the agro-processing sub-sectors almost naturally fall into a kind of cluster and linkage formation, between growers/small-scale farmers and processors in an agricultural zone, for example. Out-grower schemes - small-scale producers supplying to (large) processors or traders, e.g. in the sugar, coffee, honey, or fruits and vegetable (FV) industry - are part of such processes. However, these 'natural networks' need strategic coordination, support for cluster upgrading strategies and a specific support services infrastructure (e.g. for training and technology support). This is especially true, since the agro sector is dominated by SHFs who operate at a subsistence level; only a very small fraction is engaged in non-subsistence, market-oriented commercial production (UBOS 2006, 2003a). Consequently, the number of large-scale commercial farming enterprises remains low (e.g. compared to Kenya); the floriculture farms and a few traditional plantations of tea and sugar are owned mostly by Asians, Ugandans of Asian origin or other foreign investors.

Some of these important clustering steps were taken more recently by both the public and the private sector, e.g. in the context of NAADS activities. Clustering trends are emerging in some localities in the production of honey, FV, oil seeds, beans, sunflowers and maize. The challenge will be to strengthen this kind of model development, address the weaknesses and replicate the approach with other players in other areas, include small-scale processors in the projects, and develop policies and support measures (Wiegratz et al. 2007b). Such initiatives should be developed further so that the businesses grow into coordinated clusters. Efforts have to be increased to allow the general public and PSD community to benefit from lessons learnt and policy implications. Again, there is a role for the public sector to help in overcoming market and institutional failures that affect the provision of training and extension services in a cluster development context.

The usual precautions apply: some agents in the private sector might not be very enthusiastic about working in cluster PPPs for training, given the speed of public sector responsiveness, for example. There is also a related 'hidden cost' (e.g. comply with the 'hidden agenda' of the development agency, or reporting requirements, which might not be clear at the beginning of the arrangement) for the private sector in some of its interactions with cluster partners (GOU or donors) (van Bussel 2005). Training subsidies might reach only the lucky few and could affect efforts of firms to undertake and invest in their own training (ibid, Ribbink et al. 2005). However, these issues can certainly be worked out.

For the SME part, clustering is a way forward to establish and replicate several homogenous small-scale production units with affordable technologies (e.g. small meat processing units) that can collectively produce the quantities required to penetrate markets and establish linkages with up-market players (the UIRI approach).[282] This group of small-scale producers could then get technical assistance, mentoring and other support for upgrading efforts so that, eventually, even regional export markets could be targeted. Box 25 gives some insights into SME clustering efforts. They are firmly based on improvements in networking and cooperation patterns, and trust.[283]

---

282 SME clusters could for instance work on guaranteeing consistent quality by following the same 'script' of production.

283 See Oyelaran-Oyeyinka and McCormick (2006) regarding the incidence and role of clusters as a form of industrial organisation in Africa; the book's Ugandan case study focuses on the fish cluster (Kiggundu 2006).

Box 25: Organised SME-clusters needed in many developing countries

"Mere concentration of enterprises operating in the same sector is, however, no guarantee of success, since the advantages associated with clustering do not always emerge automatically. In many developing countries, SME agglomerations are a widespread phenomenon. On the outskirts of many cities, significant numbers of micro- and small-scale enterprises often operate close to one another and produce similar goods. While in metalworking, woodworking and textile clusters of this kind are common, few of them share the virtues of successful cluster models. In most of the cases, cooperation among firms is accidental or non existent. Although working and often living in close proximity, entrepreneurs do not share business information, discuss common problems or organize joint activities. SMEs have only sporadic relationships with providers of business development services (BDS) and are not accustomed to presenting articulated calls for action to local policy makers. These clusters are characterized by low levels of trust, latent conflicts and cut-throat competition among firms. As a result, they are locked within a vicious circle of stagnation and poverty. The transition from this stage of disorganization and stagnation to one of organization and achievement is difficult. The building of trust, constructive dialogue among cluster actors, exchange of information, identification of common strategic objectives, agreement on a joint development strategy and its systematic and coherent implementation require substantial efforts and commitment to common goals. Above all, this requires: time to invest in reciprocal knowledge and coordination, development vision beyond the daily routine, long-term commitment".

Source: *UNIDO (2001, 10-11).*

Value chains: Capabilities for value chain development are often missing

Uganda is generally marginalised in the global production of non-agro goods - especially in sub-sectors which have undergone the mentioned fragmentation of production (e.g. apparel/ textile, or footwear) - and has consequently not been exposed to most of the trends that gained momentum in global manufacturing in the last 15 years.[284] Except for the few better-organised agricultural VCs in Uganda, the level of chain management in DVCs is wanting. This is also related to firms lacking capabilities for organisation and coordination of higher-value-added activities at a competitive level for competitive markets. Related weaknesses include the level of: (1) firm specialisation, industrial organisation, chain management and collective action in numerous sub-sectors, and (2) public sector ability to facilitate the development of such systematic production and trade systems. This has made it difficult for firms to supply competitive goods in the more advanced market segments.

In some sectors (e.g. flowers, fruits and vegetables, fish, coffee), pooling of local and global sources of competitiveness, growth, innovation, learning and upgrading takes place. In this respect, sections of the private and public sector accumulate relevant experience and knowledge regarding (a) the (gainful) integration into dynamic global sectors and (b) the strategies and efforts (including collective action for capability building) needed to compete in global markets (Wiegratz et al. 2007a). Learning from participating in international markets and responding to specific export market requirements is also reported for the organic export sector, e.g. in relation to product quality, production techniques, traceability and farmers'

284 Note, there is generally a low level of FDI inflows to Africa that are *driven by global production networks*, due to low degree of production complementarities with especially advanced Asian economies (Santiso 2006).

behaviour (Gibbon 2006).[285] Overall, Uganda has yet to capture more vehemently the non-tangible benefits of effective relationships with foreign partners in terms of learning or capability building and other spillovers (Wiegratz 2008).

A key challenge for increased production and exports of Ugandan firms is to continue identifying and undertaking *beneficial* modes of integration into evolving global market structures, improve their positions within these arrangements, identify feasible LLL-opportunities, undertake the necessary collective action measures, and ensure that the required local capabilities at the level of firm, industry and SIs are developed. Both insertion and upgrading in GVCs have to be done *at competitive levels*. Even in low requirement sectors (e.g. low technology), deepened integration will be fairly demanding in terms of technology, capabilities, networks, cooperation, trust, and management systems. Simultaneous and interlinked dynamics need to be managed, e.g. the co-evolution of technological and organisational innovation (UNIDO 2004b). This assessment holds especially for the modern agro/food-processing type of industry: Processing tends to be more technology-, skill- and capital-intensive than before. Similarly, capabilities related to managing and upgrading standards and conformity infrastructure are vital: The observations below largely apply to Uganda's case and related HRD matters.

> "Not only is there greater scrutiny of production and processing techniques, but there are also stricter traceability and labeling requisites across the food supply chain ...While many in the developing countries perceive the increasing requirements as a potential and significant barrier to trade, the ability to raise capabilities in this field also presents a major opportunity for upgrading and catching-up with other high-value food-exporting developing countries. Unfortunately, while costs are immediate and easy to account for, the benefits from compliance tend to be much more difficult to ascertain ... In order to continue to trade, developing countries need to enhance private firms' ability to comply with these requirements as well as strengthen the institutional infrastructure, that helps demonstrate compliance ... [Sanitary and phytosanitary]-related risks are often not limited to one stage of production or processing. Dealing with such complex challenges in a dynamic context requires more than adopting good practices and new technologies - it involves raising domestic capacity to interact with the international system, enhancing the knowledge base, building legitimacy and trust in the domestic institutions and guiding the direction of search, experimentation and market-building for a growing business innovation system" (UNIDO 2005c, 10).

It is important to note, that once integrated in export chains, firms need to rapidly upgrade their capabilities (1) to match advantages provided by earlier entrants, (2) to compete with other firms from low-wage (yet higher capability level) regions that are simultaneously entering global production and developing their capabilities, and (3) to try to avoid the 'footloose nature' of activities (de-investment) that has been characteristic for the entry points of some chains. This requires creating strong incentives and SIs, including new and/or more responsive training facilities to build capabilities in enterprises and sub-sectors. The critical

285 Gibbon notes in his analysis of interview answers by 20 firms in the organic export business: "Each of the four operators who spontaneously introduced the subject of operational benefits from organic exporting have conventional exporting as their main business. Three of them used exactly the same expression, 'it's given us a discipline we lacked' to introduce their discussion. The disciplines that they went on to refer to were improved *product quality* on the basis of closer attention to *production techniques* (2 mentions), better understanding of how to provide *internal traceability of supply* (1 mention), learning how to do proper *crop estimates* (1 mention) and *'simply learning more about how farmers behave'* (1 mention)" (2006, 29, emphasis added).

level and mass of capabilities and capacities needed for inclusion of firms in (especially export) VCs is generally increasing due to technological progress, various upgrading activities of the existing players, or changes in VC organisation.

Past deficiencies in developing firm-level capabilities for improved participation in VCs have hindered the country's integration and catch-up process in GVCs and enlarged the gap between the existing and required capabilities for future engagements. Again, Ugandan entrepreneurs and managers will have to improve their VC performance with regard to the following issues (a) binding different activities (e.g. planning, producing, and selling) and connecting them into inter-company relationships that enable companies to target large and more beneficial markets, (b) synchronising information, production, cash flows, and (c) creating trust-based relationships, between and in different links in the chain, and between producers and immediate customers and suppliers (UNIDO 2004b). The severe difficulties in addressing these issues will be discussed below. Given the outlined agenda and the implicit need for flexible and fast but, at the same time, decisive responses to the business challenges and opportunities, Uganda will have to establish a framework that encourages - more than to date - continued restructuring and change (Rodrik 2004, 1, Kaplinsky 2005a, 12). "In a world of rapidly changing global specialisation, and even more rapidly changing technology, no country can hope to sustain income growth without the capacity to change" (Kaplinsky 2005a, 12).

Utilise upgrading potential in domestic and regional value chains

There seem to be significant – and, in comparison to GVCs, at times better - prospects for upgrading and learning (moving into higher-value-added activities such as marketing, branding, product development, and chain organisation, and building or deepening related capabilities) in the domestic and regional VCs. Not only are they in some respects less demanding and complicated export markets (than, say, the EU), but advanced local firms typically have a certain information and transport cost advantage there. Research in India and Brazil has shown that domestic/regional VCs sometimes allow for substantial functional upgrading: Local firms specialising in the (often riskier, smaller or poorer) national market are likely to develop their own designs, brands and marketing channels, including related capabilities, after which they penetrate neighbouring and global markets. One explanation might be that local VCs are likely to be less captive than global VCs, allowing local firms more space to build expertise, and develop and market their own product (Schmitz 2004, 5). By 2008, these domestic and regional dynamics seem to play out strongly in Uganda. Lall's analysis of the export composition of African exports by destination confirms certain upgrading advantages in local and regional markets:

> "Exports to industrialized countries are more primary-product intensive than those to developing countries as a whole, and even more than exports to other African countries. ... African exports have higher shares of 'pure' manufactures than to other regions, with LT and MT products taking about equal shares. This is line with expectations that exports by African countries to countries at similar levels of development would be more complex than exports to industrialized countries; however, manufactures play a very small role in intra-African exports and even less in exports to other developing countries" (2005, 18-9).

Despite the upgrading prospects for local firms in domestic and regional markets, Lall recommends a realistic approach regarding (1) the typical averse characteristics of some regional markets (relatively small, slow-growing, volatile, insecure and poorly linked by infrastructure) which might limit export prospects in *some* sectors, and (2) the competitiveness requirements (price, quality, technology) that local entrepreneurs face, also in their home/ regional markets, due to supply from non-African firms (ibid). Note that some of Uganda's major problems are linked to issues of supply-side response (e.g. volume and inconsistency) than to market access and demand. The domestic and regional market option requires a substantial level of adequate and effective support for firms' efforts in terms of specialisation, clustering, HRD, VC organisation, collective action on various competitiveness fronts (testing, standard compliance) as well as advances of traditional and emerging markets, marketing channels (upgrading of municipal, open air markets), business practices and levels of mutual trust. Advancements in this agenda can be beneficial to domestic and foreign firms alike.

Development of domestic value chains in Uganda

The following paragraphs provide a more detailed picture of the state of DVCs in Uganda (partly adopted from Wiegratz et al. 2007b). Regarding the term DVC, note that the market for products or services produced in a DVC can be in-country or abroad. To begin with, small-holder farmers (SHFs) are mostly producing without due consideration for market requirements and operations of the entire DVC; they often sell to random buyers who come along the villages/roads (spot markets). Challenges regarding market access for SHFs and appropriate coordination and cooperation systems between them and their buyers remain constraints to smallholder agricultural development. SHFs are constrained as follows:

- They are often organised in a scattered way and are not properly linked to the Lfs of DVCs. Lfs of DVCs in Uganda are buyers such as commercial lead farms, agro-processors and exporters who, for instance, coordinate out-grower schemes.
- Smallholder agriculture remains governed mainly by market forces: The farmers' relationships and interaction with Lfs are limited (thus the flow of information from the Lf to SHFs) and can hardly be used to plan, improve farm production and farmers' skills. Most SHFs thus lack product-market combinations to govern them in producing according to the requirements of specific markets.
- There is a limited number of buyers in the country who are engaged in developing a stable, long-term, trust-based and mutually beneficial business relationship with SHFs, and are willing to invest in farmers' capacity development (see Wiegratz et al. 2007b for related case studies). Most buyers are short-term oriented and only interested in the mere business transaction, with often low regard for quality issues.[286] Malpractices of buyers (and their small-scale agents) are widespread and discourage farmers.[287]

286 Very short-term oriented business actions gained ground in the pre-1986 years of conflict. Apparently, this pattern continues to impact business culture in Uganda to-date. However, also the short-term focus of an emerging neoliberal business culture in the 1990s ('free' markets, making a quick profit anyhow, low regard for: inter-actor relationships, fairness, propriety, justice, product quality) contributes to the current state of business practices and norms in the agricultural sector (author's PhD research).

287 The author's use of the word 'malpractice' (or 'deficits' in business norms and practices) implies a certain value judgment by the author (e.g. some degree of critical assessment of - in our context of agricultural trade - of outright deception, dishonesty, lying, misuse of trust, weighing scale or product quality manipulation, produce theft, or other forms of stealing), and actors, readers, or other analysts may disagree. Labelling them as 'deficits' (and identifying them as a 'problem') is an attempt to point out, among others, that (a) they (are likely to) have adverse development effects, assumed or real, and (b) involved actors themselves (the 'victims' and, at times, the 'perpetrator') highlight malpractices as a problem (Wiegratz et al. 2007a, 2007b, author's PhD research). Also, the term 'malpractices' is used in this book as a kind of proxy for related political,

The few existing studies on DVCs in Uganda have revealed the relevance of the analysis of VC governance strategies of domestic Lfs (those coordinating out-grower schemes, and building long-term-oriented trade relations with SHFs) in order to promote production, trade and investment in the country better; in particular, upgrading commercially viable production and trade systems and related HR (see below).

The BSMD body of work: Findings of pioneering research on DVCs

The pioneering research work and experience of the previously mentioned BSMD programme, which focused on DVC development (hereafter: DVCD) in mainly export-oriented agro-sectors, highlight relevant issues. The related studies reveal earlier observations about the importance of skills, capabilities and SoC related to chain development and management, and the related weaknesses in the Ugandan agro-sectors (BSMD 2005, van Bussel 2005, AT Uganda et al. 2005, Bear and Goldman 2005, McGuigan et al. 2005, Ribbink et al. 2005).[288]

The studies point to deficits of VC actors (and thus VCs) in Uganda in terms of trust, networking, as well as business organisation, behaviour, ethics and practices. There is a low level of long-term relationships, trust, cooperation and contract use, and a high level of ad hoc and informal arrangements and opportunistic business behaviour, with examples of cheating, false promises and misinformation of different VC players (farmers, brokers, traders, and processors). Thus many VCs are fragmented and characterised by spot market practices, a low quality culture, and unreliable supply quantities. This affects long-term-oriented and sustainable DVCDs adversely, particularly product volume, quality, consistency as well as knowledge transfer, joint action, specialisation, economies of scale, and productivity (van Bussel 2005).[289]

---

social, economic and cultural processes which underpin the practices and are manifold, complex and not yet researched in detail. Further research might point out that other terms (e.g. moral economy, Thompson 1971, 1980 and Scott 1979, or economic disengagement, Baker 2000) are more helpful to investigate the related topics. Finally, some practices (e.g. those related to gross injustices, malpractices that target the weak in a society) are critiqued because of the author's personal (moral/political-economic) standpoint.

288 These studies have used a supply chain approach; however, this comes close to the VC approach. The terms VCs and supply chains are used interchangeably in this book; related insights are usually relevant for both. The related BSMD documents, tools, and guidelines can be downloaded from: www.bsmd.vanbussel.biz. The author is grateful to Peter van Bussel, the BSMD project manager, for the helpful discussions and comments on matters of value chain development and related issues of business practices in Uganda. See also the valuable *Uganda specific VC studies* by Mbabazi (2005) on the milk industry, Asiimwe (2002) on the coffee sector, Ponte (2005) on standards in the fish export industry, Gibbon (2006) on certified organic cotton export firms, and Muhumuza et al. (2007) on governance in a timber value chain. Asiimwe's insightful work reveals the political and socio-economic dimensions of changes in the organization and prevailing practices in the coffee sector in the post-independence period.

289 It is important to note that what this author discusses under 'malpractices', here in agricultural commerce, has been an issue in Uganda in both colonial and postcolonial decades. In other words, this element of business culture emerged some time back and has been reshaped (by domestic and foreign actors) ever since. In the available literature, the terms discussed in this regard include the following: excessive profiteering, smuggling, black market, parallel market, secondary economy, power brokers, ill-gotten wealth, magendo operations, illegality, breakdown of law and order, erosion of morals, corruption (including cuts, kick-backs, air supply, ghost soldiers/teachers) (Green 1981, Kasfir 1983, Jamal 1991, Mamdani 1995, Kabwegyere 1995, Tangri and Mwenda 2003, Thompson 2003, Asiimwe and Nahamya 2006). Thompson (2003) shows how import and pricing practices in colonial times were element of (political-economic and moral) debates in

According to the studies, strategies of Lfs regarding SHFs typically aim at *lowering costs* and *offsetting supply instability* in terms of quantity or quality. To understand these strategies one has to explore VC issues such as: (1) Lfs' perceptions of market problems and solutions, (2) investment along VCs (e.g. cold chains), (3) technology, knowledge and monitoring requirements, (4) relationship building in the VC for mutual commercial advantage, (5) patterns of training, technical assistance and other extension services given to SHFs by the Lf or other VC actors, and importantly, (6) Lfs' calculations of different options in terms of costs (investment, coordination, monitoring, training of SHFs) and benefits of SHFs incorporations into the VC.[290]

A significant finding is that LFs which organise and coordinate DVCs face risks and the initial costs of including SHFs feasibly in their VC; in the structural context of a small base of commercial farmers ('critical mass problem'), opportunistic behaviour and other inadequate business practices, a vast informal sector and a considerable level of poverty-related skills and knowledge deficits. The level of organisation and collective action of SHFs was relevant in determining the LFs' (a) *coordination costs* and (b) *risks* (e.g. regarding input supply, trust and market dynamics), two important determinants of VC dynamics between LFs and SHFs. Farmer mobilisation and organisation as well as training and other technical assistance - which was partly supported by donors - has helped in reducing coordination and supervision costs and risk for the Lf (Ribbink et al. 2005, van Bussel 2005).[291] Box 26 presents some findings of the BSMD study on successful supply chains in Uganda (Ribbink et al. 2005). The three most vital success factors in the context of formation and management of VCs with SHFs in Uganda are: (i) access to markets, (ii) strong VC linkages, and (iii) mutual trust and commitment between VC partners. Related problems include: the small scale of operations in the agricultural sector, and the risk for domestic Lfs of integrating new out-grower farmers into their VC (ibid). See also Box 27.

---

the public (which centered around notions of fairness, unfairness, or acceptable, inacceptable). The political economy of the relationship and practices of trade between farmers and (private/ public) buying actors and institutions was part of the debate (and conflict) in colonial Uganda and thereafter (e.g. Shepherd 1955, Bunker 1991, Brett 1993, Bibagambah 1996, Mamdani 1999, Asiimwe 2002). Further note that, no doubt, commercial malpractices are (probably) part of every country's business culture; the issue is to study the details (e.g. reasons, extent, form, changes, interpretations) and implications of malpractices for a particular time and in a particular place. In Uganda's case, it is noteworthy that malpractices have remained a considerable feature of the post-conflict, liberalised economy; this continuity needs further research.

290 In their response to rising requirements in export markets, firms have to optimise economies of scale in fixed investment and quality monitoring along DVCs, for example (Gibbon 2003).

291 One of the relevant findings by Gibbon (2006): Asked about the main challenges specific to organic export production, additional staff supervision/monitoring costs was one of the most often mentioned aspects. Mentioned, yet at lower frequency was also requirement for additional literate workers and lack of availability of technically qualified staff (ibid, 27-8). See also findings of Bear and Goldman (2005).

Box 26: The importance of relationships in supply chain management

The experiences and lessons learned in domestic supply chain management - as analysed by Ribbink et al. (2005) for firms in the coffee, dried fruits and fresh vegetable sectors - offer valid insights into current development challenges in agro-industries, including the benefits, costs and rationale of certain SC interventions. "If we were to select the three most important success factors [for the value chains analyzed] they would be: 1. the access to high value markets, which provide high returns and thus financial incentives to all the supply chain partners, 2. the strong vertical linkages in the supply chain and 3. the high level of mutual trust and commitment between the partners. Of course, the pre-financing that the lead firms provide is also important, but without trust, adequate use of these funds and inputs or access to markets it would be wasted. Technical assistance provided to suppliers both by the lead firm and by third parties are also very important, both for their direct effect and because they strengthen the vertical linkages and commitment between the chain partners. Likewise a clear understanding of the rationale for the partnership [as well as the role of the respective actors in the chain] is essential for mutual trust and commitment ... The success factors are not a given, but require constant attention and monitoring by the lead firm ... The main problems seem to be the relatively small scale of operations compared to the costs of managing the supply chain and meeting all the quality requirements. At the same time the risk involved in expanding the supply base by working with more [supply chain partners is significant] ... It is better to grow slowly but surely, as all three supply chains have done, than to expand quickly".

Source: *Ribbink et al (2005, 34-5).*

Box 27: Scant use of contracting in the agricultural sector

"Generally, farmers are not organized. Individual farmers produce very small quantities and sell in bits, as they need cash. Because of low volumes, farmers are price takers with no market power. Where farmers' organizations exist they deal primarily with production issues rather than marketing. The legacy of the cooperative movement collapse in Uganda has left behind a distinct lack of trust among farmers, especially when it comes to financial management. Even so, the local cultures often rely on informal arrangements, especially between family members and people from the same community. Traditionally asking for a contract is interpreted to mean that you do not trust the other party. It is an insult. From the perspective of the traders, markets in Uganda are thin. As a result, prices are often quite volatile. The future is unknown and thus traders are generally unable/unwilling to commit to prices and quantities in advance. Lastly, contracts are seen as complicated and costly. Many farmers and traders do not understand the language used in contracts or know how to draw one up".

Source: *AT Uganda (2005, 1-2).*

Widespread deficient business practices in DVCs in Uganda

BSMD studies (Bear and Goldman 2005, AT Uganda et al. 2005, van Bussel 2005) on local sourcing strategies in agro-sectors (e.g. in the FFV sector) reveal that the majority of firms apply *horizontal (or extensive) business strategies* and operate merely on *spot markets*. This strategy is characterised by sourcing firms having loose contacts with many buyers (agents) and suppliers (e.g. SHFs) across the country with whom they do business with in a rather opportunistic, risky, short-term-oriented fashion with low levels of contract use, joint planning and coordination. This strategy reduces prospects for the following: incentives to consistently produce quality products, productivity, cooperation, learning, and capability building in the DVC. Due to its low use of contracting, the strategy leads to high transaction and aggregation costs in doing agro-business. Only a few firms *apply intensive or vertical sourcing strategies* that are based on a firm's strong and long-term collaboration with a few buyers and suppliers. This strategy generally allows for joint investment, coordination, and learning and training of VC actors and thus the exploiting of market opportunities, also in more difficult and niche-product segments or export markets (ibid). The dominance of extensive strategies is widespread according to a study covering 17 sub-sectors:

> "[M]ost farmers ... sell purely on the spot market with no prior agreement or contract ... Therefore, the bulk of the supply, particularly in the wet markets, comes from opportunistic producers, traders and brokers that have an extensive sourcing strategy. Once traders receive an order they start searching for supplies or the other way around, when they come across produce they start searching for a buyer. This searching is costly and rather uncertain because very little information is available and most producers have only small quantities of goods available. Quality issues are then put at a lower priority than finding a buyer or supplier. Consequently, losses are high as all sorts of false promises are being made and contracts are not being used" (van Bussel 2005, 5).

A field survey related to the development of a contract template notes that only a few farmers interviewed expressed the need for contracts. "The attitude is, 'This is the way it has always been done.' Where there is a contract/agreement it is generally initiated by the buyer rather than the seller. The seller has little or no input in the terms of the agreement" (AT Uganda et al. 2005, 1). Further,

> "[t]he lack of contracting results in very high aggregation and transaction costs in doing business in the agriculture sector in Uganda. There are substantial risks for both farmers and traders. Parties to the transaction have little recourse in the event that unscrupulous trading partners abscond without meeting their end of the bargain. Without documentation, farmers can do very little when traders take the product and fail to pay. The case studies were filled with bad stories of producers who were cheated when buyers disappeared with their hard earned products" (ibid, 2).

The prevalent lack of contracting practices and the deficits in enforceability of contracts (Gibbon 2006)[292] - and the incomplete understanding of related matters in the first place - is a hurdle for export-led growth and rural development through inclusion of SHFs in VCs. GOU and donors have paid little direct attention to this issue. The efforts of *some* agencies towards better SHF organisations are a step in the right direction, as they generally foster use of formalised agreements, reduce transaction costs in the VC and facilitate long-term relationships between SHFs and market intermediaries (AT Uganda et al. 2005, 2).

The above findings of deficient business links and practices in DVCs offer a major explanation for deficits in PSD in Uganda, especially for the problems of productivity, innovation, learning, HRD, cooperation, economies of scale, business organisations, specialisation as well as competitive and consistent supply for domestic and export markets.[293]

---

292 Gibbon notes: "Many operators [in the certified organic export sector] felt that most undertakings applying to outgrowers were hardly worth the paper they were written on in any event, since their enforcement was difficult or even impossible. Mentions of enforcement mechanisms in respect of commitments made by exporters were also notable for their absence" (2006, 22).

293 For instance, regarding rejected export consignments due to product standards problems, or, generally, business losses and failures due to inconsistent supply and non-compliance to standards.

Few farmers benefit from embedded services within DVCs

The BSMD work has also pointed to the importance of considering and strengthening those business services that are provided or could be provided in a commercially viable and thus entrepreneurial manner within a developed DVC: by buyers, input suppliers, business partners and acquaintances (e.g. bankers and lawyers). These services are provided to SHFs alongside or within normal business transactions within a VC. They are therefore called *embedded business services*, which can take the form of advice, information, knowledge, skills, training, learning, technical advice, innovation stimulus, quality feedback and control mechanisms, technology, credit, extension services or systems of administration, communication and management (van Bussel 2005, 8-12, 17).[294] Embedded services are usually based on a certain business rationale for providers; e.g. marketing, customer care, market development, price premium, improved and long-term supply, reduced coordination cost and risks in dealing with producers (ibid).

Such services can be offered in an informal and random, or a formal and structured manner. In Uganda, the former is the typical case while the latter can be found in relation to some larger companies. In both cases, a strong, lasting and market-oriented business relationship is a key requirement for the provision of such services. "This requires business people to be honest, transparent and willing and able to communicate effectively. It further also requires mutual investments and appreciation of long-term benefits. Moreover, businesses have to be able to rely on and trust each other" (ibid, 12). While, in general, SHFs can access business support through embedded services if they have long-lasting relationships with their buyers, "many businesses do not benefit as much as they probably could from these services because of weak business linkages. This is partly due to poor business behaviour and their opportunistic business approach" (ibid, 2). The low level of bridging social capital (e.g. links with actors outside one's own group, see Knorringa and van Staveren 2006) and trust in the country could have a significant impact on the scope, strength and benefits of such wider embedded support networks, thus inter-firm relationships and HRD for agro-sector development more generally. Note, the importance of strong inter-actor relationships for agribusiness development is increasingly recognised in SSA; the publication 'Trading up: Building cooperation between farmers and traders in Africa' (KIT and IIRR 2008) is one of the most vital publications in this regard, with a range of insightful case studies.[295]

Besides, the private sector in Uganda will have to continue identifying those products where the profits can finance and thus justify the costly and long-term-oriented establishment and management of competitive VCs, including the provision of embedded services. Importantly, costly skills development of chain actors generally helps in reducing coordination/supervision costs and risk for Lfs who wish to establish reliable supplier networks. Nevertheless, public support for VCD aspects is recommended.

---

294 These services are *in part* similar to strategic or operational BDS provided on a stand-alone and for-fee basis (e.g. entrepreneurship/skills development training). The latter is often highly subsidised (up to more than 50% of costs) and has outreach and sustainability deficiencies. Other non-embedded services and support can be obtained from enterprise-development organisations, government, NGOs, development agencies, and training institutions or from private relationships, e.g. family, relatives and friends (van Bussel 2005, 1-2, 8-12, Gibb 1988).

295 See also Kaplinsky and Morris (2003) for general remarks on high- and low-trust value chains.

The insights of this set of BSMD studies - and the follow-up studies by Wiegratz et al. (2007a, 2007b) - have apparently not yet reached mainstream policy circles, SIs or the producers in general (with few exceptions). While VC organisation and efforts to increase efficiencies in production systems (including related capabilities of farmers) have been, to some extent, a field of intervention for donors and GOU (ibid, Ribbink et al. 2005, van Bussel and Nyabuntu 2007), policy-related changes have overall not been significant to date.

Further challenges in upgrading of export-oriented DVCs

The unclear (but partly improving) policy situation regarding VCD matters undermines competitiveness prospects of key VCs in Uganda, for instance in the export-oriented agricultural and food products, which mainly go to high income countries (three-quarters of the formal agro-food trade) with high standard requirements. Studies in the fish sector chain reveal the gap in terms of production standards and related capabilities along the chain. Factories in the industrial processing and exporting part of the chain operate at the high level of international production standards and market requirements (food safety and quality standards) and use modern processing techniques. On the other hand, the general features of the fishing, maintenance and transport methods, and landing sites that determine the quality of the raw material for processing and exports instead - except for a number of upgraded landing sites and beach management units (BMUs) - are not acquiescent with basic hygiene requirements. This creates a considerable risk for the sector in terms of prospects of sanctions by the EU and/or international customers regarding Ugandan products due to non-compliance to standards in certain 'weak links' along the chain (Ponte 2005, USAID 2005, WB 2006b).

Ponte's remarks give an idea of the problems in the fish VC and the difficulties in solving them. These remarks help to anticipate the HR dimension of VCD. Positively, several of the fish processors have been setting up active linkages with BMUs, including the provision of cold-chain facilities. Many aspects raised below have relevance for other export-oriented agro-sectors, e.g. issues of traceability, quality control, demonstration of standard compliance and chain coordination in the upstream parts of the chains (SHF level):

> "[T]he fish safety management and traceability systems are in practice applied to only half of the Ugandan value chain - from landing site to export. And even in this case, the systems only apply to a very limited number of landing sites. Given the volumes exported, it is unreasonable to expect that all (or even a sizeable proportion of) fish is landed at these sites. Also, it is not clear at all whether the EU itself complies with the food safety system 'by the book' within its boundaries. The problem is that if the EU insisted on effective implementation in the other half of the value chain (from catch to landing site), the very nature of artisanal fishing on Lake Victoria would be in peril. A possible 'second crisis' would result in a very different kind of fish industry at the catch level – one operating larger boats and fleets, more concentrated, and possibly foreign-owned or financed. The implications in terms of employment and incomes for lakeshore communities would be far reaching. There are immense hurdles in applying HACCP [Hazard Analysis and Critical Control Point] principles, Good Hygiene Practices (GHPs) and traceability on fishing boats. Rather than trying to achieve this, the industry and regulators should pressure the EU to allow a special regime that applies to artisanal fisheries. Otherwise, it will be at the mercy of EU oversight (or purposive negligence of the situation) as it is the case currently ... [Further], even within the half of the value chain that is apparently functioning properly in terms of food safety management, cracks and inconsistencies are emerging. The quality of landing site inspections is reported to be unsatisfactory. The costs of continuing to test every export consignment are exacting. The export quality assurance system is in theory run

on an ex-post recall basis, but in practice is privately based on commercial principles of redress of quality claims (price adjustments), not regulatory ones (seizure of consignments). While this is a reasonable development in view of previous experiences of Uganda with EU food safety authorities, it defies the very principle of risk minimization upon which food safety regulation is based" (2005, 73).

The above insights demonstrate that the growth, export and industrialisation strategies of GOU and the private sector imply significant challenges in terms of developing basic and advanced local *systems* of production and trade, and related hygienic and agricultural practices, capacities, skills[296], know-how/know-why, as well as social capital along the DVC. This exercise - which has started with some government and donor funded projects in some issue areas - has to be expanded. Most likely, it has to go down to the level of smallholder fishermen, farmers and intermediate traders and even their families (e.g. basic hygiene to meet requirements for 'farm-to-table' traceability) if access to and success in certain consumer markets are to be retained and/or expanded.[297]

"Uganda has developed pockets of enhanced SPS/quality management capacity that have evolved in response to export market requirements (such as for fish) or acute SPS problems (such as certain animal diseases), typically supported by donors. But it lacks a broader strategy to utilize agro-food standards to enhance its international competitiveness and to protect human, plant, and animal health" (WB 2006a, xiii).

This exercise is complex: it goes in the direction of transforming domestic production, trade and logistics systems, including standardising and harmonising related systems to perform good practices for agro-food safety and agricultural health, and food safety systems. As said above, these systems are currently often affected by fragmented chains and adverse business practices. An agenda to upgrade DVCs involves the poorer players at the upstream part of the chain and could thus help the poor to profit from export-led growth: What is at stake is the *role* and *form of participation* of Ugandan SHFs in GVCs (Gibbon 2003, Ponte 2008) and related implications for forms of industrialisation as well as poverty reduction effects in Uganda. Certainly, economic agents along the chain will have to collaborate more with each other and coordinate their planning, production, technology, information sharing (including joint and timely problem sharing and solving) and management systems in order to increase systemic efficiency and produce a consistent product (van Bussel 2005, 3, 7). This agenda faces challenges in the Ugandan socio-economic setting but also political-economic context.

One important point here is the link between business practices and HRD: The dilemma here is that efforts in formal education (UPE etc.) or technical training can have limited positive effects if the above problems at the level of business systems and practices, and their root causes, cannot be resolved. The status quo can mean that *further on-the-job learning and skills development and the related application in daily business activities of knowledge and skills obtained in the ETS are severely constrained by an opportunistic and short-term business perspective that is dominating large sections of the world-of-work.* Respective production and trade structures

296 From hygiene to record-keeping skills as well as capabilities to deal with improved production techniques for post-harvest handling, processing, and packaging storage, and a number of interactive capabilities.

297 A WB study on prospects of Ugandan exports notes: "Increasing requirement for traceability by the European supermarkets makes it even more difficult for small-farmers to participate in horticulture exports" (2006b, 83).

set incentive and opportunity structures for day-to-day learning. More generally, deficient business practices in the private sector limit opportunities for engaging in and gaining from what Biggs et al. (1995) call *private and collective learning mechanisms*, which are so essential for firms' productivity enhancement.[298]

Other findings on value chain governance in Ugandan context[299]

Ugandan firms in Global Value Chains with European buyers

Wiegratz et al. (2007a) carried out a GVC study on issues of *governance* and *upgrading* in business relationships between Ugandan firms (UFs) and their buyers in Europe (EBs for European buyers), in particular the UFs' experiences in terms of integration, coordination, cooperation, challenges and upgrading in the GVCs.[300] UFs were producers, traders, and - in the case of tourism - tour operators. The study is the first one of its kind in Uganda regarding: (1) the application of the GVC framework and (2) the carrying out of in-depth interviews with VC actors about their business relations and coordination, in particular with buyers in Europe about trade with their Ugandan counterparts.

Selected findings

The study reveals the numerous and complex challenges UFs had to tackle (often in partnership with the EBs) to enter into and compete in GVCs: for instance, it took time to establish a set of relationships with both domestic and foreign actors in the chain, to understand market processes and standard requirements, to master a new technology and new processes, or to attain an adequate level of product quality. The persistent challenge for UFs, to develop appropriate HR, was significant across all sub-sectors. Further, UFs had to (proactively) search for the GVC arrangements that suit them best, according to their levels of development and stimulus needs.

There were variations in governance forms in the relationships studied: from arm's-length to network and hierarchical governance patterns, for various reasons. The report shows that the *organisational setup* of the GVCs with EBs, and thus *forms* of UF-EB relationships, matter (both positively and negatively) for UFs' export undertakings, hence for economic development in Uganda. The detailed accounts of the respondents allow a good understanding of the specifics of this point, e.g. when, how and why governance matters. The respondents noted a range of changes in the division of labour and governance patterns in certain GVCs, including:

298 In Biggs et al. (1995), "[t]wo types of learning mechanisms are distinguished: private and collective. Private learning mechanisms may be internal to the firm, such as in-house training and R&D, or external, involving relationships with buyers and suppliers, interactions with other firms through subcontracting, industry networks, and hiring local or foreign consultants. Collective mechanisms, on the other hand, consist of technical support services provided by NGOs, business associations, the government or donors" (WB 1996).

299 This section is adopted from the summaries of Wiegratz et al. (2007a, 2007b); the summaries were compiled by the author with support from the co-authors.

300 EBs were from the UK, Netherlands, Belgium and Germany. Key areas for research and analysis included: (a) linking strategies of UFs and EBs and rationale of the trading relationship, (b) discussions and activities in the early phase of the relationship including GVC entry requirements and challenges for UFs, (c) forms and dynamics of GVC governance including UF-EB cooperation, (d) UFs' upgrading and related assistance received from support institutions, and (e) prospects of the relationships, including support needed from GOU and other SIs.

(a) enhanced local value addition activities or (b) a move from arms-length towards more thick (e.g. network-like) relations between UFs and EBs. Such changes - which are driven by various forces - can imply new benefits and challenges (due to new requirements) for the UFs. Further GVC restructuring, e.g. to reduce costs and improve the efficiency of the GVC, is anticipated in some sub-sectors.

Main driving forces for the GVC arrangements include: quality requirements, contractual obligations and related threats of penalties for deficits (from EBs or other actors along the GVC), technology, standards, regulations, investments, increase in global supply and competition, market dynamics, air freight availability and costs, volume requirements, or levels of mutual trust and local expertise. Another major driving force is high labour costs in Europe, which partly motivated (i) the setting up of EB-UF VCs in the first place (e.g. flower industry), and (ii) the ongoing outsourcing of particular activities from the EB to the UF once the GVC is running (examples exist in almost all sub-sectors). A number of EBs said they welcome and encourage enhanced local value addition in Uganda.

In addition, while some UFs noted a worsening negotiation position (bargaining power), mainly due to oversupply in the market and a significant increase in production and transport costs, many UFs reported an improvement in their negotiation position with the EBs. A main reason for this improvement was strengthened HR - or, the knowledge, information, capabilities, skills, and experience that the UFs accumulate over time while they operate and learn in GVCs. Improved local HR of the UFs - because better HR contributed to improved performance and reduced risk of failure of the UFs - also tended to result in more network forms of governance, which were characterised by an advanced UF-EB relationship and more interactive and intense coordination and cooperation. The more network-like form often had a positive impact on UFs' performance and growth. The finding suggests a prime role for the HR factor with respect to UFs' advancements in GVCs, towards a relation with buyers that is characterised by more interactive, relational and beneficial forms of economic exchange, partnership and dialogue.

Regarding switching to another business partner, some respondents reported that switching is easy and related to low costs. There are other cases that point to considerable switching difficulties and costs; these are related to various relationship dimensions such as: (1) loyalty, mutual understanding, reputation, contractual obligations and the VC set-up (organisation, relationships, investment in the partner's capacity), and (2) finding a new partner and starting from scratch (building the trust/understanding between actors, adjusting to new buyer' requirements).

Upgrading of the UFs took place in terms of products/services as well as production and delivery processes; there are also cases of technology acquisition and new quality management systems. Main driving forces for upgrading were: VC requirements, competition, demand changes, and industry standards. Further driving forces were: EB demands, UF performance problems, UF strategy and enhanced local capabilities.

For some UFs, the positive upgrading effects contributed to market consolidation, productivity, customer satisfaction and loyalty, as well as profitability, and thus progress towards enhanced sustainability of their businesses. Yet, not every UF reaped upgrading benefits. Most EBs noted that UFs' upgrading (of products, processes, and practices, including communication and reliability) was considerable to date and often had a high impact on

UF-EB business. EBs noted that upgrading can benefit UFs, especially in terms of staying in business, thus gradually improving the relation with the EB and jointly developing and making use of market opportunities over time. More consistent business, reduced costs, better sales, contracts, and prices were also among the benefits identified; however, UFs' upgrading benefits could be limited or non-existent due to competition, oversupply, demand changes and price pressures.

Regarding the feasibility of upgrading, UFs mainly stated that upgrading is costly but necessary, especially in order to improve their competitiveness, comply with standards and stay in business. Some UFs reported that advantages related to successful upgrading eroded after a relatively short period of time, which made it necessary to undertake new upgrading initiatives. For many UFs, however, upgrading was vital to stabilize and consolidate the business operations, including the links with EBs. It helped in: (i) operating closer to requirement levels, (ii) carrying out more efficient production and trade activities, and (iii) achieving more consistent quality supply, fewer losses, better margins, enhanced learning processes, and a reputation as a good supplier. Thus, while upgrading does not necessarily come with higher prices, it can still be seen to be vital in building and maintaining export competitiveness. Yet, upgrading is costly and requires expertise; thus it calls for state support

Cooperation between Ugandan firms and European buyers

There are significant differences within and between sub-sectors studied in terms of the level and form of cooperation between UFs and EBs; the differences have considerable consequences for the speed and depth of advancement of particular UFs, hence the competitiveness of the EB and GVC as a whole. Cooperation can feed information, knowledge and know-how into the operations of the UF on a regular basis. Strong cooperation forms which assisted the UFs to upgrade products and processes (and sometimes technology) were particularly important in the kick-off phase of a new export sub-sector; especially in the cases of fish, flowers and FV - all of them non-traditional export sub-sectors that started from a low or zero export base only some years back. UF-EB cooperation was essential to speed up the learning and growing of the UFs and thus the development of these sub-sectors as a whole. One could learn from these experiences, that there is potential for cooperation of UFs with foreign buyers which can help PSD in Uganda.

On the other hand, not all UFs reported well-built structures of cooperation with the EBs, and there are a number of significant challenges and conflicts in some EB-UF arrangements. Yet, many UFs gave a positive assessment of the current level of cooperation with their EBs; many EBs also assessed the cooperation level with the UFs to be good or very good. These overall positive assessments could imply that relationship-related learning and improvement efforts of both UFs and EBs bear fruit and have facilitated cooperation to date.

UF-EB cooperation was typically based on some form of social relationship (as opposed to more arms-length, anonymous interactions), and a certain level of trust, loyalty, joint objectives and thus incentives to continue or deepen the relationship. Interviews showed that deteriorating production and logistics conditions in Uganda (e.g. electricity and air freight) which lower the volume traded and increase costs and uncertainty in export business, not only lower the competitiveness of both the UFs and EBs (hence, the GVC) but can undermine UF-EB relations and cooperation. Such deteriorating trends can delay or wipe out the materialisation of *planned* cooperation benefits (cooperation deepening), and even lower *existing* cooperation levels (up to EBs considering terminating the relationship). The benefits lost to the UFs due to a souring or discontinued relationship with cooperative EBs go beyond export revenues: it involves losses in areas such as product development, provision of advice and technology, sharing of information, knowledge, and ideas, as well as learning via repeated dealings with these buyers; such relationship damages could be hard to fix. Thus, while soft competitiveness factors (trust, communication, cooperation, see below) are crucial for UFs to foster and benefit from EB cooperation (in most GVCs studied), it is worthy of note that hard competitiveness factors - business volume, quality, price, production/transport conditions and costs, political stability, socio-economic factors - are relevant to maintaining and improving relations and cooperation with EBs.

Relevance of soft competitiveness factors for succeeding in business with European buyers

The study revealed that soft issues such as trust, communication and cooperation are core issues in GVCs, for both UFs and EBs. The study sums this up - from the view of the UFs vis-à-vis the EBs - as the relevance of firm-level soft competitiveness factors (SCFs), which include the following: trust (e.g. being trustworthy and able to develop and deepen trust with EBs), honesty, transparency, coordination, reliability, loyalty, responsiveness, communication, relationship management, social skills, business practices and ethics as well as proactive behaviour and eagerness to learn in the business relation with the buyer. UFs' deficiencies in the above categories can have damaging effects, e.g. when UFs are opportunistic and ill-treat EBs; and vice-versa. There are significant examples of cases where UFs have (developed) a strong SCF set, e.g. in matters of interaction, communication, responsiveness, trust and transparency.

Results across sub-sectors revealed that UF-EB business relations can grow over time, beyond arms-length into a network and close social relationship with a considerable level of mutual trust, understanding and commitment which, in turn, strengthens both the GVC (thus EB) and the UF. Consequently, - and as the report's examples of cooperation successes and failures reveal - UFs need social and interactive as well as entrepreneurial and organisational capabilities and respective business ethics, practices and know-how to initiate, manage and enhance, where desired, both the relations and cooperation with foreign buyers, and increase the cooperation benefits for both parties involved. Another basic but important message of the findings is that entering and advancing (and, leaving) relationships with particular foreign buyers in a proper manner is an important competency of engaging in export trade. Those UFs that cannot sufficiently reap cooperation benefits might find it more difficult to advance competitively than UFs that are 'cooperation champions'; and UFs that cannot make adequate relationship decisions - when and how to enter and leave a relationship with a buyer, or deepen cooperation - might advance more slowly.

There is a dimension of learning related to the above issues; often, UFs had to improve their business practices, e.g. learn how to communicate properly, be responsive to the issues raised by the buyer, or develop trust. One could therefore say that the strength of the cooperation champions is related to both their 'initial endowments' (the communication skills that the entrepreneur/staff have at the beginning of the engagement in export business) and day-by-day learning. UFs might find it useful to move beyond measuring their performance in conventional categories only (product quality, return on investment, energy efficiency), and include relationship categories.

The research revealed further that network-type relations require not only strictly technical but also (and equally important) 'soft' capabilities. Local firms that develop or possess the HR needed to enhance responsiveness, reliability, communication, flexibility and trust vis-à-vis the foreign buyer can establish the precondition for advanced and transformed GVC relations (towards more 'equal partner' and more beneficial network types). This, in turn, seems to improve the likelihood that UFs reap increased benefits from their integration into GVCs.

Markedly, respondents suggested that 'getting it right' in GVCs (developing a mutual understanding/trust, improving the VC efficiency, making good business) can take several years. It is thus important that UFs survive the early years (to reap the benefits of the later relationship periods) and keep a commitment, where appropriate or possible, to their GVC, so as to accumulate product-specific HR. Uganda has a vital interest in committed UFs - and the domestic VCs they govern - staying in export business over a longer period (rather than collapsing) because of the considerable time dimension of the underlying processes of: (i) building up the HR and (ii) setting up and improving relationships in the GVC and 'getting it right'.

Significantly, comments of EBs in the FV sub-sector indicate that buyers who are frustrated (due to UFs' dishonesty, cheating, low responsiveness, switching) talk about their negative experience among industry colleagues in their home countries or Europe generally; and cause negative reputation effects for Uganda as a sourcing country. Very important to note as well is that some UFs in the FV industry reported problematic behaviour by certain EBs, who cheat by claiming they have never received the produce or inventing quality defects of the delivery (in order to eventually pay the UFs less than agreed), breaching the contracts (if there are any), not paying the full amount for the delivery, or disappearing after delivery of the produce without making any payment.

Overall, the research reveals: (1) The pattern of evolution of GVC governance impacts on economic dynamics in Uganda. (2) Network relations tend to be accompanied by various cooperation activities which assist UFs to upgrade and perform better. These activities are usually less evident and advanced in arms-length market relationships, whether in the (anonymous) auction type of buyer-seller relationship or short-term-oriented and/or low-trust VCs that are characterised by low switching costs, and low complexity of transaction. (3) Network types of relations require from UFs not only technical but especially entrepreneurial, organisational, and interactive capabilities. Note, the above findings should not be read in a deterministic way. There will always be examples that point to other mechanisms at work in the context GVCs.

Implications for HRD: Wiegratz et al. (2007a) discuss further implications of the findings for (i) the private sector, (ii) the state and development agencies (NGOs, donors, etc.) as well as learning institutions, and (iii) future research - these will not be reproduced in detail here (see also Wiegratz 2008). A few remarks are sufficient: The behavioural (and competency) issues in GVCs discussed above highlight a particular challenge that is often overlooked in the debate about exports by African firms: the challenge regarding local business ethics, values, behaviours and practices, including honesty, communication or reliability as well as ability to effectively engage in business relations, and leverage resources, knowledge and, generally, cooperation from the buyer. Trade proponents have to analyse and address related issues of performance of UFs in SCFs. Attention should be paid not only to the economic, but also social, cultural and political (local and global) factors impacting on the relevant empirical outcomes. Research is needed on the state of relevant institutions (norms, rules, values, practices) in the Ugandan economy; those institutions that are regarded as prerequisites for the establishment and running of a more or less stable, competitive or 'modern' market economy. This agenda points to the embeddedness and thus economic sociology and political economy of markets (Polanyi 1957). Given the above, more research is needed on the (i) needs and possibilities of cooperation between UFs and foreign buyers, (ii) principles, rationalities, practices and implications (costs, benefits, changes) of cooperation, and (iii) potential cooperation stimulus measures that could be implemented by the state and the BMOs.

Further, the state should look into ways of protecting UFs from the ill-treatment of certain foreign buyers, and also the fact that foreign importers are sometimes deceived by certain UFs. Related industry action seems to be needed as well. Further, the state should learn about and support more (e.g. in terms of training and technology) the various upgrading, relationship and cooperation efforts of the exporting UFs. Related questions are: how can reliable UFs be helped to demonstrate trustworthiness to foreign buyers (and 'earn' trust over time via good performance), so that the buyer engages in the relationship, and enhances cooperation efforts? How can the reputation of trustworthy UFs in a sub-sector be shielded against the negative effects of the actions of untrustworthy UFs? How can UF-EB trust be enhanced by regulatory measures and inspection services in the foreign part of the GVCs? Trade promotion and respective training agencies need to support (especially newcomer) UFs in gaining the HR that allow them to develop a more informed mode of dealing with the challenges of linking up and developing a beneficial and long-term relationship with (trustworthy) buyers. This could help young sub-sectors and firms, especially, to strengthen the organisational setup, day-to-day operations and overall performance of newly established GVCs, and thus limit costly (learning-by) mistakes.

The respective institutions of the ETS and LIS might thus have to put more emphasis on the soft (or relationship) side of business, and facilitate training and learning of current and future economic actors in Uganda (e.g. with the help of different learning networks, courses, or self-help tools, see Wiegratz 2008). Training courses could cover the following topics: active relationship management, including active trust building and loyalty enhancement, negotiations, transparency, and proactive behaviour and communication in a VC setting, and dealing with matters of conflict, opportunism, power asymmetries, as well as control and trust between GVC actors. Such training can help boost UFs' understanding of and performance on the 'soft' side of GVC trade. The suggested trainings could involve sessions in which UFs share their experiences and lessons learnt in interacting with foreign buyers and other GVC actors or stakeholders, such as technocrats. Such training seem almost non-existent at the moment. This increases the overall learning costs of UFs: in an environment of limited formal and informal sharing of business information and experience (and limited case study reports on such business matters), each new GVC entrant from Uganda has to go through the entire learning curve and pay the costs.

Finally, again, patterns and dynamics of business culture and political economy (in the global and local economy) are closely linked. This has implications for the role of institutions of the ETS, the LIS as well as the political, economic and cultural sub-system; their 'performance' has consequences in the world-of-trade, as shown above.

Governance of buyer-farmer business in domestic agro value chains

Similar to the above GVC study, research in Wiegratz et al. (2007b) applied the VC framework to analyse the governance of DVCs in the agricultural sector in Uganda. It focuses on exploring how agricultural produce buyers set up, coordinate and monitor - that is govern - the DVCs with their supplying smallholder farmers (SHFs); particularly how buyers, or Lfs of the respective DVCs, govern the latter's activities and performance and thus the division of labour in the DVC. Governance includes (1) setting the requirements for farmers in terms of product quantity, quality and delivery, or production processes, (2) monitoring compliance, and (3) assisting farmers to meet the set requirements. The research was concerned with: the rationale and functioning of the business relation between the LF and SHFs, related benefits and costs as well as lessons learnt, farmers' upgrading as well as opportunities and challenges which will have to be addressed by the VC actors or call for assistance from, for instance, GOU and respective SIs.

The study explores five case studies of Lf governance of DVCs: Bee Natural Products (BNP/honey), Sulmafoods (fruits and vegetables), Outspan (sesame and chilli), Ibero (coffee), and the dairy firm Jesa.[301] Depending on the sub-sector, the LFs interviewed are processors or traders who sell their products on domestic and/or international markets. The main selection criterion for Lfs to be included in the study was that the LF was known to engage directly with SHFs and in a more long-term and developmental manner, which could include provision of training, advice, pre-finance, or inputs. Interviews were conducted with Lfs' personnel, SHFs as well as support institutions and industries (SIs/SIDs) that interacted with (and supported) the Lfs and SHFs and thus - in some way - carried out governance functions in the DVC.[302]

Selected findings

Governance activities of the lead firm and results regarding farmers

All Lfs studied have undertaken *efforts* to establish and maintain direct and constant relations with their farmers and build farmers' production capacities and group organisation. *Reasons* that explain the above include: (a) the desire to strive for sufficient product quantity and quality in the context of an often weak supply base due to low farmer capacities, (b) control of diseases and pests in the production area, e.g. cattle diseases, (c) meeting standards of the target market, e.g. traceability requirements in the case of organic agriculture (OA), (d) putting into practice the LF's Corporate Social Responsibility (CSR) plans, (e) publicity and marketing needs of the Lf, (vi) statutory regulation, (f) market dynamics such as enhanced competition,

301 The DVCs of the dairy firms Sameer and Paramont were also studied in the research period. This work was funded by a different agency and is therefore not part of Wiegratz et al. (2007b). The intention is to publish all seven cases together in a book. The text in this section refers to the five case studies only.

302 SIs are non-commercial players such as government and donor agencies/programmes and NGOs. SIDs are commercial partners of the LFs and SHFs and supply some of the inputs used by SHFs.

and (g) interest in local development around the LF's rural base (processing plant, own farm, supplying farmers). Most Lfs realised that having good relations with SHFs and their local communities and creating interest in the Lf's business project and prospects (a win-win situation for the Lf and SHFs) is a precondition for meeting production objectives. Some of the Lfs tried actively to develop attitudes and behaviours among farmers and community members that would directly and indirectly benefit the Lf (higher farmers' supply, information provision, and loyalty levels) and, in turn, the supplying farmers.

Findings reveal that Lfs had to consider social aspects such as the *community's sentiments* in order to be accepted, secured and grow in a rural setting. A factory is a booster of trust and confidence as it indicates to the farmers and stakeholders a more formal business approach and long-term commitment of the Lf to the locality, especially compared to on and off 'middlemen'. Moreover, it is evident that *standards* (organic, fair trade, quality), or market requirements in general - which *necessitate* Lfs and farmers to be in close contact (beyond spot transaction) have fostered relations and cooperation between the two parties. Lfs' governance activities have offered *significant benefits to SHFs* in the form of: (i) training, advice, inputs and encouragement on matters of production and group dynamics (organisation, management, activities, and leadership). A *mix of technical and non-technical training topics* was essential for successful VCD, so was the identification of successful farmers amongst the group of SHFs. Lfs often designated such farmers as *lead farmers* (LFAs), who act as role models and champions of innovations the Lf would like to see adopted by other SHFs. LFAs also helped to build and deepen trust and loyalty between farmers and Lfs and were effective in supporting farmer-to-farmer learning.

Besides, *farmers noted as positive*: (ii) the provision of production inputs and equipment as well as related services by the Lf[303], (iii) linking farmers to SIs/SIDs and other farmer groups for training, finance, input supply or professional advice, (iv) providing a stable market and thus an incentive for farmers' upgrading, (v) helping to address farmers' risks, and (vi) allowing farmers to have access to premium prices. Lfs further assisted farmer groups in handling internal control systems necessary to meet foreign buyers' requirements, hence assuring of a market for the produce. Lfs such as Jesa also deducted a farmer's financial obligation to the cooperative (or any other VC player, e.g. a bank, or input supplier), which could also be a useful arrangements in other DVCs.

These reported measures by Lfs are a result of advanced relations (network type governance) between buyers and farmers that differ from the purely transaction-based (arms-length) approach common in Uganda. Network relationships with a Lf can offer better earning and upgrading conditions for SHFs than arms-length spot-market relationships can. More generally, production and trade dynamics as well as learning at the level of SHFs and Lfs are related to forms of relationships between VC actors and forms of VC governance.

Farmers in the case studies *appreciated the relationship with their Lfs, despite existing challenges* in each of the relationships. Farmers stressed the point of learning from the Lf and benefiting directly and indirectly from its presence. There are cases where, following the success of the pioneer group of farmers in dealing with the Lf, other farmers expressed their desire to join the VC, though limited markets do not always allow the Lf to take extra farmers on board.

303 Services were offered by Lf with/without charge, at subsidised prices, or related to soft loans.

The *upgrading results* of the interaction and cooperation between Lfs and farmers were usually significant: farmers (though not all) have increased their skills, operated with better processes, expanded their fields, achieved higher productivity, increased quantity and improved quality (the latter resulting in fewer rejects by the Lfs), have better group organisation, coherence and activities, or developed a more business-oriented mindset, e.g. in terms of long-term planning. Farmers' upgrading record showed that farmers can improve their production practices and products yet face a more substantial challenge in terms of technological advancement.

Farmers reported that they have advanced significantly regarding the above improvements, compared to farmers who are not in the DVC of the respective supportive Lf and do not generally have more developed relations with buyers. To a significant extent, the better performance of farmers who work with the Lfs is due to regular interaction with a buyer who gives farmers more than just payment for their product, but *sets supply standards* and *assists* farmers (directly and indirectly) to meet the standards. The socio-economic benefits for SHFs, due to their participation in these DVCs and upgrading and hence increased incomes (through better and more regular payment and less quality related rejects) were considerable. The differences noticed above offers an important insight to DVC proponents: positive effects in terms of development of both farmers and DVCs can be achieved if proponents would support Lfs, their farmers and other VC partners in matters relevant to VCD.

Overall, the case studies showed that different forms of governance require different degrees of farmer capabilities. Network relations with Lfs came with requirement for SHFs to enhance their skills in agronomic practices, post-harvest handling, sorting, or storage. Lfs offered assistance to raise the required skills, yet also demanded that the SHFs improve their work practices over time. Further, SHFs needed skills for intense communication, trust building, and transparency vis-à-vis the Lf; they also needed to show loyalty to stabilise the VC and allow VCD. Integration into such relational modes of governance requires a high degree of relevant capabilities. Further, enhanced skills and collective actions of SHFs reduced the Lf's costs and risks of coordination and monitoring. For instance, training provided to farmers (by the Lf and its partners) reduced the monitoring costs of the Lf in the later period; through better skills and performance as well as self-governing capacities of the farmers. Enhanced farmer group structures reduced coordination costs for the Lf. Governance costs were also reduced by enhanced opportunities to transmit knowledge and information between Lf (and its partners) and SHFs efficiently, which were a result of better farmer group organisation (thus farmers acting increasingly with one voice), improved communication practices of farmers, and increasing use of mobile phones.

Given that the Lfs studied were usually the only 'developmental buyers' with the most explicit governance system in the studied localities; one can assume that the above-mentioned positive developments would have been less significant and slower (or lacking) in the *absence of these Lfs* and their governance efforts. GOU and its partners thus have to become more vigorous about promoting VCD through enhancing Lf-SHF systems. Note also: *business practices that fall short* of commitment, cooperation, trust and long-term perspective in business with VC partners - seemingly the common practice in the agricultural sector - can *undermine or slow down* VCD in the country.

Besides, Lfs still reported *deficits among farmers in terms of*: adoption of improved agronomic practices and environmental management, technology advancement, group organisation and governance, understanding VC matters and applying a more long-term business perspective, risk-taking behaviour, as well as trust, loyalty and honesty. Due to their investment in the farmers' capacity and the need to obtain the farmers' output, Lfs often favour a continuation-approach with the farmers; thus they find it hard at times to punish and (temporarily) exclude defaulting or disloyal farmers from the VC. Lfs highlighted the importance of farmers improving on the soft factors in VC business: communication, commitment, trust, responsiveness, and eagerness to improve. Lfs appreciate farmers who can govern themselves. It was also noted that enhanced farmers awareness about commercial agriculture (after training) does not guarantee that farmers apply it successfully.

The findings indicate that Lfs have to be ready to (continue to) invest in SHFs *also in the future*, in terms of: innovation, improved inputs, promotion of best agronomic practices, certification costs, or linkage building with SIs and SIDs to mobilise assistance. Such continued support can yield positive returns in the long run. There are high expectations - among farmers and VC stakeholders such as SIs and SIDs - that Lfs further increase the scope of their support and enhance VC governance. Farmers' suggestions imply that there is room for governance improvement in every VC studied, in addition to improvements on price issues.

To fulfil some of these expectations and take DVC governance to a higher level, Lfs will have to show a continued good, and in some issue areas, improved performance on various fronts (not just price). This can help to maintain or enhance the contentment and loyalty of the farmers. In order to finance the support measures for farmers, Lfs need to be strong in market expansion (marketing). Some of the expectations that are directed towards the Lf (e.g. in areas of pre-finance or input provision) are related to the fact that the weak or uncommitted (public and private sector) SIs do not provide services or assistance.

Various challenges in the domestic value chain governance systems

Farmers emphasised that the Lfs' measures and behaviour are generally different from *other buyers or agents* operating in the different areas. Other buyers tend to purchase the produce (sporadically) but do not develop farmers' production or group capacities. These buyers often prefer to interact with individual farmers instead of groups, and limit these interactions to the buying season only. Other buyers are also rather informal (less visible; e.g. they have no factory or field office) and less trustworthy than the Lfs studied. The study thus differentiates between *'developmental'* (Lfs studied) and *'non-developmental' buyers*. Based on the interviews, part of the deficient characteristics of non-developmental buyers are as follows: (1) being less concerned with enhancing farmers' product quality and volume (due to characteristics of the buyer's product, target market and business vision), (2) not caring about farmers, (3) not seeing investment in farmers' capacities as their role: not as an investment in a sustainable and long-term-oriented DVC but a 'waste' of the buyers' resources, (4) being overwhelmed by the numbers of farmers in their supply system, (5) lacking the competencies and/or motivation to address loyalty and trust issue in the DVC, or (6) fearing that providing SHFs with support might strengthen farmers' technical capacities and thus bargaining power.

In this context, there is an important effect: the ill-treatment of farmers by some non-developmental buyers (e.g. various forms of deception) affects farmers' perceptions and attitudes vis-à-vis developmental buyers who are interested in establishing relationships. It makes the latter's task more difficult and costly. This negative effect (externality) in terms of possibilities and 'costs' of trust and relationship building between VC actors should be of concern to stakeholders who wish to promote (quality product) DVCs.[304] The state should look into this effect and establish if it is necessary for it to intervene. It seems more effective (and beneficial in the long term) to regulate buyers' behaviour (and that of other actors) in the first place than to deal with the direct and indirect costs of their 'improper' actions for the process of VCD afterwards. VCD proponents need to promote more cooperative and long-term-oriented behaviour among buyers (and VC actors in general); though this is, of course, difficult in the prevailing capitalist ('free market') political economy in Uganda.

Despite the upgrading efforts and related results of both Lfs and SHFs, some Lfs faced a *supply problem* (farmers produce too little or sell to other buyers); while other Lfs faced a *market access problem* (supply is sufficient but the Lf lacks a strong market or buyer). Moreover, almost all Lfs suffer (actually or potentially) from the *loyalty problem*: Farmers who benefit from the Lfs' support - in the beginning of and often later on in the relationship - sell to other on-off buyers who can pay a higher price for the produce because they had not invested in farmers' capacities (or supported farmers in other ways) in the first place. The *'loyalty cycle'* is as follows: while Lfs can reap some loyalty benefits from the initial: (1) 'eye opening effect' of introducing a new business to farmers (e.g. modern beekeeping) and/or (2) assistance provided, this initial boost can fade to some extent over time with farmers' loyalty levels - for various reasons - declining. Loyalty levels rise again at times, e.g. when the farmers 'get burned' in their transactions with cheating buyers. Given the competition for farmers' produce, Lfs will have to find new ways of boosting or refuelling the farmers' loyalty in later phases of the relationship, often through better prices and/or other measures. Most Lfs search for market niches in domestic and foreign markets that allow them to give SHFs a premium price above the prevailing local price, to increase farmers' loyalty and supply. Organic markets are an example in this respect.

Some Lfs faced a *problem of deficient payback practices by farmers* and difficulty in *enforcing contracts and agreements* with defaulting farmers. Enforcement of 'supply and payback' contracts doesn't seem to be feasible with SHFs in the current setting. Farmers' refusal to pay back the Lf through selling their produce to the Lf and adhering to an agreed deduction scheme constrained relationship building and further development of the DVC. The *limited enforcement efforts or successes* of the Lfs are related to the following: (a) limited staff capacity of the Lf to enforce contracts, (b) fear of losing reputation among farmers by being rigid and running after defaulting farmers, (c) need for Lfs to keep farmers in the VC to ensure higher supply (in a low supply-high demand environment), (d) lengthy and costly court processes and (e) in one case (BNP), pressures from politicians who decampaign the Lf (e.g. undermine its operations). Overall, it was not clear whether enforcement is uneconomical (in a broad sense, including reputation costs) for the Lf or if other (e.g. political and cultural) reasons

304 Ongoing PhD research by the author suggests that currently dominant business practices in a liberal setting have severely hampered the motivation and need for farmers to produce quality products. Many produce buyers (and their commercial customers) don't mind low-quality products. Informants have suggested that different buyer practices are needed to stimulate *quality* production.

play also a role in explaining enforcement levels and patterns. The issue could, for instance, be related to management deficits (low staff levels) or general problems of (young) Lfs that make limited profits which cannot cover such enforcement activities.

The described problem is particularly severe in the BNP case, as acknowledged by BNP and its supporting partners (e.g. GOU and NGOs); it was estimated that about 50% of the farmers who have received inputs on a loan basis from BNP are not straightforward in terms of repayment. This should worry proponents of VCD in Uganda: Lfs face considerable risks in extending financial services to farmers. Again, the state has to think about possible support measures. BNP approached public SIs like NAADS to assist in issues of price negotiations, farmers' loyalty in VC operations and repayment for inputs, and partnerships in the DVC in general. Generally, SIs such as NAADS could carry out sensitisation seminars for politicians and other stakeholders, to raise awareness about and discuss VC matters in communities. In the same case, the Lf and farmers called for intervention by GOU in price setting and sensitisation of farmers about relationships and loyalty matters in DVCs.

Lfs stressed the high level of initial and continuous *training efforts* needed to keep the farmers motivated, committed and knowledgeable. *Costs for training and monitoring* of farmers typically constituted the majority of a Lf's *governance costs* - because these activities required considerable field staff and logistics in the context of many scattered SHFs with low production capacities. Infant Lfs, in particular, experienced the challenges of cost recovery due to scant capital outlay. Most Lfs solicited the support of stakeholders (SIs/SIDs including NGOs, or donor/state agencies) to enhance assistance provision to farmers and/or lower the financial burden on the Lf. Overall, Lfs tried to recover the costs of VC governance through: (1) higher prices of the final product they sell, (2) increased volume traded and (3) involving farmers in payment (via deduction) for services and inputs. As the VC system with farmers expanded (thus the governance workload), some Lfs, for various reasons, did not *expand* their *staff system*, including staff levels, remunerations, and qualifications as well as rules of engagement of staff with farmers adequately.

Lessons learnt from interacting with farmers as noted by Lfs' managing directors (MDs) and supervisors (SVs) pointed to technical and non-technical dimensions, for instance the importance of: (a) being transparent and patient, (b) investing in farmers so that their produce can be obtained, (c) treating farmers with respect and developing a social relationship, (d) fulfilling promises made, (e) taking group dynamics into account, (f) communicating well with VC partners and having feedback circles, (g) enhancing reputations as buyers, and (h) possessing communication, training and leadership skills (e.g. being able to guide, advise and counsel farmers). SVs, particularly, reported that they had to learn how to interact better, pass on information, make joint decisions and be patient in the relationship with farmers.

Formation and dynamics of farmer groups was another major issue in DVCs. All farmers interviewed were organised in groups. Frequently, the Lf had initiated the group formation process. The group arrangement brought many advantages for farmers, such as: (i) sharing of equipment and certain labour costs, (ii) collective crop production, from clearing the farm land to harvesting and (iii) learning from each other. Due to group processes, the output per farmer increased. Enhanced group organisation and management also boosted coordination, including communication, with the Lf. Lfs' SVs reported that enhanced group cohesion of farmers is linked to issues of common interest among farmers and between farmers and the

Lf, as well as training, sensitisation about market requirements, and incentives provided by the LF. The characteristic of the particular group leadership is another factor determining success or failure of a group.

The overall *weak group structure* of most farmer groups was a major challenge for SHFs and the Lfs that interact with them. To mobilise the collective action of farmers, not just for production matters but also for financial and other business operations, is difficult. Advanced trust levels and cooperation practices amongst farmers are required to foster members' collaboration in such matters. Indeed, all Lfs called for improved farmer organisation. This issue area - including the adverse impact of weak farmer organisation on VCD - should be of major concern for VC actors and stakeholders (e.g. GOU and donors). Farmers' organisation deficits limit the impact of the support (e.g. training and technology) provided by GOU and the Lfs. These findings point to the *importance of revived collective action by farmers* in Uganda (cooperatives and other farmer institutions). Better group organization and governance enhances the performance of the farmers (thus Lf/DVC) and reduces the Lf's governance costs, thus potentially allowing the latter to increase prices for farmers. There was willingness by some Lfs to enhance business and cooperation with farmers when farmers become better organised. Better group organisation can furthermore increase farmers' bargaining capability and power. Note that very few of the Lfs studied had *group-oriented rewards and sanctions* in their VC that would foster group development. Group performance should be emphasised more and incentive schemes which target groups, not just individual farmers, should be used. There are general *weaknesses in most Lf governance systems* in terms of designing and implementing a system which *rewards and sanctions* farmers' performance and non-performance.

Further, *bulking of produce (farmers' collective marketing)* still faced challenges, such as lack of stores in villages and inadequate business practices. The experiences of bulk marketing reveal that *VCD is a process* in terms of: (1) learning of all actors and (2) gradual improvement of the systems and practice in the VC. With time and successful, repeated interactions, practices in the DVC can be improved. Farmers need time to practice, learn about and gain trust in collective marketing (compared to the practice of individual sales to spot buyers); and Lfs need time to practice and learn about other issues. VC actors need to invest in mutual trust building; any hiccups (operational and other problems) in a buying season, caused by any of the VC actors, prolong and destabilise the trust-building process.

Handling trust and relationships in the domestic value chain

Trust was another major issue in VCs studied: Many respondents - both farmers and Lfs - referred to trust as the basis of the mutual business relationship. The Lfs usually had a high *awareness* of the importance of trust and tried to develop trust with farmers; especially in the absence of any (enforceable) contracts. Where contracts do not exist to guide expectations, the level of trust has to compensate for the insecurity of the arrangement. There were varying levels of trust: weak, fair and strong; declining, unchanging and improving.

Farmers showed awareness of the role of trust in the VC (often due to experience with the Lf) and highlighted *actions* that target developing trust with their Lf, e.g. improving quality and quantity of the produce, applying the Lf's advice, practising what was learnt in the training, being patient with Lf's deficits and believing in the Lf, complying with contract provision, selling to the Lf on credit, selling only to the Lf and informing the Lf when they sell to other buyers (e.g. when Lf cannot take produce), reserving produce for the Lf rather than selling to other buyers at higher prices, communicating to the Lf about internal dynamics in the farmer group, or issues of supply and demand in general. Farmers referred to a mix of tangible/technical (quality, quantity) and non-tangible/social (patience, belief) dimensions when reflecting on their active trust-building efforts.

A number of groups reported that during their relationship with Lfs they *have learnt about* the importance of relationships, loyalty, honesty and trust in business or the relevance of working with a 'developmental buyer'. When assessing the costs and difficulty of *switching* the buyer, groups referred to indirect (loyalty) and direct (price, market, future business) costs. Farmers who have a perspective of several seasons into the future apparently tend to weigh the loyalty factor higher in their decision to switch buyers or not, than more short-term-oriented farmers who focus predominantly on price. Many of the issues raised above point to significant learning steps in the context of development of SHFs and VCs in general. Notably, learning involves a mix of technical and non-technical aspects.

Respondents indicated that *Lfs built trust and relationships* with farmers in the following ways: providing an assured market (regular high-level transactions improve relations) and taking all or most of the farmers' produce, buying from and working with a group for a longer time and fulfilling promises over that time (having a clean record in terms of keeping promises and avoiding outright deception); by paying a more than average local price, paying regularly, being flexible in terms of payment methods and other matters, providing assistance (in forms of inputs, advice, visits, training, pre-finance, or problem solving). Important in the context of Lfs' trust and relationship building with farmers is, finally: (1) giving incentives to improve farmers' performance and exposure, (2) increasing farmers' identification with the Lfs' project, (3) being transparent, reliable and physically visible and approachable (trying to accommodate farmers' concerns), (4) being part of farmers' social life, and (5) being concerned with farmers' development and well-being. In all the case studies, regular payment was one of the strongest factors that binds farmers to a Lf; thus, Lfs should try to minimise incidences of late payment and/or late collection of the produce.

Regular *face-to-face interaction* between the Lf (including field staff) and farmers both in good and bad times (periods of high/low demand) was crucial for establishing, maintaining and enhancing relations in DVCs and maintaining or boosting the farmers' motivation and confidence in the Lf. It is thus important that buyers are willing to invest in a *good field presence* (including field staff training and remuneration). *Training farmers* was also effective in increasing farmers' commitment and loyalty regarding the Lf, and improving the farmers' understanding of VC matters. Besides, there were examples of trust in the VC being improved by using an advanced *machine* for quality control or weighing when farmers supply their produce to the Lfs. Such machines can be useful governance tools in agricultural VCs; they help to stabilise the Lf-SHF relationship. A machine which measures the parameters of concern (e.g. milk quality or coffee weight) correctly is perceived to be neutral or fair and provides valuable information and feedback to farmers (e.g. on their produce quality). In summary, Lfs have to *do well*[305] in *various* relevant trust dimensions (regular payment and other issues) to win and retain the trust of farmers.

Interestingly, the level to which a Lf's actions are seen as *'fair'* also depends on the fairness (behaviour) of other buyers in the locality. Besides, some farmers could not assess the 'fairness'

305 Perform well as VC governors and act with some considerations of the farmers' interests in mind; be pro-farmer.

in the relationship with the Lf since they had no information about the price structure in the VC. Indeed, the case studies show that it is *important for the stability, growth and sustainability of the VC* that farmers are aware of the benefits (and costs) of being in a constant relationship with a 'developmental buyer', and their own role in and contributions to this arrangement, so that the VC stabilises, if possible, in a situation where positive expectations about each other are fulfilled; thus enhancing trust, causing both parties to benefit from the long-term advantages of steady VCD.

In addition, *Lfs emphasised* that the following *farmers deficits* undermine the establishment of high-trust DVCs, and makes DVC governance more costly and risky: the price focus (switching the buyer for the sake of a few shillings thus not honouring agreements with the Lfs), deficits in loyalty and honesty after farmers have received inputs from the Lf on credit and are supposed to engage in repayment via deductions from payment for supplied produce, unpredictable behaviour and short-term business orientation, as well as the low organisational level of farmers.

However, Lfs were *not always successful* in developing and deepening trust and relationships with farmers sometimes due to their *own deficits*. Farmers indicated that *Lfs' deficits* in the following categories undermine relations and trust: timely payment of farmers, price levels (compared to non-developmental buyers), nature of price negotiations with farmers (giving farmers a voice), flexibility, timely and logistical arrangements to collect the produce, communication, as well as field staff treatment by the Lf and staff turnover. On the latter point, Lfs have to realise that (1) treating their field staff badly (low job security/remuneration, actual/perceived unfairness) and (2) a high staff turnover at Lfs (no matter what the reasons) can undermine relations with farmers. Farmers can become afraid and lose confidence and trust in the Lf when field staff change too often. Relations are also undermined by Lf's buying agents who cheat either farmers about prices/payment or the very Lf (by misusing company money, taking produce to a competitor).

One case study pointed out that farmers (especially LFAs) and other stakeholders of the VC (such as SIs) closely follow Lf's changes in field staff; personnel changes may upset farmers. In such situations, to restore confidence, Lfs - after they have resolved the matter that led to a staff leaving his/her position - need to communicate to farmers the actual events, underlying reasons, the company response and the way forward. For that, Lfs need public relations competencies, which some of the Lfs studied seemed to lack. Not communicating, especially in times of VC governance crisis, creates a vacuum for rumours and uncertain expectations on the farmers' side, which can affect trust levels and make trust building more difficult and costly in the future.

Further, Lfs have to take into account that *relations between (good) field staff and farmers* are valuable and an asset to the company: field personnel are important on the technical front (giving farmers training and advice) and the trust front. Field staff can be creators (or destroyers) of trust. The issue of field staff thus needs to receive sufficient attention and support from the Lf's management. Changes in field staff need to be communicated to farmers to keep their confidence in the relationship and business with the Lfs.

There are, moreover, *external factors* that affect the Lfs' success in trust formation with farmers: (1) competition for farmers' produce and related VC 'interference' from other buyers who try to capture the produce after the Lf has developed farmers' capacities, (2) 'price wars' with other (often non-developmental) buyers, and (3) decampaigning of the Lf by other buyers and their political allies. The competition for produce by other buyers was a major issue for Lfs who have developed the farmers' capacities. Codes of conduct for buyers are in the making in the FV industry, and aim to bring more stability to the industry; this initiative should be followed up. Overall, there were expectations among respondents that buyers (in certain sectors) are under business pressure to enhance their relationships with farmers in the near future: to meet targets in terms of quantity, quality and standards. The Lfs' learning process to date in terms of VCD in the country needs to be analysed further and made available to the learning community in Uganda.

The role of government, support institutions and support industries

There was a *close link* between the nature and level of success of state measures on the one hand, and the level of effectiveness and success of measures of the DVC actors and SIs in promoting VCD, on the other. *State decisions impacted* on: (a) relationships between DVC actors, including the division of labour in the DVC, and thus (b) the structure of incentives/profits of each actor. The *efforts and results of the state* in supporting the VCs studied have been *mixed*. Characteristics of public sector operational regulations, guidelines and implementation levels (or lack and gaps thereof) are sometimes a *challenge* to Lf's efforts to achieve effective VCD. Respondents also noted that some government decisions and interventions were insufficiently researched and/or suffer from ad-hoc methods and corruption in the state system.

Government policies and programmes have at times also *helped* the DVC, the Lf and/or the farmers, in terms of training, equipment provision, infrastructure improvement and general security. Also, *public intermediaries* such as a local government production officers can be essential in helping the economic actors to set up and improve the DVC. The analysis also revealed the difficulty of GOU (in partnership with farmers and the Lf) to establish lasting arrangements to ensure its PPP meets the set targets. Some of the public support tools for VCD being used at present in the experimental context of VCD need *clarification in terms of rules of engagement for the state*. There is need: (i) to spell out and sensitise various public employees about their roles in VCD and (ii) to train, and counsel and organise exchange of experiences between them.

In other cases, state support in crucial issue areas is largely *nonexistent*, which leaves the Lf with a significant burden regarding the development of both the DVC and the farmers. Some Lfs noted that by 'doing the work others should be doing' they extend their scope of activities beyond core functions (buying produce and training farmers in essentials), to developing farmers' capacities (at times from scratch). The more committed Lfs, especially in new sectors, risk becoming overwhelmed by the governance activities they have to carry out to develop the DVC sufficiently. This is due to the weak capacities of farmers and the low effective support provided by SIs. Lfs thus appeal to the responsible authorities to play their part more effectively in future.

Getting other stakeholders involved in the development of farmers' capacities was a major strategy of all Lfs to reduce their governance burden and costs. Such partners were NGOs, development agencies, state institutions and input suppliers. In this sense *Lfs take on a linking and mediatory function* for farmers. There are examples of good cooperation between Lfs and SIs/SIDs which benefit farmers, the Lf and the DVC. Further, SIDs such as input suppliers - due to their commercial and partly developmental interests - can provide (besides products for sale) 'extras' such as advice and training regarding the use of their products and related general issues such as animal health. At times, actors of the SIDs fill the gaps left by the weak public support system. Government should reconsider and clarify the future role it wants to play in the Lf-SHF-SID-system.

Some non-state support programmes and SIs made useful interventions. In many cases, the support from SIs was essential for the Lf to build the DVC with farmers. It is thus important that both public and private sector *SIs keep designing and effectively implementing relevant interventions for VCD*. Interviews with SIs reveal that it is possible to carry out interventions which foster direct relations and thus interaction between Lfs and farmers; these interventions can stabilise or increase the prices farmers obtain for their produce. Market requirements (e.g. traceability and quality-based competition) were used as a pushing factor for VC relationship-building purposes. The study also revealed the importance of joint product priorities of GOU and Lfs to promote a particular product in a geographical area.

Overall, SIs and SIDs (including agro-consultancy firms) can fulfil an important *linking and mediatory function* between farmers and buyers, which makes their ability to fulfil their function an important factor in VCD. Donors should thus be concerned with involving local SIs/SIDs in their work, so that meaningful interactions between VC actors and stakeholders can take place and continue after the project. Some state/donor interventions face a sustainability problem in this regard.

Further, there were examples where *two or more SIs effectively partner* with a Lf and other VC actors to complement one another and improve the performance of the DVC actors and the entire DVC, and address different issues like food security and standards, welfare of children, sustainable agriculture, environment conservation, and poverty reduction. This collaborative approach can be more effective than 'stand-alone' projects that only address one aspect. Overall, VCD promoters like the state and donors have yet to learn to design and implement programmes that include the different VC actors and improve issues *along* the DVC. Importantly, uncoordinated (or an inappropriate mix of) interventions from different development agencies (including NGOs) can confuse farmers and cause setbacks in the VC in general. There were also incidences where the design and implementation of development programmes showed *poor awareness of prevailing DVC issues* and/or *low cooperation with the Lf*, for various reasons. Farmer-oriented interventions that do not adequately consider the existing VC context (e.g. the Lf-SHFs relations and respective strategies) may leave the farmers worse off in the future, when the effects of interventions produce inadequate results, or circumstances change. In some cases there was little interaction between the Lf's field staff and the coordinators and implementers of government programmes.

Some SVs noted that the *level of commitment towards developing strong farmers* to supply future markets is higher among Lf's field staff than the private service providers (PSPs) who work on short-term/seasonal contracts, get paid for their services and move on (e.g. NAADS' PSPs). This highlights the issue of *sustainability levels* of: (1) embedded services in VCs, vis-à-vis (2) external short-term service provision. NAADS and other public SIs have to consider how to incorporate the developmental Lfs to a greater extent in their activities, and how to strengthen the provision of meaningful embedded services to SHFs, also via Lfs and other VC actors (or governors). Overall, *LFs seem to be always looking for partnerships with effective SIs* that would like to engage in assistance to farmers. Lfs, at times, face difficulties to find appropriate partners, also to outsource functions such as marketing, transport and farmers' training.

Overall, VCD-related support measures by GOU, donors and SIs (and to some extent SIDs) in a specific location often need greater coordination. The option of promoting and investing in partnerships between VC actors and external VC promoters is both a chance and challenge. The Lfs have to continue shouldering part of the related actors' coordination, but *without the efforts of the powerful state and (often donor co-founded) SIs*, coordination of support measures remains illusory. No doubt, *public SIs have to create meaningful relations with VC* actors and use these relations for VCD promotion. This is likely to constitute a significant challenge to public servants who have officially retained a distance from such forms of interaction with private sector actors in recent years. In the absence of, or transition period towards, meaningful relations between the state (and its SIs) and VC actors, more support might have to be provided to private sector SIs so that their role in VCD is enhanced.

Moreover, as argued earlier, in the context of its economic diversification agenda, GOU has to consider to a greater extent the *contribution of those Lfs who are pioneers* in: developing the supply base of a new sub-sector in a particular geographical area (e.g. by training farmers in a new activity) and demonstrating to following actors that this new commercial activity is possible and viable in this area. Without state support, the pioneer firm (Lf) will invest less than desired in capacity building (including technological upgrading) of farmers, which slows down a sub-sector's development, hence diversification. The pioneer will scale back these investments because it knows subsequent buyers will later trade with farmers and thus benefit from the demonstration and capacity-building effect and out-compete the pioneer in price, because these buyers have not invested in VCD (e.g. farmers' training). Again, not all buyers are willing to cooperate in support activities that benefit farmers, because they don't want to invest in long-term development; they feel the state should do that. That is why GOU should seek to *enhance cooperation* with those VC actors (Lfs and others) that are not purely short-term commercially oriented (money for product) but also somehow developmental (which is long-term commercial, in a way) in their orientation towards VCD.

GOU will have to *clarify its conception of and involvement in PPPs in DVCs*; the scope of support provided to Lfs, farmers and respective SIs. GOU needs to spell out guidelines for its engagement in partnerships with a particular Lf: not only on matters of farmers' production (training and equipment for farmers) but also sales and marketing (loyalty, contracts, prices). GOU has to work out meaningful regulations and step up its support with regard to VCD. More regular practical support of VC actors to ensure effective assistance and actors' learning will require effective local support structures with staff who interact meaningfully with the VC players. In any case, future policies need to support (or allow for) enhanced buyer-farmer relations and cooperation. GOU should address the issue of *buyers whose malpractices undermine* continuous, consistent and speedy VCD. If GOU attended to business practices in the agricultural sectors, it would break new ground in the post-1986 era, given the administration's overall liberal (read hands-off) stand on regulating market actors and dynamic due to its politics of 'non-interference' with market forces. The remainder of this discusses further, related issues and implications for HRD.

Competitive advantage from better interaction in inter-firm relationships

As Uganda's firms try to integrate successfully into advanced VCs and make the DVCs and thus inter-firm operations more efficient and valuable, they will experience a trend that occurred in many countries and industries worldwide: a *significant increase* in the *volume* and *value of interactions* (Johnson et al. 2005). Consequently, there is room for creating *competitive advantage from better interactions* - which competitors might find difficult to copy (Beardsley et al. 2006). In this context, the increasing importance of *'tacit' interactions* (vis-à-vis transformative and routine transactional activities) is emphasised. Below, we review some vital aspects of this topic, which - at various levels - could have increasing relevance for Uganda's general economic development agenda too.

> Tacit interactions typically involving *complex, collaborative problem-solving activities* in a specific business situation including "the [pursuit, capture, and] exchange of information, the making of judgments, and a need to draw on multifaceted forms of knowledge in exchanges with coworkers, customers, and suppliers" (ibid, 53). In other words, tacit interactions entail "the searching, coordinating, and monitoring activities required to exchange goods, services, and information ... Such interactions involve talented people armed with experience, judgment, creativity and the ability to connect the dots in problem solving, all of which make their work more effective and more likely to achieve desired outcomes ... [The power of tacit capabilities] lies in the collective company-specific knowledge that emerges over time ... Furthermore, innovations in tacit interactions are by nature the result of decentralized experimentation, trials, and learning" (ibid, 54, 57, 59).

The point is, firms that rely significantly on tacit interactions (e.g. in their VC operations) need to make those workers who are chiefly involved in these activities *more effective* and thus boost their productivity and thus the overall effectiveness of the firm's tacit interactions; this is a relatively new management approach and research terrain (ibid, 54-5).

> "Executives recognize that they must manage these workers differently. Managing for effectiveness in tacit interactions is about fostering change, learning, collaboration, shared values and innovation. Workers engage in a larger number of higher-quality tacit interactions when organizational barriers (such as hierarchies and silos) don't get in the way, when people trust each other and have the confidence to organize themselves, and when they have the tools to make better decisions and communicate quickly and easily ... The focus of managerial action is to establish conditions [including incentive structures and mechanisms that reward collaboration, group-based initiatives and knowledge sharing within the organisation; a culture built on trust] that allow tacit interactions [and the related processes of learning and knowledge creation] to emerge and florish rather than trying to engineer connections from the top down" (ibid, 56-8).

The brief elaboration of the issue of tacit interactions clearly demonstrates that the evolving debate on productivity determinants and drivers in Uganda has to be broadened and become more specific if it is to offer useful, new insights for both policy makers and practitioners who wish to see the country succeed in a global economy that is structured, and is increasingly based on various forms of complex 'networks' (e.g. design, production, marketing, distribution) and activities (searching, coordinating, monitoring, cooperating, communicating).

This is a major frontier for *new forms of competitiveness improvements*, or, alternatively, competitiveness losses, if rivals are more determined, capable and faster to exploit the productivity and business enhancement opportunities in the areas discussed above. In other words, the ability to undertake such (tacit or intangible) activities impacts on the level of economic rents that Ugandan firms can secure or protect from erosion, for instance in VC arrangements, as the quote below illustrates.

> "The key shift we are witnessing in an increasingly globalized and competitive world is a transition from rents accruing from tangible activities to those arising from intangible activities in the value chain. Intangible activities are increasingly knowledge and skill based, and imbedded in organizational systems; the knowledge they incorporate is thus tacit in nature, implying growing barriers to entry. The intangibles are to be found in all links - for example, the control of logistics in the production phase and the conceptual phase in advertising" (Kaplinsky and Morris 2003, 12-3).

Uganda does not have a significant body of research work that explores these issues at firm, VC, cluster or sub-sector level. This undermines the catch-up process of the economy, including related HRD improvements. In other words: The status quo of the knowledge deficits probably 'feeds into' the next generation of competitive disadvantage (and capability gaps) of Ugandan firms vis-à-vis their competitors in both production and trade; it undermines value-capture and upgrading prospects in a 'network economy'.

Further implications for PSD and HRD in the context of VCD

Tapping into 'new territory': limited knowledge and experience for VCD assistance

From the findings in this chapter, we can conclude that implementing changes that address some of these deficits in the DVCs in Uganda means tapping into 'new territory'. There is relatively little knowledge and experience available (e.g. in the consultancy community) that allows the development of successful DVCs (van Bussel 2005, 13). Microfinance institutions also report that they lack trained staff that understand agricultural markets (especially the agro-enterprise business model and related issues of technology and risks) (Tanburn and Kamuhanda 2005, Byaruhanga 2005a, 2005b). Van Bussel's observations point to shortcomings in existing capacities for VCD:

> "Very little is known by businesses and business advisors as regards the systems that need to be put in place to develop successful supply chains. Specifically, there is a clear lack of supply chain development and management skills ... The consultants, employed by BSMD to guide the businesses in their effort to develop their supply chains, tackled the issues ... together with the business involved. The results were mixed. The partners and consultants had neither straightforward solutions nor practical examples or frameworks to guide in handling these issues. More disappointing however was that some of the advisors with specific expertise could not provide appropriate support. For example, two professional business consultants struggled to develop templates and model business plans. Further, an experienced financial advisor was not able to prepare understandable financial forecasts of different business options and the subsequent financial statements for the businesses in a chain. None of the local business consultants BSMD has met had practical experience in supply chain development" (2005, 13-4).[306]

306 On contract use within supply chain transactions, the AT Uganda et al. report notes "[m]any farmers and traders do not understand the language used in contracts or know how to draw one up" (2005, 2). Gibbon's analysis of organic operators points to the limited use of consultancy services which could be related to deficits in utilising specialised consultancy services: "[o]nly five of all operators interviewed [about 20] had paid for consultancy services partly or mainly aimed at their organic operations over the previous two years. The total services paid for were equivalent to 158 person days, of which 120 days were accounted for by a single company. The topics of the consultancies were advice on project planning, project management and staff training; design of processing plant; quality management; and general trouble shooting duties during inspections. Even in some of these cases it is not clear whether operators paid the full cost of the service. This low uptake may have several different causes. Certainly the volume of free consultancy services that companies can access through EPOPA programmes is high. Secondly, the absorptive capacity of most operators for consultancy services is probably low. Many appear to be unfamiliar with how to go about identifying consultancy needs and suitable consultants, and perhaps also lack

Van Bussel observes that development agencies (as well as state institutions) experience difficulties in understanding, engaging with, utilising and supporting the complex and informal existing business systems and embedded services of firms in the agricultural sector (2005, 12).

> "BSMD agro business survey revealed that although 73% of the development agencies [surveyed successfully] indicated that they address supply chain or business linkages issues, only 27% of them work with the different businesses in a supply chain and no specific programme or systematic support is known of which helps and includes all businesses in a chain to establish or develop their entire supply chain ... [N]o organisation supports the development of services of professional service providers, such as accounting, marketing or law firms, that are potentially important service providers" (ibid 14, 19).

As seen above, the challenge of ensuring the ability to export within globally-integrated VCs (and their stringent quality specifications) does not only concern the larger, established sectors, but also the niche market exporters, e.g. in organic agricultural products[307], and sections of the public sector, including regulatory, training and technology SIs. These exporters will have to (continue to) set up systems that permit traceability of products and inputs (in some cases: 'farm-to-table'), quality control, standards compliance, and formalised sales agreements with SHFs and other chain players. Currently, the fish industry, for example, can typically only trace raw material inputs up to trading intermediaries, at times also one more step upstream (collection boat operators). Businesses that supply a liberalising domestic market face pressures to improve their inter-firm relationships within the chains and formalize business transactions.

One question in this regard is how effective the private and public sector will interact at local and national level in the various issue areas to develop respective capacities, capabilities

---

the know-how to get the most out of consultants. Thirdly, lack of resources to pay for consultancy services on a commercial basis is another important factor" (2006, 25-6). The Swedish funded EPOPA (Export Promotion of Organic Production in Africa) programme "has concentrated on subsidising certification and providing technical assistance for setting up internal control systems (ICSs), training of project personnel and marketing" (ibid, 2). Finally, during his PhD research, this author interviewed several NGO, donor and government officials who, while emphasizing the importance of trust in economic development in Uganda, appeared to have done no or hardly any conceptual (or empirical research) reading on the topic. One NGO organised sector platform-building workshop, which aimed to build relationships and trust between farmers and traders in a particular agricultural product in Eastern Uganda, made the impression of business as usual (e.g. Kampala-based consultants and NAADS officials occupying most talking time) rather than making a more substantial departure from previous forms of mainstream development interventions. The latter impression confirms findings by van Bussel and Nyabuntu (2007).

307 A good illustration of challenges is given in Gibbon's account on the certified organic export sector: there "has been ... a steady increase in numbers of operators which will be sustained into 2006 and 2007. This seems to reflect a combination of factors including growing awareness of opportunities in the sector, the availability of donor support especially for certification, and the very sharp downturn in the conventional vanilla market. The newer players tend to be smaller and financially and managerially weak, as well as to be facing more substantial challenges than the earlier generation of operators. They are generally obliged to organise outgrowers from scratch, as opposed to establish relations with existing producer organisations, and they generally work in international markets that are more immature. They cannot afford to recruit well-qualified staff and they cannot take advantage of economies of scale in certification and field operations. These challenges seem to be most testing for those operators that also lack experience of conventional exporting. It may be that their casualty rate will be high when they reach the end of their cycle of donor project funding, and that the sector will contract in terms of numbers of operators after the present phase of expansion is concluded in 2007" (2006, 31).

and systems along the chains and sort out the various conflicts between actors in and outside particular chains? Moreover, how effectively will Uganda be able to take advantage of GVC trends? The implementation status, in economic affairs, of the decentralisation policy of GOU since 1997 also comes into play here: Required capacities and resources at local level for engaging in such broad and complex transformations, including capability formation, are seldom adequately at hand. Yet, the former systems of interaction between the districts and the center (in terms of information, reporting, and policy awareness) have diminished in some crucial areas; though, for instance, the MTTI is presently trying to revive them.

According to the BSMD study on local sourcing strategies, useful support for development of improved sourcing systems in agro-industries could be related to: (1) research on commercially-viable sourcing strategies and related market dynamics, (2) exchange of information, ideas, chain management approaches and experiences between firms, with SIs and other key stakeholders, and (3) mechanisms for learning and training, as well as establishment of long-term business relationships between farmers and their buyers (Bear and Goldman 2005). Other recommendations from the BSMD study on 'Successful Supply Chains in Uganda' are summarised in Box 28.

Box 28: BSMD recommendations with respect to supply chain development in Uganda

Private Sector

- "Maintain a strong focus on high value exports.
- Carry out a careful selection of business partners, according to a set of criteria that is based on experience.
- Nurture long-term relationships throughout the chain, built on mutual trust and transparency, and ensure that all businesses in the chain understand each other's tasks and responsibilities and the implied interdependency.
- Lead firms should invest in building a close relationship with suppliers and vice-versa. For instance, lead firms can assist farmers to access extension services, develop and implement a quality management system with clear and measurable standards, and develop an effective communication system. Suppliers should provide reliable information about production capacities and inform their buyers about possible changes that could affect their operations.
- Promote a business attitude among farmers based on contracts, purchase orders, and production and quality targets, by engaging farmers in the production monitoring system and administrative systems, by sharing information about market requirements, by training and by savings mobilization.
- Draw up and agree upon a code of practice to establish clear trading rules e.g. to counteract 'poaching' of goods between competing companies.
- Look for strategic alliances with other exporters, both at home and abroad.

Government of Uganda

- Improve the effectiveness of extension services in the agricultural sector. For example by promoting the establishment of supply chains and targeting farmers that are part of a supply chain in a systematic way, instead of individual farmers that are not linked to a supply chain.
- Low level of education of farmers is a problem, this suggests a need for vocational training not only to improve farming skills, but also entrepreneurial skills and to raise the status of farming as a profession.

- Stimulate private-private partnerships, by removing bureaucratic barriers and providing fiscal incentives to new supply chain initiatives.
- Stimulate the involvement of specific government agencies in the development of supply chains.
- Stimulate practical research activities aimed at supply chain development.
- Organize platforms for public and private actors to discuss problems in the private sector and find common solutions.
- Invest in basic infrastructure (roads, railways, telecommunication, and electricity).
- Offer fiscal incentives for sustainable use of natural resources.
- Offer fiscal incentives for innovative or high-risk investments.
- Establish a commercial code that includes property rights and fair judicial processes.

Support agencies

- Facilitate the linking of local businesses with national, regional and foreign companies, to build up trade relations or set up joint ventures.
- Facilitate the development of training and technical assistance to farmers to help them improve their performance and entrepreneurial development.
- Reduce the amount of paperwork involved in support to private sector as the costs in time and money spent on proposals and reports can be quite high and is generally not covered by the donor agency.
- Be more business-like in supporting the private sector, by focusing on those farmers that show potential, by charging clients for services and by setting targets that can be objectively measured.
- Avoid market distortion which may result from subsidizing certain producers at the expense of other producers.
- Support the initial start-up or experimentation costs of a new supply chain, only in certain specific cases where these activities would otherwise not take place and with a clear exit strategy within a limited time-frame.
- Facilitate the certification of producers and related conversion processes by promoting the development of a more competitive market for service providers and more cost-efficient certification procedures.
- Continue research into successful supply chains to learn from experience within private sector and stimulate replication of successful cases".

Source: *Ribbink et al. (2005, 36-7).*

The outlined agenda requires developing long-term-oriented inter-actor linkages and network forms of production and trade. This includes joint learning and upgrading efforts which involve knowledge sharing. Further, it requires the establishment, where appropriate, of systems of (commercial/income) incentives, compliance, surveillance, enforcement and risk management, and the development of the related capabilities (e.g. in sanitary control). Business practices need to be more conducive to joint learning and continued skills formation. These necessities apply to the current formal and informal sector. Changes have to be at levels appropriate and sufficient to supply domestic, regional and international markets and comply with their respective standards. Note that quality problems have led to incidences of rejection of Ugandan products by regional buyers. Certainly, a number of actors play a crucial role in the above agenda.

HRD at core of domestic value chain development

Due to the transformational requirements within VCs, HRD has to be analysed in a comprehensive manner which touches technical *and* social skills, matters of trust/mistrust, and business culture and political economy generally. Building the required HRD can permit the development of the required socio-economic structures in a sustainable way, complying with social and other standards in the target markets, and enabling sectors to respond in a proactive rather than defensive manner to challenges and opportunities of competitiveness and sustainable development. A proactive, concerted and comprehensive approach which anticipates market and other dynamics would (a) enable sectors to be 'early-entrants' instead of 'latecomers' in some industry aspects (standards, certifications) thus improving competitiveness along those lines, e.g. case of ecolabelling in the fish industry (Ponte 2005), or (b) would allow larger stakeholder groups to benefit from market developments, such as Fair/Ethical/Organic Trade labels. Currently, a very small percentage of Ugandan products (coffee, tea, flowers, fish) are sold under 'specialty' certifications.

Indeed, there is a broad range of required support measures for capability formation and systematic development of production and trade networks in the context of VCD. Steps in that direction are under way, e.g. in the area of codes: the Uganda National Bureau of Standards has developed a number of codes of practice related to standards and quality, the floriculture industry has advanced experience with codes of conduct, fish processors have a code of production practices in place (focusing on quality and technical standards), the cotton industry is working on resolutions (McGuigan et al. 2005, 13-4), and NAADS is active in VCD and cluster development. However, the vast majority of SHFs have not been reached by GOU/donor projects. Moreover, many initiatives are highly dependent on external support (raising issues of sustainability) and are often reactive in nature (to events or external forces and demands). Yet, tackling and transforming broader systems require a more proactive and long-term perspective. According to various experiences, VCD can take up to five (and more) years (van Bussel 2005, 15).

It is the author's impression that large sections of GOU, NGOs, donors and the private sector have yet to more comprehensively appreciate (and act upon) the rationalities and dynamics of VCD and its link to the HRD theme; for instance, that raising technical, entrepreneurial and social capabilities of SHFs participating in VCs decreases the coordination and training costs and the related risk for the Lf (this makes chain establishment and expansion more attractive); or, that participation of local firms in GVCs can bring learning benefits. The VCD agenda has at its heart complex matters of (and, thus, also challenges and opportunities for) HRD; improved infrastructure or financial market development alone will not do the job. The PSD debate in Uganda needs to reflect more strongly on HRD-in-VCs-aspects.

Adjustment needs for training provision

From the above it follows that training and other support measures have to be linked increasingly to market structures and business linkages issues, such as understanding and dealing with VCD and related issues of management dynamics, input sourcing, handling conflicts, establishment and strengthening of mutually beneficial business-to-business links, standard compliance or specialisation and joint growth strategies that are based on cooperation and linkage structures. A recent report on building cooperation between farmers and traders in Africa concludes neatly: "Effective partnering [between value chain actors] requires a set of skills which may need to be trained, such as cultural sensitivity, creativity, flexibility, willingness to compromise, diplomacy, commitment, patience, negotiation, results-orientation, strategic thinking, and interpersonal communication" (KIT and IIRR 2008, 234).

Where appropriate, training and similar activities - those related to farmers, who are often the main target group of GOU/development agencies - should involve other commercial stakeholders in the VC as well: input suppliers, service providers, brokers, traders, retailers, agro-processors, marketing firms, advisors, exporters, foreign and potential buyers as well as SIs. This can strengthen and upgrade the whole system - existing (and potential) business relationships and thus inter-firm cooperation patterns within VCs - through tapping of collective action externalities and efficiencies. Better linkages to markets and higher sustainability prospects are then more likely. Considering VC dimensions helps to design training that can be more specific to respective buyer requirements, e.g. different buyers might have different product requirements. Importantly, entrepreneurship-training agents should consider the above issues as well.[308] Yet, most small enterprise development agencies in the agricultural sector in Uganda underestimate or neglect these chain aspects (van Bussel 2005, van Bussel and Nyabuntu 2007).

It is also vital to recognise the meaning of and/or support (a) the improved provision of *embedded BDS* which include training, logistics, financing, legal advice, network formation, market research, and information management, that come with normal transactions within a chain (see below), and (b) the development of commercial codes, codes of production and trade, business principles and ethics, producer certification, and quality standards that can foster inter-firm linkage building. For instance, "'skill development' through training programmes will in itself not be an adequate way of ensuring growing shares in global production networks. These skills have to be harnessed into teams, meeting focused objectives which can be realised in the market. These teams are simultaneously embedded in firms, which are in turn embedded in value chains" (Kaplinsky and Morris 2001, 44). A recent evaluation report on a GTZ/PEVOT project on Local skills development (LSD) in self-organised and self-financed *learning groups* (LGs) in rural areas points to the adverse consequences of training initiatives that do not take some of the considerations discussed above into account:

> "[I]mportant factors of feasibility of the training projects have often not been taken into account. Main difficulties were market opportunities. Markets are too far or not lucrative for the products of the LG. Transport is rare or expensive. Some LGs did not consider sufficiently the lack of local infrastructure like electricity, which was the case for the hairdressers or welders. They had to adapt first or there were not enough clients for the services provided at local level. Local availability of inputs had not been checked and were too expensive to get elsewhere" (PEVOT 2005, 27).

A VC perspective and related basic analytical tools (e.g. chain mapping and critical success factors analysis) can help to clarify important market structures and related challenges, *identifying* and *prioritising* knowledge and skills requirements and related gaps according to different chains (and thus *different requirements of buyers*), and pointing to different opportunities to improve these HR deficiencies in a more market-oriented and/or embedded

308 See also Humphrey (2005, 31-7) for similar points.

way (Humphrey 2005, 31). For instance, a critical success factor analysis that is informed by a VC perspective - e.g. analysis of buyers' assessment of critical success factors at producer level (buyer requirements) - can help firms to better understand "the requirements of buyers, or the areas where they are exceeding, meeting, or failing to meet these requirements" (ibid). Field research pointed to cases of different perceptions that suppliers have regarding (i) vital requirements and priorities of their buyers (such as delivery reliability, price, quality, financial stability innovation, flexibility, packaging, or conformance to specifications) and (ii) to which *extent* they meet those. Using tools such as buyers' feedback on producer deficiencies can help prioritising producer-level training and upgrading efforts (ibid, 55).[309]

On embedded services: Based on van Bussel's synthesis of the three-year-long (2002-05) BSMD project (van Bussel 2005) one might ask: How could public and private sector SIs help to develop and improve VCs which can provide linkage and specialisation opportunities for currently isolated (disconnected) MSEs? How could embedded service structures - professional services offered by the private sector itself - be understood better in the first place, and then be developed and/or strengthened? What is the impact of subsidised services provision by GOU/donors on embedded services? How (and to which extent) should subsidised support be offered to and channelled through VC Lfs, which are in a relatively better position to pay for embedded services and offer them to their suppliers in the chain? How can incentive structures and productivity in the VC be improved, not only *within* individual firms/production units but also along the VC, and thus in *inter-firm* relations? In this respect, van Bussel, referring to the BSMD experience, suggests the following to tackle the existing defects in business operations and services markets, including related training aspects:

> "[D]evelopment agencies ... should help commercial BDS providers to upgrade existing and develop new services and delivery mechanisms. Development agencies therefore require focusing on systemic change ... Specifically, [they] ... should concentrate more on the development, testing and promotion of improved market-oriented systems, tools and approaches that enable firms to access the support they need to improve their businesses ... The ultimate purpose would be, for example, to develop methods, standards and guidelines that the private sector can use and adapt to continue and repeat proven services and approaches profitably ... Doing business: developing products, exploring market opportunities, production, providing business services, etc, is in principle the task of the private sector. Development agencies should help companies to undertake this task themselves more effectively ... This [outlined agenda, however,] involves taking a long-term perspective, a holistic view, coordinated approaches and a shift from an output-orientation towards an impact orientation" (ibid, 3, 21-2).

Certainly, one would have to complement the above perspective on PSD support with the approaches and findings discussed earlier in this book, for instance Lall's argument about HRD-relevant market and institutional failures in the catch-up process (risks, costs, externalities, and coordination failures) which require decisive public sector support, especially for capability and technology accumulation. Van Bussel rightly indicates, however, that BDS providers could broaden and upgrade their BDS by relating them to the development and provision of embedded services, e.g. develop training that firms can use for developing their retail outlets, or help professional advisors (e.g. marketing experts or conflict mediators) to adjust their services to VCD perspectives. GOU and donors could support such innovations, which would be justified by a situation where these new activities face market failure issues mentioned

---

309 See Wiegratz (2007a) for an application of this technique to the Ugandan case.

above and/or require skills which are not yet available in conventional BDS agencies (ibid, 19-20).[310] Importantly, the BSMD experience demonstrates that the agenda of VCs, inter-firm linkages and cooperation, trust, embedded service provision (including training) and a market-in perspective in training design has potential to be beneficial with view to reaching and upgrading the many MSMEs (ibid, 15) and thus fostering an important part of the HRD and the related pro-poor growth agenda. The notes below are valid for Uganda:

> "The impact of supply chain interventions will most probably include improved farm-level production; an increased stability in household incomes due to stronger linkages, better knowledge of and response to market requirements; a stronger focus on improving productivity 'end-to-end' or 'farmer-to-market', increased supply chain efficiencies, long-term market-orientation within the private sector, both in perception and practice; and a business service sector responding to activities from these supply chains and therefore better targeted. All this is contributing to business growth and increased competitiveness" (ibid, 25).

Van Bussel also points to certain dilemmas in upgrading (value addition) efforts at the lower end of DVCs: the farm level. In this view, attempts - by GOU, NGOs, donors and others - to sideline or eliminate the functions of specialised agents in or related to a VC (input suppliers, middlemen, traders and marketing agents) might well be inefficient and risky and result in ineffective parallel market structures and thus not the expected benefits for farmers:

> "Traders and middlemen are fulfilling highly specialized and resource consuming functions in the market, including innovations in sourcing, bulking and marketing of produce that other players either would prefer not to undertake or are incapable of undertaking. Either way they do play an important role that should not be underestimated" (ibid, 7).[311]

The statement exemplifies the need to consider respective VC structures carefully, and to strengthen the functioning, upgrading and thus competitiveness of whole systems. This can, where appropriate, also include VC players taking on new functions within the specific, or a different chain, e.g. farmers becoming more involved in processing and VC coordination and thus 'sidelining' previous VC partners. As noted, the relationship with foreign VC actors in GVCs (LLL-approach) can be a crucial aspect of accelerated learning and upgrading in a latecomer context.[312] Finally, the state has to take on a meaningful role in nurturing VCs.

HRD proponents need to reflect on value chain structures and dynamics

We have explored the perspectives of VCs and the related issues of governance, upgrading, embedded services and business practices with some length because they constitute a new terrain for HRD-related activities. Some points made above emphasise the *organisational,*

310 See also Poulton et al. (2006) for remarks on measures (and the respective roles of the state) to improve, for instance, coordination within crucial agricultural VCs (pro-poor agricultural growth).

311 As always, one has to keep in mind that the behaviour and performance of traders and middlemen (and other actors) can differ from case to case, and thus require a case-specific assessment of the merits and fault of traders, state agencies and officials (e.g. related to agricultural extension, police and judiciary), and other VC actors such as farmers, transporters, brokers, etc.

312 Different governance forms could emerge (including rules of entry for SSA firms) in those GVCs that are led by firms from China, or India, in contrast to GVCs led by European (super-)markets (Kaplinsky 2005b).

managerial, cultural, and *behavioural (rather than purely 'technical') aspects of VCD* and thus *related HR outcomes and training needs.* The discussion complements and explains earlier findings, e.g. the low level of specialisation, supply-side response, and productivity. It is vital for HRD proponents to consider how they can respond to these realities, and adjust their approaches accordingly. Certainly, since VCs are dynamic, change is constant and thus flexibility of various kinds, including ability to respond to change, is an important implication for those who wish to debate HRD in the context of competitiveness and economic development.[313]

The perspective suggested in this chapter could be less directly suitable to mainstream approaches of the 'constraints-list' kind which often operate along single-issue solutions. Clustering, VCs and (the politics and sociology of) business culture are broader themes which - if tackled successfully - allow exploitation of opportunities and potential for economic development through multiple positive effects. The changes advocated for above are indeed often *systemic* changes.

313 The point is attributed to Victor Richardson.

11

Analysis of Government Strategies for Economic Development

The Poverty Eradication Action Plan 2004/05-2007/08

Objective: Uganda to become an industrialised middle-income country

In this chapter, the author analyses core economic strategies of GOU and discusses their implications for and links with the theme of HRD. Though there will be ever new/revised strategies of GOU in the coming years, it is vital to understand and analyse the evolution of thinking and arguments in these important and historical documents up to the time of research. Such a review also points to deficits in the arguments and priorities which, - if not discussed and where appropriate revised, might continue to appear in consequent documents and thus hamper HRD and PSD in the future.

The Poverty Eradication Action Plan (PEAP, see MFPED 2004) is Uganda's national planning framework, the purpose of which is to provide an overarching framework for guiding public action to eradicate poverty. Within this framework, the different sectors (education etc.) develop their plans. Since 1997, when the PEAP was first drafted, Uganda has been pursuing a policy of poverty eradication with a focus on export diversification, industrialisation, and increased household income. The PEAP was revised in 2000 and 2004 to accommodate changing circumstances and emerging priorities. The PEAP 2004/05-2007/08 sets the goal for Uganda to boost growth to 7% p.a. over the medium term, and to become a *middle-income country* within twenty years, with enhanced ability to compete favourably in international markets over the long-term (within twenty years).

Key strategies identified are (1) *accelerated industrialisation* through enhanced private investment and competitiveness and better exploitation of the agricultural potential (commercial agriculture, agro-processing industry), and (2) *improved participation of the poor in the growth process* through advancements and better income opportunities related to (a) smallholder agriculture and (b) non-agricultural self-employment in the medium term, as well as (c) wage employment in the long run (ibid, 1-11, 25). Government's perspective is as follows:

> "In order to achieve middle-income status, Uganda needs to industrialise by enhancing its competitiveness. Industrialisation in Uganda will depend on using the resource base and hence on equipping farmers to understand the technical and quality requirements of commercial production. Government will therefore ensure the provision of public goods to support both agriculture and industry. In order to reverse the recent marked increase in inequality, Government will aim to increase the ability of the poorer households to participate in economic growth through self-employment inside and outside agriculture and wage employment" (ibid, xv). In other words, "Uganda's strategy for poverty reduction ... combines increased agricultural incomes from smallholder farming [which is expected to boost business for locally oriented non-

> agricultural entrepreneurs in rural areas, who are assumed to depend on incomes raised from agriculture] with increased opportunities for wage employment coming from the growth of formal enterprises in agriculture, industry and services" (ibid, 25). Moreover, "[c]orresponding to the shift in labour force is a shift in the structure of the economy. Over time, two major shifts are expected; towards industry, and towards exports" (ibid, 25).

The new PEAP can be seen as an attempt to balance investments between the productive and social sectors, different to the PEAP 2000's emphasis on social investments. "[W]e have ... observed slow growth in the productive sector and therefore this PEAP emphasizes a strategy that is linked to both sectors" (ibid, 4). In this context, the document notes the *limited direct impact* of public spending under the last PEAP on the *economic/income* situation of poor households and thus on poverty. GOU spends a relatively small amount of money on the economic sectors in the first place: the agricultural sector gets less than 5% of the budget. Of course, spending on education and health services has its benefit in terms of access for the poor.

> "[b]ut it did not directly increase the incomes of the poor, and the income benefits to public servants mostly went to people above the poverty line. Some of the increases went into salaries, public administration and defence. None of these has a dramatic direct impact on poverty, except in the case where increased defence expenditure leads to improved security. Finally, there were increases in agricultural spending (especially under the Strategic Exports Programme); these may not yet have borne fruit, partly because of time lags for investments such as coffee trees to mature, and partly because of efficiency issues. Also, data on public services suggest that the interventions in production, such as extension and demonstration gardens, did not yet successfully target the poorest. The increase in education has had a significant impact. However, this impact has been mainly experienced by the better-off households. This may be because the impact of UPE on adults' education comes with a lag. For this reason, it is hoped that the long-run impact of UPE will be to spread economic opportunities more widely and hence reduce inequality" (ibid, 17, emphasis added).

The above assessment of only moderate results of the PEAP in changing the economic situation of poor households is important. It might signal that: (i) the authorities feel there is need to implement a different (e.g. broadened) set of interventions for economic development, (ii) the level of change required for designing and operating a different, and more effective, pro-poor policy and programme mix is significant, and consequently, (iii) the country, including GOU, faces some 'unknown territory' (more of the same will likely not suffice) in this endeavour. The above statement confirms a range of vital arguments of this book, including the call for a broader view on requirements for PSD and related HRD issues.[314]

The challenges and pillars addressed in the PEAP

Against this background, and the dynamics in the early 2000s (increased poverty and inequality, environmental degradation, etc.), the PEAP highlights **four challenges** for the coming period: restoring security (e.g. by improving regional equity), restoring sustainable growth in the incomes of the poor, fostering human development, and using public resources transparently and efficiently to eradicate poverty (e.g. enhancing quality rather than quantity

314 For some further background on the (politics of the) PEAP and related matters see: Muwanga-Zake and Ndhaye (2001), Foster and Mijumbi (2002), Bird (2003), Francis and James (2003), Brock et al. (2004), McGee (2004, 2000), Piron and Norton (2004), Ssewakiryanga (2005, 2004a, 2004b), Hickey (2005, 2003), Booth and Nsabagasani (2005), CPRC Uganda (2005), Lwange-Ntale (2006), and OPM (2008, 2007), EPRC (2009).

of public services). The framework is grouped under **five pillars**: (1) economic management, (2) production, competitiveness and incomes, (3) security, conflict-resolution and disaster-management, (4) good governance, and (5) human development. The identified crosscutting issues are gender (e.g. ensuring women's participation in the economy/growth process), environment, HIV/AIDS, hygiene and sanitation, employment (e.g. wage employment, working conditions and wages), population growth, social protection, income distribution and regional equity (ibid, 1-6). Although all five pillars of the PEAP play an important role regarding economic and social development, the three main pillars that are more directly relevant to HRD are pillars 1, 2, and 5. Key priorities identified under these pillars are:

- **Economic management:** maintenance of macroeconomic stability, fiscal consolidation, boosting private investment and high, sustained private sector-led growth, improving trade policy management with key measures in this respect being: (a) removal of bureaucratic barriers to investment, (b) improvement in transport infrastructure and utility services, (c) *modernisation/commercialisation of agriculture*, with emphasis on *value-addition*, (d) actions to improve rural access to finance and to *strengthen SME development*, (e) enhancing environmental sustainability, (f) security in Northern Uganda, (g) enhancing *gender equality*, and (h) continued focus on HIV prevalence reduction and mitigation of its impact;
- **Production, competitiveness and incomes:** *modernisation of agriculture*, preservation of the natural resource base, infrastructure, *enhancing private sector skills* and *business development* and tackling labour productivity with respective supply/demand-side constraints being addressed through main policy frameworks (Plan for Modernisation of Agriculture/PMA, Medium Term Competitiveness Strategy/MTCS, Strategic Exports Programme/SEP, see below);
- **Human development:** improving efficiency/performance of primary as well as post-primary education (focus on *quality* and the ultimate objective of *learning*), including better targeting of public expenditure for those who would not otherwise afford it (especially girls), particularly regarding secondary/tertiary education which needs expansion, supporting a *vocational ETS* that is *flexible* and *matched with the economy's needs* and becomes an *alternative* to academic education in the last two years of secondary education, improving health outcomes as well as access to and quality of water, increasing people's ability to plan their families better, and using *community-based approaches* to strengthen social protection for vulnerable groups (ibid, xvi-xxv, 34).

Analysis of selected PEAP aspects and important links to the HRD debate

Primary sector focus

It is evident from the content and rationale of pillars 1 and 2 that government's main concern and strategic entry point for immediate economic development in the *context of poverty reduction* is the *primary sector*: its commercialisation, including necessary linkages to the secondary (agro-processing industry) and tertiary sector. The PEAP 2004 can thus be seen, to large extent, as an agro-based rural development strategy. The PEAP *assumptions* behind this rationale are that this focus (1) will best target the majority of the poor in rural areas and improve their situation, (2) will (supposedly) create spillovers to the rest of the economy (industry, trade and services) through increased incomes in the agricultural sectors that raise demand for non-agricultural products and services in rural but also urban areas, and (3) is further justified due to a (supposedly) responsive attitude of the agricultural sector to provision of public goods such as research, extension and marketing support (e.g. through collective action arrangements, such as cooperatives and the like). The link to the industrial and services sectors is projected to develop through strategies of agro processing and marketing (ibid, 1-11). Skills development is incorporated in the core agenda mainly in relation to *commercialisation of agriculture* and *upgrading of MSMEs*.

Although this strategic agenda has some gaps in terms of conceptual considerations and programmatic focus, it is a vital strategy and its implementation is important, including the emphasised development of agriculture and agro-industry and other natural resource-based sectors. This entails the outlined improvements on the various productivity and HRD fronts and in the area of SIs. Related state interventions are more designed towards the agricultural/ commodity sector than manufacturing or services. Vital is also government's commitment regarding a combined strategy of the development of both informal smallholder farming and the formal sector (including the agro-processing industry). Significantly, the PEAP recognises the *adverse role* of *population expansion* for the *economic growth prospects*:

> "Population growth: is a major issue for poverty reduction. New analytical work has been conducted for this PEAP on the effects of population growth for incomes, motivated by the discovery in the 2002 Census that population growth was higher than had previously been observed. The results of this analysis strongly suggest that the very large families that have been observed over the years in Uganda are now becoming an impediment to the speed of economic growth and social and structural transformation. There is evidence that many people, particularly women, would like smaller families ... [In summary:] Per capita growth will depend on population growth. Per capita growth will be accelerated if Uganda enters the demographic transition by achieving smaller family sizes" (ibid, 7, xvi).

Comprehensive value chain concept needed to grasp HRD dimensions fully

Importantly, although not always explicitly stated in the document, the PEAP's conceptualisation of interventions in productive sectors is basically informed by a *VC approach*; though to a limited extent. The conceptual oversight is to separate 'value addition' as a sort of extra activity that takes place mainly in the industrial realm (e.g. add value to a commodity by processing it), whereas the VC concept describes the full range of value-added activities at *every chain stage* involved in bringing a product from its conception and production (e.g. the farm, storage, transport, and later the processing factory and marketing) to its use and disposal. The organisational setup, efficiency and effectiveness of the *whole VC*, including logistical efficiency (transport, cold chain, warehousing) and characteristics of business linkages between VC actors (farmers and traders/processors) impacts on the VC's productivity, competitiveness, value addition/capture and thus profits. Such economy-wide aspects are somewhat blurred by placing value-addition mainly (or only) in the processing stage of agricultural produce. Though in practice, more recent state programmes have applied a more holistic view of possible interventions (post-harvest handling, storage) along the chain. Note, that measures for moving up-market (processing and marketing of crops) are usually formulated in the PEAP (and other government documents) from the perspective of the farmer and agricultural sector. The perspective of the agro-processing industry is hardly mentioned in this context. Also, VCs in services and manufacturing sectors can differ in important aspects from agro-value chains, including respective HR dynamics and needs for state support, or industry action.

There is furthermore relatively little said in explicit terms in the PEAP, or the value-addition debate in the country in 2008, on strategic issues of 'value capture' (and related power asymmetries in respective GVCs) beyond aiming at better market price information tools or processing commodities in the country (which is, of course, very important). The 'value capture' perspective (see chapter on VCs) can help in the formulation of different public and private sector strategies for the Ugandan case. Important to note however: The 'Good African Coffee' initiative of the Ugandan entrepreneur Andrew Rugasira contains elements of a value capture strategy; responding to existing power imbalances in the coffee GVCs by processing coffee in Uganda, branding and marketing the coffee directly (e.g. to supermarkets in the UK, partly via partners/outsourcing), setting up coffee houses in the UK (London) and South Africa etc.[315] There needs to be follow-up research on this important business case, also to support it further and to emulate it in other suitable sub-sectors.

Moreover, there is only some loose reference in the PEAP to other VC issues; for instance, a *lead firm perspective* is mentioned - yet without further elaboration of possible implications or interventions. "Uganda's production systems are based on small holdings. This demands that value addition facilities ... [be] based on cooperatives or farmer associations or based on a lead firm that provides appropriate scale of value addition facilities and applies economies of scale in product marketing" (MFPED 2004, 68). The PEAP also refers to a VC perspective with respect to priority actions related to the Strategic Export Plan (SEP) and Zoning Plan: "Implement SEP and the Agricultural Zoning Initiative in a manner that focuses activities along the commodity value chain" (ibid, 57). The question remains: What does this mean in practice? Earlier, we mentioned van Bussel's (2005) observation about the severe problems experienced in developing VCs in Uganda. In this context, do the authorities, or the PEAP authors, (already) know 'what works' in VCD? Or, are they willing to start experimenting with the approach? The lines below suggest that the latter might be the case: "A review of the [SEP] ... has recommended the need to ... supporting identification of interventions with analytical work along the entire market chain and minimising the production bias in the current activities" (MFPED 2004, 56). Hence one of the questions is: what can be learnt in this respect from the international literature on VCD and the experiences of other African countries and Uganda (Fold and Nylandsted Larsen 2008, Gibbon and Ponte 2005, van Bussel 2005, Wiegratz et al. 2007a, 2007b)?[316]

There is some other reference to related VC issues which can be interpreted as a 'mandate' to continue efforts in the area: "In the case of extension, the private sector does conduct effective extension on out grower crops such as tobacco, and NAADS is exploring the best way to cooperate with the private sector on out grower schemes" (MFPED 2004, 93). The point is that such statements are *not clarified further*, and thus remain somewhat loose. If not explored further and discussed, a limited VC, or agro-commercialisation and industrialisation perspectives can result in a narrow interpretation of related dynamics and intervention needs, which omits issues such as relevant capability formation, business linkages and practices, market institutions, organisational efficiency, farmers' learning and upgrading, or upgrading of agro-processing firms (Lfs).

Further, the use of the VC concept in the PEAP seems inadequate to capture important issues of and opportunities for entry into non-resource-based industries, especially GVCs in modern manufacturing, where single players only carry out specific functions and thus do not produce end products (e.g. in the textile sector). If entry into such non-agro sectors is to

315 See http://www.goodafrican.com/.
316 See also the special edition on GVCs in *Economy and Society* (37, 3).

be targeted, the VC concept currently used by relevant institutions in the country needs to be broadened or reformulated, which has HRD implications of the nature discussed earlier.

Further, the term 'learning' (e.g. on-the-job) is not mentioned in the context of PSD (where it would be vital), but in the education and public sector development sections. Also, there is not much detail on strategies to address non-farm skill gaps in the large informal entrepreneurial sector, e.g. in terms of technological learning and capability building. In fact, the industry (both agro and non-agro-based) or services sub-sectors also need support to apply new technology, move upmarket and seek engagement in higher-value-added activities in more dynamic markets. There is little in the PEAP that indicates how to promote this kind of process and related HR measures, e.g. industrial firms which enter new functions (develop new production or design capabilities, e.g. in the textile industry) or VCs, and upgrade their technology and production processes.

In summary, the approach of ensuring higher demand and returns for the agricultural products of the poor through agro processing (and helping the poor to participate more in wage employment) therefore needs to be broadened by a more integrated approach towards VCD in the country. This has to identify and tackle opportunities for improving VCs, including improving farmers' performance via enhanced linkages and cooperation between farmers and lead firms. The implicit and explicit references in the PEAP to VC matters justify policy makers and other stakeholders applying the VC approach in their interventions. The challenges in this respect are likely to be: to link the VC approach to issues on the ground in terms of existing policies and programmes which are embedded in other concepts, and to broaden the scope of interventions informed by a VC perspective and increase their effectiveness over time. Issues such as better business links, organisational VC efficiency, standard compliance, investment in VC logistics, farmers and buyers cooperating and learning from each other, or building inter-actor trust will become increasingly relevant issues in this respect.

The above aspects are only partly encapsulated in the PEAP, which is unfortunate, since this is the national planning framework. Some issues are discussed in related plans, such as the cooperatives and area marketing cooperative enterprises, the marketing and agro-processing strategy (MAPS), the agricultural zoning, the clustering of commodity sectors, or district market information system development. Notably, the implementation of the PEAP and related plans is set against the background of a number of ministries and institutions which were short on capacities, capabilities and funding at the time of research (2006) and/or have considerable deficits in terms of both performance record and relationships with the private sector, the LIS, and the districts. In the recent past, many plans for PSD in Uganda which involved PSD-related public institutions had significant implementation weaknesses. Issues such as lessons learnt, or the commitment, responsibility, and accountability of respective stakeholders remain unsure. Against this background, parts of the PEAP and related plans appear very ambitious.

The post-2006 developments show that GOU is increasingly working with the VC approach in the development of Uganda's agro sectors. NAADS has engaged in a number of partnerships with farmers and agro processors (see Wiegratz et al. 2007b). Some studies have been commissioned, and VCD terminology has entered the expert and public debate on economic development in the country. The forthcoming PEAP (or National Development Plan) is likely to have more reference to VC matters. This author trusts that the VC approach, though it has some limitations, will help to design and carry out vital support interventions in the future.[317]

Industrial Competitiveness: Vital dimensions yet to be addressed in practice

It appears that the scope of action suggested by the PEAP does not yet offer a *sufficient* recipe for the kind of industrialisation that can bring Uganda, as envisaged, into the range of a *middle-income country*. The PEAP is, overall, fairly limited regarding strategies for improvement and transformation of the manufacturing or services sector *within a competitive global economy*, e.g. on capability formation, collective action or clustering. Spillover effects to the whole economy are foreseen to come from agriculture rather than industry (ibid, 51). Besides a number of general industrialisation statements at the beginning of the document, and the relevant commitment to implement the industrialization policy in the medium term[318] and deliberations on related issues (infrastructure, finance), there is only one page on 'science, technology, and industrialisation' in a 260-page document.[319] Maybe this outcome is due to Uganda's level of industrialization.[320] It could also be explained by the PEAP being a Poverty-Eradication document, and not a strategy paper for industrialisation, competitiveness or economic development as such. Yet, the PEAP could also reflect the main understanding of the core agents involved in economic policy making regarding the economic status quo and options available for the country.[321]

The impression is that deliberations are guided by a sequential understanding of the future path of export-led economic and industrial development and the links between sectoral growth and poverty reduction (rural development is the key in the medium term).[322] GOU

317 See Wiegratz et al. (2007a, b) and Wiegratz 2008b) for details.

318 The industrial policy was approved by cabinet in early 2008. The MTTI prepared a draft version some years ago titled 'Policy Framework for Industrialization in Uganda 2004-2009' (MTTI 2004). There was, however, need for further clarification, and analysis of salient matters. In this context, UNIDO provided some technical assistance for an industrial competitiveness analysis, see UNIDO (2007).

319 In the first sentence on 'increasing competitiveness' the industrial sector is omitted completely (see quote below). This is surprising given the earlier key statement of the PEAP, that Uganda was to become a middle-income country mainly through industrialisation. "The fact that Uganda is landlocked and has a small domestic market demands that she develops an export oriented economic development strategy based on high value low volume commodities and services" (MFPED 2004, 86).

320 The economic development strategies could be designed mainly by experts with an agricultural background.

321 Consider, for instance, this view: "In Uganda's case, ... [her comparative and competitive] advantages are largely in agriculture and agro processing. Labour in Uganda is not cheap as in India or China, and high transport ... make it unlikely that Uganda can quickly become competitive in the assembly of goods from imported components. Manufacturing in Uganda is likely to focus mainly on production for the domestic market, and to some degree the regional market, except where it is processing products based on natural resources in Uganda - agriculture, forestry and fisheries. Uganda may also be able to develop a comparative advantage in some services, but will face stiff international competition in this area" (MFPED 2004, 48-9).

322 An example of the *sequential view* is as follows: "In the medium run, poverty reduction depends on expanding incomes from smallholder agriculture, for two reasons. First, the incomes of the poor depend directly on agriculture. Secondly, farmers spend part of the incomes generated from crop sales, on non-agricultural goods and services. Most self-employed non-agricultural producers sell their products locally and therefore depend on the demand generated by the incomes raised from agriculture. Therefore, when agricultural incomes fall - as they did between 2000 and 2003 - people in non-agricultural self-employment experience difficulties. There is international evidence that in low-income, agricultural economies, poverty responds much more to rural than to urban growth,

might consider putting more emphasis on strategies for a compatible *parallel* and integrated development of a competitive advanced formal sector in general and manufacturing export sector in particular (including non-traditional agro-industries, or even 'pure' manufacturing). To date, export diversification into product segments that are *unrelated to the country's inherited/ original natural resource endowment* and could *coexist* with traditional (resource-based) sectors seems not to have been considered sufficiently; the agricultural starting point and the rural development perspective dominate, as the quote below illustrates.

> "Because of the country's geographical position and strong (though vulnerable) natural resource base, one of the main forms of industrialisation will be value-addition by processing agricultural products. For this to happen, the country's farmers need to understand the technical and quality requirements of commercial production. The incomes generated as a result will represent a crucial infusion into rural areas, where most poor people in Uganda live. While manufactured exports will depend on agricultural inputs, manufacturing for the domestic market will depend on the demand for manufactured goods, and this in turn depends on rural incomes ... Government's strategy in the short run is therefore aimed at strengthening both agriculture and manufacturing" (ibid, 1).

In support of the agenda of the statement above, related Government plans, as expressed in the PEAP, are to target infrastructure, extension services, financial systems, the regulatory environment as well as education and skills development of workers and farmers (ibid).

It is important to note at this point that deliberations on economic development in Uganda seem to overly rely on the 'business environment' and 'cost of production' perspectives; instead of incorporating more strongly issues such as capability and technology accumulation, HRM, productivity, or organisational and thus political-economic aspects of sub-sector development. This is, to some extent, understandable given the severe infrastructure constraints of the country (power, roads, etc.). However, it is harmful to underplay, or sideline non-infrastructural aspects of economic development. While Uganda - including her policy makers - will have to make further improvements on the infrastructure and investment climate side, she will also have to engage more robustly with the 'capability agenda' at some point to enhance diversification, productivity, technology use and efficiency.

However, the quote below could well reflect the common thinking in policy circles: enterprise competitiveness and efficiency is mentioned; yet how to achieve it is not spelt out in detail.[323] Competitiveness is understood *mainly* in terms of costs of production inputs and transportation and related provision of public goods.[324] For the Ugandan competitiveness and HR context, there is too little emphasis on *building the 'new'/'modern' endowments* that create competitive advantage, such as *improved technical knowledge* and *human capital*, in particular social, productive and technological capabilities for firm-level advancements, especially in terms of technological, operational and managerial upgrading.

---

and that agricultural growth is needed in order to generate broader rural growth. This concern is particularly important because of the increased inequality in incomes that has been evident since 1997. Expansion in incomes from smallholder agriculture is the best way of reversing this trend. In the long run, an increasing proportion of incomes will be raised from wage employment. While wage employment provides only a small proportion of incomes for the poor at the moment, its importance will increase in the future. To boost wage employment, labour-intensive activities in the formal sector need to grow. This depends on profitable private investment" (MFPED 2004, 25).

323 For instance, through conceptual backing, or core pillars of related policies and measures.

324 At least, as discussed in the PEAP section on increasing competitiveness.

> "[A]n export oriented economic development strategy ...can only be achieved if the country is able to exploit Uganda's comparative advantage and promote enterprise competitiveness ... For Uganda's products to be competitive in regional and international markets, they must be produced in the most efficient and effective manner ... For Uganda to be competitive, it needs to work on the factors that influence the cost of production and transportation. Some of these factors have to do with the businesses themselves and others have to do with the public sector. Companies have to work hard to cut costs of production linked to the structural nature of their businesses; these vary from one company to another. However, in most surveys on business operations in Uganda, the major constraints are largely public in nature, including infrastructural (roads, rail, air), utilities (electricity, water), legislative, and administrative (corruption, taxation) constraints" (ibid, 86-7).

Importantly, the statement mentions promoting *enterprise competitiveness* and production efficiency and effectiveness. Also, the PEAP section on *'productivity of workers'* mentions the key role of skills in competitiveness improvements (ibid, 84). Elsewhere, there is recognition of *competitiveness based on firm-level abilities* to be *efficient* and to *innovate* and *adopt technologies.*

> "Competitiveness will be achieved by increasing the ability of Ugandan enterprises to be profitable and increase their share of the market, both domestic and external, and by satisfying the needs of the consumers. Key to this will be the firms' level of productivity and their *ability to both innovate* and *adapt to new technologies.* Thus by improving the competitiveness of Uganda's private sector we improve the ability of firms to respond to the demands of the marketplace" (ibid, 52, emphasis added).

These are very crucial statements. They point to the core of arguments made in this book: increased focus on productivity, learning and capability building at firm level, and other aspects (including a strong and responsive BTVET system) that increase a firm's ability to respond flexibly and successfully to competition dynamics. HRD ought to be incorporated center stage in such an agenda. Significantly, the statements might indicate the *beginning* of a *broadening* view and debate on competitiveness requirements and policy packages for PSD in Uganda.[325]

To date, apart from some important exceptions (e.g. the work of UIRI and NAADS), the actual policy and programme priorities are still focused rather on the macro than certain meso and micro competitiveness aspects. The 'business climate' and 'cost of production' agenda prevails. Further implications of targeting improved enterprise competitiveness in non-primary sectors - including matters of technological abilities or operational efficiencies - have *yet to be acknowledged and translated* into actual policies, support structures and practices. In the past, state support for vital aspects of firm-level productivity, and innovation or technological upgrading was rather weak and fragmented. The commitment to enterprise competitiveness might thus imply a more substantial shift in the understanding and the way of providing Government support for economic development: towards firm/farm and sector-level support that actually addresses *enterprise abilities* in terms of technology, efficiency, organisation and productivity.

HRD proponents have to engage more intensively in the competitiveness and PSD debate and exchange ideas with the 'business climate' proponents who (at times) tend to underplay the role of capability building, technology and the like. In this context, this author agrees that framework conditions, investment climate, and infrastructure improvements are among the

325 The overall fragmentations throughout the PEAP document of the arguments on competitiveness pillars might be due to drafting procedures, not different conceptual approaches or preferences of the authors.

crucial preconditions for economic development, especially in a post-conflict LDC economy. The argument in this book highlights, however, that the measures towards increased diversification, competitiveness and growth have to include the relevant dimensions at level of firms/farms, sub-sectors and SIs more prominently. This includes functioning factor markets (regarding productive capabilities) and support systems and thus an effective and up-to-date training system. In short, certain aspects of the investment climate agenda and the local capability building and learning agenda are *interlinked*[326] and *needed* for enhanced economic development in Uganda. However, the policy mix of the recent past in Uganda suggests preference for the problem analysis of the 'business climate' agents. It is important for HRD proponents to recognise the varying levels of concern for and nature of implications of *different PSD approaches* regarding HRD. For that reason we shall continue discussing related aspects in the remainder of the book.

We note that the PEAP also refers to some strategies for PSD (such as the MAPS) and other government efforts to increase competitiveness the economic services sector institutions (MTTI, MEMD and affiliated institutions) which all have certain linkages to matters of HRD: marketing skills, market information, farmer education and organisation, extension services, export promotion, or product development, standards and quality (ibid, 86-92). Still, taken together, the planned efforts don't seem to address HRD issues in a sufficient, comprehensive, and systemic manner; this would mean targeting the series of *interconnected changes* that are required in the Ugandan context to boost HR and competitiveness. The other question is whether these initiatives (i) will actually take off adequately, (ii) will go beyond the generic (sensitisation and workshop) level and avoid being overly fragmented on implementation, and (iii) can thus have adequate impact on HRD on the ground.

Finally, we present some key measures suggested in the PEAP that are linked to the context discussed above; these measures give an impression of current state plans. Efforts are needed to set in motion the related activities and changes on a sufficient scale, especially at the level of implementing institutions. Actions need to have realistic potential if they are to reach firms and farms. Accordingly, PEAP priorities over the medium term for S&T, industrialisation and export diversification which have potential HRD links, include:

- "Establish a system of incentives including Innovation Awards to scientists that generate innovations of promise in addressing Uganda's development needs,
- Strengthen the institutional capacities for incubation centres, technology prototypes and piloting for commercialisation building on the mandate of UIRI.
- Implement the industrialisation policy.
- Provide a set of interventions, within the framework of the MTCS and the PMA, that promote enterprises based on scientific innovations and add value to Uganda's exports. These will be transparent and, as discussed ..., will not involve firm-specific incentives.
- Strengthen institutional ability to respond to export challenges, through the institutionalisation of quality management in industry, enforcement of standards, quality assurance and procurement of market information" (ibid, 50, 69).

The plans for incentives and support structures that generate innovations are commendable, as are the priorities in the areas of incubation centres, value adding, and quality management.

326 There seems little research on how, in Uganda's case, these aspects are related in practice. Note, however, the low ranking of India or China in indexes such as the World Bank's 'ease of doing business'.

With respect to the above priorities on innovative activities one has to consider the argument made earlier: *innovative* and thus *productivity enhancing activities* of most firms in a catch-up economy such as Uganda are likely to be linked to identifying, acquiring, and mastering (adopting/imitating) *existing* technologies in the production process, and undertake continuous learning-by-doing efforts to master this process better so as to *improve* the firms' products or processes. Certainly, there are cases where undertaking scientific research in the sense of general research or 'pure' R&D (innovating on the world's technology frontier) is necessary and appropriate. Yet, the adaptation and imitation aspects in mastering existing technology seem to be a very relevant concept at *present* to deal with improvements needs of most Ugandan firms. Importantly, it can help the productivity catch-up process. Below, we shall discuss other PEAP priorities that are directly linked with HRD-for-PSD.

The role of government and the private sector in economic development and poverty reduction: Implications for HRD

Government interventions seen to be appropriate for promoting incentives, ensuring provision of public goods and reducing inequality

It is essential to explore the remarks in the PEAP on the role of the GOU and the private sector in PSD and poverty reduction; they indicate the *challenges* and *opportunities* HRD proponents will face in promoting their agenda and interventions. Note that the PEAP 2000 version was less concerned with issues of the productive sectors; thus, the deliberations in the PEAP 2004 presented below can be seen as a major government statement about its understanding of these issues in the post-1990s era.

> "The state is responsible for ensuring a basic framework of legality, rights and freedom and intervening in the economy to *promote economic efficiency, equity and growth*. Interventions are appropriate for three main reasons: - Promoting the *right incentives* to encourage private production - Ensuring that *public goods* are supplied - *Reducing inequality* ... [which is] particularly relevant in a context where income inequality has been increasingly sharply ... One of the objectives of the PEAP is to develop consensus on how to interpret these principles in Uganda ... [T]he PMA and the MTCS provide frameworks for the public sector's role in supporting economic production. This PEAP re-emphasises the *importance* of *some public goods*, such as agricultural extension, while exploring the option of public funding for private provision in a number of areas" (ibid, 8, emphasis added).

Regarding the above statement, it is important to note that GOU recognises the significance of offering incentives and public goods and carrying out interventions to promote efficiency, equity and growth for pro-poor development. This perspective is vital in the context of vast market failures and a young, fragile private sector. *In principle*, the view expressed in the quotation above would cover most HRD-related considerations and suggestions made in earlier chapters of this book, which were often justified with incentives and arguments about public goods (read: need for responses to market failures). However, while the use of terminology and principles in the statement above and in sections of this book is similar (and this is important in the first place), it is evident that the main economic policy agenda in Uganda to date does not cover fully vital parts of the agenda of latecomer catch-up economic development in a LDC, as identified in this book.

The PEAP's deliberations on provision of public goods in the context of HRD-for-PSD typically refer to research, extension service and support to marketing in the agricultural sector (ibid, 51).[327] One might argue that this alone is insufficient; it is therefore crucial to respond to the invitation of the PEAP authors to jointly "interpret these principles in Uganda" (ibid, 8) and contribute to the understanding and application of related issues, especially with reference to HRD (positive externalities of training, innovation, clustering, inter-firm cooperation). Of course, in the end it is crucial how the support activities informed by these and other views will be translated into practice; after they passed the discussion and the strategy or policy formulation level.

Firm-level competitiveness: Discussing appropriate interventions

A related point is the debate about *firm-level interventions* in Uganda. Due to certain 'misuse' of this concept in Uganda's economic development in the recent past - with individual investors receiving state support which was perceived by competitors and the general public to be suspicious - the term *firm level* seems to be associated to some extent with the notion of *firm specific*. For instance, in the PEAP, GOU distances itself from firm-specific incentives and interventions: "Government will continue to avoid domestic protection and firm-specific interventions" (ibid, xviii). Further, in the competitiveness section, the PEAP states:

> "Supply constraints for businesses have to be addressed in a holistic manner and for the entire private sector rather than for selected enterprises, which would undermine competition and discourage foreign direct investment. Smart subsidies can be offered to businesses in a way that is accessible to all firms on an equitable basis, such as establishment of industrial parks with common utility supplies (water, electricity and telecommunications) and infrastructure (roads, sewerage line, waste disposal facilities), thus reducing the costs that individual businesses would incur in accessing them" (ibid, 87).[328]

The statement seems to limit the choices and mix of support intervention measures; it might well indicate that most of the interventions will halt at the level of business environment (infrastructure, utilities, legislative and administrative constraints; just like business surveys on major business constraints would suggest). Apparently, *this* perspective does not really identify a "valid role for policy in *influencing allocation* at the *activity, firm* or *technological level*" (Lall 2004a, 10, emphasis added).[329] Although, the position taken in the PEAP seems to largely neglect that there is a case for forms of 'selectivity' in terms of (policy) intervention in the industrialisation process, practices elsewhere would suggest otherwise, e.g. the experience of the successful countries in East Asia. The point seems to be how Governments should or can intervene, and then how they actually do it (ibid, 23, see Box 29). There seem to be perception shifts under way among major donors regarding the usefulness of 'backing' winners (vs. 'selecting' winners/companies); it is increasingly seen as a useful practice. This recognition

---

327 Certainly, this position is influenced by findings such as the following: "Research on returns to public expenditure ... has shown that the impact of spending on agricultural research and extension on income poverty is higher in Uganda than that of spending on roads, education or health" (ibid, 53).

328 Elsewhere, it is stated: "Government does not intend to pursue a policy of firm-specific interventions. Firm specific interventions are undesirable because they are widely perceived to be inequitable (thus eroding the certainty of the investment climate and increasing its risks), inefficient (Government is less well equipped than the private sector to 'pick winners') and create a climate for lobbying rather than entrepreneurship. Government's policy is to create a level playing field for all investors, whereby private incentives are not distorted by public policy, to minimise economic cost and risk, to reduce barriers to production and to address market failures through sector-wide interventions" (ibid, 49).

329 See Lall (2004a, 10-11) for further elaborations on gaps in this neoclassical position on technology.

seems to have gained momentum due to (academic) arguments about externalities and low supply responses in a trade reform context.[330] It will be important in the Ugandan case to utilise such an apparent opening of discourse on the international level for a revitalisation of debates on appropriate support measures for economic development in the country.

Box 29: How to intervene in the industrialisation process: Examples from the East Asian Tigers

"[T]he contrast between the success of industrial policy in the Tigers[331] and its failures elsewhere ... shows ... that the outcome depends not on *whether* governments intervene but *how* they do so. On 'how to intervene', the differences between typical import-substituting strategies and those used in the Tigers lay in such things as:

- Selectivity (picking a few activities at a time) rather than promoting all industrial activities indiscriminately and in an open-ended way.
- Picking activities and functions that offered significant technological benefits and linkages.
- Forcing early entry into world markets, using exports to discipline and monitor both bureaucrats and enterprises.
- Giving the lead role in productive activity to private enterprises but using public enterprise as needed to fill gaps and enter exceptionally risky areas.
- Investing massively in skill creation, infrastructure and support institutions, all carefully coordinated with interventions in product markets.
- Using selectivity in FDI to help build local capabilities (by restricting FDI or imposing conditions on it) or to tap into dynamic, high technology value chains.
- Centralizing strategic decision making in competent authorities who could take an economy wide view and enforce policies on different ministries.
- Improving the quality of bureaucracy and governance, collecting huge amounts of relevant information and learning lessons from technological leaders.
- Ensuring policy flexibility and learning, so that mistakes could be corrected en route, and involving private sector in strategy formulation and implementation (Lall and Teubal, 1998)".

Source*: Lall (2004a, 23-4, emphasis in original).*

In this context, note that there are, for instance, no regulations in Uganda's current Investment Code that require foreign and domestic investors to meet certain performance and local-content targets, or enter technology transfer arrangements. Technology transfer or technical service arrangements need to be registered, a procedure that is somewhat linked to certain criteria such as training provision, or access to know-how. Implicitly, the use of local materials and local staff is encouraged. It is not very obvious how closely the UIA follows up these criteria and related issues such as training and development of local workers and cadres.

The approach taken in the PEAP is unlikely to allow sufficient room and incentives for necessary HRD-for-PSD measures at national, but particularly at sub-sector and firm level.

330 Information was given by an international PSD expert.

331 The discussion is based on the group of 'mature Tigers': Hong Kong (China), Singapore, Taiwan Province of China and the Republic of Korea. Note that besides the policy/governance factor, also a good dose of "external support, and luck (in terms of industrializing at a moment when windows of opportunity were wide open)" (Altenburg et al. 2006, 4) need to be considered in explaining the success of these countries.

Some policy-makers and experts might argue that skills deficiencies and HRD is not highly ranked as business constraints in Uganda, anyway. One consequence of the lower 'ranking' of HRD as a constraint can be observed in current deliberations about public spending in FY 2006/07: the energy challenge seems to absorb most public funds for PSD (besides other spending issues such as roads, or USE), so little is left for direct HRD in the private sector, at least, in terms of capability building and deepening. Against this background, the issue of prevailing business practices and norms, inter-firm linkages and trust might hardly make it on the core agenda in the near future. The content of presentations and discussions at the recent national competitiveness meetings in 2007 and 2008 confirm this expectation. Again, issues of education and health are on the agenda of other Government-donor circles, outside the PSD-competitiveness-circle.

Related issues must be clarified about the notion of 'firm-level interventions': First, it remains unclear whether the understanding of GOU (or, more concretely, of main players in the MFPED) would support firm-level interventions of the kind that, for instance, UCPC undertakes (improving firms' resource use and technology handling). Second, it remains unclear how the statement relates to the Rodrik argument of supporting the 'new'/'non-traditional' in the economy: the efforts of entrepreneurs who experiment with new products, business models or capabilities and thus engage in the discovery of the production potential of Uganda in a context of information externalities in a transforming, diversifying economy. From a HRD perspective, *initial entrepreneurs* would need to be provided with rents or support for efforts which target *new activities* (or particular aspects thereof), especially those linked to 'new' technology (if they have potential for diversification, and spillover and demonstration effects). Yet, to what extent could the public sector successfully engage in such a highly complex and discretionary process on a broad base in the first place?

Thirdly, the implications of avoiding domestic protection and the like are unclear. Taking liberalisation to the extreme is harmful to the latecomer industrialisation project. The latter brings about severe needs among firms and farms regarding learning to use technology efficiently, building inter-firm linkages and developing and deepening related local capabilities in a long process to catch up with established foreign firms and farms which had already undergone the learning process, thus enjoying their first-mover advantage (including higher-productivity) over the Ugandan latecomers. Such entrepreneurship is unlikely to take place at sufficiently high level in a liberalised context without any significant support that helps to develop and deepen capabilities in new areas and activities (Lall 2004a, 11-3).

Government's liberal stand on protection can be found in a statement on page 49 in the PEAP. It makes no reference to learning costs or other HRD requirements in the catch-up process and could therefore count, according to Lall's discussion of these matters (2004a), as a neo-classical position vis-à-vis the structuralist (or evolutionary) economy' view ('technological capability approach'). Does GOU really prefer to (implicitly or explicitly) adopt, for Uganda's situation, the (moderate) neo-classical recipe that underplays externalities, risks, and skills deficiencies in the area of technology accumulation (import and use of technology)? Box 30 gives an overview of characteristic premises of this policy recipe. As Lall points out, the debate around forms of market failures and appropriate state responses to correct them is linked to political economy hypotheses about state capacities and capabilities to carry out related selective measures effectively (cost of intervention/government failures vs. costs of market failure) (ibid, 10). The status quo of PSD support in Uganda is thus also an expression of the balance of power on this question between the positions of various domestic and foreign players (from the public and private sector, academia, donor community, etc.) who influence policy making in the country.

Box 30: The neo-classical model on firm-level technology accumulation and related implications

"[On technology, both the moderate and the strong neoclassical position, to put it simply,] used, implicitly or explicitly, the basic neoclassical model in which all markets affecting technology are 'efficient'. In the theoretical sense, 'efficiency' has stringent requirements: product markets give the correct signals for investment and factor markets respond to these signals. At the firm level there are no scale economies or externalities. Firms have perfect information and foresight and full knowledge of all available technologies. They choose the right technology if faced with free market prices. Having selected the right technology they use it instantaneously at 'best practice'. There are no significant learning processes, no risks, no externalities and no deficiencies in the skills, finance, information and infrastructure available to them. In this model, any policy intervention that affects the prices facing enterprises is by definition distorting, and moves society away from the optimum allocation yielded by free markets. The critical assumption for industrial policy is the one on *learning and capability building* and dropping it yields very different conclusions for policy ... But showing that there may be market failures in importing and using technology cannot establish a case for selectivity. It is also necessary to show that such failures are important in practice and not theoretical curiosities, and to establish that governments can effectively remedy them in real life, that government failures are not necessarily more costly than market failures".

Source: *Lall 2004a (10-11, emphasis in original).*

From the Box above, several questions emerge: Are Ugandan firms really able to use imported technology instantly at 'best practice' level so they can compete successfully with their efficient, experienced competitors in a technology-driven global economy? Or, would they need supportive measures for the costly and lengthy technological capability-building process that would allow them to close (initial) efficiency gaps in the use of new technology? Experience from UCPC's work suggests the latter: there are examples of Ugandan firms that use the sector's international state-of-the-art technology yet experience much lower productivity levels than firms in Europe which use similar equipment; in some cases local firms operate at efficiency levels of one-quarter to one-fifth of those of the European firms due to skill deficiencies in the way workers and managers handle the technology-related production process (including input use), among other reasons.

Box 31 gives various reasons why an overly liberal position might well harm Uganda's transformation and industrialisation ambition, especially if it is not accompanied, or balanced by, a set of explicit support measures. The arguments in the Box are related to the capability building agenda and are extended versions of those presented earlier.[332] They should be considered by those who express interest in HRD strategies and policies for Uganda's economic development context. Related concerns about an overly liberal policy mix were

332 Similar arguments can be made in relation to 'selectivity' in technology support, innovation financing, FDI promotion, or IT infrastructure development (Lall 2004a, 27). See also Altenburg and von Drachenfels (2006) on what they call a 'new minimalist approach' in PSD (which includes the disregard of selective supportive interventions).

also raised, for instance, in a study on Uganda's policy reforms, industrial competitiveness and regional integration.

> "In a liberalized trading environment, competitiveness is a major objective and challenge for the private sector as well as the government. Our study suggests that to overcome the existing obstacles to international competitiveness [of Ugandan manufacturing firms], it is not sufficient for the government to rely on a relatively open trade regime. Cautious progression in trade openness needs to be accompanied by a number of policies that constitute an industrial strategy" (Siggel and Ssemogerere 2001, 32-3).

Box 31: Selective interventions in the context of local technological capability building

"[E]xposure to full import competition is likely to prevent entry into activities with relatively difficult technologies [especially when there are related high, unpredictable learning costs and widespread externalities]. Yet these are the technologies that are likely to carry the burden of industrial development and future competitiveness. Why do these interventions have to be *selective*? Offering uniform protection to all activities makes little sense when learning processes and externalities differ by technology, as they inevitably do. In some activities the need for protection may be minimal because the learning period is relatively brief, information easy to get and externalities limited. In complex activities or those with widespread externalities, newcomers may never enter unless measures are undertaken to promote the activity. The only complex activities where investments may take place without promotion are those based on local natural resources, if the resource advantage is sufficient to offset the learning costs. However, the processing of some resources calls for strong industrial capabilities and for a learning base; thus, both Sub-Saharan Africa and Latin America have large resource bases but advanced processing has only taken root in the latter, based on decades of capability building in import-substituting regimes.

It is important to reiterate that infant *industry protection is only part of industrial policy*, and *by itself can be harmful and ineffective*. This is so for two reasons. First, protection cannot succeed if it is not offset by competitive pressures on firms to invest in the capability building process. In fact, by cushioning the costs of capability building, protection removes the incentive for undertaking it. One of the reasons why industrial policy failed in most developing countries is precisely that they failed to overcome this dilemma. But it is possible to do so, by strengthening domestic competition, setting performance targets and, most effectively, by forcing firms into export markets where they have to compete with best practice. Infant industry protection only works well where it is counterbalanced by such measures. Many such measures also have to be selective, since the costs of entering export markets differ by product. Thus, differentiated export targets, credits and subsidies were often used in East Asia. The second reason why industrial policy is far more than protection is the need for *coordination with factor markets*. Firms need many new inputs into their learning ... Unless factor markets can respond to these needs, protection cannot allow them to reach competitive levels of competence. And factor market interventions also *have to be selective as well as functional* ... The *deepening* of capabilities suffers similar problems. The more complex the functions to be undertaken, the higher the costs involved and the greater the factor market coordination required. Getting into production may be easy compared to design, development and innovation. Neoclassical theory accepts that free markets (implicitly in industrial economies) may fail to ensure optimal private innovative activity because of imperfect information. However, developing countries face an additional problem. It is generally easier to import foreign technologies fully packaged than to develop an understanding of the basic principles involved [in] the basis of local design and development. 'Internalized' technology transfer takes the form of wholly foreign-owned direct investment. This is an effective and rapid way to access new technology, but it may result in little capability acquisition in the host country apart from production skills. The move from production to innovative activity involves a strategic decision that foreign investors, because of the skills and technical linkages involved, tend to be unwilling to take in developing countries ... There is, in other words, a risk of market failure in capability deepening because of the learning costs involved, similar to initial capability building. To ensure socially optimal allocation, it may be necessary to (selectively) restrict technology imports in 'internalized' forms (via FDI) and promote those in 'externalized' forms (licensing, equipment, imitation...)".

Source: *Lall 2004a (11, 13-4, emphasis in original). See moreover Altenburg et al. (2006).*

More discussion needed: HRD for more advanced firm operations

As outlined, the PEAP highlights the importance of only a few of the relevant issues. Problematically, it does not examine in detail the few it does mention, at least as far as industrialisation is concerned, for example. Interestingly though, it recognises, as mentioned, that firm-level abilities being efficient and innovating and adopting technology are key to competitiveness: "Key to ... [competitiveness] will be the firms' level of productivity and their *ability to both innovate* and *adapt to new technologies*. Thus by improving the competitiveness of Uganda's private sector we improve the ability of firms to respond to the demands of the marketplace" (MFPED 2004, 52, emphasis added). This statement is largely in line with the approach taken in this book and could be linked to the long list of HRD matters discussed earlier in the book. In contrast to the PEAP, however, this book has tried to examine - and this is important - possible *implications* of such statements about firm-level competitiveness requirements. The book also puts forward a view that discusses the actual *prerequisites and prospects* and of latecomer firms' ability to compete in liberal markets and respond to competition; such issues are underplayed in the PEAP.

More discussion is needed with and among core policy-makers (including researchers, NGOs, general public and private sector representatives) about their understanding of the implications of the PEAP statements (and similar statements contained in consequent government strategies and frameworks) as set out above. It might well be that, currently, there is no clear consensus in GOU/public service about related matters, including among those that have to undertake daily, case-to-case decisions and interventions on behalf of the state, both in the capital and the districts.

However, note that a recent UNCTAD report refers to a range of reports at international level that focus on competitiveness and the related aspect of domestic capability building and notes that none of the cited reports "goes into detail about the policies and support programmes that are necessary for strengthening productive capacity *at the enterprise level*, particularly that of ...SMEs" (2005c, 5, emphasis added). In other words, the theme of capability building at enterprise level - including through firms interacting with SIs - for increased productivity and competitiveness seems not yet to be broadly adopted by the different (state and donor) development agencies in the area of PSD.

The envisaged role of the private sector: productive investment, social activities and collective action

Finally, how does PEAP conceptualise the role of the private sector vis-à-vis government? The PEAP makes three main points: First, productive investment should mainly come from private sector agents and have a commercial impulse. In this respect, GOU, through its *leverage on incentives* in the economy intends to *encourage investment that results in pro-poor growth*. Second, the formal private sector does/can also contribute to the PEAP through its social activities (e.g. commercial sponsorships). Third, GOU recognises the importance of private-sector collective action and social organisation and commits itself to collaborate with and support, for instance, producer organisation with a view to promoting PSD (MFPED 2004, 9). The latter point is particularly noteworthy as it highlights the need for combined efforts towards improved collective action in various forms.

> "Over time, it is hoped that producer organisations will be strengthened. Services such as information about marketing opportunities, which benefit an industry as a whole, can be usefully provided by such organisations. Producers' organisations in grain trading and horticulture

already play an important role, and Government will collaborate with such organisations in promoting private sector development" (ibid, 9).[333]

It is important that GOU acknowledges the importance of collective action by producer organisations and clusters; it remains to be seen how vigorously the respective stakeholders will engage with each other to foster the capture of collective efficiency gains. Again, it would seem vital to engage in a debate with GOU to interpret the issue of *incentives for pro-poor-growth-oriented investments;* many of the remarks offered in this book with respect to transformation and HRD dynamics are linked to the vital issue of incentives. In the next section we briefly explore the PEAP priorities that deal with HRD in more detail.

Review of further PEAP sections with direct link to HRD

Skills development as well as E&T play a role in *four more sections* of the PEAP: the MSMEs, labour market and productivity of workers in pillar 2 as well as education and skills development and health in pillar 5. We will discuss all of them except health. Other societal benefits aside, conditions of health of the LF (human capital) are vital for productivity and economic development. They have become part of HRM measures in some firms in Uganda including those that export according to certain social standard requirements. Management of health risks, e.g. HIV/AIDS, plays an increasing role in both the public and private sector. Government's health programmes are thus a vital complementary part for poverty reduction and PSD.

Skills for development and expansion of MSMEs

With respect to MSMEs, the PEAP refers to findings (Ellis and Bahiigwa 2003) who point to the importance of non-farm economic activities (especially in MSMEs) for poverty reduction.[334] The PEAP notes that those enterprises are constrained by lack of entrepreneurial skills (MFPED 2004, 71). Accordingly, they also need: (a) better coordination and group formation, in the form of farmers associations, cooperatives or clusters, and, (b) business support services that enhance the growth of the upcountry MSMEs in particular. The link between clustering and HRD is recognised: "The growth of clusters will also allow Uganda to develop a workforce with diverse areas of expertise directly enhancing international competitiveness and income levels" (ibid). Finally, GOU considers subsidizing BDS provision by the private sector: "This reflects the conviction that inadequate entrepreneurial and managerial skills represent an important constraint on the private sector" (ibid). The above points - although not explored further in the PEAP - are in line with some of the findings of this book. Other concerns are neglected or underplayed; for instance, the scale and characteristics of the entrepreneurship

---

333 Concretely, the PEAP states in regard to the SEP: "Commodity sector associations such as the Uganda Fish Processors and Exporters Association (UFPEA) and the Uganda Flower Exporters Association (UFEA) can play an important role in the achievement of SEP objectives. Future emphasis will be put on supporting such associations so that they can play a leading role in identifying constraints and implementing the agreed interventions" (MFPED 2004, 56). Importantly, these intentions have to go beyond the rhetorical level.

334 "[R]ural households whose main source of income was non-farm activities are better-off than households whose main source of income was agricultural production. For rural areas, where poverty is most prevalent, the main non-farm activities are MSMEs...covering a variety of activities or sectors including general retail trade, agro-processing and other services including the food and drink industry (restaurants and bars), transportation and construction ... [The] growth of MSMEs is an important way of fighting poverty, both in rural and urban areas" (MFPED 2004, 70).

trend and related skill deficiencies are not explored further. Issues like business norms and practices (business culture, social capital, and related aspects of political economy), or industrial capabilities, are not included. Part of the implementation is supposed to be coordinated and monitored by the MTCS Secretariat which, by the time of research (2006), is one of the weaker PSD agencies in the country; an arrangement which might lead to little change in the status quo on the above points.

Labour market and labour productivity

The PEAP expresses the need to foster the supply of more skilled labour. This is supposed to boost workers' productivity and wage earnings as well as competitiveness:

> "In view of the high growth in Uganda's labour force ... characterised by a low educational profile, there is a need to intensify efforts to increase the supply of a more educated workforce into the labour market. Such a workforce will have higher productivity and hence earn higher wages. In this respect, the supply of skilled and semi-skilled manpower by both public and private education and training institutions will be accorded a high priority for increasing the country's competitiveness" (ibid, 84).

This is a strong and important statement that needs to be nurtured by HRD proponents. It contains ideas for concretisation and implementation of the agenda. In this regard, it is vital to engage in deliberations about the more complex reasons behind, for instance, the low-productivity finding, as elaborated earlier (incentive systems, experience premium, management deficiencies, casualisation of labour, learning environment, business culture and political economy); E&T-related interventions alone will not do. However, priorities and assumptions in the PEAP regarding labour productivity and labour market issues are as follows:

- Adequately finance and equip public technical and vocational training institutions to allow them deliver the required manpower for enhancing production and competitiveness; with public institutions most likely being the major providers of E&T, and the private institutions foreseen to complement state efforts in creating new skills and developing training schemes in emerging technological areas,
- The National Council for Higher Education advises public and private universities and tertiary institutions on skills needed to enhance production, competitiveness and, subsequently, incomes,
- Encourage the private sector to establish collective agreements that are performance-related to enable employers in the private sector to link wages to productivity,
- Establish a Labour Market Information System to provide relevant information,
- Consult with the private sector on the revision of minimum wages for estate workers,
- Consider revision of the Workers Compensation Act and the role of labour inspections in the protection of workers' welfare,
- Advance reforms of the pension system,
- While Government should cease to be the main provider of formal employment, it will, where appropriate (1) refer to labour-intensive production techniques/methods in the provision of public goods (roads etc.) in localities with high visible underemployment, and (2) promote community participation in infrastructure development/maintenance
- Support priorities for the educational system (see below) (ibid, 84-6).

In this part of the PEAP, there are some arguments and suggestions with links to those made in this book; they need further reflection and, where appropriate, expansion in the next PEAP (or national economic development strategy) to include relevant issues: for instance,

(a) manpower for enhanced competitiveness (this notion would fit in with almost the entire package of this book), (b) the support for creation of new skills and development of training schemes in emerging technological areas (here one could easily argue for support of training modules related to new embedded business models such as VCD), or (c) collective agreements that are performance-related and allow linking wages to productivity (here the arguments about incentive systems and social capital play a role). The aim to involve communities in infrastructure development and maintenance could also point to HRD implications. The few examples show the way in which HRD proponents can interpret and enhance the PEAP agenda with a view to broadening the understanding and increasing the effectiveness of required HRD measures.

Education and skills development

The PEAP points to the link between education, human capital accumulation and higher incomes and sustained growth. Education in Uganda has positive rates of return for all levels of education: "Based on incomes alone, social returns to primary are highest at 24%, followed by tertiary (13%) and then secondary (10%)" (ibid, 153). Accordingly, education also helps in (i) slowing down the population growth (women with education above the primary level have lower fertility rates than those with no education or only primary education), and in (ii) building civil institution and a democratic society, empowering women and protecting the environment (ibid).[335] GOU is committed to universal secondary education (USE), to eliminating gender disparity in primary education (PE) and post-primary education and training (PPET), and to focusing resources on those who would not be able to access education without public interventions, especially in secondary and tertiary education where there is no universal access at present (ibid, 153-4). Significantly, "[s]upport to post primary education to increase access, quality and relevance is being intensified to sustain the gains from UPE" (ibid, 154). The strong statement in favour of PPET is remarkable and needs to be debated in terms of implementation into practice. The following quotation summarises important aspects of the GOU view:

> "The education sector ... faces the twin challenges of delivering primary education, according to the aspirations of UPE, and strengthening the performance of higher levels of education. The medium term strategy is therefore to improve the quality of education [at PE level foremost: literacy, numeracy and life skills], expand post primary education and skills development opportunities, further decentralise post primary education services and increase the participation of the private sector in the provision of post primary education. This strategy is underpinned by the awareness for the *need to adopt a national approach to human resource development that is based on the manpower requirements of the national growth path*" (ibid 154, emphasis added).

One of the key sentences in the PEAP which has major implications for the debate on a HRD concept for Uganda is the last one in the above quote; it expresses concern for the development of a national approach to HRD which is in conjunction with the national growth and therefore transformation trajectory. If this is to be taken at face value, the debate about a HRD concept would have to deal with relevant findings presented in this book (from issues such as the

335 Notably, elsewhere the PEAP refers to a study by the International Food Policy Research Institute (IFPRI) on public expenditure and poverty reduction, which suggests that "the return to infrastructural spending in terms of income poverty is higher than that of health and education, though lower than that for agricultural extension and research" (MFPED 2004, 97, see Fan et al. 2004)

informal sector to the export-oriented VCs and so on). The last sentence in the above statement can also be interpreted as a *call* by the PEAP (there is 'need to adopt') to respective experts, among others, to start the process of HRD concept formulation.

Where is BTVET placed in the current plans? Over the next ten years, GOU targets a reduced transition rate from PE to BTVET (currently at 10%), while the rate from PE to SE is projected to increase (from 50% to 80%). On the other hand, S4 leavers should increasingly enter BTVET (10% to 50%) instead of continuing to S6 (from 77% to 40%).

> "Thus, most children would proceed from primary school to secondary school, and after 4 years 40% would continue to higher secondary school, while half would proceed to vocational education. Progress in implementing this strategy will depend on the level of resources available and on the efficiency with which resources are targeted at those who could not otherwise go to school, as well as efficiency improvements such as an increase in post-primary class size" (ibid, 154).

This outlined PPET agenda creates both a challenge and opportunity. The further transformation of the ETS remains a top area for intervention and investments by the public and private sector, arguably with lots of room for future success but also failure. Similar to the economic arena, much of the E&T terrain to be tapped in the next years will be 'new territory', while the existing structures and practices cannot and should not be disregarded (building on what exists in communities).[336] The combination of the two - a new territory in both the economic system and the ETS - results in a highly complex, risky, and experimental context with some tensions between short-term and long-term perspectives. The goal to link the ETS, particularly PPET, more closely to labour market dynamics is ambitious. Especially if the technocrats (e.g. in the MOES) continue to be relatively detached from the very 'new' realties and trends in the private sector. The example of ethics, norms and morality which anti-corruption experts, not the E&T experts, have put on the national agenda illustrates this point.

To what extent do the experts in MOES consider and utilise findings of the many studies on growth, VCs, industrialisation, or the global economy which might be relevant for their work? How do they link the E&T agenda with prevailing issues in the informal sector or the learning and capability building process in firms and farms? Is there a link between a BTVET sector that is considered to remain "generally out of touch with the needs of the labour market" (Tanburn and Kamuhanda 2005, 59) and performance of the public service, e.g. the ministry responsible for BTVET (MOES)? If the MOES wishes to equip students with "competencies they need to join the workforce" (2005, 6): How central (and thus adequately financed) will be the place of relevant education and skills development in the school system? How much do the experts know about the details of the salient issues in PSD and the emerging frontiers of the world-of-work in Uganda, considering that they make statements in the PEAP such as the one below on the very ETS (assuming MOES/BTVET department had a stake in the drafting of the text): "The private sector provides an *unknown* but significant volume of training of *various* kinds" (MFPED 2004, 160, emphasis added)? In any case, sufficient commitment to HRD-for-PSD is crucial to adequately boost PSD with the help of a more responsive BTVET system.[337]

336 The author owes this qualification to a UNESCO colleague.

337 A couple of interviewees expressed concern about the level of cooperation and commitment from e.g. the BTVET department for sector-specific skills development.

These issues aside, Box 32 provides some insights on the MOES perspective on links between education and workforce competencies as formulated in the Education Sector Strategic Plan (ESSP) 2004-2015: Indeed, it refers to a range of complex and very relevant points in this regard. This would make a corresponding follow-up and implementation over the medium and long term of the insights and goals presented in Box 32 even more important. Possibly, this is likely to create a major challenge for the ETS.

Box 32: The Education Sector Strategic Plan (ESSP) 2004-2015

The ESSP of the MOES reveals the following view on education goals: "It is not enough that children enrol in school. Uganda needs citizens who can actively participate in their democracy, families that care for the health and welfare of their members and communities, and a *workforce comprised of competent professionals, technicians, and labourers who can modernize the economy in the context of globalization*" (MOES 2005, 8, emphasis added). The most elaborated statement of the ESSP on workforce issues is probably the one it makes in relation to competencies of post-primary students: "The modern workforce, toward which Uganda is heading in important industrial and agricultural sectors, will require a different set of competencies than those taught today. To succeed in the workplace, young people will require the ability to follow written directions that assume an understanding of abstract concepts. They will need to go beyond the basics of reading, writing, mathematics, and problem solving, and many will need the ability to use computers at a basic level. Enterprises in every sector, including modern agriculture, industry and the public sector, will require entering employees who know how to solve problems using rigorous methods of problem identification, hypothesis formulation, data collection and analysis, and reporting. Factory jobs and work in agriculture-based enterprises will demand the ability to reason beyond repetition of mechanical operations, to make decisions about treatments under varying condition, to understand a business plan, to communicate clearly in writing, to read complex instructions, and other such tasks. Every person should be able to think critically - to make informed and competent judgments about what others assert and about his or her own choices and to clearly communicate information and opinions" (ibid, 10). What is apparently missing in the above statement is the notion of teamwork/social capital or social skills.

Significantly, with respect to setting education goals for different levels of the ETS, the ESSP aims at the following (ibid, 16-21):

- Primary-level pupils mastering basic literacy (reading and writing), numeracy, and basic life skills;
- Post-primary students prepared to enter the workforce and further education: Against this background, the ESSP states that at PPE level, "the bifurcated system between academic preparation for higher education and vocational training for technician jobs is not appropriate for Uganda's national development needs [in the context of globalisation]. A key objective of this plan ... is to help students acquire competencies they need to join the workforce and to continue their education (ibid, 6). Of further significance: "If Uganda is to transform its subsistence economy into modern agriculture, industrial, service, and public sectors, most of the population will eventually need competencies with broad application: the ability to: (i) Communicate effectively both verbally and in writing, (ii) Follow written instructions (manuals and diagrams) that assume an understanding of abstract concepts, (iii) Use advanced mathematics, including fractions, decimals and line graphs, (iv) Solve semi-structured problems by formulating and testing hypotheses, and (v) Understand how computers work" (ibid 19). Accordingly, these competencies are to date not sufficiently reflected in the general secondary and BTVET curricula/exams - over the term of the ESSP such competencies for workforce and further education are going to be emphasised more.
- Tertiary graduates prepared to be innovative, creative, and entrepreneurial in private and public sectors: With highest priority to S&T, mathematics, and other subjects critical to national development, and further focus on computer literacy, (applied) research and publications.

Source: *MOES (2005).*

Post-primary education and training (PPET)

According to the PEAP, plans to intensify efforts to increase access to and upgrade quality of PPET have become major issues in the context of an increasing transition rate from PE to PPE in the recent past (from 35% in 1997 to 50% in 2002) resulting in estimates that more than 400.000 pupils (2003) completed PE and demand secondary education (MFPED 2004, 158). Another main concern is the contribution of envisaged improved PPE outcomes for economic development, in particular competency level in the workforce. "[Currently,] only a minority of the students [at PPE level] are achieving what is expected. Too many are leaving school without the knowledge and skills they need to participate as citizens and productive workers" (MOES 2005, 9). With regard to vocational training, the PEAP states:

> "Vocational education needs to be well matched with the economy's need for skills. This objective will be pursued by: Establishing and operationalising the Uganda Vocational Qualifications framework (UVQF) to increase flexibility, accessibility, attractiveness, affordability and relevance, both to trainees and employers. Offering modularised courses. Ensure BTVET institutions are accessible to students with disabilities. Conclude community polytechnics ... pilot project" (MFPED 2004, 160). Format quote

This agenda is well chosen, particularly the stronger focus and inclusion on competencies for participation in the economic sphere. The findings and recommendations of this book could help the experts to adjust the vocational education and training (VET) agenda in the future. Further, the PEAP also points to the need to appropriately balance resource-spending within PPE between academic and vocational education (ibid). These and other remarks on vocational training (VT) will be quoted in some length to allow proper understanding of the state's position:

> "[T]he participation rates [in the labour market] of graduates from vocational training are good, and *communities* expressed *more appreciation for vocational than academic secondary education* (PPA2 2002)[338]; this corresponds with the importance of non-agricultural self-employment as a route out of poverty. However, these objectives can also be pursued by enhancing the vocational component of secondary education. The secondary curriculum is being reviewed to make it more responsive to national labour demands, and 56 secondary schools are being vocationalised. The Education Sector Plan envisages that vocational education will become a[n] alternative to academic education in the last two years of the secondary level, rather than an alternative to the early years of secondary education. The introduction of short modularised courses should also make it possible for adults *to acquire skills over their lifetime*" (ibid, 160-1, emphasis added).

Certainly, from the above, VT is experiencing significant attention from the authorities in the PEAP. The political and policy dynamics in 2006 support this impression: SE and training plays a significant role in the NRM manifesto; the state administration, with the help of the private sector, is attempting to fulfil the promises made during election campaigns. In addition, the quoted preference of communities for vocational training is noteworthy, so is the inclusion of a concept of lifelong learning. Community feedback also points to the severe burden to households of financing SE: "Some parents … said that paying the high financial cost of secondary school education was one cause of moving from the better-off well-being status into poverty, because it erodes the ordinary persons' asset base" (MFPED 2002, 144).

338 PPA2 refers to the second Participatory Poverty Assessment report for Uganda, see MFPED (2002).

How the implications of this PPET agenda will be translated into practice, remains to be seen, e.g. in terms of teachers' qualifications and curricula change. Box 33 reflects on perceptions of VT vs. SE at community level: consequently, most community members preferred vocational education.

Box 33: Attitudes towards traditional vocational and secondary education as pointed out by the Second Participatory Poverty Assessment Report

"Community attitudes towards vocational and secondary education were mixed. Most community members especially youths including female youths in some cases, orphans, PWDs [people with disabilities], IDPs [internally displaced persons), the poorest, local leaders and key service providers such as teachers, all preferred vocational education. Such attitudes were expressed in 24 of the 60 sites across 9 of the 12 districts. Some of these people preferred vocational education to be introduced to those schools because, then the students would be more mature and therefore choose appropriately a suitable vocational profession. Altogether, people cited three major reasons for preferring vocational education. They explained that vocational education is more affordable than secondary education and it provides a vital alternative when one cannot access secondary education due to high financial costs. They also argued that vocational education provides a vital alternative form of education to those children who are less capable in academic-oriented subjects that require a lot of reading. Therefore, they felt that vocational education is good because it imparts skills that can enable one, especially one with low or average level of education (i.e. up to diploma level), to be self-employed rather than be a job-seeker. However, some parents ... were worried about the availability of job opportunities for graduates of vocational training, given their potential influx on the market once vocational education becomes universal. Also, some community members from the poor category [the well-off categories] and from insecure areas in northern Uganda preferred secondary education [mainly because of perception of better career prospects. This] ...is mainly because secondary education exposes children much more to opportunities for higher education, and therefore many more opportunities for a high-income job in the future. The latter attitudes were expressed in 11 of the 60 sites in 6 of the 12 districts" (MFPED 2002, 142-3).

The latter points suggest continuing efforts to make VT a viable income-generating tool for the youth and raising awareness about career paths and prospects with VT skills. Also, focusing on allowing mobility to grow within the ETS - so that students can create their education and training profile flexibly - seems appropriate. It could be that the currently low prospects of 'white collar' or any formal wage jobs for the majority of graduates of tertiary institutions in the context of slow formal sector growth and widespread informalisation of work will lead to a relative decline in the differences in income and career prospects between secondary and tertiary graduates, and thus between education and training paths.

Other key priority actions with relevance to HRD

Other key priority actions of GOU over the medium term with relevance to HRD include (MFPED 2004, 52, 162, 175).

- Tertiary education:
  - Curriculum reform to emphasise S&T in a broad higher education context,
  - Use of a credit system to *increase mobility amongst disciplines* and *institutions*,
  - Review financing to focus on financing students rather than institutions,
  - Strengthened affirmative action on admissions to favour students with disabilities,
  - Operationalisation of a loan system accessible to all qualified students and an open university - both of which will increase access for the poor.
  - Target government scholarships for S&T,
  - Support research.

- Sports
  - To nurture its contribution to social capital and national unity. Key aspects of the strategy include the integration of physical education and performing arts into the school curriculum (this has been done for PE already).
- HIV/AIDS education
- Functional adult literacy (FAL)
- Gender
  - The PEAP points to the significance of "intra-household relations for agricultural productivity" (ibid, 6): the different working and spending patterns of the male and female members, or the structures of subordination including control over income.[339] Thus, actions that contribute to reducing gender inequality are priorities: organise women's groups and empower women, including support to ensure female participation in extension services (most of NAADS group members are women) and education.

Three comments on the above agenda are, first, increased capabilities in S&T are not a supplement for other learning, analytical, problem-solving and social skills that are needed by the economy. To compete in and contribute to the world-of-work, most university graduates need to have the latter set of skills; while the S&T agenda is highly relevant, it concerns a smaller part of the tertiary sector. Second, the reference made to sports and social capital is noteworthy and correct. Other aspects of the formation of (positive) social and cultural capital need to be identified and nurtured. Third, the gender agenda is a crucial part of the HRD agenda in a transformative LDC economy. In the next section we consider other growth and competitiveness-oriented programmes and reflect on their links to HRD.[340]

Further government strategies for economic growth and PSD

The three key programmes for economic growth and transformation

To foster economic growth and development, government put in place, in the early 2000s, the following three key policy programmes through which it strives to deliver the supply-side reforms (reducing supply-side barriers) that are considered necessary to achieve accelerated and sustained economic growth: the Medium Term Competitiveness Strategy (MTCS) and the Plan for the Modernisation of Agriculture (PMA). Both were launched in August 2000 to deliver pillar one (economic growth and structural transformation) and three (increasing the ability of the poor to raise their incomes) of the last PEAP. The Strategic Exports Programme (SEP) was established in September 2001 to complement the other two programmes.

The programmes mentioned are founded on the overarching idea that (1) reducing existing barriers to investment (thus, improving the business environment), such as poor transport and utilities infrastructure, excessive bureaucratic red tape, weak judicial processes, corruption,

339 "Recent participatory research has concluded that lack of control over productive resources by women remains one of the root causes of poverty. ... Yet they are responsible for meeting family needs. It is clear that although women are subordinated in a number of different power structures based on e.g. class, geographical location, ethnicity all of these are gendered and unless there is awareness of these structures women will not be able to change them. Ultimately, the empowerment processes should lead to protest against all structures that subordinate women" (MFPED 2004, 29).

340 Due to the scope of the study, the Education Strategic Investment Plan (ESIP) will not be discussed further; its main positions are captured in the PEAP, and the discussions of the same in this book.

shallow financial markets, as well as *weak farm-level organisation and marketing skills*; and (2) *boosting output productivity* are key for PSD and accelerated growth. Understanding the basic programme concerns and plans helps to determine where HRD measures are placed, or could be placed in the near future within this web of government programmes and implementation challenges. Essentially, the next paragraphs reveal the difficulties likely to be experienced in placing a comprehensive HRD agenda in a programme and implementation system that is, to date, fragmented and which has some conceptual gaps, in addition to being, in parts, poorly implemented. One of the impediments to advancement on the HRD-for-PSD agenda might well be current weak inter-ministerial cooperation, which is inadequate for such a multi-faceted and relevant theme.

The Medium Term Competitive Strategy for the Private Sector (MTCS)

Background: Objectives and intervention areas

The objective of this government strategy for PSD, sub-titled Making Institutions Support Private Sector Growth (2000-2005), was to improve the general business environment, to increase private investment and saving, and enable the private sector to compete better in domestic, regional and international markets, in the process contributing to growth, increasing incomes and reducing poverty. It sought to enhance firm productivity and profitability by reducing the cost of doing business and creating an environment where private investment became viable. Improved business conditions should support the private sector in that it (1) can make profits, (2) will have a higher capacity to create more jobs, (3) operates in a free and fair competitive environment, (4) is attractive to private investment, and (5) has a strong export base. In this respect, better coordination of and support from state institutions and donors was regarded vital (MFPED 2000, MTCS Secretariat 2005, for an implementation assessment, GOU 2003a).

As removing business constraints was the central idea of the MTCS approach, it identified key constraints affecting the private sector, and outlined priority actions (88 in number) to remove constraints. The planned measures of this crosscutting programme were grouped into the eight output areas: (a) infrastructure provision (water, transport network, telecommunications); (b) financial sector (access to capital, risks of lending, promotion of savings, financial services for SMEs); (c) commercial justice (contract enforcement and debt collection); (d) institutional reforms (regarding corruption, public procurement, administrative procedures, tax administration, public investment and export promotion institutions); (e) export sector-specific impediments (tax structure, export credit facility, quality standards); (f) business environment for *MSEs* (policy formulation, dialogue, *skills development*); (g) globalisation/regional issues (regional integration, global trade opportunities); and (h) *human capital development*, health and environmental issues (MFPED 2000, xi-xii, MTCS 2005).

MTCS position on HRD: HRD critical for increasing standards of living

The strategy has two main sections on skills development and HRD: *skills development and training* and *human capital requirements*. The former section emphasises the *lack of technical skills* which *hampers* firm *productivity* and economy-wide *growth*; one of the various consequences of this deficiency being that skilled labour has to be imported from neighbouring countries and elsewhere for some industries (MFPED 2000, 49). Further, the MTCS acknowledges that

> "[T]he current vocational education and training system is *no longer adequate* for the demands placed on it by a fast growing economy. This mismatch reduces overall productivity of the economy and reduces the standard of living of individual workers ... Given the importance of *entrepreneurship, institutional technical skills training*, as well as *apprenticeship training* in building a viable private sector, it is imperative that Government in partnership with the private sector and other stakeholders in the education industry, agree on a framework to develop the skills base ... [Based on study findings and suggestions from key stakeholders] Government shall implement key reforms to ensure technical skills development to support private sector growth. The necessary reforms, some of which of a long term nature include legal and regulatory issues, fiscal as well as institutional" (ibid, emphasis added).

The MTCS gives the following reasons for the inadequacies of the current BTVET system:

> "[A]bsence of a vocational education and training policy, the few vocational training and education facilities which in most cases lack equipment, and a limited number of trainers. Generally, there is a critical shortage of training materials in all vocational training colleges. The shortage of tools, equipment, materials and poor infrastructure is adversely affecting the quality of training programmes and those of the trainers. Consequently, the trainees do not meet the needs of the private sector and always perform at high cost to the employers, given the low productivity" (ibid, 49).

These are significant statements on problem issues and reform agenda items, which can provide general guidance for deliberations on a HRD agenda for Uganda on related themes. As pointed out in this book, government's policy perspective as well as implementation agenda lacks some vital interlinked HRD issues and dynamics: drivers of productivity at organisational and incentive level, management deficiencies, inadequacies in entrepreneurship, in-house training, or sector-specific training for the upcoming sectors, VCD or business practices and norms. The MTCS further elaborates on the reform agenda:

- GOU shall enact new national vocational education and training legislation and promote training of entrepreneurs, including legislation for the establishment of an autonomous body, the Uganda Vocational Education and Training Authority (UVETA) with charges to co-ordinate, integrate, harmonise and regulate VT efforts on behalf of GOU.
- The key requirement for resolving the fiscal constraints of VET facilities on a sustainable basis in the medium to long term is to ensure demand-led skills training, provided on a cost-recovery or profit-making basis. In the short-term, the Industrial Training Decree of 1972 will be reviewed (for better financial viability and industry relevancy of the training). Once the VET facilities have been established or upgraded, beneficiaries will be obliged to contribute towards their training.
- Priority in government spending shall be given in the short term to the rehabilitation of existing facilities and training of trainers, with support from donors. In the medium to long term, a framework shall be developed in collaboration with stakeholders, to ensure wider access to training, advice and extension services by MSEs. Activities could include: (1) countrywide training-of-trainers programme in small business management, (2) establishment of at least one rehabilitated and strengthened private or public vocational institute in each district, which focuses on delivering training to SSEs in the district, (3) creation of mobile training facilities in selected regions to deliver training, targeting mainly the remote areas, or (4) countrywide community-based skills training for micro entrepreneurs organised in groups (ibid, 50).

One comment on the above is that, in addition to rehabilitation of facilities, it will be important to bring the training closer to *real life*, this is the *market and employment context* of economic actors. How can training - especially informal training - help the learner to better deal with his/her professional and social life context? This is especially the case for the many entrepreneurs (firms/farms) in the upcountry areas who often suffer from insufficient outreach of training activities by SIs. Besides improving the income situation, suitable training could help the entrepreneur become a more informed and knowledgeable economic actor who, for instance, is better able to network with other entrepreneurs in the area (or VC). For that reason, training services need adjustment (e.g. downgrading to the need of the informal entrepreneur within basic VCs). The call for constant learning and upgrading requires an interactive and consistent relationship between economic actors, training providers and so on. We make these qualifications with van Bussel's observation in mind about the difficulties in finding training and service providers for the new area of VCD (2005).

Tackling such challenges (new territories in skills development) involves translating into practice the ambition of making the BTVET system more relevant to private sector realities. A related impediment to the efforts to establish a better BTVET system, especially in the upcountry areas, is the inadequate regional coverage of business membership organisations (BMOs), due to a range of problems such as: weak internal organisation, leadership and management; low membership coverage; weak financial situation; limited BDS delivery capacity and other challenges in BDS provision; and insufficient cooperation patterns among BMOs and between BMOs and other service providers.[341]

In the section on *human capital requirements* the MTCS emphasises the link between quality (formal and informal) education and human capital development at large *and* productivity and growth of the economy, as well as the well-being of the population (MFPED 2000, 56).

> "*Education* is central to *adaptation* of *new technologies* and *innovation*. Besides, the acquisition of technical skills through formal and informal training, education is necessary to support a vibrant private sector. Moreover, education and training are a prerequisite to developing an effective consultative process and building dialogue on issues of national interest. Thus *human capital development is critical for raising the standard of living*" (ibid, emphasis added).

In this context, the introduction of UPE is recognised as a positive step which, however, has to tackle a number of quality deficiencies. Moreover, the ESIP (1998-2003) will guide sector investment in the medium term; but reforms, according to the MTCS document, also have to cover other areas:

> "[A]part from the reforms in revitalising technical/vocational education ..., Government, in consultation with the private sector need to agree on the *program to develop specialised skills tailored to private sector needs* and how such programs can sustainably be financed. In the meantime, Government is committed to improving the quality of education through increased financial allocations for *education infrastructure* and for the accumulation of *instructional materials*" (MFPED 2000, 56, emphasis added).

The recognition of the HRD factor in economic growth and development is notable, and the logic of the suggested agenda plausible. The aspects of *implementation* and *coherence* - across sectors, regarding the education sector strategy, the PSD, competitiveness, industrialisation, trade policy and so on - is crucial. It remains to be seen whether the central government and stakeholders can actually foster collaborations with the private sector with a view to speeding up firm-level capability formation, especially with the sections of the economy that do not seem to be very keen to work with (sections of the) public administration, for various reasons. The weak implementation record of the MTCS (see below) suggests caution in this regard. Further, the MTCS priorities since the year 2000 (as expressed in documents, debates,

341 BMO comments are based on an assessment of BMOs in Uganda by Leny van Oyen (UNIDO consultant).

commissioned studies, workshop agendas, action matrixes, and recommendation lists) allow us to conclude that HRD-for-PSD is not high on the agenda (any longer). The MTCS successor, now called Competitiveness and Investment Climate Strategy (CICS, 2006-2010), has almost totally ceased being concerned about prevalent HRD issues.[342]

Scant special focus on HRD during MTCS Phase I implementation

The implementation of each of the Strategy's actions was supposed to be carried out by the relevant state agencies as part of their mandate. A coordination unit was suggested to facilitate, monitor and communicate the implementation progress; yet it was not allowed to act as an implementer itself. This unit, the MTCS Secretariat, was only established in 2003. Guided by a PPP MTCS steering committee, the Secretariat's function was to coordinate implementation, to identify and resolve constraints to progress, to build private sector linkages and to benchmark progress against agreed programme outputs. Up to the end of the MTCS period, the Secretariat seemed understaffed.

Overall, the implementation of the strategy's first phase did not meet the high expectations of the agenda as outlined, pointing to a considerable implementation gap. The long-lasting inadequacies in ownership of the strategy and lack of existence of a single over-arching coordination and monitoring body (including lack of adequate benchmarks in the first place) have been identified as main reasons for the underperformance and mixed output results. However, progress is reported in a range of MTCS agenda items, such as infrastructure/ utilities, telecommunication, financial sector, commercial justice and anti-corruption. Some of this was achieved independently, or semi-independently from the MTCS instruments, e.g. through other donor activities (GOU 2003a, MTCS Secretariat 2005). There seems little concrete activity on HRD-for-PSD that falls under the MTCS implementation record. The following are identified deficiencies of the MTCS first phase:

- Beside the initial private sector engagement in the identification of the business constraints, its participation and involvement declined quickly and the strategy was regarded by wide sections of the private sector as just another government document that would not have a strong impact;
- Insufficient PPP mechanisms as well as overall stakeholder coordination;
- Insufficient response and commitment from the respective ministries, which preferred to follow their own agendas and strategies rather than support the MTCS;
- Insufficient capacity, capabilities (especially regarding issues of coordination and communication) for implementation within the public sector;
- Private sector associations that were supposed to implement MTCS, or steer and participate in PPPs experienced performance and management problems, for instance, the PSFU;
- Linkages between implementation of MTCS, PMA, and SEP remained unclear and led to duplication and synergy losses (ibid).

'Business environment perspective' limits more intense focus on HRD issues

Two further issues are important: **First**, the MTCS document lacked a comprehensive concept of competitiveness. The different levels and drivers of competitiveness and the dimensions of the global economy were inadequately conceptualised. It is noted generically in the MTCS document, however, that competitiveness has to do with costs and the quality of products,

342 Note that the MTCS secretariat is now called CICS Secretariat. See for more information: www.cics.go.ug.

or with productivity, efficiency, clustering and linkage building. How that translates into the Ugandan context remains unclear. The strategy seems overly based on and inspired by a cost-and-constraints kind of understanding of competitiveness that tends to show concern chiefly for improvements of matters relating to an 'enabling business environment'. Competitiveness at firm level (say, in product development, or operational efficiencies in firms and VCs), is thus not addressed adequately (and cannot be). Tackling related challenges (e.g. increasing levels of innovation and efficiency) is generally seen as private sector responsibility. The government's role, in this paradigm, is limited to creating an 'enabling environment', by improving the policy, legal and regulatory framework and removing public sector constraints to enhanced firms' competitiveness.

Besides, due to its overwhelmingly domestic focus, the strategy provides insufficient consideration of (1) factors and determinants of competitiveness arising from changes in the global economy, and (2) practices in strategy and policy in other developing and developed countries, especially the newly industrialising economies in East Asia, that have often dramatically improved their competitiveness and exports, also through decisive actions on the HRD front (beyond general education).

This understanding and application of the competitiveness concept in the MTCS is worrying: Without a broader understanding of competitiveness, a strategy like the MTCS automatically risks leaving out important aspects of the issue at stake, e.g. the implications from competitiveness trends in global markets, the importance of and challenges related to VCD and VC governance (and thus relations between VC actors), related support systems, the role of global buyers, standards, business relations and trust, tacit knowledge accumulation, upgrading and other aspects of HRD. To include these aspects in the MTCS would have been central for supporting the PSD process more vehemently, also through improved HR.

The limited PSD perspective prevails in the MTCS successor, the CICS. The 'business environment' and 'costs of production' perspective *prevails.*[343] This is at the expense of a *more adequate* focus on issues of HRD and business/technology SIs, especially for capability formation and productivity enhancement.[344] A central thrust for the CICS is a strengthened partnership between GOU and the private sector (business sector/civil society) to remove bottlenecks and foster PSD.[345] Further, promotion of sectors with high growth potential is planned through support given to respective cluster initiatives. The CICS does not clearly

343 In particular, focus on infrastructure, utilities, financial services, investment/trade matters and other aspects of the business environment and cost of doing business menu (business regulation, registration, etc.).

344 Currently, the suggestions, conceptual backing and priorities of the MTCS draft regarding interventions for PSD-related HRD are relatively inadequate. They are quite far from: (1) tackling some basic HR problems that were identified in this and other reports, (2) acknowledging the specific situation (challenges and opportunities) for HRD in a latecomer, catch-up economy, (3) creating new endowments for competitiveness in the areas of know-how, social capital and business culture or industrial, technological, managerial and organisational capabilities. However, plans to collaborate with Enterprise Uganda to enhance business skills training for SMEs are commendable. Yet, there need to be efforts in MTCS phase two to enhance technological capabilities.

345 The new MTCS theme is envisaged to be Enhancing Competitiveness through Public Private Partnership.

spell out how farmers will meet the market requirements to become and remain competitive. Most likely, VC issues will, however, arise during implementation of CICS cluster initiatives. It would have been vital for CICS to show greater concern for aspects of HRD and SIs that help building local capabilities for enhanced business operations, productivity and inter-firm collaborations (at the level of firm, farms and sub-sectors).

Implementation weaknesses in first phase point to challenges that await tackling
Second, there is reason to believe that the CICS Secretariat will face a severe challenge if it attempts to improve the mechanisms and results of the envisaged PPPs in the various priority areas of the next phase due to current inadequacies in (a) inter-ministerial cooperation, (b) line ministries and SIs (capacity and capabilities), (c) private sector organisations, and (d) state-private sector interactions.

On the whole, the MTCS and its Secretariat did not play a very decisive role in the reform process - say, as an impulse-giving, coordinating, and monitoring unit. The deficient interaction pattern with stakeholders, including the private sector and line ministries raises concerns regarding the strength of future arrangements. The role of the MTCS Secretariat in promoting HRD issues appears to have been low overall. No specific evaluation report seems to exist on the MTCS first-phase results and lessons learnt; this makes assessment of the particular HRD-related efforts within the MTCS structures, processes and budgets difficult. As with some other issue areas which experienced progress in the period of concern, improvements in the area of skills development and training in the country might have been the result of the independent work of line ministries and/or other institutions, without particular or significant impetus and coordination arising from the MTCS structures.

Overall, it is likely that the relatively poor implementation record of the MTCS cluster and productivity agenda of the early 2000s has harmed HRD-for-PSD. Can this snapshot of past MTCS processes and performances realistically suggest positive change on HRD matters for the second phase? The next sections look at the PMA and SEP.

The Plan for the Modernisation of Agriculture (PMA)

Background: Objectives and implementation frameworks

Since the beginning of the PMA in 2000, efforts were directed towards establishing place institutional arrangements and implementation strategies to help the agricultural sector to move from subsistence farming to commercial production, improve productivity and increase rural incomes. GOU considers the modernisation of this sector to be the fastest way - compared an import substitution approach - to accomplish both structural transformation of the economy and reduction of (rural) poverty. It regards institutional reforms to improve provision of public services and goods as a critical part of the strategy. Outlined interventions that touch on HRD issues are in the areas of agricultural research and extension services as well as education (for commercial agriculture), farmers' associations, technology dissemination, or gender issues. The importance of an effective BTVET system is acknowledged. A review of the BTVET system in Uganda explains, regarding the PMA:

> "In a participatory process, poor farmers have identified *lack of skills in primary production* and *financial management* as one of the major obstacles facing productivity. This is therefore an area that the PMA highlights. The PMA identifies business skills as a needed area of intervention for semi commercial farmers. The plan ... [recognises that the aim of *increased*] *off farm employment* ... is best *served with a good BTVET system*. It is also recognised that the training has to be demand

driven, so the stake of the farmers and by extension the MAAIF has to be addressed by them through the agricultural training schools and other private providers ... Based on the interviews held, it was apparent that any development of community polytechnics and demand driven training provision required opportunity for self-employment after training ... The NAADS ... is also responsible for skills development in entrepreneurship, financial management, marketing, storage and agro-processing" (Wirak et al. 2003, 20, emphasis added).

Implementation frameworks for the seven PMA priority areas have been designed and are by now mostly operational. The seven areas are:

- National Agricultural Advisory Services (NAADS): Farmers' associations at sub-county level are provided with resources to enable them to articulate their priorities and contract private sector advisory service providers; the latter is a shift towards provision of extension services by commercial private providers. Also, resources are made available for technology development, and dissemination, as well as capacity development of farmers' associations takes place under NAADS.
- National Agricultural Research System (NARS): The reformed National Agricultural Research Organisation (NARO) is supposed to be an umbrella body that comprises both public and private sector research entities and provides mechanisms for greater participation by lower-level structures (communities, farmers' associations and local governments) in defining and funding research priorities through competitive research grants.
- Marketing and Agro Processing Strategy (MAPS): MAPS aims to enhance the provision of market information to farmers and traders, to improve farmer organization and to introduce quality standards and improved post-harvest technologies. A market information and dissemination service is being established as a part of NAADS; NARO is conducting research into improved post-harvest technologies, and is training farmers in optimal storage management practices; the Uganda Commodity Exchange (UCE) is trading in grains and other agricultural commodities complemented by a Warehouse Receipt System (WRS).
- Physical infrastructure (road development and energy for the rural areas)
- Sustainable natural resource utilisation and management
- Micro finance outreach plan
- Agricultural education: Orient stakeholders to view agriculture as a business, and develop appropriate skills among producers but also among marketing agents, processors, exporters and service providers for the commercialisation of agriculture.
- Cross-cutting issues: Concern for empowerment of women in agriculture and the impact of HIV/AIDS on agricultural productivity and patterns of household production, support for community programmes that deal with such issues (GOU 2003a, 30-34).

Aspects of the implementation experience relevant to HRD[346]

The PMA offers a list of valid ideas to help boost agricultural development and productivity across the board. The conceptual and operational focus on farmers' capacities and productivity brings the PMA closer to the farm and firm level, and crucial issues, such as research, technology, marketing, skills development, and, importantly, organisation of sectors and thus inter-actor relationships and trade practices. In the first years of implementation, however, there was insufficient capacity, capability and commitment to translate the insights and ideas from the planning level into praxis and to work on the critical issues consistently so as to ensure the PMA has a lasting impact on the ground. The extent of impact and lessons learnt from some interventions remain uncertain (GOU 2003a). Deficiencies in the implementation of this ambitious plan that have been identified for the PMA are similar to that of the MTCS: Inefficient

346 Part of this section is adopted from Wiegratz et al. (2007b).

monitoring and benchmarking due to lack of a single monitoring mechanism, which has now resulted in design of a Monitoring and Evaluation Framework; implementation problems due to awaiting institutional reforms within GOU at the local level, for example, and funding problems (GOU 2003a, 34). Interventions were thus spread too thinly and inefficiently across sectors and issue areas. A recent evaluation report summarises the situation as follows:

> "The overall logic of the PMA still holds good, but there have been confusions over the function of the PMA, *insufficient emphasis* on *some* of the *constraints identified,* and *weaknesses* in the *implementation* which should be addressed. In particular, ... there is a need for *greater differentiation amongst* the *target groups.* More importance should be placed on *improving performance along the value chain* for traditional food crops, a key activity for resource-poor risk-averse farmers, including women. Access to land is an important constraint for many women farmers, which has not yet been addressed effectively under the land policy. There is need for greater *support* and *capacity building* for both *private sector service providers* and *local government officials.* The time is now ripe ... to address these issues, and to provide a more specific set of *time-bound targets* and *indicators of success.* This should also make clear the *poverty focus* of the PMA ... It is widely recognised in Uganda that the *rate of rollout of the pillars* has been *highly variable.* This has led to frustration for some stakeholders. It has also meant that *potential synergy amongst the pillars has not been achieved.* The geographic distribution amongst the pillars has exacerbated this. In some districts, there appears to have been a deliberate policy to spread out available services and resources, to achieve an equitable result, at the *expense of effectiveness and efficiency* ... Chief amongst [the report's suggestions for re-arrangement of pillars to improve performance] ... is mainstreaming of *marketing issues* within all pillars, development of *more differentiated strategies according to target groups,* and *greater coordination of pillars at district level*" (OPM 2005, i-ii, emphasis added).

Further, the requirement to strengthen private sector service providers is recognised in the above quote and also in the following quote from the report's recommendation section: "The need for capacity building of service providers should be addressed as a priority - this has been the slowest disbursing component of NAADS" (ibid, v). Capacity needs for extension and research related to agricultural upgrading were also noted elsewhere: "The long-term success of these reforms will depend on a growing critical mass of qualified researchers and extension workers" (Muhumuza et al. 2005, iv).

The quotes from the OPM report generally imply that it is well understood that: (1) the performance of all actors along the VC matters, and (2) that more effective support systems are needed. The emphasis on marketing of farmers produce goes to the core of the VC argument for better links between farmers and buyers. The report furthermore makes a crucial observation regarding the positive effect of interventions that focus on *group formation, technology,* and *input supply;* this is actually a call for *better integrated DVCs,* where buyers, farmers, SIs and input suppliers strive for better linkages and cooperation. The quote reveals that improvements of the farmers' situation can be achieved via support measures, under specific conditions, a finding that is confirmed by Wiegratz et al. (2007b).

> "To assess progress in achieving intermediate and final outcomes of the PMA, the Evaluation undertook a [small] household survey, supplemented by district visits. This showed that there was significant activity going on at district level. The household survey, which was qualitative in nature, also showed progress in terms of *improved technologies* and *increases in marketed output,* though it is *not possible to attribute this directly to any particular element of the PMA.* In focus group

> discussions with women's farmer groups, participants were very clear that their wealth status had increased as a result of *joining these groups*, which were receiving services from NAADS. The team feels that, although the process is slow, *where technology is appropriate* and the *relevant inputs are available*, adoption rates are significant, and there are positive outcomes. However, more emphasis should be being placed on monitoring of outcomes and impact, to enable effective assessment of progress" (OPM 2005, iv, emphasis added).

Regarding implementation challenges, the difficulties of executing new approaches in agro-related programmes (with HRD components) for a transforming economy are also revealed in a recent analysis of the NAADS programme (Tanburn and Kamuhanda 2005). There are problems related to: (a) linking interventions with market dynamics and thus managing the commercial rather than mainly the technical side of the agro-diversification process, and (b) bringing on board the competencies required for the implementation and concrete capacity-building process. In addition to that, (c) some support provision remains very short-term oriented, and (d) services are not used by significant sections of farmers. Regarding (d), the analysis also looked at relationships between farmers and NAADS by socio-economic characteristics of farmers. Of the five categorised groups, only two were cited to have beneficiary relationship with NAADS: the *progressive middle-class farmers* (who "dominate leadership positions in farmer groups and farmer forums", "beneficiaries from NAADS but who could do without it") and the *active poor farmers* ("attend meetings but do not participate as much as progressive farmers do"). Regarding NAADS services, the other three groups were 'not interested' (commercial estate farmers), 'generally not interested' (commercial farmers, "can pay for services whenever there is need"), or 'do not bother' (inactive poor farmers, "think such programmes are not made for them") (ibid, 52). Nyabuntu (2006) also gives an overview of relevant challenges of NAADS implementation:

> "[a]gricultural commercialization ... is the most challenging single component facing the NAADS programme ... Market linkages remain poor and smallholders continue being production oriented and not market oriented. Commercialisation is constrained by: Absence of market linkages and long term relationships between farmers and private sector traders ... Lack of partnering between farmers, private sector and NAADS. It is true that there have been some private sector/NAADS partnerships. The scale of this is very negligible compared to NAADS coverage ... Lack of market oriented advisory services. Farmers are not yet producing for the market. General advisory services cannot lead to commercialisation. Advisory services must target a certain market and must be oriented to the requirements of that market" (ibid, vi).

Box 34 offers further examples of NAADS implementation challenges that can serve as illustrations for general HRD challenges in the Ugandan agro sectors.[347]

347 See also Bahiigwa et al. (2005), and Hickey (2005, 2003). See Daily Monitor (2009) regarding a recent value-for-money audit from the Auditor General. According to the newspaper, the report states that two-thirds of the 600 interviewed farmers were dissatisfied with the training provided by NAADS. Respondents complained about the effectiveness of the training and criticised the work of the private service providers who were hired by NAADS to conduct the training. Farmers' training attendance was reportedly low. See Wiegratz et al. (2007b) for a couple of examples of relevant work that NAADS is doing.

Box 34: Difficulties in undertaking interventions for commercial diversification of agricultural sector

"The [NAADS] programme aims at commercialising Uganda's agricultural sector through the use of private service providers. NAADS has been a major shift in approach to the provision of services in the agricultural sector. For the first time, Government is hiring private service providers. Farmers select enterprises (crops) in which agricultural extension services are needed, and they also participate in selecting the service providers. Presently NAADS is the most prominent agent for service delivery in the agricultural sector, with a budget for the first 7-year phase of $108 million, although it has not yet received all of these resources. By mid-2005, NAADS was covering 280 sub-counties in 29 districts, out of the total of 900 sub-counties and 56 districts. This means that 69% of sub-counties remain under the old extension system of public civil service ... Actual implementation [of the programme] takes place in sub counties where farmers choose three crops that they consider to be the most profitable and marketable. Two other factors considered in crop selection are financial outlay and risks, but profitability and marketability are given higher weights in making the decision. *While a step in the direction of marketability, the process still does not involve people who understand markets and current demand. Marketing therefore remains a problem and continues to constrain agricultural commercialisation. Marketability is based on farmers' perceived markets and not on actual identified markets* ... The NAADS programme was designed on the premise that 'Many past efforts in agricultural development have had limited success and long term effectiveness because of lack of ownership by the key stakeholders-farmers' [NAADS 2000, 13] however, service provision remains an *imitation of the old system*:

- *There is no link in practice with market demand.* Farmers are supposed to choose crops for which there is a viable market, but they lack the information and contacts to make informed decisions about this

- Not all the NAADS coordinators at district and sub-county levels have the competencies that they need to manage the whole process

- Service providers are contracted for a very short period. In most cases, the contract is for less than the growing season of annual crops. Service providers do not get time within the short contractual period to visit each farmer's field. Moreover, the ToR [terms of reference] for service provision does not require service providers to visit farmers' fields.

In terms of funding, farmers contribute 2%, district local government 5%, and sub-counties 5% of the costs for service provision. The rest is contributed by donors (80%) and central government (8%). The insignificant contribution by farmers is because farmers are poor and remain poor even after producing and harvesting their crops. However, this low level of contribution by the ultimate service users brings with it a number of problems, not least that service fees are likely to be higher than farmers will be able to afford. It also means that, even now, they are not really the customers, but still rather the beneficiaries. Experience suggests that contributions of over 50% of service charges from public funds mainly distorts the market by driving up prices, rather than stimulating demand in the longer term ... [In sum, the] government's agricultural extension 'flagship', NAADS, has signalled an important shift towards provision of extension services by private providers on a commercial basis. Problems remain, however, since NAADS still lacks significant links to actual markets, remaining focused on the technical rather than commercial aspects of diversification. In addition, it requires only a very small cost contribution from farmers, meaning that sustainability will only be achieved far into the future (if at all)" (Tanburn and Kamuhanda 2005, 51-2, 57, emphasis added).

Note also the observation of the OPM evaluation report on PMA which reveals difficulties of undertaking successful agricultural training in primary education: "According to the PMA annual report 2003/2004, in four districts 247 primary schools have started agriculture-related teaching or formed agriculture 'clubs' [PMA 2004, 17-21, quoted in OPM 2005, 19]. School gardens established through the NSCG [non-sectoral conditional grant] are supervised by extension workers. According to sub-county extension workers met during field visits, commitment to the gardens by teachers and students is low. Teachers are reluctant to take on the extra work of managing and maintaining the gardens, and students regard the work as a punishment rather than as education. Integrating agricultural education within the curricula for primary schools is a challenging task. However, the Evaluation feels that this is an important component of the education pillar and should be continued" (OPM 2005, 19).

These documented observations by researchers on the deficits and weaknesses of recent state efforts reveal that: (1) a number of years after the kick-off of the PEAP and PMA there seems to be, overall, limited progress in the agro-sector in terms of organisation of economic actors and improvement of inter-actor relations (or DVC governance in general). (2) Tackling the difficult agenda of DVCD is therefore a core challenge for the aspirations of the PMA and other programmes and the economic transformation agenda of the country in general.

That aside, it is positive to note that the debate and efforts related to commercialisation of agriculture in Uganda are increasingly sensitive to (or even structured around) the VC approach. An increasing number of government and donor programmes have started subscribing to the VC approach and have undertaken first steps to design and implement related support measures.[348] VCD-related measures are gaining prominence in the country's development circles. Recently, NAADS re-emphasised its commitment to the approach: NAADS currently supports buyer-farmer systems and enters partnerships with firms such as the honey processor Bee Natural Product and Mukwano. These are moves in the right direction.

As indicated in the above discussion of the implementation experiences to date, the challenge is: (a) to move from theory to practice in a meaningful way that serves the purpose of the programme and (b) to enhance the institutional collaborations (between different state institutions, and the state and the private sector) to the level that is required for successful DVCD. In the context of current features of DVCs in Uganda, the issue is *how* the state wants to support VCD effectively. The related issues have significant dimensions of political economy and economic sociology. Furthermore, VCD is a terrain that is relatively unknown to public sector officials (and also donor personnel) who have, in the recent past, rather focused on regulatory reforms or carried out single-issue interventions (e.g. training farmers, giving seeds) that do not sufficiently address the challenge of *building VC systems including linkages between VC actors* (see for details Wiegratz et al 2007b). However, there is relatively little detailed analysis available regarding results, experiences and lessons learnt of these interventions; however, see ibid for an attempt in this direction.

348 This is evident from government's new Rural Development Strategy (RDS) which was launched in FY 2005/06: The RDC plans to facilitate linkage building between producers (farmer groups) and processors/produce buyers, or delivery of inputs through market mechanisms, including produce-dealer and processor credit. The goal of the RDS is poverty eradication by increasing household incomes through advanced agricultural productivity, value addition, and market access. A linkage programme implemented by Enterprise Uganda which has so far supported parts of training of farmers in the context of out-grower schemes of a brewery and sugar factory is also noteworthy. Others are NPA, MTTI, DANIDA, UNIDO or USAID.

The Strategic Export Programme (SEP)

Background: Objectives and interventions

Government's main concern in promoting exports is to *capture additional value* from traditional exports and *diversify into higher-value non-traditional exports*. To promote the production, processing and marketing of selected strategic exports GOU introduced the SEP in 2001.

"The SEP constitutes a specific intervention based on the premise that even when the macro-economic and micro-economic policy environment are conducive, the private sector may not perform as expected due to some specific bottlenecks that might require government intervention" (GOU 2003b, 5). The SEP objectives are as follows: "(1) to stimulate investments in strategic areas, particular for value addition, that are likely to have multiplier effects on the entire economy, (2) to remove specific bottlenecks that impede the private sector's ability to take advantage of emerging trade opportunities under initiatives such as AGOA, EBA and other initiatives such as by Japan, Canada and in the Middle East" (ibid).

The programme (2001/02-2005/06) was intended to triple the national export earnings, thereby removing the current trade deficit. It initially focused on eight sectors: coffee, tea, livestock, fish, cotton, horticulture, Irish potatoes and Information and Communications Technology (ICT). Other sectors were added later, e.g. petroleum exploration, cocoa, commodity trading and risk management (WRS and Agricultural Commodity Exchange). The interventions included: *training and skills development (export marketing, data entry, and clean seed production)*, import of machinery (processing machines), distribution of agricultural inputs (planting material and stock), formulation of laws and regulations, and initiatives to attract investment or obtain certification schemes (GOU 2003a, 2003b).

SEP implementation constraints - an example of a general problem experienced by PSD strategies in Uganda

According to a progress report, the SEP has so far demonstrated that:

> "(a) There is potential for achieving rapid economic growth and structural transformation through strategic intervention. (b) Technology based interventions such as the ICT have potential for increasing employment opportunities and export earnings in a relatively short period. (c) Prospects for value addition for commodities are high. These may not involve processing in the usual form but could take the form of appellations and certification of selected brand names and packaging" (GOU 2003b, 3).

The report also documents major constraints experienced by the programme: (1) insufficient resource allocations, budget cuts and reallocations, all together creating financial uncertainty, (2) no initial involvement of stakeholders, especially from the private sector (but also donors), implying that the SEP was at first viewed with suspicion; overall deficient private sector involvement throughout the SEP implementation process, and (3) SEP resources and funds often being used for routine activities, e.g. staff salaries or transportation and office operational costs (ibid). The negative consequences of insufficient programme activities have been severe in many of the selected sectors.349 Such implementation problems usually have various negative side-effects, e.g. on FDI (2003b).

In addition, the monitoring and evaluation arrangement for SEP was poor, involving the lack of an impact assessment and cost-benefit analysis; without which it is difficult to determine which of the interventions have a high/low impact regarding the desired outputs, and why. It is one thing to provide production inputs, as it was done in the SEP, it is a different thing (and can be more sustainable) to work with economic actors to transform the way they operate their firms/farms and use the inputs/technology and thus improve their input-output ratio (productivity). This aspect does not appear to have received much attention. Finally, coordination with the interlinked growth strategies - PMA and MTCS - was not undertaken (2003a, 37). There have been discussions on how to change the situation. Obviously, the SEP faces challenges to ensure integrated, coordinated and consistent interventions as well as the necessary support from the main actors in the future. Similar to its sister programmes, it had lost some credibility and pace by the mid 2000s; as a result of a combination of factors (funding, coordination, or cooperation inefficiencies) that hampered meeting ambitious targets.

More to the point, some agencies that are supposed to contribute to the SEP are underfunded in their own core functions and programmes in the first place, not to mention for extra activities designed under the SEP. The Uganda Export Promotion Board (UEPB) is an example; in the early 2000s it only received around 30% of its required budget. This money covered mainly the salaries and office expenditures, but was inadequate to undertake e.g. SEP implementation activities. Consequently, UEPB - with donor support - designed a parallel strategy to the SEP without, it seems, strong consideration of lessons learnt or gaps of the SEP: the National Export Strategy. Indeed, in Uganda, many PSD strategies exist in a somewhat parallel and conceptually different or overlapping system of frameworks (including problem analysis) and related strategies, policies and programmes. These often target the same (partly weak) private sector actors, and count on the same (partly weak) SIs to participate and contribute to the implementation. Ineffective use of scarce resources and strategy fatigue are some of the outcomes. One of the latest plans is the Plan for Zonal Agricultural Production, Agro-processing and Marketing (GOU 2004a, 2004b); see Box 53 (Appendix 29) for a review. The SEP was meanwhile brought within the MTCS with the intention of aligning it with the MTCS and PMA. The MTCS/CICS Secretariat now promotes a perspective of addressing the problems of each export sector through vertically integrated sector strategies (MTCS 2005) which by itself is a positive conceptual improvement.

---

349 There was considerable scaling down of the planned activities in field interventions in particular, e.g. in the cotton lint, textiles, and garments sector with respect to production-related mobilisation and sensitisation activities. The delays in payment or late decisions about budget cuts have led to distortions in the implementation process, or have not allowed a significant impact in some areas. Sometimes budget cuts were undertaken while implementation was already under way, which led to frustration, loss of momentum of mobilisation and sensitisation activities and thus confidence in SEP. Further, insufficient flexibility in the management of these resources didn't, for instance, allow assistance to farmers in the horticulture sector (fruits, flowers, vegetables) to cope with frequently changing market demands, e.g. with respect to required changes in the type of packaging material. In the ICT sector, insufficient resources have resulted in non-establishment of the ICT incubation centre (GOU 2003b).

A national HRD framework? Implementation challenges are likely

Government has recognised the unsatisfactory overall coordination and monitoring of the implementation of all three programmes, above all of the MTCS - its main programme for reducing investment barriers. With regard to the two key programmes that are designed to enhance productivity, namely the PMA and the SEP, GOU has recognised similar needs for improvements, stressing issues of implementation, monitoring, evaluation, stakeholder involvement, institutional reforms, transparency, cross-programme coordination, and funding. Against the background of the implementation problems, GOU is aware that focusing not only on *processes* but also on *outcome delivery* is critical for the future of its growth strategies; otherwise, the risk is that stakeholders, including investors and donors, lose confidence in the state commitment to PSD (GOU 2003a, 39-42). Indeed, both processes and results need urgent strengthening in all growth-related programmes. For reasons explored above, advancements in HRD-for-PSD remained limited within this fragmented programme structure and its implementation deficits.

The key impression is that some of the very areas of interventions required for PSD that go *beyond* macro-economic stability or market liberalisation[350] have experienced a range of relevant *implementation problems*. This includes efforts to develop and improve productive and social capabilities for PSD.

It is, therefore, difficult to assess if and how a comprehensive appreciation of HRD issues and determinants for PSD could be worked out meaningfully and successfully. Or, even further, if and how a realistic national HRD concept that has ownership and a good chance of implementation could be developed. The generally appreciative perspective of GOU on the HRD front - especially in terms of formal education - is an important beginning. No doubt, the HRD theme will gain further momentum in one way or another. In the near future, PSD (and HRD) stakeholders might even reach a consensus regarding a formulated strategy and action agenda. However, whether *sufficient, continuous and concerted actions* transpire at the implementation level and can be translated into concrete outputs is another issue altogether.[351] The review of the implementation difficulties in the early 2000s of the three key economic growth and transformation programmes illuminated important indications of complex challenges in relation to execution of significant PSD support interventions in Uganda. In the mid-late 2000s, implementation problems are still being reported. For instance, NAADS and NUSAF (Northern Uganda Social Action Plan) were affected by a number of cases involving the improper use of money and a poor implementation record in a several locations.[352] In 2007, President Yoweri Museveni suspended NAADS activities over reports

350 The market liberalisation reforms of the telecommunication and finance sectors, for instance, have been undertaken with some success.

351 Note the following IMF assessment: "The government's commitment to reforms appears to have eroded despite a well-articulated PEAP ... Incentives to implement bold reforms appear to have receded in a post-debt relief era, indicating 'reform fatigue' on the part of the authorities" (2006, 24). Nevertheless, it is possible that implementation performance improves in the new government period (2006-2011).

352 EPRC (2009) research on public expenditure in the agricultural sector also revealed severe spending and implementation inadequacies. See also OPM (2007). This author cannot offer a political-economic analysis of public expenditure patterns in Uganda in this book. Note, however, that, for instance, technically 'improper' use of public finance can be politically and/or culturally appropriate (e.g. to facilitate political support networks or comply to social norms); see the debate

of mismanagement for a period of time to allow investigation into the programme activities. Following this assessment, new guidelines for NAADS were worked out and the programme is now running again (GOU 2008a, NV 2008a).

The highlighted experiences and insights can assist proponents of a national HRD framework or programme to develop *appropriate* strategies which consider the political, economic, cultural and institutional reasons for such implementation challenges.[353] In the next chapter we shall look at evidence of HRD efforts in the formal private sector in Uganda.

---

on the neopatrimonial state (e.g. Erdmann and Engel 2006). See also Blundo and Olivier de Sardan (2005) for an insightful analysis on the state and everyday corruption in Africa. For research on politics, power, institutions and the supply of public goods in Africa, see also http://www.institutions-africa.org/.

353 It is important to note that various implementation difficulties have been a characteristic of economy-related interventions of different Ugandan governments in both colonial and post-colonial times (see e.g. Carswell 2007, Thompson 2003, Asiimwe 2002, Asiimwe and Nahamya 2006, Jamal 1991).

12

HRD Activities in the Formal Private Sector

Background of the chapter

Previous chapters of the book offered a range of insights on the level of skills available in sections of the Ugandan economy. For instance, besides the discussion of the study done on training needs of MSMEs (EU and GOU 2003), an analysis of matters of technology adoption, business growth, and microfinance in the SSE sector (Byaruhanga 2005b) revealed the low level of technical, innovative, managerial and other capabilities of employees in many small firms, as well as the deficits in terms of firms' management and organisational setup. This, it was argued, impacts negatively on the incidences and quality of training in firms, including learning-by-doing mechanisms. We also reviewed training efforts in the meat, textile, carpentry and flower sectors. It was generally argued that deficiencies in social capital, including trust, adversely affect the formation of productive skills and capabilities, both within a firm and in inter-firm relationships. This finding points to relevant yet under-researched characteristics of the business culture in the country: in terms of training, learning and cooperation. We also examined certain firms' characteristics that had a direct or indirect link to the HRD theme.

Initially, the author had planned to include a more detailed analysis of HRD perceptions and practices of firms in Uganda. During the period of research for GTZ/PEVOT in early 2006, about 50 firms were contacted by e-mail. A contact list and introductory letter were provided by PEVOT. The e-mail approach was selected by the author and PEVOT as the chosen channel of communication with firms for *this* study (its scope and purposes), given the limited funds and time available and the fact that the author was requested to analyse the available reports and data in particular, as well as government strategy documents, while interviewing only some experts. Against this background, the author took notice of some more extensive studies on BTVET and PPET and related employment matters in Uganda (Bennel and Sayed 2002, Liang 2002, Wirak et al. 2003, Nalumansi et al. 2003a, J.E. Austin Associates and UMACIS 2004), as well as the employment policy draft 2004 of the MGLSD (2004). The authors of these studies had carried out many interviews with sector experts. This author therefore sought to complement and link with those reports, instead of 'updating' them by going through the same lengthy interview procedure. Consequently, this book contains no particular analysis of the BTVET system in Uganda.

Thus, for this research, firms were requested via e-mail to provide inputs on the following four issues: (1) trends in firms' demand for certain skills and competencies, including supply-side conditions for their provision, (2) current focal points of firms' HRD efforts as a reflection of certain issues and challenges, including competitiveness forces that firms are facing, (3) examples of training practices, including interaction with the ETS, and (4) expectations regarding future trends in the above categories. The feedback from firms was very low, which could be related to, among others: (a) means and ways of author's communication[354], (b) workload of HRD experts and managers, (c) survey fatigue, and (d) election time during contact period.

Still, there seems to be plenty of reason to undertake such a particular study in the future, and it could focus solely on HRD practices and issues at firm level. Based on a firm understanding of the HRD environment in Uganda and in the light of findings and information presented in this book, such a broader study could provide relevant insights on firm-level efforts, and difficulties and achievements in developing HR. This research could also investigate firms' experiences with the ETS and discuss future possibilities regarding improving the latter. As said earlier, as much as this book advocates increased attention on the informal sector, including agriculture, it also suggests that development (including poverty reduction) effects will have to come from a further upgrading of the formal sector. Presumably, the latter can apply technology to its business processes more easily and/or significantly than semi-subsistence/informal businesses can, thus advancing productivity, output and growth. In general, the formal sector can also benefit considerably from the global pool of resources (knowledge and technology) while trying to meet the requirements of competitive markets. Without a more advanced formal sector (which is linked to the informal sector, agriculture etc.), there might be continuation of the current pattern of Uganda's integration into the global economy (marginalisation, exports of mainly unprocessed agricultural products) and little catch-up in technology use and productivity. In other words, opportunities remain underexploited. It is thus relevant for practitioners and policy-makers alike to understand HRD realities in the private sector.

HRD matters raised by an agro-processing firm

The view provided by a firm that operates upcountry in the agro-processing sector is by no means representative, yet it is informative (Box 35). It indicates the evolving and transformational character of HRD in the country and refers to a range of related achievements and deficiencies. Furthermore, the firm applies a HRD strategy that *mixes local* and *international* sources for improvements in HR areas. The improvement of the capabilities of staff is done both locally (in-house training with the help of national experts) and internationally (sending staff abroad for extra training, hiring international experts to conduct in-house training, use of online learning possibilities). The *combination* of *internal* and *external sources of learning* can be regarded as an innovative way - but of course not the only one - of dealing with the challenges and opportunities of the current HRD phase in Uganda. The firm relies on various partnerships for HRD and applies forms of the LLL-approach to benefit from foreign sources of information, knowledge, technology and skills. Box 35 (as well as Box 3 regarding the training mix in the flower sector) demonstrates the value of this mixing strategy.

354 There was only one e-mail sent to each firm and follow-up efforts undertaken only when firms replied to the initial e-mail. Instead, face-to-face interviews or questionnaires and a direct-contacts approach, by going through the associations (FUE, UMA, or PSFU), would have been more appropriate. Yet, this was not pursued further by the author due to time and manpower restrictions (funding for about two months) and the main method (desk research) of the GTZ study.

As noted at the beginning of this book, marrying effectively the available internal and external sources of productivity, competitiveness and growth is *one* of the key strategies for competitive late-comer economic development. It can help to address input gaps and technological constraints that impede this process at firm, sector or national level. Box 35 also points to the need for increased levels of productivity, commitment and loyalty - or, a mix of technical and social skills - as objectives of HRD. The example of Unilever Uganda also reveals the role of external relationships, here with the parent company/headquarters, and for staff training (here in managerial skills) in Uganda (Box 54, Appendix 30). It further points to more limited efforts of this firm, and others of a similar nature, in areas such as local technological capability formation.

Box 35: Reflections of a larger agro-processing firm on HRD matters in Uganda

(1) Trends in firm's demand for certain skills and competencies, including respective supply-side conditions: "Within Uganda HR is a *relatively new concept* and only seriously embraced by the major companies and international organisations. There is no focussed HR organisation, only a number of small associations offering services mainly on a consultancy basis. For HR qualifications the only real options are new university courses in HRM such as that operated by the Makerere University or overseas distance learning programmes such as the Chartered Institute of Personnel and Development in UK. Most HR practitioners in Uganda have become involved in the discipline through necessity rather than planning or training. There is a strong demand for a *solid local institute* offering local training and qualifications. HR specialities that *need improvement* are *strategic planning, manpower planning* and *performance management*. Overall, throughout the country the skills level continues to be low with anecdotal evidence suggesting that graduates from the main university (Makerere University) are not of the same calibre as they used to be due to changed entrance criteria as from a decade ago. Trades skills tend to be taught on the job and are hence spasmodic and generally at a low level. Management training is generally unplanned and there is a definite cultural submissiveness to elders/seniors which makes the concept of proactive management alien".

(2) Current focal points of firm's HRD practices as a reflection of certain trends and challenges: "The main preoccupations of HR departments include the *recruitment* and *selection* of qualified experienced specialists and managers and the *provision of welfare facilities*. Linked to the *brain drain* of good graduates to Europe and USA there is a shortage of competent graduate calibre staff despite the numerous young people holding degree qualifications. There is need to improve levels of *productivity, commitment* and *loyalty*".

(3/4) Examples of firm's training practices; expectations regarding future trends: "Within the company there is a strong emphasis on management development, Distance Learning for professional qualifications and *growing our own qualified people* through a 4 year apprenticeship City & Guilds London accredited programme. Technical courses are provided on site by local experts and where necessary overseas trainers are imported. Throughout the year, staff attend courses abroad, e.g. in South Africa or in the UK on technology matters and management. There are numerous training providers in Uganda offering services on a whole range of areas and of differing quality; main providers that are available within the country are Uganda Institute of Management, the Management Training Advisory Centre, the Federation of Uganda Employers, and the British Council. There is a *new wave of HR Consultancy firms* that are trying to offer 1-3 days workshops/seminars within the country. Some of these are locally arranged while others are initiated outside Uganda but conducted within the country. There is need to *evaluate* their *effectiveness*. In current conditions it is likely that the strategy of continuing to 'grow our own' whether it be trades people or managers will need to continue".

Source: *Response from firm to author's study questions, emphasis added.*

Findings of the Employer of the Year Award Survey Report 2004

Background

There is a series of reports available on HRD practices in Uganda which is relevant to the context of this book. These publications are related to the annual Employer of the Year Award (EYA) of the FUE. With a view to enhancing organisational growth and profitability, the EYA seeks to identify, promote and encourage Uganda's top employers who carry out *best* HR-management (HRM) and business practices or who have *improved* most significantly in the various categories. For some years now, the international consultancy firm Ernst&Young has produced the EYA reports, and undertaken related firm-level surveys and analyses. Usually Ernst&Young provides further analytical feedback (audits) to participating organisations and firms only (thereafter termed: organisations).

The objectives of the EYA are: (1) trend identification, (2) understanding leading HRM practices, (3) organisation-level analysis of HRM practices, (4) feedback on HR status (e.g. gaps) and solution mix for participating organisations, (5) benchmarking of performance of peer organisations, (6) recognising leading practices as well as efforts to improve practices, and (7) awareness creation and promotion of a 'people first' culture in participating organisations (FUE 2005a, 1-28).

We will briefly review the 2004 report of the EYA titled Achieving Organisational Results through a People First Culture. It expresses specific appreciation of needs related to fostering behavioural changes in firms and organisations (ibid, 1, 5). Relevant findings of the analysis of the *voluntarily participating* national and foreign organisations are provided in Box 36. Participating firms and organisations were from different sections of the Ugandan economy and society. Out of 78 organisations and firms (size: at least five employees) which submitted questionnaires, 55 were eventually audited. Note there can be a bias in the results as some organisations with a rather weak HR record might well have excluded themselves from participating in the survey in the first place. Overall, this report - the survey results, the listing of best HR practices of the award winners etc. - can serve as indication of the HR reality in the *advanced* section of the formal private and public sector. Note, to the best of the author's knowledge, the EYA related data is the first and so far only firm level data set on this topic in the country.[355] There is hardly any research available on HRM practises in other sections of the economy.

355 There is another data set on HRD issues which was collected by the EPRC in a field survey for UNIDO in 2005 in relation to analysis on industrial competitiveness and industrial HRD (UNIDO 2007).

Human resource management in the formal sector: findings and practices

Box 36 provides insights regarding the level of HR practices in the (advanced) formal sector. The variety of relevant findings and results presented speak for itself; we will not discuss it in detail. Furthermore, many issues that are raised regarding firm activities (and related achievements and gaps) have in one way or another already been discussed in earlier chapters of the book: productivity, performance incentives, business ethics and behaviour, training, learning, or the management of world-of-work and world-of-life, consideration of staff' value systems.[356]

Box 36: The Employer of the Year Award 2004 survey - Selected key findings and leading practices

From the report summary: "*Human Resource Practices* ... More companies are becoming aware of and, concerned about the overall investment in human resources (HR), and the return on it. Many are looking for help to modify, or even transform their HR function - focusing more energy on a strategic approach to HR, including managing costs, improving business performance, and outsourcing the non-core pieces. Less than half of all companies link reward programs (compensation, benefits, and work-life balance) with corporate strategy. Critical HR programs are not effectively managed in today's complex and rapidly changing regulatory environment. Because some companies incur labour costs amounting to more than half of revenues, pressures to continually reduce costs are conflicting with organisations' need to attract, retain, and reward critical talent in order to sustain their competitive advantage. Only one-third of workers feel they are on track when it comes to planning and saving for retirement ....

Local Challenges in HRM People in organisations do not generally understand the role of HR, and do not recognise this as a profession of its own. Some organisations have an administrative focus on HR, which is only part of what HRM does. It is common that the HR function reports to Finance and Administration irrespective of the difference in objectives/goals. Human Resources Departments are not always led by competent Human Resource people. There is limited investment in HR systems, and cost constraints provide limitations. Many organisations lack information about what HR systems should be adopted, and how they can contribute to the business. HR is not yet fully viewed as a strategic partner. ...

Comments on Best Practice in Uganda Most organisations have limited information on what best practice is and therefore lack guidelines on what they should be doing. Sharing of HR information with colleagues is not common practice. There are many sound systems in existence, with limited technical knowledge which lead to systems not being as strong as they should be. There was not a high proportion of innovation in the systems and procedures we reviewed. Based on our observation of HR practices in many of the organisations in Uganda, we believe that there is a need for improvement and added focus in the following areas: The HR function needs to be placed at a senior level within strategic management and should be separate from the administration function; Employee participation and consulting; Grading, Job evaluation and pay structuring; Enhancement of performance systems; Implementation of systems to monitor business ethics; Innovative HR practices, and Capacity building of organizational leaders to be able to handle HR issues" (FUE 2005a, 1-5)

The following are further selected key results and assessments from the report (taken from ibid, 12-27, the selected text is presented as it appears in the original except for some formatting done by the author in terms of text selection and presentation to allow condensed reading of this information box):

Human resource function: The activities of HR managers vary from one workplace to another and are affected by such factors as the size and structure of the organisation. In all the surveyed organisations, human resources are a centralised corporate function. However, in several

356 See Munene (1995) on HRM practices in the health and education sector in rural Uganda. See Ahikire (1994) for an account of labour conditions in the Ugandan garment industry. See Grierson (2002) for case studies of enterprise-based training in Kenya and Zambia.

organisations the HR function is blended with office administration activities, with usually one individual being responsible for both functions. The focus of the HR function in all organisations primarily covers the following objectives: (1) Create and manage human resource strategy, (2) Manage deployment of personnel, (3) Develop and train employees, (4) Manage employee performance, rewards and recognition, (5) Ensure employee well being and satisfaction, (6) Ensure employee involvement in achieving organisational goals, (7) Recruitment and resourcing.

Changing role of HR: In addition to the traditional functions performed by HR specialists, the role of HR professionals is undergoing a significant change to meet an organisation's demands for improved quality, reduced costs, and constant innovation. The HR role has extended to provide learning and to train and develop employees who are capable of responding to changing priorities.

- 10% of the surveyed organisations outlined a broad HR strategy.
- In 5% of the surveyed organisations, the HR head is a member of the top management committee.
- 10% of the surveyed organisations have indicated that the human resource plan is becoming an integral part of the business plan.
- In 50% of the organisations, HR managers are responsible for learning/organisational development.
- 30% of the surveyed organisations have indicated that they have a well-documented HR policies and procedures manual.
- 10% of the surveyed organisations acknowledged that their HR policies have been properly communicated to all employees.
- At least 5% of the participating organisations have a well established HR database, which integrates employee details and provides data on personal information, promotions, transfers, employee performance, and development needs.

Leading practice: Leading organisations in HR have installed monitoring software to track the progress of HR development activities. A few organisations have developed qualitative and quantitative KRAs (key result areas) for their human resources functions. In two organisations the HR department has assessed the level and efficiency of service provided by distributing a questionnaire to its internal customers. A sample of senior managers from all functions is selected to respond on the effectiveness of HR systems.

Organisation structure

Grade structures: 25% of the surveyed organisations have indicated that they have a clear and well defined grading structure. Grade structure divides employees into 3 to 4 categories, namely workers, staff, officers/executives, and management. The average number of grades at the managerial cadre varies between 4 to 5 grades in the surveyed organisations. Some organisations have indicated that they do not foresee a reduction in the individual grade structures implemented across the organisation in the near future.

Leading practice: Some organisations have gone through a process of management restructuring to improve functioning, strategic alignment and productivity. Strong market competition, cost reviews and manpower alignment were the main reason for the organisational reviews. For instance an organisation introduced a business-process reengineering program to overcome the problems of manufacturing inefficiencies, poor production and huge overtime. This involved restructuring of the organisation at all levels. It shifted from a functional organisation to a business unit structure base as well as centralised shared service units. The business heads have a higher span of control and greater flexibility in operations. This exercise has made some jobs in the middle and junior management levels redundant. The organisation designed a detailed reorganisation implementation plan along with a phased manpower reduction plan.

Organisational culture

Institutionalising vision and values: 10% of the organisations agreed that they have taken active measures in institutionalising vision and values. Common examples of systems used by the organisations to strengthen and instil values are stated below: (a) Conducting vision workshops to educate employees on their organisations' vision. These workshops are used to gain commitment to the vision from employees and align their personal career visions to the corporate vision, (b Setting up a vision compliance committee to set standards, conduct educational programs and enforce disciplinary mechanisms, (c) Employee feedback survey is used to measure the clarity and support on the organisation's values and visions, (d) None of the surveyed organisations have indicated that they use an employee feedback survey as a part of institutionalising their vision and values amongst employees, (e 5% of the surveyed organisations have indicated that they translate their values into leadership competencies, which are assessed during the objective-setting process.

Communicating vision: Vision communication is increasingly becoming a constant corporate need. The vision is communicated to employees primarily through meetings, newsletters, training modules and placards/posters.

Key issues

Organisational culture assessment: In the last two years, few of the surveyed organisations have conducted an organisational culture survey. In a majority of the cases this survey is either designed by an external consultant, or provided by the parent organisation as part of their worldwide survey, or developed and managed by the HR department of the organisation.

Building a learning and risk-taking culture: Leading organisations have adopted steps to foster a learning and risk-taking culture, which will help tap the knowledge and potential of all employees and improve quality. Practices followed by such organisations to build a learning culture include the following: (i) Benchmarking leading practice: Organising periodic workshops to identify leading practices within their organisations, (ii) Cross-functional exposure: Employees are rotated across various functions to acquire multiple skills and constantly upgrade knowledge, (iii) Small-group activities: Cross-functional teams that work on improvement projects within the business, (iv) Building learning goals. A risk-taking culture is fostered by organisations using the following: (1) Stretch targets: In one of the surveyed organisations, management is asked to define objectives that are not easily achievable, to encourage risk-taking, (2) Supportive culture: Management should perpetuate a secure and supportive climate in which employees are not penalised for making mistakes, (3) Rewards: Employees should be rewarded for unique contributions that have a significant impact on quality, cost, lead-time, profits, and products.

Leading practice: Need to strengthen corporate culture and communication systems as one of the primary focus areas. A periodic employee satisfaction survey is conducted to assess employees' perceptions on various parameters under various functional areas. Managers attend several leadership and other behavioural courses to strengthen their perception of corporate culture and its effective implementation. A well-designed suggestion scheme is instituted to encourage employees to suggest innovative work practices.

Job evaluation

Job reviews: Some organisations indicated that they actively conduct systematic job reviews. The frequency of job reviews varies: Some organisations conduct a structured annual review to assess new jobs and validate existing ones. Other organisations conduct a bi-annual or a semi-annual review. Some had indicated that they perform the review less than once in every two years. Others have never performed any job review.

Leading practice: Leading organisations use the job evaluation system to record the nature and content of all jobs, outline the jobholders' accounts, and summarise the qualifications required for competent performance of the position. The organisation uses job descriptions for grading, salary, benefits, appraisal, and career progression.

Compensation strategy: Few of the surveyed organisations have indicated that they have a well-defined compensation strategy in place. Compensation is largely grade driven. Some of the surveyed organisations strategise to position their compensation package among the top three in their respective industry. The primary factors that influence the remuneration strategy are market levels, performance of employees, performance of the company, team performance, and profitability of the business. Most of the organisations have indicated that they are moving towards a greater proportion of variable compensation as compared to fixed components in the total compensation package offered to their employees.

Performance-based pay systems: Some organisations have a profit-sharing scheme whereby employees at the managerial level receive bonuses based on corporate profit performance. The systems for performance pay practised are: (i) Lump-sum bonus, (ii) Functional incentive scheme, (iii) Special incentives: Some organisations have indicated that they actively pursue various special incentive schemes as part of their performance based pay system.

Leading practice: Some of the organisations have introduced team performance based bonus payment systems.

Training and development

Identification of training needs: Few of the surveyed organisations indicated the presence of a well defined system to identify training needs for each employee: (a) On-the-job training: This is one of the most common forms of training used by many organisations, (b) Internal training: Most organisations actively pursue internal training workshops as an integral part of their training process, (c) External training: Some organisations have indicated that they use external training consultants for the creation of customised programs that are ongoing and to fulfil the training needs of large numbers of employees. Other organisations have alliances with local colleges that offer short-term training courses, (d) Job rotation: Job rotation is identified as an important training area in developing multiple skills among employees. Banks actively practice this to create generalists who understand the complete organisational picture and their specific role in it, (e) Job enlargement: Few organisations enhance employee skills and knowledge by exposing them to larger responsibility and control by increasing their job content, (f) Induction training: Some organisations actively conduct induction training programs for new recruits at the entry level to acclimatise them in the organisation.

Training budget: Most of the surveyed organisations have indicated a general increasing trend in the training budgets implemented in their organisations. Focus on developing employees with appropriate technical skills has been cited as the primary reason for an increasing budget trend. Total training costs incurred by companies as a percentage of their respective operating costs range from 0.01% to 28%. The average expenditure incurred for training and other related activities is approximately 3% of total operating costs.

Training assessment: Most of the organisations have stated that an assessment of value addition (through the respective training imparted) to the employee and consequently to the job is a major concern in their organisation.

Leading practice: Leading organisations ensure that their in-house training is designed by design and content experts who are operations and line employees, to ensure that training is focused and relevant. Many organisations use external training consultants to design and deliver customised training or conduct open seminars. Organisations value the interaction and networking that open seminars offer to employees.

Executive development programs: Some organisations have developed management programs for its employees at middle and senior management levels to equip them to effectively assume new and different responsibilities as their roles evolve. Leading organisations train employees on various cultural traits that are valued by the organisation the most, e.g.: openness, interpersonal skills, ethics/integrity, team spirit, involvement, and judgment. Competency development based training programs are becoming more and more popular and necessary amongst leading organisations.

Performance management

Few organisations have a well-defined performance evaluation system. The trends and practices in performance management are covered under the following sections:

Assessment process: Most organisations lack a well defined competency profile for various levels of employees. Few organisations indicated that the key competencies on which their employees are assessed are defined by top management and are based on vision and corporate goals. Few of the surveyed organisations have a formal goal-setting system in which the top management team outlines the corporate goals, which are then translated into divisional/functional/team goals and integrated further with individual employee objectives. Other organisations lack clearly designed processes for aligning individual performance with the stated corporate objectives.

Method of appraisal: (i) Self-appraisal: 5% of the organisations stated that they practice employee self-appraisal, (ii) Joint appraisal: 25% of all organisations stated that they have a system of joint-appraisal implemented as an integral part of the employee appraisal process, (iii) Superior's/managers' review: 90% of the organisations have a second-level review by the superior's supervisor, who validates the ratings given by the employee's superior, (iv) 360-degree appraisal process: Non of the organisations use a 360-degree appraisal technique in which the assessment is done not only by employees' superiors but also by their subordinates, peers, and internal customers, (v) Frequency of appraisal: An appraisal process is conducted annually by most of the organisations. Some of the organisations have interim semi-annual and quarterly reviews.

Performance rewards and promotion: Performance bonus: 50% of the surveyed organisations offer a performance bonus to their employees. Types of performance bonus: (1) Linked to base salary: 50% of the organisations offer increments as a percentage of base salary. The percentage is based on organisation performance and cost-of-living index. This percentage remains constant for all levels, (2) Budgetary allocation: Some of the organisations practice the system of budgetary allocation, (3) Lump-sum payment: Other organisations offer a lump-sum reward for different performance ratings at different grades. 25% of the organisations surveyed have direct linkages between performance appraisal and performance rewards.

Succession planning

5% of the organisations have a well-defined strategy for succession planning for key management positions.

Leading practice: Leading organisations link succession planning to its management development program.

Source: *FUE (2005a).*

A problem of using the report is that the writing and data presentation style does *at times* not really give insights into the *relative* significance of certain practices and trends: Sometimes the report provides percentages numbers, but too often it uses words such as 'few firms', 'some', 'many', or 'leading organisations' without further definition of the percentage equivalent of these categories or reference to respective graphs and tables (all in all, the report has only one graph: the number of participating organisations and firms). Importantly, the reader's own assessments and interpretations of the findings can be very different if 'few' stands for 5%, 10% or 25%; this ambiguous reading of the survey results limits the confident use of these important findings of this report, e.g. for policy-oriented research and analysis and public debate. This comment applies even more in a context where detailed statistics are powerful tools for understanding and shaping realities (and thus calling for action) depending if a data situation is perceived to reflect a rather *worrying* or a *normal* state of affairs. This said, how should one interpret, for example, the following interconnected statements which were written on one page in the report on the issue of compensation strategy?

> "*Few* of the surveyed organisations have indicated that they have a well-defined compensation strategy in place ... *Some* of the surveyed organisations strategise to position their compensation package among the top three in their respective industry ... *Most* of the organisations have indicated that they are moving towards a greater proportion of variable compensation as compared to fixed components in the total compensation package offered to their employees ... *Some* organisations have a profit-sharing scheme whereby employees at the managerial level receive bonuses based on corporate profit performance ... Leading practice[:] *Some* of the organisations have introduced team performance based bonus payment system" (ibid, 21, italics added). Or, what would this mean in a research and policy context: "*Few* of the surveyed organisations indicated the presence of a well defined system to identify training needs for each employee" (ibid, 22, emphasis added).

In short, it would be helpful if Ernst&Young (in cooperation with FUE) provided an improved version of its data set and assessments on HRM practices that is more applicable to research and analysis, including public administration and policy making (e.g. include appendices with detailed results and tables). On the other hand, future FUE reports on the EYA should improve the application of quantitative and qualitative methods. An earlier EYA survey in the year 2002, undertaken by another consultancy firm, offers statistics in a more user-friendly form (FUE 2003, see below).[357]

However, from the information available we can state that the spread of certain HRM practices among firms varies. For example, (1) only 5% of the organisations surveyed have a well-defined strategy for succession planning for key management, and (2) 10% of the surveyed organisations have outlined a broad HR strategy. Further, 10% have taken active measures to institutionalise vision and values, with 5% having translated their values into leadership competencies which are assessed during the objective-setting process. On the other hand, (3) 30% of the responding firms have indicated they have a well-documented HR policies and a procedures' manual, and (4) in about 50% of the organisations HR managers are responsible for learning and organisational development. Elsewhere the report states that (5) *few* organisations conducted an organisational culture survey in the two years prior to the survey, or (6) *leading* organisations have adopted steps to foster a learning and risk-taking culture, and (7) *some* of the organisations have introduced the concept of team performance-based bonus payment system. Further, *most* of the organisations have indicated a general increasing trend in the training budgets implemented in their organisations primarily due to technical skills training (FUE 2005a, 13-7, 27).

The exercise above demonstrates that the survey gives highly relevant insights into a range of salient HRD topics. A follow-up of these results by other stakeholders in the HRD system, including relevant sections of GOU, is recommended. For this stage of the HRD debate, and given the mentioned problem of data analysis and presentation, we prefer to present the key results and leave it to the reader to make his/her own assessment of the different issues raised. Certainly, the publications related to the EYA survey can be seen as vital inputs for a HRD debate and related interventions in the country, at least as far as the formal sector is concerned.

One of the many notable report findings is that the descriptions of advanced HR practices of the award-winning firms - as presented in 'major reasons for winning the award' (ibid, 28-40) - reveal that best practices firms undertake efforts to accommodate the private interests

357 Of course this book also uses words like 'many' and 'some', but we did not really carry out primary research on HRD per se.

of their staff - such as reconciling home, community and work life, including concerns for education and health issues and value systems - and thus motivate staff and gain commitment.[358] Accordingly, the winning company of the 'indigenous award', for instance, (a) provides full treatment for staff and their families for those with HIV/AIDS, (b) gives condoms to all staff and provides anti-malaria plants, (c) has introduced a school fees scheme ranging from 200,000-400,000Ush per employee per term, and (d) emphasises the emotional (invisible, soft) aspect of relating with their staff (ibid, 34). Some other award-winning firms have arrangements on education and health issues for family members of staff, or participate in community activities (corporate social responsibility).[359]

Note, another FUE survey (100 organisations, 9 sub-sectors) on employment issues states that 63% of the organisations had a HRD policy which typically covered staff training, code of conduct, standing orders and terms and conditions of employment. Other findings of this survey include: of the organisations surveyed 44% had a career succession policy, 69% a policy on occupational safety, health and environment, and 46% a policy on HIV/AIDS (2005b, 18-20). Consider, however, the observation of another FUE EYA report about the low implementation level of HRM systems and tools in many organisations in Uganda (2003, 22).

Despite the weaknesses in data presentation of FUE (2005a), it is safe to make the following points with respect to the overall results of the reviewed EYA survey 2004: There are indications of advancement in the HRM area in the section of the economy that *participates* in the EYA competition. An Ernst&Young member of the survey team for the EYA 2005, who was interviewed by the author, stated that HRM awareness and practices in the organisations visited have *improved*, pointing to an increasing recognition of the importance of a people-centred business and organisational approach. There are examples of many positive initiatives (including FAL for illiterate or semi-skilled staff) that reflect this seemingly positive trend in awareness. Nevertheless, there are severe gaps in many HRM categories where only small sections of the sample surveyed for the EYA undertake particular HRM measures; for instance, only 10% of organisations outlined broad HRD strategies, and most organisations lack a well-defined competency profile for various levels of employees. These deficits hinder the building of a strong HR at company and industry level.

One interesting question regarding the state of HRM in the economy is, of course: How would an extended firm sample impact on the results, for instance, within an academic research rather than award-related consultancy study? There are reasons to expect HRM practices to worsen in a broader sample, yet to what extent? It would also be useful to compare the EYA survey data - if made available and usable - over the years to track the pace and significance of change, or the spread of best practices. Generally,

Findings of the Employer of the Year Award Survey Report 2002

Differences in HRM between local and multinational organisations

In this section we take look at the *EYA Survey Report of the year 2002* (FUE 2003) which had 102 participating organisations and firms (hereafter: organisations) and was produced by a

358 See also discussion of Jackson (2003) earlier in the book.
359 We will not review CSR-related activities of firms in HRD areas (e.g. education, sponsorships, and sports).

local HR consultancy firm (Partner in Learning and Action/PILA Consultants). Interestingly, the report makes some observations on the influence of *origin of the organisation* surveyed (multinational vs. indigenous) on the results. While there was no particular impact of origin on issues such as communication climate, medium of communication, or implementation of training policy, there were differences in two areas: employee guidelines and performance management (ibid, 15-9). Regarding the former:

> "Multinationals more than indigenous organisations had established employee guidelines. They also used them more systematically than indigenous ones ... Interpreted, this finding means that multinationals are more likely to have, to use, to update and to distribute among employees terms and conditions of service, orientation procedures health, and safety guidelines and documented discipline procedures" (ibid, 15).

Accordingly, local organisations in most cases lack the capacity to draft such guidelines internally; they seem to need external professional support (from consultants etc.) to tackle the issue of drafting and implementing employee guidelines and so on (ibid).

Performance management

The report findings underline the importance of the earlier discussion on inability of many local firms and organisations to meaningfully and successfully undertake performance management and incentive setting. We elaborated why this can be an important explanation for the productivity problem in Uganda. Table 43 shows the relative gaps between local and multinational players.

Table 43: Performance management and organisation's origin

Performance Management	Organisational Origin	
	Multinational	Indigenous
1. Competence-based management	More likely	Less likely
2. Performance appraisal system	More likely	Less likely
3. Operating plans	More likely	Less likely
4. Status-based pay	Less likely	More likely

Source: *FUE (2003, 16).*

The table reveals a trend in the sample: organisations with indigenous origin are *less likely* to apply competence-based management methods and performance appraisal systems or operate with organisational, departmental, and individual plans. They are *more likely* to use a status-based pay approach and position-based management approach that is less geared towards allowing dynamic incentives to work for increased performance (ibid, 16-8).

> "Among the several indicators of performance management that we surveyed during the employer of the year study was competence-based management by which we were looking for organisations that are shifting from position-based to competence-based personnel administration ... Our findings from the survey indicate that multinationals rather than indigenous organisations are more likely to be operating competence-based management while indigenous organisation are more likely to be continuing to use position-based management ... A systematic use of appraisals is more likely to be found among multinational organisations than in indigenous organisations ... The other means of performance we looked at were the operating plans. We asked respondents to indicate whether or not annual organizational plans, departmental plans and individual

plans exist. Our findings indicate that such plans are more likely to be found in multinational rather than in indigenous organisations … This is in keeping with the aggressiveness of these organisations which allows them to succeed in foreign lands. Survival in the intense competition in which these organisations operate means that they manage performance as a way of life … In direct opposition to this way of managing performance, indigenous organisations are more likely to use status-based pay, undermining the self-motivation and the individual urge to exceed targets that are associated with the kind of positive and meaningful rewards you find in [some of the award] winning organisations" (ibid).

This is a remarkable finding, which has apparently not been applied further in a significant manner, e.g. by GOU, researchers or donors. Also, the WB study team which pointed to productivity problems and low use of bonus systems in the manufacturing sector (WB 2004) did not go deeper into the theme or comment on firm-level realities that impacted on the productivity findings. The FUE report, however, further elaborates on the problematic level of *actual utilisation of HRM tools* in Uganda:

"It is generally understood that employers in the Third World are unwilling or unable to put effort into managing the performance of workers. This may be so because performance management is a process rather than a product although it uses known products such as appraisal format, various types of operating plans including annual business plans, strategic plans, departmental plans and individual operating plans. Once the products are available their actual utilization is the management of performance [or, the effort an employer puts in making employees productive]. This is what managers in the Third World apparently find so hard to do. Our experience in Uganda for instance, shows that few indigenous organisations consistently use systematic and competence based appraisals. Quite often employees are promoted or dismissed at the whim of their superiors and not on the basis of competence based appraisal results" (FUE 2003, 16).

It is difficult to compare the reports for EYA 2002 and EYA 2004 on some salient points since the two different consultancy companies responsible for the writing applied a different style in terms of data presentation and analysis. However, we can cite the EYA 2004 survey (2005a) statements on performance management: Accordingly, few of the surveyed organisations have well-defined compensation strategies in place, while about half of the sample offered a performance bonus to their employees[360], and every fourth organization had direct linkages between performance appraisal and performance rewards in place. Most players indicate plans to move towards a greater proportion of variable compensation in the total compensation package offered to employees (ibid).

In this context, the write up of the OD (organisation development) specialist provides useful insights on matters of performance management in organisations in Uganda (Box 55, Appendix 31). Discussed are various factors that impact on performance management at individual, team and organisational levels. The account highlights characteristics such as deficient competencies in people management and performance management, low appreciation of HRM aspects, and shortcomings in systematic and continued application of appropriate HRM tools and practices. The systematic use of HRM tools was seldom pursued further by organisations, even when tools were introduced in (or even developed for) the respective organisation by the OD specialist.

There are related weaknesses in many organisations regarding organisational cultures, recruitment practices, induction systems, and appraisal systems. In most cases, tools and

360 No further differentiation is given, e.g. by staff group, functional level, or indigenous vs. multinational origin of the organisation.

good practices were not used at all, or not used in a continual, systematic and effective way. For instance, it is not common practice to articulate performance targets and performance standards in job descriptions and contracts. Such information is usually found in competence profiles of jobs in an organisation but very few organisations in Uganda have competence profiles for jobs in their organisations. It is further very difficult to institutionalise the practice of systematic staff appraisal in organisations. Actual performance-oriented staff development, capacity building and in-house training are often neglected (while focus is on obtaining paper qualifications); so are performance-oriented remuneration. It is also observed that HRM deficits in organisations (including salary structure) are among the factors that lead sections of staff to work harder and perform better in their second (side) jobs. Hence there is a low work centrality in the first job. Other factors that negatively affect performance orientation in organisations are problems regarding performance-oriented leadership, communication and behaviour (e.g. in teams) (ibid).

No doubt, such shortcomings significantly undermine performance-oriented work in organisations, particularly in the public sector, where, in relation to a number of HRM aspects, the deficiencies seem to be more severe than in (sections of) the private sector. As we have argued earlier, the continued HRM weaknesses in the public sector (e.g. regarding aspects of performance management) are highly problematic because of the state's prime role as a provider of formal employment, especially for better-educated Ugandans. The state's HRM systems and practices have a significant impact (indicator, perception shaping) on the nature of HRM dynamics in the country as the whole.

Further report findings and recommendations

Another notable finding regarding the FUE 2003 report is that organisational differences such as size (small, medium, large) or sector origin (NGO, private sector, public sector) had no potential or actual impact on questionnaire outcomes in survey topics such as (1) employee guidelines, (2) performance management, and (3) quality of work life. Yet, *organisational size mattered* in aspects of (4) *general working environment* and *quality of work life*: this included the empowering and competence-building climate, such as employee benefits, communication, training systems, and the occupational health and safety climate (16-19, Table 44). Small organisations, for instance, paid overall less attention to health and safety matters than their medium and large counterparts. Medium size enterprises were less successful in communication measures and training systems, with large firms scoring best in these categories. "What this might mean is that large sized organisations had the resources to introduce opportunities for learning and communication and small organisations were able to create systems to reach most or all their employees because of small numbers" (ibid, 19).

Table 44: Quality of working environment/work life and organisation's size

General Working Environment & Quality of Work Life	Organisational Size		
	Small	Medium	Large
1. Employee benefits	No difference	No difference	Superior
2. Medium of communication	Better	*Least*	Superior
3. Communication climate	No difference	No difference	No difference
4. Training systems	Better	*Least*	Superior
5. Occupational health and safety climate	*Least*	Better	Superior

Source: *FUE (2003, 19, emphasis added).*

Given the importance for our book of the findings and implications offered by this FUE report we shall quote parts of its summary and conclusion on performance and competence in Uganda at some length. The quote points to (i) the deficits regarding usable and realistic instruments for performance management, (ii) the capability deficiencies in effectively applying HRM tools at competitive levels, and (c) the low actual use of HRM systems and tools in many Ugandan organisations:

> "[T]he questionnaire used to assess the employer of the year was deliberately skewed towards process rather than structure. It is our experience that many organisations in Uganda have formalized HR and other subsystems that they never use. This includes strategic plans, business plans, and job descriptions. Reasons for the rampant failure to utilize these structures and therefore to manage competences and performance, often come from these products being unusable [and unrealistic: bearing little resemblance with the reality on the ground, ibid 31] because they are hurriedly and poorly constructed without a solid understanding of the underlying theory why they should be designed in one way and not in another. … The results indicated that the origin of the firm or organisation ensured that the participating organisation was more likely to practice competence management. The direction was in favour of multinationals. Our observation here was that multinational organisations put effort into creating the instruments for competence management and provide the required resources in terms of time and expertise to implement these instruments. We noted our experience as consultants in this area that many indigenous firms do not make time for systematic appraisals for instance. They consider time spent in appraisal for instance as time spent away from 'real work'. The real problem however is that many organisations have appraisal forms that are not usable because they rarely reflect what the individual 'appraisee' really does" (ibid, 22).

Related recommendations of the report are presented in Box 37. The issues presented throughout the EYA 2002 report signal the potential for improvement in Ugandan organisations, both in the private and public sector. Closing the gaps in HRM practices among firms operating in Uganda would mean allowing firms with lower HRM capabilities (and less economic resources) to catch up in terms of best HRM practice in the country. This is likely to enable local firms to catch up in terms of productivity and competitiveness.

Box 37: The Employer of the Year Award 2002: Selected recommendations

"Public sector organisations need to recognise that modern HR management has reversed the relationship between HR and administration. That is, increasingly administration as a function is distributed among line managers and disappearing as a separate function. In the mean time, professional HR is gaining a place at the top decision making table in its own right. As a way forward we recommend that FUE ... mount[s] a campaign in public organisations. One of the objectives would be to sensitise Public Sector Managers and Administration on the importance of emancipating the HR function so that HR officials and managers begin to permanently sit in the top decision making committees along with chief planners, finance managers, university secretaries and so on ... [W]e further observed that managers in the Third World are unwilling to put efforts in managing performance. We indicated that this may be so because they have no readily usable and realistic instruments ... The other reason we raised is that performance management is a process that takes place on daily basis just like decision making and it is appropriately a management function. What we find however, is the lack of effort norms translating into the inner need to put more and more effort into one's work. It is probably the lack of effort norm compounded by irrelevant and often invalid performance management instruments that is hindering the development of performance management tradition in our organisations. Our recommendation is for private sector firms and public sector organisations to put effort into generating realistic appraisal instruments using competent consultants and providing time to conduct the appraisal interview. We recommend a move away from one generic interview format for all employees to a behaviourally competence based one that is specific to each job family. We recommend a shift from the practice of using supposed core competences such as innovativeness, leadership, cooperation and so on to utilising key result areas that are systematically derived from job or competence analysis of each job family. We found successful efforts among participating organisations indicating that what we are recommending is already happening although in too few organisations".

Source: *FUE (2003, 31).*

We have argued that the positive impact of technical skills development in training institutions, for instance, remains limited as long as the world-of-work is insufficiently oriented towards incentives and performance management, interpersonal cooperation, and competence-based recruitment. In other words, weak HRM structures and practices are limiting the economic development impact of existing HR improvements (e.g. in education). HRM weaknesses also contribute to a stagnation or decline of HR levels, e.g. when graduates cannot practice and improve their skills properly. The impression is that only a few actors in the development community undertake efforts to tackle this systemic problem of deficient HRM practices in sectors and firms, or appreciate it in the first place.

It is not straightforward to expect positive changes to happen at an adequate level (beyond the 'pockets of good practices') in the near future, given the official framework for PSD in Uganda in the recent past - characterised by a focus on the macro-economy, investment climate, and cost of production - the underplaying of HRM aspects in both the public debate and in the world-of-work, the deficient practices in many public institutions, and the general difficulties faced in enhancing HRM in Ugandan organisations.

Adjustment of the official PSD focus is needed to improve efforts towards the enhanced ability of Ugandan firms to operate in a more performance-oriented manner, which includes improved 'people management'. Better-functioning local firms are needed to handle change and competition in today's globalised world and to take better advantage of the benefits of the country's latecomer status, for instance in terms of tapping into the global pool of knowledge or technology (applying ICT) and accelerating local learning and upgrading processes. Without proper recruitment and retention practices (e.g. with regards to educated, skilled and talented young specialists) or knowledge management systems in place in the world-of-work, the productive outcomes of the improved knowledge and skills available in the country will be lower. In fact, improved HRM in firms and institutions will be needed to ultimately utilise (to a greater extent) the HR that have been and are being built in the ETS with substantial efforts and investment from the various sides. The central issue here is the level of actual impact of the generally increased HR level in the country. If, in the global context, Ugandan firms *learn* and *improve* relatively slower than their (regional and international) competitors abroad, they lose ground and cannot catch up.

Against the above, related future support measures could consider the shortcomings and dynamics (including existing advancements and efforts) discussed in this chapter and in relevant parts of Chapter 2 (productivity and performance management). This book argues that better HRM can lead to enhanced productivity and more meaningful PSD in Uganda, and can thus improve the job, earnings and on-the-job capacity development prospects of graduates of the ETS. Again, it is hard to think of practical reasons why this issue does not feature prominently in the development agenda of the country, which is shaped by (powerful) donors too, of course. The existing PSD agenda has expressed concern about productivity, firm competitiveness, entrepreneurship, exports, firm growth, job creation, and poverty reduction. The impression is that the link between these agenda items and HRM (working conditions, workers' treatment, or performance management) is underplayed or sidelined in the dominant discourse.

Note that it is plausible to assume a certain link between local HRM deficits and brain drain dynamics; a theme that needs to be explored in the current context of economic development in Uganda. See Ijsselmuiden (2006) (Appendix 32) for an illustration of this point for the health (research) system.

Good HRD practices need to spread across the economy

Against the above background, the stimulation of HRM-related demonstration and spillover effects should be a major issue for the Ugandan economy: How can good and best HRM practices (and related knowledge and expertise) spread effectively across the economy? How can the know-how accumulated by the firms that won FYA awards (e.g. the winner in the productivity and performance management category), or have otherwise performed well, be strategically utilised to a higher degree in the economy, e.g. help other firms to apply the champions' practices? The bottom line is that improved HRM practices are needed within the modern formal sector and in the thousands of SMEs operating in the informal sector; the issue is how to get there (mixture of measures). Related challenges are manifold. They include the downscaling of respective HRM consultancy services (e.g. on organisational techniques) to the needs of SMEs. Further, there are 'expert rounds' operating in FUE and other BMOs/SIs[361]; most likely, these circles include the crème of enterprises in Uganda. Capturing spillovers is crucial in this context: it is the knowledge, inspiration and best practice models of these

361 Note, for instance, the Human Resource Managers Association of Uganda (http://www.hrmau.org/), or the British Council Management Forum (www.managementexpress.org).

firms and organisations that needs to spread more systematically and quickly, for example, through inter-firm learning networks, cooperation between firms and SIs, and workshops. This will not happen automatically, but will require particular efforts, from GOU and SIs such as EUg, UCPC, and UWEAL. In this respect, stronger in-house HRM capabilities can help firms to benefit from exposure to best HRM practices (absorption capacity).[362]

Significantly, HRM is quite a recent theme in Uganda. It is embedded in the context of a latecomer catch-up economy with all its market and institutional failures and other particulars, as discussed earlier. This makes improvements on this important frontier regarding competitiveness, productivity and development such a challenge, yet, at the same time, a rewarding opportunity. Correspondingly, the need of firms and organisations to start and/or continue improving their HRM practices is significant. Continued local learning efforts in HRM are paramount for the award-winning firms (which might now have to manage newly-upcoming HRM areas such as change management) and other fields.

Clearly, more in-depth analytical research is needed on some HRM aspects mentioned in the FUE report and in this book. For instance, future research could investigate the cultural, social, economic and political underpinnings of the (varying) HRM practices in the different firms in the country. This research can also include related business practices in inter-firm networks, e.g. aspects of training, informal learning and mutual treatment in buyer-farmer relationships (Wiegratz et al. 2007b). Questions could include: how did the process of fostering a culture of learning evolve over time in specific firms (experience, success and critical factors)? Are gender-linked phenomena significant in HRM in Uganda, e.g. in behavioural terms? Have some firms taken the route of decasualising their (production) workers? What is their experience: has decasualisation enhanced team work, productivity, and the on-the-job learning of workers? How are industrial firms' practices in terms of treatment of their out-growers related to the firms' links with the political system? To answer *some* of these vital questions, players other than those of the up-market consultancy category need to make their analytical contribution to allow broader capture and analysis of relevant dynamics.

Related research findings and reflections can help economic actors who face similar challenges. It can also help public administration and public SIs to appreciate more (1) the actual HRM efforts in the private sector, and (2) the state's actual and potential role in this process. It can also raise awareness among relevant actors about the state of HRM in the country and the development consequences. In the next chapter, the views of some donors regarding HRD in Uganda are presented.

362 Note in this context that, to date, one problem with some (economic development related) associations of professionals in Uganda is that the (leading) members are working mainly for elite constituencies in Kampala (and/or tend to pay more attention and focus on headquarters issues) and might thus not be aware of or sufficiently interested in improving the existing HRM situation in the wider economy, e.g. in upcountry firms, (informal) SMEs, or large (foreign-owned) factories. For instance, addressing gross injustices in the economy (e.g. treating staff badly in relation to payment and working conditions in companies and organisations, or day-to-day economic malpractices) is often not very highly placed on the agendas of associations.

13

Donor Activities in HRD, Especially for PSD

Introduction and background

Similar to the case of the private sector, the research attempted to gain the views of development partners (hereafter: donors[363]) on HRD in Uganda. For reasons explained above, the e-mail approach was the main contact method; phone call follow-up was made only in very few cases. The two relevant donor issue groups approached - through introductory e-mail from PEVOT and several follow-up e-mails from the author - were the Education Funding Agencies Group (EFAG) and the Private Sector Donor Group (PSDG). Thus, around 60 experts were contacted. For the case of EFAG, the author gave a presentation of the study rationale and the relevant study questions in the EFAG February 2006 meeting. Donors were requested to give inputs on the following three issues:

- Perception of HRD issues in the Ugandan economy, in particular those of relevance for PPET,
- Current focal points of PPE and training support, and experiences (e.g. proportional focus on general secondary and tertiary education vs. vocational training and HRD in the private sector), and
- Expectations regarding future HRD trends in Uganda and plans to respond to trends.

The overall inputs from both donor issue groups was low (five respondents), although, for instance, the author's presentation in the EFAG meeting raised interest regarding the study. This low turnout is not unusual, and could be explained by high workload and low incentive or commitment to contribute to the research.

Review of donor views on HRD matters

The answers from the responding development agencies are presented in Box 38. They reveal concern for the strategic role of HRD in the context of the country's transformation process. Reference is made to HR as a key factor for advancements in nation building, societal development as well as competitiveness and economic development. Respondents also highlighted that despite achievements in the recent past in HRD (e.g. access to education), the existing gaps remain severe and the challenges ahead thus diverse and significant. More effective measures for improved HRD are called for in the ETS and the health sector as well as at the level of firms, farms and sectors. Access, content, relevance and quality of formal and non-formal education are among the major problems identified. Highlighted are also the retention challenge and the mounting deficiencies in providing adequate E&T in conflict and post-conflict areas, including non-formal education to help school leavers,

363 This includes (international) development agencies that implement programmes financed by their member states.

out-of-school children and the youth. The issue of *adequate* E&T options for the respective local socio-economic context is important here. Overall, there is concern about issues of (1) implementation and lessons learnt so far, as well as (2) priorities, sequencing and suitable intervention approaches[364] for the coming years of HRD in the country.

PPET/VET, including on-the-job training and workforce development, is recognised for its increasing relevance in enabling the country and its firms to advance on the competitiveness and national development fronts. The question is whether existing capacity of the private sector, to offer and undertake training is sufficient, e.g. in terms of in-house and sectoral training, or skills formation within value chain arrangements. In fact, there are numerous HRD stakeholder-groups and HRD-related systems that require upgrading of skills and capabilities: besides pupils and students, teachers, health workers and firms (workers, managers) need skills too. Furthermore, pressures are acknowledged regarding different views of GOU and ETS donors on spending priorities and intervention approaches.

Importantly, HRD has different time dimensions: short-term as well as mid to long-term gaps and tasks need to be tackled. Deficiencies at a given time (e.g. in improving various aspects that together can push HRD) put at risk the achievement of development goals that require *interconnected, simultaneous* changes. As one respondent stated with regard to the activities and improvements under way; "there is both quite a lot and not enough". Finally, regarding the aspect of firm-level learning in applying foreign technology efficiently, the view of the Japan International Cooperation Agency (JICA) is instructive: "Uganda ... faces the new challenge of new technology coming into the country. Although new technology undoubtedly increases productivity, training is necessary to enable workers to acquire skills and knowledge to deal with it".

Box 38: Responses from donors and development agencies on HRD matters in Uganda

DFID (Department for International Development): "DFID does not have an educational sector programme in Uganda. DFID contributes funding to the sector via our support to the budget as a whole, but we have signed a 'partnership agreement' with the Netherlands whereby they represent us in all 'donor-only' and 'donor-GOU' discussions in this sector. In return DFID represents Dutch interests in the health sector. It is designed to promote donor coordination. This means that we are somewhat removed as a donor from the ongoing debates around PPET that are taking place and do not have specific projects in the education sector. We do however, training and capacity building in various forms: The DFID funded Business Services Market Development (BSMD) project undertook work on supply chain development. This project is now at an end, but the key objective was to take a market development perspective rather than seek to provide support to a number of training institutes through projects often characterized by low outreach, low sustainability and a supply driven approach. In essence, we tried here to follow a perspective of 'making service markets work for the poor'; what GTZ/PEVOT and some other agencies are doing in the training area supports such efforts. Our BSMD research emphasized that policy makers and donors should be thinking more about why it is that markets aren't operating effectively when it comes to training, why is it that the demands of the labour market aren't being met by the educational sector".

JICA: "*Perception of HRD issues relevant to PPE in Uganda:* HRD is the key to nation building. This philosophy could also be said to be rooted in Japan's own development experience, and through providing international cooperation in East Asia. Not only for individual capacity development but also for sustainable socio-economic development of Uganda, quality education is a cornerstone.

364 Approaches that have a chance to bring about the envisaged (sustainable) improvements in the relevant HR areas.

Although there remains the quality issue in the PE sub-sector, nearly all the children have access to primary education. This requires more attention to the PPET in order to absorb the increasing number of graduates of primary schools and to further accelerating educational development in the country. Developing outstanding human resources/people that/who will be leaders in nation building is an important factor to ensure the success of medium- to long-term development efforts by Uganda itself, and the importance of PPET in this context is ever increasing. JICA has been supporting the GOU initiatives to improve the quality of PPET, in the field of secondary and vocational training.

Current focal points of PPET support, and the experiences made: JICA has recently started to provide technical assistance for the Secondary Science and Mathematics Teacher's (SESEMAT) Project. The project provides secondary level mathematics and science teachers with in-service training aimed at enhancing teachers' capacity as well as attitudinal change toward their profession. In addition, through sensitizing key stakeholders such as head teachers, local education administrators and parents, the project creates an enabling environment where teachers easily obtain the necessary support. Since teacher development requires long-term and continuous commitments, in-service training will be institutionalized in conjunction with various stakeholders. One of the unique approaches taken by the project is to focus on classroom activities, where primarily learning takes place. The project promotes an activity-based and student-centered approach, which enhance understanding of concepts and principles of the subjects. Teachers are encouraged to perform experiments by improvising, using locally available materials.

In the field of VET, in order respond to the needs of the labour market and trainees, providing relevant training is a critical issue. As Japan is known for its advanced technology and manufacturing in the world, JICA has been supporting the Nakawa Vocational Training Institute since the 1970s through the technical assistance in the skills and knowledge of technology and management as well as installing necessary facilities and equipment. The Institute has successfully been playing the major role in development of the skilled labour force. Aiming to be the center of excellence in the East African region, the Institute started the new training program in 2003 whose participants are invited from Kenya, Tanzania, Eritrea, and Zambia as well as within Uganda. Through the program, the participants are expected to bring back their learning to their countries and to contribute to socio-economic advancement. In the near future, the Institute will fulfil a new function, to be a focal point of instructors' training in order to further enhance the quality of training at relevant institutions in the whole country.

Expectations regarding future HRD trends in Uganda and plans to respond to them: The macroeconomic performance in Uganda is dependent on substantial donor support. For the sustainable social and economic development, it is necessary for the GOU to strengthen country's competitiveness in the regional and global market through the HRD. Agriculture is still the most important sector, its share is decreasing and other economic activities such as manufacturing and construction are gaining more significance. Just like other countries, Uganda also faces the new challenge of new technology coming into the country. Although new technology undoubtedly increases productivity, training is necessary to enable workers to acquire skills and knowledge to deal with it. Without proper training, it will only threaten the low-skilled workers, causing unemployment among them. Nakawa Vocational Training Institute offers skills training at advanced levels under the technical assistance of JICA. In addition, the Institute provides upgrade training on the request from private sectors such as Nile Breweries, Uganda Breweries, and Coca-Cola Company.

In the education section, we recognize a certain tension between national priority to focus on PPE, responding to the president manifest of UPPET for socio-economic development and international trend to achieve MDGs, which is to achieve UPE in terms of both quantity and quality".

Netherlands: "Basically, HRD is extremely needed in Uganda. We have come to conclude in the education sector that UPE and great increases in enrolment have actually been to the detriment of quality. Often, literacy and numeracy at grade 7 are still limited and many students don't make it to secondary school. Even if they have received follow-up education, either general or vocational, the skills and knowledge are still at a disappointing level. The result is that Uganda doesn't have a truly qualified labour force. Much of the extra training and education will have to be done by the employers. GOU plans to introduce free USE: However, we fear that it will be underfunded and lead to more quality loss. The depletion of the limited number of well trained personnel and middle management by HIV/Aids and other diseases such as TB and malaria is a major loss and cost factor for companies in Uganda. The spread of the pandemic would justify a rate of training of 3 people for 1 function. Of course, this meets with objections of cost efficiency. Although Uganda has made great strides in combating for instance HIV/Aids, the prevalence seems to be on the rise gain. There are no measures to compensate companies. We believe that the low quality of HR in Uganda is an impediment to economic growth. In the horticultural sector, the Netherlands will be involved in establishing a separate training and education facility".

SCOPE Programme (Strengthening the Competitiveness of Private Enterprises, USAID funded): "From the perspective of competitiveness, Uganda needs to shift its HRD focus to workforce development. Questions with regard to proportional focus on secondary/tertiary education versus vocational training can probably best be answered first on a sector basis and then aggregated into an overall plan. And, it is most likely to require strategies that link an immediate vocational training 'fix' with a series of short to longer term adjustments in secondary and tertiary education systems. ICT is a good example of a sector where this kind of approach to workforce development can yield huge gains. Actually there is both quite a lot and not enough".

UNICEF (United Nations Children's Fund): "We emphasize concern about limited access to early-childhood education. While generally access to primary education has increased over the years, the poor quality of education continues to be a persisting problem leading to high wastage (high repetition and drop-out rates, very low achievement rates) in terms of financial and human resources. Additionally, many children of school-going age in specific parts of the country like the Karamoja sub-region and conflict-affected North, continue to be excluded from the formal education system. There is urgent need for the provision of basic education for the out-of-school children that takes into consideration their gender, age, socio-cultural and economic contexts through relevant, flexible and gender responsive non-formal education programmes. The importance of incorporating accelerated learning modalities into non-formal education with a view to mainstreaming school-age learners into the formal education system was stressed. Other options, especially for those learners who are far above the primary school age, must be established, e.g. livelihood and skills-building training opportunities and transition into secondary, post-primary education.

In the current GOU/UNICEF programme of cooperation (2006-10), programme focus is primarily on the conflict and post-conflict districts of Northern, Eastern and Western Uganda. While the education programme prioritizes early childhood and primary education (formal and non-formal), addressing the issues of access, completion and quality in a holistic way and taking into account the special needs (and this includes psycho-social needs) of children and teachers suffering from the effects of protracted conflict and displacement. Through other programme interventions including life skills, especially those relating to HIV/AIDS, for orphans and vulnerable children and protection, children, girls and boys, of secondary school age are reached. UNICEF acknowledges the existence of gaps, especially in programming for the education and training of children at the post-primary level, calling for better linkages with non-traditional partners. In this regard, the role of the private sector in HRD in these areas needs to be better understood. Overall, efforts to improve the ETS will need to improve on: relevance, resource utilization, coordination/collaboration and achievements. Given the severity of deficiencies in the UPE sector in some areas, the move into SSE has to be undertaken carefully: Overlooking or underplaying what already exists on the ground would not be advisable: 'Building on what exists' has to be considered as an important guiding principle".

Source: *Agencies' written responses to author's study questions (submitted in the first half of 2006).*[365]

365 See also Box 57 (Appendix 34) for HRD-related views and interventions of the GTZ programme PEVOT.

Inadequate attention to aspects of capability formation for PSD

Beyond what we have learnt from Box 38, the following is important to note: In the past few years, major donors have given high priority to the UPE programme which was introduced in 1997. This intervention per se is justified for several reasons, one being the low level of education among the population. Basic education (numeracy, literacy and functional skills) is a prerequisite for the participation of people in society and the economy. Household analysis suggests a positive relation between years of education attained and earnings; in farming, non-farm self-employment and wage-employment. PE seems to encourage households to enter non-farm income-generating activities (especially self-employment) and reallocate labour out of farming (Appleton 2001).[366] However, to have reasonable or even advanced performing and earning prospects, 'new entrants' (in non-farm activities) need skills and know-how that go beyond basic general education, especially against the background of a generally low (technical and managerial) skills base in the country. Further, if educational levels are actually achieved (see debate on education quality and high drop-out rates[367]), basic education *can* help farmers, workers, entrepreneurs and firms. For instances, firms can undertake *on-the-job training* (both inside and outside the firm) of the workforce faster, cheaper and more productively with already appropriately educated workers who have higher so-called absorptive capacities. If combined with training, basic education can help in (1) using technology and production inputs more efficiently, (2) enhancing economic transactions, cooperation and teamwork, and (3) fostering the entrepreneurship drive. Overall, productivity can be improved.

Finally, another argument being made is that public spending on UPE *benefits children of poor households* relatively more than spending on higher levels of education that would subsidise the relatively better-off households (Kappel et al. 2004).[368] "Yet, it remains unclear which level of education plays the most essential role for pro-poor growth. Is it primary education leading to an improvement in the basic knowledge level of the population at large? Or is it

366 The Appleton analysis of effects of education on household earnings is based on a 1992 Integrated Household Survey (prior to UPE).

367 Note that only about 23% of the first intake of the UPE programme graduated in 2003 (PEVOT 2006). In 2008, the public debate about the quality of education in UPE schools gained further momentum as PLE (Primary Leaving Examination) failure rates increased, and overall performance in some subjects dropped. On UPE-related challenges (e.g. quality deterioration) see, for instance, Bategeka et al. (2004). See Mamdani (2007) on problems related to the commercialised university education system in Uganda. On education in Uganda, see also Ssekamwa (1997), Kasozi (2003), or UNESCO (2007).

368 Matching enrolment numbers with data on public education spending in Uganda, Kappel et al. note: "Public spending on primary education has a pro-poor distribution in the sense that children from poorer households benefit more than children from richer households. For secondary and tertiary education, this does not hold. Benefits accrue clearly to children from richer households. Public spending on tertiary education is most pro-rich, as the richest 20 percent of the population receive about 60 percent of public subsidies. Looking at all educational levels, it turns out that public spending on education does not have a pro-poor distribution, an equal one at best. Yet, the bias towards higher consumption quintiles cannot be ignored. In order to secure that indirect pro-poor growth is taking place the conclusion suggests itself that this bias should be reduced in future. Taking into consideration that primary education alone does not seem sufficient to enable the poor to improve their (self) employment situation, this would be even more important" (2004, 78-9).

tertiary education forming a highly educated but small part of the population that can form a capable and innovative leadership group in economic and political terms" (ibid, 78-9)?

Indeed, a crucial issue in development efforts is how to balance spending so as to address different impact factors, e.g. on productivity, competitiveness, growth and development, that benefits large sections of the population and future generations. The impression of the author is that certain aspects of HRD that are highly relevant for (especially non-farm) private sector activities have received too little attention from donors and government counterparts for a long time, pointing to imbalances in the PSD approach that is applied in Uganda. In other words, several important drivers of competitiveness at micro and meso levels have been insufficiently addressed; e.g. technology, capabilities, learning and inter-firm cooperation. The support for technology and training SIs (including BTVET) and thus local capability formation and learning processes in the private sector has been insufficient.

Some changes in the scope of support for PSD in Uganda seem to have come under way more recently: more recognition is given to PPET and training of firms and entrepreneurs for advanced private sector activities by GOU and sections of the donor community. This broadened view on vital pillars and determinants of HRD and competitiveness - and the role of support interventions - is overdue; especially in the case of BTVET, firm and sector-level capability formation, and the development of SIs for enhanced productivity. Note that in many cases PPET has the potential to help the poor, such as women, early school leavers, non-farm entrepreneurs, and farmers more directly and immediately than some other measures, which only attempt to target long-term (macro) change, do.[369] Informal and formal LSD, for instance, can improve productivity and incomes in non-farm activities. Adequate PPET can also support firms' efforts to improve technology use, management, productivity and competitiveness.

Due to the limited scope of this book, issues of UPE and general secondary and tertiary education will not be discussed further. Instead, we shall continue to reflect on donor efforts to build HR for PSD beyond general education.[370] Different training and capacity building initiatives in the past, of *varying financial scale, project length,* and *conceptual merits* include those in areas of: (a) business skills and entrepreneurship, (b) training for women, youth, farmers and SMEs in the various occupations and skills areas (technical, commercial, or collective action skills), (c) value chain development, business-linkage formation, clustering and public-private partnerships, (d) export-oriented skills, including standards awareness and compliance, (e) product quality management, (f) capacity building in MFIs, (g) LSD in conflict and post-conflict areas, (g) establishment of centres for private sector promotion and business information, (h) capacity building in various business membership organisations (BMOs) and other private sector institutions (both headquarters and upcountry outlets), public sector institutions (e.g. ministries and affiliated institutions), and vocational training

369 Attempts to change macro-level issues (e.g. introduce a new policy) can take a long time to 'bite', and attempts may be undermined by conceptual contradictions, personnel change, political dynamics, or elite capture. At the implementation stage, a policy can remain on paper or fall victim to elite capture etc., resulting in little positive change for the targeted beneficiaries. Of course, there are political-economic and other reasons why targeting 'long-term change' of the Ugandan society is preferred by, for instance, donors.

370 Besides the interventions discussed in earlier sections of this book.

institutions (including polytechnics), (i) respective activities in tertiary institutions (research and analysis, scholarships), and (j) HRD-related efforts in the health sector (including HIV/AIDS programmes in the workplace).

Many of the related initiatives offer an essential input for enhanced PSD in Uganda. Nevertheless, the point made earlier holds: In the context of Uganda's post-conflict[371], late-comer and catch-up development (and the related shortcomings in HR), there appears to be an astonishingly inadequate level - compared with spending on social, infrastructural and other priorities[372] - of consistent and comprehensive support in the 1990s and early 2000s. Support is inadequate for knowledge and know-how transfer, training, as well as capability formation and learning processes for improved firm activities, productivity and competitiveness in both the formal and informal sectors. This includes firm and sub-sector level assistance as well as the strengthening of particular SIs (including training institutions) that are part of the local LIS. The justification for such support interventions was discussed earlier in this book. In comparison to other issue areas, donor support for private sector focused HRD (basic/further training, learning, technical support) - although it exists - seems *relatively* fragmented, uncoordinated, under-financed and poorly documented. In part, this situation could be a result of local and international trends regarding reform sequencing (social sectors, infrastructure, investment climate, etc.) and respective development approaches and priorities. Technology, productivity, skills, know-how transfer, technical support and collective action for PSD were not very high on the agenda of the donor mainstream in the 1990s. Maybe this was all too meso and micro, and too much 'market interference', for the dominant champions (or 'hard-liners') of a more macro and 'hands-off'-oriented policy and support intervention mix for PSD in Uganda.

371 And, related a significantly low level of HR, including technical and managerial skills in the post-conflict period due to the loss of HR in the turbulent earlier decades.

372 The education sector spending of GOU stands - also due to substantial donor support - at about 344mUS$ in FY 2004/05 (GTZ information).

14

Support for Capability Formation for Accelerated Economic Development

Agenda of progress in productivity, competitiveness and HR requires closer engagement with the private sector and the support system

Despite a range of vital interventions, there seems, overall, too little appropriate and substantial support *on the ground* - provided by GOU and donors (and the public and private sector SIs) - for those firms which try to adopt (basic and advanced) technology or business models for their production and business processes, which try to learn how to respond to competition challenges and market changes, including issues of process or product development, organisational change or value chain development, and which engage in capability formation of their own staff, or their suppliers. As elaborated earlier, various training and learning needs exist across the transformative economy: *building* and *deepening* of *industrial, technological, managerial, organisational or social capabilities* to actually undertake value addition in competitive markets is relevant for the large, export-oriented firms and the SME sector, in agriculture, the manufacturing and the services sub-sectors, in foreign and in local firms.

A key aspect of a pro-productivity intervention would be to help firms master existing technologies in their production and/business systems, and build industrial, technological, organisational and social capabilities. This would include ensuring appropriate outputs from the HR factor markets, and appropriate support from institutions charged with aspects of training, technology operations and productivity. It should be evident from the findings presented in this book that improvement in productivity and PSD can hardly be achieved without increased focus on a range of capabilities, and stronger impact of respective SIs. General business and entrepreneurship training is vital, but so is - especially in the context of Uganda's industrialisation vision - industrial or generally technical training, which seems particularly inadequate in the country.

Having technology or innovation-related schemes for upper-end firms is vital (assuming the schemes are administered by a competent and vibrant institution), yet insufficient if there (1) is too little on offer for the many smaller enterprises that want to grow, and (2) too little concern for building and strengthening technical SIs. The findings on adverse impacts of technological skills gaps in SSE (Byaruhanga 2005b) have revealed the adverse consequences of this support deficiency: lower expansion and reduced success of firms.[373] In short, to date there has been too little PSD support that *effectively* boosts the process of technology transfer and incorporation, which can significantly enhance productivity levels

373 Another perspective: Post-harvest losses are another example of the negative consequences of inadequate investment in technology and related capabilities for its operation: "It is estimated that over 35% of food grown in Uganda is wasted through post-harvest losses. Cost-effective technologies for preservation, transformation, storage and transport of this food could increase food security and income opportunities for the poor" (Muhumuza et al. 2005, 38-9).

of local firms, in particular in non-farm sectors. The UIRI would operate under this agenda. Efforts are under way to strengthen the institution. An effective UIRI would be very useful to foster technological capability formation. As Ssemogerere points out, the UIRI can, for instance, be an opportunity for SMEs to "opt for an initial learning process' commensurate with their productive capacity, marketing ability and financial means and ...then upgrade to more complex undertakings as resources and experience are acquired" (2005, 53). Institutional strengthening and regional outreach in this regard are needed to enhance UIRI's role in the process of knowledge creation, transfer and absorption (ibid). However, effective support and training institutions are just as much needed in other skill areas, e.g. for the tourism and agricultural sectors.

Further, there has been little adequate support for new skills aspects related to issues of diversification, including the development of social, organisational and interactive skills in the context of value chain operations (van Bussel 2005, Wiegratz et al. 2007b). 'New' HRD territories such as HRM have also received inadequate attention by mainstream PSD circles of state, private sector and donor representatives.

This situation of inadequate HRD support in some issue areas - and the underlying choice of other core areas for PSD support - is astonishing against the background of the prevailing economic and social structures and dynamics (large semi-subsistence economy, labour market, skills level) as well as the economic development agenda (agro-based industrialisation) in Uganda. The requirements of the diversification, competitiveness and growth agenda of a latecomer LDC economy in general, the loss of quality HR in the pre-1986 period and the rather slow and unsteady progress in some of the relevant issue areas for PSD in the post-1986 period (technology use, TFP, labour productivity, know-how, business practices) should have made policy-makers and donors rethink their priorities some time ago: towards giving *more focus* to capability building, training (BTVET), organisational development, and technology transfer etc., and thus adopting some suggestions of the (technological) *capability building approach*[374] for PSD.

Important to consider is HRD implications of the continued process of divergence between those countries (Uganda being one of them) that further fall behind relative to the group of advanced, developed and dynamic developing countries, regarding levels of technology use, technical efficiency, and TFP. A more vital focus on the adoption of technology, its efficient operation (moving along the learning curve), and thus formation of related capabilities is needed for LDCs such as Uganda if it is to undergo needed technological upgrading successfully (Isaksson et al. 2005, 61).

Furthermore, two areas of major concern for an agenda that stresses productivity, competitiveness and growth suffer from market and institutional failures: the investment in technology and related HR. This suggests a major role for the state and development partners to "take charge of the externalities at work" (ibid). Carrying out this task needs to go *beyond* vital efforts in health and formal education and go further towards *stronger engagement* with the *training* and *learning pillar of HRD-for-PSD*, and thus engage with firms and farms, entrepreneurs and farmers and agents of the support system, including those from the ETS.

374 As presented, the approach points to the cumulative nature and path-dependency of learning and capability building, and the importance of constant technological efforts (Lall 2004a) - which makes delays in the process costly, especially against the background of increasing threshold levels for capabilities required to enter and participate in production and trade for advanced markets.

It is important to note that the call for adequate support for employment-oriented HRD does not merely include adequate financing but, rather, adequate *efforts* (including policy responses) in areas such as know-how and skills transfer, joint learning, on-the-job learning, interpersonal and interinstitutional interactions, organisational and social capital formation, support systems, capturing of spillovers, the support of pioneering firms, and working out LLL-strategies with actors from abroad.

The argument for a *broadened* approach to PSD and thus a *more balanced mix* of intervention which gives increased attention to the development of enterprises including SMEs - and thus ensures that firms have the capabilities they need to operate, compete and grow - is supported by interdependence between the accumulation of labour and technology (ibid). A relatively high spending on formal basic and academic education appears odd in a context of relatively low support for sub-sector and firm-level HRD that can lead to productive and advancing firms which increasingly use technology and, in turn, acquire technical and advanced skills from the ETS in order to improve their productivity and competitiveness.

A lack of promotion of strong local capabilities and respective SIs can lead to increased difficulties for latecomer economies: "Some upgrading [of technologies, capabilities and activities] does take place over time, but it is likely to be slower and more limited than without promotion. Given the speed at which technologies are changing and path-dependence and cumulativeness in capability building, it can lead to latecomers being mired in low growth traps from which market forces cannot extract them" (Lall 2004a, 24-5). A related slow growth *and* advancement of the private sector (in terms of technological and functional upgrading, and shift to higher-value-added activities) will continue to have an adverse impact on the labour market, against the background of (1) significant graduate and youth cohorts seeking wage and salary employment or opportunities to undertake meaningful self-employment in a thriving economy, (2) the high levels of poverty and inequality, or (3) the state's need for tax revenue.

Significantly, both the PEAP and the MTCS have addressed the issue of *enterprise competitiveness* and have pointed to the importance of improving *firms' productivity* and *ability* to innovate and adapt to new technologies as well as to respond to the demands of markets. These are themes that are linked to capability building, know-how transfer and various HRD issues more generally: to education *and* training. Of the two, especially the latter cannot take place meaningfully without a higher involvement of firms and farms and strong institutions of the training, learning, innovation, technology and general business support system. The examples presented in this book, and others which were not discussed, show that support for enhanced capability building in firms, farms and sub-sectors is a paramount task in the context of Uganda's economic development; it can yield significant results.

The UCPC record, for instance, is commendable and can offer many important lessons: The intervention has targeted firms from different sectors and with different sizes; from the exporting textile company in Kampala to the small scale brewing entrepreneur in the North. It also fits with the argument put forward by Lall and Rodrik: give support to firms that (intend to) apply or undertake a specific activity, skill, technology, or business solution which is 'new' to the local economy (and has potential for diversification, spillover and demonstration effects) so that technological upgrading, product diversification and productivity enhancement can take place.

Without the subsidised UCPC services in terms of training and advice, firms would face the full level costs, risks, uncertainty, (import) competition and externalities that come along during the long process of learning and capability building related to entering into new activities; especially those activities linked with relatively advanced technologies. Without UCPC (and the know-how of its trained staff which was also built over time), firms would even find it difficult to locate a competent partner in Uganda for training and advice in technological and organizational matters of productivity enhancement. A firm might therefore not have undertaken the Cleaner Production investment and production process adjustment, thus remaining at lower productivity and competitiveness levels. The UCPC then is an incentive to firms to overcome a stalemate which hampers investment in technology, productivity-enhancing measures and diversification; its intervention helps to strengthen firms in many aspects: technology use, productivity, environmental sustainability as well as organizational efficiency and HRD. Cost reductions achieved with the help of the UCPC training and advice can be spend on better worker conditions and salaries (pro-poor effect), as happened in some firms that had undergone the training.

Surprisingly, the Centre has been running with less than a handful of permanent technical staff. Certainly, the UCPC - especially, given its enlargement plans - needs to be one of the core partners for initiatives aimed at increased efforts towards higher productivity levels in the Ugandan economy, especially in (agro-) industry and services sectors. Firms urgently need to improve their ability to master new technology efficiently. The question remains whether the Centre's approach and experiences (and those of similar institutions) can influence meaningfully the policy and programme choices of the powerful mainstream actors in Uganda (MFPED, CICS, World Bank, etc.).

More to the point, the contribution in the recent past of the three major *public* SIs, Uganda Industrial Research Institute (UIRI), Uganda National Bureau of Standards (UNBS), and Uganda Export Promotion Board (UEPB) to productivity and competitiveness-related efforts of firms have been commendable but at the same time also limited due to constraints regarding finance and technical staff (Ssemogerere 2005, xv). The work of EUg, UGT, UNBS and other SIs reviewed above is also commendable. An argument could be made that is similar to the supportive discussion of the UCPC interventions. It is, in sum, vital that these SIs operate (more) effectively - this includes adequate managerial and technical expertise - and increase their HRD impact on PSD. Indeed, there are many issue areas in the training context that need strong and specific SIs. Overall, firm and sub-sector level interventions that target capability building and that can lead to increased technical efficiency, technology use, productivity and performance in advanced and new activities, and improved business practices, need to be increased significantly and thus financed and staffed better. The actual support interventions need to target the formal and the informal private sector as well as state institutions that play a role in PSD.

It cannot be overstressed that more efforts are needed to help firms and farmers understand, measure, calculate and interpret productivity indicators, and subsequently improve their productivity through a range of efforts. Also, actors of the ETS, the business and technology support and the policy system need to enhance their capacities in this regard.[375] The BTVET

375 The OECD has a range of useful information (data, studies and manuals) on productivity. See OECD (2001), www.oecd.org and http://www.oecd.org/document/20/0,2340,en_2825_30453906_31526868_1_1_1_1,00.html.

system has to play a major role in the process of training and HR support for adequate PSD. A cautionary note remains regarding the implication weaknesses in certain PSD issue areas of the public sector in Uganda (at least, if measured by the recent past); it is hoped that implementation can be enhanced in future. Importantly, also, the private sector will have to enhance its efforts for effective HRD.

However, to date, the establishment of the UCPC and the few other examples of (direct) support for firm and sector level HRD, especially in relevant technological, innovative or managerial *capabilities* for *non-farm activities*, appears the result of priorities of a minority group in the government-donor-nexus. The same seems to be the case with regard to efforts to strengthen the learning and training-support system, especially for non-farm activities. Without doubt, more adequate HRD interventions and support systems for advanced farm production are also needed.

Overall, we recognise that there is a division of labour in the donor community, and that many other interventions for social and economic development that are not related to technology and human capital accumulation are justified as well. It is also understandable that, given limited resources, there is a certain degree of reform sequencing. However, the consistent mantra of 'more infrastructure and more adequate finance' which turns up prominently in almost every major mainstream PSD report in Uganda suggests that capability building is neglected, also for political (e.g. ideological) reasons; the Washington Consensus had its impact in Uganda too. Considering the HRD-related findings and arguments presented in this book, we propose to adjust the PSD agenda so that HRD-for-PSD aspects are covered more appropriately in future.

Rethinking prerequisites for accelerated economic development in Uganda

Maybe the situation of particular HRD gaps in the PSD support mix is linked to an initial belief, prominent during the 1990s among GOU and certain donors in (1) a smooth and vibrant process of private sector-led growth with entrepreneurs ably exploiting market opportunities which open up in a liberalizing, growing economy, and (2) liberal assumptions about market functioning, incentives and failures. Related beliefs in the operations of markets and 'market forces' appear to have shaped the understanding in these circles regarding the respective tasks of GOU and donors in the recovery and transformation process in Uganda. In many economic issue areas, the state shifted from a control, regulation and involvement-oriented mode of operation ('hands-tied') to 'hands-off' forms of engagement with the (young) private sector.[376]

It seems that this view of the role of economic actors (the market) and the state in a LDC has underplayed the role of government (and donors) in taking charge of externalities and other market failures (at the level of firms, sub-sectors and SIs) in the difficult and costly capability-building process involved in transforming a post-conflict LDC economy that has to diversify, grow and become more productive *within a competitive environment*. It certainly underplayed the role of the state in fostering (more long-term-oriented) inter-actor relationships, cooperation,

376 GOU applied a private sector-led approach in a post-conflict and stressed (transformation, liberalization) economy and operated with understaffed line ministries which often had inadequate staff capacities for the interactive 'competitiveness era' of the 2000s.

trust, and collective action in the economic realm (including shaping the business culture and political economy), e.g. among farmers and between traders and farmers. One can reason that the crisis in relationships and interactions between economic actors - for instance, the value chain governance crisis in parts of the agricultural sector characterised by low-trust and low-cooperation VCs and significant incidences of malpractices - is related to the neoliberal policy mix and growth paradigm dominant since the 1990s.

A position that is articulated, at times, by some state/donor officials is that certain larger firms that supply less competitive domestic and regional markets make enough profit to finance in-house skills development or technology acquisition themselves. While this might be true for some firms, this perspective leaves out many other business situations in Uganda that are very different and where firms with growth ambitions (yet, for instance, tighter current profit margins) are in relatively greater need of functioning SIs and technology support programmes. Further, more serious attention from those who wish to support diversification and export-led growth in Uganda needs to be given to the argument of existing market and institutional failures in exploring new, non-traditional areas, especially in competitive export markets where foreign competitors have a first-mover advantage and are often aided by strong, effective SIs in their home or host countries. The point here is to support and stimulate the relatively ambitious and difficult capability and learning processes that lead to the transformation of the economy, in particular. Market processes alone will not always lead to required investments. And even larger firms will find it useful to have SIs (that advanced competitors abroad might also enjoy) for the sake of competitiveness.

Against the background of an economic development agenda that emphasises and strives for pro-poor development, agricultural commercialisation and industrialisation, export growth, innovation, FDI and diversification, it is inadequate to give relatively little attention to the *vast* market and institutional failures in the process of local capability formation (especially in new and difficult activities) in a latecomer economy. In Uganda, the status quo in terms of actual (as opposed to expressed) PSD support is costly and rather unhelpful for achieving the country's economic development and poverty reduction ambitions. It is exacerbated by the current low levels of technical, managerial and organisational capabilities in many firms, especially in the informal sector, and their low HR-related training and learning efforts; and the current output inadequacies of graduates of the ETS in terms of functional and social skills, which makes it necessary for firms to educate and train staff further via on-the-job and institutional training.

Compared to other expenditure items on the government and donor bill, it seems this major part of building the country's HR was left largely to firms, entrepreneurs, farmers, students, employees and trainees themselves. They have to undertake their private training and learning efforts in the context of an overall weak and inadequate support system (including weak BTVET system[377]), high costs of education and training, and the structural conditions of a latecomer, or late-latecomer and liberalising economy. There is evidence that this situation often overwhelmed farmers and agro-processors in the past and lowered their capability building efforts; the state's support system for capability and technology accumulation was, in some (not all) cases, absent, for instance in the dairy industry (Wiegratz et al. 2007b). This

377 To date, many training institutes seem to offer mainly a narrow range of rather traditional occupational skills.

author argues that the high rate of business failure in Uganda, the problems with business practices and value addition are related to these inadequacies in the PSD support mix. Many Ugandans, including the 'newcomers', face a tough reality in terms of training and learning; yet, they need both to enhance their chances of competing with established foreign firms, in both domestic and export markets.

Maybe some donors prefer to invest in (what they hope will lead to) *systemic* changes; thus they choose to commit themselves to fostering the development of strategies and policies, frameworks, PPP dialogue arrangements, infrastructure and health systems, good governance structures, or ministerial-level capacity building. There are good reasons for such support, especially when it can be carried out effectively and with some success. However, systemic interventions, in the sense of making a considerable and hopefully sustainable impact, can also be achieved through (1) developing pillars of the (technical) training, innovation and learning system (read: build SIs), (2) supporting HRD for a specific sub-sector's development (e.g. modern dairy or meat sector, honey and flowers) or for the establishment and improvement of domestic- and export-oriented value chains, (3) upgrading a firm's ability to apply technology, or (4) increasing the interaction between firms and specific SIs. In other words, support that is more closely linked with how entrepreneurs, managers, workers, farmers, extension workers, traders are able and equipped to deal with day-to-day working issues - especially in technological, organisational and marketing areas - can make a valuable direct contribution to people's lives and careers. Importantly, supporting concrete changes in the world-of-work and in the related PSD support system can help to gather crucial experiences and lessons learnt; information that can subsequently be channelled into making policies and support programmes in the future.

In short, up to now the identification of problems of GOU and major donors has not paid enough attention to the question of market failures in the formation of new capabilities at firm, farm and sub-sector levels. Consequently, there is a risk that the effects of related disincentives are underestimated and the competencies and experience of the private sector to offer and/or undertake the training of its workers, technicians, managers, field staff, out-growers, and farm group members are overestimated. This risk is particularly severe regarding new activities, technologies, business solutions and systems in the (new) higher-value-added activities and sectors that the country diversifies (or plans to diversify) into.

In this context, consider competency deficits in the private sector for training certain new PSD aspects: Take, for example, the difficulties experienced with the BSMD project in VCD. Local business consultants had generally little experience, knowledge and competencies to adjust their services to this salient yet *new* topic, and to help design and implement appropriate support interventions. This problem was still acute at the time of completing this book in 2008, also in the national and international development agencies. Yet, as reported, DFID has stopped the BSMD project, without considerable follow-up activities. Activities by other donors/agencies (e.g. UNIDO, DANIDA, USAID) and more recently GOU (NAADS, PMA, EUg, MTTI, NPA) in VCD matters are notable and to some extent (very) praiseworthy.[378] Some

378 DANIDA's Business-to-Business (B2B) programme or DANIDA's and USAID's work to link farmers and buyers, for instance, appear to make a positive contribution. See also the activities by NAADS and EuG mentioned earlier. See Wiegratz et al. (2007b) for other examples of VCD interventions. Unfortunately, these programmes are very rarely analysed in detail (e.g. by anthropologists or political economists) for academic (and, in turn, policy) purposes.

of them, however, appear, in part, unlinked to some of the most crucial BSMD lessons-learnt (especially on the importance of and difficulty in strengthening VC actors' relationships and embedded services); hence, there seems little accumulated learning and experience exchange in this vital PSD area. This delays the process of developing more adequate policies and programmes for VCD. Some of the core economic programmes of GOU are *in practice* still scanty in terms of VCD activities; the CICS is an example.

Research is limited on VCD intervention experiences in Uganda to date; however, van Bussel and Nyabuntu (2007) and Wiegratz et al. (2007b) point to a number of weaknesses of existing VCD programmes in the country. Further, there are only a small number of appropriate skills development offers to address the broader training and learning needs associated with VCD. Hardly any programme considers in-depth the political-economic[379], organisational, managerial, and behavioural (not just purely 'technical') aspects of VCD, or addresses the development or strengthening of entire VC systems through involving different VC players in the training (ibid).

There is an underestimation of the spillover effects (society/economy wide gains) of private entrepreneurial activity into new areas. Rodrik's writing describes the societal contributions made by investors who 'discover' a competitive and profitable business opportunity and thus newly position a country in global markets. In these cases, the social benefits in terms of diversification, jobs and capability formation in the local economy (through demonstration, information and knowledge spillovers) are typically greater than the private benefits that the initial investor captures. Such entrepreneurship - and the spillovers - will flourish better in an economic system that offers adequate capabilities and backing from SIs. It seems these considerations were not the main concern of those who shaped policy and spending priorities in Uganda during 1990s and thereafter. Their decisions might have been based on the assumptions that (a) entrepreneurial activities are undertaken (entirely) for private benefits, that, (b) markets correctly reward entrepreneurship according to consumer preferences and benefits, and (c) markets provide sufficient information and incentives for skills or technology accumulation. Correspondingly, people who strive for employment have to finance the training and thus training structures mainly themselves - they be rewarded by incomes, it is assumed. These assumptions, as argued in this book, are questionable and unhelpful in the Ugandan case.

Instead, Uganda's development agenda of the recent past has been dominated by arguments about the importance of producing public goods such as basic education and infrastructure; related societal benefits and/or market failures and externalities were probably more obvious (or visible) to influential policy makers.[380] This author believes this view underplays the insight that "market forces ignore the growth-enhancing potential of externalities" (Isaksson et al. 2005, 45) just as well in inter-linked areas such as *entrepreneurship* and *investments* in *technology* and *capability building*. In other words, the market failures and public goods related to the process of capability and technology accumulation need to be taken into account in the policy arenas for HRD and PSD in Uganda.

---

379 International Alert (2008, 2006) activities regarding economic development in Northern Uganda, funded by SIDA, are exceptions.

380 The author is grateful to Fred Muhumuza (MFPED advisor and EPRC research fellow) for a related comment. Of course, every reform mix has political reasons as well, which this book will not however examine.

As indicated above, it is important to realise that the insufficient focus on HRD-for-PSD has partly to do with the dominant PSD policy approach applied in Uganda to date: This approach seems to rely overly on a concern for certain aspects of the business environment (business regulations, starting/closing a business, contract enforcement, property rights protection, difficulties of hiring/firing, 'ease of doing business') and costs of production (utilities, access to finance). Correspondingly, there is inadequate support for the development and deepening of crucial skills and capabilities and the required SIs. However, continuing with the almost exclusive focus on macro-economic framework conditions, the investment climate, business environment and infrastructure might not be enough to change the micro- and meso level status quo (in areas such as HR) that determines *local firms' abilities (managers, workforce)* to operate business affairs more competitively, respond to market changes, upgrade their productivity levels (through better utilisation of technology and improved processes, products, organisations, HRM methods; in short innovation), or utilise the outputs and services from *effective factor markets* and *SIs*. Productivity is driven by the application of more efficient technologies in business and production processes, and the application of related knowledge, know-how and skills. The productivity challenge is thus much more than overcoming the deficits in terms of roads, energy and affordable finance. The problem is not merely finding money for and building or maintaining a road.

From the above it follows that, the PSD approach dominant up to now in Uganda is insufficient to stimulate and enable entrepreneurial activity to enter new, technologically more advanced business areas, characterised by significant externalities and requirements for skills and SIs. The same applies to the issue of support for the SMEs. These concerns underline the role of HR in taking advantage of technological change and diversification opportunities for economic and social development, and thus advances in the country's catch-up process. The vital role of a functioning and responsive ETS for this agenda is evident.

New initiatives: Towards a broader view on support for PSD?

Against this background, some new GOU and donor initiatives appeared around *2005/06*. Examples are the government's Innovation and Industrialisation Fund, the emphasis on secondary education, including BTVET, and on better quality in UPE, the scholarship schemes adjusted towards science subjects at the tertiary level, the efforts to strengthen government institutions of the (innovation and learning) support system such as UIRI, the NAADS training and technology transfer activities in the agro-sector[381], and projects related to the Prosperity-for-all Programme, the Millennium Science Initiative (MSI) and the development of the ICT infrastructure in Uganda.[382]

The Innovation and Industrialisation Fund, for instance, supports R&D activities, especially by SMEs. Emphasis is placed on development and commercialisation of suitable prototypes and R&D in the processing of agricultural products. Efforts towards commercialising business ideas that are supposed to lead to the development of industrial processing enterprises must

381 NAADS (National Agricultural Advisory Services) has tried to institute a number of important measures to promote farmers' capability, technology accumulation and collective action (farmer groups); the results are mixed and the authorities have tried to improve the outcomes of the programme. See Nyabuntu (2006) and Wiegratz et al. (2007b) for a review and case study material.

382 Note also the establishment of the Innovation Fund some years back by UNCST.

be based on appreciation of a longer-term business undertaking, pointing to the importance of quality entrepreneurship and the long-term existence of initiatives and SIs.

Further, GOU has decided to more state sponsorships at university level for science subjects. The objective is to increase the share of students taking science and technical subjects so as to develop HR for the country's strategic economic development priorities. Currently, the tertiary system concentrates on relatively inexpensive programmes: For instance, four-fifth of tertiary enrolments at undergraduate level is in arts and humanities and one-fifth is in subjects related to S&T (Muhumuza et al. 2005).[383] There are also plans to give greater support to BTVET over the next years - in the context of an increased focus on secondary education. GOU also passed the BTVET Act 2008 to promote and coordinate business, technical, vocational training and education, establish the related institutional framework, establish the Uganda Vocational Qualifications Framework (UVQF) and provide for the financing of BTVET (www.btvet-uganda.org).

The initiatives under the MSI project - coordinated by the WB with the UIRI and UNCST, among others, as main local partners - consists of two components: (1) a competitive fund to support research, education and training in science and engineering, as well as linkages to the private sector; (2) an outreach, policy, and institutional strengthening component (WB 2005c).[384] Indeed, more support to UIRI - as envisaged by the MSI project - is crucial in the context of arguments put forward in this book (technology, capabilities, and productivity).

The cooperation between the Makerere University (MUK) Faculty of Computing and Information Technology (CIT) and the US IT firm Cisco to form an academy and enhance students' ICT knowledge and skills is remarkable. This is an example of a LLL-strategy at work; though the cooperation has commercial underpinnings, it has helped to develop crucial capabilities and networks. The positive dynamics are significant: in 2007, the MUK Faculty of Cisco Academy was given an award for being the best Regional Academy in the global CISCO network of academies; it "was singled out from amongst other Academies in over 164 countries as the Regional Academy that has clearly contributed to the development of the program for the entire Europe and Emerging Markets (the latter comprising of Middle East and Africa)" (Makerere University 2007).

Another encouraging example in the context of the development of the Ugandan food industry: staff and students of MUK's Department of Food Science and Technology (DFST) have in the past years developed a variety of innovative technologies and novel value-added food products from materials produced by farmers in Uganda. The products include: bushera

383 This policy has caused debate among the Ugandan public; a main concern is that arts and humanities also deserve strong state support. This book will not enter this debate due to the research limits.

384 The project is about US$30m. The core item under component one is a competitive grant fund that supports three areas: (1) research connected to graduate training, (2) undergraduate degree programmes in S&T disciplines, (3) research activities defined by the private sector. Under component two activities include: outreach activities that raise the profile and public understanding of the role of S&T, e.g. 'social marketing' of science by high-profile researchers to primary and secondary school students, a National Science Week, activities to pilot remedial science education and 'science-for-the-non-scientist' courses at tertiary level. Further, institutional strengthening is envisaged for the UNCST and the UIRI as principal agencies involved in S&T policy making, implementation, and service delivery. One of the activities of a restructured UNCST would be develop a S&T Human Capital Development Report (WB 2005c).

beverage, smoked beef, nutrient-enhanced cookies, katunkuma pickles, omulondo liqueur, banana juice, nile perch gelatine, and orange-fleshed sweet potato flour. These products can be taken up by interested industries. In 2008, DFST assessed the feasibility of some of the developed products and found that many had great market potential. An incubation programme was launched, with support from I@MAK, to promote commercialisation of the products developed by DFST so far. Incubatees have been identified to commercialise bushera, smoked beef and nutrient enhanced cookies; they will use facilities at DFST and get technical support from the department.[385]Further, MUK's Department of Technology is a main actor in an initiative (funded by SIDA and the Rockefeller Foundation) to develop several clusters in Uganda.[386] The donor support for MUK in terms of research, training, equipment, and construction of buildings has been commendable and has had led to positive results.[387]

There are also signs that Ugandans from the Diaspora are increasingly being recruited to take over leadership positions in the ETS and the political system in areas crucial for economic development and apply their knowledge, experience and networks; as recently happened in the ICT sector. The government's efforts to attract FDI (and the technology and capabilities that come with it) have remained high. Further positive developments are that the country, now after years of preparations, has a trade policy and an industrial policy, while a textile sector policy and a standards policy (including a national food safety/SPS policy) are in the making. Work on constructing industrial parks throughout the country is on its way; warehouses for farmers' produce are being constructed; there are efforts to limit the import of counterfeits and revive collective action under cooperatives societies, now called SACCOs (savings and credit cooperative organisations). A number of farmer groups are becoming stronger, in the oil seeds and the honey industry, for example. It remains to be seen how significant and sustainable the positive effects of the trends mentioned above will be.

A technology project that looks promising (at least in terms of objective and design) is the Technology Acquisition Fund (TAF), a matching grant scheme managed by the PSFU under the BUDS (Business Uganda Development Scheme) programme.[388] The Fund is designed to help exporting firms with, among others, technological skills development (Box 39). For the first two years (2005-2006), about 1.5mUS$ in total was allocated to the TAF with prospects of an increased budget after a first evaluation of the scheme in 2007.[389] Note the proportions of the TAF: The total amount of the WB PSCPII (Private Sector Competiveness Programme) for the entire period (2005-2010) stands at about 70mUS$ with a major share of it going into construction of the Industrial Park at Kampala, Namanve. The 1.5mUS$ of the TAF will likely cover only about 30-50 firms.[390] The maximum grant might be too small to stimulate implementation of larger technology projects.

385 Information was received from DFST.

386 Sectors in the pilot phase include local agglomerations of metal fabrication, production of salt or pineapples, fashion design, handicrafts, and management.

387 As said, this book does not assess the efforts of GOU and donors in the education sector.

388 The TAF applies the matching grant principle for cost sharing: up to 50% of activity costs, maximum grant level per firm: 50,000US$. TAF was designed by GOU, WB and PSFU officials, among others, and will utilize money from a World Bank loan to GOU under the PSCPII: 2005-2010.

389 The author obtained the information from an interview with the PSFU scheme manager in charge.

390 Calculation example: With 20 firms receiving the maximum grant of 50,000mUS$, and the rest receiving 25,000mUS$ each the scheme would only have 40 beneficiary firms.

Box 39: Background to the Technology Acquisition Fund

The TAF is a matching grant facility managed by PSFU, to assist exporting firms in raising skills, standards and the quality of products across export supply chains.

Objectives of TAF

- To support the competitiveness of Uganda's exports in the international market,
- To improve on the quality of Uganda's export products, along an export supply chain
- To increase the skills along an export supply chain,
- To increase the level of export items from Uganda.

Activities eligible for support

Export firms can be supported with any of the following eligible activities:

- Procurement of patents or manufacturing rights,
- Procurement of prototypes,
- Technology transfer to facilitate the physical development of new products,
- Acquisition of new quality-control equipments,
- Staff training and other related training costs,
- Compensation to large firms for part of the costs incurred in providing on-the-job training to workers from MSMEs within the export supply chain,
- Acquisition of international standards (including ISO 9000),
- Consultancy costs,
- Development of new agency contracts.

Technology Acquisition Fund is available to

- Privately-owned export-oriented enterprises duly established and operating under the laws of Uganda,
- Enterprises that are part of export supply chain,
- Enterprises with evidence of export orders,
- Enterprises that are VAT and income tax compliant,
- Enterprises with an adequate business concept or proposal showing clear projected increase in sales revenue, the description of financial resources required for implementation, the anticipated sources of funds, the proposed time frame, benefits expected to be derived, etc.

Source: *Private Sector Foundation Uganda.*

The TAF is a commendable move, and should be scaled up as soon as possible. Currently its target group does not include firms that mainly or only operate and grow in domestic markets. Besides BUDS, other agencies (with other target groups) should also be considered to implement related schemes and tools to advance technological capability formation in the context of technology-transfer stimulation. The crucial importance of respective technological learning efforts should be kept in focus: "Unlike the sale of a good, where the transaction is complete when physical delivery has taken place, the successful transfer of technology is a prolonged process, involving local learning to complete the transaction" (Lall 2005, 11). In other words, the adoption of existing technologies from elsewhere by a Ugandan firm is "only the beginning of the learning curve" (Isaksson et al. 2005, 61). Thus, there is need in this context for firms to undertake technological efforts and for the technology, learning and training support system to provide sustainable, constant and competent institutional support. Clearly, there is in the first place, need for capacity building in many SIs. Given that technological learning is ongoing and thus long-term in nature, one cannot overstress the importance of building and strengthening SIs rather than relying on on-off and short-term projects that hardly pass their accumulated know-how in project design and implementation on to the wider learning and support system. Hence, initiatives like the TAF must maximise the learning, demonstration and spillover effect to the economy and the national LIS and ETS; that is one of the major justifications for such subsidies.

The upcoming initiatives, activities and trends mentioned above - and others that were mentioned earlier in the book e.g. the relatively new business linkages programme under EUg - are commendable. These activities - including the commitment expressed by GOU for stronger support of the BTVET system - constitute vital steps: towards technological capability building and learning, the establishment of an LIS that supports PSD, and a better coordination of factor markets, that provide firms with adequate education and skills. The recent activities might signal a certain move by GOU - and thus some political and technocratic backing - towards a broadened perspective on PSD support measures.

In some of the new programmes, several challenges certainly exist, e.g. in terms of target group, spending design, administration and implementation. A higher level of meaningful interaction between the public and private sectors is required in this context. Further, the new R&D/scientific initiatives must consider that many firms in DCs - probably also the majority in Uganda - are in particular need of a better *learning system* than a *'pure' innovation or research system*, since they are concerned "with mastering and using existing technologies rather than with innovating on the [technology] frontier" (Lall 2002, 7, fn 3). This qualification on the nature of firms' innovative efforts (including R&D) and thus support needs is important in the context of technological capability building initiatives. Of course, more basic research and new local technology development is required, as well, where appropriate.

Further, the interrelationships between skills formation and PSD (capital and technology accumulation) have to be kept in focus, including the demand and supply side of markets for education, knowledge and skills. *Without accelerated development of a larger and more advanced private sector (which builds its competitive advantage on HR, technology, or innovative activities)*, many of the students that enjoy S&T sponsorships, or are in courses such as marketing, supply chain management or ICT today will probably be unemployed, or might be forced to go abroad (brain drain) upon graduation. An advanced private sector is unlikely to emerge without broadening of the current PSD support agenda of the GOU-donor-nexus and taking capability and technology accumulation into account more seriously. The efforts to refocus sections of the tertiary system towards economic development priorities must go hand in hand with efforts to advance the current few industry-university linkages, including private sector focused research partnerships. This can help both the ETS and the private sector.[391]

It is noteworthy that the success of some Asian economies is founded on considerable return migration of entrepreneurs and highly skilled manpower to their respective host economies. The question is whether Uganda (both GOU and the private sector) is doing enough to encourage return migration of qualified Ugandans living abroad, and whether Uganda has an adequate strategy to foster knowledge and technology flows from the Ugandan Diaspora or other cross-border networks?[392] Altenburg et al. (2006) reflect on the cases of India and

391 The MSI Programme addresses the issue of research for the private sector.

392 By late 2008, there were signs that GOU was applying a more strategic approach to involve the

China, and make the interesting point that "[p]erhaps poor countries should now send their most promising cadres (students, young professionals, attachés) for study and work to the centres of learning and innovation in China and India rather than to OECD countries. It may prove to be cheaper and more effective" (ibid, 30).

Despite the recent improvements and initiatives, the overall impression, however, remains: there is much more adjustment and change necessary (at the level of policy making etc.) to make HRD a significantly higher priority in the context of support measures for accelerated PSD in Uganda. Vital aspects of HRD-for-PSD are still not given adequate consideration (at least at policy and implementation level) by major players who drive policy and spending priorities in Uganda (GOU-donor nexus). This is the case, even though numerous studies have identified HR-related evidence from across the economy that the HR status quo is harmful and changes are overdue. Given severe problems regarding certain matters on the business environment agenda (electricity, roads) and other emerging priorities that the GOU plans to address in the near future, there is a risk that the agenda of economic-development-oriented HRD in its various forms will rather be (further) underemphasised and marginalised, and not receive increased attention, efforts and resources. For instance, there seem to be few signs that the donor community is ready to engage in a discussion about adequate measures for PSD-oriented HRD, beyond PE/SE, generic sensitisation workshops for the private sector and the like. One explanation for the status quo could be that government's priority agenda has indicated only first signs of a renewed and increased intention to scale up support for private sector-related capability formation. However, various implementation questions (leading ministry, capacity deficiencies, political economy) for an adjusted PSD agenda with an increased HRD focus in the future remain unsolved to date.[393] Another reason for the rather slow change towards a more strategic HRD focus in PSD could be that the main (generally liberal) approach and policy mix for PSD in Uganda remains largely unchanged to date, a decade after the recovery and stabilisation period of the 1990s.

In other words: GOU, donors and other stakeholders appear to be obliged to meet prior commitments and related (political and cognitive) priorities which have yet to be completed, and advanced further (see plans on SE, focus on business environment and investment climate). It seems it is not so straightforward and unproblematic for main policy-makers and practitioners to acknowledge and shift to (or incorporate) certain new themes and 'new territories' in PSD and HRD which need urgent and lasting attention at present and in the near future, especially if they are placed somewhat outside the mainstream PSD agenda. As noted, Uganda already ranks relatively highly in the World Bank's Ease of Doing Business Index[394], ahead of countries like China, India, Vietnam, Brazil, Rwanda, or Egypt. The 'new territories', as this book has argued, are among others: capabilities, technology, productivity, HRM, business culture (SoC) and VCD.

Ugandan Diaspora in boosting private investment in the country. A Diaspora Investment Summit under the theme *Back to my Roots - Uganda My Home* was organised by the UIA and the business community in Uganda in December 2008. For more information on this Summit and the Ugandan Diaspora in the UK see http://www.ubpa.org.uk/. See also http://www.ugandainvest.com/.

393 In this context, a WB report notes the current absence of an overall PSD approach: "Uganda lacks an effective high-level institutional framework devoted to PSD. There is also no overall GOU PSD strategy although there have been overlapping initiatives aimed towards supporting PSD, most notably the ... MTCS ... [and the] SEP" (2006a, xiv).

394 Uganda ranks in position 72nd, which is in the first half of the ranking that comprises 155 countries (WB 2006c).

For these reasons, the discussion on how (and why) to open up and better balance the support agenda for PSD and economic development in the Ugandan context deserves attention; especially regarding utilisation of specific opportunities and engagement with challenges for HRD in the context of efforts to achieve accelerated economic growth and the PSD of a latecomer economy. The quote below on the question of how to mix spending on 'pure' innovation on one hand, and application of imported technology on the other, exemplifies general aspects of such a discussion:

> "Poor countries ought not to engage in a vertical integration of the stages of developing new-to-the-world technology. What they mostly need is to absorb mature technology. Granted, international technology does not come cheap, but it is still cheaper for a latecomer to buy the technology already invented by others than to re-invent the wheel. This argument rests on two points. One ... advantage of backwardness is the situation of a country well behind in terms of technology. Such a country can make a lot of progress by merely catching up, i.e., without innovating. The other point is that the cost of innovating is proportional to backwardness. Innovating is relatively more expensive for countries currently at low levels of productivity. Inversely, investing in technologies that have been developed elsewhere but are better than the ones currently in use is relatively cheaper. There is no need to take either side in this argument. The two options are not mutually exclusive; on the contrary, they can be combined. The only question here is to find the right proportion: In total investment what share should go to innovative activities and what share to imitative activities? But it is an important question. ...[F]or a poor country, [we suggest,] the most central policy issues in the realm of technology is to what extent to invest in domestic R&D, given that there are opportunities to acquire imported technologies" (Isaksson et al. 2004, 28).

Finally, as this book has tried to argue, HRD involves more than addressing issues of general education and health and (technical) skills. Box 58 (Appendix 35) presents a snapshot of newspaper clippings from the final days of writing this book: the range of HRD-related news goes from successful operations of a training institute that offers value addition and food processing courses, successful regional market expansion of the largest dairy processor in the country, and efforts to regulate fishing practices, to reports about cattle theft, fraud in the Ugandan banking system, farmer and buyer tensions, and the problem of counterfeits.

15

Summary, Conclusion and Recommendations

The discussion in this book revealed a range of issues that are related to understanding of the economic and social dynamics that impact on HRD realities and prospects in Uganda. One of the main assumptions that guided the discussion was the belief that core prerequisites for enhanced economic development, competitiveness and growth of a latecomer and catch-up LDC such as Uganda are closely related to aspects of HRD. A comprehensive set of knowledge, know-how, skills and experiences is required in order to respond to and benefit from current structures and the dynamics of a liberalising global, regional and domestic economy, first, and undertake the desired structural transformation of the Ugandan economy, second. That is, to continue and strengthen the catch-up trends and limit or stop the falling-behind dynamics in the various salient issue areas.

The findings and themes presented in **Chapters 1-10** point to the main challenges and opportunities in this context. To begin with, the country undergoes ***structural transformation*** towards services and industry. At present, both sectors together make up about two-thirds of the GDP and almost entirely drive GDP growth. The agricultural sector, which consists mainly of (semi-)subsistence and smallholder farmers, is experiencing a decreasing share of GDP and a weak growth performance (with consequently low contribution to GDP growth). The Ugandan post-1986 growth episode - which started from a low base - has been significant. In recent years, there has been a slowdown in the growth process - although figures are still positive and above the SSA average - pointing to the need to realise new sources of growth. The effects of stabilisation and economic policies (e.g. liberalization) of the 1990s seem largely captured. The role of ODA in the recovery and growth process has been very significant, and has remained so up to now; this reveals problems related to nurturing new sources of growth. The formal sector is still small and growing slowly; the informal sector is large. Consequently, few people are in paid wage/salary jobs, while a large percentage of the LF is self-employed or work as unpaid family workers. Formal sector employment is characterised by a relatively high level of casual labour, for instance about 50% in the manufacturing sector.

There has been a rise in overall ***exports***, also due to the expansion of non-traditional exports (such as fish, flowers, and tourism). The structure of exports, however, reflects the overwhelming role of resource-based products (primary products and processed food) and a relatively poor technological upgrading record towards export products with higher technology content. With imports sharply on the rise, the trade imbalance is significant and was increasing at the time of research. Increasing the scope of regional trade should be one of the country's priorities, another one is finding an adequate diversification response to the rise of China and India in the global economy and the related competition pressures in both home and export markets. Increasing the competitiveness of Ugandan firms, including the know-how, capabilities and skills of their staff and suppliers is an essential requirement in this context.

Of concern is the low level of ***TFP and labour productivity***, with the latter being very low for the manufacturing sector in Uganda, compared to that of Kenya, Tanzania or the Asian economies. Positively, data suggests that technical efficiency levels in the industrial sector have improved considerably in the recent past. However, the trend in growth of average labour productivity in the post-1986 period, though above zero, has yet to develop a consistent upward movement. This will need efforts to improve further the pool of qualified HR and the operations of the ETS and LIS. The negative impact of the pre-1986 years of political and economic turbulence, that resulted in massive HR losses and slumps in average labour productivity, needs to be considered in this context. Regarding the need to adopt and master new technology competitively, there should be increased efforts to support firms' and farms' learning processes - and to provide and upgrade the required capabilities - so that the efficiency levels during the initial period of use of the new technology decline less severely and improve faster.

Overall TFP growth appears to have contributed relatively little to post-1986 GDP growth in Uganda and experienced, moreover, a declining impact in more recent years. Instead, the high dependence on capital accumulation (with significant support from external finance) questions long-term potential and sustainability of GDP growth. TFP needs to be enhanced, to allow higher per capita output and income as well as to catch up with the leading and dynamic TFP performers worldwide. Significantly, TFP can be boosted through (1) improved knowledge about and handling of technology and production processes, in short, through incorporating new technology in production and learning how to use it efficiently, and (2) diversification into high-productivity sectors. It is manifest that technological, managerial, organisational and social capabilities play a major role in this context; so do capabilities related to firms' HRM. The related HRD deficiencies of local firms are significant, and undermine the productive operation of plants.

Other deficiencies that affect significant sections of the economy adversely are related to areas of ***business practices*** (including trust, fairness, inter-firm cooperation, networking, clustering) and the underlying structures of ***political economy*** and ***business culture*** in Uganda (and the global economy at large). The development of long-term-oriented VCs in the agro-business sector, for instance, suffers from the above characteristics, especially the low use of contracts, poor business practices and ethics, weak cooperation patterns, and a drive towards low product quality in parts of the sector.

Skills deficiencies among ***smallholder farmers*** make their systematic incorporation into export-oriented value chains a risky and costly venture for exporting companies (e.g. regarding training, supervision and coordination). Many farmers need upgrading from (semi-) subsistence towards basic commercial production and trade practices, including a higher degree of efficiency, consistency, quality, organisation and collective action at farm and VC level. Buyers and farmer groups who try to build better relationships and enhance cooperation (e.g. in matters of training) do not always receive sufficient support from the state. Their trust-based business relations are also under threat of 'interruption' by traders who merely want to buy produce from farmers without providing training and other support, or who ill-treat farmers by cheating in one way or another, thus making subsequent trust building by other traders more difficult and 'costly'. Generally, business practices of (export-oriented) *traders and processors* are also in need of improvements vis-à-vis interaction with both farmers and buyers abroad. Overall, there are signs that some actors in the agricultural sector realise the importance of inter-actor relationships and related aspects of respect, fairness, joint communication, planning, negotiations, and honesty.

The upgrading of production and trade and related relations and practices along ***value chains***, and the development of capabilities of and relationships between the various actors, and the enhancement of required state support and regulation, will probably gain importance in Uganda's agricultural sector for some time to come. At least, if Uganda wishes to pursue vehemently its chances to achieve an export-led (agro-industry based) growth, which will help to improve the livelihood of the poorer economic actors (more inclusive development), and bring about the aspired economic and social transformation. VC-related improvements are necessary against the background of increasing market requirements for products and services as well as stiff competition due to (1) increasingly efficient and strong global competitors, and (2) new liberalisation rounds in the regional and global economy. No doubt, the HRD requirements in competitive agro VCs are increasing. Related state-supported HRD can help VC actors to move into upgraded, higher-value-added economic activities, and poorer producers to participate and benefit more in the expected export-led growth and transformation dynamics.

Importantly, there is a notable ***entrepreneurship drive***, with people and households diversifying their income-generating activities into non-farm activities, though often only on a small-scale base, with a focus on local markets and employing very few people per business. Entrepreneurs are driven by necessity (poverty) and business opportunities. The household diversification into non-farm activities (often informal services, trade, and manufacturing), and out of agriculture, has probably helped to limit the poverty problem. Importantly, the transformation and diversification drive into non-farm activities has led to a situation where many people are 'newcomers' in the very area in which they are trying to make their living as entrepreneurs or employees. They have little or no training in their current economic occupation. Skills surveys among SMEs and entrepreneurs reveal low levels of business, managerial, and technological skills, which has adverse effects on enterprise upgrading and growth.

Of further significance is that even the more qualified entrepreneurs seem to find it difficult (or not attractive) to enter industrial or other processing activities that are related to relatively high levels of technology investment, export and import competition, networking, institutional support, or skills formation; they rather seem to operate in sectors with lower requirements, such as the local service industry (transport, estates, finance). These aspects limit the positive impact of entrepreneurial dynamics in the country on job and growth creation as well as overall economic diversification and development. Conversely, tackling these issues, including the vital HRD part of training and learning, can result in improvements on various fronts of economic and social development.

As part of a ***latecomer economy*** on the global industrial scene, Ugandan firms face the paramount challenge of having to catch up with established players (from advanced economies) who enjoy first mover advantages (capability accumulation, learning curve), and often also superior SIs (ETS) of their respective home economies. In particular, Ugandan firms have to catch up in terms of technology, know-how, education, skills and capabilities, business organisation and practices, networks and productivity. Often, Ugandan firms have to catch up against a moving target because competitors elsewhere improve their operations, HR, and value chains faster. If Uganda and her firms cannot improve sufficiently in terms of level and tempo in the various categories mentioned above, they could face a continued widening of gaps (technology, capabilities, productivity, income) and a lowering of future development prospects. Deficiencies in the Ugandan ETS and LIS undermine the ability of local economic actors to catch up with established competitors or respond to dynamic competitiveness challenges and opportunities in markets. This holds for the international but also the regional and domestic market, with the latter being liberalised further, which increased import competition in certain sections. In addition, a range of market and institutional failures typical of the catch-up process in latecomer economies, particularly LDCs, hamper the process of PSD. These failures slow down and delay progress in terms of local technology and capability accumulation, and diversification into new activities.

Current challenges and opportunities are thus in areas of innovation and learning, productivity, mastering technology that is new in the local context, operating capacities (including HR) in enterprises and VCs efficiently, attracting appropriate FDI, improving business practices, strengthening the system of SIs, utilising the global pool of knowledge and information, and encouraging know-how transfer. Other relevant areas are: developing domestic VCs and providing improved embedded services and training, making the most of changing structures of global value chains (integrating into, advancing in and benefiting from), taking advantage of exposure to export markets for HRD, improving entrepreneurial activities in the formal and informal sector, undertaking market-oriented upgrading at firm and farm level, or overcoming market and institutional failures in HRD, building long-term business relationships (with higher levels of trust, cooperation and learning), exploiting the advantages of collective action, and improving the working and income conditions as well as health status of workers and other actors in the economy, such as farmers. The transformation, growth and poverty reduction agenda of the country, and the dynamics of the global economy, imply that improvements in the above categories are highly desirable. Currently, characteristics in some issue areas are encouraging; in others they are rather poor. The present-day HR deficits are also related to the significant loss of human capital and the erosion of the institutions compromising the ETS in the turbulent pre-1986 history of the country.

In summary, there are various reasons why a stronger supply side response from the private sector towards increased investment in new activities and the supply of competitive products has not materialised; deficits in relevant capabilities is among the main ones. The transformational and competitiveness dynamics require upgrading of capabilities in almost all sub-sectors to allow competitive businesses of a different scale to emerge, to keep going and to grow in the different markets. Vital in this context are improvements in the local LIS in general, and the ET/BTVET system, including SIs for business, technology and VC matters, in particular. A better LIS can enhance the abilities of firms and farms to upgrade products, processes and organisational methods and improve the use of technology. The adjustment requirements at the level of public and private SIs, as well as public administration, are also substantial. Improvements in the dimensions mentioned in this summary (and throughout the book) are crucial, given Uganda's economic development aspirations, namely to become an export-oriented, middle-income, industrialised country within the next 20 years, and to reduce poverty in the course of this process. Many important examples of improvements in businesses and farms and in the related capabilities of economic actors exist in present-day Uganda; some examples were presented in this book. The insights and lessons learnt should be utilised to develop the capability stock in the country further.

The current and near-future challenges of HRD and PSD as outlined in this book seem considerably different from the ***PSD agenda*** that was at centre stage of efforts by GOU and donors during the 1990s. The official PSD mainstream agenda was adjusted slowly in the early 2000s to incorporate new issue items and, more importantly, to implement interventions meaningfully. The 'new' challenges - which are often not really new but sometimes scarcely acknowledged, explored and/or poorly tackled in their root causes - are more related to the micro and meso level of economic activities and are, in part, of a rather long-term nature. Moreover, it appears there insufficient knowledge and experience available in state institutions and the private sector and donor realm to engage adequately with some of the 'new' problems, for instance regarding matters of productivity, value chain development, business culture, inter-actor linkage building and collective action, or human resource management. Indeed, some salient matters related to HRD in Uganda have to date not been explored, and are thus poorly understood (related determinants, processes and impacts) by the PSD research and policy community. Playing down and thus insufficiently addressing the obvious further is not a good option; it only delays required improvements further and thereby also the economic catch-up process.

Given the ***basic level of a number of fundamental problems of HRD in Uganda*** at the moment (e.g. in the large informal and agricultural sectors), it seems difficult (or unreasonable) in the near future, to respond too closely to the technocratic call for 'world class human resources'[395] - be it in the public or private sector. The problems are, in many cases, relatively basic, according to the findings of this book: Field studies show that the majority of MSEs never participated in formal training. Most persons engaged in non-crop household enterprises have never undergone informal/formal training. Furthermore, about six out of ten participants in the labour market are self-employed, mostly in an informal and often semi-subsistence fashion. The proportion of unpaid family workers in the LF is also high. Those in wage/salary employment are few and the majority of them operate in casual, temporary employment structures. About two-thirds of the LF (with low HR levels) work in subsistence agriculture; about one-third of the LF falls in the 'working poor' group. About 1.8% of the LF in the rural area has an educational level of S4+; and about 10% of the national LF obtained vocational training. The country's HR base - although in many ways improving in the recent past - still ranks low in international comparison; the decline in HR and E&T structures during the period of turbulence in the pre-1986 period played a role in causing these deficiencies. Thus, it is important to provide (and finance) basic or first-step training and learning opportunities for the many hardly-trained economic actors in the Ugandan economy and build advanced capabilities from there.

Moreover, as stated already, the economy and thus the realm of further, on-the-job training and learning are affected adversely by a short-term business perspective, wanting

395 See the NPA's HRD and Capacity Building Master Plan for Uganda (Draft), for an example in this respect.

business practices and little use of trust-based business relationships; all of this hinders HRD. A world-of-work characterised by opportunistic and short-term business behaviour erodes long-term business perspectives and undermines (1) the application of the knowledge and skills obtained in the formal or informal ETS, and (2) processes of on-the-job training, knowledge transfer, joint learning, mentoring, training and cooperation. This hampers the development and appropriate use of social and productive skills of entrepreneurs and staff which, in turn, stands in the way of further PSD and HRD. For the near future, a realistic and effective response to this situation, one which considers the situation of the majority of the population and some of the core upgrading requirements of the economy, is therefore, in most cases, likely to be different from what is required to build *world class* HR. More HRD-related efforts are needed to deal with the more basic (commercial, technical and social) skills needs of firms, entrepreneurs, workers, and farmers.

There are, no doubt, also many businesses (and public sector organisations) in Uganda which require technology, business processes, and capabilities to be at or close to international/ regional (best practice) level. More advanced requirements tend to apply, for instance, to the globally integrated vale chain operators, e.g. the flower growers, fish processors, tourism operators, or agro-traders and processors and their supplying farmers, and enterprises in services such as ICT and other technology support. These actors ought to operate and upgrade at international/regional best practice level and it is reasonable to expect them to do so. Support for their efforts to develop and deepen capabilities (at level of firms, farms, value chains) is recommended, as these businesses are often prime forces in the modernisation and growth of the economy. They operate in demanding markets and may face competition from firms elsewhere who are able to utilise the services of strong SIs.

Arguably the boom in education in Uganda since the 1990s has created expectations for better and more meaningful jobs and incomes - beyond the subsistence or 'working poor' level - in all sections of society. However, global structures and dynamics in the last decade - such as increased competition and labour-saving technological change, sustained protectionism in the North, global warming, the rise of China as a manufacturing powerhouse, and a widening technology and capability gap between richer and poorer countries - have in part prevented the economic and political conditions for these hopes from materialising. More efforts towards the accumulation of capabilities and technologies to strengthen economic activities are thus required, among others, to respond to some of these structures and dynamics and influence their materialisation and effects in the Ugandan economy. This said, there is indeed need for Uganda - just as for her neighbours Rwanda, Tanzania or Kenya - to achieve the ***dual goals*** of developing and deepening capabilities for (a) poverty reduction (and thus broad-based social and economic development) and (b) enhanced economic competitiveness (and catching up) of firms, farms and value chains (Tikly et al. 2003). The challenges related to these dual goals apply to the actors and institutions of the ETS and the LIS.

Importantly, under conditions of what some analysts call 'compressed development' (Whittaker et al. 2008), characteristics and processes that are conventionally associated with different 'stages of development' (Rostow 1960) now occur simultaneously in so-called would-be developers (e.g. LDCs/latest developers). Features such as industrialisation and deindustrialisation, malnutrition and obesity, institutions (e.g. norms, values, attitudes, and practices) of agrarian, industrial and post-industrial societies, the necessity of promoting basic education and developing (highly) advanced knowledge and skills, are overlapping in most recent developers,

> "rendering the concept [of 'stages' of development] empirically problematic if not meaningless. 'Stages' may still inform the analysis of development, but mainly as a historical comparison to processes that are now likely to occur simultaneously rather than sequentially. This means that different 'stages' of development interact and influence each other in real time, a situation which not only presents new policy choices, but also policy dilemmas which early and even late developers did not confront and do not appear to recognize ... [C]ompressed development has created 'policy stretch' in LDCs and ... necessitates a changed role for the state. The overall result is likely to be greater unevenness, disjointness, and inequality compared with early and late developers, which experienced more comprehensive and integrated industrialization at the national level" (ibid, 9, 3). make a quote design

Against this background, a major problem to date has been the ***deficient implementation level of core growth and competitiveness strategies of GOU***. Besides not adequately including crucial issue areas that need support in the first place, the strategies (and related programmes) often fail to reach the ground in a sufficient manner, e.g. the SMEs or the agricultural sector. One could anticipate that the public sector performance in certain areas in PSD will probably remain weak in the next few years. Core structures and capabilities of the public service are still geared - not surprisingly - towards the PSD agenda of the 1990s and its (ideological) successors in the 2000s: to recovery, stability, liberalisation, and, lately, improving the business environment. Hence, there are awareness, skills and know-how deficiencies in the 'new terrains'. The very inner government-business circle aside, the relationships between public and private sector actors are often weak.[396] Besides pockets of improved practices of interaction, a 'join hands' mode of operation (e.g. at technical level) seems to be at a state of emergence and experimentation. A successful catch-up process in HRD, technology and other PSD areas requires substantial PSD interventions by the public sector and advanced relationships and interaction patterns between the public and the private sector. Uganda will have to improve in this regard if she is to address market and institutional failures and other issues affecting HRD, economic development and competitiveness in a timely and effective manner.

The discussion in **Chapters 1-10** entailed most of the core arguments and findings of this book. From this basis, the remaining parts of the book reflected on (1) selected government strategies for economic development (competitiveness and PSD) and government's take on the HRD theme, (2) private sector activities in HRD, (3) donor activities in HRD, and (4) implications of findings for the PSD-related HRD agenda of the country.

In **Chapter 12**, we reviewed information on ***HRM practices*** in organisations operating in the country: good and best practices exist in this respect, as well as encouraging efforts in both the private and public sectors to improve HRM. Experts have noticed improvements towards a greater recognition of the importance of people management. Many organisations, however, reveal significant shortcomings in their HRM awareness, skills, and practices. These include a number of issues such as recruitment systems and practices, induction and appraisal systems, staff development, staff retainment, team leadership, communication and knowledge management, organisational culture, salaries and benefits structures. For instance, HRM tools

396 The relevant political and economic reasons for this state of affairs of the public sector are not discussed in this book.

for performance management, including the setting and implementing of incentive schemes to reward on-the-job performance by individual employees, teams or the whole organisation, are significantly underutilised. These deficits contribute to lowering overall work attitudes, efforts, and productivity at different levels - worker, team, and whole organisation. This, in consequence, makes firms less able to: (a) handle competition in today's globalised world, (b) take advantage of the benefits of the country's latecomer status, and (c) successfully undertake catching up strategies. In brief, Ugandan firms will, ceteris paribus, lose ground if, due to HRM deficits, they learn and improve relatively slower than their competitors.

From a ***public investment perspective,*** it is important to consider that poor HRM in the private and public sector undermines important education and training efforts that are currently being undertaken by individuals, households, groups, firms, the state, and international donors. Not only does poor HRM lessen the rate of return to education, it is also likely that it contributes to the considerable brain drain that the country is experiencing. Importantly, improved HRM is needed to translate all the efforts of pupils, students, trainees, teachers, and family members towards higher knowledge and skills levels into actually enhanced economic and social development. The level of HRM in firms is unlikely to improve (automatically) as a result of market forces and incentives alone as they exist in Uganda today.

Firms, workers, GOU, SIs (of the ETS and LIS), and donors need to: (a) give greater recognition to the HRM dimension as they strive for HRD, productivity, competitiveness, PSD, growth, and poverty reduction, and (b) tackle the HRM deficits in the country, e.g. by helping to: spread HRM know-how, instruments and good practices to more firms, farms and SIs (managers, head of departments, SMEs, or farmer groups), and find ways to translate the HRM commitment of firms into actually improved practices that impact on the performance of staff and teams.

In Chapters 11-14, we reviewed major ***Government strategies and policies*** of the early 2000s for PSD, and poverty reduction and the statements therein about challenges and opportunities for economic development, PSD and HRD. Significantly, Uganda envisions becoming a middle-income country with enhanced ability to compete favourably in international markets over the long term. Key strategies include accelerated and competitive industrialisation, enhanced exports, and improved participation by the poor in the growth process. The PEAP 2004/05-07/08 notes moderate outcomes - in terms of direct impact - of prior PEAP periods with respect to production and improvements of the economic situation of poor households. Prior PEAP versions are seen to have over-emphasised issues of the social sector; hence, the new PEAP seeks to increase the focus on matters relating to productive sectors. This author argued that this renewed agenda might signal that (1) the authorities feel there is need to implement a different set of (PSD) interventions; (2) the level of change required for designing and operating a different yet effective pro-poor and pro-PSD policy and programme mix is significant; and consequently, (3) the country, including the GOU, face some 'unknown territory' in this endeavour. We have interpreted related statements in the PEAP as a call for a broader view on requirements for successful PSD and HRD in Uganda.

The three PEAP pillars directly relevant to HRD are pillars 1, 2 and 5 (economic management; production, competitiveness and incomes; and human development). The impression of the author is that, regarding economic development, the PEAP is essentially informed by a rural-development and primary-sector perspective, which might be justified by the underlying assumptions regarding the PEAP's main concern, the poverty theme. However, since the PEAP was Uganda's *national* planning framework at the time of researching for this book, the outlined strategic agenda has relevant gaps in terms of conceptual considerations, programmatic focus etc. These include deficient acknowledgement of several salient matters of industrial development, commercialisation of agriculture, and, as a consequence, certain aspects of HRD. There are a number of important PEAP statements (on analysis and interventions) that need further debate and clarification, or there is the risk of incomplete and restricted interpretation and discussion of the country's opportunities (possible pathways) and challenges for economic development; in the context of latecomer development and catch-up within an ever-dynamic and competitive global economy. A restricted debate could result in a narrow interpretation of HRD dimensions, dynamics, and related needs for interventions and support.

It appears that the scope of action suggested by the PEAP does not offer a sufficient recipe for the kind of economic development that can bring Uganda, as envisaged, into the range of a middle-income country. The PEAP text is limited on prospects for improvement and transformation of the private sector (e.g. manufacturing) within a competitive global economy, e.g. with regards to capability formation, productivity, or clustering. Overall, the outlined plans don't seem to address certain HRD issues in the private sector in a sufficient and comprehensive manner required to boost HR and related aspects of competitiveness more significantly.

It is important to note that ***deliberations on PSD in Uganda*** rely too heavily on the 'business environment' and 'cost of production' perspectives. Competitiveness is understood mainly in terms of costs of production inputs, transportation and the related provision of public goods (infrastructure etc.). For the Ugandan competitiveness and HR context, there is too little emphasis on building new endowments that create competitive advantage, such as improved HR. While Uganda - that is, her policy makers - will have to make (further) vital improvements to the infrastructure, the investment climate and the business environment, she will have to engage more robustly with the 'capability agenda' to enhance prospects for economic development in general, and diversification, technological and organisational upgrading, as well as productivity, in particular. Notably, the capability agenda goes beyond general education.

This author suggests that the PSD and HRD agenda needs to incorporate more comprehensively aspects of enhancing (entrepreneurial, industrial, technological, design, organisational, social, negotiation, interactive and institutional) capabilities, which can boost the productivity of workers, teams and organisations, and help firms in their efforts to respond to competitiveness challenges and opportunities. This will have to be accompanied with increased concern for functioning SIs (for training and learning) that build and deepen capabilities. However, there are reasons to anticipate that the overriding impact of the conventional PSD agenda (business climate, physical infrastructure) may lead to a continued sidelining of substantial support measures for capability formation for the coming years, with adverse affects for HRD in Uganda.

On the positive side, the PEAP notes that competitiveness is based on firm-level abilities to be efficient and to innovate and adopt technologies. The expressed commitment to enterprise competitiveness needs to be translated into provision of government support for PSD: towards firm and sector-level support that actually addresses enterprise abilities in terms of technology use, productivity, product development, and value chain development. It is not clear to what extent such an approach will be implemented in the coming years. GOU has expressed concern about improved abilities of firms in non-farm activities; the implications of this agenda in terms of policies and support measures have yet to be fully understood and translated into practice. There is need for discussions on how the GOU and concerned partners can boost the abilities of firms and farms. In the past, GOU's support of vital aspects of productivity, innovation or technological upgrading was rather weak and fragmented. There is need to develop and implement appropriate support measures, and to learn about their impact. HRD issues would have to be incorporated at center stage.

It will be both a major opportunity and challenge for HRD proponents to engage in the debate on the role and contribution of capabilities and respective SIs in the context of improved technical and organisational efficiency, productivity, innovation, and technological upgrading at firm and farm levels. A core issue will be *how* the relevant HR can be developed and strengthened. The future HRD response needs to address - in the context of latecomer development - relevant market and institutional failures in the process of capability formation, technology accumulation, and, ultimately, economic diversification.

We discussed the PEAP's view on the ***role of the Government and the private sector*** in aspects of PSD and poverty reduction. Related PEAP positions may well define the discursive entry and resistance points for HRD proponents vis-à-vis the mainstream government-donor-policy circle when discussing HRD. This is so because, to date, GOU is, in terms of PSD, committed mainly to the (conventional) policy recipes of the investment climate and business environment agenda. The views and debates at this principal level of PSD approaches and related policy recipes define what is considered a public good in Uganda and thus the role of the state (regarding support interventions and regulation) and the private sector (issues to be shouldered by firms, entrepreneurs, employees, students, etc.). We have elaborated why the PSD approach and policy recipes applied so far in Uganda could have underestimated the size, scope and nature of support needed to develop HR for PSD adequately. Also, the approach taken in the PEAP seems not to allow sufficient room for a significant range of HRD measures to support firms and farms better; especially if (policy) principles are not adjusted further at the implementation level. Importantly, we recognise that the content of PSD recipes favoured and applied in Uganda is affected by the 'dialogue' with donors (and thus politics), first, and, the restricting effect of external systems (trade regimes etc.), second. The interests, views, and actions of the main actors in the domestic political economy also explain the policy mix; however, this was not researched by this author.

Since some aspects of HRD-for-PSD have so far received insufficient attention in the context of support interventions, proponents need to engage more intensely in debate if they want to avoid underemphasising these issues and related forms of support (e.g. LIS). Limited success in this regard would undermine the prospects for improvements in major PSD issues, especially those related to the particular conditions of a latecomer economy and the catch-up required in terms of levels of capabilities, business organization, technology, productivity, and diversification.

Besides these concerns, the common tenor in the PEAP and other documents for PSD and economic growth indicates that HRD in general is recognised by the authorities as a crucial matter: the arguments for support of general education (UPE etc.) are well established in Uganda. There are recent plans and measures to focus more on aspects of PPET (access and quality), including BTVET. The expansion and transformation of the ETS will remain an area for intervention and investments by the public and private sectors. Correspondingly, there are significant possibilities for success but also for failure. ETS reforms take place in a complex and experimental context, regarding dynamics and changes in both the economic and education systems. It is vital that ETS reform efforts are enhanced, and adequate improvements are made in the coming years.

All major economic development strategies launched since 2000 outline ***issues of skills development as an area of concern and an area for intervention***. They typically point to the importance of the BTVET system and related reforms, the training needs of MSMES, and in agriculture; related statements should give HRD proponents a vital entry point into the process of policy and programme making.

We can conclude that some aspects of HRD are (highly) acknowledged by the authorities, and these aspects have ultimately received actual support. However, there are gaps in the implementation (effectiveness, efficiency, coordination, and monitoring) of Government's PSD programmes in the recent past. It is vital to take into account this track record, related difficulties (and their causes) and lessons learnt when conducting discussions for enhanced national efforts in the HRD area and related matters of productivity, technology, and value chains. This can help in designing and implementing interventions in the future that have better prospects for a greater impact.

Regarding the main focus of ***donor support***, we argue that HRD-related efforts in some areas must be enhanced significantly, thus broadening the scope of support for both HRD and PSD. There needs to be increased attention on a number of HRD and PSD matters that have so far received insufficient attention. Focusing mainly on education and giving inadequate attention to the complementary formation of capabilities (in both non-farm and farm activities) and related factor markets, incentives and SIs, can result in a significant vacuum situation that hinders a relatively continuous HRD process in the country. This can affect the catch-up and development ambitions of the country adversely.

Donors who shared their views with the author highlighted the relevance of HRD-for-PSD. There seems to be widespread understanding among respondents regarding (1) the vital role of HRD (education, training, and health) for the country's development, and (2) the difficulty and complexity of the tasks ahead in terms of achieving actual improvements. Donors acknowledged that significant achievements have been made, particularly in terms of access to PE. Recent policy initiatives to improve access to and quality of PPET are generally welcomed. The relevance of PPET, including on-the-job training and workforce development beyond general education, for poverty reduction based on economic development, is recognised increasingly.

The following are seen as challenges to be tackled in the near future: Improve access, retention, content, relevance, adequacy, and quality of formal and non-formal E&T. Provide adequate formal and non-formal E&T as well as enhance chances for informal learning in conflict and post-conflict areas. Find appropriate roles for the state and the private sector to engage in TVET and HRD. Make efforts in E&T and health promotion more effective so as to obtain better results, e.g. better trained and more productive workforce, better ability of the poor to earn incomes, more inclusive interventions, etc. Donor representatives responsible for PSD and ETS matters actually face a similar situation: a commitment to certain development goals, a rather mixed success record so far, and substantial challenges and opportunities ahead.

With a view to achieving tangible improvements in poverty reduction, donors express an interest in tapping into existing experience and lessons learnt derived from the implementation of HRD-related initiatives in Uganda and elsewhere. Realising that better outcomes along the entire HRD spectrum requires a set of interconnected changes (due to the cumulative and path-dependency character of HRD), the donors also articulated the need to discuss priorities, and the sequencing and approaches of interventions. Indeed, significant inconsistencies, gaps and breaks in support can be costly in the long-term process of HRD.

Against this background, ***this book argues*** for an increased focus on development of a range of capabilities and related SIs (for training, learning, technology operations, know-how and technology transfer, and business support). Enhanced efforts and investments in this regard can significantly improve the ability of firms, entrepreneurs and farmers to undertake higher-value-added activity, develop and improve products, respond to market dynamics, network, learn and upgrade, and diversify and grow. This kind of HRD support is a crucial dimension for almost all development aspirations of the country: diversification, transformation, industrialisation, knowledge economy, competitiveness, productivity, technological upgrading, and advanced integration into the world economy, and thus PSD, growth, poverty reduction and social development. In addition, there are indications of an increasing threshold level in terms of technologies and capabilities needed for participation in global production and trade. Uganda needs to enhance the pace of HRD to match these rising HR requirements for advanced economic activities, especially of high-value-added activities. In sum, the economic catch-up and development agenda of the country clearly requires stronger HRD support.

Finally, E&T for economic development can work. Support interventions have resulted in positive impacts in Uganda and other developing countries. Indeed, human resources in Uganda have improved in the last two decades due to the enormous determination, efforts, and investments of a range of actors (e.g. teachers, parents and families, pupils and students, the state, NGOs, and donors). The Ugandan people have mobilised remarkable energy and financial resources to gain more education and skills. The activities of GOU and donors were, in relative terms, mainly directed towards education (and health). Training and learning - and thus the development of a set of capabilities for improved economic activities - have yet to feature on the agenda more prominently. The many examples presented in this book illustrate the need and usefulness of such an agenda. Detailed recommendations will be presented in the remaining section below.

Final recommendations and comments: Towards a strengthened support mix for HRD

The arguments made in this book and the subsequent recommendations below can be seen as a call for continued and increased efforts to strengthen HR levels in firms and farms, and the institutions comprising the support system, that are relevant in this venture. In this context, based on the findings presented in this book, some recommendations and suggestions are given below for key stakeholders from the public and private sectors as well as the donor community, that are committed to the agenda of upgrading the capabilities of actors in the economy and improving the respective support systems (ETS, LIS and BTVET). The following observations, recommendations and suggestions are developed against this general understanding. They are an attempt to highlight issues and implications that might help to strengthen interventions that target the various HRD dimensions, systems and support structures. They could thus serve as inputs for those who are in charge of or in other ways involved in strengthening HRD in Uganda. What follows below is a synthesis of recommendations made in the studies that the author has been involved in (Wiegratz 2006a, 2006b, 2008, Wiegratz et al. 2007a, 2007b, and Ssemogerere and Wiegratz 2006).

Against the background of the arguments and findings presented in this book, this author has argued for concerted effort to enhance HRD for economic development in Uganda. While the efforts of GOU and other development partners have so far been directed mainly towards education and health, it is timely and crucial to scale up initiatives directed at assisting entrepreneurs, firms and farmers operating in the informal and formal sectors to develop the necessary HR to become and remain competent and competitive players in local, regional, and international markets. Therefore, the overall recommendation is to enhance efforts to develop, deepen, and apply relevant local capabilities (including knowledge, know-how, skills, and experience) for economic transformation, productivity, innovation, and competitiveness. These include entrepreneurial, industrial, technological, production, managerial, organisational, learning, social, linkage, interactive and institutional capabilities. Improvements in the respective SIs, incentives regimes, and factor markets are vital. Specific recommendations are as follows:

Regarding the BTVET sector in particular

- There is need for the ETS (including the BTVET) as well as the business and technology support system to respond appropriately to the goals of developing and deepening capabilities for (1) poverty reduction (including social development), and (2) enhanced economic development.
- Increase the relevance, openness and effectiveness of the BTVET system for all economic actors in the country. Increase responsiveness to changing economic realities and related skills needs in both the informal and formal sector, including the exporting sector. The BTVET has to be relevant to progressive firms and entrepreneurs who enter into non-traditional activities. BTVET reform proponents need to improve their links with the private sector, and better capture the concerns of a wider range of firms (beyond the current government and PPP-committee level, which always attract only a section of firms).
- Continue strengthening the competency and modular training approach. Such an intervention is supported by arguments in favour of capability building and deepening in a diversifying catch-up economy that has to tackle a learning process that is rife with market and institutional failures.
- For the informal sector, affordable, flexible and relevant BTVET, in many cases non-formal and relatively short-term, is potentially a vital response. Importantly, the BTVET system needs to support career shifts of Ugandans at different levels.
- Competency-based training in the BTVET system needs, in order to be more effective, counterpart firms that are conversant with instruments of HRM, e.g. competency-based recruitment, personnel development, and organisational development. Hence, HRM-related capabilities in the private sector need strengthening. This includes the larger, progressive SMEs. Appropriate tools for HRM training and HRM application are needed.
- Keep track of PSD dynamics and make use of existing good practice in skills development existing in the private sector (e.g. in-house training) to improve the BTVET system continuously.

- An appropriate approach is required to ensure timely skills development in new skills areas. For instance, the support mix given to economic actors who enter new areas where activities have potential for diversification as well as spillovers and demonstration effects contains a significant HRD category: new capabilities. Proponents of the BTVET system and HRD in Uganda might consider how to proactively help in this entrepreneurial undertaking (and the related training efforts) so as to foster the diversification process, which is vital for both capability building in the initial phase of entry into new activities, and later capability deepening. A systematic approach is needed for this activity of skills building in 'new territories'. Such entrepreneurs need appropriate partners for training, consultation and mentoring.
- In this context, regional cooperation with partner institutions in neighbouring countries could be advanced with a view to the pooling of training resources and competencies. Some examples of regional pooling of training competencies and capacities and joint training initiatives exist already, also as an integrated part of some donor programmes.[397]
- Ensure that the mix of capabilities that trainees can acquire through the BTVET system includes (as appropriate) aspects of productivity, entrepreneurship, management and organisation, business ethics, effective interaction and communication, social skills and attitudes (cooperation, networking, teamwork, trust building), and also capabilities for innovation and self-guided lifelong learning.
- Foster the process of formation of *social capabilities* in the LF (including managers) for enhanced PSD. Improved network and interaction patterns are required in most economic sectors; its formation and impact on economic development in Uganda needs to be understood better. The BTVET and other actors of the ETS need to play a larger role in developing social skills (for trust building, conflict resolution, or negotiation) of the future LF. Include topics such as collective action, trust building, fairness, and morality in entrepreneurship E&T.
- Adapt the services and modes of delivery of the BTVET sector to the needs and situations of its different user groups, with special attention to the living, working, and learning situation of the rural poor and the informal sector. Adapt systems and instruments of training (and BDS provision) suitable for people working in the informal sector. For instance, certain training and consultancy services need to be adjusted (upgraded or downgraded) to the 'new territories and realities'. This includes PSD and HRD in the Northern Region.
- Improve links with the private sector to track the impact of improved BTVET programmes and to support spillover effects of HRD-relevant experiences, knowledge, and skills. Use feedback gathering (strengths and weaknesses of graduates of particular training institutions) as a method to improve (a) interaction with stakeholders and (b) the effectiveness of BTVET. Undertake sector skills audits and analyse how graduates of improved BTVET programmes perform in organisations.
- Strengthen the linkages with other support programmes and establishments, including technology and business SIs, BMOs or training initiatives of development agencies, to enhance synergies, mutual learning, and support. Enhanced cooperation is particularly important in rural areas.
- Establish stronger links vis-à-vis interventions by GOU and donors that foster entrepreneurship dynamics. Higher quality entrepreneurship (with long-term business perspective) is vital to ensure that firms and entrepreneurs display greater concern for skills, training, and HRM than they do at present. This can also strengthen their demand for adequate skills in the labour market.
- The UVQF Secretariat, the BTVET Department of the MOE and other organisations of the BTVET establishment could enhance practices of sharing their work with the general public (including the research and PSD/HRD policy community); for instance, knowledge and information on the work done (approach, experiences, impact, way forward).[398]

---

397 E.g. regional training approaches are applied by UNIDO to develop and deepen industry specific skills in sectors that are vital to several countries in the region. A respective SI from one of the different countries has the responsibility for training coordination and implementation; e.g. UCPC leads a training initiative for the regional fish industry.

398 There was no substantial information or analysis available on the BTVET website: http://www.education.go.ug/btvet.htm. See for instance the compilation of reports available at the website of the MTTI: http://www.mtti.go.ug/reports.php.

- Strengthen efforts for the promotion of vocational training: sections of society have reservations vis-à-vis VET and only see it as the last resort. This points to the need to strengthen the relevance of VET for the LF (especially in semi-urban and rural areas). Raise awareness in the population about working opportunities for graduates with relevant VET; and graduates' experience with their obtained skills set in 'real life', including related changes in income, attitudes, confidence, and social skills.
- Reforms of the ETS need not only enhance the building of functional skills but also work-related ethics, values, attitudes and social skills. The desired mix of ethics and values is not merely an economic but a cultural, social and political question.
- Make transition from BTVET to tertiary level easier so that a significant disincentive for students to opt for BTVET system can be lowered.[399]
- Strengthen linkages between the BTVET system and the health system, including training initiatives (by the state, NGOs, etc.) that are oriented towards issues of health of workers and their families and communities.

From the above, it follows that BTVET proponents and practitioners need to clarify and articulate the position regarding the following questions:

- How do you intend to collaborate and conduct dialogue, in a timely fashion, with the progressive and newly upcoming sectors, e.g. with the exporting firms, or with respective associations which might not be included in current BTVET/MOES circles?
- Some firms operate in dynamic and competitive GVCs and face significant HRD challenges: the HR requirements are often new to the local economy, which some firms master in an exemplary manner. How do you keep track of those developments and various implications for the BTVET system?
- How do you keep track of frontier HRD themes and their implications for the evolution of the ETS (BTVET system)? Such themes include inter-firm management of value chain operations, social capital, business ethics, or productivity.
- How do you improve spillovers from the HRD-relevant experiences and knowledge of these modernising (traditional and new) sectors and firms, so that benefits to other sectors which will have to go through similar processes - e.g. due to their integration into GVCs - can be enhanced, and thus reduced learning costs and rapid movement on the learning curve be achieved?
- How do you respond to and support the diversification dynamics in the economy; the risk-taking entrepreneurs who enter into non-traditional activities? What is the concrete role of and contribution of the BTVET system to the diversification process? How do you proactively respond (e.g. develop training tools, manuals for firm-level in-house training, application of new concepts) to upcoming skills needs and/or firms' efforts to build new skills (say, in cleaner production, value chain organisation, organisational, interactive and learning skills)? How do you ensure identification and integration of new skills sets (e.g. Cleaner Production) into the BTVET?
- How do you position yourself regarding sector-specific initiatives of respective firm and business associations? Do you see a role for actors of the BTVET system in helping to overcome sector-specific collective action issues for advanced HR (in the context of market and institutional failures, e.g. information externalities and coordination failures)? How do you encourage inter-firm cooperation in training?
- How do you learn about HRD practices and issues of those sections of the private sector that are not well presented in institutions such as FUE or UMA? How do you bring them closer to the BTVET and business/technology SIs? How do you collect their feedback on skills sets of trained graduates? How do you help the BMOs or other associations to be more active and effective in HRD?
- How do you channel relevant information from the micro level - from the different corners and frontiers of HRD challenges and efforts - back to the meso and macro levels (the strategy, policy and institution building levels)?

399 See also: "BTVET must be opened for the academic route (no 'dead end')" (Nalumansi et al. 2003, 2).

- How do you strengthen the role of the BTVET system and the various SIs in the local process of creation, transmission and absorption of knowledge for HRD and productivity growth?

Other recommendations for the BTVET sector and beyond

The web of organisations of the BTVET and the SIs that can help firms in their day-to-day upgrading and learning efforts needs a significant boost to accelerate firms' advancements in capabilities, technology use, and productivity.

Support innovation and learning efforts for enhanced upgrading

- Support firms and farms' innovation and learning efforts for enhanced upgrading of products, processes (including technology), organisation and value chains. Constant formal and informal efforts in this regard are central prerequisites for HRD and economic development in Uganda. Making the necessary support available to economic actors requires an adequate local training, learning, and technology support system. Target specific BTVET and BDS needs for the issue areas of VC development (including VC embedded training), clustering, networks, collective action, productivity, and business culture. Develop or improve respective training tools, manuals, and services.
- Ugandan firms will have to *innovate more* in order to advance their productivity. For most of them, innovation will mean to *incorporate* (adopt or imitate) and *master already-existing technology in their production system* (instead of undertaking radical innovation and generating new-to-the-world techniques). This process requires continuous local technological efforts and learning (HR upgrading) and thus needs substantial support from and utilisation of the local LIS (especially technology support system). Respective BTVET trainees need to acquire innovative and learning capabilities; they need the ability to improve products and processes through experimentation, trial and error processes, and joint learning.
- Enhance technological capability formation efforts in processing SMEs. Increased *process/ technical efficiency* of firms (better handling of production inputs and technology) could be a major focus for HRD efforts at firm level, e.g. on-the-job training and learning-by-doing of management, technicians, and workers. Capability-enhancing support interventions can help to increase the technology use, performance and profit level of firms. Savings can be used, among other methods, for improved workers' benefits (pro-poor effect).
- Skills upgrading needs exist for training in relation to aspects of new business models that entrepreneurs wish to implement. In this context, taking business models that have been successfully tested in the Kampala area to other regions in Uganda (including through franchising, for example) can involve significant training aspects. The upcountry BTVET (including business/technology SIs) but also BMOs and their counterparts in Kampala, need to support such processes so as to develop local skills and improve private sector activities in other areas of the country. Also, certain functional, social and interactive skills required in sections of modern industry (e.g. services/hospitality sector) can be deficient among staff in the beginning; hence a special training effort is needed.
- The plans of GOU to build business incubation centres should be followed up: There are vital linkage possibilities and synergies waiting to be explored and captured through partnerships between the BTVET system and incubation centres (as well as firms and institutions that will be operating in upcoming industrial parks).
- Particular attention - incentives and support for training - should be paid to entrepreneurial efforts that (1) try to increase productivity, and (2) target non-traditional activities which are new to the economy and have the potential to instigate new areas of specialisation and create spillover and demonstration effects.
- Given the deficits in skills output of the current BTVET system and the loss of vital HR pre-1986, firms face the challenge of having to undertake a significant further training of staff, including short-term training to build or advance certain skills.[400] Besides finances, this undertaking needs an adequate partner from the BTVET system which can offer the needed training package in a flexible arrangement; this seems to be a problem for some firms, especially in the relatively

400 For example, in a restaurant business: safety/health issues, service orientation, customer behaviour, customer care, kitchen production issues; also to fulfill required industry standards, e.g. occupational health and safety.

new activities/sectors. GOU, the private sector and the BTVET sector need to consider a more adequate response to this situation. Consider, for instance, establishing a (topped up) local skills development fund[401], strengthening respective SIs or engaging trainers/consultants who can help in the training of a particular skills set needed in specific or across sub-sectors (e.g. food, restaurants, tourism). Skills audits might be needed to determine skills needs and preferred modes of training intervention. Foster too the establishment of learning networks and skills pooling among entrepreneurs.

- Follow up on impact of training and R&D incentive package that UIA offers to investors. The particular incentive design might need improvements to better cater for a pro-capability building, pro-diversification and pro-productivity agenda. More awareness building in the private sector on such incentive categories might be required. Moreover, the current threshold level of the investment code seems to exclude many SMEs from related support packages, including incentives for training, innovative activities (R&D) and technology acquisition. Incentives for the purchase of technology and equipment appear to need strengthening as well; this can support both productivity and HRD efforts.
- Explore possibilities of more appropriate financing schemes for support of technology acquisition by MSMEs, and enhance relevant training. Related improvements would be vital to encourage a higher level of HRD efforts by firms, especially in the formation of industrial and technological capabilities.
- Undertake efforts to increase spillovers (know-how etc.) from the presence and practices of progressive firms in the country, including (larger) foreign firms, to other firms and sections of the economy. This can improve capability formation and productivity, especially among MSMEs. Consider boosting spillovers in areas of HR and technology. The FDI inflow can best be used for spillovers in a local context with (increasingly) strong local capabilities as well as competent and responsive SIs for training, technology mastery, and product development. This can bring much-needed improvements in HR and productivity. Related instruments for the creation of spillovers could be: learning networks, or supplier-development programmes. In this respect, link advanced firms with relevant SIs (UIRI, EUg, UCPC, UGT, TEXDA, etc.) and other actors from the LIS and BTVET system. Experts who work in locally-operating foreign firms should be encouraged to train local cadres within the structures of the BTVET and LIS.
- Institutions of the BTVET system need to exploit access to a global pool of knowledge, know-how and information (LLL-strategy) better.

Training for farmers, actors in the informal sector and disadvantaged groups

- Provide more adequate BTVET for both farmers and those economic actors who have moved out of the poverty-laden agricultural sector and face the risk of low performance, business collapse and poverty in a non-agro activity. Adequate training of farmers and farmers' groups is crucial, e.g. to improve prospects of poverty reduction, VCD, exports, agro-processing and environmental protection.
- The training implications of urbanisation and the release of labour from agriculture for development of social (besides functional) skills in non-agro sectors need to be kept in focus accordingly.
- Increase training of women and youth to find employment or start up and run businesses. Support skills training that strengthens the livelihood strategies of (chronically) poor people.
- There appears to be a problem of attracting talented and/or highly skilled local manpower (e.g. with tertiary education) to rural areas: Therefore, engage with and learn from firms (e.g. in agro-processing) and public sector institutions in rural areas that have managed to attract and retain talent through particular HRM methods (e.g. specific career and training plans).
- People with disadvantaged socio-economic backgrounds (in terms of education, socialisation, experience, poverty) might be held back by particular 'deficiencies' in practical, social and emotional skills when they try to enter the advanced formal urban sector. Their trades might therefore need some special focus to enhance their skills and thus increase their chances of

401 EUg and BUDS/PSFU are already operating matching grant principle schemes related to skills development. There is need to target more firms/entrepreneurs, and different skill sets.

getting or retaining jobs.[402] The private sector is unlikely to bear this particular training burden alone, especially if adequate training programmes are not offered by the BTVET system. Consider training programmes that focus on a variety of aspects.

Cooperation with actors abroad

- Accelerate the development of HRD for economic development through North-South and particularly South-South cooperation in areas of know-how, technology transfer, inter-firm cooperation, capabilities, knowledge, and FDI. This could involve foreign firms working in Uganda, local firms using foreign experts, skilled Ugandans working abroad, exchange programmes, or the use of so-called 'integrated experts' hired from abroad with the explicit mandate of know-how transfer and capacity building in both firms and SIs. Integrate the returning entrepreneurs/workers from the Ugandan Diaspora abroad into such initiatives. Exploit knowledge and skills of Ugandans learning or working abroad for upgrading local LIS.[403] Increase local firms' awareness about respective measures.
- Carve out opportunities for study, training, further learning and work in the dynamic Asian economies (especially China and India) as well as cooperation with these countries in matters of technology transfer and inter-firm linkage building. The technological level (intermediate technological level, capital intensity) and respective forms of technological innovations in such economies *can* be more relevant (vis-à-vis highly capital-intensive technology from developed countries) for the Ugandan context of economic, technological and HR development.
- There seems to be increasing interest by some European countries to fund technical assistance of European senior/retired experts in SSA. Consider showing high responsiveness to such initiatives to foster know-how and capability formation in the local economy.

Human Resource Management

- Consider the shortages in the area of HRM at firm and organisational level (micro-level management of competencies and performance at individual, team and organisational level) and their implications for the wider economic and social development agenda of the country.
- Improve HRM capabilities and practices in firms, including MSMEs, e.g. in matters of recruitment, personnel development, performance management, learning environment, organisational development and organisational culture. Improve tools for aspects of HRM training and HRM application in different sectors of the economy. Increase the spillover and demonstration effect of good HRM practices across the economy. Respective approaches (firm-level support and advice, mentoring, handholding) and lessons learnt could be adopted from the work of FUE, UCPC, UGT, UIRI, MCP, or EUg.
- Learning-by-doing processes at the workplace are a vital source of productivity improvements in the production/business processes. They complement more formal training. Improved skills should be systematically encouraged at firm level such that trained employees can make a better performance impact, and find an environment to develop his/her competencies further. Training, both in-house/in firms or in the ETS, needs to enhance competencies of workers and managers that are relevant in engaging in and nurturing the effects of informal learning-by-doing processes. Also, support the private and public sector in the creation of a better learning environment for their personnel at the workplace, so that skills effects of learning-by-doing processes and personal interaction (e.g. teamwork, staff-customer interactions) can be

402 Of course, in this and many other areas of HRD that were discussed in this book, one has to be careful with using words like *weaknesses* or *deficits* because, first, sometimes, these words only hint to an issue but do not give justice to its complexity, and, second, such assessments depend one the (e.g. cultural and analytical) position of the writer or observer, and others might disagree. Further, in the author's view, the intention of the recommended social skills trainings is not to make the trainees more neoliberal selves, but rather to give them (analytical) skills that enhance their ability to read and approach (changing) social situations at their workplace in a confident way. In the same way, some young professionals (e.g. in leadership positions) from relatively rich families might also have socialisation-related weaknesses in social and emotional skills and need training, e.g. regarding perspective-taking and empathy, listening (e.g. to criticism, suggestions), reflecting on and adjusting their behaviour.

403 See illustrative newspaper article in Box 56 (Appendix 33).

nurtured. Learning processes need to be supported by firm level HRM systems. This requires adequate people management competences at different levels of the organisation.

- Enhance the training of managers (and senior staff) of enterprises, especially locally-owned enterprises which tend to display lower productivity performance than the foreign-owned firms. Offer training in organisational issues, process efficiency, teamwork and other salient HRM matters to allow managers and senior staff (heads of departments etc.) to operate firms and capacity at competitive levels. Training in areas of HRM and social capital could be a relevant and realistic start to tackle private sector deficiencies in terms of productivity, performance management, business practices and collective action.
- BTVET actors might consider cooperating with FUE regarding the survey of the EYA. The survey, especially if improved further in future, can serve as an important source of information for the HRD debate and related initiatives. More vigorous expansion of survey coverage to SMEs could be considered.
- The EYA survey efforts could be combined with the search for best/most improved practices of training institutions from the BTVET system. Or, an independent survey and award system could be established. Spillover effects of award systems should be encouraged, including related networks between participating firms.

Casualisation of world-of-work

- Discuss implications of casualisation and informalisation of employment and develop measures to respond to these trends. Reward private sector efforts and investment in employment, capability building and deepening, and HRM. HRD efforts need to take advantage of the fact that the share of wage/salaried jobs, including permanent job arrangements, is notably higher in the urban private sector.
- Address the problem of local cadre development in some businesses that rely overly on imported experts/labour.

On value chains

- Overall, where appropriate and desired, (a) foster inter-firm linkages, cooperation, communication and understanding in the entire VC (between producers, exporters, importers, etc.) thereby fostering VC organisation and operational efficiency, (b) develop long-term-oriented, trust-based, fair and sustainable VCs, (c) address contentious business ethics and practices (deception of business partners, fraud, theft), (d) enhance level of technology use, logistics (cold chains, dryers, irrigation systems), skills and productivity of VC actors and related service provision, (e) support farmers' organisations, and (f) enhance research on VC matters and exchange of information and experiences between various VC actors and VC stakeholders (see also Bear and Goldman 2005, van Bussel 2005). Regarding (c) the work of institutions such as UNBS, local governments, schools, churches, media, or the police is important.
- Public policies, regulations, incentives and support measures need to focus on the promotion of enhanced and sustainable production and trade *systems* and related HR and technology aspects. Where appropriate, they need to be more sensitive to strategies of actors such as lead firms (often larger buyers/exporters who coordinate formal or informal out-grower schemes) and farmer groups. Some lead firms undertake significant investment in the VC and organise and coordinate the inputs and activities of the various VC participants (e.g. farmers), support the latter via training, technology transfer and so on. Farmers' VCD concerns also need to be considered carefully. The agricultural sector (value chains, markets) needs to operate better, more predictably and fairly, for the larger-scale farmers but especially for the many small-scale farmers who often face(d) traders/middlemen whose harsh trading practices are discouraging, demotivating, and impoverishing farmers. Government and other stakeholders should consider how they can complement and enhance inter-actor cooperation in VCs.
- Government and other stakeholders should consider how they can complement and enhance inter-actor cooperation systems in VCs.
- Public regulations and services (e.g. inspections) need to be evaluated and adjusted both in Uganda and abroad in the export destination countries to enhance VCD, for instance to minimise trade risk of outright cheating/ill-treatment in VCs and thus help to build strong relationships, including trust and cooperation in VCs.

- Where possible, improve bargaining power of weaker actors in the chains. Given the status quo, this would generally mean support for Ugandan exporters vis-à-vis foreign buyers, farmers (and their cooperatives) vis-à-vis traders/middlemen, traders vis-à-vis processors, and workers vis-à-vis employers. In certain industries look into protection of interests of Ugandan exporters abroad, especially vis-à-vis importers who (try to) deceive them. Such issues also need industry initiative (or public private partnership). Uganda's advocacy efforts in international trade negotiations could take such issues into account.
- Shield Ugandan firms that try to develop VCs in the long-term and operate on trust-based-relations in VCs, against the negative effects of the actions of firms who cheat farmers or foreign buyers and who free-ride on the developmental efforts (training of farmers, knowledge and technology transfer) of their competitors in the early phase of sector development in a geographical area. Specific codes of conduct for industry might be needed in certain agro-sectors. Effective sector-specific use of quality standards for domestic consumer markets and enhanced consumer awareness and preferences for Ugandan quality products might help to enhance market-pull effects for skills developments in VCs.
- Pay attention to and address where appropriate not only the economic, but also political, social, cultural/institutional, and emotional factors impacting on the relevant structures of and practices in VCD; in other words, the embeddedness of VCs. The nature of embeddedness impacts on both PSD and HRD. GOU and other (cultural, economic, and political, domestic and foreign) actors, including donors, need to consider their roles in the current state (and development consequences) of business culture - including the level of trust, propriety, fairness, justice, dignity, and morality - in the economy and country at large. A trader's particular connection with the political and bureaucratic system might impact on his/her trade practices with farmers. And, of course, the structures and dynamics of the global and regional economy impact on trade practices in Uganda - and thus possibilities for inter-firm learning and cooperation, and development of skills.
- There is a close link between the nature and level of success of state measures, and the level of effectiveness and success of measures of the economic actors and SIs in promoting VCD. Also, state decisions impact on: (i) relationships (including power imbalances) between VC actors and the division of labour in the domestic VC, and thus (ii) the structure of incentives/profits of each actor. GOU could consider its role in terms of VCD, and how it wishes to impact on VCD (as a promoter, mediator, or partner in PPPs) and foster advanced VCs and accumulation of technology and capabilities therein. Other stakeholders, e.g. development agencies and SIs, have to think about similar issues. Note that uncoordinated (or an inappropriate mix of) interventions in VCs from different agencies (including NGOs) can hamper HRD in VCs. See Wiegratz et al. (2007b) for a more detailed discussion of these points.
- Address injustices in the Ugandan economy (in terms of malpractices, payment and working conditions). It remains to be seen if there is political support in Ugandan society (especially among major political and economic actors) to check more vehemently deceitful business practices (e.g. in the agro-sector), or particularly inhumane working conditions (Sender 1999).[404] Indeed, *who* accumulates and *how* (Cramer 2008) in Uganda's economy remains a crucial issue for the country's development prospects, including matters such as HRD.
- *Where appropriate*, training efforts should be embedded within normal business transaction structures between actors along the chain and/or linked to market opportunities. Thus, avoid 'isolated' training, if possible. However, at the same time, the state needs to enhance its direct involvement in the accumulation of capabilities and technology.
- Different players in the chain (farmers, buyers, input suppliers, SIs) can be involved in or consulted about training efforts. This can also enhance cooperation and knowledge spillovers. For instance, consider the assessment of the local and foreign buyer regarding critical success

404 Vogel (1996) discusses that 'progress' under capitalism tends to come with exploitation and other suffering of human beings (human rights violations, attack on human dignity). Sender (1999) makes the point that a softer (restraint, more 'human') capitalism has currently little/no political base in Africa; yet, economic development in a particular country might strengthen classes/groups such as workers who might then pressure for better working conditions. See also Cramer (2007, 2008) on related points.

factors at producer level to prioritise skills areas that need upgrading, e.g. innovation, quality management, logistics, and communication capabilities. The perceptions of a buyer on crucial characteristics of a product/service can differ significantly from those of the actual producer. Such 'misunderstandings' (perception discrepancies), if not addressed, might lead to mistaken views of producers regarding product (and thus skills) characteristics needed to be successful in the market. Consequently, training and upgrading efforts might be ineffective; it does not increase producers' competitiveness in *relevant* areas.

- Support LLL-strategies of Ugandan firms in terms of technology and capability accumulation and enhance related training, learning, and technology support.
- Give foreign buyers of Ugandan agro-products incentives and support to visit local business partners in the country and engage more in the training of business partners (exporters and farmers) but, where appropriate, also in capacity building of respective SIs or students and trainees in the ETS in general. Strengthen relations between the ETS/ILS and foreign and local economic actors who can share their views on VCD matters with students etc. (presentations, public talks, or lectures, small training sessions). Some foreign buyers regularly visit Uganda; however, they don't seem to have been approached by ETS actors of the ETS. The same argument can be made for buyers' involvement, where appropriate, in assessment/design of policies and programmes for PSD and HRD.
- A functioning feedback system between foreign buyers and Ugandan institutions would probably help in tracing GVC dynamics and develop appropriate responses in a timely manner.
- Intensify efforts to identify: (1) areas of cooperation needs and possibilities between Ugandan exporters and foreign buyers; and, (2) how cooperation could be stimulated, where desired and appropriate, by supporting policies and institutions. Further, (3) understand the principles of cooperation dynamics and what they mean for Ugandan firms, and (4) grasp the rationalities, practices and implications (costs, benefits, changes) of cooperation between Ugandan firms and foreign buyers.
- Support VC actors to stay in business for a longer period, so that they not only improve VC operations but also accumulate experiences and capabilities, deepen inter-business relationships and reap cooperation benefits (which tend to arise especially in later phases of trade relationships).
- If training is done without existing business transactions it needs to be designed with a detailed understanding of local/foreign market conditions and VC operations.
- VC tools can help to map out market structures (challenges and opportunities), identify related knowledge and skills requirements and respective gaps on the side of the trainee, and prioritise action needed - according to different markets, buyers and problems (e.g. low inter-actor trust and cooperation). See Riisgaard et al. (2008), Bolwig et al. (2008) and Ponte (2008) on VC-related action research in the context of small-scale producers and poverty.
- Local consultancy services that can assist in the establishment and/or strengthening of domestic VCs need to be developed and improved. VCD-related capacities of development agencies, SIs and policy/regulation setting bodies also need strengthening.
- Training efforts can help producers meet VC requirements. Training can also help improve the governance of domestic VC operations; this is the coordination of the value-adding activities and thus the division of labour and interactions between the actors along the chain. Training can, for instance, enhance VC management and coordination capabilities and thus the operational efficiencies of chains.
- Where appropriate (necessary/desired), focus on improving the trust level between chain players (support towards high-trust VC) so that more long-term-oriented inter-firm relationships (e.g. between farmers and buyers) can be developed. First, this can help to exploit the development benefits of cooperative business relations (collective efficiency, relational rents, joint innovation and learning); and, second, constitute a more appropriate response to the requirements of present-day production and trade in global economy in terms of consistency, uniformity, speed, flexibility, efficiency, reliability, innovativeness, technology or standard compliance.
- VC actors need training for enhanced capabilities, not only in technical, but also non-technical (or 'soft') areas such as capabilities for matters of VC coordination and management,

negotiation, conflict management, networking, trust building and management, coalition building and collective action, organisation, flexibility and willingness to compromise, commitment and reliability, dealing with failures, interpersonal communication, leadership, and cultural sensitivity. Training tools and manuals for firms, farmers, traders and BTVET institutions need to be developed and/or adopted from abroad.

- Trade-related training - especially for new and small exporting firms but also for University students of trade, for example - needs to put more emphasis on the 'soft' side of (export) business. Courses could cover active relationship management (including trust and loyalty enhancement), transparency, and proactive behaviour and communication in a VC setting, and dealing with matters of conflicts, opportunism, power imbalances, as well as control and trust between VC actors. Such trainings can help boost firms' understanding of and performance on the 'soft' side of VC operations. More case study and class discussion-based teaching is needed. Training could involve sessions in which Ugandan entrepreneurs share their experiences and lessons learnt in interacting with foreign buyers and other VC actors or stakeholders, such as technocrats. Training based on experience sharing about soft issues of exporting seem almost non-existent at the moment. This increases the overall learning costs of UFs: in an environment of limited formal/informal sharing of business information and experience (and limited case study reports on such business matters), each new GVC entrant from Uganda basically has to go through the entire learning curve which involves a significant level of costly 'learning by mistake'. Instead, lecturers and learning group participants could, for instance, develop guidelines or self-help-tools for a firm's reflection and action on related topics.
- Regularly monitor *new* skills requirements that arise with participation and upgrading of local firms in (global) value chains and draw implications for the ETS and ILD, e.g. the role of tacit interactive capabilities. Different BTVET actors as well as economic actors themselves need to be involved in this; also actors from the research system. This applies to the next few recommendations too - hence the topics will not be listed again under 'research required'.
- Study HRD efforts of firms and farms operating within advanced (export-oriented) VCs, and HRD-related strategies, benefits, costs, risks and limitations.
- Observe HRD dynamics in cases where the (foreign) VC lead firm transfers activities to the local player at the lower chain end, and understand the HRD implications. Learn about different VC governance forms and their implications for local HRD in GVCs led by Asian (e.g. Chinese or Indian) vs. European firms, for instance.
- Understand in-house and inter-firm learning processes of firms that participate in VCs for domestic and/or foreign markets. In the case of involvement in GVCs, understand how firms undertake forms of LLL-strategies in partnerships with foreign firms. Such an appreciation can enhance strategies of Ugandan firms to better benefit from the global pool of knowledge, know-how, information and technology, or technical assistance measures in GVCs, and lead to increased knowledge of the dynamics of global economy more generally. The BTVET system and the business/technology SIs can develop related training and support measures for local firms' upgrading and LLL-efforts.
- Understand how local affiliates (partners, representatives) of international companies learn and upgrade the skills of their staff within the relationship with the parent company abroad.
- Understand the role of tacit knowledge as well as interactive capabilities, networks, culture, as well as organisational requirements in the context of the increase of *intangible activities*, including *tacit interactions* in VC operations, e.g. complex searching, coordinating, monitoring, problem-solving activities. Improving abilities of Ugandan firms to undertake intangible activities and tacit interactions is vital to gain and sustain competitive advantage. Firms and their managers need to make workers who undertake such activities more effective, boost their productivity and thus the overall firm and VC productivity. Specialised HRM consultancy can help firms manage the organisational aspects of such a competitiveness strategy.
- More efforts are needed to upgrade the skills and practices along VCs in those sectors likely to contribute to Uganda's aims of improving the livelihood of the poor by achieving economic development. The political aim of linking export-led, agro-industry based economic growth and transformation to the nation's poverty reduction strategy has implications for HRD in these sectors. Pro-poor growth will require, among other actions, that the poor sections of producers participate in and benefit from export-led growth and transformation dynamics. In order to do so, their specific skills-development needs and learning situations need to be

taken into account. Further, the relationship between characteristics of concrete production and trade practices and thus of the political economy and business culture in and around specific VCs matters, on one hand, and HRD and poverty reduction, on the other, need to be studied and addressed where desired (see also Ponte 2008).

- Particularly challenging, yet vital, is the skills-upgrading process (and socio-economic changes that would likely come with it) in export-oriented agro VCs, especially in chains that are built around semi-subsistence production and trade practices. Such chains can face problems to meet requirements for advanced markets in terms of coordination, trust and standards (traceability).
- For the case of relations between local traders/processors and farmers, the role of field staff in training and relationship building cannot be overemphasised. Relations between (good) field staff and farmers are valuable to an agro company: field staff are important on the technical front (giving farmers training and advice) and the trust front. Field staff can be creators or destroyers of trust. The issue of field staff (recruitment, retainment, further training, working conditions) and their work with farmers needs sufficient attention and support from the firm's management. The experiences and know-how of field staff in terms of farmers' training is hardly tapped by the ETS. Training and learning networks for field staff need to be enhanced.
- For further exploration of the VC approach in relation to HRD in the Ugandan context: Consider the findings of the BSMD project, the experience of some sectors and firms that have strategically applied the VC approach (flowers etc.), the two VC studies by Wiegratz et al. (2007a, 2007b) as well as the literature presented in this book.

Public awareness, advocacy and (discourse) coalitions for HRD

- HRD proponents need to get more involved in the (policy) debate on PSD, competitiveness and growth. There are related efforts and also successes in this respect, yet overall the HRD-for-PSD agenda remains insufficiently presented in or promoted by the economic policy mainstream. HRD proponents might need to enter the debate on PSD policies more vigorously and build stronger partnerships with those SIs and development agencies that could contribute to the economic policy debate in favour of HRD. Further, partnerships are needed between HRD proponents and those BMOs that face a challenging HRD agenda in the foreseeable future. Overall, there are significant advocacy complementarities and synergies waiting to be nurtured, and experiences to be exchanged. To allow the HRD arguments to gain greater currency, relevant PSD agents from the public and private sector and donor community have to buy into the argument for a significant up-scaling of particular HRD efforts. For that to happen, stakeholders need to recognise the range of respective deficiencies and the importance of tackling them, in the first place.
- Raise public and expert awareness about the crucial role of HRD-for-PSD and the risks involved in neglecting it, e.g. the need for public and private investment in HRD-for-PSD in order to achieve Uganda's development goals.
- Raise public and PSD expert awareness about market and institutional failures as particular challenges for both HRD and technology acquisition in a LDC and catch-up context and the kind of support required. Such arguments are hardly present in the current debate on HRD and PSD. The same holds, though to a lesser extent, for the theme of development of an appropriate LIS, in particular SIs that interact with firms to improve issues at various competitiveness fronts, including HR.
- Point to the link between current policies and incentive regimes for technology and capability upgrading and respective firm-level efforts. Examples of firm and sub-sector-level training and learning are needed to give the HRD theme more weight in the relevant policy circles by showing the authorities *concrete* results, the impact and importance of training and learning efforts for competitiveness, growth and development of firms and sub-sectors. It could also reveal the adverse impacts of related deficiencies in the ETS and business/technology support system.
- It seems generally useful to put together, in brief, write-ups and training examples for the purpose of updating, information sharing, demonstration, learning ('what works', 'lessons learnt'), and collaboration. This can include training interventions by the private sector (supplier development programmes, training by BMOs), the BTVET system, other SIs,

NGOs, GOU, or development agencies. This can help: (a) to spread good practices (especially regarding innovative and vital training forms), and (b) to point to, not only the impact, but also the difficulties of various training efforts in the country and thus give a realistic picture of actual HRD-for-PSD in Uganda. Such overview reports for documentation and analysis could be done every two years.

- The Ugandan surveys of the Global Competitiveness Index have ranked poor work ethics as a top constraint for increased competitiveness. HRD proponents could utilise this finding to introduce, intensify and/or broaden the debate with conventional PSD circles on HRD issues such as industrial relations, working conditions, casualisation of work, business and working culture, and HRM in the Ugandan economy.
- The PEAP and the MTCS have addressed the issue of enterprise competitiveness and pointed to the importance of improving firms' productivity and ability to innovate and adapt to new technologies as well as to respond to demands of markets. Technical skills deficiencies were identified as a main reason for the low productivity levels of firms. These are themes that are strongly linked to training in firms and SIs.
- Develop suggestions on how to strengthen the policies, incentives and institutional support system for local technological efforts, learning, productivity enhancement and capability building of firms (within and beyond the BTVET system reforms). Engage more strongly in the debate on enhancing ethics, norms and values in society (e.g. schools) that are required for a more dynamic but also equitable and just economy. Links to entrepreneurship education, industrial relations issues can be nurtured.
- HRD contributions to the PSD debate need to result in increased actions. HRD experts need to undertake, not only advocacy efforts in policy circles, but also engage with GOU, donors, firms and farms, NGOs etc. on how to translate general commitment for HRD-for-PSD into practice. Foster pro-poor multi-stakeholder partnerships for policy dialogue and action on HRD.
- Finally, debates about the advantages and disadvantages of the economic paradigm(s) applied in Uganda (and actual or likely outcomes) should not be limited to abstract economic statistics (about GDP growth) and modeling (about so-called market efficiencies and price 'mechanisms'), but be extended to other economic, social, cultural and political dimensions of economic development and therefore matters such as principles, norms, values, beliefs and actual practices that underpin the different economic paradigms. Thus, this author recommends to reflect on the (obvious and 'hidden') economic, social, cultural and political implications (including shortcomings) of the neoliberal paradigm which has been applied in the recent past to reengineer Ugandan society and economy.
- Reflect on the normative base of the day-to-day activities and interactions in and the overall structure of the Ugandan economy. Which norms should be given priority, why and to what extent? How much attention is (and should be) given to norms, values and principles that effectively result in social and economic inequality, injustices, economic and social tensions, (chronic) poverty, ownership of economic assets and power in the hands of a few, short term gains at the expense of long term costs and suffering (see e.g. the development of the Lake Victoria commercial fishing industry over the years).

Inter-agency cooperation

- Keep track of established and emerging industry-university linkages and related lessons learnt; see examples of flower sector, UCPC, UGT, SIDA cluster programme, Cisco-MUK). Important impulses for competency profile and module development at the UVQF - and the BTVET system in general - could emerge from these partnerships, especially if other HRD institutions could be involved and information, experiences, ideas, training manuals and tools shared. Potential partners would be UGT, UCPC, UIRI, MCP, TEXDA, APEP, EUg, or UWEAL.
- For instance, the BSMD project on supply chain development brought to light many salient issues for HRD in the agro-sectors, and the economy at large. It would have been vital for BTVET proponents to elaborate with the BSMD team on implications of the programmes' findings and experiences for the ETS and LIS in the country. BSMD experts could have been invited to write a brief paper on these aspects or address certain BTVET stakeholder groups on their pioneering experience and provide insights on supply chain development and business practices and their HRD implications.

- It appears that the BTVET system can also increase cooperation with local and international experts and programme managers that implement HRD-for-PSD-related activities for UNIDO, JICA, EUg, UGT, UIRI, UWEAL, and Horizont3000, for example. Such synergies need to be captured more vividly and channelled to key BTVET stakeholders (issue of knowledge creation and management). In this context, related knowledge could also be shared more widely with the international research and development community.
- Enhance the cooperation level between SIs such as EUg, UCPC, MCPC, UIRI, Horizont3000, TEXDA, and UGT. Many of these SIs are present in upcountry areas. Some of them have already established links to BMOs, the BTVET as well as the university system. Some SIs have yet to strengthen their presence and work in the upcountry areas. There seem to be good prospects for respective synergies and mutual learning - and thus improved training provision - if the actors are aware of, responsive to and supportive of the relevant outreach processes.

Research[405]

- Enhance research efforts in HRD matters in the country and improve the take-up of national and international research results into policy making for BTVET sector reform and HRD-for-PSD. This could involve improved cooperation in and coordination of research efforts, improved access to research findings and regular production of relevant policy inputs based on national and international lessons learnt, best practice case studies, etc.
- Currently, information and knowledge resources that could stimulate the public debate, policy making and programme formulation are underutilised or underdeveloped in certain thematic areas. Improvements in this respect could be of value for a range of stakeholders, including the private sector or the PSD research and policy-making community. One of the government ministries could be committed to upload relevant reports that have a link to HRD in Uganda on its website.
- Enhance cooperation of the public and private sector to research institutes, university departments or development agencies that undertake research in related areas, so as to optimise utilisation of available data and information as well as coordination of research undertakings (knowledge management, synergies).
- Understand, analyse and document learning processes of firms, entrepreneurs, managers, workers, traders, and farmers; especially, against the background of particular conditions of training and learning in a latecomer, catch-up economy. Over the next few years, a series of studies is needed on the following: productivity, capability formation, learning culture, learning systems, HRM, teamwork and cooperative behaviour, personal development processes of firms' staff (including change in attitude, behaviour, and values) and, generally, business culture, including inter-firm cooperation in training and learning. Also, more research on matters of labour market and industrial relations is required. There is need for a better understanding of related dynamics, including their implications for HRD strategies, policies, and programmes.
- Analyse relevant sub-sectors (e.g. textile) regarding the link between the country's liberal trade policies and the development (in firms and the ETS) of indigenous HR for that sub-sector.
- Investigate the nature of tensions (trade-offs) between specific HRD issues and other priorities of the state (e.g. policies for trade, consumer satisfaction, poverty reduction, social welfare), and the private sector.

- Analyse efforts of *local capability development* and *deepening* (the two can be very distinct, e.g. in their dynamics and incentive setting) including the respective role of culture and political economy. Hence, undertake efforts to analyse:
- The different forms of local technological efforts and learning, especially adoption, modification and imitation of existing technology in Ugandan firms and related capability building dimensions (dynamics, risks, benefits, incentives).
- The linkages between skills training in the ETS, HRM practices and performance output in firms (BTVET impact studies).[406]

---

405 Issues grouped under research 'speak', of course, not only to academicians but also policy makers and actors from the ETS and the private and public sector.

406 For instance, to find out if graduates from modular training courses have fulfilled the employment-related skills requirements of firms, research could concentrate on questions such as: How did the

- The process towards a higher level of firm specialisation and related VCD, clustering, and industry collective action and their implications for HRD.
- The impact of levels of trust, networks, cultural and social/cultural norms, values, and practices on inter firm-relationships, e.g. on forms of joint action and thus related HRD categories (level of learning from suppliers, buyers, and market interactions).
- The standard and nature of training undertaken by enterprises to equip 'fresh' graduates from the BTVET system with needed skills; related insights are to be channelled back to the BTVET system.
- The process in which local firms link, leverage and learn (LLL-approach) from foreign partners and related HRD effects such as knowledge and know-how transmission, technology flows, and best practices. Respective implications for firms' strategies, for public policies, the BTVET system, and theLIS.
- The evolution of social skills development in the context of the rise of modern sector activities, for instance in the formal service sector. What did graduates have to learn in this respect? How do they assess the role of the family, traditions, ETS and politics in the context of social skills formation? Feed findings back into ETS and the public debate.
- Learn about the role of the highly talented/skilled workforce in the rural context (capacity building etc.), find out their motivation to contribute to rural development, their learning benefits, and their problems. The findings should be used for related measures, e.g. to support talent recruitment and retaining programmes in rural areas. Advise new (foreign) investors in upcountry areas accordingly.
- Document good practices and problems regarding sector-specific changes in interaction patterns between firms and SIs for learning and training. It might be that efforts, such as changing the curricula, improving teacher's capabilities or upgrading training facilities, are insufficient if the level of interaction between firms and training SIs is not deliberately enhanced (industry-training system). Develop adequate strategies for better industry-BTVET interaction throughout the country.
- Similar themes (learning processes, networks, role of norms and values, collective action) should be analysed in the context of economic activities of poorer groups in the context of the rural informal sector, household enterprises, micro/small firms, agricultural activities, and local learning groups.
- Impacts of women and youth training should be studied; especially in the context of gender disparities and (cultural, social, economic, political) practices that hinder or support the process of knowledge and skills formation among females/the youth. What are the interrelationships between training interventions and existing community or household-level conditions and practices? Does training change cultural practices? If yes, what are the consequences?
- Study the (cultural, social, economic and political) responses of the youth to the employment crisis in the country.

Regarding research on HRD in VCs, we have already highlighted several issues that need follow-up research (see the recommendation sections on value chains in Chapter 10). Below is a furthermore a list of research topics that were suggested in Wiegratz et al. (2007b) for the study of relationships between lead firms (buyers) and farmers in domestic VCs.

- The challenges for lead firms in setting up and enforcing systems of rewards and sanctions for good and poor performance of farmers,
- The relationship between rewards, sanctions and the performance of farmers' groups in the VC,
- The relationship between the lead firm's training and support activities and farmers' loyalty levels,
- The role of lead farmers in matters of training and relationship management between a farmer group and a buyer,

---

improved/new competencies impact on the firms' processes and performance (productivity)? Did the new graduates trigger any spillover effects different from the 'traditional' graduates? Were there differences in technical and behavioural factors?

- The role and 'effectiveness' of all other VC 'governors' including (1) supervisors as links between buyer's management and farmers, (2) consultancy firms, and (3) local government and SIs,
- Effectiveness of different methods for farmers' training and generally for managing interpersonal relationships in domestic VCs,
- Trust links in the DVC: different actors - their role, behaviour and impact regarding distrust as well as high/low trust in different links in the VC,
- The link between a farmers' group's geographical distance from Kampala, its economic options and the nature of relationship between farmers and buyers and related HRD effects,
- The practices and rationale of cheating buyers ('sub-standard buyers'),
- The motivation of non-developmental buyers to only engage in arms-length trade with farmers vs. the different approach of the more developmental-minded buyers who engage in farmers' training, technology transfer, etc.,
- Possibilities of state measures to limit ill-treatment of farmers by certain buyers,
- Problems of farmers' groups to cooperate internally on specific issues,
- The sustainability issue of public support for VCD,
- Experiences of SIs who have engaged in explicit VCD in the past, e.g. NAADS, and
- Details and results of PPPs for VCD between the state, buyers and farmers.

Finally, on the embeddedness and constitution of (concrete/real) markets and actors and aspects of business culture:

- Study concrete and real markets and actors (Carrier 1997, Callon 1998, Watson 2005a, 2005b, Beckert 2007b, Harrison 2005b) and their political, cultural, and social (not merely economic) embeddedness and constitution. Further, investigate the political, cultural, and social preconditions of (functioning, growing, equitable, developmental) markets in the Ugandan context, and link the findings to issues of HRD. What would constitute a more developmental business culture in the Ugandan context? Of course, one has to debate what 'developmental' would mean in the context of Uganda 's development.
- Study the pluralism of 'practical norms' (which tend to be informal, latent, invisible and implicit and therefore different from more accessible, formal social, official, professional norms) that actually shape and govern the behaviour (including motivations, options/constraints, decisions, justifications) of economic, bureaucratic and political actors in a particular context (Olivier de Sardan 2008). Analyse actors' perspectives, and the implications for development issues.
- Study whether 'deficits' in agricultural or business practices are not merely linked to skills 'deficits', but are (in part) expressions of moral sentiments about the local political economy that the actors face (e.g. farmers' dissatisfaction with the organisation, principles, outcomes and legitimacy of neoliberal rural economies. See Thompson (1971, 1980) and Scott (1979, 1985) for related studies in other contexts. See also Bernstein (2007), Carrier (2007) and Sayer (2005) for examples of recent writings on the 'moral economy'. Study also whether criminal and unlawful activities by individuals or groups in the so-called criminal secondary economy are, in some cases, forms of disengagement (evasion/mitigation of, or withdrawal) from relationships of domination (economic/political, state/non-state) which they see as unacceptable and illegitimate (Baker 2000).
- Study trends of moral codes and moral actions (including moral sensitivity, knowledge/reasoning, motivation and character) in specific action contexts in Uganda and analyse the development implications (Nunner-Winkler 2007, Rest et al. 1999). Study how different economic and other actors handle and negotiate the normative tensions (e.g. moral dilemmas, conflicting moral obligations) of living and working in a neoliberal(ising) economy and society, e.g. situations in which there are conflicts between (1) different moral obligations (ensuring survival of a very poor family, refraining from stealing from and harming another person, complying with religious principles that prescribe behaviour), or (2) between moral concerns and other non-moral values and interests (ibid). Study changes in values and norms in the different groups in society (differentiate by e.g. age, gender, education, religion, class, profession, location, family background). Study the moral considerations (e.g. norms) that shape the motivations, decisions and behaviour of economic actors in various contexts.

- Trace the evolution of (rural and urban) business culture (norms, values, attitudes, beliefs, relationships, and, importantly, practices of economic transactions) from the pre-colonial to colonial and post-colonial times. Analyse the political, social, cultural and economic (as well as foreign and domestic) dimensions of the changes in business culture and examine the broader development implications.
- Study the interrelationships between social norms, cultural values, political economy, actors' attitudes/beliefs and economic practices.Study the link between actors' character traits and behaviour.
- Study the impact of external agents (donors, transnational companies, church groups, media) on business culture and other aspects of society in Uganda.
- Study actors (individuals and groups) whose business strategies and practices are in some ways different from the surrounding mainstream business culture, e.g. whose business relationships with other actors are long-term oriented and based on, for instance, fairness, propriety, fellow-feeling and trust. Study also actors who work with strategies based on low-trust/mistrust and deception. Study (groups of) actors who change their business attitudes and strategies, e.g. who try to increase (or lower) the level of trust and honesty in their business transactions. Consider context factors in any of the above investigations.
- Study the developmental consequences of (the history of) economic and social injustices and inequality in the country.
- Study how socio-economic and cultural changes in rural and urban communities and families impact on economic and HR dimensions of development. Study rural-urban differences in (a) knowledge production and distribution, (b) in inter-personal relating, (c) moral action, and (d) business culture. Trace respective spillovers (e.g. in business culture, political economy or moral reasoning) from urban to rural areas and vice versa.
- Study livelihood practices of poor households and their links to HRD matters.

References

Ablo, E. and R. Reinikka (1998) 'Do Budgets Really Matter? Evidence from Public Spending on Education and Health in Uganda', *Policy Research Working Paper*, No. 1926, The World Bank, Washington D.C.

Abramowitz, M. (1986) 'Catching-up, Forging Ahead, and Falling Behind', *Journal of Economic History*, 46, pp. 385-406.

Ahikire, J. (1994) 'Worker Struggles, the Labour Process, and Control in United Garments Industry Limited', in M. Mamdani and J. Oloka-Onyango, eds., *Uganda: Studies in Living Conditions, Popular Movements, and Constitutionalism*, Journal für Entwicklungspolitik, Book Series, Vienna.

Akella, J., J.M. Manyika, and R.P. Roberts (2003) 'What High Tech Can Learn from Slow-Growth Industries', *McKinsey Quarterly*, 2003/04.

Altenburg, T. and C. von Drachenfels (2006) 'The 'New Minimalist Approach' to Private-Sector Development: A Critical Assessment', *Development Policy Review*, 24 (4), pp. 387-411.

Altenburg, T., H. Schmitz, and A. Stamm (2006) 'Building Knowledge-based Competitive Advantages in China and India: Lessons and Consequences for Other Developing Countries', Paper presented at the Workshop 'Asian and Other Drivers of Global Change', Global Development Network Annual Conference, St. Petersburg, 18-19/01/2006.

Amsden, A.H. (1992) *Asia's Next Giant - South Korea and Late Industrialization*, Oxford University Press, New York.

Appleton, S. (2001) 'What Can We Expect from Universal Primary Education?' in R. Reinikka and P. Collier, eds., *Uganda's Recovery: The Role of Farms, Firms, and Government*, The World Bank, Washington D.C., pp. 371-405.

Appleton, S. and S. Ssewanyana (2003) 'Poverty Analysis in Uganda 2002/03', Economic Policy Research Centre (EPRC), mimeo, Kampala.

Asiimwe, G. (2002) *Marketing Systems and Peasant Production in Uganda: A Historical Analysis, 1900-1994*, Shaker Publishing, Maastricht.

Asiimwe, G. and W.K. Nahamya (2006) *A Historical Analysis of Produce Marketing Co-operatives in Uganda: Lessons for the Future*, Network of Ugandan Researchers and Research Users (NURRU), NURRU publications, Kampala.

Asowa-Okwe, C. (1999) 'An Evaluation of Trade Unions and Social Conditions of Industrial Workers in Uganda', Centre for Basic Research (CBR), *CBR Consultancy Report*, CBR, Kampala.

AT Uganda Ltd., CARE International Uganda, CEFORD, SATNET, SNV, VEDCO, World Vision Uganda (2005) Contract Template Field Studies, *Report of the Business Services Market Development (BSMD) Project*, Kampala.

Autio, E. (2005) *Global Entrepreneurship Monitor 2005: Report on High-Expectation Entrepreneurship*, Babson College (US), London Business School (UK) and Global Entrepreneurship Monitor, London.

Bahiigwa, G., D. Rigby, and P. Woodhouse (2005) 'Right Target, Wrong Mechanism? Agricultural Modernization and Poverty Reduction in Uganda', *World Development*, 33 (3), pp. 481-96.

Bair, J., ed. (2009) *Frontiers of Commodity Chain Research*, Stanford University Press, Stanford.

Baker, B. (2000) *Escape from Domination in Africa - Political Disengagement and its Consequences*, James Currey and Africa World Press, Oxford and Trenton.

Bank of Uganda, Uganda Investment Authority, Uganda Bureau of Standards (BOU et al.) (2004) *A Report On Private Sector Investment Survey 2003*, Kampala.

Barkan, J.D. (2005) 'Uganda: An African Success Past Its Prime', in Woodrow Wilson Center, Challenges and Change in Uganda -Proceedings of Presentations Made at a Conference on 'Uganda: An African 'Success' Past its Prime?', 02/06/2005, Washington D.C.

Barkan, J.D., S. Simba Kayunga, N. Ng'ethe, and J. Titsworth (2004) *The Political Economy of Uganda: The Art of Managing a Donor-Financed Neo-Patrimonial State*, Background paper for the World Bank, Washington D.C.

Bartels, F. (2005) 'The Evolving Nature of FDI Industrial Organisation: Challenges for Policy and Practice', *UNIDO Working Paper*, 01/05, UNIDO, Vienna.

Barya, J.-J (2001) 'Trade Unions and the Struggle for Associational Space in Uganda: The 1993 Trade Union Law and Article 40 of the Constitution', *CBR Working Paper*, No. 63, CBR, Kampala.

Bategeka, L., M. Ayoki and A. Mukungu (2004) *Financing Primary Education For All Uganda*, EPRC and Institute of Development Studies, Kampala and Sussex.

Bear, M.A. and R.H. Goldman (2005) *Enhancing Local Sourcing of Fresh Fruit and Vegetables in Uganda's Domestic Market*, BSMD Report, Kampala.

Beardsley, S., B. Johnson, and J. Manyika (2006) 'Competitive Advantage from Better Interactions', *McKinsey Quarterly*, 2006/02.

Becker, K.F. (2004) *The Informal Economy: Fact Finding Study*, Swedish International Development Cooperation Agency (SIDA), Stockholm.

Beckert, J. (2007a) 'The Great Transformation of Embeddedness: Karl Polanyi and the New Economic Sociology', Max Planck Institute for the Study of Societies (MPIfG), Cologne/Germany, *MPIfG Discussion Paper*, Nr. 07/1, Köln: MPIfG.

Beckert, J. (2007b) 'The Social Order of Markets', *MPIfG Discussion Paper*, No. 07/15, Cologne (see also related article in *Theory and Society*, 2009).

Belshaw, D. and P. Lawrence (1999) 'Agricultural Tradables and Economic Recovery in Uganda: The Limitations of Structural Adjustment in Practice', *World Development*, 27 (4), pp. 673-90.

Bennel, P. and Y. Sayed (2002) *Improving the Management and Internal Efficiency of Post-Primary Education and Training in Uganda*, Institute of Development Studies (IDS), University of Sussex, Brighton.

Bernstein, H. (2007) 'Capitalism and Moral Economy: Land qQerty Research Group and Brooks World Poverty Institute, University of Manchester, 2-4/07/2007.

Bernstein, H. and L. Campling (2006a) 'Commodity Studies and Commodity Fetishism I: Trading Down', Review Essay, *Journal of Agrarian Change*, 6 (2), pp. 239-64.

Bernstein, H. and L. Campling (2006b) 'Commodity Studies and Commodity Fetishism II: 'Profits with Principles'?', Review Essay, *Journal of Agrarian Change*, 6 (3), pp. 414-47.

Bevan, D., C. Adam, J. Okidi, and F. Muhumuza (2003) PEAP Revision 2002/03: *Discussion Paper on Economic Growth*, Investment and Export Promotion, Kampala.

Bibagambah, J.R. (1996) *Marketing of Smallholder Crops in Uganda*, Fountain Publishers, Kampala.

Biggs, T., M. Shah, and P. Srivastava (1995), 'Technological Capabilities and Learning in African Enterprises', *World Bank Technical Paper*, No. 288, Washington D.C.

Bird, A. (2003) *Country Case Study 8: Design and Implementation Features of MTEFs and their Links to Poverty Reduction in Uganda*, Overseas Development Institute (ODI), London.

Bird, K. and I. Shinyekwa (2003) 'Multiple Shocks and Downward Mobility: Learning from the Life Histories of Rural Ugandans', Chronic Poverty Research Centre (CPRC), *CPRC Working Paper*, No 36, Institute for Development Policy and Management (IDPM), Manchester.

Blake, A., A. McKay and O. Morrissey (2002) 'The Impact on Uganda of Agricultural Trade Liberalisation', *Journal of Agricultural Economics*, 53 (2), pp. 265-381.

Blundo, G. and J.-P. Olivier de Sardan (eds.), with N.B. Arifari and M.T. Alou (2005) *Everyday Corruption and the State: Citizens and Public Officials in Africa*, Zed Books, London.

Bolwig, S., S. Ponte, A. du Toit, L. Riisgaard, and N. Halberg (2008) 'Integrating Poverty, Gender and Environmental Concerns into Value Chain Analysis: A Conceptual Framework and Lessons for Action Research', Danish Institute for International Studies (DIIS), *DIIS Working Paper*, No. 2008/16, Copenhagen.

Booth, D. and X. Nsabagasani (2005) 'Poverty Monitoring Systems - An Analysis of Institutional Arrangements in Uganda', *ODI Working Paper*, No. 246, London.

Bourdieu, P. (1984) 'The Forms of Capital', in J.G. Richardson, ed., *Handbook of Theory and Research for the Sociology of Education*, Greenwood Press, New York, pp. 241-58.

Brett, E.A. (1993) *Providing for the Rural Poor - Institutional Decay and Transformation in Uganda,* Fountain Publishers, Kampala.

British Broadcasting Corporation (BBC) (2006) 'Fishy feet smell sweet in Uganda', BBC news online, 03/05/2005, http://news.bbc.co.uk/2/hi/africa/4965018.stm.

Brock, K., R. McGee, and J. Gaventa, eds. (2004) *Unpacking Policy: Knowledge, Actors and Spaces in Poverty Reduction in Uganda and Nigeria,* Fountain Publishers, Kampala.

Brock, K., R. McGee, R.A. Okech, J. Ssuuna (2003) 'Poverty Knowledge and Policy Processes in Uganda: Case Studies from Bushenyi, Lira and Tororo Districts', *IDS Research Report 54,* Brighton.

Brock, K., R. McGee, and R. Ssewakiryanga (2002) 'Poverty Knowledge and Policy Processes: A Case Study of Ugandan National Poverty Reduction Policy', *IDS Research Report 53,* Brighton.

Brown, S., R. Lamming, J. Bessant, and P. Jones (2000) *Strategic Operations Management,* Butterworth Heinemann, Oxford.

Bunker, S.G. (1991) *Peasants Against the State: The Politics of Market Control in Bugisu, Uganda, 1900-1983,* University of Chicago Press, Chicago.

Bush, R. (2007) *Poverty and Neoliberalism: Persistence and Reproduction in the Global South,* Pluto Press, London.

Business Services Market Development (BSMD) (2005) *Agro Trading Principles and Agro Contracts: Guidelines, Contract Template,* BSMD Report, Kampala.

Byaruhanga, J. (2005a) *Transformation of Micro-Finance Schemes from Subsistence Living to Small-Scale Enterprises in Uganda: Analysis of Policies for Integration of Science and Technology into the Clients' Activities*: Policy Paper for Uganda, Report for UNESCO, Kampala.

Byaruhanga, J. (2005b) *Research Summary Report: Impact of Existing Policy Environment on the Technological Capability of Micro and Small Scale Enterprises,* Report for UNESCO, Kampala.

Callon, M., ed. (1998) *The Laws of the Markets,* Blackwell, Oxford.

Cammack, P. (2006) 'The Politics of Global Competitiveness', *Papers in the Politics of Global Competitiveness,* No. 1, Institute for Global Studies, Manchester Metropolitan University.

Carrier, J.G. (2005) 'Making Rough Places Plane: Moralities and Economies in Environmental Conservation in Jamaica', Paper for Conference on 'Moral Economy', Lancaster University, 25-27/08/2005.

Carrier, J.G., ed. (1997) *Meanings of the Market - The Free Market in Western Culture,* Berg Publishers, Oxford.

Carswell, G. (2007) *Cultivating Success in Uganda: Kigezi Farmers and Colonial Policies,* Fountain Publishers, Kampala.

Chang, H.-J. (2002) *Kicking Away the Ladder: Development Strategies in Historical Perspective,* Anthem Press, London.

Chen, M. (2004) 'Informality at Work: Re-Conceptualizing the Employment Challenge', Paper presented at the 50th Anniversary Conference Reviewing the First Decade of Development and Democracy in South Africa, Durban, South Africa, 21-23/10/2004.

Chronic Poverty Research Centre Uganda (2005) *Chronic Poverty in Uganda - the Policy Challenges,* Summary, CPRC-Uganda, Kampala.

Citigroup (2006) Uganda: *Attractive Rates with Election Behind Risk, Fixed Income Quantitative Strategy - Emerging Market Strategy.*

Collier, P. and A. Hoeffler (2002) 'Aid, Policy, and Growth in Post-Conflict Societies', *Policy Research Working Paper,* No. 2902, World Bank, Washington D.C.

Collier, P. and R. Reinikka (2001) 'Beyond Recovery', in R. Reinikka and P. Collier, eds., *Uganda's Recovery: The Role of Farms, Firms, and Government,* The World Bank, Washington D.C., pp. 453-60.

Competitiveness and Investment Climate Strategy (CICS) Secretariat (2008) 'Measuring Competitiveness: The Global Competitiveness Survey', *CICS Policy Brief,* No. 08/06, http://www.cics.go.ug/docs/CICS_policy_brief_on_Competitiveness_Dec_08.pdf (accessed 29/12/2008).

Cramer, C. (2008) 'Trajectories of Accumulation - Through War and Peace', Paper for the Heterodox Economics Seminar (CES-Matisse, University of Paris 1) & International Initiative for Promoting Political Economy (IIPPE), 19/02/2008, http://matisse.univ-paris1.fr/fr/IMG/pdf/CramerTrajectories.pdf (accessed: 27/08/2008).

Cramer, C. (2007) *Violence in Developing Countries: War, Memory, Progress,* Indiana University Press, Bloomington.

Daily Monitor (2009) 'NAADS a waste of money - report', 16/02/2009.
Daily Monitor (2007) 'NAADS: Transforming lives through partnerships', 18/05/2007.
Daviron, B. and P. Gibbon (2002) 'Global Commodity Chains and African Export Agriculture', *Journal of Agrarian Change*, 2 (2), pp. 137-61.
Daviron, B. and S. Ponte (2005) *The Coffee Paradox: Commodity Trade and the Elusive Promise of Development*, Zed Books, London.
Deyo, C., R.F. Doner, and E. Hershberg, eds. (2001) *Economic Governance and the Challenge of Flexibility in East Asia*, Rowman and Littlefield Publishers, Lanham.
Deininger, K., G. Kempaka, and A. Crommelynck (2002) 'Long-term Welfare and Investment Impact of AIDS - Related Changes in Family Composition: Evidence from Uganda', *EPRC Research Series*, Kampala.
Deininger, K. and J. Okidi (2001) 'Rural households: Incomes, Productivity, and Nonfarm Enterprises', in R. Reinikka and P. Collier, eds., *Uganda's Recovery: The Role of Farms, Firms, and Government*, The World Bank, Washington D.C., pp. 123-75.
Development Partner (2003) Consultative Group Meeting, Kampala, April 2003, www.u4.no/document/showdoc.cfm?id=51 (accessed 01/03/2006).
Dijkstra, A.G. and J.K. van Donge (2001) 'What Does the 'Show Case' Show? Evidence of and Lessons from Adjustment in Uganda', *World Development*, 29 (5), pp. 841-63.
Directorate for Ethics and Integrity (DEI) (2004a) *National Strategy to Fight Corruption and Rebuild Ethics and Integrity in Public Office 2004-2007*, Kampala.
Directorate for Ethics and Integrity (2004b) *Anti Corruption Progress Report on Government's Strategy and Plan of Action to Fight Corruption and Rebuild Ethics and Integrity*: May 2001-October 2004, Kampala.
DiMaggio, P. (1988) 'Interest and Agency in Institutional Theory', in L. Zucker, ed., *Institutional Patterns and Organizations: Culture and Environment*, Ballinger, Cambridge (MA), pp. 3-21.
Docquier, F. and A. Marfouk (2006) 'International Migration by Education Attainment, 1990-2000', in C. Özden and M. Schiff, eds., *International Migration, Remittance and the Brain Drain*, World Bank and Palgrave Macmillan, Washington D.C., pp. 151-99.
Dolan, Ch. (2009) *Social Torture: The Case of Northern Uganda, 1986-2006*, Berghan Books, Oxford.
Dolan, Ch. (2007) Uganda Strategic Conflict Analysis, SIDA, Stockholm.
Dolan, C. (2004) 'On Farm and Packhouse: Employment at the Bottom of a Global Commodity Chair', *Rural Sociology*, 69 (1), pp. 99-126.
Dolan, C. and J. Humphrey (2004) 'Changing Governance Patterns in the Trade in Fresh Vegetables between Africa and the United Kingdom', *Environment and Planning*, 36 (3), pp. 491-509.
Dolan, C. and J. Humphrey (2000) 'Governance and Trade in Fresh Vegetables: The Impact of UK Supermarkets on the African Horticulture Industry', *Journal of Development Studies*, 37(2), pp. 147-76.
Dorgan, S., J. Dowdy, and T. Rippin (2006) 'The Link between Management and Productivity', McKinsey research article, February 2006, http://www.mckinseyquarterly.com/ article_page.aspx?ar=1725&L2=1&L3=24 (accessed 04/04/2006).
Dunn, D. (2002) 'Economic Growth in Uganda: A Summary of the Post-Conflict Experience and Future Prospects', IMF Mimeo, Washington D.C.
Durlauf, S.N. (2002) 'Symposium on Social Capital: Introduction', *Economic Journal*, 112 (November), F417-F418.
Durlauf, S.N. and M. Fafchamps (2004) 'Social Capital', in S. Durlauf and P. Aghion, eds., *Handbook of Economic Growth*, http://www.economics.ox.ac.uk/members/marcel.fafchamps/homepage/soccaphandbook.pdf (accessed 05.07.2006).
East African Business Week (2006) 'Rwanda to make mobiles', *East African Business Week*, 2 (2).
Economic Policy Research Centre (2009) Agriculture Sector Public Expenditure Review, Phase Three: Efficiency and Effectiveness of Agricultural Expenditures, Draft, Kampala.
Ellis, A., C. Manual, and C.M. Blackden (2006) *Gender and Economic Growth in Uganda: Unleashing the Power of Women*, World Bank, Washington D.C.
Ellis, F. and G. Bahiigwa (2003) 'Livelihoods and Rural Poverty Reduction in Uganda', *World Development*, 31 (6), pp. 997-1013.

Erdmann, G. and U. Engel (2006) 'Neopatrimonialism Revisited: Beyond a Catch-All Concept', German Institute of Global and Area Studies (GIGA), *GIGA Working Paper*, No. 16, GIGA, Hamburg.

Ernst, D., T. Ganiatsos, and L. Mytelka, eds. (1998) *Technological Capabilities and Export Success - Lessons from East Asia*, Routledge Press, London.

Esser, K., W. Hillebrand, D. Messner and J. Meyer-Stamer (1996) 'Systemic competitiveness: A New Challenge for Firms and Government', *CEPAL Review*, No. 59, pp. 39-53.

European Union and Government of Uganda (2003) *Meeting MSE Training Needs: An Assessment of the Demand for and Supply of Business Management and Skill Training among Micro- and Small Enterprises in Uganda: A Case Study from Kampala, Mpigi and Wakiso District*, Kampala.

Fafchamps, M. (2002) 'Social Capital and Development', University of Oxford, Department of Economics, *Economics Series Working Papers*, No. 214.

Fan, S., X. Zhang, and N. Rao (2004) 'Public Expenditure, Growth and Poverty Reduction in Rural Uganda', International Food Policy Research Institute, Development Strategy and Governance Division, *DSGD Discussion Paper*, No. 4, Washington D.C.

Federation of Uganda Employers (FUE) (2005a) Employer of the Year Award 2004: Survey Report, produced by Ernst&Young, Kampala.

Federation of Uganda Employers (2005b) *Terms and Conditions of Service Report 2005*, Kampala

Federation of Uganda Employers (2003) Employer of the Year Award 2002: Survey Report, produced by PILA (Partners in Learning and Action) Consultants, Kampala.

Ferguson, J. (1999) *Expectations of Modernity: Myths and Meanings of Urban Life on the Zambian Copperbelt*, University of California Press, Berkeley and Los Angeles.

Ferranti, D. de, G.E. Perry, D. Lederman, and V.E. Maloney (2002) 'From Natural Resources to the Knowledge Economy: Trade and Job Quality', World Bank, Latin American and Caribbean Studies, *Viewpoints*, Washington D.C.

Financial Times (2006) 'FT Interview: President Thabo Mbeki', *Financial Times*, 24/05/2006, http://news.ft.com.

Fine, B. (2003) 'Social Capital for Africa?', *Transformation*, 53, pp. 29-52.

Fine, B. (2002) 'It Ain't Social, It Ain't Capital and It Ain't Africa', *Studia Africana*, 13, pp. 18-33.

Fine, B. (2001) *Social Capital versus Social Theory: Political Economy and Social Science at the Turn of the Millennium*, Routledge, London.

Finnström, S. (2008) *Living with Bad Surroundings: War, History, and Everyday Moments in Northern Uganda*, Duke University Press, Durham.

Flanary, R. and D. Watt (1999) 'The state of corruption: a case study of Uganda', *Third World Quarterly*, 20 (3), pp. 515-36.

Fligstein, N. (2001a) *The Architecture of Markets: An Economic Sociology of Capitalist Societies*, Princeton University Press, Princeton.

Fligstein, N. (2001b) 'Social Skill and the Theory of Fields', *Sociological Theory*, 19, pp. 105-25.

Fold, N. (2002) 'Lead Firms and Competition in 'Bi-polar' Commodity Chains: Grinders and Branders in the Global Cocoa-Chocolate Industry', *Journal of Agrarian Change*, 2 (2), pp. 228-47.

Fold, N. and M. Nylandsted Larsen, eds. (2008) *Globalization and Restructuring of African Commodity Flows*, Nordic Africa Institute, Uppsala.

Foreign Investment Advisory Service (FIAS) (2003) *Uganda: Administrative Barriers to Investment*, Washington D.C.

Foster, M. and P. Mijumbi (2002) 'How, When and Why does Poverty get Priority? Poverty Reduction Strategy and Public Expenditure in Uganda', *ODI Working Paper*, No. 163, London.

Foucault, M. (1991) 'Governmentality', in G. Burchell, C. Gordon, and P. Miller, eds., *The Foucault Effect: Studies in Governmentality*, Harvester Wheatsheaf, Hemel Hempstead, pp. 87-104.

Francis, P. and R. James (2003) 'Balancing Rural Poverty Reduction and Citizen Participation: the Contradictions of Uganda's Decentralization Programme', *World Development*, 31 (2), pp. 325-37.

Franklin, J., ed. (2004) *Politics, Trust and Networks: Social Capital in Critical Perspective*, London South Bank University, London.

Fukunishi, T., M. Murayama, T. Yamagata, and A. Nishiura (2006) *Industrialization and Poverty Alleviation: Pro-Poor Industrialization Strategies Revisited*, UNIDO, Vienna.

Fukuyama, F. (2003) 'Still Disenchanted? The Modernity of Postindustrial Capitalism', Cornell University, Center for the Study of Economy and Society (CSES), *Working Paper Series*, No. 3 Ithaca.

Gauthier, B. (2001) 'Productivity and Exports', in R. Reinikka and P. Collier, eds., *Uganda's Recovery: The Role of Farms, Firms, and Government*, The World Bank, Washington D.C., pp. 235-67.
Gereffi, G. (2005) 'The Global Economy: Organization, Governance, and Development', in N.J. Smelser and R. Swedberg, eds., *The Handbook of Economic Sociology*, 2nd ed., Princeton University Press and Russell Sage Foundation, Princeton, NJ, pp. 160-82, http://www.soc.duke.edu/~ggere/web/Global_Economy_chapter_Handbook_2005.pdf (accessed 10/03/2006).
Gereffi, G. (2001) 'Shifting Governance Structures in Global Commodity Chains, with Special Reference to the Internet', *American Behavioral Scientist*, 44 (10), pp. 1616-37.
Gereffi, G. (1999) 'International Trade and Industrial Upgrading in the Apparel Commodity Chain', *Journal of International Economics*, 48, pp. 37-70.
Gereffi, G. (1994) 'The Organization of Buyer-Driven Global Commodity Chains: How US Retailers Shape Overseas Production Networks', in G. Gereffi and M. Korzeniewicz, eds., *Commodity Chains and Global Capitalism*, Praeger, Westport, pp. 95-122.
Gereffi, G., J. Humphrey and T. Sturgeon (2005) 'The Governance of Global Value Chains', *Review of International Political Economy*, 12 (1), pp. 78-104.
Gereffi, G. and T. Sturgeon (2004) 'Globalization, Employment, and Economic Development: A Briefing Paper', Sloan Workshop Series in Industry Studies, Rockport, Mass., 14-16/06/2004, see also, Massachusetts Institute of Technology (MIT), Industrial Performance Center (IPC), *MIT IPE Working Paper*, No. 04-007.
Gereffi, G. and O. Memedovic (2003) *The Global Apparel Value Chain: What Prospects for Upgrading by Developing Countries*, UNIDO, Vienna.
German Technical Cooperation (GTZ) (2006) *PEVOT Progress Report*, Kampala.
German Technical Cooperation (2005a) Labour Market Information System Report in Uganda, Kampala.
German Technical Cooperation (2005b) 'Trying to be useless! The German butcher, Karl Reindl, was placed by CIM to train his own successor', *Newsletter: The GTZ in Uganda*, April 2005, article prepared by A. Penny.
German Technical Cooperation (2005c) 'Sparking Innovation', *Newsletter: The GTZ in Uganda*, October 2005, article prepared by A. Penny.
German Technical Cooperation (2005d) 'The Contribution of Vocational Education to Pro-Poor Growth', Memo, Eschborn.
Gibb, A. (1988) 'Towards the Building of Entrepreneurial Models of Support for Small Business', Durham University Business School, *Occasional Paper*, No. 9046.
Gibbon, P. (2006) 'An Overview of the Certified Organic Export Sector in Uganda', *DIIS Working Paper*, No. 2006/13, Copenhagen.
Gibbon, P. (2004) 'Value-Chain Governance, Public Regulation and Entry Barriers in the Global Fresh Fruit and Vegetable Chain into the EU', in S. Maxwell and R. Slater, eds., *Food Policy Old and New*, Blackwell, Oxford, pp. 71-80.
Gibbon, P. (2003) 'Value-chain Governance, Public Regulation and Entry Barriers in the Global Fresh Fruit and Vegetable Chain into the EU', *Development Policy Review*, 21 (5-6), pp. 615-25.
Gibbon, P. and S. Ponte (2005) *Trading Down: Africa, Value Chains, and the Global Economy*, Temple, Philadelphia.
Gichure, C.W. (2006) 'Africa, Business Ethics', in P. Werhane and R.E. Freeman, eds., *The Blackwell Encyclopedia of Management - Volume 2: Business Ethics*, 2nd ed., Blackwell Publishing, Oxford.
Giddens, A. (1990) *The Consequences of Modernity*, Stanford University Press, Stanford.
Goldstein, A., N. Pinaud, H. Reisen, and X. Chen (2006) *China and India: What's in it for Africa?*, OECD, Paris.
Government of Uganda (GOU) (2009) President Yoweri Museveni's State of the Nation's Address on New Year's Day, printed in *New Vision*, 02/01/2009.
Government of Uganda (2008a) 'President directs on NAADS funds', 21/3/2008, http://www.statehouse.go.ug/news.php?catId=1&item=183 (11/10/2008).
Government of Uganda (2008b) Speech of President Yoweri Museveni on the 46th Independence Anniversary, 09/10/2008, printed in *New Vision*, 10/10/2008.
Government of Uganda (2006) Budget Speech, Financial Year 2006/07, Theme: Enhancing Economic Growth and Household Incomes through Increased Production and Productivity, delivered at the meeting of the first session of the 8th Parliament of Uganda, 15/06/2006, by Dr. E. Suruma, Minister of Finance, Planning and Economic Development.

Government of Uganda (2004a) 'Increasing Incomes through Exports: A Plan for Zonal Agricultural Production, Agro-processing and Marketing', Executive Summary, Kampala.

Government of Uganda (2004b) *Increasing Incomes through Exports: A Plan for Zonal Agricultural Production, Agro-processing and Marketing*, Kampala.

Government of Uganda (2003a) *Strategies to Promote Economic Growth*, Progress Report, Kampala.

Government of Uganda (2003b) *Government Interventions to Promote the Production, Processing and Marketing of Selected Strategic Exports*, Progress Report (September 2001-March 2003), Ministry of Agriculture, Animal Industry and Fisheries, Ministry of Finance, Planning and Economic Development, Ministry of Trade, Tourism and Industry, Kampala.

Government of Uganda (1992) *Government White Paper on the Education Policy: Review Commission Report*, Kampala.

Granovetter, M. (1985) 'Economic Action and Social Structure: The Problem of Embeddedness', *American Journal of Sociology*, 91, pp. 481-510.

Green, R. (1981) 'Magendo in the Political Economy of Uganda: Pathology, Parallel System or Dominant Sub-Mode of Production?', *IDS Discussion Paper*, No. 64, Sussex.

Grierson, J. (2002) 'Enterprise-based Training in Africa: Case Studies from Kenya and Zambia', International Training Centre of the ILO, *Occasional Papers*, Turin.

Hale, A. and M. Opondo (2005) 'Humanising the Cut Flower Chain: Confronting the Realities of Flower Production for Workers in Kenya', *Antipode*, 37 (2), pp. 301-23.

Hansen, H.B. and M. Twaddle, eds. (1998) *Developing Uganda*, James Currey, Oxford.

Hansen, H.B. and M. Twaddle, eds. (1991) *Changing Uganda: The Dilemmas of Structural Adjustment and Revolutionary Change*, James Currey, London.

Hansen, H.B. and M. Twaddle, eds. (1988) *Uganda Now: Between Decay and Development*, James Currey, London.

Harriss, J. (1997) "Missing Link" or Analytically Missing?: The Concept of Social Capital', *Journal of International Development*, 9(7). 9, pp. 919-37.

Harrison, G. (2005a) 'The World Bank, Governance and Theories of Political Action in Africa', *British Journal of Politics and International Relations*, 7 (2), pp. pp. 240-60.

Harrison, G. (2005b) 'Economic Faith, Social Project, and a Misreading of African Society: the Travails of Neoliberalism in Africa', *Third World Quarterly*, 26 (8), pp. 1303-20.

Harrison, G. (2005c) *The World Bank and Africa: the Construction of Governance States*, Routledge, London.

Hasunira, R. (2004) *Factors Influencing Investment in Research and Development (R&D) in Selected Manufacturing Firms in Uganda*, MA Dissertation, submitted to Makerere University, Faculty of Economics and Management, Kampala.

Hay, C. and D. Wincott (1998) 'Structure, Agency and Historical Institutionalism', *Political Studies*, 46 (5), pp. 951-57.

Henderson, K. (2005) 'The Uganda Floriculture Industry: Past, Present and Future', PP-Presentation, http://www.psfuganda.org /docs/FLOWER INDUSTRY.ppt (accessed 20/04/2006).

Henson, S. and W. Mitullah (2004) 'Kenyan Exports of Nile Perch: The Impact of Food Safety Standards on an Export-Oriented Supply Chain', *World Bank Policy Research Working Paper*, No. 3349, World Bank, Washington D.C.

Hess, M. (2008) 'Governance, Value Chains and Networks: An Afterword', *Economy and Society*, 37(3), pp. 452-59.

Hickey, S. (2005) 'The Politics of Staying Poor: Exploring the Political Space for Poverty Reduction in Uganda', *World Development*, 33 (6), pp. 995-1009.

Hickey, S. (2003) 'The Politics of Staying Poor in Uganda', *CPRC Working Paper*, No. 37, IDPM, Manchester.

Holmgren, T., L. Kasekende, M. Atingi-Ego and D. Ddamulira (2001), *Aid and Reform in Uganda*, World Bank, Washington D.C.

Humphrey, J. (2005) *Shaping Value Chains for Development: Global Value Chains in Agribusiness*, GTZ, Eschborn.

Humphrey, J. (2004) 'Upgrading in Global Value Chains', World Commission on the Social Dimension of Globalization, *Working Paper*, No. 28, Geneva.

Humphrey, J. and H. Schmitz (2002) 'Developing Country Firms in the World Economy: Governance and Upgrading in Global Value Chains', Institute for Development and Peace (INEF), *INEF Report*, No. 61, Duisburg.

Humphrey, J. and H. Schmitz (2000) 'Governance and Upgrading: Linking Industrial Cluster and Global Value Chain Research', *IDS Working* Paper, No. 120, Brighton.

Humphrey, J. and H. Schmitz (1998) 'Trust and Inter-Firm Relations in Developing and Transition Economies', *Journal of Development Studies*, 34 (4), pp. 32-61.

Ijsselmuiden, C. (2006) 'Reversing brain drain can be easy: If research institutions start to reward talent and enthusiasm, not seniority', *Sunday Monitor*, 25/06/2006.

Inspectorate General of Government (IGG) (2008) Third National Integrity Survey, Kampala.

Inspectorate of Government (2004) Report to Parliament, July-December 2004, Kampala.

Inspectorate General of Government (2003) Second National Integrity Survey, Kampala.

International Alert (2008) 'Building a Peace Economy in Northern Uganda - Conflict-sensitive Approaches to Recovery and Growth', *Investing in Peace*, Issue No. 1, author: J. Banfield.

International Alert (2006) *Mobilising the Ugandan Business Community for Peace - Scoping Study: Summary Report*, Report for the Embassy of Sweden in Uganda, author: J. Banfield.

International Monetary Fund (IMF) (2006) Uganda: Ex Post Assessment of Performance under Fund-Supported Programs and Public Information Notice on the Executive Board Discussion, Washington D.C.

International Monetary Fund (2005) Uganda Selected Issues and Statistical Appendix, Washington D.C.

International Food Policy Research Institute (2004) 'Strategies for Sustainable Land Management and Poverty Reduction in Uganda', *Research Report*, No. 133.

Isaksson, A. (2005) UNIDO Productivity Database Version 2.0, UNIDO, Vienna.

Isaksson, A., T.H. Ng, and G. Robyn (2005) *Productivity in Developing Countries: Trends and Policies*, UNIDO, Vienna.

Jackson, T. (2004) *Management and Change in Africa: A Cross-Cultural Perspective*, Routledge, London.

Jackson, T. (2003) 'Management and Change in Africa: A Cross-Cultural Perspective, Key Results', http://www.africamanagement.org/Resources/KeyResults.pdf (accessed 01/03/2006).

Jamal, V. (1998) 'Changing Poverty Patterns in Uganda', in H.B. Hansen and M. Twaddle, eds., *Developing Uganda*, James Currey, Oxford.

Jamal, V. (1991) 'The Agrarian Context of the Ugandan Crisis', in H.B. Hansen and M. Twaddle, eds., *Changing Uganda: The Dilemmas of Structural Adjustment and Revolutionary Change*, James Currey, London.

J.E. Austin Associates, Inc. and UMACIS (2004) *Skills Enhancement for Enterprise Productivity and Export Competitiveness, Uganda: Second Private Sector Competitiveness Study*, Kampala.

Johnson, B., J. Manyika and L. Yee (2005) 'The Next Revolution in Interactions: Successful Efforts to Exploit the Growing Importance of Complex Interactions Could Well Generate Durable Competitive Advantages', *McKinsey Quarterly*, 2005/04.

Kabwegyere, T.B. (1995) *The Politics of State Formation and Destruction in Uganda*, Fountain Publishers, Kampala.

Kakembo, F. (2003) 'The Education Challenge in the Industrialization of Uganda', Paper presented at the International Conference on Industrialization in Uganda, Kampala, 14-16/08/2003.

Kanyandago, P. (2003) 'Rejection of the African Humanity: Search for Cultural Reappropriation', in M. Falaiye, ed., *African Spirit and Black Nationalism: A Discourse in African American Studies*, Foresight Press, Lagos, pp. 30-50.

Kanyandago, P. (2000) 'From Scarcity to Abundance: Reflections on Using African Values to Combat Fraud', *Business Ethics - A European Review*, 9 (4), pp. 248-58.

Kanyandago, P. (1999) 'A New Role for the Church in the Fight against Fraud', in G.J. Rossouw and D. Carabine, eds., *Fraud and the African Renaissance*, Uganda Martyrs University Press, Nkozi, pp. 109-26.

Kanyandago, P. (1994) 'Violence in Africa: Pastoral Response from a Historical Perspective', in D.W. Waruta and H.W. Kinoti, eds., *Pastoral Care in African Christianity*, Acton Publishers, Nairobi.

Kaplinsky, R. (2006) 'Revisiting the Revisited Terms of Trade: Will China Make a Difference?', *World Development*, 34 (6), pp. 981-995.

Kaplinsky, R. (2005a) 'China, Globalisation and Neo-liberal Dogma', Paper for the Queen Elizabeth House (QEH) 50th Anniversary Conference, Oxford, UK, 04-06/07/2005.

Kaplinsky, R. (2005b) 'The Sun Rises in the East', Commission for Africa - Report Response, http://www.commissionforafrica.org/english/report/reactions/08-04-05_rr_ids_raphie_kaplinsky.pdf (accessed 01/04/2006).

Kaplinsky, R. (2004) 'How Does It All Add Up? Caught Between a Rock and a Hard Place', Sloan Workshop Series in Industry Studies, Rockport, Massachusetts, 14-16/06/2004.

Kaplinsky, R. (2000) 'Spreading the Gains from Globalization: What Can Be Learned from Value Chain Analysis?', *IDS Working Paper*, No. 110, IDS, Brighton, UK.

Kaplinsky, R., D. McCormick, and M. Morris (2006) 'The Impact of China on Sub-Saharan Africa', Asian Drivers Research Programme, IDS, Brighton.

Kaplinsky R. and M. Morris (2008) 'Do the Asian Drivers Undermine Export-oriented Industrialization in SSA?', *World Development*, 36(2), pp. 254-73.

Kaplinsky, R. and M. Morris (2006a) 'Dangling by a Thread: How Sharp Are the Chinese Scissors?', Asian Drivers Research Programme, IDS, Brighton.

Kaplinsky, R. and M. Morris (2006b) 'The Asian Drivers and SSA; MFA Quota Removal and the Portents for African Industrialization?', Paper presented at the Workshop 'Asian and other Drivers of Global Change', Global Development Network Annual Conference, St. Petersburg, 18-19/01/2006.

Kaplinsky, R. and M. Morris (2003) 'Governance Matters in Value Chains', *Developing Alternatives*, 9 (1), pp. 11-18.

Kaplinsky, R. and M. Morris (2001) *A Handbook for Value Chain Research*, International Development Research Centre (IDRC), Ottawa.

Kaplinsky, R. and J. Readman (2001) *Integrating SMEs in Global Value Chains - Towards Partnership for Development*, UNIDO, Vienna.

Kaplinsky, R. and J. Readman (2000) 'Globalization and Upgrading: What Can (and cannot) be Learnt from International Trade Statistics in the Wood Furniture Sector?', IDS and the Center for Research in Innovation Management, University of Brighton, Brighton.

Kappel, R. J. Lay, and S. Steiner (2005) 'Uganda: No more Pro-Poor Growth?', *Development Policy Review*, 23 (1), pp. 27-53.

Kappel, R., J. Lay and S. Steiner (2004) *The Missing Links: Report on Uganda's Economic Reforms and Pro-Poor Growth*, Report for GTZ, Eschborn .

Kapur, D. and J. McHale (2005a) 'The Global Migration of Talent: What Does it Mean for Developing Countries?', Center for Global Development (CGD), *CGD Brief*, October 2005.

Kapur, D. and J. McHale (2005b) 'Give Us Your Best and Brightest: The Global Hunt for Talent and Its Impact on the Developing World', CGD Brief, Washington D.C.

Kasekende, L.A. and M. Atingi-Ego (1999) 'Uganda's Experience with Aid', *Journal of African Economies*, 8 (4), pp. 617-49.

Kasfir, N. (1983) 'State, Magendo, and Class Formation in Uganda', *Journal of Commonwealth and Comparative Politics*, 21 (3), pp. 84-103.

Kasozi, A.B.K. (2003) *University Education in Uganda: Challenges and Opportunities for Reform*, Fountain Publishers, Kampala.

Keefer, P. (2000) *Growth and Poverty Reduction in Uganda*: The *Role of Institutional Reform*, World Bank mimeo, Washington D.C.

Keller, M. (2006) 'The Development of Obligations and Responsibilities in Cultural Context', in L. Smith and J. Voneche, eds., *Norms in Human Development*, Cambridge University Press, London.

Kiggundu, R. (2006) 'Learning to Change: Why the Fish Processing Clusters in Uganda Learned to Upgrade', in B. Oyelaran-Oyeyinka and D. McCormick, eds., *Industrial Clusters and Innovation Systems in Africa: Institutions, Markets and Policy*, United Nations University Press, New York, pp. 158-88.

Kiggundu, R. (2004) 'Learning to Close Deficiencies in Local Innovation System: Case Studies of Fisheries in Uganda', in SIDA/SAREC, eds., Proceedings of Regional Conference on Innovation Systems and Innovative Clusters in Africa, Bagamoyo Tanzania, 18-20/02/2004, pp. 449-76.

Kiiza, J. (2006) Institutions and Economic Performance in Africa: A Comparative Analysis of Mauritius, Botswana and Uganda', *UNU-WIDER Research Paper*, No. 2006/73, Helsinki.

Kiiza, J. (2004) *Business-Politics Linkages in Uganda – Implications for the PEAP*, Report for DFID Uganda, Kampala.

Kiiza, J. (2000) 'Market-Oriented Public Management in Uganda: Benchmarking International Best Practice?', *Ufahamu*, XXVIII (1), pp. 94-124.

Kiiza, J., G. Asiimwe and D. Kibikyo (2006) 'Understanding Economic and Institutional Reforms in Uganda', in J. Mensah, ed., *Understanding Economic Reforms in Africa: A Tale of Seven Nations*, Palgrave Macmillan, Basingstoke, Hampshire, pp. 57-94.

Kinyanjui, M.N. and M. Khayesi (2005) *Social Capital, Micro and Small Enterprises and Poverty-Alleviation in East Africa*, OSSREA, Addis Ababa.

Kirumira, E. and F. Bateganya (2003) 'Where Has all the Education Gone in Uganda? Employment Outcomes among Secondary School and University Leavers', IDS, Brighton.

KIT and IIRR (2008) Trading Up: *Building Cooperation between Farmers and Traders in Africa*, Royal Tropical Institute, Amsterdam, and International Institute of Rural Reconstruction, Nairobi.

Knorringa, P. (1999) 'Agra: An Old Cluster Facing New Competition', *World Development*, 27 (9), pp. 1587-1604.

Knorringa, P. and I. van Staveren (2006) 'Social Capital for Industrial Development: Operationalizing the Concept', Summary, UNIDO, Vienna.

Kogut, B. (1985) 'Designing Global Strategies: Comparative and Competitive Value-Added Chains', *Sloan Management Review*, 26(4), pp. 15-28.

Krippner, G.R. and A.S. Alvarez (2007) 'Embeddedness and the Intellectual Projects of Economic Sociology', *Annu. Rev. Sociol.*, 33, pp. 219-40.

Kyomugisha, C. (2001) 'The State and Small Scale Industrialisation in Uganda', *CBR Working Paper*, No. 69, CBR, Kampala.

Lall, S. (2005) 'Is African Industry Competing?', University of Oxford, Queen Elizabeth House, *Working Paper Series* (QEHWPS), No. 122.

Lall, S. (2004a) 'Reinventing Industrial Strategy: The Role of Government Policy in Building Industrial Competitiveness', *G-24 Discussion Paper Series*, UNCTAD, Geneva.

Lall, S. (2004b) 'The Role of Industrialization in Achieving the Millennium Development Goals in Least Developed Countries', in UNIDO, *The Role of Industrial Development in the Achievement of the Millennium Development Goals*, Proceedings of the Industrial Development Forum and Associated Round Tables, 1-3/12/2003, Compendium Edition, UNIDO, Vienna, pp. 80-3.

Lall, S. (2003) 'FDI, AGOA and Manufactured Exports from A Land-Locked, Least-Developed African Economy: Lesotho', *QEHWPS*, No. 109.

Lall. S. (2002) 'Social Capital and Industrial Transformation', *QEHWPS*, No. 84.

Lall, S. (2001a) *Competitiveness, Technology and Skills*, Edward Elgar, Cheltenham.

Lall, S. (2001b) 'Competitiveness Indices in Developing Countries: An Economic Evaluation of the Global Competitiveness Report', *World Development*, 29(9), pp. 1501-25.

Lall, S. (1994) 'The East Asian Miracle Study: Does the Bell Toll for Industrial Policy?', *World Development*, 22 (4), pp. 645-54.

Lall, S., M. Albaladejo, and J. Zhang (2004a) 'Mapping Fragmentation: Electronics and Automobiles in East Asia and Latin America', *Oxford Development Studies*, 32(3), pp. 407-32.

Lall, S., M. Albaladejo, and M.M. Moreira (2004b) 'Latin American Industrial Competitiveness and the Challenge of Globalization', Inter-American Development Bank (IDB), *INTAL-ITD Occasional Paper*, No. SITI-05.

Lall, S. and C. Pietrobelli (2002) *Failing to Compete: Technology Development and Technology Systems in Africa*, Edward Elgar, Cheltenham.

Lall S. and M. Teubal (1998) ''Market Stimulating' Technology Policies in Developing Countries: A Framework with Examples from East Asia', *World Development*, 26(8): pp. 1369-85.

Lawson, D., A. McKay and J. Okidi (2003) 'Poverty Persistence and Transitions in Uganda: A Combined Qualitative and Quantitative Analysis', Global Poverty Research Group (GPRC), *GPRC Working Papers*, No. 4, Manchester.

Liang, X. (2002) Uganda Post-primary Education Sector Report, *Africa Region Human Development Working Paper Series*, World Bank, Washington D.C.

Luetkenhorst, W. (2005) 'UNIDO: Business Linkages, Supply Chain Management and SMEs', in UNIDO, ed., UNIDO and Global Compact - Sustainable supply chains, Vienna, pp. 15-29.

Lutwama J. (2004) *Constraints to Employment Growth in the Formal Manufacturing Sector in Uganda*, MA Dissertation, Makerere University, Kampala.

Lwanga-Ntale, C. (2006) 'Does Chronic Poverty Matter in Uganda?', *CPRC-Uganda Policy Briefs*, No 1, CPRC-Uganda, Kampala.

Makerere University (2007) 'CIT Cisco Academy Won International Award', http://cit.ac.ug/cit/award507.php (accessed 06/10/2008).

Mamdani, M. (2007) *Scholars in the Marketplace: Reform at Makerere University 1989-2005*, Fountain Publishers, Kampala.

Mamdani, M., ed. (1996a) *Uganda - Studies in Labour*, Council for the Development of Social Science Research in Africa (CODESRIA), Dakar.

Mamdani, M. (1996b) *Citizen and Subject: Contemporary Africa and the Legacy of Late Colonialism*, James Currey, Oxford.

Mamdani, M. (1995) *And Fire Does not Always Beget Ash: Critical Reflections on the NRM*, Monitor Publications, Kampala.

Mamdani, M. (1994) 'A Critical Analysis of the IMF Programme in Uganda', in U. Himmelstrand, K. Kinyanjui, and E. Mburugu, eds., *African Perspectives on Development Controversies, Dilemmas and Openings*, James Currey, London, pp. 128-36.

Mamdani, M. (1999) *Politics and Class Formation in Uganda*, Fountain Publishers, Kampala.

Masiga, F. (2008) 'Uganda will still struggle even with better roads, more energy', *Daily Monitor*, 07/10/2008.

Matembe, M. (2003) 'Integrity: Developing Political Will and Commitment', Paper given by the Minister of State for Ethics and Integrity, Mrs Matembe, Workshop on 'Managing Integrity in Customs', Global Forum III on Fighting Corruption and Safeguarding Integrity, Seoul, South Korea, 29/05/2003, http://www.wcoomd.org/ie/En/Topics_ Issues/CustomsModernizationIntegrity/Speech%20of%20Mr.%20Douglas%20Browning,%20US%20Customs%20and%20Border%20Protection%20%20.PDF (accessed 01/03/2005).

Mather, C. and S. Greenberg (2003) 'Market Liberalisation in Post-Apartheid South Africa: the Restructuring of Citrus Exports after 'Deregulation'', *Journal of Southern African Studies*, 29 (2), pp. 393-412.

Mathews, J.A. (2006) 'Catch-up strategies and the Latecomer Effect in Industrial Development', *New Political Economy*, 11 (3), pp. 313-35.

Mbabazi, P. (2005) *Supply Chains and Liberalisation of the Milk Industry in Uganda*, Fountain Publishers, Kampala.

Mbabazi, P. and I. Taylor, eds. (2005) *The Potentiality of 'Developmental States' in Africa: Botswana and Uganda Compared*, CODESRIA, Dakar.

McGee, R. (2000) 'Meeting the International Development Targets in Uganda: Halving Poverty and Achieving Universal Primary Education', *Development Policy Review*, 18, pp. 85-106.

McGee, R. (2004) 'Poverty Knowledge in Central-level Policy Processes in Uganda: Politics, Voice and Legitimacy', in K. Brock, R. McGee, and J. Gaventa, eds., *Unpacking Policy- Knowledge, Actors and Spaces in Poverty Reduction in Uganda and Nigeria*, Fountain Publishers, Kampala, pp. 113-33.

McGuigan, C., F. Zake, D. Luswata-Kibanda, P. Nyabuntu, and J. Ssemwanga (2005) *Developing and Promoting Trading Principles for the Ugandan Agro Business Sector*, BSMD Report, Kampala.

Meagher, K. (2007) 'Manufacturing Disorder: Liberalization, Informal Enterprise and Economic "Ungovernance" in African Small Firm Clusters', *Development and Change*, 38 (3), pp. 473-503.

Meagher, K. (2005a) 'Social Capital or Analytical Liability: Social Networks and African Informal Economies', *Global Networks*, 5 (3), pp. 217-38.

Meagher, K. (2005b) 'Social Networks and Economic Ungovernance in African Small Firm Clusters', Paper for the Queen Elizabeth House (QEH) 50th Anniversary Conference, Oxford, UK.

Medium Term Competitiveness Strategy (MTCS) Secretariat (2006) *Medium Term Competitiveness Strategy 2nd Edition* (2006-2010), Draft May 2006, Kampala.

Medium Term Competitiveness Strategy Secretariat (2005) *Medium Term Competitiveness Strategy 2nd Edition* (2005-2009), Draft March 2005, Kampala.

Menocal, A.R. and S. Mulley (2006) 'Learning from Experience? A Review of Recipient-Government Efforts to Manage Donor Relations and Improve the Quality of Aid', *ODI Working Paper*, No. 268, London.

Meyer-Stamer, J. (2003) 'Obstacles to Cooperation in Clusters and How to Overcome Them', *Developing Alternatives*, 9 (1), pp. 19-24.

Ministry of Agriculture, Animal Industry and Fisheries (MAAIF) and Ministry of Finance, Planning and Economic Development (MFPED) (2004) *Plan for Modernization of Agriculture - Eradicating Poverty, Government Strategy and Operational Framework*, Kampala

Ministry of Education and Sports (MOES) (2005) *Education Sector Strategic Plan 2004-2015*, Kampala.

Ministry of Education and Sports (2002) *Options for Post Primary Education and Training in Uganda Increasing Access, Equity, and Efficiency*, Report of the Task Group for Post Primary Education and Training, Kampala.

Ministry of Education and Sports (1998) *Education Strategic Investment Plan: 1998-2003*, Kampala.

Ministry of Finance, Planning and Economic Development (2008) *An Annotated Inventory of Poverty-Related Research Studies in Uganda (2000-2007)*, Kampala.

Ministry of Finance, Planning and Economic Development (MFPED) (2007) Budget Speech Financial Year 2007/08 - Re-orienting Public Expenditure Towards Prosperity For All, Kampala.

Ministry of Finance, Planning and Economic Development (2006) Data Set from the Macroeconomic Policy Department, February 2006, Kampala.

Ministry of Finance, Planning and Economic Development (2004) *Poverty Eradication Action Plan 2004/5-2007/8*, Kampala.

Ministry of Finance, Planning and Economic Development (2002) *Uganda Participatory Poverty Assessment Process (PPA)*, National Report, Final Draft, December 2002, Kampala.

Ministry of Finance, Planning and Economic Development (2000) *Medium Term Competitive Strategy* (MTCS) 2000-2005, Kampala.

Ministry of Finance, Planning and Economic Development (MFPED) and United Nations Development Programme (UNDP) (2008) *Assessing the Macroeconomic Impact of HIV/AIDS in Uganda*, Summary Report, Kampala.

Ministry of Finance, Planning and Economic Development (MFPED) and Centre for Basic Research (CBR) (2007) *Moving out of Poverty: Understanding Freedom, Democracy and Growth from the Bottom Up*, Kampala.

Ministry of Gender, Labour and Social Development (MGLSD) (2004) *The National Employment Policy*, Draft July 2004, Kampala.

Ministry of Tourism, Trade and Industry (MTTI) (2004) *Policy Framework for Industrialization in Uganda: 2004-2009*, Draft, Kampala.

Möllering, G. (2006) *Trust: Reason, Routine, Reflexivity*, Elsevier, Oxford.

Möllering, G. (2005) 'Understanding Trust from the Perspective of Sociological Neo-institutionalism: The Interplay of Institutions and Agency', *MPIfG Discussion Paper*, No. 05/13, Cologne.

Moncrieffe, J.M. (2004) *Uganda's Political Economy: A Synthesis of Major Thought*, Report for DFID Uganda, ODI, London.

Moran, T.E., E.M. Graham, and M. Blomström, eds. (2005) *Does Foreign Direct Investment Promote Development?*, Institute for International Economics, Washington D.C.

Morris, M. (2003) *Using Value Chain Analysis as a Policy and Strategy Intervention Tool*, School of Development Studies, University of KwaZulu-Natal, Durban, South Africa.

Morrissey, O., N. Rudaheranwa, and L. Moller (2003) 'Trade Policies, Performance and Poverty in Uganda', Executive Summary, Report for Uganda Trade and Poverty Project (UTPP), Kampala.

Morrison, A., C. Pietrobelli, and R. Rabellotti (2006) 'Global Value Chains and Technological Capabilities: A Framework to Study Industrial Innovation in Developing Countries', Paper for the GLOBELICS (Global Network for Economics of Learning, Innovation, and Competence Building Systems) Conference 2006, 'Innovation Systems for Competitiveness and Shared Prosperity for Developing Countries', India, 4-7/10/2006, http://www.globelicsindia2006.org/ Andrea%20Morrison.pdf (accessed: 20.10.2006).

Mugaju, J., ed. (1999) *Uganda's Age of Reforms - A critical Overview*, Fountain Publishers, Kampala.

Muhumuza, F., S. Kutegeka and A. Wolimbwa (2007) 'Wealth Distribution, Poverty and Timber Governance in Uganda: A Case Study of Budongo Forest Reserve', ACODE (Advocates Coalition for Development and Environment), *Policy Research Series*, No. 26, Kampala.

Muhumuza, F., J. Daly, S. Farley, and M. Crawford (2005) 'The State of Science and Technology in Uganda', Background paper for the Uganda Millennium Science Initiative Project (UMSIP), World Bank, Washington D.C., Draft, Citation allowed by main author.

Mukasa, S., N. Tanzam, H. Kabuchu, and S. Vusia Kayonga (2004) *Uganda: Poverty and Gender Assessment: Strengthening Linkages between Poverty and Gender Analysis in Uganda*, Danish Development Cooperation, Copenhagen.

Munene, J.C. (1995) 'Organisational Pathology and Accountability in Health and Education in Rural Uganda', in P. Langseth, J. Katorobo, E. Brett, and J.C. Munene, eds., *Uganda: Landmarks in Rebuilding a Nation*, Fountain Publishers, Kampala, pp. 133-54.

Munene, J.C., H. Schwartz, and G.M. Kibanja (2005) *Escaping from Behavioural Poverty in Uganda - The Role of Culture and Social Capital*, Fountain Publishers, Kampala.

Munene, J.C and S. Schwartz, eds. (2000) *Cultural Values and Development in Uganda,* Royal Tropical Institute, Amsterdam.

Musisi, N.B. and C.P. Dodge (2002) *Transformations in Uganda,* Makerere Institute of Social Research and Cuny Centre, Kampala and Washington D.C.

Muwanga-Zake, E.S.K. and S. Ndhaye (2001) 'The HIPC Debt Relief Initiative - Uganda's Experience', World Institute for Development Economics Research (WIDER), *Discussion Paper,* No. 2001/94, Helsinki.

Myanuzi, F. (2003) *Where Has all the Education Gone in Tanzania? Employment Outcomes among Secondary School and University Leavers,* IDS, Brighton.

NAADS Secretariat (2003) *NAADS Poverty and Gender Strategy for the Delivery of Improved Agricultural Advisory Services,* Kampala.

NAADS Secretariat (2000) *Master Document of the NAADS Task Force and Joint Donor Groups,* Kampala.

Nalumansi, S., S. Müller-Maige, S. Oluka, G. Rösch, and D. Moll (2003) *Skilled Manpower in Uganda: A Study on the Need for Modern Business, Technical and Vocational Education and Training (BTVET) - Matching Social Needs and Economic Requirements,* Summary Report, Report for EU in cooperation with GTZ, Kampala.

Namara, A. (2001) 'The Invisible Workers - Paid Domestic Work in Kampala City Uganda', *CBR Working Paper,* No. 74, Kampala.

National Planning Authority (2005) *Human Resource Development and Capacity Building Master Plan for Uganda,* Draft outline, Kampala.

Nelson R. and S. Winter (1982) *An Evolutionary Theory of Economic Change,* Harvard University Press, Cambridge (MA).

New Vision (NV) (2008a) '2007 exports fetch $3.4b', 10/10/2008.

New Vision (2008b) 'MPs, civil society hail NAADS assessment', 17/06/2008.

New Vision (2008c) 'Govt told to plan for increasing population', 13/10/2008.

New Vision (2006a) 'Government to review primary curriculum to fight graft', 28/03/2006.

New Vision (2006b) 'Government proposes to integrate religious values in curriculum', 03/04/2006.

New Vision (2006c) 'The MTCS and competitiveness for economic growth', 29/05/2006.

Nkata, I. (2007) TEXDA Tracer Study, Report for TEXDA/UNIDO, InterAfrica Corporate Limited, Kampala.

Noland, M. and H. Pack (2003) *Industrial Policy in a Era of Globalization: Lessons from Asia,* Institute of International Economics, Washington D.C.

Nyabuntu, P. (2006) *Assessment of Effectiveness of Farmer Groups as Viable Institutions for Farmer Empowerment and Poverty Reduction in the Implementation of the Plan for the Modernization of Agriculture,* Report for DENIVA, Kampala.

Nkonya, E., J. Pender, P. Jagger, D. Sserunkuuma, C. Kaizzi, and H. Ssali (2004) 'Strategies for Sustainable Land Management and Poverty Reduction in Uganda', *International Food Policy Research Institute Research Report,* No. 133.

Nunner-Winkler, G. (2007) 'Development of Moral Motivation from Childhood to Early Adulthood', *Journal of Moral Education,* 36, pp. 399–414.

Okidi, J.A., S. Ssewanyana, L. Bategeka, and F. Muhumuza (2007) 'Uganda's Experience with Operationalizing Pro-Poor Growth, 1992-2003', in T. Besley and L.J. Cord, eds., *Delivering on the Promise of Pro-Poor Growth,* World Bank and Palgrave Macmillan, New York, pp. 169-198.

Okidi, J.A., S. Ssewanyana, L. Bategeka, and F. Muhumuza (2004) *Operationalising Pro-Poor Growth: Case Study on Uganda,* EPRC, Kampala.

Okidi, J., P.O. Okwi and J. Ddumba-Ssentamu (2003) 'Welfare Distribution and Poverty in Uganda, 1992 to 2000', *EPRC Occasional Papers,* No. 22, Kampala.

Okidi, J. and G. Kempaka (2002) 'An Overview of Chronic Poverty and Development Policy in Uganda', *CPRC Working Paper,* No. 11, IDPM, Manchester.

Olivier de Sardan, J.-P. (2008) 'Researching the Practical Norms of Real Governance in Africa', Africa Power and Politics Programme (APPP), *APPP Discussion Paper,* No. 5,London.

Oloka-Onyango, J. (2004) 'Economic and Social Human Rights in the Aftermath of Uganda's Fourth Constitution: A Critical Reconceptualization', *CBR Working Paper,* No. 88, Kampala.

Organisation for Economic Co-operation and Development (OECD) (2005) *Main Science and Technology Indicators,* Paris.

Organisation for Economic Co-operation and Development (2001) *Measuring Productivity: Measurement of Aggregate and Industry-Level Productivity Growth*, Paris.
Organisation for Social Science Research in Eastern and Southern Africa (OSSREA) (2008) *Assessment of Poverty Reduction Strategies in sub-Saharan Africa: The Case of Uganda*, Addis Ababa.
Oxford Policy Management (OPM) (2008) *Evaluation of Uganda's Poverty Eradication Action Plan*, Oxford.
Oxford Policy Management (2007) *Uganda - Agriculture Sector Public Sector Expenditure Review*, Phases 1 and 2, Oxford.
Oxford Policy Management (2005) *Evaluation Report: The Plan for the Modernization of Agriculture*, Oxford.
Oxfam (2008) *Turning up the Heat: Climate Change and Poverty in Uganda*, Kampala and Oxford.
Oyelaran-Oyeyinka, B. and D. McCormick, eds. (2006) *Industrial clusters and innovation Systems in Africa: Institutions, Markets and Policy*, United Nations University Press, New York.
Plan for the Modernisation of Agriculture (PMA) Secretariat (2004) *Annual Report 2003/04*, Kampala.
Pietrobelli, C. and R. Rabellotti (2004) 'Competitiveness and Upgrading in Clusters and Value Chains: The Case of Latin America', Prepared for the DTI/UNIDO conference 'An Institutional Approach to Competitiveness: The Critical Role of Institutions at the National and Regional Level', Pretoria, South Africa, 7-11/06/2004.
Piron, Laure-Hélene with Andy Norton (2004) 'Politics and the PRSP Approach: Uganda Case Study', *ODI Working Paper*, No 240, London.
Polanyi, K. (1957) *The Great Transformation*, Beacon Press, Boston.
Polaski, S. (2006) *Winners and Losers: Impact of the Doha Round on Developing Countries*, Carnegie Endowment for International Peace (CEIP), Washington D.C.
Ponte, S. (2008) 'Developing a Vertical Dimension to Chronic Poverty Research: Some Lessons from Global Value Chain Analysis', *CPRC Working Paper*, No. 111, Manchester.
Ponte, S. (2005) 'Bans, Tests and Alchemy, Food Safety Standards and the Ugandan Fish Export Industry', *DIIS Working Paper*, No. 2005/19, Copenhagen.
Ponte S. and P. Gibbon (2005) 'Quality Standards, Conventions and the Governance of Global Value Chains', *Economy and Society*, 34 (1), pp. 1-31.
Porter, M. (2000) 'The Current Competitiveness Index: Measuring the Microeconomic Foundations of Prosperity', in *Global Competitiveness Report 2000*, Oxford University Press, New York/ Oxford.
Porter, M. (1990) *The Competitive Advantage of Nations*, The Free Press, New York.
Poulton, C., J. Kydd and A. Dorward (2006) 'Overcoming Market Constraints on Pro-Poor Agricultural Growth in Sub-Saharan Africa', *Development Policy Review*, 24 (3), pp. 243-77.
Prahalad, C.K. (2004) *The Fortune at the Bottom of the Pyramid: Eradicating Poverty Through Profits*, Wharton School Publishing, Philadelphia.
Promotion of Employment-oriented Vocational and Technical Training (PEVOT) (2006) *'Non-formal Skills Development in Uganda'*, Briefing Paper, June 2006, Kampala
Promotion of Employment-oriented Vocational and Technical Training (2005) Local Skills Development Pilot Project (LSDP) - Evaluation Report on LSD Activities in Mityana, Bbowa and Rukor', Kampala.
Rasiah, R. and H. Tamale (2004) 'Productivity, Exports, Skills and Technological Capabilities: A Study of Foreign and Local Manufacturing Firms in Uganda', UN University, Institute for New Technologies, *Discussion Paper*, No. 2004-1.
Reinikka, R. and J. Svensson (2005) 'Fighting Corruption to Improve Schooling: Evidence from a Newspaper Campaign in Uganda', *Journal of the European Economic Association*, 3 (2-3), pp. 259-67.
Reinikka, R. and N. Smith (2004) *Public Expenditure Tracking Surveys in Education*, International Institute for Educational Planning, UNESCO, Paris.
Reinikka, R. and J. Svensson (2004) 'Local Capture: Evidence from a Central Government Transfer Program in Uganda', *Quarterly Journal of Economics*, 119 (2), pp. 679-705.
Reinikka, R. and J. Svensson (2003) 'Survey Techniques to Measure and Explain Corruption', *World Bank Policy Research Paper*, No. 3071, Washington D.C.
Reinikka, R. and P. Collier, eds. (2001a) *Uganda's Recovery: The Role of Farms, Firms, and Government*, World Bank, Washington D.C.

Reinikka, R. and P. Collier (2001b) 'Reconstruction and Liberalization: An Overview', in R. Reinikka and P. Collier, eds., *Uganda's Recovery: The Role of Farms, Firms, and Government*, World Bank, Washington D.C., pp. 15-47.

Rest, J.R., D. Narvaez, M.J. Bebeau, and S.J. Thoma (1999) *Postconventional Moral Thinking - A Neo-Kohlbergian Approach*, Lawrence Erlbaum, Mahwah, New York and London.

Ribbink, G., P. Nyabuntu, and S. Kumar (2005) *Successful Supply Chains in Uganda: A study of Three Successful Chains in the Coffee, Dried Fruit and Fresh Vegetables Sectors*, BSMD Report, Kampala.

Riisgaard, L., S. Bolwig, F. Matose, S. Ponte, A. du Toit, and N. Halberg (2008) 'A Strategic Framework and Toolbox for Action Research with Small Producers in Value Chains', *DIIS Working Paper*, No. 2008/17, Copenhagen.

Roberts, M. and J. Tybout (1997) 'Producer Turnover and Productivity Growth in Developing Countries', *The World Bank Research Observer*, 12(1), pp. 1-18.

Robison, R., ed. (2006) *The Neoliberal Revolution: Forging the Market State*, Palgrave Macmillan, London.

Robison, R. (2005) 'How to Build Market Societies: The Paradoxes of Neoliberal Revolution', *New Political Economy*, 10 (2), pp. 247-57.

Robinson, M. (2007) 'The Political Economy of Governance Reforms in Uganda', *Commonwealth & Comparative Politics*, 45 (4), pp. 452-74.

Robinson, M. (2005) 'The Political Economy of Turnaround in Uganda', paper prepared for the Low Income Countries under Stress (LICUS) Initiative, Research Project on 'How do LICUS/Poor Performing Countries Achieve Turnaround?', Draft, The World Bank, http://www1.worldbank.org/publicsector/PREMWK2005/poleconomy/materials.htm (accessed 01/03/2006).

Rodrik, D. (2004) *Industrial Policy for the Twenty-First Century*, UNIDO, Vienna.

Rostow, W. (1960) *The Stages of Economic Growth: A Non-Communist Manifesto*, Cambridge University Press, Cambridge.

Rubongoya, J.B. (2007) *Regime Hegemony in Museveni's Uganda: Pax Musevenica*, Palgrave Macmillan, New York.

Sachs, J. and D. Bloom (1998) 'Geography, Demography, and Economic Growth in Africa', *Brookings Papers on Economic Activity*, Vol. 2, Washington D.C.

Santiso, J. (2006) 'China & India: What's in it for Africa', Presentation, *OECD Breakfast Series*, Washington D.C., 22/05/2006.

Sayer, A. (2007) 'Moral Economy as Critique', *New Political Economy*, 12 (2), pp. 261-70.

Sayer, A. (2005) 'Approaching Moral Economy', in N. Stehr, C. Henning and B. Weiler, eds., *The Moralization of the Markets*, Transaction Books, New Brunswick, New Jersey, pp. 77-97.

Schmitz, H. (2005a) 'Asian Drivers of Change in the Real Economy', Paper for Asian Driver Workshop, IDS, Brighton, May 2005.

Schmitz, H. (2005b) *Understanding and Enhancing the Opportunities of Local Producers in the Global Garment and Footwear Industry: What Does the Value Chain Approach Offer*?, GTZ, Eschborn.

Schmitz, H. (2005c) *Value Chain Analysis for Policy-Makers and Practitioners*, ILO, Geneva.

Schmitz, H. (2004) 'Local Upgrading in Global Value Chains: Recent Findings', 50th Anniversary Conference Reviewing the First Decade of Development and Democracy in South Africa, Durban, South Africa, 21-22/10/2004.

Schmitz, H. (1998) 'Responding to Global Competitive Pressure: Local Co-operation and Upgrading in the Sinos Valley, Brazil', *IDS Working Paper*, No. 82, Brighton.

Schmitz, H. (1995) 'Collective Efficiency: Growth Path for Small-scale Industry', *Journal of Development Studies*, 31 (4), pp. 529-66.

Schmitz, H. and P. Knorringa (2000) 'Learning from Global Buyers', *Journal of Development Studies*, 37 (2), pp. 177-205.

Schmitz, H., and K. Nadvi (1999) 'Clustering and Industrialization: Introduction', *World Development*, 27 (9), pp. 1503-14.

SciDev.Net (2006) 'China to Share Farming Expertise with Poorer Nations', SciDev.Net (London) news, 22/05/2006, source: http://allafrica.com.

Scott, J. (1985) *Weapons of the Weak: Everyday Forms of Peasant Resistance*, Yale University Press, New Haven, CT.

Scott, J. (1979) *Moral Economy of the Peasant: Rebellion and Subsistence in Southeast Asia*, Yale University Press, New Haven, CT.

Selassie, A.A. (2008) 'Beyond Macro-Economic Stability: The Quest for Industrialization in Uganda', *IMF Working Paper*, No 08/231, Washington D.C.

Sender, J. (1999) 'Africa's Economic Performance: Limitations of the Current Consensus', *The Journal of Economic Perspectives*, 13 (3), pp. 89-114.

Shepherd, G.W. (1955) *The Early Struggle for Freedom and unity in Uganda: I K Musazi and the farmers' Cooperative Movement*, John Day Company, New York.

Shonhiwa, S. (2006) *The Effective Cross-Cultural Manager – A Guide for Business Leaders in Africa*, Zebra Press, Cape Town.

Siggel, E. and G. Ssemogerere (2004) 'Uganda's Policy Reforms, Industry Competitiveness and Regional Integration: A comparison with Kenya', *Journal of International Trade and Economic Development*, 13 (3), pp. 325-57

Siggel, E. and G. Ssemogerere (2001) 'Uganda's Policy Reforms, Industry Competitiveness and Regional Integration: A Comparison with Kenya', *Discussion Paper*, New Industrial Realities and Firm Behaviour in Africa, CSAE (Centre for the Study of African Economies) and UNIDO International Forum, 2001. www.csae.ox.ac.uk/conferences/2001-NIRaFBiA/pdfs/siggel.pdf (accessed 01/03/2006).

Smith, J. (2007) 'What's New About 'New Imperialism'', http://www.ragingwave.com/index_files/What%27s%20new%20about%20%27new%20imperialism%27.pdf (accessed 05/10/2008).

Snyder, M. (2000) *Women in African Economies - from Burning Sun to Boardroom: Business Ventures and Investment Patterns of 74 Ugandan Women*, Fountain Publishers, Kampala.

Ssekamwa, J.C. (1997) *History and Development of Education in Uganda*, Fountain Publishers, Kampala.

Ssemogerere, G. (2005) *Productivity Performance in Developing Countries: Country Case Studies: Uganda*, UNIDO, Vienna.

Ssemogerere, G. (1999) 'Employment and Labour Markets during Adjustment - the Case of Uganda', in W. Van Der Geest and R. Van Der Hoeven, eds., *Adjustment, Employment and Missing Institutions in Africa - The Experience in Eastern and Southern Africa*, James Currey, Oxford.

Ssemogerere, G. and J. Wiegratz (2006) 'Is Export-Led Growth a Possibility? A Qualitative Assessment of Uganda's Export Policies over the Last 15 Years 1990/91-2005/06', Paper presented at the 'National Policy Conference on Sustaining Growth in Uganda', Kampala, 30-31/10/2006.

Ssewakiryanga, R. (2005) 'The Making of Uganda's Poverty Eradication Action Plan - Politics and Processes, in W. Eberlei, P. Meyns and F. Mutesa, eds., *Poverty Reduction in a Political Trap? The PRS Process and Neopatrimonialism in Zambia*, UNZA Press, Lusaka, pp. 293-321.

Ssewakiryanga, R. (2004a) 'The Corporatist State, the Parallel State and Prospects for Representative and Accountable Policy in Uganda', in K. Brock, R. McGee and J. Gaventa, eds., *Unpacking Policy- Knowledge, Actors and Spaces in Poverty Reduction in Uganda and Nigeria*, Fountain Publishers, Kampala, pp. 74-93.

Ssewakiryanga, R. (2004b) 'Donor-Dependent Decentralization and the Political Economy of Aid in Uganda', *CBR Working Paper*, No. 91, Kampala.

Ssewakiryanga, R. (ed.) (2004c) 'The State and Policy Making', *CBR/ENRECA Occasional Paper Series*, No. 06, Kampala.

Stamm, A. (2004) *Value Chains for Development Policy: Challenges for Trade Policy and the Promotion of Economic Development*, GTZ, Eschborn.

Stiglitz, J.E. (1998) 'Toward a New Paradigm for Development: Strategies, Policies and Processes', UNCTAD Prebisch Lecture, Geneva, reprinted in H.-J. Chang, ed., *The Rebel Within: Joseph Stiglitz and the World Bank*, Anthem World Economics, London 2001, pp. 57-93.

Stiglitz, J. E. (1996) 'Some Lessons from the East Asian Miracle', *The World Bank Research Observer*, 11(2), pp. 151-177.

Sturgeon, T.J. (2006) 'The Governance of Global Value Chains: Implications for Industrial Upgrading', Global Value Chains Workshop on 'Industrial Upgrading, Offshore Production, and Labor', 9-10/11/2006, Social Science Research Institute, Duke University, www.cggc.duke.edu/pdfs/workshop/ SturgeonGVCDuke.pdf (accessed 10/12/2006).

Sturgeon, T. J. (2000) 'How Do We Define Value Chains and Production Networks', MIT IPC, *Globalization Working Paper*, No. 00-010, Cambridge, MA.

Svensson, J. (2002) 'Who Must Pay Bribes and How Much? Evidence from Cross-Section of Firms', *Institute for International Economic Studies Seminar Paper*, No. 713, Stockholm University, Stockholm.

Swedberg, R. (2003) 'The Economic Sociology of Capitalism: An Introduction and Agenda', Cornell University,http://www.economyandsociety.org/publications/wp5a_swedberg_03.pdf (accessed 01/03/2006).

Tanburn, J. and R. Kamuhanda (2005) Making Service Markets Work for the Poor: The Experience of Uganda, BSMD Report, Kampala.

Tangen, S. (2002) 'Understanding the Concept of Productivity', Proceedings of the 7th Asia Pacific Industrial Engineering and Management Systems Conference (APIEMS2002), Taipei, http://www.woxencentrum.nu/documents/publications/papers/pap_Tangen2002-Understanding The Concept Of Productivity.pdf (accessed 01/03/2006).

Tangri, R. and A.M. Mwenda (2006) 'Politics, Donors and the Ineffectiveness of Anti-Corruption Institutions in Uganda', *Journal of Modern African Studies*, 44 (1), pp. 101-24

Tangri, R. and A.M. Mwenda (2003) 'Military Corruption and Ugandan Politics since the Late 1990s', *Review of African Political Economy*, 30 (98), pp. 539-52.

Tangri, R. and A.M. Mwenda (2001) 'Corruption and Cronyism in Uganda's Privatization in the 1990s', *African Affairs*, 100 (398), pp. 117-133.

Taylor, M. (2007) 'Rethinking the Global Production of Uneven Development', *Globalizations*, 4 (4), pp. 529-42.

Taylor, M., ed. (2008) *Global Economy Contested: Power and Conflict across the International Division of Labour*, Routledge, London.

Thoen, R., S. Jaffee, and C. Dolan (2000) 'Equatorial Rose: The Kenyan- European Cut Flower Supply Chain', in R. Kopiki, ed., *Supply Chain Development in Emerging Markets: Case Studies of Supportive Public Policy*, MIT Press, Boston.

Thome, W. (2006) 'Training for CHOGM is also for the future', *New Vision*, 17/06/2006.

Thompson, E.P. (1980) *The Making of the English Working Class*, Penguin Books, London.

Thompson, E.P. (1971) 'The Moral Economy of the English Crowd in the Eighteenth Century', *Past and Present*, 50, pp. 76-136.

Thompson, G. (2003) *Governing Uganda: British Colonial Rule and its Legacy*, Fountain Publishers, Kampala.

Tiberondwa, A.K. (1998) *Missionary Teachers as Agents of Colonialism in Uganda*, Fountain Publishers, Kampala.

Tikly, L., J. Lowe, M. Crossley, H. Dachi, R. Garrett, and B. Mukabaranga (2003) 'Globalisation and Skills for Development in Rwanda and Tanzania', *DFID Education Paper*, No. 51, London.

Transparency International (2004) Transparency International Corruption Perception Index 2004, Press release, 20/10/2004, http://www.transparency.org/pressreleases_archive/2004/2004.10.20.cpi.en.html (accessed 04/05/2005).

Uganda Bureau of Statistics (UBOS) (2007a) *Labour Force Report*, Kampala.

Uganda Bureau of Standards (2007b) *Nature, Distribution and Evolution of Poverty & Inequality in Uganda*, Kampala.

Uganda Bureau of Standards (2006) *Report on the Labour Market in Uganda, February 2006*, electronic version, Kampala, see also UBOS, *Labour Market Conditions Report*, Kampala.

Uganda Bureau of Statistics (2005) Statistical Abstract, Kampala.

Uganda Bureau of Statistics (2004) *Where are the Poor? Mapping Patterns of Well-Being in Uganda 1992 and 1999*, together with International Livestock Research Institute, Kampala and Nairobi.

Uganda Bureau of Statistics (2003a) *Uganda National Household Survey 2002/2003: Report on the Labour Force Survey*, Kampala.

Uganda Bureau of Statistics (2003b): *A Report on the Ugandan Business Register 2001/2002*, Kampala.

Uganda Cleaner Production Centre (UCPC) (2008) *Uganda Cleaner Production Centre - Summary of Achievements (2001-2008) and Future Prospects*, Kampala.

Uganda Investment Authority (UIA) (2004) *Strategic Plan 2004-2009*, Kampala.

United Nations (UN) (2004) *Common Country Assessment Uganda*, Kampala.

United Nations (2001) *Public Service Ethics in Africa, Volume 2*, UN Department of Economic and Social Affairs, Division for Public Economics and Public Administration, New York.

United Nations Conference on Trade and Development (UNCTAD) (2005a) *World Investment Report 2005: Transnational Corporations and the Internationalization of R&D*, Overview, Geneva.

United Nations Conference on Trade and Development (2005b) *World Investment Report 2005 Transnational Corporations and the Internationalization of R&D*, Full Report, Geneva.

United Nations Conference on Trade and Development (2005c) 'Improving the Competitiveness of SMEs through Enhancing Productive Capacity', Proceedings of Four Expert Meetings Geneva.

United Nations Conference on Trade and Development (2005d) *World Investment Report 2005: Country Fact Sheet Uganda*, Geneva.

United Nations Conference on Trade and Development (2004a) *An Investment Guide to Uganda: Opportunities and Conditions*, Geneva.

United Nations Conference on Trade and Development (2004b) *World Investment Report 2004: The Shift towards Services*, Geneva.

United Nations Conference on Trade and Development (2004c) *World Investment Directory: Country Profile Uganda*, Geneva.

United Nations Conference on Trade and Development (2003) *Africa's Technology Gap: Case Studies on Kenya, Ghana, Uganda and Tanzania*, Geneva.

United Nations Conference on Trade and Development (2001) *World Investment Report 2001: Promoting Linkages, Overview*, Geneva.

United Nations Conference on Trade and Development (1998) *World Investment Report: Trends and Determinants*, Geneva.

United Nations Development Programme (UNDP) Uganda (2008) 'HIV/AIDS has made Uganda poorer', http://www.undp.or.ug/news/115 (accessed 30/12/2008).

United Nations Development Programme (2007a) *Uganda Human Development Report 2007: Rediscovering Agriculture for Human Development*, Kampala.

United Nations Development Programme (2007b) *Millennium Development Goals -Uganda's Progress Report 2007*, Kampala.

United Nations Educational, Scientific and Cultural Organization (UNESCO) (2007) *Study on National Research Systems - A Meta-Review*, Regional report on Africa, Paris.

United Nations Educational, Scientific and Cultural Organization (2005) Country Profile Uganda, Statistics on Science and Technology, http://www.uis.unesco.org/profiles/EN/ GEN/countryProfile_en.aspx?code=8000 (accessed 01/04/2006).

United Nations Industrial Development Organization (UNIDO) (2007) *Uganda - Integrated Industrial Policy for Sustainable Industrial Development and Competitiveness Report*, Vienna.

United Nations Industrial Development Organization (2005a) 'Industrial Development, Trade and Poverty Alleviation through South-South Cooperation', Issue Paper submitted by Secretariat for General Conference, 11th Session, 28 November-2 December 2005, Vienna.

United Nations Industrial Development Organization (2005b) Uganda Integrated Programme Textile Component: Tracer Study, Vienna.

United Nations Industrial Development Organization (2005c) 'Industrial Development Report 2005: Capability Building for Catching-up: Historical, Empirical and Policy Dimensions', Executive Summary, Vienna.

United Nations *Industrial Development Organization (2005d) Industrial Development Report 2005: Capability* Building for Catching-up: Historical, Empirical and Policy Dimensions', Full report, Vienna.

United Nations Industrial Development Organization (2004a) *Industrial Development Report 2004: Industrialization, Environment and the Millennium Development Goals in Sub-Saharan Africa: The New Frontier in the Fight against Poverty*, Vienna.

United Nations Industrial Development Organization (2004b) *Inserting Local Industries into Global Value Chains and Production Networks: What Opportunities and Challenges for Upgrading?* With a focus on Asia, China raising competitiveness and phasing out of the Multi-Fibre Arrangements, Vienna.

United Nations Industrial Development Organization (2003a) 'Clustering, Innovation and Regional Development: What Works!', UNIDO Workshop on Cluster-Based Economic Development, Background paper, Vienna.

United Nations Industrial Development Organization (2003b) *A Path out of Poverty: Developing Rural and Women Entrepreneurship*, Vienna.

United Nations Industrial Development Organization (2002) *Industrial Development Report 2002/2003: Competing through Innovation and Learning*, Vienna.

United Nations Industrial Development Organization (2001) *Development of Clusters and Networks of SMEs: The UNIDO Programme*, Vienna.

United Nations Industrial Development Organization (2000) *Public-Private Partnerships for Economic Development and Competitiveness*, prepared by M.J. Enright, Vienna.

United States Agency for International Development (USAID) (2005) *Uganda's Fisheries Competitiveness Plan, July 2005*, Draft, Part of the SCOPE Project 'Building Uganda's Global Competitiveness in Agribusiness 2005-2010', Kampala.

van Bussel, P. (2005) *Business Services Market Development: Experiences and Lessons,* BSMD Report, Kampala.

van Bussel, P. and P. Nyabuntu (2007) *Recommendations and Suggestions for a Strategy and activities to Develop Value Chains,* Report for SNV Uganda, Kampala.

Vogel, J. (1996) 'The Tragedy of History', *New Left Review,* 220, pp. 36-61.

Wade, R. (1990) *Governing the Market,* Princeton University Press, Princeton.

Walter, T., P. Rosa, S. Barabas, W. Balunywa, A. Sserwanga, R. Namatovu, and S. Kyejjusa (2005) *Global Entrepreneurship Monitor* (GEM) Uganda Executive Report 2004, Kampala.

Walter, T., W. Balunywa, P. Rosa, A. Sserwanga, S. Barabas, and R. Namatovu (2004) Global Entrepreneurship Monitor, Uganda Executive Report 2003, Kampala.

Watson, M. (2005a) *Foundations of International Political Economy,* Palgrave Macmillan, Basingstoke.

Watson, M. (2005b) 'What Makes a Market Economy? Schumpeter, Smith and Walras on the Coordination Problem', *New Political Economy,* 10 (2), pp. 143-61.

Weatherspoon, D.D. and T. Reardon (2003) 'The Rise of Supermarkets in Africa: Implications for Agrifood Systems and the Rural Poor', *Development Policy Review,* 21, pp. 333-55.

Whittaker, D.H., T. Zhu, T.J. Sturgeon, M.H. Tsai, and T. Okita (2008) 'Compressed Development', *MIT IPC Working Paper,* No. 08-005, Cambridge, MA.

Wiegratz, J. (2008) 'Beyond Harsh Trade!? The Relevance of 'Soft' Competitiveness factors for Ugandan Enterprises to Endure in Global Value Chains', *African Journal of Business and Law,* 2 (1), pp. 2-22.

Wiegratz, J. (2006a) An Analysis of Selected Aspects of Economic Development and Competitiveness in Uganda: Implications for Human Resource Development, Background Report for GTZ, Kampala.

Wiegratz, J. (2006b) *Capabilities for Catching-up: Economic Development and Competitiveness in Uganda: Implications for Human Resource Development with Particular Focus on Technical and Vocational Education and Training in Uganda,* GTZ PEVOT, Kampala.

Wiegratz, J., P. Nyabuntu, and C. Omagor (2007a) *Competing and Learning in Global Value Chains - Firms' Experiences in the Case of Uganda: A Study of Five Export Sub-Sectors With Reference to Trade between Uganda and Europe,* Uganda Programme for Trade Opportunities and Policy (UPTOP), Kampala.

Wiegratz, J., P. Nyabuntu, and C. Omagor (2007b) *Case Studies of Lead Firm Governance Systems in the Context of Commercialization of Smallholder Agriculture in Uganda,* UPTOP, Kampala.

Williams, D. and T. Young (1994) 'Governance, the World Bank and Liberal Theory', *Political Studies,* 42 (1), pp. 84-100.

Williamson, T. (2003) 'Targets and Results in Public Sector Management - Uganda Case Study', *ODI Working Paper,* No. 205, London.

Wirak, A., B. Heen, E. Moen, and S. Vusia (2003) *Business, Technical and Vocational Education and Training (BTVET) for Employment and Private Sector Development in Uganda,* Report for the Royal Norwegian Embassy in Kampala and Norwegian Agency for Development Cooperation, Oslo.

World Bank (WB) (2006a) *Uganda: Diagnostic Trade Integration Study, May 2006, Volume 1,* electronic version, Washington D.C.

World Bank (2006b) *Uganda: Diagnostic Trade Integration Study, May 2006, Volume 2,* electronic version, Washington D.C.

World Bank (2006c) *Doing Business in 2006: Creating Jobs,* Washington D.C.

World Bank (2005a) 'Comments on Minister Suruma's Budget Strategy Paper: With a Focus on the Agriculture Proposal', PowerPoint Presentation, World Bank staff Uganda, Kampala.

World Bank (2005b) *Pro-Poor Growth in the 1990s: Lessons and Insights from 14 Countries,* World Bank, Washington D.C.

World Bank (2005c) *Project Information Document: UG-Millennium Science Initiative (FY 06),* Appraisal Stage, Washington D.C.

World Bank (2004a) *Republic of Uganda - Country Integrated Fiduciary Assessment,* Washington D.C.

World Bank (2004b) *Competing in the Global Economy: An Investment Climate Assessment for Uganda,* study done with UMACIS (Uganda Manufacturers Association Consultancy and Information Service), Washington D.C.

World Bank (2003) *East Africa Investment Climate Assessment Survey,* Washington D.C.

World Bank (1996) *Sub-Saharan Africa: Assessing Technological Capabilities and Firm Productivity,* Findings, Africa Region, Nr. 58, Review of Biggs et al. (1995), http://www.worldbank.org/afr/findings/english/find58.htm (accessed 01/05/2006).

World Bank (1993) *The East Asian Miracle,* Washington D.C.

World Bank (1982) *Uganda: Country Economic Memorandum,* Washington D.C.

World Intellectual Property Organization (WIPO) (2005) PCT *Statistical Indicators Report, Highlights,* February 2005, Geneva.

World Intellectual Property Organization (2003) *Member Country Profile Uganda, http://*www.wipo.int/about-ip/en/ipworldwide/pdf/ug.pdf (accessed 05/07/2005).

Yumkella, K. (2005) *Towards Pro-Poor Sustainable Industrial Development: A Shared Vision for UNIDO, UNIDO, Vienna,* http://www.unido.org/file-storage/download/?file_id=38781 (accessed 01/03/06).

Zalk, N. (2004) 'The Role of Dynamic Products in Global Integration: Implications for South Africa', *Trade and Industrial Policy Strategies,* Working Paper, No. 2-2004.

Zak, P.J. and S. Knack (2001) 'Trust and Growth', *Economic Journal,* 111 (470), pp. 295-321

Appendices

Appendix 1

Box 40: Selected recent drivers of competitive advantage in the global economy

"Patterns of competitive advantage are changing as exports grow in response to two forces: innovation and the relocation of activities, processes or functions to lower cost areas. Both play a role in most industries, but their importance differs by technology and physical characteristics.

- Some products (e.g. pharmaceuticals) grow rapidly mainly because of rapid innovation; there is little relocation to take advantage of low wages because of the continuous processes involved in production and the extremely stringent technical demands on the intermediate inputs.
- Some products (e.g. electronics) benefit from both innovation and relocation – they enjoy rapid demand growth, substitute for older products and also have low-technology assembly processes that can be placed in poor countries.
- Some products (like apparel) are driven primarily by relocation. The overall growth of production and technical change are relatively slow.
- Some products (like automobiles) have discrete, 'separable' processes that can undergo relocation. However, their technological complexity and 'weight' (critical components are, unlike electronics, heavy in relation to their value) means that distances across which processes are fragmented are fairly small (Lall, Albaladejo and Zhang, 2004).

Products for which neither innovation nor relocation are relevant tend to grow slowly in trade. One of the secrets of rapid export growth is therefore to enter product segments where the process of relocation is very active and demand is growing rapidly. This was just what the East Asian Tigers managed to do. Fragmentation and relocation are dynamic processes, and, with new technologies, new forms are appearing constantly. The service area, for example, is experiencing a veritable explosion of relocation. Functions like call centres, back-office services and even R&D are being relocated in low wage countries, though most of these are concentrating in India and China".

Source: *Lall (2005, 8).*

Appendix 2

Box 41: Three kinds of innovation: Radical innovation, adaptation and imitation

"For the sake of clarity, it may be useful to distinguish three kinds of innovation: radical innovation, adaptation and imitation, where only the first one is innovation in the strict meaning while the latter two are the result of technology diffusion and appear as innovations to the recipient countries. In practice these three innovations often take place in an interrelated manner. Radical innovation is the generation of new-to-the-world techniques. Radical innovation is sourced in inventions that are generated by technological creativity. This creativity comes from coupling a strong R&D sector, with ties to industry, commerce and services, to a strong basic scientific research capacity, complete with universities, modern laboratories, public finance support, government agencies, and civil societies such as scientific academies. Of course, to build up and maintain these assets, heavy technological investments and expenditures are needed. To cover the costs of the innovation system and the risks inherent to innovation, the market structure must authorize profit margins. The key to these margins is productive flexibility and product differentiation.

There is kind of technological change that relies on adaptation. Well-established techniques are incorporated in the production system after modifications to fit the commercial and technical needs of the host environment. The adjustment to local circumstances requires the existence of a technological system comprised of scientists, engineers, technicians and managers specialized in the D side of R&D. It also demands support institutions and an open economy. Imitation is the straightforward incorporation of techniques used by others. Imitation presents little risk since the techniques can be observed in operation before incorporation in the host environment. The requirement that imitation places on the recipient is to possess a productive system large enough to allow specialization and stable enough to ensure experience. Imitation demands little in the way of a country's own technological assets since the techniques come from abroad. It requires, however, institutions that guarantee the financiers that made their acquisition possible, and the managers that operate them.

Although the three kind of innovation will be active simultaneously in just about any economy, their relative contributions change in the direction of less imitation and more innovation as the economy is more technologically advanced. Numerous pieces of evidence ...have documented that, when innovation takes on more and more importance, the economy's requirements of skills and technological assets inflate incommensurably with the previous regimes of imitation and adaptation".

Source: *Isaksson et al (2005, 51-2).*

Appendix 3

Box 42: Pro-productivity public interventions: The sails that will propel productivity (if the wind blows)

In order to enhance productivity in developing countries, "[w]hat must be brought in the first place is technology. Technology is partly a public good; it is not easy to accumulate enough of a public good because those who pay for it are fewer than those who use it. Hence, public intervention to stimulate the transfer of technology is justified. These interventions have two targets in their sights.

Since technology is knowledge about how to do things, the first target will be located on the knowledge (the logos) side of technology. The question here is how to influence the process whereby intellectual capital is acquired, generated and used. Free markets are of little use in regulating this process because of the non-rivalry attribute of knowledge. Instead, the patent and science ... are to be in charge of generating knowledge and distributing it. The second target derives from the fact that knowledge by itself cannot do anything to stir productivity. It is only when knowledge meets matter (the 'techne' side of technology), when it gives birth to better modes of organization, better processes, better equipments, better labour skills, better products, better supplier relations and so forth, that productivity is enhanced. The second target is the process whereby technology is embodied in the production system.

In both areas, externalities and imperfect competition have been found to play a major role. It ensues that the free play of market forces cannot deliver proper incentives to accumulate technology. Market forces should play a role, certainly, but the requirements of social welfare have to be delivered by policies, and these policies must be about the generation of incentives leading to socially efficient outcomes. Both knowledge acquisition and its implementation in the form of activities that put new techniques to use can be pursued by long-term supply policies. The three sails that will propel productivity (if the wind blows) are the National Innovation System, the education system, and the communication and energy infrastructure. ... Possessing the three sails is a critical condition for productivity, but all it does is to provide a potential to catch the wind of opportunities. The actual utilization of that potential may vary to a rather large extent according to the skills with which these sails are deployed ... The art of productivity policies is to elicit the right ingredients and to mix them so as to serve the economy a cocktail on which it would not want to pass".

Source: *Isaksson et al (2005, 129-32).*

Appendix 4a

Table 45: Catching up and falling behind relative to the USA, 1960 and 2000

Catching up	Change	No change	change	Falling behind	Change
Luxembourg	64	Australia	4	Ethiopia	-5
Taiwan, Province of China	50	Kenya	2	Uganda	-6
Ireland	49	Sweden	1	Bolvia	-7
Hong Kong SAR of China	48	Colombia	1	Seychelles	-7
Barbados	47	Guinea-Bissau	1	South Africa	-7
Cyprus	43	Algeria	0	Philippines	-7
Singapore	33	Turkey	0	Mexico	-7
Mauritius	31	Malawi	0	Chad	-7
Italy	26	United Kingdom	0	Nepal	-8
Korea, rep. of Spain	25	Peru	0	Paraguay	-8
Gabon	25	Uruguay	-2	Argentina	-8
Botswana	24	Ecuador	-2	Bangladesh	-8
Portugal	24	Trinidad and Tobago	-2	Fiji	-8
Belgium	21	Tanzania, United Rep.	-2	Burundi	-8
Japan	20	Guyana	-2	Benin	-9
Finland	20	Indonesia	-3	Jamaica	-10
Austria	20	Panama	-3	Mauritania	-10
Norway	19	Denmark	-3	Burkina Faso	-12
Cape Verde	18	SriLanka	-3	Guinea	-13
Israel	16	Iran, Islamic Rep. of	-4	Mali	-13
Greece	16	Zamiba	-4	Senegal	-14
Tunisia	15	Canada	-4	Cameroon	-14
France	14	Cote d'lvoire	-4	Togo	-14
Thailand	11			Honduras	-15
Syrian Arab Rep.	11			Madagascar	-16
Malaysia	11			Papua N. Guinea	-17
Brazil				Congo D. R.	-18
China	11			Costa Rica	-18
Zimbabwe	10			Rwanda	-19
Congo	10			Niger	-19
Haiti	10			Nigeria	-19

Dominican Rep.	10			Angola	-19
Chile	9			Gambia, The Switzerland	-19
Iceland	9			Jordan	-20
Morocco	9			Central Afr. Rep.	-21
Netherlands	9			New Zealand	-23
Egypt, Arab Rep.	8			Comoros	-25
Ghana	8			Mozambique	-26
India	6			El Salvador	-29
Pakistan	5			Lesotho	-36
				Nicaragua	-37
				Venezuela	-38
				Sierra Leone	-38
				Equatoria Guine	-49

Source: *Isaksson et al (2006, 65).*

Appendix 4b

Figure 20: World Technology Frontier, 1960 and 2000, World

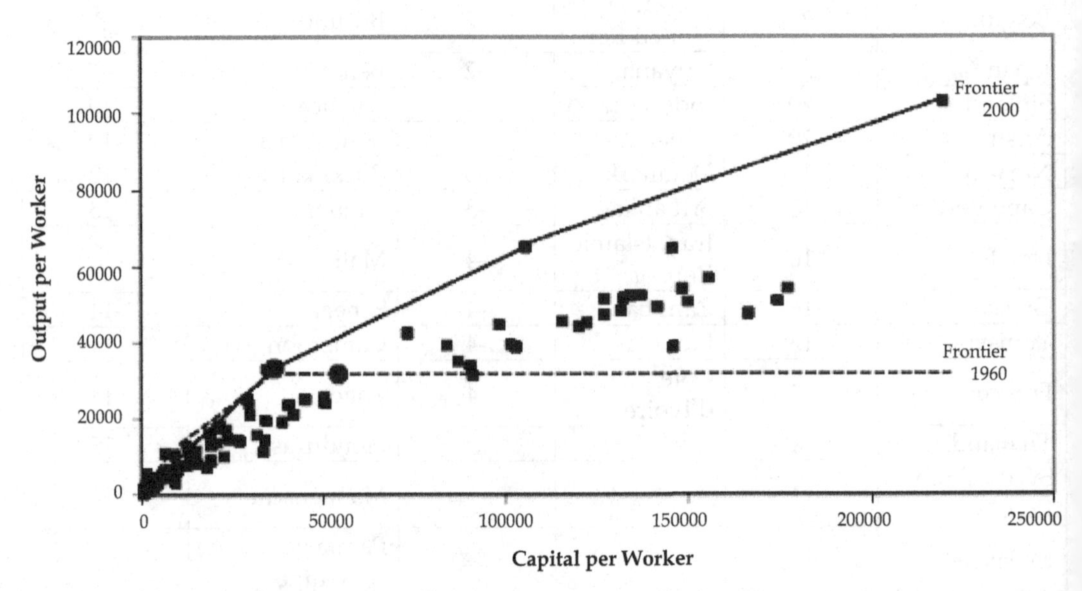

Source: *Isaksson et al (2005, 75).*

Related explanations and interpretations: The figure shows "the shift of the technology frontier by drawing the frontiers of 1960 and 2000 in the same space. The distance between the two frontiers measures the extent of technological progress. The shift of the frontier is nothing less than spectacular. One segment has not moved (the segment corresponding to the Less Developed Countries) but the top segment exhibits a counter clockwise shift that lifts top labour productivity over $100,000 by a sevenfold increase in capital per worker. So a vast new technological space has opened up, populated exclusively by the industrialized countries plus Hong Kong, Israel, South Korea, Singapore, and the Taiwan province of China. Appallingly, the other countries still occupy the technological space already chartered in 1960. An additional interesting finding is that the production relationship seems to have tilted so that the slope of the 2000 frontier is steeper than that of 1960. In other words, technological change has not been neutral regarding capital and labour; it has been labour saving. One important implication of such a tilt is that the time of diminishing marginal returns to capital is being postponed. We can conclude that capital intensity has a strong bearing on technological change" (ibid, 55).

Appendix 4c:

Figure 21: World Technology Frontier 1960

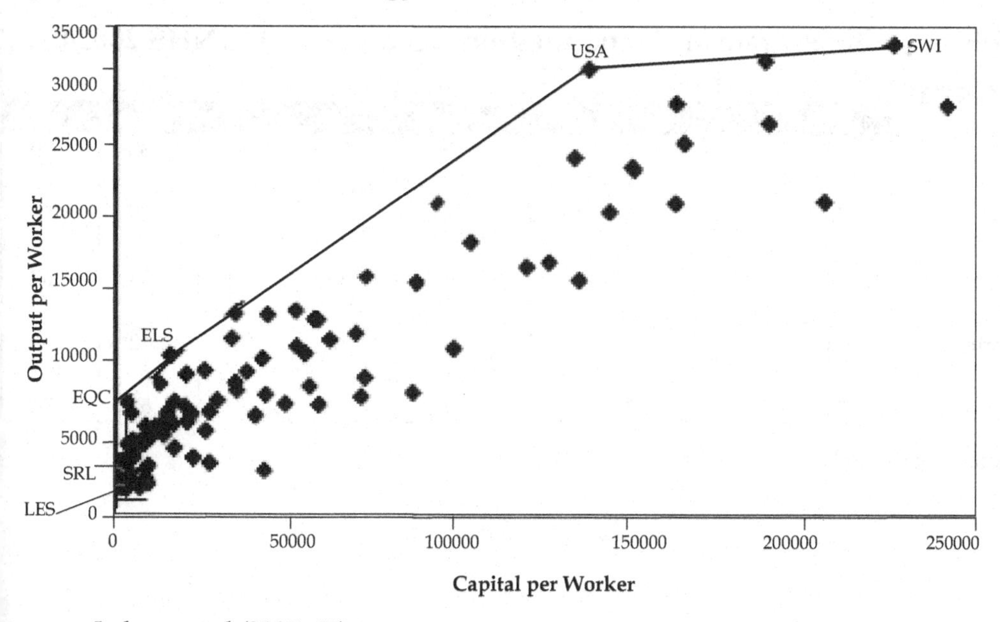

Source: *Isaksson et al (2005, 67).*

Appendix 5

Table 46: Educational attainment of the population, aged 10+, (%), UNHS 2002/03

Category	Rural			Urban			Total		
	M	F	T	M	F	T	M	F	T
Total	100	100	100	100	100	100	100	100	100
No Education	9.1	21.2	15.4	2.6	8.3	5.7	8.1	19.1	13.9
P1-P6	59.2	58.5	58.9	38.6	39.0	38.8	56.2	55.5	55.8
Primary 7	12.2	8.6	10.3	13.6	13.6	13.7	12.5	9.4	10.9
S1-S3	16.7	10.7	13.6	31.4	30.7	31.0	18.9	13.9	16.3
S4-S6	2.5	0.8	1.5	5.4	2.8	4.1	1.8	0.9	1.3
Above S6	0.3	0.2	0.3	8.2	5.6	6.7	2.5	1.2	1.8

Source: *UBOS (2003a, 9).*

Appendix 6

Table 47: Literacy rate of the population, aged 10+, (%), UNHS 2002/03

Category	Rural			Urban			Total		
	Male	Female	Total	Male	Female	Total	Male	Female	Total
Uganda	74	60	67	90	84	86	77	63	70
Central	78	73	75	92	90	91	82	79	80
Eastern	70	52	61	85	75	80	72	54	63
Northern	71	40	54	82	63	72	72	42	56
Western	74	67	73	87	80	83	79	69	74

Source: *UBOS (2003a, 10).*

Appendix 7

Table 48: Distribution of unemployed persons, aged 14-64, by education attainment, residence, region and sex, (%), UNHS 2002/03

Background characteristics	Unemployment rate			share of youth to total unemployment		
	M	F	T	M	F	T
National	2.6	4.2	3.5	51	62	58
Residence						
Rural	1.7	2.0	1.9	47	66	58
Urban	7.6	17.0	12.2	57	60	59
Region						
Central	4.3	9.4	6.9	56	64	61
Eastern	2.2	2.6	2.4	47	63	56
Northern	0.8	1.2	1.0	34	29	31
Western	2.3	2.1	2.2	50	71	60
Education						
No schooling	2.2	1.6	1.7	34	40	38
Primary	1.8	3.3	2.6	63	66	65
Secondary	4.6	11.3	7.4	56	66	62
Above secondary	4.5	8.5	5.9	17	50	34

Source: *UBOS (2006, 43)*

Appendix 8

Table 49: Unemployment rates, aged 10+[407], by sex, residence and region, (%), UNHS 2002/03

	Unemployment rate (%)		
	Male	*Female*	*Total*
Region			
Kampala	10.0	22.5	16.5
Central (excluding Kampala District)	2.5	5.2	3.9
Eastern	2.1	2.4	2.3
Northern	0.9	1.1	1.0
Western	2.2	1.9	2.1
Total	**2.5**	**3.9**	**3.2**

Source: *UBOS (2003a, 34).*

407 Note the difference in age category in the UBOS 2003 report. However, the proportions - especially the Kampala effect - are applicable.

Appendix 9

Table 50: Distribution of unemployed youth, aged 15-24, by educational attainment, residence, region and sex, (%), UNHS 2002/03

	Male	Female	Total
Total	7.5	8.8	6.3
Residence			
Rural	5.8	7.5	4.2
Urban	19.3	16.6	22.8
Region			
Central	13.0	12.6	13.4
Eastern	5.7	7.9	3.8
Northern	5.0	6.1	4.0
Western	5.2	7.1	3.4
Educational attainment			
None	6.6	9.5	4.9
Primary	5.9	7.4	4.5
Secondary	11.9	11.2	12.9
Above Secondary and above	20.0	20.1	20.0
Number	**85,097**	**61,501**	**146,598**

Source: *UBOS (2006, 46).*

Appendix 10

Box 43: Culture/gender disparities that affect poverty determinants (including E&T) of females

According to Mukasa et al. (2004), culture and gender disparities affect a range of issues in Uganda, including proportion/share (of total) of women in land ownership, formal LF participation, wages, literacy rate, share of total tertiary enrolment, maternal mortality ratio, credit distribution, sickness, membership in parliament, participation in governance and development structures, chairperson of district land boards, and applications for processing of land certificate titles. The following are findings from Mukasa et al. (2004, presented in Ellis et al. 2006) on related cultural practices that impact on the above categories; indeed, these practices also affect the process/pathway of knowledge and skills formation of Ugandan females:

"Women are economically dependent on men. Land inheritance is mainly patrilineal. Women work largely at home and have limited job opportunities. No emphasis is placed on preparing them for the workplace. Training is often skewed toward culturally appropriate fields, regardless of their income-earning potential. Less value is placed on women's work. Literacy rates reflect the low value placed on the role of women outside the home. Grooming of women for marriage is a factor in limiting schooling and therefore literacy. Gender allocation of roles also affects girls' progression in formal education, the main channel for literacy. Poverty interacts with negative attitudes about girls' education. For many, investment in girls' education is an investment in the family or clan of the girl's husband or father. Early marriage also keeps tertiary enrolments low.

Women have no control over sexuality and resources, [and] limited access to information. Harmful practices and taboos against women and children as well as early marriage contribute to high maternal mortality rates. Lack of credit limits women's economic independence and affects gender relations. Women have no control over their sexuality or bodies. Women are exposed to heavier workloads and face exposure to hazardous conditions. Leadership is the preserve of men. Women are not socialized to play political roles, have limited skills, and are not highly valued. Women have limited participation in governance structures. Ownership of land and participation in public life are male preserves. Applying for a land title is costly. Women lack exposure to land issues, have limited opportunity to inherit, are subject to land grabbing when widowed, and have limited knowledge of land rights and information on procedures."

Source: *Ellis et al (2006, 22-3) based on Mukasa et al (2004).*

Appendix 11

Table 51: Working poor by sex and occupation

	Working population			Below poverty level			Rate		
	Male	Female	Total	Male	Female	Total	Male	Female	*Total*
Legislators, senior officers	8	2	10	0	0	0	0	0	0
Professionals	79	40	119	3	3	7	4.4	8.0	5.6
Technicians and associates	118	69	187	18	0.6	18	15.1	0.8	9.8
Clerks	73	46	120	7	3	10	9.2	6.1	8.0
Service/sales workers	670	657	1,326	135	84	219	20.2	12.8	16.5
Agriculture and fisheries	2,242	3,128	5,370	1,033	1,329	2,363	46.1	42.5	44.0
Crafts/ related trade workers	249	130	379	55	48	103	21.9	37.0	27.1
Plant/ machine operators	144	13	157	29	4	33	20.2	33.6	21.3
Elementary occupation	582	213	795	15	69	223	2.6	32.4	28.1

Source: *UBOS (2006, 41).*

Appendix 12

Table 52: Currently employed persons, aged 10+, by industry, residence and sex, (%), UNHS 2002/03

Industry	Rural			Urban			Total		
	M	F	T	M	F	T	M	F	T
Agriculture hunting and forestry	68.0	83.5	75.8	11.7	18.9	15.1	60.1	75.4	67.8
Fishing	1.8	0.1	0.9	0.8	0.0	0.4	1.7	0.1	0.9
Mining and quarrying	0.4	0.2	0.3	0.5	0.3	0.4	0.4	0.2	0.3
Manufacturing	6.3	3.9	5.1	13.5	12.6	13.1	7.3	4.9	6.1
Electricity, gas and water	0.1	0.0	0.0	0.3	0.3	0.3	0.1	0.0	0.1
Construction	1.9	0.0	1.0	6.3	0.1	3.3	2.5	0.0	1.3
Sale, maintenance, repair of m/vehicles & personal h/hold goods	11.1	6.3	8.7	30.2	31.2	30.6	13.8	9.4	11.6
Hotels and restaurants	1.4	2.6	2.0	1.7	12.2	6.7	1.4	3.8	2.6
Transport, storage and communications	2.5	0.1	1.3	11.8	0.4	6.4	3.8	0.1	1.9
Financial intermediation	0.0	0.0	0.0	0.2	0.1	0.2	0.0	0.0	0.0
Real estate, renting and business activities	0.3	0.1	0.2	2.2	1.0	1.6	0.5	0.2	0.4
Public administration and defence	0.8	0.1	0.4	5.3	1.1	3.3	1.4	0.2	0.8
Education	3.3	1.4	2.3	3.6	4.7	4.1	3.3	1.8	2.6
Health and social work	0.6	0.6	0.6	1.6	2.3	1.9	0.7	0.8	0.8
Other community, social & personal service activities	1.2	0.7	0.9	7.7	4.4	6.1	2.1	1.2	1.6
Private households with employed persons	0.0	0.5	0.4	2.4	9.8	5.9	0.6	1.7	1.2
Total	**100**	**100**	**100**	**100**	**100**	**100**	**100**	**100**	**100**
Numbers ('000)	3,972	4,060	8,033	646	582	1,228	4,618	4,642	9,260

Source: *UBOS (2003a, 21). Reference period: seven days prior to survey.*

Appendix 13

Table 53: Main occupation of employed persons, aged 10+, (%), UNHS 2002/03

Main Occupation	Cent.	East	North	West	Total		
					M	F	T
Managers and administrators	0.1	0.1	0.1	0.1	0.2	0.1	0.1
Professionals	1.1	0.8	0.6	2.5	1.8	0.9	1.4
Associate professionals	3.4	2.1	2.2	2.4	3.6	2.0	2.8
Clerks	0.5	0.3	0.3	0.3	0.4	0.5	0.4
Service workers and market sales workers	15.6	11.6	9.8	14.7	14.8	14.4	14.6
Agricultural and fishery workers	62.4	74.1	74.7	67.1	57.9	74.2	66.1
Craft and related workers	5.7	3.0	6.4	3.9	6.9	3.1	5.0
Plant machine operators and assemblers	0.9	0.5	0.4	0.8	1.3	0.1	0.7
Elementary occupations	10.3	7.5	5.6	8.2	13.0	4.8	8.9
Total	**100**	**100**	**100**	**100**	**100**	**100**	**100**
Numbers ('000)	2,203	2,429	1,658	2,401	4,618	4,642	9,260

Source: *UBOS (2003a, 22). Reference period: seven days prior to survey.*

Appendix 14

Table 54: Main and secondary occupations of employed persons, Aged 10+, (%), UNHS

Main Occupation	Number engaged in main activity ('000)	Number engaged in secondary activity ('000)	Percentage engaged in secondary activity
Managers and administrators	12,500	4,500	36.2
Professionals			
Associate professionals	126,600	5,600	4.5
Clerks	257,100	33,700	13.1
Service workers and market sales workers	40,100	1,800	4.6
Agricultural and fishery workers	1,353,000	628,600	46.5
Craft and related workers			
Plant machine operators and assemblers	6,118,500	997,600	16.3
Elementary occupations	463,100	268,000	57.9
Not reported	65,100	4,000	6.4
Uganda ('000)	822,900	277,000	33.8
	745	2,000	-
	9,260	2,224	24

Source: *UBOS (2003a, 23). Reference period: seven days prior to survey.*

Appendix 15

Box 44: Structures of monthly wages/earnings, by educational attainment, industry and occupation

Education	**Mean Income**
No formal education	25,000
Primary education	74,000
Secondary education	99,000
Specialised training and above	237,000
Industry Major divisions	**Median wage**
Agriculture, hunting and forestry	22,000
Fishing	77,000
Mining and quarrying	22,000
Manufacturing	60,000
Electricity, gas and water supply	160,000
Construction	75,000
Sales	60,000
Hotels and restaurants	33,000
Transport, storage and communications	80,000
Financial intermediation	500,000
Real estate, renting and business	100,000
Public administration	140,000
Education	100,000
Health and social work	100,000
Other services	20,000
Occupation major group	**Median wage**
Legislators, senior officials and managers	450,000
Professionals	150,000
Technicians and associate professionals	105.000
Clerks	100,000
Service workers and shop and market sales workers	50,000
Agriculture and fishery workers	20,000
Crafts and related trade workers	75,000
Plant and machine operators and assemblers	80,000
Elementary occupation	30,000

Source: *UBOS (2006, 16-7).*

Appendix 16

Box 45: Distribution of job advertisements in newspapers[408]

"**Distribution of job advertised by major industrial divisions** [T]here was a downward trend in jobs advertised from 57,289 in 2001 to 14, 051 in 2003 ... The trend again improved in 2004 with 29,462 jobs advertised. **In 2001**, social and personal services, health and social work, Public administration, hotels and restaurants, manufacturing and agriculture, forestry and fishing showed high demand for labour with job adverts ranging from 9,593 to 4,038. **In 2002**, the major divisions of hotels and restaurants, public administration, education and social and personal services had tremendous job advertisements ranging from 16,996 to 1,464. **In 2003**, only two major divisions are worth mentioning, that is public administration and social and personal services with 7,672 and 4,626 jobs advertised respectively. **In 2004**, public administration and Transport, Storage and Communication had a lion's share of the total 29,462 jobs advertised, accounting for 81 per cent. One can conclude, therefore, that following the trend of jobs advertised that the economy is growing in sectors with low investments, low technology and high returns. ... **Distribution of jobs re-advertised by major occupational groups** ... [T]he skills in the upper occupational groups are not easily filled for one reason or the other. Among the possible reasons is lack of skilled manpower to fill the vacancies, unattractive remunerations, job specifications, etc. In 2001, out of a total of 606 vacancies re-advertised, legislators, professionals and associate professionals occupational groups constituted 97 per cent and the remaining 3 per cent [were] shared among the remaining occupational groups."

Source: *UBOS (2006, 59-61, emphasis added).*

Appendix 17

Table 55: Monthly earnings for paid employees in (non-crop) household enterprises, by sex, residence, region, in Ush, UNHS 2002/03

Background characteristics	Less than 25,000	25,000-49,999	50,000-74999	75,000-99,9999	100,000 and above
National	**63.9**	**22.5**	**7**	**4**	**2.6**
Sex					
Male	63.4	22.3	7.3	4.2	2.7
Female	72.4	25.9	1.7		
Residence					
Rural	65.5	21.5	7.1	3.7	2.2
Urban	46.1	33.7	6.3	7.3	6.6
Region					
Central	63	20.9	7	6.4	2.7
Eastern	64.9	26.3	4.9	0.3	3.6
Northern	46.5	34.2	11.6	7.2	0.5
Western	74	15	7.6	1.3	2.1

Source: *UBOS (2006, 29).*

408 "A vacancy [was] ...entered only once even if it appears more than once in the same newspaper or different newspaper" (UBOS 2006, 60). Advertisements in New Vision, Monitor and the East African were analysed.

Appendix 18

Table 56: Average monthly earnings for paid employees in (non-crop) household enterprises, by residence, region, industry, sex, in Ush, UNHS 2002/03

Background characteristics	Male	Female	Total
National	**28,793**	**13,816**	**27,519**
Residence			
Rural	22,582	15,734	22,294
Urban	38,392	13,326	34,725
Region			
Central	24,522	11,507	24,028
Eastern	22,627	5,464	21,763
Northern	25,894	30,797	26,609
Western	22,537	7,601	22,094
Industry			
Other agriculture	22,227	24,333	22,387
Fishing	71,660	-	71,660
Mining & quarrying	18,500	5,333	13,563
Manufacturing	16,402	10,710	15,773
Construction	49,200	-	49,200
Sales, trade and repairs	23,525	10,900	23,137
Hotels	15,811	26,000	17,664
Transport, storage and communications	73,511	9,000	72,167
Other services	13,188	50,000	15,353

Source: *UBOS (2006, 30).*

Appendix 19

Box 46: Diversification in practice: Skills needs among suppliers in the tourism sector in Uganda

"Tourism services

Travel agents and tour operators (including car hire companies) are ... primary trade tourism service providers after attractions, accommodation and airlines. In 2003, there were 162 tour operators and 151 travel agencies in Uganda, of which 143 and 151, respectively, were based in Kampala.1 Of the 160 or so registered tour operators, only 35 are current members of the Association of Ugandan Tour Operators (AUTO),2 all of whom are linked to medical facilities in Kampala including private clinics and emergency evacuation facilities. Only 16 are formally licensed (by MTTI) tour operators, conforming to standards set out in the existing tourism legislation. Local tour operators and travel agents in Uganda play a very small role in being the main distribution platform for tourism products compared with neighboring countries. In Kenya and Tanzania, tour operators and travel agents provide between 20-30 percent of business to lodges and resorts, while in Uganda they provide only 7 and 3.5 percent, respectively ...

Table: Sales Channels in Hotels (% of annual Sales)

	Kenya	Tanzania	Uganda
Airlines	6.17	36.71	1.58
Travel Agencies	29.20	23.18	3.42
Tour Operators	27.41	19.53	7.05
Walk-in business	32.04	19.53	77.68
Other	5.17	40.50	10.26

Source: 2003 East Africa ICA Data [see World Bank 2003].

Weak skills and service delivery among suppliers in the tourism sector in Uganda

Firms in the tourism offer supply chain (for example hotels, in-bound tour operators and transport providers) in Uganda are all small and relatively underexposed and inexperienced with international tourism. With a few exceptions, operators in Uganda are not actively working with international agents or independently marketing their products and services in key target market ...

Many of Uganda's tour operators and accommodation owners have a 'shop-keeper' mentality with regards to sales of tourism products; they sit on their inventory and wait for customers, they do not generate demand. This can be attributed to the quick re-entry Uganda made into tourism in the mid-1990s triggered by the high demand for gorilla tourism. International tour operators were able to sell trips to Uganda because of the high demand ... [to see] gorillas; Ugandan companies capable of transporting clients to and from the airport, to hotels and to the gorillas were needed at the time. Many of the operators who started their businesses then were able to fit quickly into the supply chain that was demanding these ground handling operations. Partly as a consequence of this external focus, the foreign visitors in the domestic market (both resident and visiting for business or VFR [Visiting friends/relatives]) have largely been ignored as a potential source of business, particularly by tour operators. There is a need to both study the needs and size of this market and help tour operators exploit this opportunity ...

As tour operators have matured during the past decade, they have gradually tried to take on more of the supply chain, getting involved both with marketing and supplying accommodation. Their skills in these areas are weak as they have little exposure. The same is true of the companies that entered the tourism supply chain through providing accommodation; many of these owners did not come from a tourism background but were opportunistic and provided a vital piece of infrastructure needed at the time. With the exception of hotels and lodges that have hired international management, operating skills are weak throughout the accommodation sector. Even hotels with international managers have neglected other departments (such as sales and marketing) and opted to hire locally (and pay poorly) where the necessary skills are absent.

Visitor and industry surveys conducted during the preparation of a Tourism Skills Needs Assessment Study in 2003 for gaining a comprehensive picture of the current and future training needs of the tourism sector found that overall, visitors had a positive impression of Uganda and felt that the standard of service was acceptable. Where standards were considered to be lower than acceptable or average they were made up for in friendly service. The most commonly identified training needs across all areas (including the Immigration Dept., taxi drivers, restaurants, hotels, lodges and tour guides) were:

- Customer Relations
- Communication Skills
- Foreign Language Skills
- General Tourism Information

According to the industry operators interviewed for the present study, training should focus on the development and training of existing staff. The most urgent training requirements are in the areas of: food preparation and production; health, hygiene & safety; computer skills, including administration and front office programs; customer care and customer relations; salesmanship and marketing; supervisory skills; product knowledge. ...

Recommendation ... Skills

Tour operators (and to a large extent sales staff attached to hotels and lodges) in Uganda lack basic sales and marketing skills which ... [affects] their ability to enter and perform in international markets. Targeted sales and marketing training is required covering the following aspects of destination management:

- Identification of profitable market segments
- Creation of appeals that resonate with visitor benefits
- Establishment of strategic alliances and public-private partnerships
- Preparation of action-oriented marketing plans
- Recognizing opportunities in tourist spending patterns
- Tracking preferences of target visitors
- Adding value to natural and cultural attractions
- Linking attractions together
- Bench marking and countering competitor strategies
- Measuring the performance of marketing campaigns
- Determining returns on marketing investments

In addition, there is a need to strengthen skills in food preparation and production; and in health, hygiene and safety.

[FN:] 1 Based on the 2003 MTTI Baseline Survey of Tourism Enterprises (including tour operators, travel agencies, restaurants, airline offices, crafts and souvenir shops, and recreational facilities). 2 AUTO membership requires members to pay annual subscriptions of Sh500,000".

Source: *WB (2006b, 115-6, 122).*

Appendix 20

Box 47: Challenges in skills development in a small business in the hospitality sector

"Educational background: Most of the staff from the training institutions in our sector are not motivated, they lack enthusiasm, energy, and attitude. This is because they go to these institutions as the last resort. The culture is that when there is no money to pay school fees or when somebody does not make it to a higher institution, they opt for hotel management. In interviews for new positions, for instance waiters jobs, there is rarely a candidate who expresses that working in the hospitality business was actually his/her own decision based on actual motivation to be part of this industry; often, family members made the initial decision to opt for a training institution. Secondly, the society has a negative attitude towards these courses; people who go for these courses are looked at as failures. The work of such service jobs is not highly regarded. This kind of attitude has caused stigma on the waiters and other cadres in the hotel industry and negatively impacted on the staff's self-esteem and attitude. Indeed, the deficiencies in Human Resources caused by our cultural and educational systems are immense. Because of that, it is really difficult, really hard work and takes a lot of time and patience for us entrepreneurs to improve the skills of our staff. It would help a great deal if society and the education system would change so that practical and social skills, adequate attitudes, a culture of work and work ethics, and a sense of job responsibility, pride and confidence are more widespread.

Skill Development: Skill development in small business is very challenging. Most of the students who graduate from these institutions are equipped with theory but lack the practical part of it. For instance, customer feedback shows that customer service of our waitresses and waiters is currently our major weakness; we are trying to address that issue together with the staff. We potentially have to do a lot of further training, and do indeed as much as we can because competent staff is a crucial in our business. But there are other pressing expenditures emerging all the time; recently we had to purchase a generator because of the level of power cuts. Unfortunately, there are no training institutions in the market that are flexible and can provide hands-on information and further training. Also, there are no consultants in the market who are well trained especially in food & production. We sometimes have to hire experts from up-market international hotels in Uganda or Kenya to train our staff in specific skills. We need more support to efficiently and effectively deal with our Human Resource Management issues. Enterprise Uganda does the training at a cost but this is mainly in customer care and other generic business courses like book-keeping, marketing etc. There is also new competition for personnel emerging due to the upcoming CHOGM. The international hotels are attracting some of our best staff; to replace them and train the new employees afresh will be costly and timely.[409] The tourist industry is growing. Some of these issues related to Human Resources and training need urgent attention by the relevant Government institutions."

Source: *Managing Director of an upmarket restaurant business in Kampala. Text produced for this research.*

Appendix 21

New Vision, 17/06/2006: 'Training for CHOGM is also for the future'

By Prof. Wolfgang Thome (President of Uganda Tourism Association at the time of writing)

"A recent article on CHOGM and its substantial merit for Uganda raised the political temperature, but as the pro summit voices grew into a chorus the anti summit voices faltered quickly, not having any substance to offer. Thank God Ugandans are overwhelmingly mature people who swiftly made up their mind on what benefits the summit would bring to the country, after all, infrastructure would last for decades to come. In the remaining 15 months, as meetings and committees now sit to prepare for the challenges the summit will pose in logistical terms, a grey area has begun to emerge. We often hear comments and complaints about the service levels in restaurants or hotels and the lack of finesse in service delivery by their staff. Training personnel already employed in existing hotels and hospitality businesses, leave alone training yet more 'new' staff to fill the vacant positions in the many new hotel ventures now coming up, will pose a substantial challenge for the vocational and tertiary education sectors, to produce qualified staff capable ... [of giving] services commensurate to the expectations of our visitors.

The Hotel and Tourism Training Institute in Jinja, the only public national institution of its kind, has developed in-service training modules, to give refresher courses to staff already working in hotels and restaurants, both at the Institute and at the hotels. For long ... the HTTI [has] struggled with inadequate infrastructure, insufficient funding and lack of a purpose built campus. It is still awaiting to be allocated land by government on which a new campus for between 1,000 – 1,500 students can be built. The domestic demand for well trained hospitality, hotel and tourism personnel has risen sharply over the past years and regional demand has been growing exponentially. Kenya Utalii College is perpetually full so Uganda has an opportunity to step into the gap and meet regional and domestic training needs. But this will not be achieved in time for CHOGM. HTTI must seek alternatives to meet the demand for in-service courses and training for new entrants into the work force, so that adequate human resources will be available to the hotel sector for employment.

Organisers of CHOGM 2007 should note that human resource development and vocational training will be a cornerstone towards hosting a successful summit next year. Sad news for the new five star hotel structures and the money spent on building them, if we do not have trained and qualified

409 Uganda was the host country for the Commonwealth Heads of Government Meeting (CHOGM) in 2007. The event significantly spurred (local and foreign) investment into the country's hotel industry.

Ugandans to work in these places. Training for CHOGM is an investment not only for a successful summit but also for the future of the hospitality, hotel and tourism industry in this country. Well trained Ugandan professionals will set us apart from other destinations, where less emphasis is given to this important field, leaving us the space to excel where others don't. It is therefore my humble submission, that sufficient funds be set aside under the CHOGM budget to enable HTTI to meet the need and demand for training of personnel ahead of the summit next year, unless we are ready to import waiters, room stewards, barmen, cooks and other hotel workers at the expense of young Ugandans, while foreigners are hired because they have qualifications. Let us now give some real hope to our young generation by providing them with the skills to find and retain work in the world's fastest growing economic sector and make good [use] of the projections of opportunities the summit will bring to our country."

Appendix 22

Box 48: Features of technological learning in developing countries

"1. Technological learning is a real and significant process. It is vital to industrial development, and is primarily conscious and purposive rather than automatic and passive. Firms using a given technology for similar periods need not be equally proficient: each will be at the point given by the intensity of its capability building efforts.

2. Firms do not have full information on technical alternatives. They function with imperfect, variable and rather hazy knowledge of technologies they are using. There is no uniform, predictable learning curve for a given technology. Each faces risk, uncertainty and cost. Differences in learning are larger between countries at differing levels of development.

3. Firms may not know how to build up the necessary capabilities - learning itself often has to be learned. In a developing country, knowledge of traditional technologies may not be a good base on which to know how to master modern technologies. For a latecomer to a technology, the fact that others have already undergone the learning process is both a benefit and a cost. It is a benefit in that they can borrow from the others' experience (to the extent this is accessible). It is a cost in that they are relatively inefficient during the process (and so have to bear a loss if they compete on open markets). The cost and risk depend on how new the technology is relative to the entrant's base of knowledge, how developed factor markets are and how fast the technology is changing.

4. Firms cope with these uncertain conditions not by maximising a well-defined function but by developing organizational and managerial routines (Nelson and Winter, 1982). These are adapted as firms collect new information, learn from experience and imitate other firms. Learning is path dependent and cumulative.

5. The learning process is highly technology specific, since technologies differ in their learning requirements. Some technologies are more embodied in equipment while others have greater tacit elements. Process technologies (like chemicals) are more embodied than engineering technologies (machinery or automobiles), and demand different (often less) effort. Capabilities built up in one activity are not easily transferable to another. Different technologies involve different breadth of skills and knowledge, some needing a narrow range of specialization and others a wide range.

6. Different technologies have different degrees of dependence on outside sources of knowledge or information, such as other firms, consultants, capital goods suppliers or technology institutions.

7. Capability building occurs at all levels - shop-floor, process or product engineering, quality management, maintenance, procurement, inventory control, outbound logistics and relations with other firms and institutions. Innovation in the conventional sense of formal R&D is at one end of the spectrum of technological activity; it does not exhaust it. However, R&D does become important as more complex technologies are used; R&D is needed just for efficient absorption.

8. Technological development can take place ... [at] different depths. The attainment of a minimum level of operational capability (know-how) is essential to all activity. This may not lead to the development of deeper capabilities, an understanding of the principles of the technology (know-why): this requires a discrete strategy to invest in deepening. The deeper the levels of technological capabilities aimed at, the higher the cost, risk and duration involved. It is possible for an enterprise to become efficient at the know-how level and stay there, but this is not optimal for its long-term capability development. It will remain dependent on other firms for all major improvements to its technologies, and constrained in what it can obtain and use. The development of know-why allows firms to select better the technologies they need, lower the costs of buying those technologies, realise more value by adding their own knowledge, and to develop autonomous innovative capabilities.
9. Technological learning is rife with externalities and inter-linkages. It is driven by direct interactions with suppliers of inputs or capital goods, competitors, customers, consultants, and technology suppliers. Others are with firms in unrelated industries, technology institutes, extension services, universities, industry associations and training institutions. Where information and skill flows are particularly dense in a set of related activities, clusters of industries emerge, with collective learning for the group as a whole.
10. Technological interactions occur within a country and abroad. Imported technology provides the most important input into technological learning in developing countries. Since technologies change constantly, moreover, access to foreign sources of innovation is vital to continued technological progress. Technology import is not, however, a substitute for indigenous capability development - the efficacy with which imported technologies are used depends on local efforts. Similarly, not all modes of technology import are equally conducive to indigenous learning. Much depends on how the technology is packaged with complementary factors, whether or not it is available from other sources, how fast it is changing, how developed local capabilities are, and the policies adopted to stimulate transfer and deepening".

Source: *Lall (2004a, 12-3).*

Appendix 23a

Box 49: Training boosts production, confidence and collective action in the leather industry

The following information is related to a training intervention (assisted by UNIDO) in the leather industry in the 1990s, in particular to the Training and Common Facility Centre (TCFC) that supported the emergence of *Crane Shoes* factory in Kampala. The TCFC is now a centre point for entrepreneurs/firms for processing and product innovation. Crane Shoes is a registered brand utilised by trained footwear and leather goods manufacturers in Uganda. The brand is managed/run by TCFC and used by TCFC as well as by entrepreneurs who produce products under TCFC supervision/mentoring (TCFC info, see also Box 50). In the remaining part we use information from the UNIDO and the BBC website respectively, which is related to a BBC article:

UNIDO: "Will Ross's report for BBC News, Kampala, that 'Fishy feet smell sweet in Uganda' (see article below) gave us a welcome update on an Austrian-funded UNIDO Project that ran in Uganda between 1996-1999. The Fishy Feet story centres around Mr. Ross's visit to a Crane Shoe factory in Kampala where he saw the skin from Lake Victoria's Nile perch being used to make fashionable shoes and sandals. UNIDO leather specialist Aurelia Calabro, who managed the project, reports the BBC story has already prompted enquiries from Sweden and USA on Crane Shoe products. In early 1993, when UNIDO started its work with the leather industry in Uganda, there were around 270 unorganized MSMEs that had problems obtaining suitable raw materials and components. There was no formal training available, local producers did not have the confidence of the market and were struggling against competition from imported secondhand shoes from Europe, USA and Canada. A Training and Common Facility Centre (TCFC) was established in 1996 and extension services introduced within the UNIDO Integrated Programme (IP). A Mobile Training Unit was brought into operation to reach those MSMEs in remote areas. Over 200 people have been trained under the TCFC programme. In all, over 70 percent of the leather products MSMEs have been assisted. Since it is connected to all leather manufacturers in the country, TCFC is now the meeting point for those interested in the leather sector. In 1998 TCFC registered the Crane Shoes brand with the Uganda Leather Association. Quality control of the products is done by the independent TCFC. Every Ugandan shoemaker who is producing shoes according to the Crane Shoes standard can use this brand and its labels." Source: UNIDO.

BBC article on Crane Shoes: "Fishy feet smell sweet in Uganda, By Will Ross, BBC News, Kampala: When I searched for sandals at the Crane Shoes factory in the Ugandan capital's modest industrial area, I left with fish on my feet. For years fillets of Lake Victoria's Nile perch have been exported to Europe and beyond. But now Crane Shoes in Kampala is making use of the previously discarded skin of the fish. Since it was introduced to the world's second largest fresh water lake around 50 years ago, many smaller species have disappeared, having been gobbled up by the Nile perch. These fish can grow up to 200kg and 2m in length - one serious pair of shoes in the making. 'They are popular with expatriates and ministers,' says John Byabashaija, the executive director of Crane Shoes, as he admires the latest Nile perch design. So far he hasn't found an Imelda Marcos-like benefactor - the former Philippines first lady apparently owned more than 3,000 pairs of shoes - but he is hopeful. 'Ugandan ladies have started to develop the culture of shoe buying,' John Byabashaija says with a smile before leading me into the workshop. These shoes are made to measure - Ugandan style. Shoe-maker Innocent Rwabukye places a sheet of A4 paper on the floor. I stand on it, he draws around my foot with a biro and then displays a lengthy menu of fish skins which have been dyed in the tannery; pink, dark green, purple, light blue - in fact a different colour for each day of the week. And no, they don't smell of fish. 'They'll be ready this time tomorrow as long as we have power,' Innocent tells me as he starts gluing the scaly fish skin to a strip of leather which will make the strap of the sandal. ...[T]he industries are being hit hard by lengthy power cuts [that are common due to the country's electricity supply crisis]. ...The factory uses machines to cut and score the leather. With almost all the 30 staff employed on a casual basis, incomes are also affected by the power cuts.

The factory was set up as a project under ... Unido. John Byabashaija spent a few months in Italy learning about the quality shoe industry before returning to run the factory which now produces more than 1,000 pairs each month bringing in close to $20,000. 'As a child I used to admire people who wore shoes. Growing up in rural Bushenyi in the west of Uganda, I didn't wear shoes until I was 15,' Mr Byabashaija tells me, before admitting that with more than 30 pairs in his wardrobe, he now takes a little longer to leave the house in the morning. Inside the Crane Shoes factory, the staff are not sticking to foot fashion; belts, wallets and bags are also crafted. In one corner is a pile of black shiny military boots, while across the other side of the room one of the women in the workshop, Jovia, has a special order - a photographer with interesting taste wants his camera protected in a goat skin case. I even tried on a cowboy hat made from black and white calf skin - although I was put off by the thought of straying too near a bull in such an ostentatious, hairy hat. The following day I leave the factory with fish on my feet and pause on the way out. 'Hmmm, these shoes would go well with that cowboy hat - then again maybe not.'"

Source: *BBC news online, 03/05/2005, http://news.bbc.co.uk/2/hi/africa/4965018.stm.*

Appendix 23b

Box 50: The Training and Common Facility Centre (TCFC) for the leather manufacturing sector

"In 1996, the ULAIA (Uganda Leather and Allied Industries Association) - which is the owner of the TCFC - was established with support and assistance of UMA and UNIDO. Stakeholders of ULAIA are organisations, firms and entrepreneurs involved in the leather manufacturers' sector, like butchers, flayers, meat processors, hides and skin traders, tanners, shoemakers and leather goods manufacturers. In the 1990s, the import dumping of second-hand shoes pushed most shoemakers out of business; many enterprises did not survive then or had to downsize their activities to shoe repairing. That's why, in 1997, ULAIA established the TCFC. ULAIA believed that better training and improved access to proper facilities would improve the competitiveness of the firms and entrepreneurs in the sector. The TCFCs objective and mission includes supporting local MSMEs in the leather products manufacturing sector with training, technical assistance, facilities, machines to rent, subsidised tools and equipment for the start-up, material supply in Kampala as well as for upcountry shoemakers through the TCFC-Extension Service Van.

TCFC-Training Activities

Since it was established, the TCFC has trained 380 entrepreneurs in any of the following courses: Basic Shoemaking, Advanced Shoemaking, Basic & Advanced Leather Goods, Business Skills, and Project Proposal Writing. Moreover, the TCFC works with 20-30 entrepreneurs every day. Sometimes, the company TCFC Crane Shoes - which is run by TCFC - sub-contracts orders to these entrepreneurs. Indeed, the role of TCFC Crane Shoes is to support the sector through training and the establishment of small and medium sized workshops, and to offer good quality products to the domestic and international market.

In 1999-2000, the TCFC ran its Extension Service Van for up-country shoemakers; this provided, once a month, technical assistance and material supply to shoemakers in Kisoro, Kabale, Ntungamo, Bushenyi, Fort Portal, Kasese, Mbarara, Masaka, Jinja, Iganga, Mbale, Kumi, Soroti and Lira. Services included the following:

- Supplying of tools and lasts: All shoemakers appreciated this. The quality of the shoes could not be improved without these tools and lasts.
- Supply of quality materials: Through the Van upcountry shoemakers received the required quality materials necessary for their work. The Van could reach every upcountry shoemaker to supply the materials requested at the previous trip. This encouraged the entrepreneurs to stay in business. Due to the supply, a standard of good quality shoes and leather goods was maintained.
- Extension Service: Upcountry shoemakers had easy access to technical support, materials, hand tools and basic equipment. This helped to re-establish most of the shoemakers who had ceased business before.

The Van services were discontinued because it did not cover costs in completion of the project. The system now in place is a bi-monthly entrepreneurs' meeting to discuss problems related to footwear manufacturing and suggesting ways forward regarding issues such as competing with second-hand and synthetic leather shoes. In such meetings the TCFC updates entrepreneurs with current information. The supply of quality materials, hand tools and basic equipment is now done at TCFC where all types are stored. Materials from TCFC are purchased by entrepreneurs who were trained or who use the Centre facilities.

Other TCFC activities:

- Renting out of facilities: The facilities were put in place to assist shoemakers who do not have enough capital to start their own facilities; they are still appreciated by the users.
- Renting out of machinery: This activity helps the trained shoemakers to produce required quality shoes. This improves both quality and quantity, and in consequence the turnover.
- Marketing: Marketing has been done through different media, i.e. radios, TVs, and newspapers. This has helped entrepreneurs and the center to get clients.

The level of competitiveness with second-hand shoes is not as stiff as it was in 1999-2001, since the taxes were increased and competition is now levelled. The threat is from plastic shoes from the Far East, which are however of no/low quality. We think with time people will realise this."

Source: *Management TCFC CRANE SHOES, text produced for this research.*

Appendix 24

Table 57: UNCTAD Human Capital Index: Low Index Group, 1995 vs. 2001

Human Capital Index: Low Index Group				
Ranking	**1995**		**2001**	
81	Indonesia	0.349	Iran	0.355
82	Syrian Arab Rep.	0.34	El Salvador	0.354
83	Paraguay	0.339	Paraguay	0.351
84	Namibia	0.337	Indonesia	0.347
85	Mauritius	0.324	Algeria	0.347
86	China	0.318	Sri Lanka	0.337
87	Nicaragua	0.313	China	0.298
88	Albania	0.308	Oman	0.288
89	Zimbabwe	0.298	Nicaragua	0.277
90	Botswana	0.297	Honduras	0.272
91	Oman	0.29	Namibia	0.251
92	Vietnam	0.275	India	0.247
93	Honduras	0.262	Yemen	0.239
94	Morocco	0.251	Zimbabwe	0.229
95	India	0.247	Morocco	0.222
96	Guatemala	0.224	Guatemala	0.215
97	Nepal	0.173	Syrian Arab Rep.	0.212
98	Nigeria	0.169	Bangladesh	0.18
99	Cote d'Ivoire	0.166	Nepal	0.17
100	Zambia	0.157	Cameroon	0.167
101	Cameroon	0.152	Kenya	0.161
102	Bangladesh	0.148	Cote d'Ivoire	0.157
103	Yemen	0.146	Nigeria	0.153
104	Kenya	0.137	Ghana	0.148
105	Ghana	0.136	Zambia	0.13
106	Pakistan	0.122	Pakistan	0.104
107	Mauritania	0.103	Mauritania	0.098
108	Haiti	0.102	**Uganda**	**0.095**
109	Madagascar	0.097	Eritrea	0.092
110	Senegal	0.083	Benin	0.09
111	**Uganda**	**0.083**	Haiti	0.083
112	Benin	0.077	Senegal	0.081
113	Eritrea	0.077	Malawi	0.08
114	Malawi	0.066	Madagascar	0.071
115	Tanzania	0.056	Tanzania	0.063
116	Angola	0.044	Djibouti	0.055
117	Djibouti	0.043	Ethiopia	0.044
118	Ethiopia	0.028	Angola	0.025
119	Mozambique	0.015	Mozambique	0.019

Source: *UNCTAD (2005b, 291).*

Appendix 25

Box 51: Ease of Doing Business Ranking: Uganda in 72nd position

Ease of doing business ranking			
1. New Zealand	40. Botswana	79. Russia	118. Croatia
2. Singapore	41. Czech Republic	80. Greece	119. Brazil
3. United States	42. Portugal	81. Macedonia, FYR	120 Venezuela
4. Canada	43. Jamaica	82. Ghana	121 Syria
5. Norway	44. France	83. Moldova	122 Afghanistan
6. Austria	45. Kiribati	84. Kyrgyz Republic	123 Sao Tome and Principe
7. Hong Kong, China	46. Armenia	85. Uruguay	124 Ukraine
8. Denmark	47. Kuwait	86. Kazakhstan	125 West Bank and Gaza
9. United Kingdom	48. Marshall Islands	87. Bosnia and Herzegovina	126. Zimbabwe
10. Japan	49. Vanuatu	88. Paraguay	127 Mauritania
11. Ireland	50. Palau	89. Costa Rica	128 Algeria
12. Iceland	51. Oman	90. Yemen	129 Benin
13. Finland	52. Hungary	91. China	130 Cameroon
14, Sweden	53. Solomon Islands	92. Serbia and Montenegro	131 Madagascar
15. Lithuania	54. Poland	93. Turkey	132 Senegal
16. Estonia	55. Nepal	94. Nigeria	133 Cambodia
17. Switzerland	56. Micronesia	95. Lebanon	134 Haiti
18. Belgium	57. Panama	96. Malawi	135 Angola
19. Germany	58. Tunisia	97. Lesotho	136 Sierra Leone
20. Thailand	59. Nicaragua	98. Azerbaijan	137 Eritrea
21. Malaysia	60. Pakistan	99. Vietnam	138 Uzbekistan
22. Puerto Rico	61. Mongolia	100. Georgia	139 Rwanda
23. Mauritius	62. Bulgaria	101. Ethiopia	140 Tanzania
24. Netherlands	63. Slovenia	102. Morocco	141 Egypt
25. Chile	64. Papua New Guinea	103. Dominican Republic	142 Timor-Leste
26. Latvia	65. Bangladesh	104. Bhutan	143 Burundi
27. Korea	66. Colombia	105. Guyana	144 Guinea
28. South Africa	67. Zambia	106. Belarus	145 Cote d'Ivoire
29. Israel	68. Kenya	107. Ecuador	146 Mali
30. Spain	69, United Arab Emirates	108. Iran	147 :ap PDR [sic]
31. Maldives	70. Italy	109. Guatemala	148 Congo, Rep.
32. Austria	71. Peru	110. Mozambique	149 Togo
33. Namibia	**72. Uganda**	111. Bolivia	150 Niger
34. Fiji	73. Mexico	112. Honduras	151 Sudan
35. Taiwan, China	74. Jordan	113 Philippines	152 Chad
36. Tonga	75. Sri Lanka	114 Iraq	153 Central African Republic
37. Slovakia	76. El Salvador	115 Indonesia	154 Burkina Faso
38. Saudi Arabia	77. Argentina	116 India	155 Congo, Dem. Rep.
39. Samoa	78. Romania	117 Albania	

Source: *World Bank (2006 c, 92).*

Appendix 26

Box 52: Tendencies of rising entry barriers for newcomers in global industry

"The success of [a very few developing countries: the first generation NIC's Korea, Taiwan, formerly independent Hong Kong and partly Singapore in catching up with the technological frontier and appropriating significant innovation rents] ... has triggered an intensive and controversial debate on the role of the state in the development process in general and the effectiveness of industrial policy in particular.[1] This debate is not concluded. Different interpretations persist especially with regard to the role of infant-industry protection, the use of trade-related investment measures (TRIMs), the application of 'horizontal' vs. selective policies, and the need for government to target 'strategic' sectors vs. market-driven resource allocation. However, most scholars concerned with technological upgrading agree that entry barriers for newcomers tend to rise for a number of reasons. **First**, technologies become more complex and increasingly require not only world-class capabilities in different technological fields but also the capacity for systems integration. Countries with well-established and diversified innovation systems thus have a strong advantage over latecomers lacking certain 'ingredients' of mature innovation systems as well as the experience of interactive problem-solving. **Second**, globalization tends to increase scale requirements. **Third**, product cycles become ever shorter as the speed of innovation accelerates. **Fourth**, new international rules on trade, investment, and property rights protect proprietors of technologies better and strongly confine developing countries' possibilities to employ trade policy, mandatory technology sharing, local content and equity requirements, subsidies and other 'distorting' elements for their own technological development. Strategies of infant industry protection, aggressive product piracy and reverse engineering, which have been pursued in earlier catch up-processes, can largely be ruled out for contemporary development processes. While some industrialists argue that such policies have anyway done more harm than good,[2] others claim that the new global trade, investment and property rights regimes have 'kicked away the ladder' that developing countries needed to climb up from factor-cost to knowledge-based competitive advantages.[3]

[FN:] [1] Ernst/Mytelka/Ganiatsos (1998); Lall (1994); Wade (1990); World Bank (1993). [2] E.g. Moran/Graham/Blomström (2005). [3] E.g. Chang (2002)."

Source: *Altenburg et al (2006, 3-4, emphasis added).*

Appendix 27

New Vision, 28/03/2006: 'Government to review primary curriculum to fight graft'

"The Government is to review the existing primary school curriculum and integrate it with religious values which promote honesty, respect and fairness, reports Carol Natukunda. Under the proposal, Religious Education, which is currently incorporated in Social Studies (SST), will become an independent examinable subject. State minister for ethics and integrity Tim Lwanga yesterday said making religion part of the curriculum would help in fighting corruption. "We have had dialogue with some religious leaders and discussed the proposal to have a code that will harmonise the conduct of the various churches and religious institutions. We would like to ensure that there is some sort of uniformity. We believe religious education contains a good package of ethical values required to mould the young into the type of society Ugandans are yearning for," he said. Lwanga was addressing a stakeholders' workshop at Imperial Botanical Beach Hotel in Entebbe. Lwanga said the proposal followed a meeting with the education ministry, Uganda National Examinations Board, National Curriculum Development Centre, Education Standard Agency, Uganda Joint Christian Council and Uganda Christian Religious Teachers Association."

New Vision, 03/04/2006: 'Government proposes to integrate religious values in curriculum'

"The Government's proposal to review the primary school curriculum and integrate in it religious values has brought mixed reactions. Under the proposal, Religious Education, which is currently incorporated in Social Studies (SST), would become an independent examinable subject, in order to promote good morals among children. Legislators say this would halt the deteriorating behaviour in society, and encourage self-discipline and integrity starting at a lower education level. "We are experiencing cultural erosion. Our fore parents were brought up in a society that highly cherished respect, honesty, responsibility, transparency, fairness and truthfulness. But these values have deteriorated," said Prime Minister Apolo Nsibambi in a speech read by primary education state minister Nyombi Tembo at a workshop at Imperial Botanical Beach Hotel, Entebbe recently. Tim Lwanga, the state minister for ethics, said integrating religion in the curriculum would help fight corruption at all levels. There was concern that although ethical values were part of the School Curriculum, teachers were not teaching them because they were not examinable at the end. However, some educators had diverse views. Dr. Stephen Schwenke, a lecturer of ethics and public management at Makerere University, said religious education could not be an appropriate method to teach moral values. "Using religion to justify and explain one's moral values relies on the belief of a particular religion. You would not challenge a student, because they would say, 'this is my belief! We should look for national and secular values in the Constitution, which are based on a common ground." Prof. Senteza Kajubi, the vice-chancellor of Nkumba University, said there was need to explore alternatives available. "Ethics is not a dominance of religion. We have to break boundaries and explore the alternatives." Annet Nanteza, a teacher at Lakeside Junior School in Entebbe, said Ugandan teachers were not motivated to teach ethics, "Because they had too many demands on their limited time. Materialism has taken over teachers, because of the little salary. If I didn't have supper, for instance, and somebody offered it on provision that I promote his son, why not?" "How does a teacher, whose morals have degenerated, teach against what he is doing? Don't worry, that children are not listening to you, but worry that they are watching what you are doing," Nanteza said."

Appendix 28

Table 58: Generic characteristics of low-trust and high-trust value chains

Length of trading relationship	Low-trust chains short term	High-trust chains long term
Ordering procedure	Open bidding for orders, with prices negotiated and agreed before order commissioned	Bidding may not take place or likely winner known in advance; prices settled after contract awarded
Contractual relationship	Supplier starts production only on receipt of written order	Supplier more flexible about instructions and will start production without written order
Inspection	Inspection on delivery	Little or no inspection on delivery for most parts
Degree of dependence	Supplier has many customers, and customer has multiple sources	Few customers for supplier and single-or dual sourcing by customer
Technical assistance	Expertise rarely pooled and assistance only when paid for	Extensive unilateral or bilateral technology transfer over time
Communication	Infrequent and through formal channels; narrowly focused on purchasing department	Multi-channeled, including engineers personnel department and top management frequent and often informal
Price determination	Adversarial, with hiding of information	Non-adversarial; with "open books"
Credit extended	Punitive or no credit extended	Easy access to letters of credit, longer payback period, easy terms
Outsourcing payment terms	Long delays in paying agents and informal economy producers	Payment on receipt of finished goods

Source: *Kaplinsky and Morris (2003, 15).*

Appendix 29

Box 53: The Plan for Zonal Agricultural Production, Agro-processing and Marketing

The zoning plan aims at increasing household incomes, especially in the rural areas, by raising volume, value and profitability of household agricultural production through transformation of the agricultural sector and parallel investment in agro-processing industries. In this respect, it acknowledges the limited progress so far in the country's effort to connect the industrial and the agriculture sector. The primary premise of the plan is the development of strong linkages between agriculture and industry, in particular the agro-processing industry; with the view of producing exportable, high-value agricultural products that promise high profitability and socio-economic returns and thus ensure consistency of export growth and sustainability in production. It is projected that more complex industries would launch from this base. The outlined interventions tackle both the production and the market side of the matter, and target crops, fisheries and livestock sectors, related agro-processing and agribusiness enterprises and issues of market access (GOU 2004a, 4-9).

The plan highlights as main constraints the following: Lack of critical supply capacity in agriculture, Inadequate or non-existent processing capacity, Failure on market requirements/ standards, especially on quality, Inadequate market information, Lack of affordable and accessible export finance, Inadequate market infrastructure in almost all production areas, Fragmented business enterprises, Non tariff barriers, an Inadequate export database, and Insufficient national export development competencies. With regard to the latter, the plan points to inadequate skills for negotiating and executing exports, including planning, management, and marketing and the lack of an established framework to build these export business skills (GOU 2004b, 25-28). The mentioned lack of framework for export-oriented skills development is a significant problem. Again, note that even if such issues would be addressed in the near future in one or the other growth or competitiveness programme, the low implementation profile of many state institutions in the past makes it advisable to keep expectations of results at adequate levels.

The crucial restriction of lack of critical supply capacity (production volumes etc.) informs the key strategic intervention of the plan, which is to zone the country into agricultural and related socio-ecological areas of comparative/competitive advantage, and subsequently foster geographical specialisation in commercial agriculture. A zone typically focuses on the same crop or livestock and is usually characterised by a similar socio-economic background and quite homogeneous ecological conditions, farming systems and practices. A zone may cut across districts and may be divided into sub-zones to respond to specific development requirements. Ten zones as well as corresponding profitable/viable enterprises with high export potential for the respective zones have been mapped/singled out to promote specialisation. The enterprises were selected according to (1) value of the product on the export market, (2) market availability and access, (3) agro-ecological suitability of the enterprise to the respective zones, (4) existing production, processing/marketing infrastructure, knowledge, skills, support institutions, and systems for input supply.

The zoning approach acknowledges that the agro-processing capacities to be established/ supported under this plan require reliable supplies of high quality inputs and raw materials which, according to the premise, can be assured through an integrated, market-led and scientific agricultural production, processing and value addition strategy. The interventions for both zones and respective enterprises are based on consideration of economic and ecological factors. The approach is integrated in the sense that, with a view to fully exploiting the potential of an area, the strategies link the agricultural zoning to issues like technology, farmer organisation and mobilization, advisory/support as well as social services, agro-processing, input supply system, skills, quality, marketing, market access and exporting. The strategies are classified as follows:

- Organising agricultural production (strategies that go hand in hand with zoning activities and the selection of products to be grown in each zone, including issues of farmer organisation, input sourcing, advisory services), • Improving agricultural output (input supply system: e.g. networks of certified input suppliers/stockist, procurement of improved planting materials),

• Preserving the environment, • Minimizing post-harvest losses (provision of intermediate warehousing and cold chain infrastructure at the zonal level, advisory services and training),• Extracting valuable derivatives by processing; • Increasing shelf-life by processing; • Improving quality of processed and unprocessed goods (develop the quality infrastructure), • Identifying high value markets and products (strengthen the market research function and information structure); • Penetrating new markets and increasing market share in existing markets (encourage producers to attend trade fairs, exhibitions etc.) • Availing export development finance.

Following the general focus of the plan, the strategies apply to four themes: (a) agricultural production, (b) agro-processing, (c) market access and entry, and (d) policy and regulatory framework (GOU 2004a, 10-13). Specific strategies include: (i) Support for enterprises with established markets will be given to: • Existing enterprises seeking to expand or needing resources to meet planned outputs, • 'Sick' but viable export-oriented firms that need to rehabilitate existing production facilities or factors, • New or pioneering enterprises, (ii) Attracting investments in agro-food sector, especially to locate them into the Kampala Industrial and Business Park (KIPB) Namanve, (iii) Research support for agro-processing to close the gap between research findings and their application and adaptation and to ensure resources for agro-processing R&D, and (iv) Improving and applying quality assurance regulations to upgrade the infrastructure on Technical Barriers to Trade, and Sanitary and Phytosanitary training and skills development in agro-processing is regarded as central (GOU 2004b, 65-70). Within this strategic setting, GOU at both central and district levels, commits itself to undertake activities at the framework level (infrastructure in the various zones); at the same time encouraging the private sector to undertake the complementary investment at the enterprise level (firms/farms). The plan recognises the need to address related topics that determine the plan's success, e.g.: (1) Integrate the strategies into the post-conflict programmes for Northern Uganda so as to accelerate resettlement and restoration of economic activity in the region; (2) Establish a coordination agency to ensure implementation of the strategies; (3) Provide substantial funding under the Medium Term Expenditure Framework (MTEF) and establish funding mechanism for the private sector through UDB; (4) While this plan focuses upon exports, consider designing a plan to develop local markets and ensure food security (GOU 2004a, 13-4).

Brief assessment: The zoning plan offers a rich problem analysis and a list of important observations and solutions; it highlights the need to build the prerequisites that allow stronger linkages between industry and agriculture and considers the various layers and actors that need to be taken into account by the interventions. The underlying VC approach brings out a good, integrated and comprehensive set of strategies. The plan therefore deserves serious consideration in future moves towards a more commercial agricultural sector and stronger agro-processing industry. Yet, the plan faces certain challenges. One problem is that the plan offers an enriching analysis only up to a certain point. In some important aspects, it remains at a general level and is not sufficiently linked to detailed plans regarding implementation. In particular, the plan does not analyse explicitly the status of implementation of similar plans, particularly the PMA and the SEP, and does not reveal the areas of complementary activity. This would have strengthened belief that the zoning plan builds explicitly upon the lessons learned in the recent past, and would thus be advanced on implementation issues, often the most critical part in such an ample project. For instance, a critical account of the problematic nature of export-oriented agro-processing in the country needs to offer more detailed insights regarding the relevant current weaknesses of government agencies, including SIs. Consequently, the plan bears weaknesses regarding its action plan, e.g. in the area of interventions for capability formation at enterprise level. To some extent these details can be worked out in the implementation phase.

However, the plan needs to tackle the problem of a deficient domestic LIS in many agro-processing sectors, including areas of insufficient knowledge flows (due to low level of interaction) between industry, research and policy. Further, little concrete is said about building capacities and capabilities for production at firm level. Accordingly, relevant sections of the plan are somewhat biased towards confidence in the effects of offering more (market, product etc.) information, promotion and the like; consequently giving little space to issues like technological capability building, knowledge adaptation/mastering with a view to improving production processes, products etc.; and related challenges of interactions between stakeholders. More to the point, one of the two main ministries in this zoning exercise, the MTTI, is short on capacities and capabilities by the time of research (2006), in the first place, which undermines the MTTI's working relationships with the districts and the private sector. Positively, GOU is currently trying to address the capacity problem in MTTI. The UEPB also lacks adequate funding, among others. The districts are supposed to design development plans that match the ideas of the zoning plan; yet the progress in this respect has been slow since the plan's launch. Deliberations about the pattern and institutional setting for public and private sector-interaction are needed.

Appendix 30

Box 54: Training and skills development by transnational corporations: Unilever Uganda

"Unilever Uganda Ltd. is one of the leading foreign investors in Uganda, specializing in the manufacture [, marketing] and distribution of [both locally produced and imported household products - in] foods, detergents, soaps and related products. Its sales were $15 million in 1997 and were expected to grow to $20 million in 1998. Unilever Uganda is part of the global Unilever group and has strong linkages with Unilever subsidiaries in India, Kenya, South Africa and the United Kingdom. The company has a long history in the country, dating back to 1960 as a subsidiary of East African Industries Ltd. based in Kenya. Later it was partly nationalized under the Obote Government and became a distribution outlet for its mother company in Kenya. In 1996 Unilever bought 100 per cent of the shares, and now the company reports independently to London.

The benefits of this company's presence to Uganda's transfer of technology and skill development depend largely on Unilever Uganda's relationship with the parent company. Unilever is a world leader in personnel development. Rigorous reviews of managerial staff are carried out every year to identify existing capabilities, gaps in capabilities, and measures to fill these skill gaps. [Training focuses on uplifting the skills and competencies, through both internal and external courses, and on-the-job training. With the central resource available within Unilever, the company is able to 'UNIleverage' the knowledge pool existing within Unilever.] ... Under the Management Trainee Program, selected young graduates are sent on a six-month training programme to prepare them for managerial posts within the group. In the programme of internationalization of managers, Ugandan managers and management trainees are seconded for international postings, and overseas managers are sent to local operations. Local managers and staff members are thus exposed to modern management techniques developed by subsidiaries of the global Unilever Group. [Working through the local distributors, who are SME's, the company distributes its products throughout the country, with an underlying theme of 'Availability, Visibility & Affordability everywhere'. To achieve such an objective the Company puts a lot of focus on developing and training of not only company's own staff, but also the staff of the key distributors - specifically in finance management, stock control, management information and selling skills.] ... Technology is sourced from the parent company, and almost no research and technological efforts are carried out locally. Interaction with local science and technology is only occasional. Sourcing of intermediate inputs from local firms still occurs to a limited extent, essentially for packaging materials, calcium carbonate (a key ingredient in Vim detergent), and a few others".

Source: *UNCTAD (2003, 95, based on information in UNCTAD 1998). Information in brackets was provided by Unilever Uganda for this research.*

Appendix 31

Box 55: Experiences and observations by an organisation development (OD) specialist on performance management in organisations[410] in Uganda

"At the theoretical level, it is very often said that in organisations one of the key roles of management is getting the best out of people (out of the employees). Despite this claim, however, in many organisations in Uganda in which the author has done some OD work, the main factor that lead to low and sometimes extremely low performance of employees is the fact that the management lacks skills and knowledge/competence in human resource management (HRM), especially with regards to performance management.

Lack of competence in HRM in organisations is a very tricky problem for organisations: It is a vicious circle type of problem. The immediately observable problem in the said organisations is that the performance of the employees tends to be low/very low because the management does not have the competence to get the best out the employees. But the more intrinsic problem is that organisations where the competence in HRM is lacking are not able to recruit, develop and retain managers who can help solve the problem: The existing management in such organisations does not know which competences/qualities to look for when recruiting management staff or any other staff. Nor does such management know how to develop management staff capacity in HRM in general and in performance management in particular. Further, management that is not competent in HRM cannot put policies, structures and practices in place that are required for getting the best out of people. This problem is indeed a catch-22 type of problem for many organisations in the country.

In addition, many organisations in Uganda do not have what one would call appropriate organisation cultures for achieving and maintaining high levels of performance at individual, team and whole organisational levels. The term 'appropriate organisation culture' is in this context used to mean, 'a way of thinking and doing things that is in line with the vision and mission of the organisation and at the same time optimises the use of available resources (including HR) in achieving set objectives'. Such systematically-conceptualised rational organisations with corresponding rules, procedures and practices are still very few in the country. Lack of appropriate organisation culture renders organisations less (or even pathetically little) performance-oriented. On average this problem exists in differing degrees in various types of organisations in the country. Generally, it is more evident and prominent in the government sector than in the NGO and private sector types of organisations. Lack of competence in HRM affects directly the quality of performance management in organisations and consequently the performance of the organisations at the individual and group (team) and organisational levels.

Below the author describes a few experiences and observations he has made in Uganda in the course of carrying out various OD exercises, including facilitating strategic planning, developing HRM instruments and practice, conducting job analysis (developing competence profiles for jobs in organisations) and job evaluations, salary-grading exercises, and team building. The experiences described below cover the three levels of performance management mentioned above: individual performance management, group (team) performance management and general (whole) organisation performance management.

1. Frequently observed problem areas in performance management at the individual employee level

Inadequate staff recruitment systems and practices

To a large extent, in many organisations recruitment is still done on the basis of paper qualifications and not on competences required to perform the given tasks of the job in question. This is very difficult to change, because when an organisation consultant tries to address this problem, he/she is unintentionally or even unknowingly questioning the legitimacy of the appointment/position

410 The term 'organisations' here refers to firms as well as public sector institutions/organisations.

of some existing members of staff, including some of the management staff themselves. The management whose competence to fulfil certain positions is questions may be the very people who appointed the consultant. This sometimes leads to a situation where the consultant's recommendations are only partially implemented/never implemented. In some cases, the consultant is never engaged again by the organisation as long as the same people are in charge.

It is obvious that in order to achieve and maintain high levels of performance, organisations require, in the first place, managers who can get the best out of people. However, in the process of recruiting management staff, people management competences (knowledge and skills in HRM) often aren't considered. This is particularly the case when organisations recruit executives such as finance managers, marketing managers, production managers, or programme managers of various kinds. The applicants' competence in people management is not so much focused on in the process of recruitment, although it is known that these managers will be operating as heads of departments and thus supervise a number of people working under them directly.

As a consultant, one tries to help organisations to appreciate the importance of people management skills in organisations and therefore the importance of looking for such skills when recruiting management staff. However, technical competences and other issues tend to preoccupy the minds of interviewers during recruitment processes. One of the reasons for this is that some interview panels put in place by organisations may not have someone who is able to find out whether or to what degree a particular candidate for a management post has the required HRM skills for the job in question.

Recruitment and promotion into management jobs based on considerations other than competence

In many organisations in Uganda, particularly in government organisations, recruitment and promotion into management jobs is often based on other considerations than competence. Many posts are offered to people as a 'thank you' for what they or their parents, relatives or friends did for the appointing authority or an individual member of it. In other cases, jobs are offered to people due to loyalties or attachments of some kind to the appointees. It is very disheartening when young people, for instance, complain to a consultant, saying: 'I cannot be appointed or promoted to that post, not because I am not competent enough or qualified for it, but because I do not know any influential [recruitment relevant] people in or outside the organisation.' It is often a fruitless exercise and difficult for an OD consultant to get the appointing authorities to focus on competences required in the respective jobs when recruiting, appointing or promoting staff. This is particularly the case in government organisations; not only for top/middle management jobs, but also for jobs at lower levels.

In organisations where considerations other than competence is required for appointing and placing people in jobs is the order of the day, an OD consultant is very often seen to be too theoretical and unrealistic in his/her attempts to establish a system and develop instruments for performance-oriented staff recruitment and development. The practice in the organisation may have more to do with persons being recruited because of the influence of the people they know or are attached to, than with their competences. Those people involved cannot see this practice changed for any reason.

Lack of appropriate staff induction systems and practices in organisations

Many organisations do not have effective induction systems. Some of them hardly have staff inductions worth the name. Thus it takes too long for staff to really get to know their place of work, or where and how to get what they need in order to do their work. Although in many cases staff are given job-descriptions and work contracts, in none of these documents nor anywhere else are the performance targets and quality performance standards articulated.

Management tends to appreciate it very much when a consultant draws their attention to such deficiencies in their organisation and the importance of setting and communicating performance targets and performance quality standards to new staff from the very beginning. In some cases consultants are even asked to work out/produce a staff induction manual for the organisation.

However, in many cases, the manual is not systematically used (as an instrument of staff performance management) when new staff is recruited.

Lack of or inadequate staff appraisal systems, instruments and practices in organisations

In many organisations there is no systematic and sometimes no staff appraisal practices at all. In cases where staff appraisals are carried out, it is done very unprofessionally and ineffectively. In some cases it even turns out to be counterproductive. After an appraisal, for example, the appraised employees complain of not being appreciated, not being liked or even of malice by their supervisors. Neither do the supervisees come out of the appraisal sessions with a clear picture of what their supervisors really expect from them.

When a consultant draws the management's attention to this problem and suggests solutions to it, this advice is generally accepted and even appreciated. The consultant may even be asked to develop a staff appraisal system and instruments and train supervisory staff to conduct staff appraisals, using the system and instruments developed. However, many organisations, even after having done this, do not maintain the practice of continual and systematic staff appraisal practice as a normal and regular operation of the organisation. The HRM staff fail to maintain and update the staff appraisal instruments as required. In some cases even if they would like to, they fail to convince or motivate the rest of management in the organisation to carry out regular staff appraisals as may have been agreed upon.

Even when a consultant succeeds in persuading management to institute HRM, particularly staff appraisal (as an instrument of performance management and basis for staff development), as a constituent of the job descriptions and competence profiles of management staff, it may not be enough to institutionalise the practice of systematic staff appraisal in the organisation.

Staff development policies and practices not so much geared to promotion of staff performance as such

In some organisations, policies and practices for staff development are not geared to improve the performance of the individual members of staff. In some cases, individual members of staff are not particularly interested in improving their capacity to perform in their current/ expected jobs; they are more interested in obtaining formal qualifications and certificates through further training and education. Although it is generally accepted that in-house training - when adequately designed - enhances staff performance, little attention is paid to on-the-job training exercises in Uganda. It is indeed an uphill battle for a consultant to try and change this attitude in organisations.

Considerations other than competence being overriding when hiring an OD consultant

In non-performance-oriented organisations management is seldom able to develop the required terms of reference for the appointment of a consultant. This can be done by a consultant, who can work out the required terms of reference. In many cases, however, the consultant is not always selected on the basis of competence. Consequently, consultants are sometimes incapable of dealing with the problems or needs of the organisation for which they are engaged, and tend to propose changes that are palatable to their protégées in the short term, and not necessarily the best solutions to the problems.

2. Frequently observed problem areas in performance management and performance-oriented behaviour at the group and team level

Lack of the following competences tends to affect the level of performance of groups/teams (e.g. departments or units) in organisations.

Lack of performance-oriented team-leadership qualities and practices

- Failure to provide the members of the team with the orientation they need to function effectively and efficiently,
- Failure to involve the members of the team in the processes of decision making,
- Failure to assign the right people in the team to the right tasks in order to maximise the synergy effect,

- Failure to give the members of the team the support required and not facilitating their work accordingly,
- Failure to create two-way communication channels and not listening to the members of the team and not promoting listening among the individual members and sections of a given team.

When members of the team in an organisation discover these deficiencies in their teams during training exercises for team building, team management and team work, they are usually inspired to address the problem. In most cases, this makes a remarkable difference to the quality of teamwork in the organisation.

Lack of performance-oriented communication and behaviour in teams

- Members of the team don't receive the right information, in time for them to be able to do their work effectively and efficiently,
- Team performance targets and performance standards are not well defined for the members of the team, and/or not properly communicated to the members of the team,
- Members of the team don't articulate what each one needs from the others in order to be able to fulfil their roles effectively,
- Members of the team don't sufficiently appreciate each other's roles and contributions to the performance of the whole team: This is demoralising and causes lack of cooperation and support in teams.

When, during a training session, consultants guide team members to discover the deficiencies in their teams regarding performance-oriented communication and behaviour, staff are appreciative. Remarkable mid to long-term impacts on the quality of teamwork in the respective organisation/team is possible.

Poor communication management and communication behaviour in groups and group-work meetings

- Lack of preparation for team meetings,
- Poorly structured and chaired meetings, including poor time management in meetings,
- Poor timekeeping by staff who need to attend meetings: much time is wasted waiting for the latecomers.

This is an area of team management and teamwork where OD consultants in Uganda do not experience much success. The impact of the efforts made in addressing such deficiencies in teams tends to be very low. Apparently, the real problem lies in poor self-management and poor time-management of many members of staff, starting from top management down through the ranks.

3. Frequently observed problem areas in performance management at the organisational level

Very large salary differences between the top executives and the rest of the members of staff

Organisations and particularly government organisations tend to have very large salary differences between the top executives and the rest of the members of staff. Besides their salaries, top executives tend to receive various types of allowances and other benefits while other members of staff receive little or hardly any. Many members of staff earn salaries or wages that are below the existence minimum. This leads to disillusionment and taking on other jobs on the side in order to make ends meet. Paradoxically, it is not surprising to discover that the performance of people is much higher in their side-jobs than in the organisations where they are officially employed.

Consultants' efforts to reduce such unwarranted differences in remuneration, through job-evaluation and salary grading exercises have been never appreciated by any organisations the author has dealt with, not even in cases where such interventions were expressly requested. Top executives of the organisations reject the results of systematic job-evaluations and the corresponding salary grading. In addition, the consultant is never invited to conduct any other

OD exercises as long as the top executives remain working for the organisation.

In Uganda, carrying out job evaluation and salary grading exercises in a professional and systematic manner is one of the trickiest OD exercises. The consultant can only succeed in making enemies of the top executives by pointing out that the top executives do not deserve to earn as much as they do, while other members of staff, whose contributions in the organisation are comparatively high, earn so little.

Salaries and other remunerations/benefits not directly linked to performance

In many organisations, salaries tend to be linked to the formal qualifications of the employees and the positions they occupy, but not necessarily to their performance and contribution to the achievement of the goals of the organisation. Organisations in the private sector undertake relatively greater efforts to move away from this practice. In such organisations the staff, for example, cannot afford to rely so much on their formal qualifications when claiming more pay. But in government institutions this is the order of the day. And it is indeed one of the most difficult attitudes and practices in the country's organisations for a consultant to try to change.

Lack of strategic and action planning used to be one of the hindrances to high performance in organisations, but this is no longer the case

Systematic planning, particularly strategic and action planning, is becoming more common in organisations, including government organisations. But in many organisations, strategic plans are not systematically implemented. Such plans are seldom used for day-to-day planning of the organisations' activities. However, in the organisations where this is done it tends to provide the staff with information on where the organisation is headed, and provides feedback on organisational performance against the set objectives.

Lack of appropriate organisation cultures in organisations

Lack of appropriate organisation cultures in organisations is still a great and widespread problem in the country. In this context, the author tried to gather more information about the issue by instructing postgraduate students at the Makerere University Business School and the Department of Organisational Psychology (Institute of Psychology) at Makerere University to analyse the cultures of their own organisations. Postgraduate students worked in various administrative/managerial positions during the day and attended the evening courses. The results of the exercise were stunningly clear. The organisations lacking organisation cultures systematically were much less successful than those which had had the required cultures. However, the idea of establishing and maintaining appropriate organisation cultures has not yet taken root in most organisations, particularly in government organisations. When consultants raise this issue, the management of the organisations seldom understand and/or appreciate what the consultant is talking about.

In summary, many factors contribute to raising and maintaining high levels of performance in organisations. Many of these factors are related to the quality of HRM and the corresponding policies and practices in organisations. In a country like Uganda, where so many studies and observations point to a generally very low level of organisational performance, the HRM function in organisations needs to be strengthened. This means not only strengthening the HRM departments, but also the capacity of all management staff in people-management skills. The effort must, of course, be coupled with the establishment of adequate HRM policies, instruments and practices in the organisations".

Source: *Dr. Francis X. Bisasso, Organisation Development (OD) consultant and part-time lecturer in Communication and Organisation Psychology (Uganda and Germany). Text produced for this research.*

Appendix 32

Sunday Monitor, 25/06/2006: 'Reversing brain drain can be easy: If research institutions start to reward talent and enthusiasm, not seniority'

By Carel Ijsselmuiden (director of the Council on Health Research for Development, NGO, Geneva)

"Last month Uganda held its maiden President's Science Awards ceremony as a significant effort in recognising the often unsung heroes in the sciences. President Museveni pledged that the country's scientists would receive higher remuneration compared to other public servants, partly to discourage them from seeking a higher salary abroad. Like Uganda, many African and Asian countries have suffered the loss of health care workers such as nurses to northern labour markets in the past decade. The health research sector faces the same realities. There has been much debate around the issue of loss of talent and how countries can reverse it. Certainly, in low-income countries, the economic argument is a strong one. Other equally important considerations are: a stimulating work environment; flexibility of employment (for women or men with young children, or time to pursue professional interests or studies); opportunities to get training and build skills; opportunities to take on responsibility in early career. (This means ... [having] the possibility to become a project leader, manager, programme leader to participate in a multi-country team, or to travel and represent the organisation.) We need a dialogue between countries to have an equitable exchange of labour and avoid the wholesale 'poaching' of talent from the south to the northern labour markets.

Common responses have been to propose legislation or rules to encourage (or oblige) people to work in the country where they are trained. Beyond this, there is a lot of discussion and description of the 'brain drain' problem but few proposals for long-term solutions. But in this discussion about legislating against the flight of talent and improving dialogues between countries, some simple facts and solutions have not been addressed at all. Institutions and managers with a modern style and dynamic programme will attract talent, even against higher salaries abroad. Donors and research sponsors can do a lot to increasing retention of talent by appreciating how some of their actions encourage brain drain. Government leaders and their policies should engage these two groups to support a more professional approach to encouraging health research in the poorer countries.

How to do it

Leaders of southern health research organisations should learn the lessons of many northern counterparts and organise themselves ... [so that they can offer] more attractive work opportunities, especially responsibility to researchers early in their careers. To motivate their staff, leaders of research organisations should create good governance and strong policies that encourage professional management of their talent base. Today's leading organisations are based on individual performance, not seniority. The best performers are rewarded with opportunities, responsibilities and salary increases - they can be of any age (even older too!) There are also staff rotation mechanisms, such as temporary attachment to project teams, shorter-term contracts - even for senior managers - to make room for new talent in an organisation.

All this creates an environment where professionals gain experience working in different teams and where they have frequent opportunities to assume new roles and move up in the organisation. Southern research organisations that embrace professional management practices and take investment in their people seriously will come out on top. This includes government departments, universities, health research councils and NGOs. Institutions that take this on seriously will become Africa's leaders. They will build better quality partnerships, produce better quality research and attract more donor money. And, as development donors focus more on measuring the performance of the organisations they fund, those institutes that are professionally managed will receive more donor investment.

In my experience as a manager working with many African research colleagues and institutions, a big part of the issue is clearly a question of the old-style versus new-style of management. In the old style hierarchical structures, a researcher has to wait until [he is] 50 years or older before advancing to a position of responsibility. The new-style approach recognises talent and enthusiasm regardless of age. The current environment is most de-motivating and a big limiting factor for young and mid-career professionals and technical specialists - the lifeblood of a national health research system. Why would someone who can progress in a competitive, merit-based promotion system remain at home[,] where the primary reason for promotion is age or political affiliation? Clearly, working under a 'lid' means that talent moves sideways, migrating to research systems that award competence and commitment. This seems to happen mostly in the public sector. Looking at the more commercial research systems such as the Pasteur Institutes in francophone Africa, it seems clear that there is much to be gained from modernising management in national health research.

The development situation has its own 'market forces' that affect the human resources situation for health research. Through their funding and programmes, donors provide solutions to countries. But they are also a part of the problem that inhibits development of human resources for health research. Project-based funding for southern research organisations does not encourage development of a professional cadre in institutions, or of their infrastructures. The fact that overheads are usually not covered in grant financing creates fragmented institutions without the essential support services needed to make research effective. This includes a lack of sustained activities such as research support staff, IT and database development, research communication, publishing and library services, or professional staff focused on policy analysis or impact assessment. In many regions, donors continue to work with the same group of intermediaries or 'trusted contacts' year-after-year, instead of using competitive processes based on deliverables. This prevents new and younger research players from putting their ideas forward, stifling creativity and limiting the possibility for new talent to develop.

In our work to support countries in building their health research systems, the Council on Health Research for Development based in Geneva, encourages donors to support development of human resources in health research by working with wider groups of people and including more new players in projects and programmes, especially at the managerial level. Donors should encourage broader south-south and north-south partnerships that involve new groups of people, beyond the same groups that have privileged access to donors and donor agendas. They should create a more open playing field for research funding and lead by example. A research manager from West Africa explained that a team of young malaria researchers she mentors hope to remain in their country and pursue their careers at home after studying partly abroad. I expect that this is the case with the majority of young researchers. The problem is the lack of opportunities to do solid work in their country. We should also look beyond 'researchers' towards the system. A July symposium to be held in Nairobi will focus on Human Resources for Health Research. It is looking at four key topics: research environment; networking in research; engaging communities; and communication. These are topics that are usually forgotten yet they need to be addressed to make health research work - beyond health researchers. ...

> Prof. Ijsselmuiden is the director of the Council on Health Research for Development, an NGO-based in Geneva. He has spent more than 20 years working in the fields of rural health care, public health and academia managing and building research teams in South and southern Africa."

Appendix 33

Box 56: Linking with external pool of skills to enhance local human resource development

"China to Share Farming Expertise with Poorer Nations

SciDev.Net (London), news, 22/05/2006

At least 3,000 Chinese scientists will spend three years working in rural communities in developing countries to help improve their food security, China's Ministry of Agriculture confirmed on Friday (19 May). The arrangement is part of a strategic partnership between China and the UN Food and Agriculture Organization (FAO) that was agreed at the FAO's Regional Conference for Asia and the Pacific in Jakarta, Indonesia last week. 'Chinese science and agriculture have much to offer, as intensive agriculture has been practiced on very small plots of land in China for centuries,' said Tesfai Tecle, FAO assistant director-general for technical cooperation. Tecle said China's commitment to helping other countries improve food security would be a major contribution towards achieving the UN Millennium Development Goal of halving hunger by 2015. Over the next six years, Chinese scientists and technicians will be deployed for three-year assignments in host countries. They will share practical expertise relating to irrigation, agronomy, livestock, fisheries and post-harvest handling of agricultural produce. The China-FAO collaboration is part of the South-South Cooperation Initiative that the FAO launched in 1996. The programme aims to increase food production by promoting cooperation among developing countries at different stages of development. The recipient countries will be jointly selected from a list of potential beneficiaries provided by the FAO. China has already sent more than 700 experts and technicians to at least 20 countries mostly in Africa and Asia, says Zhao Lijun, an official at the Chinese Ministry of Agriculture."

Source: http://allafrica.com.

"FT interview: President Thabo Mbeki

South Africa's [former] president offered his views on trade, Iran's nuclear programme, and China's interest in Africa, during a wide-ranging interview conducted in London ... This is an edited transcript. Q: What's top of your agenda in talks with Tony Blair at the SA/UK bi-national commission? A: We will look at issues that have to do with defence co-operation, arts and culture, education and human resource development, issues to do with home affairs and the movement of people. I think the most urgent one for us is really the human resource development issue. It's clear that, in regard to whole areas of South African national life, if we want to make better progress we need more people with skills. Whether engineering skills or management skills. This is a critical area. We want to be able to reach into the UK, to the capacity of the UK to assist. The problem is everywhere. It's partly to bring people to the UK for training. Partly to have trainers come to South Africa. Partly to see whether for a limited period of time we could take retired people to mentor people on their jobs in South Africa. It might include one form of assistance or another by the British government. On retired people: if we need a 100 civil engineers to be deployed in our municipalities to assist municipal government to build capacity for water delivery, sewerage systems, roads is there a way the two governments can cooperate to find these people and fund them. The Japanese have offered to assist in this area and they say you have this ageing Japanese population. Lots of people are quite willing to assist. It's a very good offer. The advantage with the UK is the advantage of language. We have done an audit of skills shortage. We've taken a very urgent matter, which is a global problem - project managers. You have state corporations with very major plans for energy, water, transport and one of the questions they are raising is that there aren't project managers to manage what are going to be very large projects. You need those people and that kind of skill with experience to make sure these ambitious projects happen. We've done an audit. There are skills shortages coming up as people are investing more. And we've been assessing what kind of skills is needed on the government side. ...."

Source: *Financial Times, http://news.ft.com/, Published 24/05/2006.*

Appendix 34

Box 57: PEVOT's support interventions in Uganda

"The focus of the GTZ Programme PEVOT in Uganda is improvements in the area of BTVET within the PPET area. The overall objective is the formation of a more robust, modern, affordable, flexible and relevant BTVET system. The integrated various long and short-term interventions target three levels - macro, meso and micro. The PEVOT unifies and coordinates the respective activities of five other German development agencies (CIM, DED, InWEnt, KfW, SES) in close cooperation with the main counterpart, the Ugandan MoES. At macro-level, the programme supports the development and implementation of the ESSP within the MOES. Particular attention is given to capacity building (technical assistance/policy implementation, PPP) of the BTVET department, and the BTVET advisory board. At meso level, PEVOT strengthens the Secretariat of the UVQF and the UGAPRIVI with view at improving quality and relevance of vocational training programmes. At micro level, work is devoted to non-formal training and respective social capital improvement as well the support of private and public vocational training institutions/providers which includes improving training capacities through training and investment measures. Observations and experiences from work on micro and meso level are to be channelled back to the higher intervention levels and vice-versa. Special attention is given to best practices as inputs for ongoing strategy and policy consultations with the MoES and stakeholders.

Meeting the Demands of the Ugandan Labour Market

Uganda's economy, although reported as growing, suffers from lack of appropriately skilled manpower as well as from a lack of employment opportunities vis-à-vis the numbers of ever growing school leavers. The UVQF and a Competence-Based Education and Training (CBET) contribute to overcome this critical situation. PEVOT is involved in policy reforms, such as the establishment of the UVQF, which promotes a more competence-based education and training system and is the key element of the programme. Having occupational standards which describe employment or competence-based outcomes of training developed in such a way allows training providers, public or private, to concentrate on and compete for the best possible practices of training. If training providers also modularise hitherto 'long' training programmes of several years of duration, the number of shorter training courses ('modules') that can be taken in flexible combinations will allow more young people to go for one or more of such modular courses. This will open up the training system for the 'forgotten majority'. It can also be expected that in this way the unit cost of training will be reduced quite soon. Subsequently, assessment (examinations and/or testing) based on the new occupational standards will lead to more credible and more transparent qualifications (certificates and diplomas) which, when arranged appropriately and consistent with occupational areas and performance levels, will make up what is called the UVQF.

Involving the Private Sector: Without the clear commitment and involvement of private industry for relevant, demand-driven skills development, it will be difficult to close the gaps in the labour market. The active engagement of the industrial sector in TVET is seen, internationally, as an important success factor. It must also be given serious consideration by the Ugandan TVET system as it undergoes reform. Such private sector involvement should have a sustainable impact on competitiveness and employment, thus boosting the economy.

Reaching out to the forgotten Majority: PEVOT worked with the MoES to develop its LearnNet programme as a means of broadening the availability of vocational skills training around the country. LearnNet is a training model that addresses the needs of the 'forgotten majority' by providing low-cost vocational training that meets the people's greatest needs. The local communities that benefit are also expected to mobilise their own resources to increase the sustainability of the training. The programme is expected to contribute to poverty reduction and community development."

Source: *PEVOT, Kampala.*

Appendix 35

Box 58: Examples of HRD-for-PSD issues in the news during the final days of writing the book

The following articles are from the New Vision

14/10/2008

62 vocational schools for USE

By *Ganzi Muhanguzi*

THERE are now 62 free vocational and technical institutes in the country under the universal education programme, the Minister of State for Higher Education, Gabriel Opio, has announced. He urged students to take advantage of this access to free vocational training. "Many people think that vocational training is for those who are academically challenged or who fail to make it in secondary schools but this is not true," Opio said. He was speaking at the inauguration of the new Directorate of Industrial Training building at Lugogo in Kampala. "This building is a testimony to our Government's determination in improving facilities and infrastructure in such institutions," Opio said. The vocational institutes included in the universal education programme consist of 16 community polytechnics, 25 technical schools, four farm schools and one vocational training centre, along with 16 privately-owned technical institutes. Opio further revealed that the education ministry had doubled its funding to vocational training institutes in a bid to develop technical skills in the country. "Our budget allocation for business, technical and vocational education and training has increased from 3% last year to 7% this year," he said. The new building, which cost sh142m, was funded by the Ministry of Education. The ministry's permanent secretary, Francis Lubanga, thanked partners like GTZ and JICO for their support to technical education development in Uganda.

'Vocational training is the engine of our economy'

By John Kasozi

THE closure of Uganda Martyrs' Primary School in Ggaba, Kampala in 1997 was sad news to its teachers, pupils and other employees. Many teachers contemplated what their next step would be after losing their jobs. To Grace Tukahebwa, a Grade Three teacher, the loss of her job was a shock, but at the same time a blessing in disguise. Her job at the school was her only means of survival. She thought of looking for another school to teach, but the previous salary discouraged her from continuing with the profession. "The remuneration I took home could not even push me half way through the month," Tukahebwa says. "At first, my brother employed me in his shop. Later, he asked me if I could take up a course in leather craft and shoe making. I accepted the offer because he was in the same industry and was earning some good money." In 2002, Tukahebwa joined Crane Shoes and Crafts Training and Common Facility Centre in Kampala's Industrial Area. After the training, she applied to rent part of the facility. "I did not have funds to buy machinery and tools. They are expensive," she says. Today, Tukahebwa does not have any regrets. She specialised in making belts, sandals, bags, keyholders and wallets. "These products have quick returns, unlike the shoes. The materials for making shoes are expensive," she says. "Since the Government wants value-addition and women's emancipation, it should consider helping us in this male-dominated sector. We need machinery to expand," Tukahebwa says.

Innocent Rwabukye, another crafts and shoe-maker renting space at the centre, has no kind words for parents who discourage their children from doing vocational courses. "Joining this industry was not accidental. I wanted to be a shoe-maker. As I grew up, I developed a chest problem and I could not do menial work. However, after realising that shoe-making required little energy, I went for it," Rwabukye explains. "Ever since I left school in 1989, I have never undermined vocational training. I am always busy and most times, my pockets are well-oiled," he says. Rwabukye adds that his six children have never slept on empty stomachs. "I meet all my family needs and I have built a house. "My first employment was in Mbarara. In

1994, I decided to go it alone until 1999, when the demand for locally-made shoes increased. Unfortunately, I did not have the machinery and tools to make them. "In 2000, I joined Crane Shoes in Kampala to increase the quality and quantity of my products. The centre had machines and tools similar to what we used in school," he adds. Rwabukye says it took him six to 12 months to get re-acquainted with the machinery. Thereafter, he started producing products for sale. "I am now an entrepreneur. I pay rent for using the centre's machinery and space. Although I was trained to make shoes, bags, wallets, belts, table mats and carpets, I have specialised in making sandals," he explains. He says self-employment is prestigious. "You have no time to waste." Rwabukye's children are also following in his footsteps. "I identify my children's talents to ensure that they get the right vocational training. This saves them the burden of walking Kampala streets in search of employment," Rwabukye says. Three of his children took up nursing, catering and computer servicing [respectively] and are all employed. "If you do not plan with your children, you are leading them to a dungeon. The Government is the least employer and the remuneration cannot sustain its workers." He appeals to the Government to set up more vocational schools and give capital to young people to start their own jobs. "Vocational training is the engine of our economy."

Jovia Kamukama, a trainer at TCFC, says she joined the centre in 2001 for a course in making shoes and crafts. In 2005, she was taken on as a trainer. Kamukama says since 2005, the centre has trained over 2,000 people. The unisex centre admits abled and disabled people, above 18 years, from Uganda and the neighbouring countries. Companies also take their staff to the centre for training. Its training module includes skills on how to run a small-scale industry. However, Tom Mukiibi, the administrative assistant, says, the centre is faced with many problems, especially high taxes. "The taxes on raw materials should be reduced because this increases the price of our products." "Many students walk away after paying half the fees, while others default." The centre also lacks tools and machinery such as the scoring and stitching machines. The scoring machine, which costs sh1.5m, is used to make finishing or smoothening of shoes. Mukiibi urges the Government to ban synthetic shoes and bags, especially those that are imported from China. "They are below standard. Surprisingly, when the Chinese are leaving this country, they come here to buy assorted leather products." Funded by the Austrian Government, TCFC was established in 1997 by the Uganda Leather and Allied Industries Association, under the United Nation Industrial Development Organisation. The Ministry of Tourism, Trade and Industry has supported the centre since 2000 by offering the premises where they operate. The centre's product profile is made up of leather uppers, stitch down footwear, leather goods and handcrafted leather products. Its finished products are sold to Shoprite, Garden City, Banana Boat, National Theatre and other areas throughout the country.

13/10/2008

Uganda: Japan to Boost Agriculture

Charles Kakamwa

JAPAN plans to increase aid to Uganda to boost agriculture, the deputy ambassador, Kazuaki Kameda, has said. Addressing district leaders from the east at a workshop at Mbale Resort Hotel recently, Kameda said the programme would include doubling of rice production, development of irrigation schemes, introduction of new crop varieties and capacity building. He said Japan was contributing to the modernisation of agriculture in Uganda by focusing on rice production, small-scale farming and the livestock industry."The objective is to contribute to increased food security, opportunities for employment and income generation," Kameda said. The embassy said in a statement that Japan started the project in eastern Uganda in 2003 with the introduction of a new rice variety, NERICA. "The cultivation of NERICA in Uganda has increased from 6,000 ha in 2003 to more than 35,000 ha in 2007. Approximately 2,000 farmers and stakeholders have received training to raise their technical knowledge," the statement said.

07/10/2008

'I left KASPER with a business plan'

Students of Kasper in Mityana district stick labels onto processed juice bottles

By John Kasozi

THE desire to create jobs and self-employment drove them into studying at an institute that could meet their needs. Florence Acuma, 21, from Owang village in Apac district is a second year student at Kasper Institute of Development Studies in Mityana district. She says during secondary school, she longed for self-employment. "My region is blessed with lots of foods and fruits which are usually left to rot. This is money thrown away and it displeases me a lot. If many of us did a value addition course, there would be no famine in the region. We would export the fruits," she says. "By enrolling at institutes that offer value addition courses, we could rescue ourselves from problems caused by the Lord's Resistance Army insurgency," says Acuma. "I got to know about Kasper through Plants and Health, an NGO in northern Uganda, when I was looking for an institute that teaches value addition," she says. "I also wanted to create jobs in the North since most of the youth in Uganda are unemployed. The region needs to catch up with other regions," says Acuma. Besides, she looks at reintroducing and improving local breed poultry, bee-keeping, fish and dairy farming, commercial tree planting and piggery. "The revival of these sub-sectors would drive us into setting up food processing cottages. We hope the Northern Uganda Social Action Front (NUSAF) and National Agricultural Advisory Services (NAADS) will facilitate us," says Acuma.

Harriet Adoko, 22, a first year student at Kasper says she was inspired by her desire to create jobs and be self-employed. "I longed to share what I learnt about modern organic farming and adding value to foods and fruits with farmers in my district, Lira," she says. Josephine Amongi, 23, from Apac district, says since childhood, her focus has been on agriculture. "At one time, I wanted to be a veterinary surgeon and to engage in organic farming, so when I heard of Kasper, I knew this was the beginning of my dream." She says northern Uganda is still blessed with a lot of virgin land on which they can practice organic farming. "With this kind of vocational course, I can practise what I have learnt." Justin Bangindi, 24, a Sudanese from Western Equatorial State in Sudan, says he was inspired to study a food processing course when he was a student at St. John Bosco Seminary in Hoima. I came to Uganda in 2001 and went to the seminary. During my six years, I developed the desire to set up a food processing unit and also put up a vocational institute in Sudan," said Bangindi. "After that, since I had not identified an institute at which to study, I enrolled for a six-month certificate at the International Institute of Business Studies in 2006," he adds. After the course, Bangindi joined an agriculture college in Bukalasa, but because the courses did not measure up to his expectations, he went to Kasper. The institute offered practical and theoretical course units of his choice, so chances of employing himself and others were high.

Kasper offers courses in project planning and management, food processing technologies, community development and entrepreneurship skills. Others are crop science, intensive animal science and poultry nutrition, sustainable organic agriculture, environmental management, participatory market chain approach, computer studies, cleaner production and industrial extension. Bangindi, now a second year student, says he has already written his business plan. When he goes back home after completing his course, Banginda will start Atita Solidality Service, a training centre and cottage industry. "I will mobilise and train farmers in January before the rain season begins so that we can produce enough food for processing in July before the exhibition," he says. Banginda says there is no food processing cottage industry in his home area. He wants to change the face of agriculture. Robinah Nakaweesi, 26, from Mityana says: "I observed that Uganda's economy depends mainly on self-employment. This drove me into joining Kasper." "The institute has taught us to be job creators and innovators. We can also write business plans and start our own enterprises," Nakaweesi, the NAADS youth representative for Mityana Town Council, says. "For two months, 16 of us have been at Kabanyolo Agriculture Research Centre doing industrial training. We performed best among the institutes that took part in the in-service learning programmes." Prof. Moses Tenywa, the head of the centre, rewarded them with sh90,000 for excelling in the implementation of in-service learning programmes. In-service learning is offering services, while learning with others. Kasper Vocational Institute is located in Kannamba village behind the Mityana district local government offices. It offers a two-year diploma course to S.4 and S.6 leavers with at least six credits at O'level and two principle passes at A'level. The institute has a food laboratory to facilitate practical sessions and a hostel to house the students. The institute also offers tailor-made training programmes every year in January and July for four weeks.

Twenty-five students can enroll for a fulltime course every year. Peter Kasirye, the institute's director, says the school was founded in 2007. Currently, it has 20 students including six females. Last year, there were 23 students including eight females. It has eight fulltime lecturers and some visiting ones. Before it was registered as Kasper Institute of Development Studies, Kasper Food Enterprise was training farmers from Kasese, Kayunga, Lira, Gulu, Mbarara and Bushenyi districts. Other farmers were from Masaka, Butogota, Kabale, Mukono, Kampala, Mityana and Mubende districts. A total of 720 farmers have been trained at this centre. Kasirye says he has also trained foreigners including seven entrepreneurs from the Democratic Republic of Congo under Women International and 20 from Southern Sudan. He has also trained Nigerians through the National Organic Agricultural Movement of Uganda and many university students. Kasirye says students grapple with a number of challenges. "Many people have failed to put to use what they have learnt. Value addition equipment is also expensive. Only a few people can afford it." "We are also still struggling to establish linkages with some universities and institutes in the same field like the Uganda Industrial Research Institute," he said.

'Theft: Cattle-keepers new disease' 411

Cattle thefts account for the increase in the price of meat

By Joshua Kato

Cattle-keepers around the country now face many challenges. Besides diseases and the rising costs of cattle rearing, theft is now their latest nightmare. Thieves, mainly from major slaughter houses in Kampala, Mukono, Jinja, Mbarara and Luweero are terrorising the farmers. According to an investigation by The New Vision, out of every 10 trucks that unload cattle in any slaughter house, at least five of the animals on six of the trucks are stolen. In some cases, an entire truck of cattle is stolen. In the latest incident, 23 cattle were stolen from a farm in Nakasongola, but were recovered at a Kampala slaughter house, says Bruno Matovu, the owner of the animals. Between May and September, four other trucks were nabbed transporting stolen cows to various abattoirs. Cattle theft is regularly reported in Ssembabule, Nakasongola, Kiruhura and areas of Mbarara, parts of Kayunga and Gomba in Mpigi district. According to cattle keepers in these areas, animals, mainly cows and goats worth millions are lost every day to thieves, who pretend to be genuine buyers from Kampala.

For example, Matovu's cows had been sold at sh10m. This is a loss to only one farmer. On average, a cow costs between sh300,000 to sh500,000. When a farmer loses two cows in a month, he loses sh1m. "I was losing at least cows every month to thieves. That is around sh0.5m per month. Then, I decided to hire guards to look after the animals at night," says James Nsiyoona, of Gomba, a few miles away from President Museveni's Kisozi ranch. The thieves are so daring, that before President Yoweri Museveni completely sealed off his ranch, they also stole his cattle. "We thought that being near the President would save us from these thieves, but that is not the case," Nsiyoona says. There are different ways through which the animals are stolen, a loader at one of the leading abattoirs in the city explains. "As we go to pick-up animals from Ssembabule, we drop some colleagues in selected areas, say in Gomba. These colleagues steal the animals from farms well known to them at night and as we return from Ssembabule, we load the animals on the trucks, long before the

411 To clarify: This news clip combines issues of business culture (including malpractices) and political economy in the context of Uganda's economic setting. It highlights relevant aspects of HRD as discussed earlier in this book. The same holds for other articles quoted below on realities of business practices, economic and social conflicts, and related state regulations.

owners wake up to discover the theft," he says. "Sometimes those who steal the cows arrive at the village much earlier, spot the animals to be stolen, chase them to a given location and wait for the trucks," says Sulait Lwanga, a cattle dealer. In some incidences, the thieves target the cattle market day, when most of the herdsmen and the farm owners have taken some of their cattle for sale, the thieves pounce on the remaining animals.

Many cattle-keepers are investing in the expensive venture of fencing their farms. On average, a cattle-keeper needs at least 25 rolls of barbed wire, each costing about sh60,000 to fence a five acre farm. "In addition to fencing, we are hiring guards, to keep off thieves," says Emilio Rwamukaaga of Bulyamushenyi, Ngoma. These added expenses are passed onto the consumer. According to the Police, some of the stolen cattle are taken to the Sudan, where the market is more lucrative. "Many cows stolen from Ngoma and Masindi districts end up in Sudan," says Martin Amoru, the Police commander, mid-western region. A cow costs four times ... [more] in Sudan than in Uganda. In order to try and reduce losses, cattle keepers have friends in most city abattoirs who they contact whenever their animals are stolen. This is the how Matovu traced his animals on September 9. Having contacts in the abattoirs also helped Julius Byarugaba of Mawogola in Ssembabule recover his animals. "Twenty cows were stolen from my farm. I contacted my people in the different abattoirs around the city and they told me they had seen the cows in Kalerwe," he says. Byarugaba immediately came to Kampala and found his cows. According to Issa Nsubuga, the chairperson of the cattle traders at Kampala Meat Packers, it is sometimes difficult to differentiate between stolen and genuine cattle, especially if the thieves have relevant documents. Animal movement documents include a trading licence and a movement permit. Amoru says movement of cattle at night has been banned in order to enable the Police to have clear records of cattle coming from cattle-keeping areas. He says in order to stop stolen cattle going to Sudan, there are road blocks at Karuma where all cattle carrying trucks are registered.

Dunavant vows to fight CDO

By Ibrahim Kasita

Cotton farmers and local leaders in Pader and Kitgum are up in arms against Dunavant, saying the company wants to sabotage the sector. The confrontation follows remarks made by Patel Ravi, the dunavant managing director, that he would oppose the Government's policy on the sector. Ravi made the remarks during a farmers' consultative meeting held last week at Pader district headquarters. "I am not ready to listen to the Government or the Cotton Development Organisation (CDO). I will fight them," Ravi reportedly vowed. "The Government should not regulate my activities because I have done a lot to empower the people in the north." Dunavant promotes organic cotton growing in the two districts. The company was pushed out of the Lango sub-region because of the controversial project. Leaders from the two districts want the sector's regulator to closely monitor Dunavant's activities "to avoid economic sabotage." "CDO as an arm of the Government must closely monitor and regulate your activities for the good of our people if you want to remain here," Charles Kurwa, the deputy Resident District Commissioner for Pader, said. "We need peaceful economic players to rehabilitate this region. This calls for harmonised methods of work." "We have been in war for 20 years. When you vow to fight the Government, you are fighting us. Don't evoke past memories," Beatrice Akello, the female youth district councillor, said. Akello said the farmers were suffering because of Dunavant. Alfred Akena, the Pader district vice-chairman, warned: "The farmers want high yields not those war words. You must follow the Government's policies if you want to operate here."

05/10/2008

Sugarcane growers cry foul over prices

By Samuel Balagadde

Sugarcane growers need a policy to protect them from exploitation by sugar manufacturers. Wilberforce Kiwagama, the chairman of the Uganda National Association of Sugarcane Growers, said big sugar manufacturers are frustrating sugarcane outgrowers by paying them peanuts. "Every sugar manufacturing company has its offer per tonnage, yet outgrowers incur the same costs," Kiwagama said during a national consultative workshop at their offices at Old Kampala. He said Kinyara buys a tonne of sugarcane at sh32,500, Kakira sh38,000 and the Sugar Corporation of Uganda sh34,000. Kiwagama said the prices were peanuts compared to what their counterparts in the neighbouring countries earn. He said they were also being forced to move from the Ministry of Tourism, Trade and Industry to that of agriculture where they will directly be catered for in terms of loans as commercial farmers. Kiwagama said Uganda's sugarcane industry is lagging behind in the East African Community, a situation that would severely affect the country' participation in the regional market. "Sugar from outside the country is cheaper because of support of sugarcane farmers by the respective governments and sugar processing companies," he said. The commercial sugarcane farmers include Kinyara Sugarcane Growers, Mukono Sugarcane Outgrower Cooperative Society and Busoga Sugarcane Growers Association.

30/09/2008

Uganda: Fishermen to Fight Illegal Fishing

Ronald Kalyango

Fishing communities at major lakes have formed an association to fight illegal fishing methods and ensure sound fishing practices. The Association of Fishers and Lake Users of Uganda (AFALU) will be responsible for monitoring and sensitising the public about the dangers of catching premature fish. "Not so long ago we used to have a lot of fish in our lakes and fish was one of the cheapest sources of protein in Uganda. Currently many people can only afford fish skeletons locally called 'fille'," said James Kisambira, the association's adviser. Speaking during an operation to destroy illegal fishnets at Katosi Landing Site in Mukono, Kisambira said the association had deployed at all the major lakes to promote efficient and environment-friendly fishing methods. Kisambira said the association works with the Beach Management Unit (BMU) officers, the Police and fisheries officers. In Ntenjeru sub-county, Mukono district, the AFALU team recently teamed up with the Lugazi Police, local BMUs and the fisheries officers to impound 10,000 illegal fishing gear and premature fish. He said the operation's monitoring team had covered Bulebi, Sowe, Kiziru, Kikoko, Kijjuko, Bubazi, Mbale and Bugula landing sites. State minister for fisheries Fred Mukisa who was the chief guest said the country's fish exports had grown over the last 10 years."This remarkable performance has been partly attributed to an increase in export tonnage and the higher prices on the foreign market," he said. Mukisa said his ministry was taking steps to streamline fisheries management activities and to support and build the capacity of BMUs.

18/01/2009 (Sunday Vision)

Makerere-designed car at global exhibition in Italy

By Conan Businge

A prototype car designed by Makerere University students is being exhibited at the World Design Capital in Torino, Italy. The environmentally-friendly and energy efficient prototype was part of last year's Dream Exposition designs at the workshop room at Torino Museum. The first model of the vehicle, Vision 200, was partly designed by six Makerere undergraduate engineering students. While building the car in Italy, the students handled the 'heart' of the vehicle. "We handled the transmission and power-train, which are the basics for the vehicle's movement," said Steven Ntambi, who headed the students team. This involves data networking, battery and the protection system and welding on the body of the vehicle. Since Makerere University did not have enough money to build a general transportation research centre, Massachusetts Institute of Technology of the USA took over the building of the vehicle. Last year, the Design Summit invited 55 students studying different disciplines from 21 universities in 11 countries to the Massachusetts Institute of Technology to develop commuter cars. Makerere represented Africa.

The following articles are from the Daily Monitor

07/10/2008

Sameer looks to West Africa to expand market for powder milk

Dorothy Nakaweesi

Sameer Agriculture and Livestock has extended its exploits in the powder milk market to West Africa as the company seeks to become a leader in an industry dominated by foreign brands. After a successful launch of powder milk and subsequent exports in the East African region, Syria, Egypt, and Yemen, Sameer Agriculture and Livestock Limited, a company which took over former Dairy Corporation Limited almost two years ago, sees the West African market as being critical in boosting the company's sales. In an interview with Business Power, Sameer Head of Sales and Distribution Rajiv Joshi said: "We are in the final stages of discussion to start exporting powder milk to Nigeria and this will be our base to the rest of the region". Uganda started production of powder milk in January and the product has since performed well in the pioneer foreign markets of Syria, Egypt, and Yemen. "These countries don't produce milk, so they approach us to supply them with the product," Mr Joshi said. Sameer currently produces about 20 tonnes per day most of which is consumed within the East African region. This comes from close to 250,000 litres of raw milk supplied by 50,000 farmers ... countrywide. Sameer produces both skimmed and cream powder milk products in the 25kg bags which is mainly for factory and confectionary use. Nigeria presents a huge potential for milk market in Uganda since it is the largest importer of dairy products in West Africa. The company has started supplying milk powder to local supermarkets in packs of 400 grams to compete with renowned import brands like Nido.

"On a monthly basis we supply about 14 to 20 tonnes to local supermarkets," he said. Each 400g-pack costs Shs7,000. This same product size is also exported to Rwanda, Burundi and DR Congo but it is still on a small scale. Mr Joshi said on average the company has earned close to $2 million in export revenue from all the countries. "Our annual target $15 million," he said. Uchumi Manager Eric Korir said: "We have had Sameer powder milk on our shelves for the last one and a half months and I must say the sales are gradually picking up". He ... [advised, however,] that Sameer needs to improve on its packaging to compete favourably with other brands which are packed in tins if it were to win more customers. "Some consumers would be buying Sameer but because of the packaging they tend to choose the other brands instead," Mr Korir said. A tin of Nido weighing 400 grams costs Shs11, 000 at Uchumi and other supermarkets sell it at Shs12,000. Hajji Jamil Ssegujja proprietor of Saduna Wholesalers one of the importers of Nido distributed to Supermarkets said: "The reason why we import Nido is because of the local demand and the country is not producing enough". ... [Sameer] also produces a range of other products like fresh dairy pasteurised milk and Ultra Heat Treated (UHT), yoghurts in different flavours like vanilla and straw berry and ghee. The company has also expanded milk collection network. Mr Joshi said having a big network of suppliers will help them meet and increase production of all their products. The company's future plan ... [has] hit a daily processing capacity of up to 400,000 litres up from from the current 120,000 litres. Sameer's introduction of powder milk product is in line with the government's call to investors to add value on exports such coffee, cotton, fish, fruits, and vegetables among others. However, challenges like the delays at the Mombasa Port bring about the high cost of doing business and sometimes losing confidence from the importers. "We sent a consignment to Yemen on June 29 and it departed Mombasa port on August 9. International clients who are dealing in manufacturing don't wait when the products delays," Mr Joshi said. "In the long run they are losing confidence, quality of the product and the plan of the exporter and importer. If I am not paid then this will affect the production of other products." He said if there was an alternative they would have blacklisted the port, but this the only port ... [Uganda] uses.

When fishing becomes a dangerous job

Fewer fish in the lake, crime, disease and drowning of fishermen have made fishing a feared job nowadays, writes Francis Mugerwa. Mr. Robert Opita (38) sits in his canoe boat on the shores of Lake Albert. He is at Butyaba landing site, contemplating how he will go about his day's fishing activities. He would like to get a huge catch so that he can sell good quality and high quantities of fish and therefore have a better income. But he is not only worried of accidents but also about the low fish catches which have reduced the earnings of fishermen. Opita's wishes, just like those of many other fishermen, are increasingly becoming hard to materialise because of the numerous challenges they face. Lake Albert, located in the Albertine graben in the Rift Valley is one of Africa's famous lakes but accidents, decreased fish stocks, poor hygiene, lack of ready reliable market, poor fishing methods and gears, insecurity and crime in the waters have greatly hampered smooth fishing operations. "We lack modern fishing gears. The canoes are slow and unreliable when we meet strong winds in the lake," Mark Sipya (32) says. Worse still, the fishermen overload the dilapidated canoes while some attempt to over speed. On September 30, a canoe carrying 27 fishermen capsized at Kamina-Nguse landing site in which 18 people died. The mid-western Police Commander Mr Paul Martin Amoru says 13 bodies so far have been recovered while police managed to rescue six people. The desperate search for survivors by police, army and Uganda Red Cross Society is ongoing. "The accident was caused by overloading," Amoru said. He also said the strong winds which the boat encountered greatly contributed to its sinking. He says enforcing safety on the lake has become difficult. "Whereas on the road we have the Road Safety Act, in the waters we lack a specific law that mitigates lake-related accidents," he says.

This is the latest accident in the several accidents that have occurred in the lake. In April, a canoe boat at Butyaba landing site capsized and killed over 10 people who were on board. Amoru says that putting on life jackets would be mandatory for all lake users to minimise losing lives when boats capsize. He said the boat that capsized was in a dangerous mechanical condition just like many other boats on the lake. "Life jackets keep one floating till he gets people to rescue him or her," the police commander says. The fishermen here use prohibited fishing methods, to the chagrin of conservationists and various government technocrats. Amoru says many Uganda fishermen are attacked, assaulted and robbed by criminals ... "Quarrels between Ugandan and Congolese fishermen are common and often times they result in ... fights," he added. Crime ... [on the lake] is another concern for police. There are some pirates who reportedly waylay the fishermen and rob them of their money and other property in the lake. "We are going to enforce our Marine Unit which is stationed in Butyaba to curb crime in Lake Albert waters," Amoru added. The unit has a marine boat but is overstretched to monitor activities on the entire board line in Bunyoro. Conservationists are struggling with the marked decrease in fish stocks in various lakes in the country. "Fish is very scarce nowadays. It is possible to lay nets and you come back empty handed," Opita says. The Buliisa District fisheries officer Mr. Philip Ngongaha says fishermen at various landing sites in the district use beach seines locally known as kokota, poison, undersized nets and light to fish at night which is prohibited. "Indiscriminate fishing is dangerous since immature fish is also caught," Ngongaha says.

Some fishermen fish without minding about the breeding grounds of the fish, which affects the fish stocks. Sanitation at all landing sites on this lake is pathetic. Many residents lack toilets and other related sanitary facilities. This explains why cholera, bilharzia, diarrhoea, dysentery and sanitary related diseases are prevalent here. "We are sensitising them about the need to set up and utilise toilets," Dr.Charles Kajura, the District production coordinator says. Fishermen are also being sensitised on better fishing methods that prioritise restocking. The re-emergence of the water hyacinth on the lake is another concern for the fishermen. The weed is at Wanseko, Butyaba, Hoimo and Sebigoro landing sites and is reportedly spreading to other landing sites. Dr. Kajura explained that the weed has created a canopy on the water and blocks sun rays from reaching the waters which is key in fish breeding. Fish eventually suffocate and die because the weed consumes the oxygen the fish ... [need] for metabolism. It may also cause accidents when it blocks moving boats. "We are encouraging fishermen to manually extract it (water hyacinth) from the waters and offer it to cows which feed on it," Kajura said. The fisheries state minister Mr. Fred Mukisa says the government plans to improve sanitation, infrastructure, and assist fishermen with access to international markets and restock the lake. He says efforts will be made to mitigate accidents through increased inspection of the boats. Mr. Mukisa says all fishing boats and gears will be inspected and registered by fisheries' officials to ensure they do not contravene national fishing guidelines.

Bankers alarmed by increasing fraud

Elias Biryabarema

The mounting incidents of fraud in the banking industry and the rising level of sophistication and amounts of money involved have provoked the Uganda Bankers Association (UBA) to voice alarm and frustration at the fast deterioration of safety standards in banks. Since this year, there has been a rising number of robbery and fraud cases orchestrated by bank staff often in collusion with external elements. The latest of these was on September 25th when a planned raid on Stanbic Garden City branch, Kampala in which Shs7 billion would have been lost, was foiled by alert bank officials and Police which responded swiftly. Almost in the same week Police also arrested the ATM operations manager of Barclays Bank for allegedly defrauding the bank of Shs73 million through diverting money from some accounts into his, over a year-long period. Two months ago, Crane Bank also foiled an internally orchestrated scam that was under way in which millions would have been lost.

UBA Executive Director Emmanuel Kikoni said while most banks had assured them that they had instituted robust, unfailing safety standards that were being rigorously enforced, the explosion of fraud pointed ... [in] a different direction. "It's a bit disappointing and I think banks really must show their customers that their internal safety measures are working and reliable," he said. A much more acute problem in Uganda that was undermining efforts to stem fraud in banks, he said, was the lack of effective investigative capacity on behalf Police. He said most criminals end up getting bailed out of prisons and even cases collapsing, allowing them to enjoy the fruits of their scams. "Our police is failing us and certainly there is an obvious need for a toughening of efforts in this area such that those who commit these offences get justice which will deter others," he said.

Stanbic, perhaps on account of its size or because of the level of laxity in its safety procedures, has had the biggest number of heists in the industry. In one of the most notorious cases in January last year, robbers posing as staff invaded Stanbic Bank branch at Jubilee Centre on Parliament Avenue and hauled off about Shs700 million. Stanbic Bank Communications Director Daniel Nsibambi, however, said fraudsters are more likely to target the bank because of its size. "We are the biggest bank in the county and that inevitably heightens the risk exposure," he said. He asserted that the Bank was constantly updating and strengthening its internal security procedures and that that's why most of scams are foiled. Mr Richard Byarugaba, the chief operations officer of Barclays Bank suggested in an interview that the wave of fraud in the banking industry was the natural corollary to the collapse of ethics and integrity that he said is evident in the Ugandan society. "There are so many people who want to get rich quick and that attitude is going present lots of problems for everyone," he said. He was confident though that the banks' internal safety mechanisms were still strong enough to detect and foil any scams that might be attempted by criminals. His views were echoed by Mr Sam Owori, the executive director of Institute of Corporate Governance Uganda, who suggested in an interview that Uganda's corruption-infested politics was infecting the business community with its vices. "What we have is a terrible erosion of morality that started with politics and is now spilling over into private sector," he said. "People no longer pursue hard work and merit, instead they search for what brings wealth in the quickly."

Police impound fake drugs, cosmetics

Alfred Wandera & Andrew Bagala

An operation by the Police, the National Drug Authority and URA has impounded counterfeit medicinal products worth millions of shillings. The organisations have as a result placed 38 pharmacies in four districts under investigation for sale of fake products, including un registered medicinal lotions, creams and ointments betamethasone, clobetasol picked mainly from Kikuubo in Kampala, Police spokesperson Judith Nabakooba announced yesterday. Surprisingly, of the 40 pharmacies that were sampled in Kampala, Jinja, Masaka and Iganga districts, only two did not have counterfeit products, raising fears that many drugs consumed in the country may be fake and dangerous to human life. In a five-day operation from September 29 to October 5, 2008, 19 pharmacies in Kampala were found trading in fake drugs, while nine drug shops in Masaka District are also being investigated over selling counterfeit drugs. Jinja District came third with seven pharmacies dealing in fake drugs while three are under investigation in Iganga District. The operation was carried out with support from Interpol. In a press conference at Interpol head offices in Kampala yesterday, Ms Nabakooba said 10 people have been arrested as investigations continue. "Ten suspects are being investigated for operating illegal pharmaceutical businesses, having no certificates for suitability of premises, and unlicensed sellers not qualified to handle drugs," Ms Nabakooba said. Among the products impounded include body and hair gel, creams and lotions ...

Ms Nabakooba declined to mention the names of the pharmacies being investigated, saying samples of the medicines have been handed over to the Police Forensic Department for testing. Ms Kate Kikule, the head of NDA Drug Inspectorate Services, said most manufacturers of the counterfeit medicines do not state the origin of the drugs because they will be investigated. ... Some of the impounded products included medicinal lotions, creams and ointments containing betamethasone, clobetasol, chemicals that cause cancer. "Poor and ignorant villagers constitute the willing victims of the growing market in cheap counterfeit drugs. As a consequence over 2 million people treated for malaria die each year because they were treated with fake drugs in Africa," Interpol Intellectual Property Rights Project officer Stanley Ude said. Mr Geoffrey Balamaga, the URA manager of Customs in charge of Enforcement Operations, said most drugs find their way into the country through ungazetted entries at border posts, which lead to losses of tax revenue to the government.

Index